the glory
of the atonement

BIBLICAL,
HISTORICAL
& PRACTICAL
PERSPECTIVES

Essays in Honor of Roger Nicole

CHARLES E. HILL AND
FRANK A. JAMES III, EDITORS

InterVarsity Press
Downers Grove, Illinois

InterVarsity Press
P.O. Box 1400, Downers Grove, IL 60515-1426
World Wide Web: www.ivpress.com
E-mail: mail@ivpress.com

InterVarsity Press® is the book-publishing division of InterVarsity Christian Fellowship/USA®, a student movement active on campus at hundreds of universities, colleges and schools of nursing in the United States of America, and a member movement of the International Fellowship of Evangelical Students. For information about local and regional activities, write Public Relations Dept., InterVarsity Christian Fellowship/USA, 6400 Schroeder Rd., P.O. Box 7895, Madison, WI 53707-7895, or visit the IVCF website at <www.intervarsity.org>.

All Scripture quotations, unless otherwise indicated, are taken from the Holy Bible, New International Version®. NIV®. *Copyright ©1973, 1978, 1984 by International Bible Society. Used by permission of Zondervan Publishing House. All rights reserved.*

Cover Design: Cindy Kiple

Cover Image: Werner Forman/Art Resource, NY

ISBN 0-8308-2689-0

Printed in the United States of America ∞

Library of Congress Cataloging-in-Publication Data

The glory of the atonement: biblical, historical & practical
perspectives: essays in honor of Roger Nicole / Charles E. Hill
and Frank A. James III, editors.
    p. cm.
Includes bibliographical references and indexes.
 ISBN 0-8308-2689-0 (pbk.: alk. paper)
 1. Atonement. 2. Reformed Church—Doctrines. I. Nicole, Roger R.
II. Hill, Charles E. (Charles Evan), 1956- III. James, Frank A.
BT265.3.G56 2004
232'.3—dc22

2003025924

P	16	15	14	13	12	11	10	9	8	7	6	5	4	3	2	1
Y	15	14	13	12	11	10	09	08	07	06	05	04				

contents

pReface

Academics are prone to lamentation—it is an occupational hazard. About three years ago the editors were lamenting the fact that there was no *Festschrift* for our esteemed colleague Roger Nicole. To that lament we added another. As we were bemoaning the paucity of really good thinking on the doctrine of the atonement, the idea for a book began to flicker in our minds. As we massaged the idea, we began to see a vague image of a resolution for our lament. We knew that one of his favorite doctrines, one to which he had devoted considerable academic attention over his long career, was the atonement. The fact that evangelical readers have not seen much on this topic since John Stott's *The Cross of Christ* in 1986 made the project even more appealing. What better way to honor our colleague and dear brother than a book devoted to the topic of the atonement? This way we could, so to speak, kill two birds with one stone.

Eventually, we took our idea to Dan Reid of InterVarsity Press, who suggested, in so many words, that we could kill a third bird. We could stimulate renewed discussion of the doctrine of the atonement among college students, seminarians and other scholars, and honor Roger at the same time. Thus, we designed this festschrift as a textbook.

One final task was to assemble a superb team of evangelical scholars and ask them to turn their academic talents to the doctrine of the atonement. Our scholars were eager to participate, both because they wanted to honor Roger for his many years of service to the church and because they wanted to address the all-too-neglected doctrine of the atonement from their particular angle of expertise. The caliber of the contributors may be seen as a tribute to Roger's reputation and relationships.

In a career spanning over half a century, Roger Nicole has been identified with a number of important doctrines such as inerrancy of Scripture, the role of women in the church and, more recently, opposition to
open theism; but the doctrine of the atonement retains a special place
in his theological heart. These essays are offered in fond affection for a
dear friend and superb scholar.

Special thanks to two superb graduate assistants, Jeremy Alexander
and Ryan Reeves, to Rev. David Bailey for sharing his recollections of
Roger Nicole, and to John Muether for the subject index.

a tribute to roger nicole

Timothy George

I first met Roger Nicole in the early 1970s when I was a student at Harvard Divinity School and he was a professor at Gordon-Conwell Theological Seminary on whose faculty he served for forty-one years. When Nicole first came to what was then Gordon Divinity School in 1938, the campus was in the heart of Boston. In those days, Gordon was one of the few evangelical institutions where young ministers were taught to believe that the tomb was empty without being made to think that their heads had to be. Doubtless, the school's reputation for academic rigor and spiritual vitality had attracted the brilliant young Roger, fresh from his classical and theological studies in Lausanne and at the Sorbonne, in the first place. Eventually, Nicole would earn three degrees from Gordon (B.D., S.T.M. and Th.D.) as well as an additional research doctorate (Ph.D.) from Harvard University. He joined the faculty of Gordon in 1945, and by the time I met him, he had become something of a legend there.

In 1946 Roger married the former Annette Cyr. For many decades they have modeled the graces of Christian hospitality. Several generations of students and colleagues have known the largesse of their table and the conviviality of their home. Roger has always invested himself in the spiritual formation as well as the theological development of his students, and students have responded to him with great love and affection. After his retirement from Gordon-Conwell in 1986, Roger and

Annette moved to Orlando, where he continued to teach at Reformed Theological Seminary and also, on occasion, at an extension center of New Orleans Baptist Theological Seminary. David W. Bailey, one of his students from this extension center, has given the following account of Roger in the classroom:

> During his lectures, several of the students, on occasion, would weep. His keen mind (as an octogenarian!) was demonstrated in his total lack of notes (just an NIV Bible and a Greek New Testament) and his ability to teach for nearly four solid hours, at night (6:00 p.m. to 10:00 p.m.), with only a twenty-minute nap in between from which he did not need to be awakened. He was gracious in handling questions from "difficult students." We were deeply impressed by his complete transparency regarding his own Christian pilgrimage, his manifest godliness, his willingness to share with the students volumes from his own library due to the limitations of an extension center library. Such obvious brilliance was coupled with a love for stamp-collecting and mystery novels and an incredible knowledge of books. One feels both more intellectual and more Christ-like just spending time with Roger Nicole.

Another former student from Gordon-Conwell remembers that Roger and Annette always had time for the little children of their students, whom they knew by name and always welcomed with open arms. Some time ago I was invited to participate in a service of ordination for one of Roger's former students. He had asked Roger to offer the prayer of consecration. I am sure that his prayer will be remembered long after what the rest of us said has been forgotten. Here was a beloved father in God, commending to the Great Shepherd of the Flock one of his own sons in the faith with such tenderness, care and solicitude, but also with the *gravitas* of a patriarch who has walked with God and who knows that this young minister will one day be called to stand before the divine bar of accountability. Hearing that prayer, I thought: This is what it means to be a theologian of the church.

Roger Nicole is well known as a defender of the doctrine of biblical inerrancy. He is a man of the Book. But he is also a man of books. For a number of years he served as the curator of Gordon-Conwell's theological library. Often with only meager resources at his disposal, he collected, bought, wheedled, swapped and bargained, until he had amassed more than 100,000 volumes for that collection. His own personal theological library of over 25,000 volumes is now the centerpiece of the special collections at Reformed Theological Seminary. In 1968, the year after Roger completed his Ph.D. at Harvard, the university was temporarily "taken over" by student radicals who occupied administrative buildings and threatened to burn down the great Widener Library there. George Huntston Williams, the Hollis Professor of Divinity at Harvard, once told me that he and a few other professors had stayed in the library all through the night. Armed with snow shovels and a few broomsticks, these sentinels of civilization guarded the doors to the house of learning, preserving for future generations the wisdom of the ages. As it turned out, the impassioned vandalism of the students turned in another direction, but an all-night vigil of guarding the books is an instinct Roger Nicole would understand.

Roger Nicole is one of European Christianity's great gifts to the American church. His role in the shaping of American evangelical theology during the latter half of the twentieth century was enormous and deserves to be better known. Nicole was a respected member of an informal cadre of evangelical scholars—young Turks—who quite self-consciously broke with the strictures of an older, introverted fundamentalism to forge a fresher, more vibrant version of Christian orthodoxy—one that was culturally relevant, intellectually engaged, globally aware and committed to world evangelization. Among his fellow travelers were Carl F. H. Henry, Paul Jewett, George Eldon Ladd, E. J. Carnell and Kenneth Kantzer. Nicole was one of the founders of the Evangelical Theological Society in 1947. Some of his most influential writings, more essays and articles than books, have recently been published as *Standing Forth: Collected Writings of Roger Nicole.*[1]

Three things about Roger Nicole's theological style have impressed me deeply. First, he is a person who cares passionately about the issue of truth in theology. He is not afraid to pursue rigorous thinking in the service of theological truth. J. I. Packer has aptly described Roger as "a masterful systematic theologian, poised for logical-exegetical pincer movements against muddles and mistakes." One such muddle that has drawn the attention of Nicole in recent years is that form of semi-process theism commonly known as "openness of God" theology. Some Reformed opponents of this recent theology have criticized it as a form of Arminianism gone amuck. Nicole rightly sees that this new

[1]Geanies House, Ross-shire: Christian Focus Publications, 2002.

view is compatible with neither Calvinism nor Arminianism in their historic expressions, but rather represents a radical departure from the historic doctrine of God as believed and taught by Roman Catholic, Orthodox and Protestant theologians alike. I cite the openness debate as simply one example of Nicole's desire to do theology always in dialogue with the Great Tradition of the church. One sees this abundantly in the two great theological themes he has pursued throughout his long career: the inspiration and authority of the Bible, and the doctrine of the atonement.

While Nicole's single-minded pursuit of the truth has led him into the thicket of controversy on more than one occasion, he has also earnestly tried to be an irenic theologian. He believes that theology, like Jesus, should be full of grace and truth—both at once without the diminution of either. We might well place Roger Nicole's approach to theological controversy under the rubric "between compromise and contentiousness."

One of the finest expressions of this approach is Roger's remarkable essay "Polemic Theology—How to Deal With Those Who Differ From Us."[2] Drawing on his immense personal experience of doing theology in the trenches, Roger pursues three important questions for dealing with those who differ from us: (1) What do I *owe* the person who differs from me? (2) What can I *learn* from the person who differs from me? (3) How can I *cope* with the person who differs from me? To pursue what we might call the Nicolian approach to polemics is not easy. It is much easier to go after our opponents with all of our evangelical guns "loaded for bear"! But, as Roger knows so well, it is possible to win an argument and yet lose a soul—including one's own! At the end of the day, Karl Barth may well be right when he declares that there can be no real dogmatics without polemics. But no Christian theologian is exempt from the biblical command to speak the truth in love. For truth spoken without love—in harshness, anger or arrogance—will, like a boomerang, return to the speaker with vengeance.

Finally, I've been greatly impressed by Roger's courage to stand forth "against the stream" when required by conscience and conviction to do so. Some theologians are just cantankerous by nature and always seem to take the contrarian point of view. Not so Roger Nicole.

---

[2]*Founder's Journal* 33 (1998): 24-35.

By disposition, experience and training, he is a mainstream theologian who seeks to work in a consensual manner within the orthodox Christian tradition. But there are times when he has felt compelled to stand apart from colleagues, friends and constituencies in the service of a greater truth.

Let me mention just three examples. Roger is an egalitarian in his views on women in ministry and gender-inclusive language for human beings. That many conservative Christians have difficulty distinguishing radical feminism from evangelical egalitarianism he regards as a serious flaw. Thus, he supports Christians for Biblical Equality as a hopeful renewal movement within the evangelical church. Second, Roger Nicole is a Reformed Baptist who is happy to work closely with Presbyterians without accepting the logic (or illogic) of their pedobaptism. Indeed, Roger has become an important voice and influence among the growing number of Baptists who understand the Reformed roots of the Baptist tradition and want to recover the sovereignty of God in salvation, worship and the Christian life. While still a student in France, Roger came under the influence of Dr. Ruben Saillens, a convinced Baptist and a disciple of Charles Haddon Spurgeon. Roger once called him the most spiritual man he had ever known. On one occasion, Saillens said to Roger, "Nicole, why don't you get baptized? Here what counts is grace, not race." The fact that his beloved brother and theological mentor, Jules-Marcel Nicole, had also received baptism as a believer in Jesus doubtless influenced Roger's own acceptance of the baptistic position.

And, finally, although Roger has not participated personally in the Evangelicals and Catholics Together dialogue, he did endorse "The Gift of Salvation," a 1997 statement signed by Roman Catholic and evangelical theologians. Among other things, this statement declared that "justification is not earned by any good works or merits of our own. . . . In justification, God, on the basis of Christ's righteousness alone, declares us to be no longer his rebellious enemies but his forgiven friends, and by virtue of his declaration it is so." This document further stated, "We understand that what we here affirm is in agreement with what the Reformation traditions have meant by justification by faith alone (*sola fide*)." Nicole recognized that this statement was only one step in a long process of dialogue between Roman Catholics and Evangelicals. No theologian in North America is better acquainted with Reformation theology than Roger Nicole. He knows very well that major differences remain between Rome and the Reformation. But, in the footsteps of the Reformers themselves, Roger recognizes a proper place for an ecumenism of conviction. To pursue such a dialogue on the basis of biblical authority is not a sign of compromise but of faithfulness to the gospel itself.

Near the end of his life, Karl Barth likened the theologian's vocation to that of the donkey who was pressed into service as the beast of burden that carried Jesus to the cross. Roger Nicole has lived out this high calling—which indeed is sometimes a burden—with a sense of deep-welled joy, the burdensome joy of one who knows that the precious cargo he bears is the Savior of the world.

general introduction

Frank A. James III

The analytic philosopher A. J. Ayer argued that a strong case could be made that of the world religions, Christianity was the worst. He based his judgment on the fact that Christianity rests on the "allied doctrines of original sin and vicarious atonement," which, he added, "are intellectually contemptible and morally outrageous."[1] Ayer was right about one thing—historic orthodox Christianity does rest in a profound sense on these twin foundations. Ronald Wallace asserts, "The death of Christ was central to the thinking of the New Testament writers about God, man and life itself. It was the cross they spoke about first of all in the summary of the Gospel. It was toward the cross they turned to experience the power of God, the forgiveness of sins and newness of life."[2] Ayer is right about another thing: these doctrines are contemptible and outrageous to the outsider. If Christ's atonement is still powerful enough to excite the antipathy of A. J. Ayer, it is a reminder of the apostle Paul's warning that the cross is a "stumbling block" to unbelievers. It also demonstrates that the atonement is still a worthy topic of serious reflection.

This book centers on one of Ayer's outrageous doctrines—the atonement. And there is, indeed, an outrageous aspect to the atonement because it revolves around such disquieting concepts as death, blood sac-

---

[1]A. J. Ayer, *The Guardian*, August 30, 1979, cited by J. R. W. Stott, *The Cross of Christ* (Downers Grove, Ill.: InterVarsity Press, 1986), 43.
[2]Ronald Wallace, *The Atoning Death of Christ* (Westchester, Ill.: Crossway, 1981), 63.

rifice, guilt, sin, wrath and propitiation. With such notions in view, the thoughtful Christian might ask: Why must God employ such distasteful means to effect salvation? The atonement is further complicated by the idea of substitution. How can a just God permit the innocent to substitute for the guilty? The truth of the matter is that it has proven difficult for Christian theologians to adequately probe the full depth of the meaning of this doctrine within a single all-encompassing theory. Hence, there has been considerable diversity among Christians down through the ages—a diversity that, as a practical matter, has often relegated the idea of the atonement to the academic ivory tower, in part because for the average Christian it was, as it were, too hot to handle. Even for theologians this doctrine has resisted domestication. It is complex and multifaceted and has therefore defied Christian consensus.

The contributors to this volume are among the ablest theologians working today. Most of our contributors have some association with Dr. Nicole—most have worked with him as a colleague and know him personally; others know him by reputation. This group represents something of the wide swath of Christian scholarship, from North America and Europe (United States, France, Canada, England and Scotland) as well as a diversity of ecclesiological traditions—Anglican, Presbyterian, Southern Baptist, Evangelical Free and Dutch Reformed. The national and denominational variety is itself a measure of Nicole's enduring legacy. Because of this variety, there will inevitably be differences of academic opinion, but the primary goal is not unanimity but a reminder to readers that this is a topic worthy of vigorous discussion. Better than anyone we know, Dr. Nicole knows "How to Deal with Those Who Differ from Us," as he titled one of his essays. Most importantly, it was judged that above all we must carefully consider the biblical dimensions of this doctrine—even where there are different theological perspectives informing the exegesis. This biblical concern lies at the center of this book.

In carrying out this goal, the editors intend in this volume, insofar as it is possible, to reconnoiter the outer perimeters as well as some of the inner workings of this doctrine from three angles: the Bible, church history and the Christian life. In the opinion of the editors, too many biblical scholars engage in exegesis without any sense of the historical context or the theological developments. To remedy that, this book approaches the topic of atonement from multiple perspectives in an effort to get a better grasp of the idea of atonement. Of course, there are many other theological contributions to the doctrine of the atonement that we could have considered—Schleiermacher and Ritschl are but two that come to mind. But due to space limitations, we have had to make choices in our coverage. The book that follows is structured around these three foci.

If one is to honor Roger Nicole and at the same time appreciate the atonement, one first must turn to the Scriptures. He would never forgive us if we did not begin with the Book of Books. It is evident that the language and the idea of the cross is central to the biblical message of Christ. One finds various metaphors employed to communicate the essential message that Christ died for sinners. It is one thing to read the Scriptures; it is another to interpret them aright. We agree with Dr. Nicole that theology is best conceived in community and thus to do it correctly entails an ongoing dialogue not only with each other but also with theologians of the past. Theological forebears offer us not only a range of interpretations of the cross but also some sense of perspective. To gain wisdom from the past, we must interact with the best insights of our predecessors.

Reading the Scriptures and gaining insight through a dialogue with history still does not address application to the individual Christian life. Apprehending the truth is not always the same thing as internalizing it. To fail to internalize the atonement in one's own life, both behind and in front of the Sunday morning pulpit is to fail at a crucial point. If the atonement is rightly understood, it must have a practical and personal significance. Moreover, the atonement belongs in the evangelical pulpit, and if it is as valuable as we think it is, it must be preached in the church. We fundamentally agree that the aim of all theology is a changed life—or, as Martin Bucer, the Alsacian Reformer of the sixteenth century and John Calvin's mentor, put it so well nearly five hundred years ago: "True theology is not theoretical or speculative, but active and practical. For it is directed toward . . . a godly life. . . . It is theology's aim . . . that we shall ever more firmly trust in God and live a life that is increasingly holy and more serviceable in love toward our neighbor."[3]

---

[3] Herman J. Selderhuis, *Marriage and Divorce in the Thought of Martin Bucer*, trans. J. Vriend and Lyle Bierma (Kirksville, Mo.: Thomas Jefferson University Press at Truman State University, 1999), 356.

Perhaps the reason the atonement has fallen on hard times is that most Christians have not understood well its meaning or its significance for their personal lives. Somehow we have lost the connection and interest in one of the basic questions for Christians—namely, why did Jesus have to die on the cross? Was it a defeat or a triumph? The editors believe that to understand the atonement is to gain a deeper understanding of Christ and his salvation and that such an understanding will enrich the Christian life immeasurably.

The doctrine of the atonement strikes a very deep chord in Dr. Nicole's Swiss heart because he believes it lies at the center of the gospel. He would echo the words of Stephen Neill, who stated: "The death of Christ is the central point in history."[4] The doctrine of the atonement is like a pebble dropped into a theological pond—it makes ripples throughout the entire system. Historically, systematic theology has tended to understand the atonement as part of the priestly work of Christ. As our priest, Christ is our representative with God, and his special responsibility is to act on behalf of the people of God to bring them near to God. The atoning work of the great high priest is viewed from various angles in the New Testament. It may be viewed in terms of Christ's sacrifice—that he paid the penalty of death for us; or his propitiation—that he removed the wrath of God from us; or his reconciliation—that he overcame our separation from God; or his redemption—that he redeemed us from our bondage to sin. But the atonement also must be connected with its implications for soteriology. In the words of Leon Morris, "The crucifixion is rightly understood only when it is seen as God's great saving act."[5] Thus, in the panoramic view of the priestly work of Christ, not only is redemption accomplished for the people of God, but it also provides the only foundation for the application of redemption in terms of calling, regeneration, justification, adoption, sanctification and glorification.[6]

It is no wonder that theologians have waxed eloquent about the centrality of the atonement. Few, however, have reached the rhetorical heights of Emil Brunner, who said that the atonement "is the Christian

---

[4]Stephen Neill, "Jesus and History," in *Truth of God Incarnate*, ed. E. M. B. Green (London: Hodder & Stoughton, 1977), 80.

[5]Leon Morris, *The Atonement: Its Meaning and Significance* (Downers Grove, Ill.: InterVarsity Press, 1983), 11.

[6]John Murray, *Redemption Accomplished and Applied* (Grand Rapids: Eerdmans, 1955), 80-81.

religion itself; it is the main point; it is not something alongside of the center; it is the substance and kernel, not the husk."[7] To this sentiment Roger Nicole would add his hearty "Amen." And so it is that we, his colleagues and admirers, pay tribute to our friend and mentor with a book dedicated not only to Roger but to one of his favorite doctrines.

---

[7]Emil Brunner, *The Mediator* (Philadelphia: Westminster Press, 1947), 40.

abbreviations

AB	Anchor Bible
AnBib	Analecta biblica
Ant.	*Jewish Antiquities* (Josephus)
AThR	*Anglican Theological Review*
AUSS	*Andrews University Seminary Studies*
B.J.	*Bellum judaicum* (Josephus)
BECNT	Baker Exegetical Commentary on the New Testament
BNTC	Black's New Testament Commentaries
CBQ	*Catholic Biblical Quarterly*
CBC	Cambridge Bible Commentary
CO	*Calvini opera*
CTJ	*Calvin Theological Journal*
CTQ	*Concordia Theological Quarterly*
EKKNT	Evangelisch-katholischer Kommentar zum Neuen Testament
EQ	*Evangelical Quarterly*
ET	English Translation
EuroJTh	*European Journal of Theology*
ExpTim	*Expository Times*
HNTC	Harper's New Testament Commentary
ICC	International Critical Commentary
JBL	*Journal of Biblical Literature*
JECS	*Journal of Early Christian Studies*
JSNTSup	Journal for the Study of the New Testament: Supplement Series
JETS	*Journal of the Evangelical Theological Society*
JTS	*Journal of Theological Studies*
LQ	*Lutheran Quarterly*
LW	*Luther's Works*
NCBC	New Century Bible Commentary
NIGTC	New International Greek Testament Commentary
NICNT	New International Commentary on the New Testament
NIDOTTE	*New International Dictionary of Old Testament Theology and Exegesis*

NPNF[1]	*Nicene and Post-Nicene Fathers*, series 1
NSBT	New Studies in Biblical Theology
NT	New Testament
NTC	New Testament Commentary (Baker)
OT	Old Testament
OTL	Old Testament Library
RTR	*Reformed Theological Review*
SP	Sacra pagina
TNTC	Tyndale New Testament Commentaries
TZ	*Theologische Zeitschrift*
VT	*Vetus Testamentum*
WA	*D. Martin Luthers Werke: Kritische Gesamtausgabe*
WBC	Word Biblical Commentary
WMANT	Wissenschaftliche Monographien zum Alten und Neuen Testament
WTJ	*Westminster Theological Journal*

PART I

ATONEMENT IN THE
OLD AND NEW TESTAMENTS

Charles E. Hill

What can a man give in exchange for his soul?" This provocative question, posed by Jesus himself in Matthew 16:26, epitomizes the dilemma that in one form or another has plagued human hearts in every generation. Scripture tells us that all men and women, having a "sense of God" (Ps 19:1-4; Rom 1:19-20) and knowing that their lives are owed to their Creator (Rom 1:21, 25, 32), also know themselves to be offenders against his holy law (Rom 1:32). Separated from God by their sins (Is 59:2), yet their persistent, natural tendency is not to repent but to "suppress the truth by their wickedness" (Rom 1:18). What is left to the sinner but "a fearful expectation of judgment and of raging fire that will consume the enemies of God" (Heb 10:27)? "If you, O LORD, kept a record of sins, O Lord, who could stand?" asks the psalmist, remembering the depths of his despair (Ps 130:3). Yet in the next verse he speaks from the joy of his salvation and exults, "But with you there is forgiveness; therefore you are feared." The Bible brings to humanity the marvelous good news that God, though he is a holy Creator and a righteous Judge, forgives transgressions! Consistently and emphatically, it teaches that forgiveness is due to God's mercy, his own compassionate love for those whom he redeems. "As a father has compassion on his children, so the LORD has compassion on those who fear him" (Ps 103:13).

Since the Bible reveals a God who is merciful, some have concluded that there is no need for an "act of atonement" per se, an act that by its performance can turn aside God's righteous judgment on sin and regain his favor or acceptance. That one should merely "repent and believe in the gospel" is the New Testament call (Mk 1:15; cf. Acts 2:38; 16:31; 1 Jn 5:10), and this cannot be conceived of in any way as a work of "atonement" on the part of the believer. Many therefore do not regard even Jesus' death as an "atonement" for sins, certainly not as an offering made to satisfy God's justice that sins be paid for. Thomas Chubb, in *True Gospel of Jesus Christ Vindicated* (1739), gave voice to Enlightenment sentiments that still resonate with many "moderns" and "postmoderns" (see chapter eighteen below) at the beginning of the twenty-first century, when he wrote that "God's disposition to show mercy . . . arises wholly from his own innate goodness or mercifulness, and not from anything external to him, whether it be the sufferings and death of Jesus Christ or otherwise."[1] And yet, while the Bible stresses the gratuity of God's free grace in forgiving our sin, it also reveals the theological framework for the outflow of this grace, presenting other facets of the truth about how human beings are reconciled to the God we have offended through sin. This is the scriptural doctrine of the atonement—not only *that* he forgives, but also *how* and *on what basis* his mercy is bestowed on the undeserving. And when this full doctrine is comprehended, the necessity of an act of atonement for human sins is seen to be of the greatest possible importance.

Atonement in the Bible

Scripture conceives of humanity, despite being made in God's own image, as fallen in Adam (Gen 3:19; Rom 5:12-14), prone to sin (Gen 6:5), and subject to the judgment of a holy God (Rom 2:5; 3:23; Eph 2:1-3). To the first sinners, God made plain the penalty for transgressing his word: "In the day that you eat of it you shall die" (Gen 2:17). The dreadful sentence is echoed throughout the Hebrew and Greek Scriptures: "The soul that sins shall die" (Ezek 18:4, 20); "The wages of sin is death" (Rom 6:23, cf. 5:12); "Without the shedding of blood there is no forgiveness" (Heb 9:22). Though he is slow to anger, God is yet a just judge (1 Pet 2:23) who will "by no means clear the guilty" (Nahum 1:3, cf. Ex 23:7). That Jesus himself poses the question "What can a man give in exchange for his soul?" clearly implies that some kind of "exchange" is justly required by God. And yet, as the psalmist lamented,

---

[1]Cited from Alister E. McGrath, *Christian Theology: An Introduction* (Oxford and Cambridge, Mass.: Blackwell, 1994), 344.

"Truly no man can ransom himself" (Ps 49:7, cf. Mic 6:6-7). What indeed, then, can a person give in exchange for his or her soul?

We find first and foremost, as if this were a reflexive human response, the phenomenon of sacrifice, not only among the ancient line of biblical patriarchs but throughout many societies. In the covenant graciously established with Abraham and his descendents, particularly in its Mosaic form, God provided an elaborate system of cultic observances, involving the death of animals, for dealing with the sins of his covenant people. While offerings of grain, oil and wine were acceptable as sacrifices of consecration and thanksgiving, to approximate the place of a sinner's death only the lifeblood of an animal, a "clean" and unblemished animal, was permitted to be offered. The symbolic role of the animal's blood was crucial: "I have given it to you to make atonement for yourselves on the altar; it is the blood that makes atonement for one's life," Moses was told in Leviticus 17:11 (cf. Gen 9:4; Heb 9:22). Here and elsewhere is enunciated the principle of substitution that was operative in "sin offerings." For in the institution of these offerings, a ceremony of the "laying on of hands" preceded the slaying of the victim (Lev 4:4, 15, 24, 29, 33, etc.), which is best understood as symbolizing a transference of the sin and guilt of the offerer to his or her substitute (cf. Lev 16:21). A complex structure of sacrifice and ritual—not all by any means set up overtly to deal with sin—was instituted for the tabernacle and temple cultus. Through these rituals, the penitent offender might yet approach God.

Ordinarily, provisions for the individual to make atonement for his or her sin pertained only to unwitting and less serious sins; deliberate and more heinous sins could only be atoned for once a year, in the high priest's work on the Day of Atonement (Lev 16:16, 34). In the regulations for the Day of Atonement, the laying on of hands is explicitly mentioned only with regard to the "scapegoat," the goat that "bore" the people's sins away into the wilderness (Lev 16:21-22). But this element of the ceremony no doubt pertained also to the goat that was slaughtered, because both it and the bull sacrificed for the priest's sins were "sin offerings" (Lev 16:11, 15), regulations concerning which already included the laying on of hands to signify transference of guilt (Lev 4:4, 15, 24, 29, 33). The two goats must be considered together as "in reality one sacrificial object; the distribution of suffering death and of dismissal into a remote place simply serving the purpose of clearer expression, in visible form, of the removal of sin after expiation had been made, something which the ordinary sacrificial animal could not well express, since it died in the process of expiation."[2]

As centrally important as Israel's sacrificial system was, it could not by itself comprehend every aspect of humanity's dependent situation with respect to God. Alongside this cultic program for dealing with individual and corporate sin in Israel, the special covenant arrangement for the nation bound it up with its acquisition of, and tenure in, the land of promise (beginning with Gen 12:1, 7). Israel's possession of this covenant blessing came about through a national deliverance from slavery in Egypt. It was maintained through numerous acts of divine deliverance from the hand of Israel's enemies. It was lost in the painful judgment of exile and then re-established through a marvelous restoration to the land. Each of these great episodes in covenant history not only formed the national-religious consciousness for future generations but also served to expand the biblical vocabulary of atonement. The exodus was the redemption of an enslaved people from their oppression (Ex 20:2, etc.). The retention of sovereignty and blessing in the land involved the interposition of judges and kings, who delivered Israel through the conquest of God's enemies, and of prophets, who executed God's legal lawsuit against his own rebellious people (Mic 6:2, etc.). The exile was seen as (among other things) the payment of a debt to the covenant-keeping God, and restoration from Babylonian captivity signaled an end to that temporal punishment (Is 40:1-2; Jer 16:18). Without prejudicing the importance of the sacrificial system for dealing with sin, each of these great historical experiences taught Israel something more about the reconciliation of sinners to God. Each would also contribute to explaining the ultimate act of atonement when it arrived.

With respect to the sacrificial system itself, despite its centrality and the utter solemnity of its proceedings, the awakened consciousness was aware that such external offerings of the blood of bulls, goats, rams and lambs were not in the deepest spiritual sense adequate and could not ultimately be effectual (Ps 40:6; Mic 6:6-7; Heb 10:4). In the first place, these sacrifices could not appease God while the heart of the

---

[2]Geerhardus Vos, *Biblical Theology: Old and New Testaments* (Grand Rapids: Eerdmans, 1977, reprint of 1948 original), 163. See also chapters 1 and 3 below.

worshiper remained rebellious (1 Sam 15:22). Second, the truly penitent knew that there must be a deeper, condign basis for God's forgiveness of human beings, made in his image (Gen 1:26; 9:6), than the blood
of mere beasts, humanity's servants. "Truly no man can ransom himself, or give to God the price of his life, for the ransom of his life is
costly, and can never suffice, that he should continue to live on for ever,
and never see the Pit" (Ps 49:7-9 RSV). The reality of inward cleansing,
through broken and contrite hearts, continued to be experienced by the
forgiven even while the mystery of atonement was, in a sense, held at
bay. The basis for atonement with a just and exacting God, who would
by no means clear the guilty, was left in the impenetrable heights of
God's own mercy.

In the great prophecy of Isaiah, however, a momentous step in rev-
elational clarity was taken. Prior to this there were strands in the law
and poetical books (e.g., Ps 22), which had extolled the role of the righteous sufferer. But this suffering was not delineated clearly in terms of
redemption, least of all in the redemption of another. In Isaiah 40—45
an enigmatic "Servant of the Lord" is heralded, a figure who is explicitly compared to a "lamb led to the slaughter"; of whom it is said that
he "was wounded for our transgressions, he was bruised for our iniquities, upon him was the chastisement that made us whole, and with
his stripes we are healed" (Is 53:5). On him "the LORD has laid . . . the
iniquity of us all" (Is 53:10). But the question posed by the Ethiopian
eunuch centuries later, "About whom, pray, does the prophet say this,
about himself or about someone else?" (Acts 8:34), has puzzled interpreters from the first. Some in antiquity attempted, as some still do today, to identify the Servant with king Hezekiah or with some other figure from Israel's past, or, in some mysterious way, with the nation of
Israel itself. But so far no convincing evidence exists of a Jewish (non-
Christian) identification of the Servant as a suffering messiah.[3] But the
difficulties produced by those interpretations were many, and the
question received no satisfactory answer throughout the remainder of

---

[3]*Targum Jonathan* on Isaiah 52:13 identifies him as the Messiah but shifts all the references of
his suffering to the Gentiles! See Samson H. Levey, *The Messiah: An Aramaic Interpretation*
(Cincinnati, Ohio: Hebrew Union College Press, 1974), 63-67. The targumist may have been
reacting against Christian interpretations of Isaiah 53; see John J. Collins, *The Scepter and the
Star: The Messiahs of the Dead Sea Scrolls and Other Ancient Literature* (New York: Doubleday,
1995), 123-26.

Israel's experience in the period documented in the Old Testament.

The enigma stood until the fifteenth year of the Roman emperor Tiberius, when the word of God came to a Jewish preacher of repentance in the region of the Jordan (Lk 3:1). As he saw Jesus of Nazareth approaching, the prophet John was moved to cry out, "Look, the Lamb of God, who takes away the sin of the world!" (Jn 1:29, 36). The mystery hidden for ages then began its glorious unfolding. Amid several intimations to his disciples that he would soon suffer at the hands of the authorities and be killed, Jesus himself gave this indication of the meaning of his coming death: "The Son of man did not come to be served, but to serve, and to give his life as a ransom for many (ἀντὶ πολλῶν)" (Mt 20:28, par. Mk 10:45). Thus, Jesus answers his own otherwise unanswerable question, "What can a man give in exchange for (ἀντάλλαγμα) his soul?" (Mt 16:26 par. Mk 8:37). The implied answer is that a man can give nothing—but the Son of man came to give his own soul as the ransom, in exchange for the souls of many others! It is Jesus, the "Son of man," God's appointed sin-bearing Lamb, who would be Isaiah's Servant of the Lord, the one who "bore our iniquities," on whom the Lord would lay the iniquity of us all! The shedding of Jesus' blood occurred not merely to demonstrate the heinousness of sin, or to give us an example of self-giving (or of the renunciation of violence), or even simply to remind us of the depths of divine love (1 Jn 4:9; Rev 1:5). Jesus told his disciples that his blood would be "poured out for many (περὶ πολλῶν) for the forgiveness of sins" (Mt 26:28)[4]—it was the sacrifice required by a holy God to effect his people's forgiveness. It was part of what Paul passed on to the Corinthians as of "first importance: that Christ died for (ὑπέρ) our sins according to the Scriptures" (1 Cor 15:3; cf. Gal 1:4, etc.).

Thus the far-reaching meaning of Jesus' betrayal by his own people and his crucifixion—a form of execution that signified not simply human shame but supremely God's curse (Deut 21:23; Gal 3:13)—became clear. For ultimately, "it was the LORD's will to crush him" (Is 53:10). What happened to him is what God's "power and will had decided beforehand should happen" (Acts 4:28; cf. Acts 2:23; 3:18).

Thus too, the old and otherwise insoluble mystery of God's forgiving

---

[4]The three sayings of Jesus (Mt 16:26; 20:28; 26:28, par. Mk 8:37; 10:45; 14:24) form a nexus, demonstrating that the "ransom" indeed had to do with sin.

sins while an adequate atonement was outstanding was finally answered. For as the apostle Paul explains it, it was God himself who put Jesus forth to be our propitiation through his blood: "This was to show God's righteousness, because in his divine forbearance he had passed over former sins; it was to prove at the present time that he himself is righteous and that he justifies him who has faith in Jesus" (Rom 3:25 RSV). The inadequacy of the entire system of animal sacrifice is now fully acknowledged and its temporary function explained: God had "passed over former sins" until the proper and fully acceptable propitiation could at last be put forward. That propitiation was in the blood of Jesus, which Jesus himself said would be "poured out for the forgiveness of sins" (Mt 26:28; cf. Acts 20:28; Rom 5:9; Tit 2:14), and its benefits are received by the sinner through faith. God's own righteousness in requiring and obtaining satisfaction of his righteous demand for payment is thus also vindicated. The fact that sins were ultimately "paid for" by no means reduces redemption to a mere "financial transaction," nor does it detract from redemption's gracious character. For it is God himself who put forth Jesus to be the new "mercy seat," an act that on his part was entirely free, compassionate and gracious: "They are now justified by his grace as a gift" (Rom 3:24 NRSV; cf. 4:4; 5:15-16).[5]

It is easy to see why the New Testament's reflections on the atoning work of Christ are so astonishingly rich and complex. No single description, whether by metaphor or by plain speech, can comprehend the fullness of the revelation of what God has done in Christ in reconciling the world to himself. Humanity's collective relationship as well as each person's individual relationship to God are necessarily multifaceted, and, as we have seen, the history of redemption introduced specific elements (notably the sacrificial system and the deliverance from slavery and captivity) that continue as modes for conceiving of the full biblical message of the atonement. Because of this, the New Testament's several categories of expression concerning atonement should not be seen (as they often are in modern writers) as competing against one another, or as resulting in a hodge-podge of undeveloped ideas. Not only does each have its own significance, but some are closely intertwined, and most grow naturally out of God's historical dealings with Israel. The *sacrificial* realm, of course, accounts for much

---

[5]See chapter 6 below.

of the Bible's atonement language. Because of the uniqueness of his person, Jesus is both the Great High Priest who offers the sacrifice and the pure and spotless sacrifice itself (Jn 1:29, 36; Heb 9:11-12; 1 Pet 1:19; Rev 5:6, 9) that alone can finally purify the conscience of the sinner (Heb 9:14; 1 Pet 2:24). As such, he is both the expiation that covers sin (Heb 2:17) and the propitiation that turns away God's holy anger (Rom 3:25; 1 Jn 2:1-2; cf. Rom 1:18; 2:5-10; Eph 2:3; 5:6).

God's great acts of delivering his people from Egyptian slavery and from Babylonian captivity form the background to the death of Christ as a *ransom* that secures the release of the individual sinner, conceived of as a slave, a condemned prisoner or a debtor (Mk 10:45; Lk 24:24; Tit 2:14; Rev 1:5; 5:9). Because death is originally and above all a punishment for sin (Gen 2:17), and because humanity's fall came through the instigation of the devil (Gen 3:1-7), Christ's vicarious experience of the curse of death for his people, together with his glorious resurrection (1 Cor 15:14; Rom 4:25; 8:33-34), represents also a *conquest* of sin (Heb 9:26), death (1 Cor 15:21, 26; Rev 1:18), and the devil on their behalf (Heb 2:14-15; 1 Jn 3:8; Rev 12:11). This one death is also the *legal satisfaction* made in the law court of God to dispel the charges that stood against us as transgressors (Rom 3:24-25, 5:9; 8:33-34; Rev 12:10-11). Due to all these factors, Christ's death is *reconciliation*, the bridging of the sin-induced separation between God and those whom he made in his likeness (Rom 5:10-11; 11:15; 1 Cor 7:11; 2 Cor 5:18-20, etc.).

Another key aspect of New Testament atonement theology is that it is dependent upon the spiritual union that exists between Christ and his people. This union involves both representation and substitution (recognizing the former does not eliminate the latter). Christ's death is accepted in place of the redeemed, as their substitute (Mk 10:45; 1 Pet 2:24; 3:18). And yet they have also been "crucified with Christ" (cf. Rom 6:6; Gal 2:20), for he is also their representative. Because we have died with him and been raised with him, we must henceforth consider ourselves dead to sin and alive to righteousness (Rom 6:11; 1 Pet 2:24). This is a union foreshadowed in the identification between the offerer and the victim in the OT cultus (substitution), by which the latter symbolically took the place of the former. It was also operative in the identification of the high priest with the people (representation), by which it was allowed that he could represent them all in making atonement. A unique aspect of the believer's union with Christ is that while Christ serves as both our substitute and our representative, this does not eventuate in any moral passivity on the part of those he redeems. For he is also our leader and master, whom we seek to follow and imitate in order to be conformed to his likeness even in his sufferings (Rom 8:17; Phil 2:5-8.; 3:10; 1 Pet 2:21).

The Biblical Essays in This Book
The essays that follow seek to provide responsible and relevant exegesis of many of the chief scriptural passages that explain the wonderful atonement Christ has wrought through his death and resurrection.

Emile Nicole, nephew of the honoree of this volume, writes on atonement in the Pentateuch. He focuses his exegetical and theological discussion on Leviticus 17:11, a critical verse wherein God explains why the blood of animals was not to be eaten with their flesh, "for the life of a creature is in the blood, and I have given it to you to make atonement for yourselves on the altar; it is the blood that makes atonement for one's life." In recent decades, this "cornerstone of the Christian doctrine of substitutionary atonement" has been subjected to a variety of interpretations, often tending to downplay or eliminate the concept of substitution from this verse and from OT atonement theology in general. Dr. Nicole patiently assesses these newer developments and furnishes a valuable discussion of the important Hebrew term *kipper*.

In "Atonement in Psalm 51: 'My Sacrifice, O God, Is a Broken Spirit,'" *Bruce Waltke* examines what is often called "the Great Penitential Psalm," associated with David's repentance after the sin regarding Bathsheba and Uriah. Several penitential psalms, and this one in particular, are often seen as problematic to Christian theology because they appear to present a view of atonement that runs quite counter to the ceremonial norms of the Pentateuch. Dr. Waltke finds such an analysis lacking in that it fails to take seriously this psalm's form as a lament for public and grievous sin. He walks the reader through the sections of David's spiritual reflection on his experience of reconciliation to God in this psalm.

"Atonement in Isaiah 53: 'For He Bore the Sins of Many'" by *Alan Groves* considers the well-known passage from Isaiah's prophecy, Isaiah 52:13 to 53:12, a passage which became crucial for early Christian reflection on the significance of Christ's death. Groves takes up the controversial question of what is meant by "bearing guilt" and "carrying sin" in Isaiah 53:11-12. The importance of the question demands the kind of thorough grammatical and syntactical study Groves gives to it, which the advanced student and scholar will find most useful. The result of Groves's research is a fresh perspective on this fundamental atonement text. Purification by atonement, Groves says, is "central to the concern of the entire book" of Isaiah, and chapter 53 unveils a purification by atonement which is new and radical because it is to secure a purification that is not simply temporary and in need of repetition but once for all and permanent; because it is to be effective not just for Israel but for the nations as well, being the basis for a "new covenant" and a new exodus from sin; and because it will be effected by a single, righteous Israelite and will be accomplished through his suffering.

Royce Gruenler examines the Synoptic Gospels and Acts, setting their relatively few atonement-specific texts in their redemptive-historical context. In the drama of the Gospels, Jesus the Messiah has to undergo probationary tests to show himself qualified as the redeemer of God's people. He reenacts not only the exodus conquest but, as the ultimate son of Adam, also rights the actions of the first Adam, bringing about a new access to God the Father, poignantly symbolized by the rending of the veil in the temple. Gruenler moves through Mark's narrative, highlighting the "atoning invasionary warfare" of the Messiah, the Plunderer of Satan's goods, a warfare that culminates in his advance into Jerusalem, ironically hostile to its Savior King.

According to *J. Ramsey Michaels* in "Atonement in John's Gospel and Epistles: 'The Lamb of God Who Takes Away the Sin of the World,'" the accent in the Gospel of John is on "salvation positively as the giving of eternal life, not negatively as repentance or the forgiveness of sins. In itself, the Gospel of John has no explicit theology of the atonement." That is, while it is clear that Christ alone saves and that he does so by laying down his life for his sheep (Jn 10:11, 15; 15:12), it is not as clear how or on what basis he does this. Such "gaps" left by the gospel, however, are fortunately filled in by 1 John and the rest of the New Testament, which must be read along with the Fourth Gospel. In 1 John we learn that Christ's death is both an expiation for sin and a propitiation of God. The controversial passage in 1 John 2:2 is treated in a way that is very sensitive exegetically and theologically, and with a personal reflection on the author's friendship with Roger Nicole himself.

In "Atonement in Romans 3:21-26: 'God Presented Him as a Propitiation,'" *D. A. Carson* examines ten "turning-points" in the exegesis of this foundational Pauline passage that has become a focus in recent attempts to reconfigure the understanding of the atonement. The discussion is carried out with particular reference to the "new perspective" on Paul associated with scholars such as E. P. Sanders, J. D. G. Dunn, and N. T. Wright. These and others have sought to interpret Paul's thought on atonement as having more to do with membership in God's covenant people than with the plight of the guilty sinner called before the judgment seat of a just and holy God. The "newer" perspective has tended to mute, redefine or abolish notions of wrath, substitution, propitiation and justification that have traditionally made up much of the vocabulary of atonement in Christian thought. Carson's careful, nuanced and well-informed treatment provides needed guidance on this and related passages.

The substantial article by *Richard Gaffin*, "Atonement in the Pauline Corpus: 'The Scandal of the Cross,'" is also very much engaged with discussions of atonement in contemporary Pauline scholarship. Professor Gaffin demonstrates the importance, in the current climate more especially, of recognizing Paul's teaching on sin and the wrath of God for understanding the significance of Christ's death. Sin is relational (against God's holy and righteous person) and, Gaffin writes, "sin is also illegal." That is, it is inherently a violation of God's self-expressed will, making the issue unavoidably a legal or "penal" one. In keeping with the personal nature of sin, God's wrath against sin too is personal and not merely a mechanistic appendage or by-product of sin, nor can it be reduced to mere metaphor. This likewise has repercussions for understanding the significance of Christ's death "for us" and "for our sins." In the face of a widespread reluctance on the part of many interpreters to follow Paul, Dr. Gaffin seeks to allow to the apostle's "scandal of the cross" its rightful and salutary, scandalizing power.

In "Atonement in Hebrews: 'A Merciful and Faithful High Priest,'" *Simon Kistemaker* begins with a consideration of the word ἱλάσκεσθαι in Hebrews 2:17, referring to the seminal studies of C. H. Dodd, Roger Nicole, and Leon Morris. Though in the end he translates the word "to expiate" and not "to propitiate" because the direct object in this case is sin, not God, Kistemaker shows how both concepts are bound up in the word as used by the author of Hebrews. In his exposition of Hebrews 5:7 Kistemaker offers a penetrating look at the sufferings of Christ in the last days of his earthly life. He explains how the author of Hebrews ties together strands from many Gospel passages in his reflections on the meaning of Christ's high-priestly work.

Dan G. McCartney examines atonement in James, Peter and Jude. The letters of James, Jude and 2 Peter do not concern themselves overtly with the atonement, but McCartney shows how in their allusions to the subject they concur with Christian tradition expressed elsewhere. 1 Peter, however, "is dense with allusions to and applications of the atonement wrought by Jesus Christ," writes McCartney, who finds five major aspects of atonement in 1 Peter. First Peter's teaching on the atonement is occasioned by, and geared to, the practical concern of Christian suffering. Thus, Peter returns time and time again to the presentation of the suffering servant of the Lord in Isaiah 53 because he "finds the solution to the problem of Christian suffering in identification with Christ's atoning suffering."

In "Atonement in the Apocalypse of John: 'A Lamb Standing As If Slain,'" *Charles E. Hill* considers how the book of Revelation presents atonement theology by way of vision and interpretation. The chief image for atonement teaching in Revelation is the startling figure of the Slain Lamb, which also happens to be the main title for Jesus Christ in the book. "In the imagery of John's Revelation," writes Hill, "sin is portrayed in several of its horrible effects, as bondage or captivity, as incalculable debt, as defilement and as incurring legal guilt. Yet all of these aspects of sin's vicious craft are resolved for the sinner by the blood of the Lamb." It is noteworthy that Revelation's predominant context for atonement theology is doxology; that is, it occurs in songs or statements of praise to Christ or to the Father for the redemption accomplished by the Lamb for his bride.

atonement in the pentateuch

"It Is the Blood That Makes Atonement for One's Life"

Emile Nicole

In Christian theology the concept of atonement, and more specifically substitutionary atonement, is closely related to the sacrificial practice of Israel. The meaning of rites usually remains implicit in any given cultural system, which leaves open the possibility of various and conflicting interpretations. One well-known passage of Leviticus, however, lifts the corner of the veil,[1] explaining that blood must not be consumed because life is in it and God gave it "on the altar to make an atonement for your lives" (Lev 17:11). This cornerstone of the Christian doctrine of substitutionary atonement has been subject these last decades to a growing tendency to replace the traditional understanding,[2] the most frequent interpretation proposed being

---

[1]"Rarely does the Old Testament subject sacred things to such conscious interpretation," Erhard Gerstenberger, *Leviticus*, OTL (Louisville, Ky.: Westminster John Knox, 1996), 240.

[2]Thirty years ago Jacob Milgrom reacted against an interpretation he judged uniform at the time and advanced the thesis that the blood upon the altar was offered as expiation for the death of the animal itself. To kill an animal for human food would be considered as murder unless such an expiation was presented to free the Israelite from this guilt, "A Prolegomenon to Leviticus 17:11," *JBL* 90 (1971): 149-56. The thesis was adopted by some commentators like Joshua R. Porter, *Leviticus*, CBC (New York: Cambridge University Press, 1976), 139; John H. Hayes, "Leviticus," in *Harper's Bible Commentary* (San Francisco: Harper and Row, 1988), 172; and, consistently, Milgrom himself in the first part of his monumental commentary, *Leviticus 1-16*, AB (New York: Doubleday, 1991), 1,163 pages on chapters 1 to 16, and already 7 pages on the interpretation of Leviticus 17:11 (706-13). Refutation in Rolf Rendtorff, "Another Prolegomenon to Leviticus 17:11," in *Pomegranates and Golden Bells*, Festschr. Jacob Milgrom

that the blood offered upon the altar would be considered as a life force purifying the one offering from the power of death.[3] In this contribution, we intend to examine the main objections raised against the substitutionary interpretation of Leviticus 17:11. The first two sections of this chapter will deal with exegetical and more general theoretical objections. The third part will then examine the key issue of meaning of the verb *kipper* (כִּפֶּר), "to cover."

Exegetical Objections

The translation of the preposition *bêt* (בְּ) in the last part of Leviticus 17:11 in terms of price or exchange (the so-called *bêt* of price: "the blood makes atonement *for* the life"), transmitted by the Septuagint,[4] the Targum and the King James Version,[5] is now abandoned by many modern versions[6] and interpreters in favor of other solutions, like *bêt* of instrument[7] or *bêt* of essence.[8]

To make the question as clear as possible, a substitutionary understanding of the entire verse does not necessarily depend on the trans-

(Winona Lake, Ind.: Eisenbrauns, 1995), 27-28; Adrian Schenker, "Das Zeichen des Blutes und die Gewissheit der Vergebung im Alten Testament. Die sühnende Funktion des Blutes auf dem Altar nach Leviticus 1.10-12," in *Text und Sinn im Alten Testament* (Fribourg: Universitätsverlag, 1991), 174; Richard E. Averbeck, "כִּפֶּר," in *NIDOTTE* 2 (1997): 694-95.

[3]Cf. René Peter-Contesse and John Ellington, *A Handbook on Leviticus*, UBS Handbook Series (New York: United Bible Societies, 1990), 267: "It is because blood carries life that the priest can use it in the ritual of pardoning sins." Truly, in recent commentaries like that of John Hartley, WBC (Dallas: Word Books, 1992), or Erhard Gerstenberger, OTL (Louisville, Ky.: Westminster John Knox, 1996), the substitutionary interpretation is not ruled out, but rather it is associated with the life-force interpretation. Gerstenberger writes: "The background to these blood rites apparently involves legal considerations. Life forfeited through guilt— namely that of the one offering—is redeemed from the warranted punishment through the presentation of the life of another, 'through life it effects atonement' (Lev 17:11) would be the most precise expression of this doctrine. Of course, legal explanation by no means exhausts this phenomenon, since even the late collector of these sacrificial prescriptions is still influenced by ancient, even magical beliefs concerning the efficacy of blood" (242).

[4]Preposition *anti*: τὸ γὰρ αἷμα αὐτοῦ ἀντὶ τῆς ψυχῆς ἐξιλάσεται.

[5]KJV: "it is blood that maketh an atonement for the soul."

[6]Among the main modern translations, NIV: "it is the blood that makes atonement for one's life" and NJB (1985): "blood is what expiates for a life" look like exceptions.

[7]NASB: "it is the blood by reason of the life that makes atonement," RSV: "it is blood that makes atonement by reason of the life."

[8]NEB: "It is blood, that is the life, that makes expiation"; *Living Bible*: "it is blood that makes the atonement because it is life"; NRSV (1993): "for, as life, it is the blood that makes atonement"; the translation in *The JPS Commentary* (*Leviticus*, 1989): "it is blood, as life, that effects expiation." The German modern translation seems to combine *bêt* of essence and of price: "Weil im Blut, das Leben ist, schaft es Sühne für verwirktes Leben" *Die Bibel im heutigen Deutsch* (Stuttgart: Deutsche Bibelgesellschaft, 1982).

lation of this last clause. The two preceding propositions in the first part of the verse, "I have given it to you to make atonement for yourselves on the altar," clearly imply some kind of substitution. Modern interpreters who nevertheless would not attribute a substitutionary force to the preposition *bêt* in the last clause have acknowledged this.[9] But in this case, the substitutionary interpretation would depend on the meaning of the verb *kipper*, something that is not so easily demonstrated, as will be shown in the last part of this study. If the substitutionary meaning of preposition *bêt* in the last clause could be proved possible or more probable, the corresponding meaning of the verb *kipper* would be better substantiated.

Alongside a priori opposition to the concept of substitutionary atonement,[10] one major objection has been raised against the traditional interpretation when used with the verb *kipper*, that is, that the preposition *bêt* always introduces the means by which an action is performed,[11] or, in two instances (Lev 6:23; 16:27), the place where it is performed. Strong support can thus be cited for the majority instrumental understanding of the preposition: "blood makes atonement *by* the life (of the animal)."[12] Such a case can be strengthened by the observation that *bêt-pretii* would not, strictly speaking, support the translation "*for* the life (of the one offering)." The price could only be the life of the animal, not of the worshiper!

Thus, three distinctive arguments can be stated as follows, to which a fourth can be added: (1) an instrumental use of preposition *bêt* is the most frequent; (2) with the verb *kipper*, it is the only convenient option between the two otherwise attested; (3) an appeal to *bêt-pretii* implies a confusion between the price paid and the object acquired by the trans-

---

[9]Especially Baruch Schwartz, "The Prohibitions Concerning the 'Eating' of Blood in Leviticus 17," in *Priesthood and Cult*, ed. Gary A. Anderson and Saul M. Olyan (Sheffield: JSOT Press, 1991), 34-66, who argues very thoroughly to establish the substitutionary meaning of the phrase *kipper ʿal nefeš* (55-59), although he understands the preposition *bêt* as instrumental (47-48).

[10]Cf. the remark of Baruch Schwartz: "It should be noted that one of the reasons scholars have labored so arduously at proposing other interpretations of how blood serves עַל־נַפְשֹׁתֵיכֶם לְכַפֵּר and have often ignored the obvious derivations from כֹּפֶר has been their reluctance to admit that the idea of vicarious sacrifice . . . might be at work here," in ibid., 57.

[11]In sacrificial context: the animal or a part of it, such blood (Num 35:33). In other contexts: present (Gen 32:20), goodness (Prov 16:6).

[12]Cf. NASB: "it is blood that by reason of the life that makes atonement"; John Hartley, *Leviticus*, 261: "it is blood that makes atonement by the life."

action; and (4) the statement "blood atones *for* the life" would merely
duplicate the preceding sentence "I have given it . . . to make an atonement for your souls."

The first two arguments, founded on frequency, speak in terms of
probability. In any given example, without consideration of other possible elements, the preposition *bêt* with the verb *kipper* is very probably
instrumental. But this does not preclude the possibility of other meanings, especially if, in the sentence structure or the immediate context,
there are serious reasons to suspect that the most frequent meaning
would not be appropriate.

The third argument must be considered. In logical terms, the price
ought not to be confused with the object of purchase.[13] Nevertheless,
in contexts of buying or exchanging, biblical Hebrew uses the same
preposition *bêt* not only for the price paid but also for the object acquired. This can be clearly seen in the eighteenth edition of Gesenius's
dictionary, meaning II.5.b: "*for*, to indicate the price as means of purchase (the ‏ב‎ *pretii*). . . inversely, the thing acquired can also be introduce by ‏ב‎."[14] Three of the examples listed are quite convincing: Lamentations 1:11, "they barter their treasures *for* food (‏בְּאֹכֶל‎)"; 2 Samuel
3:27, "he died *for* the blood of Asael";[15] and the famous "life *for* life" in
Deuteronomy 19:21, where the preposition *taḥat* (‏תַּחַת‎) of Exodus
21:23 and Leviticus 24:18 is replaced by *bêt*. Though less clearly, this
particular use is also present in the other important lexicons: *HALOT*,
meaning 17, "price or value" cites also Deuteronomy 19:21; *DCH*,
meaning 10, notes, "at the cost of, at the risk of, in exchange *for*."[16] Several examples are particularly convincing, notably Genesis 29:18 "I'll
work for you seven years *for* Rachel (‏בְּרָחֵל‎)." *BDB* presents the phenomenon in a slightly different way: "cost or price, whether given or
received," meaning number 3.

The reality is somewhat more complex, involving two subjects and

---

[13]Note the confusion in *NIDOTTE* vol. 2, 1997, 697: "*bᵉ* of price, meaning that the blood is the price for ransoming the soul of the person who offers it." It is not the word *blood* (the price) that is introduced by preposition *bêt*, but the soul ransomed by it.
[14]"*Für*, um zum Angabe des Preises als Erwerbsmittel (das herk. ‏ב‎ *pretii*. Umgekehrt, kann auch das zum erwerbende mit ‏ב‎ eingeleitet werden)," *Wilhelm Gesenius Hebräisches und Aramäisches Handwörterbuch über das Alte Testament*, 18ᵉ ed. Udo Rüterswörden, vol. 1, ‏א‎ - ‏ג‎ (Berlin: Springer, 1987).
[15]That is: in exchange for, to pay off the blood debt caused by the death of Asael.
[16]Italics added.

two objects: (1) A gives *x* to B and receives *y* from him, or (2) B receives
x from A and gives him *y* in exchange. When A buys *y* from B, *x* is the
price given by A and received by B, but for A, *y* is not a price received.
In the examples listed above, the preposition *bêt* is not used for *x* but
for *y*, and with A being the explicit or implicit subject. This would also
be the case in Leviticus 17:11. It must also be observed that different
kinds of transactions are considered: purchase, exchange (Lam 1:10),
compensation (Deut 19:21) and even blood revenge (2 Sam 3:27). If this
be the case, is not substitutionary atonement a possibility?

Whatever the problems of grammatical vocabulary, such as *bêt-
pretii*,[17] a substitutionary use of the preposition is rather well documented. The absence of other occurrences of such a construction with
the verb *kipper* is not an insurmountable obstacle. If such a translation
be possible, does a substitutionary use of preposition *bêt* in Leviticus
17:11 become necessary? An instrumental use of the preposition
would create a logical difficulty. The obvious subject of the verb *kipper* is "blood." Therefore, "life" would be an agent of the action. In
this context, "blood" and "life" are so closely related that it can be
said that "life is in the blood" (Lev 17:11) and even "life is blood" (Lev
17:14). That being the case, to state that blood atones *by* life becomes
a tautology.

Some scholars would argue that since life is in the blood (Lev 17:11),
it may be understood as the agent of purification active in the blood
rite: "Blood atones *by* the life *which is in it.*"[18] This inference from "life
is in the blood" nevertheless departs from the common experience that
was probably at the origin of the saying. The life of an animal is in its
blood as long as it is alive. When it dies, life departs from it as the blood
flows out of its body. The same is true of human beings. Blood poured
out, far from being the power of life, is a sign and sometimes the actual
cause of death.[19] Life endangered or lost is very close to death. When

---

[17]Some would prefer beth of exchange, cf. Henri Cazelles, *VT* 8 (1958): 315.

[18]Ibn Ezra comments: "בנפש שיש בו יכפר," *The Commentary of Abraham Ibn Ezra on the Pentateuch*, vol. 3, *Leviticus* (Hoboken, N.J.: Ktav, 1986), כ [53].

[19]"Since bleeding is the way in which slaughtered creatures and murdered humans were seen
to die, this was the most logical way of saying what it was made them to die: the loss of
blood. The statement is no innovation, no great discovery, it is certainly no abstract theological principle or statement of belief. The text is merely trying to make use of a well-known
fact in order to ground its explanation for the prohibition of eating blood" (Schwartz, "Prohibitions Concerning the 'Eating' of Blood," 49-50).

the psalmist complains that his enemies "seek my life," it could be more appropriate to translate: "seek my death," at least in the French language, where *"danger de mort"* (literally: "danger of death") is the exact equivalent of English "danger of life" or German *Lebensgefahr*. With regard to death, the Old Testament is ruthlessly down-to-earth. The first part of verse 11 ("life is in the blood") cannot support a magical interpretation for its last part: the blood of the victim cannot be a power of life to cleanse the worshiper.

Would the proposition be a mere duplication of the preceding one? Two distinctive features differentiate the last proposition from the first part of the sentence: the absence of a personal suffix attached to the word (*nepeš* נֶפֶשׁ), and the prefixed preposition (*bĕ* instead of *'al* [עַל]).

The absence of the suffix endows the statement with a more general nature, which corresponds exactly to the function of the proposition introduced by the causal *ki* (כִּי) It is here that the explanation or confirmation can be found that blood indeed makes atonement for life: "I have given it . . . to make atonement for *your* lives, *because* blood makes atonement for life." The strengthening of the word *blood* by the personal pronoun (*haddām hû'* הַדָּם הוּא), *blood itself, blood indeed*) follows the same intention. The word order of the proposition confirms this interpretation: (1) the subject, which begins the sentence and is reinforced by the pronoun "blood itself"; (2) the complement "for life"; and (3) the verb "makes atonement." If the intention were to stress the power of life active in the blood, the word *life* would have to be found at the beginning: "It is by life that blood makes atonement." On the contrary, there are two clear indications (the priority of the word blood reinforced by the pronoun), which prove that an instrumental understanding of *beth* is an obvious mistake.

But why then the preposition *bĕ* instead of *'al*? The preposition *'al* most commonly accompanies the verb *kipper* to designate the beneficiary of the rite. The uncustomary use of the preposition *bĕ* allows the possibility of the substitutionary nature of the act. Described as the beneficiary in the first part of the verse (preposition *'al*), the life (*nepeš*) of the worshiper is now considered as the object of the substitution: the poured-out life (*dām* דָּם) of the sacrificial victim is substituted *for* the life of the worshiper.

A very strong exegetical case can thus be made for a substitutionary reading of the verse. Nevertheless, several objections have been raised on another level and will be dealt with in the following section.

Theoretical Objections

Notker Füglister has presented a detailed list of objections to a substitutionary reading of this verse.[20] Before each objection is individually examined, the entire list will be summarized.

1. In OT law, sin offering[21] was provided only for unwilling or minor faults, never for a crime that entailed the death penalty. Why then substitute the life of an animal for someone who was not condemned to death?

2. In the performance of sin offerings, there was no rite that symbolized the transfer of sin as on the Day of Atonement when the high priest laid *"both hands* on the head of a live goat and *confessed over him* all the iniquities of the children of Israel" (Lev 16:21).

3. All offerings, and especially sin offerings, were considered as most holy (Num 18:9). How could this be the case if the animal sacrificed were a substitute for the sinner?

4. If substitution was the working principle of sacrifice, how could a simple meal offering be accepted for sin offering (Lev 5:11)?

5. The blood of the animal, rather than its death, was emphasized in the sacrificial rite.

The first of these objections is assuredly the most impressive; an indisputable but often ignored fact. It is surprising that this characteristic limitation of OT sacrificial system remained unnoticed by NT writers who, like the author to the Hebrews, would have had a special interest in pointing out such limitations to highlight the insuperable value of the sacrifice of Jesus.[22] The catalog of the various offenses demanding sin offerings clearly limits them to unwilling or minor offenses.[23] Numbers 15:29-31 plainly states that forgiveness through sacrifice was limited to sins of ignorance, whereas deliberate

---

[20]Notker Füglister, "Sühne durch Blut - Zur Bedeutung von Leviticus 17.11," in *Studien zum Pentateuch*, ed. Georg Braulik (Festschr. Walter Kornfeld; Wien: Herder, 1977), 143-44, 146-47.
[21]הַטָּאת and אָשָׁם.
[22]Sacrifices had to be presented again and again (Heb 10:1-4); all priests were subject to death (Heb 7:23), infected by sin (Heb 7:26-28), etc.
[23]Leviticus 4:1—5:19.

transgressions remained liable to divine revenge or human justice.[24] The well-known example of David confirms these provisions: being guilty of a doubly deadly offense, he could not be permitted to offer any sin offering and could only commit himself to the sole and free mercy of God (Ps 51:18 [16]).

This objection finds its strength in the inequality between the real and the symbolic penalty that would result from a substitutionary understanding of sacrifice: death as a symbol would be out of proportion with the real guilt. Such disproportion appears even more offensive in our present cultural context, where the death penalty is less acceptable and higher value is placed on the life of animals.

First of all, it must be observed that sacrifice does not appear in OT primeval history as a divine command but rather as a human initiative. Abel, without any previous instruction, took the initiative to offer fat portions from the firstborn of his flock (Gen 4:4). After the flood, Noah chose to make burnt offerings from every pure animal (Gen 8:20). This is confirmed by the widespread usage of sacrificial practices throughout the primitive cultures of the world. It was not God who first of all demanded that animals would be killed, but it was man, used to killing animals for food and having the feeling that the death of an animal was not a trivial thing and was somehow related to divinity, who made slaughter an act of worship or at the least linked it to cultic activity. Given this fact, the purpose of sacrificial regulations in the Pentateuch was not to impose sacrificial practice upon a people who previously ignored it but to submit an already existing practice to the proper understanding of the relationship between God and his people.[25] It is in such a perspective that the connection between sin and sacrifice observed in the OT law as well as the surprising disproportion pointed out earlier are to be correctly understood.

The OT connection between sin, remission and sacrifice, considered by the author of the letter to the Hebrews as a typical feature of the system,[26] is modified by a twofold and rather disturbing limitation: the main and most frequent offerings (burnt offerings and fellowship of-

---

[24]One can hesitate over the exact implication of the expression נכרת מקרב עמו, lit. "to be cut off from one's people," but the impropriety of any sacrifice is clearly stated.

[25]This would be carried out both by new dispositions and interpretative comments like Leviticus 17:11.

[26]Cf. Hebrews 9:22: "Without the shedding of blood there is no forgiveness."

ferings)[27] have no precise connection with sin and forgiveness; and the two rather uncommon offerings pertaining to the remission of a specific transgression (the so-called *sin* and *guilt offerings*) only deal with unwilling or minor offenses or with the cleansing of certain severe cases of impurity.[28]

The core of the problem lies with the interpretation of this twofold limitation. Does this mean, as the above objection surmises, that the connection between sin and sacrifice implied by the principle of substitutionary atonement is overestimated or mistaken? There are clues that point in another direction. At least in one case, Leviticus 1:4, the verb *kipper* is used in connection with the holocaust offering. Placed at the beginning of the presentation of the first and most important sacrifice, this unique precision is certainly meaningful. Does it not suggest that all sacrifice, whether or not there be a connection with some particular sin, has to do with sin and forgiveness? This is confirmed by the observation that this unique use of the verb with the holocaust occurs in the same sentence in which the rite of laying one's hand on the head of the animal is mentioned: "He is to lay his hand on the head of the burnt offering and it will be accepted on his behalf to make atonement for him" (Lev 1:4).

There no hint whatsoever that the considerations of Leviticus 17 pertaining to the use of blood in sacrifice and its atoning value were to be limited only to sin offerings.[29] On the contrary, since they were included in the general dispositions relative to the slaughter and eating of animals and they referred to the placing of blood on the altar, a common disposition for all sacrifices,[30] it reveals the atoning aspect present in all sacrifices, be they mandatory or voluntary.

---

[27]The first to be presented in the list of Leviticus 1—7, and the most frequently evoked in historical narratives.

[28]Namely, severe skin disease (Lev 14:10-20), childbirth (Lev 12:6) and pathological discharges (Lev 15:15, 30).

[29]Against Alfred Marx, *Les sacrifices de l'Ancien Testament*, Cahiers Evangile 111 (Paris: Cerf, 2000), 20. On the contrary, Jakob Milgrom (1997, 708-10) argues that Leviticus 17:11 concerns only fellowship offering. This is more in consonance with the context of Leviticus 17 but unduly restrains the scope of a rite that concerns all sacrifices, cf. next note.

[30]Burnt offering (Lev 1:5, 11, 15), fellowship offering (Lev 3:2, 8, 13), sin offering (Lev 4:30), and guilt offering (Lev 5:9). Although the precise handling of the blood differs from one sacrifice to the other: sprinkling against the altar on all sides for the burnt and fellowship offerings, putting on the horns of the altar and pouring the rest at the base for sin offering, sprinkling against the side of the altar and draining the rest at the base for guilt offering, the contact of the blood with the altar is a constant of all sacrifices corresponding with the statement of Leviticus 17:11: "I have given it to you on the altar to make atonement for your lives."

These observations lead us to another understanding of the limitation. Does it not pertain to the symbolic, limited, and, from a Christian point of view, provisional character of the OT system? If the Israelite had been allowed to compensate a capital offence by the blood (life-death) of an animal, would it not have scandalously minimized the gravity of sin and created an illusory confidence in a real efficacy of the sacrifice? The unmerited grace of God's forgiveness would have been reduced to a trivial scale of costs in which the payment of the corresponding sacrificial tax would free the guilty party from all charges. On the contrary, it was precisely unwilling or minor sin that was dealt with by a kind of sacrificial taxation, a reminder that all sin is deadly. The special role of blood in the main sacrifices, which did not pertain to any particular sin, would have reminded all worshipers that they were sinners whose very lives depended on God's forgiveness.

Leviticus 17:11 thus brings to the fore a general principle underlying the whole OT sacrificial system, whose practical carrying out was limited by the concern for the seriousness of sin, the freedom of God's forgiveness and the will not to reduce the moral dimension of human life to the mere repetition of a ritual. The apparent unseemliness signaled by the objection can be well explained in such a way. Having now dealt with Füglister's first objection, the four others will be examined more briefly.

Why would the laying of one sole hand on the head of the sacrificed animal be less impressive or of a different nature than the laying on of both? Laying on of the hand necessarily entails some kind of identification. Füglister claims that the laying on of one hand only meant on the part of the worshiper that the offering was really his own.[31] But who could have doubted that? He brought it personally and would himself put it to death. It may be conceded that, unlike the particular ceremony of the Day of Atonement, where the symbol of the transfer of sin was obvious,[32] the symbolism here was more general. But there can be no doubt that by this gesture the animal was presented as a substitute for the human being who offered it. It must be observed that whereas the confession of sin was made on the head of the famous scapegoat, this was only half of the ritual. A first goat, chosen by lot be-

---

[31]Füglister, "Sühne durch Blut," 146.
[32]Leviticus 16:21: "He [Aaron] is to lay both hands on the head of the live goat and confess over it all the wickedness and rebellion of the Israelites—all their sins—and put them on the goat's head."

tween two, had to be previously slaughtered and offered as a sin offering for the people (Lev 16:15). The scapegoat represented the removal of sin, the sins being symbolically placed on the animal that took them away *into* the desert. It should not be forgotten that the fate of the first goat, "for the Lord" (Lev 16:8), represented, by its slaughtering and the handling of its blood, the atonement of sin through substitution.

Füglister's third objection concerns the flesh of the offerings, which had to be eaten as something *most holy* by the priests and their families (Num 18:10). In response, it must be observed that when the priests were not permitted to eat these same parts of sin-offerings,[33] they had to be taken outside of the camp and burned with the impure parts of the animal, that is, the entrails and the offal (Lev 4:11-12). The characterization of the flesh of these offerings as most holy did not imply that it had nothing to do with sin. This is obvious since they bore the very names of *sin-* and *guilt-*offerings. It pointed out rather that these offerings belonged to God and were only to be eaten by the priests and with proper reverence.[34]

The provision of mere grain as sin offering (Lev 5:11-13) must be put back into proper perspective. It was an exception among exceptions! The normal rate for an ordinary member of the community was a female lamb or goat.[35] If somebody was too poor to afford a lamb, he was permitted to bring two doves or two young pigeons (Lev 5:7). It was only as a last resort, when someone was not even able to present the two birds, that he was allowed to offer fine flour as a sin offering. Once it is admitted that such a substitution was inevitably unequal (the life of the animal could not be considered equivalent to the life of man), it can be understood that in borderline cases of extreme poverty, a grain-offering could be substituted for a living being. In any case, the objection could well be turned back on those who uphold the cleansing power of blood. If this vital force was necessary to drive away sin, how could the burning of some fine flour on the altar bring about the same result? Why not use water instead, which in several cases of uncleanness was supposed to bring about purification (cf. Lev 15:5ff.)?

---

[33]Because they have been offered by them in reparation for their own offenses. It would be scandalous if they would take benefit of their own offenses.

[34]In Leviticus 10:17, sacredness of the sin offerings and sin itself are closely related: "It [sin offering] is most holy; it was given to you to bear the guilt of the community."

[35]Leviticus 5:6. Cf. also Leviticus 4:27-31 female goat and Leviticus 4:32-35 female lamb. Chiefs and priests are imposed a much more severe rate.

It is true that the slaughter of the animal was not said to be carried out by the priest.[36] Neither was there any special emphasis on this part of the ritual. Nevertheless, it must be borne in mind that in this case it is not question of a real, but rather of a symbolic substitution. The death of the animal was symbolically embedded in the ritual in the form of blood, which is clearly consistent within the system.

We thus come to the conclusion that none of the objections put forth by Füglister can challenge the substitutionary interpretation of Leviticus 17:11. Conversely, very strong evidence can be opposed to the rival theory: if the blood of the victim were conceived as a purifying power of life, why would it be poured out on the side of the altar and not sprinkled on the one offering? Such a process was not unknown in OT ceremonial law. For instance, a sevenfold aspersion with blood was provided to symbolize the purification of healed lepers (Lev 14:7). But whereas the blood mentioned in Leviticus 17:11 would be "given, as God said, *for you,*" it was nevertheless not placed on the worshiper, but on the altar, which represented God's "space." What need would God have of such a purifying power of life? Only as acceptance of the death (blood) of the animal in place of the sinner who should have died, would the blood have any sense *for God.* It is highly significant that the sacrificial blood be described as given to man *by God* in a rite where precisely the opposite took place: man, who offered the sacrifice, gave it *to God* through the mediation of the priest. As many interpreters have noticed, this underlines the generous all-sufficiency of God: humans can only offer what he has already given to them.[37] Such a formulation also rules out any magical conception of the blood. Blood is reserved *for* God, even when used for man's sake.[38] At

---

[36]The Torah of Ezekiel sets clearly apart the Levites who may serve in the sanctuary. They may "slaughter the burnt offerings and sacrifices for the people and stand before the people and serve them" (Ezek 44:11) and by consequence of their sin "are not to come near any of my holy things or my most holy offerings" (Ezek 44:13). There is a clear-cut distinction between slaughter, which is the duty of the people, served by the Levites, and the priests who "are to stand before me [the Lord] to offer sacrifices of fat and blood" (Ezek 44:15).

[37]Cf. 1 Chronicles 29:14: "Everything comes from you, and we have given you only what comes from your hand."

[38]Even in the paschal rite, when blood was not to be poured on an altar but put on the doorframes of each individual house (Ex 12:7) and is presented as "a sign *for you*" (Ex 12:13), it would nevertheless be a sign *for God*: "when I see the blood, I will pass over you." Israelites would not be protected by a power of life, which could avert the peril of death, but by a sign intelligible by God.

this point, it is now possible to deal with the key issue of the meaning of the verb *kipper*.

The Meaning of the Verb *kipper*

Does the verb *kipper* deal with purification or with substitution? Both cases may be substantiated by etymological considerations.[39] On the one hand, the well-known substantive *kōper* (כֹּפֶר), *ransom*, points to the idea of compensation; while on the other hand, the unique use of the verb in the qal stem with the hapax *kōper* (כֹּפֶר) II., *bitumen* (Gen 6:14) evokes a material process that could rather easily be linked with purification, since the gesture of washing is almost identical with distempering.[40]

In the case of a word used so frequently in the OT (according to some sources 101 or 102 times), usage must prevail over any etymological or comparative considerations. Ritual use, by far the most frequent in the Old Testament[41] and decisive in Leviticus 17, unquestionably sways the evidence in favor of purification. The strongest proof is the use of the verb where sacred things are the direct object of the verb.[42] But it may also be said that the rite sometimes applies to human beings affected by some severe kind of defilement,[43] in which the result of the process is the recovery of a state of purity: "she/he will be clean."[44]

On the other hand, several occurrences of the verb indisputably link it to the notion of compensation. For instance, each census brought about the payment of a tax,[45] given to the Lord by each one to "atone

---

[39]Cf. especially the monograph of Bernd Janowski, *Sühne als Heilsgeschehen. Studien zur Sühnentheologie der Priesterschrift und zur Wurzel KPR im Alten Orient und im Alten Testament*, WMANT 55 (Neukirchen: Neukirchenen Verlag, 1982), 14, 394; and Baruch A. Levine, *In the Presence of the Lord. A Study of Cult and Some Cultic Terms in Ancient Israel* (Leiden: Brill, 1974), 55-67, 121, 123-27.

[40]Cf. in English, *whitewashing*. This could be related to Akkadian *kuppariu* "purification."

[41]It represents nearly 80 percent of all OT occurrences and more than 9 out of 10 in the Pentateuch.

[42]This use is rather scarce in the Pentateuch and limited to the ceremonies of *Yom kippur* with most holy place, the tent of meeting and the altar as direct object with particle אֵת (Lev 16:20, 33). Cf. the same use in Ezekiel 43:20, 26; 45:20.

[43]Like childbirth (Lev 12:7, 8), skin disease (6 occurrences in Lev 14) and pathological discharges (Lev 15:15, 30).

[44]Leviticus 12:7, 8; 14:20. Cf. also the prepositional phrase (prep. מִן) indicating the uncleanness from which one is freed by the rite (Lev 14:19; 15:15, 30).

[45]Named כֹּפֶר נַפְשׁוֹ, *ransom of his life*, Exodus 30:12.

for his life."[46] Is it necessary to separate sacrificial *(purification)* from nonsacrificial *(ransom)* uses of the verb?

Many typical features of the sacrificial use of the verb indicate that the intent of the rite could not be reduced to some kind of purification: more often than defilement, sin is what makes the rite necessary;[47] more frequently than purification, forgiveness is shown to be the result of the act;[48] offerings closely linked with the rite of *kipper*, even in cases of uncleanness, are designated as sin *(ḥaṭāʾt* חַטָּאת) and guilt *(ʾāšam* אָשָׁם); and human beneficiaries of the rite, consistently mentioned, are never the direct object of the verb and very rarely the concrete object of a blood rite. The preposition *ʿal*, or more seldom *bĕʿad* (בְּעַד), is used consistently to show the human being as beneficiary of an action, which was not performed *upon him*, as logically would be the case for purification, but for *his sake*, outside of him.

Therefore, in *kipper* rites, purification cannot be disconnected from compensation: through compensation given to God, purification and forgiveness were granted. Irrespective of various hypotheses that attempt to provide a genetic explanation for this rather disturbing connection,[49] it should be observed that it corresponds precisely to the close relationship between defilement and sin, which is typical of the old covenant in comparison with the new.

This connection is illustrated quite well by the ceremonies of Yom Kippur. All sacred places and furniture were to be decontaminated by a man wearing special clothes, almost like an atomic power station.

---

[46]Exodus 30:15,16. לְכַפֵּר עַל־נַפְשֹׁתֵיכֶם. This same phrase is used in Numbers 31:50 for the offering to the Lord of a part of the spoils by the Israelites after their victory over the Midianites. One could consider a half-shekel (Ex 30:15), a very low price in compensation for life. The owner of an ox reputed dangerous and responsible for the death of a slave would have to pay sixty times more, 30 shekels (Ex 21:32), but in some other instances the "atonement" could be more dramatic: Phinehas "made atonement for the Israelites" (Num 25:13) by killing an Israelite leader and a Midianite woman (Num 25:7-8), and after the golden calf apostasy, Moses intended to "make atonement" for the people (Ex 32:30) either by his prayer or by offering his own life in the place of the people (Ex 32:32).

[47]Note the twelve occurrences for sin and guilt offerings in Leviticus 4—7.

[48]Leviticus 4:20, 26, 31, 35; 5:10, 13, 16, 18; 6:7; 19:22; Numbers 15:25, 28. There are 12 occurrences with verb forgive (נִסְלַח), 7 with verb purify (טָהֵר).

[49]Baruch Levine, after having established a logical relation between *purification* and *compensation*, "*kōper* is rather a payment made for the purpose of erasing or 'wiping away' guilt incurred by the offense" (61), surprisingly proposes that "biblical cultic texts reflects two distinct verbal forms: (1) *kipper* I, the primary *Piel*, and (2) *kipper* II, a secondary denominative, from the noun *kōper* "ransom, expiation gift" (67).

Thus, not only ritual impurity but sin itself was to be driven out like pollution in this graphic rite of the so-called scapegoat. But sin, even though closely linked to impurity, is not to be confused with, or reduced to, a kind of defilement. Humiliation and public confession were necessary (Lev 16:21, 31). Whereas sacred things and human beings are mentioned together as objects of the rite (Lev 16:33), a distinction is maintained between them in the verbal construction: direct object with the particle 'ʾt (אֵת) for the sacred things ("he makes atonement for [ʾt] the Most Holy Place, and for [ʾt] the Tent of Meeting, and for [ʾt] the altar he makes atonement"); the preposition ʿl (עַל) for the persons ("for [ʿl] the priests and for [ʿl] all the people of the community he makes atonement"). Since they were polluted objects, sacred things were direct objects of the rite performed *upon*[50] them for purification. In contrast, human beings need not only and primarily to be purified, but to be reconciled with God,[51] which is symbolically represented by the blood rite, which takes place outside of them *upon* the altar.

Therefore, even in a cultic context, it is not possible to limit the meaning of the verb *kipper* to a mere purification rite, since it is also linked to a compensation, which implies God. This sometimes disturbing connection between sin and defilement or forgiveness and purification observed in the use of the verb can be recognized as another typical limitation of the old covenant. The *kipper* rite provided a merely provisional representation of God's forgiveness still embedded in its symbolic aspect of purification. A proper understanding of the relationship between the two testaments implies that one should not try to find the New Testament in the Old, but to read the signs in the Old Testament that point in the direction of the New.

Given the very real disproportion between animal and human life, it is possible to agree in part with Andrian Schenker, who proposed to trans-

---

[50]This is clearly the meaning of the preposition עַל when used for the altar or sacred things upon which the blood rite is preformed.

[51]The comparative study of Roy E. Gane, "Schedules for Deities: Macrostructure of Israelite, Babylonian and Hittite Sancta Purification Days," *AUSS* 36 (1998), 231-44, points out that only in Israelite ritual would human beings be objects of the purification rite (243). In Babylon, the origin of pollution is extra-human. There is no question of sins; on the contrary, the king affirms his innocence. At Ebla also, in a ritual close to the scapegoat ritual, there is no confession of sin, cf. Ida Zatelli: "There is no confession by the imposition of hands in the Eblaite ritual, but loading the goat with impurities is the essential, primitive nucleus of the rite itself" ("The Origin of the Biblical Scapegoat Ritual: The Evidence of Two Eblaite Texts," *VT* 48 [1998]: 262).

late the substantive *kōpēr* (*ransom*) as "accommodation."[52] He rightly observed that the price given could have no intrinsic connection with the offense, such as money given to avoid capital punishment in cases where the family of the victim accepted such compensation from the owner of a dangerous ox responsible for a mortal accident.[53] Acceptance of such accommodation is evidently a free act of God's clemency. However, in the case where the accommodation provided is the blood of a slaughtered animal, to claim that it would be without connection with the guilt and merited punishment of the one offering it would suppose arbitrary and inexcusable violence on the part of God. The "noble" intention to avoid a "shocking" doctrine of God's justice that demands the death of the guilty arrives therefore at the horrific conclusion of gratuitous sadism.

Conclusion

In the conclusion of his thorough analysis and critique of C. H. Dodd, Roger Nicole felt it necessary to clarify that propitiation ought not be understood "in a way that would seem to do injustice to the love, mercy and grace of God by representing him a vindictive being thirsty for man's blood."[54] We hope that this present study confirms for the reader Roger Nicole's thesis stated forty-nine years ago (in relation to the OT):

> The word כָּפַר, standing at the heart of the Hebrew sacrificial system, reveals that the worshipper felt the need of escaping the divine displeasure at sin. In this respect it appears to have had a basic propitiatory connotation, although the grammatical construction varies. The non-religious use of this verb confirms this (Gen 32:21; Prov 16:14).[55]

We believe that a more careful study of the OT sacrificial system would help readers of this new century to understand its particularities and typical limitations as specific means to enhance, preserve and anticipate a concept of propitiation worthy of the justice, love, mercy and grace of the holy God.

---

[52]Cf. his two articles in *Text und Sinn im Alten Testament* (Friburg: Universitätsverlag, 1991), "*Koper* et expiation," 120-34, and "Das Zeichen des Blutes und die Gewissheit der Vergebung im Alten Testament. Die sühnenden Funktion des Blutes auf dem Altar nach Leviticus. 17.10-12," 167-85.
[53]Exodus 21:30. Cf. also the census *tax* of a half-shekel (Ex 30:13), the *present* offered by Jacob to obtain the pardon of his brother Esau (Gen 32:21), the *incense* burned by Aaron to stop the plague in the people (Num 17:11 [16:46]), etc.
[54]Roger R. Nicole, "C. H. Dodd and the Doctrine of Propitiation," *WTJ* 17 (1955): 150.
[55]Ibid., 152.

atonement in psalm 51

"My Sacrifice, O God, Is a Broken Spirit"

Bruce K. Waltke

The removal of sin in the Old Testament has two aspects, the external liturgical sacrifices such as the sin and guilt offerings that through the shedding of blood (i.e., the giving of life) make payment in expiation for a life which is forfeit, and the internal spiritual factors involved in forgiveness.[1] The latter involves the personal willingness of God to forgive sin and the offender's willingness to renounce his wrongdoing. The liturgical laws of the Mosaic law featured the former aspect; the Prophets and the Psalter, the latter. Higher critics commonly allege that the external procedures for the removal of sin represent an older, more primitive stage of Israel's religion, and the personal aspects a later stage. Those who contend for the integrity of Scripture because of its plenary inspiration contend that this difference between the Law and the Prophets and Psalter is due to their different literary genres, not to progressive religious thinking in Israel that denied and corrected its earlier religious reflections.

When we turn to the Psalter, it seems to support the common higher critical view. The penitential psalms in particular appear to ignore or even repudiate blood sacrifice as a means of removing sin. A liturgical tradition that reaches back into the Middle Ages placed

---

[1]Cf. Leviticus 4:1—6:7; 14:5; 16:20-22; 17:11; cf. Hebrews 2:17; 9:5, 7; Numbers 8:7-10; 19:9. For special circumstances, other rituals such as trial by fire and washing by water were required (cf. Num 31:22-24).

seven psalms under the rubric of penitential psalms.[2] In these psalms
the penitent sinner pleads with God for deliverance from his deep
sense of guilt, yet none of them, aside from Psalm 51, mentions atonement. But Psalm 51, the so-called "Great Penitential Psalm," is in fact
the most problematic because it seems both to affirm and to deny the
sacrificial system. On the one hand, it mentions ritual washing in
Psalm 51:2 and makes mention of the purgation by hyssop in Psalm
51:7 and of offering sacrifices in Psalm 51:19. On the other hand, the
psalmist claims in Psalm 51:16-17 that God does not want sacrifices
and that the only appropriate and acceptable sacrifice is "a broken and
contrite heart." Some interpret this last statement to mean an absolute
rejection of the sacrificial system.[3] W. O. E. Oesterley comments:
"Wholly in opposition to the belief and practice of his times, [the
psalmist] repudiates the idea of material sacrifices."[4] Elmer Leslie
agrees: "The psalmist is at one with Amos (5:21-22), Hosea (6:6), Isaiah
(1:10-17), Micah (6:6-8), and Jeremiah (7:21-23) in his rejection of animal sacrifice as a rite that is pleasing to God. He has achieved a deeply
spiritual conception of religion. It is not sacrifice that God desires, but
a heart free from pride and rebellion."[5] A. A. Anderson thinks varying
circumstances, not an absolute rejection, "occasioned such a radical
reconsideration of the meaning of the sacrificial system."[6] Exegetes of
this school of thought usually claim that Psalm 51:18-19 is a later addition from "a less spiritually minded poet."[7] Bernhard Anderson
comments: "The psalm's language, in fact, was so sharply critical that
a later revisionist added a qualification at the end of the psalm (Ps
51:18-19), thereby justifying the use of the psalm in Temple services."[8]
These exegetes, however, do not adequately answer the liturgical references in Psalm 51:2, 7. For example, Leslie inconsistently comments

---

[2]Psalms 6, 32, 38, 51, 102, 130, 143.

[3]For scholars who hold this view, see H. H. Rowley, "The Unity of the Old Testament," *Bulle-tin of the John Rylands Library* 29 (1946): 5-7.

[4]W. O. E. Oesterley, *The Psalms: Translated with Text-critical and Exegetical Notes* (London: SPCK; New York: Macmillan, 1939), 1:274.

[5]Elmer A. Leslie, *Psalms: Translated and Interpreted in Light of Hebrew Life and Worship* (New York: Abingdon, 1939), 401.

[6]A. A. Anderson, *The Book of Psalms*, The New Century Bible (Greenwood, S.C.: Attic Press; London: Marshall, Morgan and Scott, 1972), p. 401.

[7]Leslie, *Psalms*, 402.

[8]Bernhard Anderson, *Out of the Depths: The Psalms Speak for Us Today* (Philadelphia: Westmin-ster Press, 1983), 95.

on Psalm 51:7: "We are to think here of ritual acts . . . being performed by the priest, in which hyssop . . . will be dipped in water ritually prepared for ceremonial cleansing." Anderson, with more consistency, denies that hyssop refers to a ritual act that accompanied the recitation of the psalm. According to him the hyssop is a figure, derived from the cultic life, of inward cleansing.

These explanations, which pit the psalm's teaching about the removal of sin and guilt against the Mosaic covenant, and at least to some extent against itself, are based on the common error of proof-texting. In the case cited, representative exegetes have failed to give due consideration to its form as a specific kind of lament psalm, a lament for sin. In this essay, I aim to exegete Psalm 51 in the light of its form with a focus on its teaching about atonement, the removal of sin and guilt and forgiveness.

Exegesis of Psalm 51

As is well known, lament or petition psalms typically include the motifs of an address, lament, confession of trust, petition and praise. Psalm 51, adopting this form to lament sin and petition God for forgiveness, includes an introductory petition in connection with the address (Ps 51:1-2, 2 lines), a lament in the form of a confession for sin (Ps 51:3-6, four lines), a petition corresponding to his confession (Ps 51:7-12, six lines), and praise (Ps 51:13-19, seven lines).

Superscription. Before turning to the psalm itself, the superscription provides a helpful background to elucidating its contribution toward the doctrine of the atonement. To be sure, for more than a century most critics denied the historicity of these superscriptions, but careful exegesis refutes their objections, and recent studies in the light of ancient Near Eastern parallels support the credibility of these superscripts and postscripts. My own research has led me to the conclusion that the superscript pertains to the psalm's composition and that its postscript, which has become confounded within the textual tradition with the following superscript, to its performance.[9] The superscript of Psalm 51 mentions its genre, "a psalm," its author, "by David," and the historical circumstance prompting its composition, "when the prophet Nathan came to him after David had committed

---

[9]See Bruce K. Waltke, "Superscripts, Postscripts, or Both," *JBL* 110 (1991): 583-96.

adultery with Bathsheba."[10] In that connection, David committed a blatantly defiant (*b*ᵉ*yād rāmâ*, "with a high hand"), not an inadvertent (*bišgāgâ*, "with inadvertence"), transgression. To cover up his adultery with Bathsheba, the king coldly calculated her husband's murder over a period of at least two weeks, reckoning four days for the messenger to fetch Uriah from the battlefront and another eight days for Uriah to journey to and from Jerusalem, and counting his three days in Jerusalem. The sin offering made atonement for inadvertent sin (Lev 4:1-35), but not for open-eyed sin of the high hand.[11] Moreover, both the sins of adultery and of murder carried a death penalty for the culprits.[12] Third, let it be noted that David could not make restitution to either Bathsheba or her husband. He could neither restore her purity nor his life. Yet in spite of these awesome deficits, David found God's forgiveness. The superscription infers the reason. He sinned and confronted death because, as Nathan accused him, he despised the word of the Lord (2 Sam 12:9), but now he submitted himself to the prophetic word "when Nathan the prophet came to him" and through a parable brought out David's true nature, enabling the king to experience forgiveness and life.

Address and Introductory Petition—Psalm 51:1-2. David addresses Israel's covenant-keeping God by his generic title, the one and only "God," not by his personal name "the LORD" (Yhwh), presumably because the so-called Elohistic Psalter (Ps 42—83) for an unknown reason demanded it. In his introduction, David lays hold of three of the sublime attributes that manifest God's glory.[13] Standing in the deep hole of sin and death, he looked up and saw stars of God's grace that those who stand in the noon-day brightness of their own righteousness never discern.[14] He petitioned God on the basis of his character to be gracious (*ḥānan*, bestowal of an undeserved favor), kind (*ḥesed*, help to

---

[10]See 2 Samuel 11:1—12:25. For a careful literary analysis of the Story of David and Bathsheba, see Meir Sternberg, *The Poetics of Biblical Narrative: Ideological Literature and the Drama of Reading* (Bloomington: University of Indiana Press, 1987), 190-229.

[11]Numbers 15:27-31. The Yom Kippur rite (Lev 16:16, 21) provided for the high priest to represent the sinning people who were barred from the sanctuary. See Jacob Milgrom, *Leviticus 1-16: A New Translation with Introduction and Commentary,* Anchor Bible (New York: Doubleday, 1991), 228.

[12]Leviticus 20:10, Deuteronomy 22:22, and Numbers 35:30-31 respectively.

[13]See Exodus 34:6.

[14]Cf. Alexander Maclaren, *Psalms LI to CXIV* (London: Hodder & Stoughton, 1908), 12.

the helpless because of a covenant relationship) and merciful (*raḥam*, pity for the helpless).

In the Mosaic law as well, the whole paraphernalia of worship, including sacrifice, is rooted in God's sublime, forgiving character. While God is instructing Moses on the mountain on how to worship him (Ex 25—Lev 9), the people sin by erecting the infamous golden calf (Ex 32:1-8). The omniscient God responds to their rebellion by commanding Moses to get down from the mountain. He thereupon proposes two alternative plans for dealing with their sinfulness and responds to one by Moses in order to expose the spiritual mettle of the human founder of Israel's religion. Moses rejects God's first plan of starting over again with him because it would tarnish God's reputation, making him known as an angry God, and would violate his covenant promises to Abraham, Isaac and Jacob (Ex 32:8-14). God rejects Moses' plan of offering himself as a sin offering because his justice demands that the people who sinned be blotted out (Ex 32:31—33:3). Moses and his repentant people in turn reject God's plan of sending his angel before them so as not to consume them by being in the midst of sinful people because it would signal that the Lord had rejected them and that he was not pleased with Moses (Ex 33:1-17). In that dialogue, Moses asks God for assurance of his presence by asking him to show him his glory. In the closing scene God proclaims his glory, adding to the three attributes David appeals to, his patience and his reliability (Ex 34:1-9).[15] The holy God can dwell in Israel's unholy camp because he is willing to forgive the repentant. In other words, the priestly section of the Law combines the sacrificial system of atonement with the personal dimension of God's willingness to forgive conditioned on Israel's willingness to repent.

On the basis of God's forgiving character, David boldly makes his double petition. First, he asks God to blot out (*māḥâ*, i.e., wipe the slate clean and remove God's wrath) his transgressions, one of several metaphors for forensic forgiveness in the Old Testament. And second, he requests that God "launder" him (*kābas*) so as to "cleanse" him (*ḥāṭṭāʾ*, i.e., "de-sin") and purify him (*ṭāhēr*, i.e., make him fit for temple worship). God's forgiveness is required because David has violated God's

---

[15]See R. W. L. Moberly, *At the Mountain of God: Story and Theology in Exodus 32-34*, JSOTSup 32 (Sheffield: JSOT Press, 1983).

standard of holiness. David's three words in the semantic domain of sin assume this standard: he fell short of it (*ḥāṭā²*, "sin"), rebelled against it (*pešaʿ*, "transgression") and deviated from it or perverted it and so incurred guilt (*ʿāwōn*, "iniquity").

Lament and Confession—Psalm 51:4-7. Having laid the foundation for his appeal in God's glorious character to forgive, David gives the reason for his petitions ("for I know"), and in so doing, he meets the human spiritual requirement of his recognition and confession of his sin, a feature Psalm 32 also emphasizes. In Psalm 51:3-4 (2 lines), he confesses his overt sin, and in Psalm 51:5-6 (2 lines), his moral impotence. Without excusing himself, he emphatically confesses by a synonymous parallelism his culpability and, inferentially, his renunciation of his wrongdoing: "I know *my* transgression, *my* sin is always before *me*." The proverbial truth that "he who conceals his sins does not prosper, but whoever confesses and renounces them finds mercy" (Prov 28:13) entails naming the sin. David specifies his sin in Psalm 51:14: "Save me from blood guilt." Psalm 51:4, however, employs abstract terms so that other penitent sinners may use the psalm in connection with their specific sins.

As noted, by strict definition sin is against God, so David confesses in Psalm 51:4: "Against you, you only, I have sinned," and quickly adds the reason for his theological assertion: "so that you are proved right when you speak and justified when you judge." Because sin violates God's standard, only God can forgive sin. The keen theological minds of the teachers of the law recognized Jesus' claim to deity and authorship of the Law when he said to the paralyzed man: "Son, your sins are forgiven." They thought to themselves: "He's blaspheming! Who can forgive sins but God alone?" (Mk 2:1-12). What matters on the eternal vertical axis between God and human beings is not whether people forgive sins, but whether the Lawgiver forgives them. On the horizontal axis, however, people also need to forgive one another of their wrongdoing to also restore their relationship. Sins against people and against God are inseparable.[16] Probably not everybody, including Ahithophel—perhaps Bathsheba's grandfather—forgave David.[17] In sum, in the first part of his confession, he

---

[16]Leviticus 6:1-7 [5:20-26].
[17]Cf. 2 Samuel 11:3; 15:12; 23:34.

reveals his consciousness of sin, his confession of it, and his acceptance of God's judgment.

In the second part of his confession, David traces the root of his spiritual problem to his depravity, not to excuse himself but to seek a solution. He confesses his moral impotence by contrasting his inherited sin
nature with his congenital conscience against it. He inherited both during his gestation. Concerning his original sin he laments: "See, I was
sinful at birth, sinful from the time my mother conceived me" (Ps
51:5).[18] Of his embryologic conscience he says: "See, you desired[19] truth
in the covered over place; you taught me wisdom in the closed [cham-
ber of the womb]" (Ps 51:6). Dalglish argues the organic unity of these
verses by noting the parallel structure: "see [*hinnēh*] . . . see [*hinnēh*]"
and the expressions pertaining to the semantic domain of gestation: "at
birth" and "conceived" and "in the concealed place" (i.e., the womb,
baṭṭuḥôt, lit. "covered over place"[20]) and "closed" (chamber of the
womb, *sātum*, lit. "stopped up, bottled up").[21] What the LORD desires is
moral "truth" (*'emet*, i.e., faithfulness) and "wisdom" (*ḥokmâ*), i.e.,
"spiritual discernment or the actualizing principle of right conduct,
which is to be equated with the fear of Jahweh (Ps cxi.10; Prov. Ix.10;
Job xxviii.28)."[22]

Petitions—Psalm 51:8-13. His petitions can also be analyzed into
two broad divisions corresponding to his confession. For his overt
acts of sin, he repeats his introductory petitions for forensic forgiveness and for ceremonial cleansing, using the same vocabulary, but he
chiastically reverses them. "Cleanse me (*ḥaṭṭ'ā*, i.e., "de-sin me") with
hyssop and I will be pure (*ṭāhēr*), launder me (*kābas*) and I will be
whiter than snow" (v. 7) matches Psalm 51:2. "Hide your face from
my sin"—another metaphor for forensic forgiveness—"and blot out
all my iniquity" matches Psalm 51:1. The bushy and aromatic hyssop
is a metonymy for the blood its ample leaves held after being dipped
in blood mixed with water. The law provided a guilt offering to make

---

[18]Translations of Psalm 51 are mine.

[19]Perfective tense, same as verse 5a.

[20]Plural of extension to indicate the noun is complex (Bruce K. Waltke and M. P. O'Connor,
Introduction to Biblical Hebrew Syntax [Winona Lake, Ind.: Eisenbrauns, 1990], 120,
P.7.4.1c).

[21]Edward R. Dalglish, *Psalm Fifty-One in the Light of Ancient Eastern Patternism* (Leiden: E. J.
Brill, 1962), 118-22.

[22]Ibid., 123.

atonement for, and to relieve a conscience defiled by, deceiving and
wronging one's neighbor with regard to property (Lev 6:1-7), but
none for adultery and murder. David in an ad hoc way appeals to
purgation by hyssop used in connection with cleansing the leper (Lev
14) and one defiled by death.[23] Through these rituals the one in the
process of dying and the other in the realm of death were transferred
to the realms of life by the atoning rituals involving blood. Of course,
as the writer of Hebrews argues, the animal blood that affected the
transference served as a temporary arrangement until their fulfillment in precious blood of Christ in the new order (Heb 9:6-10). "The
blood of bulls and goats and the ashes of a heifer sprinkled on those
who are ceremonially unclean sanctify them so that they are out-
wardly clean. How much more, then, will the blood of Christ, who
through the eternal Spirit offered himself unblemished to God,
cleanse our consciences from acts that lead to death, so that we may
serve the living God!" (Heb 9:13-14). In sum, the psalmist appeals to
the sacrificial system with its sprinklings of blood for cleansing. Sand-
wiched between his petitions for cultic cleansing and forensic forgiveness based on the sprinkling of blood, he asks for a priestly oracle of
absolution: "Cause me to hear joy and gladness" (Ps 51:10) a metonymy for the word of forgiveness.

The second part of his petition (Ps 51:12-14) addresses his moral impotence. The second verse of each of these verses mentions the spirit.
What he needs is a new spirit (Ps 51:10), the Holy Spirit (Ps 51:11), and
a willing spirit (Ps 51:12) to offset his congenital spiritual contradiction.
This will require a new creation: "Create (bārā᾿) for me a pure heart, O
God" (Ps 51:10). The ritual cleansing is effective only for those to whom
the Spirit applies it.

Praise—Psalm 51:13-19. Instead of presuming upon God with a section on confidence and praise, he anticipates his praise in the mood of
petition. "Let me teach (ălammĕdâ, probably a cohortative of request)
transgressors your ways (i.e., his ways of grace, mercy and covenant
kindness to the helpless, Ps 51:1), the ways God taught Moses.[24] The
praise section of lament psalms typically consists of words of praise accompanied with a sacrifice, a so-called thank offering, or (better) ac-

---

[23]Numbers 19. Dalglish, *Psalm Fifty-One*, 134-37.
[24]See Exodus 33:13; 34:6-7.

knowledgment offering. "The altar and *tôdâ* (praise/acknowledgment) go together," says Mayer.[25] The praise sacrifice (*zebaḥ tôda*)[26] is a peace offering of sacrificial animals and sometimes cereal.[27] In Psalm 51:14-16 David anticipates his words of praise, and in Psalm 51:17-18, his sacrifice. However, in the case of a woman pregnant through adultery and a grieving family due to murder, a joyous feast is entirely inappropriate: "You do not delight in [such a] sacrifice, or I would bring it; you do not take pleasure in burnt offerings [of praise to be eaten by the celebrants]. My sacrifice,[28] O God, is a broken spirit; a broken and contrite heart [upon which all can "feed"] O God, you will not despise." In this section of his lament/confession psalm, and on this particular occasion, David is not rejecting the sacrificial system or animal sacrifices for ritual cleansing but is presenting a joyous celebration of praise through feasting.

Whether or not Psalm 51:18-19 is a later liturgical addition is uncertain, but it is certainly not by a less spiritually minded person. In the future, when God's good hand of blessing again rests on the nation and builds the walls of Zion, perhaps under Solomon, he anticipates: "Then there will be righteous sacrifices, whole burnt offerings to delight you; then bulls will be offered on your altar."

Conclusion

Although the liturgical portion of the Mosaic covenant features the ritual atonement, the spiritual element, as we have seen, is very prominent as well. In addition, note the call for Israel's confession of sin before sacrifice in other liturgical instructions: Leviticus 5:1-6;[29] Numbers 5:5-12. Psalm 51 is totally consistent with this pattern of combining ritual efficacy with spiritual requirements. Moreover, as Dalglish has shown, ancient Near Eastern hymnody also combines them. Besides, three other psalms mention making atonement (*kpr*, usually translated "forgive"): Psalms 65:3 [4]; 78:38; 79:9. Commenting on the translation "forgave our transgression" (NIV) the NIV *Study*

---

[25]G. Mayer, *Theological Dictionary of the Old Testament*, 5.436, s.v. *ydh*. Cf. Psalms 26:6-7; 40:5-8; 43:4; 107:21ff.; Jonah 2:9 [10].

[26]Psalm 116:17.

[27]Leviticus 7:11-15; Psalm 69:30-31 [31-32].

[28]Reading *zibḥi*, not *zibḥê*.

[29]Cf. Leviticus 26:40; 1 Kings 8:33.

Bible says: "Accepted the atonement sacrifices you appointed and so forgave our sins."[30]

I am the one who is honored by being invited to offer this essay in honor of my highly esteemed colleague Roger Nicole, a giant in the faith.

---

[30]*The NIV Study Bible*, gen. ed. Kenneth Barker (Grand Rapids: Zondervan, 1995), 843.

atonement in isaiah 53

"For He Bore the Sins of Many"

J. Alan Groves

In studies of atonement in Isaiah, the Song of the Servant in Isaiah 52:13—53:12 is the text to which almost all attention tends to be devoted. While Isaiah 53[1] must always be considered, it does not exhaust what the broader text of the prophecy is saying about atonement. The entire prophecy is concerned with the issue of purification, and Isaiah 53 describes the atonement demanded to accomplish that purification.[2] I will not treat the question of atonement in Isaiah as a whole, or even of atonement in Isaiah 53 as a whole. Rather, I will focus more narrowly on one issue in Isaiah 53—how the phrases "to bear guilt" (סבל עון) and "to carry sin" (נשא חטא) in Isaiah 53:11-12 relate to the overall concept of atonement in Isaiah. This discussion is carried on with the understanding that the study of atonement in Isaiah 53 ultimately has its place in the broader concerns of the book. Atonement in Isaiah, therefore, neither begins with, nor is solely confined to, a discussion of Isaiah 53.

---

[1] I will use the convention of referring to Isaiah 52:13—53:12 by the shorthand of Isaiah 53.

[2] The scope of the argument that purification is the overarching theme that ties the book of Isaiah together goes beyond the limits of a chapter for this book. The argument is made in a forthcoming work on atonement in Isaiah. An outline of the argumentation and conclusions from that work is presented at the end of this article.

Complexity of Isaiah 53

In introducing his comments on Isaiah 53, Brevard Childs rightly says that it is perhaps "the most contested chapter in the Old Testament. The problems of interpretation are many and complex."[3] Historically, scholarly discussion of Isaiah 53 has focused on such issues as:

1. Who is speaking at various points—who are the "he," "we," "I" and "they"?[4]

2. What is the relation of Isaiah 53 to its context versus its relation to the other Servant Songs?[5]

3. Who was the Servant? An individual? Corporate Israel? Zion?[6]

4. Did the Servant actually die?[7] Or is the song a metaphor for the extreme suffering of a righteous sufferer?

5. Is the language that of substitutionary/vicarious atonement?[8] Is it atonement at all?

   a. What does it mean that the Servant is made a "guilt offering" (אשם in Is 53:10)?[9]
   b. What does it mean that the Servant "makes righteous" (Is 53:11)?[10]
   c. What does it mean to "bear/carry" "sin/guilt" (Is 53:11-12)?

The Focus: "Bearing Guilt" and "Carrying Sin" in Isaiah 53:11-12

As can be seen from the citations in the footnotes, these issues have

---

[3]Brevard Childs, *Isaiah*, OTL (Louisville, Ky.: Westminster John Knox, 2001), 410. See also John N. Oswalt, *The Book of Isaiah: Chapters 40-66*, NICOT (Grand Rapids: Eerdmans, 1998), 377; and David J. A. Clines, *I, He, We, and They: A Literary Approach to Isaiah 53*, JSOTSS 1 (Sheffield: Sheffield Press, 1976).

[4]Clines, *I, He, We, and They.*

[5]The other Servant Songs are found in Isaiah 42:1-9; 49:1-11; and 50:4-11. (Some argue that Isaiah 61:1-3 is also a Servant Song.) For a history of scholarship and a refutation of treating the Servant Songs as independent of their context, see Tryggve N. D. Mettinger, *A Farewell to the Servant Song: A Critical Examination of an Exegetical Axiom* (Scripta Minora 3; Lund: C. W. K. Gleerup, 1983).

[6]For those who hold to the idea of the servant as an individual, many argue for an historical person: e.g., an unknown sixth-century figure—Childs, *Isaiah*, 385, 422; Second Isaiah himself—R. N. Whybray, *Thanksgiving for a Liberated Prophet: An Interpretation of Isaiah Chapter 53*, JSOTSS 4 (Sheffield: JSOT, 1978) 25.

[7]Childs, *Isaiah*, 419; Whybray, *Thanksgiving*, 79-106; Clines, *I, He, We, and They*, 27-29. For a refutation of Whybray's argument that the Servant did not die, see Oswalt, *Isaiah*, 393, n. 25.

[8]Childs, *Isaiah*, 418; Whybray, *Thanksgiving*, 25; Oswalt, *Isaiah*, 385-86.

[9]Childs, *Isaiah*, 417-18; Whybray, *Thanksgiving*, 63-66; Clines, *Isaiah 53*, 20-21.

[10]Childs, *Isaiah*, 419; Whybray, *Thanksgiving*, 66-71; Clines, *I, He, We, and They*, 21-22.

been studied at great length.[11] Arie van der Kooij, in his review of the collection of essays in *Der leidende Gottesknecht. Jesaja 53 und seine Wirkungsgeschichte*, suggests that the use of the verbs נשׂא ("to bear") and סבל ("to bear") in Isaiah 53:4, 11-12 still needs further study in order to yield a better understanding of the servant's role in Isaiah 53.[12] In this article I am taking up van der Kooij's challenge and looking more closely at how these two phrases are used in Isaiah 53 in order to discuss their bearing on atonement in Isaiah 53. As part of the process I will interact with Whybray's extended study on "bearing guilt,"[13] because he highlights the issues so very well.[14] My scope is therefore quite narrow; I will not address the arguments for all the issues in the history of Isaiah 53's interpretation except insofar as they are relevant to the discussion of the interpretation of the expression "to bear guilt."

The two clauses on which attention will be focused are

Isaiah 53:11d: וַעֲוֹנֹתָם הוּא יִסְבֹּל ("and their guilt he will bear").

Isaiah 53:12d: וְהוּא חֵטְא־רַבִּים נָשָׂא ("and he the sin of many bore").

Interaction with Whybray's Study of "Bearing Guilt"

Whybray concludes that if the "many" for whom the servant "carried guilt" (Is 53:11b) are Jewish exiles in Babylon, then

> the Servant cannot be said to be suffering, or to have suffered, *in place* of the exiles in such a way that they escape the consequences of their sins, since, as in the case of speakers in Lam. 5:7, it cannot be said that these have escaped punishment: they are all actually suffering the conse-

---

[11]For a recent and extensive bibliography, see Wolfgang Hüllstrung and Gerlinde Feine, "Bibliographie zu Jes 53," in *Der leidende Gottesknecht. Jesaja 53 und seine Wirkungsgeschichte*, FAT 14, ed. B. Janowski and P. Stuhlmacher (Tübingen: J. C. B. Mohr, 2000), 251-71.

[12]*BO* 57 (2000): 677, 679. There have been three more extended studies of the language "to bear/carry sin/guilt": Walter Zimmerli, "Die Eigenart der prophetischen Reden des Ezechiel," *ZAW* 66 (1954): 9-12; Whybray, *Thanksgiving*, 29-57; Otfried Hofius, "Das vierte Gottesknechtslied in den Briefen des Neuen Testaments," in *Der leidende Gottesknecht*, 107-14. Whybray interacts extensively with Zimmerli (whose work is primarily on these verbs in Ezekiel), but Hofius, as van der Kooij observes, neither cites them nor interacts with them.

[13]For economy in the following discussion I will use the expression "bearing guilt" as shorthand for the class of phrases involving the verbs נשׂא or סבל with noun phrases containing עון or חטא —"bearing sin," "carrying guilt" and "carrying sin." On the meaning of עון in particular, see Whybray, *Thanksgiving*, 29, for his argument that it means both the sin and the punishment for that sin, though one of them is usually accented in actual usage.

[14]Whybray, *Thanksgiving*, 29-57.

quences of defeat and banishment. The Servant, if, as is here maintained, he is one of them, shares their suffering. Chapter 53 indeed makes it clear that he has suffered more intensely than they, and the "we" who speak there confess that, at any rate compared with themselves, he is innocent; nevertheless this is shared and not vicarious suffering. This consideration applies equally to the other passages which are to be considered . . . and should itself be sufficient to dismiss the theory of vicarious suffering [in Isaiah 53] as impossible.[15]

In contrast, I will argue that "bearing guilt" is uniquely presented in Isaiah 53 and that it is indeed vicarious. Some have questioned whether the Servant of Isaiah 53 actually died or whether he suffered terribly—almost, but not quite, to the point of death. Many compelling and well-reasoned arguments have been set forth on both sides, which I commend for further reading and study. While a discussion of the topic or an extended defense of my position is clearly beyond the scope of this chapter, I take the position here that the Servant did, in fact, die.

Atonement in Isaiah 53 and the Issue of Cultic vs. Noncultic Language
As a preamble to the discussion of the relation between "bearing guilt" and atonement in Isaiah 53, a brief treatment of the connection of the cult, that is, the ritual associated with worship and sacrifice as established especially in Exodus-Numbers, and atonement is necessary. The verb כבר ("to make atonement") is not used in Isaiah 53. Notwithstanding, Christian interpreters of Isaiah have traditionally argued that Isaiah 53 employs the language of making atonement and is therefore about atonement.[16] Since the end of the nineteenth century, this interpretation has been criticized and challenged on numerous grounds. The most common argument has been that the language in Isaiah 53 is not cultic language and hence cannot be the language of atonement.[17] In other words, atonement has come to be viewed as an exclusively cultic concept, and if language traditionally labeled "atonement lan-

[15]Ibid., 30.
[16]Childs, *Isaiah*, 418.
[17]See Childs, *Isaiah*, 418; Whybray, *Thanksgiving*, 29-57; Harry M. Orlinsky, "The So-Called 'Servant of the Lord' and 'Suffering Servant' in Second Isaiah," in *Studies in the Second Part of the Book of Isaiah*, SVT, XIV (Leiden: Brill, 1967), 56. For an argument that the language in Isaiah 53 is cultic, see Oswalt, *Isaiah*, 386.

guage" in Isaiah 53 is demonstrably noncultic in its use, then it is not the language of atonement.

Three Lines of Argument Concerning the Distinction Between Cultic and Noncultic

Three lines of argument suggest that the debate over the distinction between cultic and noncultic language in Isaiah 53 may be focused in the wrong direction. I will argue that the actual concept of כפר ("make atonement") in the Hebrew Bible suggests a sense that is not limited to cultic contexts, that Isaiah's vision of Yahweh's global presence makes the issue moot in any case, and that in Isaiah's vision, Yahweh has rejected the cult.

Not all contexts for atonement are cultic. The broader scholarly discussion concerning atonement and the cult in the Hebrew Bible has focused on the meaning of the Hebrew word כפר[18] ("ransom, substitute, cover, or wipe away").[19] Whatever the precise nuance of its mechanism, however, the result of atonement, was always to prevent or arrest the wrath of God from flaming out and consuming Israel while he dwelt in their midst.[20] Atonement as prevention against the outbreak

---

[18]The verb כפר occurs almost exclusively in the *piel* stem in the Hebrew Bible. Most of its occurrences are in ritual (legal) or in direct speech in Leviticus and Numbers—i.e., Moses or Yahweh is speaking about the need for atonement. The word is almost never used in narrative. (The concept is there, perhaps, but not the word.) In its narrative usage, making atonement is always the act necessary to arrest the wrath of God that has broken out (e.g., Num 16:46-49; 25:1-13).

[19]See R. Averbeck, "כבר," *NIDOTE* 2:689-710, for a detailed discussion of the various proposals of the meaning of כבר and a full bibliography covering the issues.

[20]In some cases in which the wrath of God (expressed in various ways) was arrested by some particular action, the narration is explicit that the action "made atonement," e.g., Numbers 16:46-49 (Aaron's censer made atonement) and Numbers 25:1-13 (Phineas's killing of the offending party made atonement). Cf. Exodus 32:30—33:6, where Moses understands that atonement was necessary lest Yahweh destroy the people by his very presence. (Moses ultimately arrested God's wrath by interceding for Israel. In context, this was atonement.) But there are instances of the arrest of God's wrath that were not explicitly said to have been accomplished by atonement: Numbers 14 (God's wrath for failing to have faith and go up into the land—a generation will die); Joshua 7 (the sin of Achan resulted in God striking Israel with defeat at the hand of Ai, and the abatement was only through the execution of Achan and his household); 2 Samuel 21:1-14 (the famine on account of Saul's sin was abated by David executing seven descendants of Saul—note that in 2 Samuel 21:3 David asked how he could make atonement; and 2 Samuel 24:1-25 (David prayed and sacrificed to halt the wrath of God, which had broken out because of his sin of taking a census). Based on the preceding discussion, I would argue that these too are cases of atonement, because the wrath of God was arrested in each instance.

of God's wrath is seen, for example in Numbers 8:19: "Of all the Israelites, I have given the Levites as gifts to Aaron and his sons to do the work at the Tent of Meeting on behalf of the Israelites and to make atonement for them so that no plague will strike the Israelites when they go near the sanctuary" (NIV).

At times, this result may be expressed in terms of forgiveness,[21] cleansing,[22] consecration[23] or redemption,[24] but in each case the bottom-line connotation of the result is the same: preventing the outbreak of Yahweh's wrath.[25] I am proposing, therefore, that atonement is best understood as made by an act that purifies something in such a manner that the outbreak of Yahweh's holy wrath is either arrested or prevented, whichever is appropriate in a particular situation.

While many contexts in which the verb כפר is used are indeed cultic, the concept of atonement as preventing or appeasing the wrath of God also appears in noncultic cases, and sometimes the act of appeasing the wrath of God is explicitly called atonement. One particular situation stands out—the action of Phineas recounted in Numbers 25:1-13, where he kills the offending Israelite and stops the ongoing outbreak of Yahweh's wrath. It is Yahweh himself who calls this "making atonement."[26] The case of Phineas alone is sufficient to disprove the blanket statement that language must be cultic to be the language of atonement.[27]

The cultic implications of the universal presence of Yahweh's glory in Isaiah. Secondly, Isaiah's vision of the universal presence of Yahweh's glory seems to make the distinction between cultic and noncultic

---

[21]Leviticus 4:20, 26, 31, 35; 5:10, 13, 16, 18; 19:22; Numbers 15:25, 28.

[22]Leviticus 12:7, 8; 14:20, 53.

[23]Consecration (sanctification) in the sense of setting something or someone aside for service to the Lord (e.g., Ex 29:33, 36-37; Lev 8:15).

[24]Redemption is another way of speaking about the result of atonement—Israel is delivered from the outbreak of God's wrath.

[25]Note that the instrument used to accomplish atonement varied as well: the blood of the sacrifice (the primary cultic solution to prevent the wrath of God); money (Ex 30:11-16, esp. Ex 30:12), and killing someone caught in sin (Num 25:13). In each case, wrath—plague, or something else that killed or could kill the people—was arrested or prevented. (This list is not to be understood as exhaustive.)

[26]Numbers 25:13. The Phineas example also suggests that other situations in which the wrath of the Lord is appeased and atonement is not explicitly mentioned can legitimately be called "making atonement" (e.g., in 1 Sam 21 the famine on account of Saul's sin is abated when some of his relatives are executed).

[27]See footnote 20 for other cases of noncultic atonement.

moot in the book of Isaiah. The breakdown in the cultic/noncultic distinction begins with Isaiah's initial throne-room experience, where the seraphim declare that the "the whole earth is full of [God's] glory" (Is 6:3). Yahweh's glory, the signature expression of his presence in the holy of holies, is *everywhere*. There is no place where he is not present, and hence where the fire of his holy wrath might not break out. All of the earth becomes the place for the "cult." Isaiah indicates this global perspective throughout the prophecy (e.g., Is 11:9; 40:5; 65:17; 66:24). The Holy One is everywhere, and holiness is demanded everywhere, not just in the temple precincts at set times.

Yahweh has rejected the cult. A third line of argument in the book of Isaiah is Yahweh's apparent rejection of the cult. At the beginning of the book, Yahweh rhetorically demands: "The multitude of your sacrifices—what are they to me? . . . Who has asked this of you, this trampling of my courts?" (Is 1:11-12). While Israel is granted no venue for response, if they had made one, it would certainly have been "Didn't you tell us to come and sacrifice?" But he dismisses their sacrifices as meaningless (Is 1:13). The implication is that sacrifices are not bringing any change in the people and that sin remains in their midst even after he has been faithful to deliver them and to bless them time and again (e.g., the great deliverance of Israel from the siege of Sennacharib in 701 B.C.; cf. Isaiah 36—37). Yahweh promises that he will cleanse Zion and her people, that he will purge her and her inhabitants of their sin and pollution.[28] Yahweh will do what the people, their sacrifice and their repentance has failed to do. Not surprisingly, therefore, the cult plays little or no positive role in Isaiah.[29]

Summary concerning cultic vs. noncultic language. Atonement can be noncultic. In Isaiah in particular, God's presence is seen to "fill the whole earth"; there is no place to go from his presence. And the cult has been rejected by Yahweh in favor of his own action to purify Israel of her impurities (Is 1:24-26). Therefore, to demand that the language in

---

[28]Isaiah 1:21-27. This promise to purify raises the expectation of some kind of atoning act on Yahweh's part.

[29]The cult is ultimately transformed, along with everything else, when Yahweh performs his "new thing" (Is 48:6) and makes an atonement that secures a purification that is global and permanent and that changes the hearts of his people (see the final section of this chapter for an elaboration of this point). In that new reality, where sin and its effects have been banished, the task of those who are priests will be bringing inhabitants to Zion for worship rather than offering sacrifices for sin (cf. Is 66:20-21).

Isaiah 53 be cultic in order for it to be atoning misses the mark. The issue in the book of Isaiah is not cultic vs. noncultic language but whether or not the language is the language of atonement, which can be noncultic in any case. As we shall see, the language of Isaiah 53 is indeed atonement language since it concerns that which purifies and shields from Yahweh's wrath.

The Real Problem with Atonement in Isaiah 53:
The Humanness of the Sufferer

The real problem with seeing atonement in Isaiah 53, however, is not Isaiah 53's language, but its presenting human suffering (and death) as the means for making atonement for others. If the sufferer in Isaiah 53 were a sacrificial animal, I suggest that there would be little or no controversy about seeing atonement in this passage. If it were said of a sacrificial bull, for example, that "he was pierced for our transgressions; he was crushed for our iniquities; the punishment that brought us peace was upon him; and by his wounds we are healed . . . the Lord has laid on him the iniquity of us all . . . for the transgression of my people he was stricken . . . the Lord makes his life a guilt offering" (Is 53:5-10 NIV), no one would think twice about this being atonement language. It is the humanness of the sufferer that is the chief stumbling block.

While almost no one denies that the text is saying that the Servant in some sense suffers for the sins and iniquities of others, many question whether or not that suffering *makes atonement*. Harry Orlinsky said that "[it] would have been the greatest injustice of all, nothing short of blasphemy, that the lawless be spared their punishment at the expense of the law-abiding. Nowhere in the Hebrew Bible did anyone preach a doctrine—which would have superseded the covenant!—which allowed the sacrifice of the innocent in place of and as an acceptable substitution for the guilty."[30]

Because the Torah knows of no atonement requiring human sacrifice, but rather condemns human sacrifice in no uncertain terms, and because the sufferer is human, Isaiah 53 clearly cannot be about atonement. If Isaiah 53 is speaking of a human sufferer making atonement, then Isaiah is most definitely departing from—indeed "contradicting"—all previous tradition. The alternative is that the human-

---

[30]Orlinsky, "Second Isaiah," 55.

ness of the sufferer makes this a unique and most terrible atonement.[31]

The real problem, then, is not the absence of cultic language. The real problem is whether or not Isaiah 53 uses the language of atonement (an action that arrests or prevents Yahweh's wrath), and if so, how the suffering and death of a *human being* to make atonement can be explained.

Observations Concerning the Use of the Language of "Bearing Guilt"

In this section I will discuss the phrase עָוֹן נָשָׂא ("bearing guilt") and in the process also interact with Whybray's extended discussion of the phrase.[32] Whereas Whybray began with functional and semantic distinctions and categories to discuss the phrase "bearing guilt," I will begin with the more formal parameters of syntax and grammar. The discussion in the following section is more technical and requires understanding of Hebrew, so some readers may want to proceed to "Summary of 'bearing guilt' in Isaiah 53."

Old Testament Usage of "Bearing Guilt" According to Syntactical Patterns

While the more common phrase נָשָׂא עָוֹן ("bearing guilt") does not occur in Isaiah 53 as such, its parallels do. It is worthwhile to examine the phrase נָשָׂא עָוֹן in the rest of the Hebrew Bible to see what light its usage sheds on its parallels in Isaiah 53.[33] I cast my net a bit more broadly than Whybray did and looked at all the combinations of סָבַל ("to bear") or נָשָׂא ("to bear") either preceded or followed by the following synonyms for sin: עָוֹן, חֵטְא and פֶּשַׁע ("sin," "guilt" or "transgression").[34] Because all of these words occur individually or in combina-

---

[31]This point will be discussed in more detail at the end of the chapter.

[32]Whybray, *Thanksgiving*, 29-57.

[33]Whybray makes a good case for this broader study (*Thanksgiving*, 31).

[34]Each of the three Hebrew nouns can be used more or less interchangeably, though עָוֹן and חֵטְא are more common. While each of them can be translated in any of the three ways mentioned, they do seem to be distributed according to particular contexts in Hebrew. The search engine *Quest 1.0* (1991) was used for the concordancing of these combinations of words. The search query: for either verb (סָבַל/נָשָׂא) within nine words of any of the three nouns for sin/guilt in any order (i.e., the verb can either precede or follow the noun). Fifty-two occurrences were returned, with only two using the verb סָבַל (Is 53:11 and Lam 5:7).

tion with one another in Isaiah 53, and because they all occur in various combinations elsewhere, their study is appropriate. The results can be systematized according to syntax and then to a corresponding meaning (see table 3.1).

Table 3.1. Summary of the syntax of סבל/נשא with nouns for "sin" / "guilt"

Category	Subject	Verb for "carry/bear"	Object Marker	Noun for "sin"	Comments
1	Various	נשא	ל	פשע in construct or + pron. sfx.	"to forgive transgression"
2	Sinner	נשא		חטא/עון + pron. sfx	"to bear one's own guilt"
3	Priest	נשא	את	עון in construct or + pron. sfx.	"to bear guilt for someone else"
4	Father/Son	נשא or סבל	ב or ( )	עון in construct or + pron. sfx.	"to bear guilt of another"
5	YHWH	נשא		עון	"to forgive"

Including the two occurrences in Isaiah 53:11-12, there are fifty-four total occurrences in the Hebrew Bible of the various combinations compiled by the software search.[35]

1. Various subjects: נשא + ל + פשע—"to forgive transgression"

In contexts where the preposition ל marks the noun פֶּשַׁע ("transgression"), the clause means "to forgive transgression."

Example: כִּי לֹא יִשָּׂא לְפִשְׁעֲכֶם "for he [the angel of the Lord] will not forgive [bear] your transgressions " (Ex 23:21)[36] The five occurrences are:

Genesis 50:17—two times {without ל in first occurrence}

---

[35]In the presentation that follows, variations to the syntactical pattern are included in "{ }" following the citation. Comments within "( )" are explanatory. Citations within "[ ]" immediately after a citation indicate English version versification where it is different from the Hebrew versification. All Scripture passages, unless otherwise noted, are the author's translation.

[36]Israel was not to rebel against the angel of the Lord because he would not forgive their sins, for the name of Yahweh was in him.

Exodus 23:21

Joshua 24:19—also includes the noun חֵטְא[37]

1 Samuel 25:28

2. The sinner is the subject: נשׂא + עון/חטא + pron. sfx—"to bear one's own guilt"

In contexts where the noun is either עון[38] ("guilt") or חטא ("sin") with a pronominal suffix[39] referring to the subject of the verb, and the noun is unmarked by preposition or direct-object marker את, the clause means "to bear one's own guilt." The back-reference of the pronominal suffix to the subject of the verb is the key to recognizing this class. The absence of the expected direct-object marker also marks this class.[40] In many of these situations an explicit punishment or penalty is cited for committing the particular sin[41]—for example, the person eating sacrificial meat that has not been consumed within the prescribed time "must be cut off from the people" (Lev 19:8).

Example: וְהַנֶּפֶשׁ הָאֹכֶלֶת מִמֶּנּוּ עֲוֺנָהּ תִּשָּׂא. "The soul who eats from it[42] will bear its own guilt" (Lev 7:18). The twenty-four occurrences include:

Genesis 4:13—עון with first common singular pronominal suffix is the subject of a participial form of נשׂא.[43]

---

[37]Because the subject of the verb is Yahweh, this case is also treated in Category 5 (cases where Yahweh is the subject).

[38]עון is more commonly used than חטא. Occurrences with חטא are noted in parentheses.

[39]In two cases, Leviticus 22:16 and Ezekiel 23:49, the noun for sin is in construct with another noun rather than a pronominal suffix. The syntactical structure of construct noun-phrases is formally parallel to that of the noun-phrase with pronominal suffix.

[40]The direct-object marker is expected in cases where the object is definite, as would be the case in all situations where the object noun has a pronominal suffix or the object noun is in construct. Its regular absence in these constructions is noteworthy, though the primary signal remains the back-reference of the suffix to the subject of the verb.

[41]See Whybray, *Thanksgiving*, 32, for further discussion on the presence of a penalty with phrases in this category of warning.

[42]I.e., sacrificial meat that has become impure because it was left too long before it was consumed.

[43]Cain complains to God that "bearing my guilt is severe [great]" (גָּדוֹל עֲוֺנִי מִנְּשֹׂא). The context suggests perhaps an emotional and psychological dimension to "bearing sin." This passage belongs in this category because the pronominal suffix refers back to Cain. While Cain is not the subject of the immediate clause, he is the referent for the suffix, and the sin that is being borne is his.

Exodus 28:43—{no suffix with עָוֹן}.[44]

Leviticus 5:1, 17; 7:18; 17:16; 19:8; 20:17, 19, 20 (חטא); 22:16—(עָוֹן in construct with אָשָׁם); 24:15 (חטא).

Numbers 5:31—{את marks עָוֹן}; 9:13 (חטא); 14:34 {את marks עָוֹן};[45] 18:22 (חטא), 23.

Ezekiel 14:10; 23:49—(חטא; in construct with "your idolatries"), 44:10, 12.

Leviticus 19:17; 22:9; and Numbers 18:32 share identical syntax, with a variation (the addition of the prepositional phrase עָלָיו) that forms a related subclass within this category of "bearing one's own guilt" where the sin/guilt of something else comes to an individual for that individual's sin of omission or neglect:

Syntactical pattern: conjunction + negative + נָשָׂא + עָלָיו + חֵטְא.

Leviticus 19:17: וְלֹא־תִשָּׂא עָלָיו חֵטְא "and you will not bear sin on account of him."[46]

Leviticus 22:9: וְלֹא־יִשְׂאוּ עָלָיו חֵטְא "and they will not bear sin on account of it."[47]

Numbers 18:32: וְלֹא־תִשְׂאוּ עָלָיו חֵטְא "and you will not bear sin on account of it."[48]

3. **The subject is a priest: נָשָׂא + את + עָוֹן in construct (or + pron. sfx.)—"to bear guilt for someone else"**

In contexts where the noun עָוֹן ("guilt") is used in construct (five times), with the noun for which someone is bearing the guilt, or is used with a pronominal suffix (three times) that refers to that for

---

[44]This is an exception (the only one in this category) to the pattern of a pronominal suffix referring back to the subject of the verb. It is included here because, as is the case in most of the other passages in this category, there is a penalty associated with the warning (i.e., the priest will die if he dresses improperly). So, while the pronominal suffix is absent, it is clear from the context that the guilt (עָוֹן) is the priest's and that its consequences fall on him.

[45]While the direct-object marker, את, marks the noun-phrase containing עָוֹן in Numbers 5:31, 14:34, the pronominal suffix in each case refers back to the subject of the verb, which is the primary syntactical key identifying this category. Grammatically, the את is to be expected in all cases where the noun-phrase is definite. Its unexpected absence in all but two cases also serves to mark this group as a unique category.

[46] The context is a warning about rebuking your neighbor so that you do not become guilty on account of his sin.

[47]The context is a warning to priests not to break Yahweh's commandments.

[48]The context is a warning to priests concerning the proper manner of offering sacrifices.

which guilt is being borne, the clause is translated "to bear guilt for something or someone else." The key identifier is that the back-reference of the noun phrase for guilt is *not* to the subject of the verb. Another key identifier is that the noun phrase with עָוֹן is marked by the direct object marker אֵת. This construction occurs primarily in contexts of priestly duties.

Example: וְנָשָׂא אַהֲרֹן אֶת־עֲוֺן הַקֳּדָשִׁים "and Aaron will bear the guilt of the holy things" (Ex 28:38). There are eight occurrences of this:[49]

Exodus 28:38—for "the guilt of the holy things."

Leviticus 10:17—for "the guilt of the assembly"; 16:22—for "their guilt" (pron. sfx. refers to Israel; + prep. phrase עָלָיו.[50]

Numbers 18:1—(two times) for "the guilt of the holy things" and for "the guilt of your priesthood"; 30:16 [30:15]—for "her guilt" (pron. sfx. refers to the wife of the man, who will bear her wrong).[51]

Ezekiel[52] 4:4—for "their guilt" (pron. sfx. refers to Israel); 4:5—for "the guilt of the house of Israel" {unmarked by אֵת};[53] 4:6—for "the guilt of the house of Israel."

4. **Subject is father (or son): נשא (or סבל) + בְ (or no marker) + עָוֹן in construct (or + pron. sfx.)—"to bear guilt of another as well as your own"**

The clauses about "the sins of the fathers visited on the sons"[54] form a unique category on the basis of content and unusual syntax. The three occurrences in Ezekiel 18 are unusual in that the noun phrase for "guilt" is marked by the preposition בְ.[55] The isolated case in Lamentations 5 is unusual on three counts: first, the verb סבל occurs

---

[49]The item for which guilt is being borne is indicated in quotation marks after the dash.

[50]In the scapegoat situation, which will be discussed in more detail below.

[51]While this case fits syntactically and is a warning to someone about bearing the sin for something or someone else, this is the only case where the subject is not a priest. The husband, the subject of the verb, will suffer the consequences of the wife's vow if he did not object when he first heard it.

[52]Whether Ezekiel, who is a priest, is functioning as a priest in this set of symbolic actions is unclear and does not affect the conclusion that his act is for someone else.

[53]The syntax in Ezekiel 4:5 is identical to that of Ezekiel 4:4, 6 except for the lack of אֵת, and hence it belongs to this class though the direct-object marker is missing.

[54]Ezekiel 18:19-20; Lamentations 5:7. See the discussion in Whybray, *Thanksgiving*, 52-56 and in Hofius, "Gottesknechtslied," 111-12. See also the related passages in Exodus 20:5, 32:31-34; 34:7.

[55]This syntax is unique to this passage and not used elsewhere in the OT.

only here and in Isaiah 53:11; second, as in category 2, the noun-phrase for guilt is unmarked; but third, unlike category 2, the back-reference is not to the subject.

This class of clauses for "bearing guilt" is different in that the subject of the verb bears both his own guilt and the guilt of the earlier generations.[56] Hence, they do not fit well with any of the other categories, nor do they match them syntactically. Perhaps the peculiar and unique use of בֿ and the unusual choice of verb are a recognition of this nuance in meaning. The data is insufficient for drawing any firm conclusions, but it is noteworthy that these cases were indeed marked syntactically.

There are four occurrences in two contexts:

Ezekiel 18:19-20—for "the guilt of the father and/or son" (בֿ marks the construct chain in each case).

Ezekiel 18:19 לֹא־נָשָׂא הַבֵּן בַּעֲוֹן הָאָב ("The son has not borne the guilt of the father").

Ezekiel 18:20 בֵּן לֹא־יִשָּׂא בַּעֲוֹן הָאָב ("The son will not bear the guilt of the father").

אָב לֹא יִשָּׂא בַּעֲוֹן הַבֵּן ("The father will not bear the guilt of the son.") Lamentations 5:7—for "their guilt" (pron. sfx refers to the fathers; the verb is סבל).

עֲוֺנֹתֵיהֶם סָבָלְנוּ ("Their guilt we have borne"; i.e., the guilt of the fathers).

5. **YHWH is the subject: נשׂא + עון/פשׁע/חטא (usually without suffix or construction)—"to forgive"**

In contexts where *Yahweh* is the subject doing, or being asked to do, the "bearing" with any of the three of the nouns for "guilt," usually *without* pronominal suffix (i.e., a general sense of guilt, transgression or sin), and unmarked by preposition or direct-object marker, the clause is translated "forgive guilt."

Example (Ex 34:7): נֹשֵׂא עָוֺן וָפֶשַׁע וְחַטָּאָה ("who[57] bears guilt, trans-

---

[56]For Lamentations 5:7, the exclamation that they are all sinners in Lamentations 5:16 settles the issue that the speaker in Lamentations 5:7 is not debating personal guilt. See also Why-bray, *Thanksgiving*, 29.

[57]I.e., Yahweh, who maintains his love to innumerable people and bears guilt, transgression and sin *to those who love him*.

gression and sin.") The eight occurrences are as follows:[58]

Exodus 34:7—plus פֶּשַׁע and חַטָּאָה

Numbers 14:18—plus פֶּשַׁע

Joshua 24:19—marked by לְ;[59] "your transgressions" (פֶּשַׁע) and "your sins" (חַטָּאָה), but without עָוֹן

Micah 7:18

Hosea 14:3 [14:2]—"all" is the modifier

Psalm 32:5—עָוֹן in construct with "my guilt"

Psalm 85:3 [85:2]—עָוֹן in construct with "your people"

Job 7:21—"my transgression" (פֶּשַׁע)

Unique Syntax Deserving Special Attention

Besides the two cases in Isaiah 53:11-12, four of the fifty-four occurrences were not treated under the five headings above. Each is unique in some fashion or other, though each arguably falls within one of the five domains already discussed.

Isaiah 64:5 [6]—in a context of poetic simile, "our guilt" is the *subject* of the verb נָשָׂא—guilt is likened to "the wind bearing away those who are guilty." Note the ironic twist of sin bearing the sinner away rather than vice versa.

Isaiah 33:24 and Psalm 32:1—both use a passive participial of נָשָׂא as a nominal in construct with עָוֹן ("the one who has been forgiven guilt"). In each case the one forgiving is Yahweh, so these arguably belong under category 5, where Yahweh is the subject of the verb.

Hosea 4:8—the only case in the Hebrew text in which the preposition אֶל marks עָוֹן.[60]

---

[58]Exodus 34:7, Numbers 14:8, Joshua 24:19 and Micah 7:18 are all related—Yahweh is the one who forgives (or does not forgive) sin, guilt and transgression.

[59]The noun-phrase marked by לְ is used in the syntax of category 1 "to forgive transgression," but it seems to be atypical when Yahweh is the subject doing the forgiving. Perhaps what sets this passage apart is that sin is not general but specified by the pronominal suffixes.

[60]The second colon of Hosea 4:8 is of uncertain translation: עַמִּי יֹאכֵלוּ וְאֶל־עֲוֹנָם יִשְׂאוּ נַפְשׁוֹ חַטָּאת ("the sin of my people they [i.e., wicked priests] consume, and to/for their guilt they bear him [i.e., my people]"). Because אֶל and לְ can be used interchangeably, this colon could be syntactically construed with category 1, "to forgive," and in that case the sense would be ironic—the priests are not only consuming the people but they are giving them false security by improperly forgiving their sin, all the while profiting from it.

In sum, with these exceptions, the distribution of the various combinations for "bearing guilt" can be categorized according to syntactical and grammatical features into five categories, which in turn have specific connotations.

The Peculiar Syntax of the "Bearing Guilt" Clauses in Isaiah 53:11-12

Having covered the syntax and context of the various cases, I now turn attention to the syntax and context of the two cases in Isaiah 53:11-12. These two clauses do not precisely fit any of the preceding five categories, but they do match one another and seem to form their own category.

Isaiah 53:11d וַעֲוֹנֹתָם הוּא יִסְבֹּל ("and their guilt he will bear"): conj. + noun-phrase for guilt + subj. + verb (סבל).

Isaiah 53:12d וְהוּא חֵטְא־רַבִּים נָשָׂא ("and he the sin of many bore"): conj. + subj. + noun-phrase for guilt + verb (נשׂא).

Except for switching the order of the noun-phrase for guilt and the subject, the syntax of these two clauses is identical:[61]

The noun-phrase for guilt is unmarked by the preposition or the direct-object marker. In both cases the noun for guilt is modified (pronominal suffix in Is 53:11 and absolute noun of the construct chain in Is 53:12), and in both cases the back-referent of the modifiers is not the subject (i.e., the Servant) of the verb "to bear." In both cases the noun-phrase for guilt precedes the verb.

Syntactically there are similarities and differences with categories 2-4:[62]

1. Like category 2—"to bear one's own guilt"—these two clauses do not have the direct-object marker marking the noun-phrase for guilt. But unlike category 2, neither subject of the clauses is the reference for the modifier in the noun-phrase for guilt.

2. Like category 3—"to bear guilt for someone else"—the back reference for the modifier in the noun-phrase for guilt is not the subject. But unlike the syntactical pattern in category 3, the direct-object marker does not mark the noun-phrase for guilt.

---

[61]The tenses of the verbs vary, as do the lexemes for the verb "to bear" and the noun for "guilt." These variations belong, not to the discussion of syntax, but to the hierarchical relations.

[62]No one is arguing that these clauses fit Category 1 "to forgive transgression" or category 5 where Yahweh himself is the subject.

3. Like category 4—Yahweh forgiving sin—these two clauses lack the direct-object marker, and the modifiers for the noun-phrase for guilt do not point to the subject. In this passage, of course, the Servant is distinguished from Yahweh and is hence not to be understood as Yahweh.

On the basis of the preceding observations of the syntax and distribution of "bearing guilt" clauses in the Hebrew text, the syntax of the two bearing-guilt clauses in Isaiah 53:11-12 are unique, and I conclude that they may therefore have a meaning peculiar to their syntax.

Four Particular Passages That Relate to "Bearing Guilt"
Before exploring what significance, if any, might be borne by the unique syntax of these two "bearing guilt" clauses in Isaiah 53, it is necessary to look at four passages that have been discussed at length in this debate about the meaning of "bearing guilt" in Isaiah 53.

1. *Ezekiel symbolically bears the guilt of Israel (Ezek 4:4-6).*[63] The situation in Ezekiel 4:4-6 appears to be similar to that of Isaiah 53:11-12. As part of a sign prophecy, Ezekiel was to "bear (נשָׂא) the guilt (עָוֹן) of the house of Israel." But there are also differences in the two contexts. Ezekiel's action was serving as a sign. As Whybray correctly points out, Ezekiel did not remove Israel's guilt by "bearing it," for Israel went into exile notwithstanding—his symbolic suffering "signifies that the inhabitants of Jerusalem will in the future themselves bear their עָוֹן, which they have fully deserved."[64] In other words, his symbolic suffering only indicates how long the exiles will suffer. Moreover, there is never an accent on Ezekiel's righteousness or on his suffering innocently for the sins of others.

2. *"Bearing guilt" and "making atonement" (Lev 10:17).*[65] Speaking about the food given to the priests, Moses linked "bearing the guilt of others" to "making atonement" when he reminded Aaron that

וְאֹתָהּ נָתַן לָכֶם לָשֵׂאת אֶת־עֲוֺן הָעֵדָה לְכַפֵּר עֲלֵיהֶם לִפְנֵי יְהוָה

---

[63]Cf. Whybray, *Thanksgiving*, 50-52.
[64]Ibid., 52.
[65]Cf. Whybray, *Thanksgiving*, 45-46.

"[Yahweh] gave it to you *for bearing the guilt* of the assembly *in order to make atonement* for them before Yahweh."[66]

The sacrifice was for making atonement and belonged to the priest because the priest had borne the guilt of the congregation in his priestly duties. As part of the process of making atonement for the people, the priest bore their guilt; that is, he removed it. Bearing and removing sin and guilt are two ways of describing the same action, and both stand at the heart of atonement. The priest, however, was never construed as innocent or suffering for others in this task. He too had to make atonement for his own guilt and was himself in constant danger of mortal consequences if he did not behave according to the commandments of Yahweh.

3. *The Scapegoat (Lev 16:20-22).*[67] The scapegoat passage has often been cited in connection with bearing guilt in Isaiah 53. The ceremony surrounding the scapegoat was a unique part of the atoning process in the annual celebration of the Day of Atonement (Lev 16:1-25). After Aaron, the high priest, had made atonement for himself and for the holy of holies, he made atonement for Israel by laying his hands on the head of the scapegoat and confessing all the guilt (עֲוֹן) of Israel and their transgressions (פֶּשַׁע), indeed all their sins (חַטָּאת), and then sending the goat off into the wilderness (Lev 16:21). Leviticus 16:22 explains that "the goat will bear (נָשָׂא) on itself (עָלָיו) all their guilt (עֲוֹן) into a solitary land."[68]

The similarities between the Servant and the scapegoat are several. First, there are the linguistic similarities. As with the Servant bearing guilt in Isaiah 53:11, 12, the scapegoat (the subject of the verb) is bearing guilt that is not his own (i.e., "their guilt" refers to Israel, not the scapegoat).[69] Second, as was the case in Isaiah 53:11-12, it was a

---

[66]The two infinitive clauses are not to be treated as functionally identical. The first infinitive means "for bearing guilt," and the second, "in order to make atonement."

[67]Cf. Whybray, *Thanksgiving*, 48-49.

[68]When Childs argues that in the language of Isaiah 53:11-12 "the servant did not obliterate the sin" and hence that "there is no parallel to scapegoat—rather the terminology is that he 'bore' or 'carried it' (ns' sbl)," (*Isaiah*, 418) he overlooked the use of "bearing sin" language in the scapegoat passage itself, Leviticus16:22.

[69]Whybray, *Thanksgiving*, 46, denies that the OT assumes a transference of guilt to a sacrificial victim. Yet he never deals explicitly with the concept of the laying on of hands in discussing either the scapegoat or the Levitical sacrifices.

living creature who bore the guilt of others. Third, the goat, like the Servant, suffered— the goat was led out into the wilderness, a place of barrenness and threat to life.[70]

There are differences as well as similarities between the Servant and the scapegoat. The noun phrase "their guilt" is marked by the direct-object marker, which is not the case in Isaiah 53. The prepositional phrase "on him" (עליו) is also absent. From the more ritual perspective, Isaiah has no parallel to the priests laying their hands on the scapegoat and confessing the guilt of the people over him. Indeed, the Servant bears guilt without any one knowing it until after the fact.

4. *Moses' offer to be blotted out to atone for the guilt of Israel (Ex 32:30-35).*[71] Although it does not use the language of "bearing guilt," the story of Moses going up to Yahweh on Mt. Sinai in order to try to make atonement for Israel's sin with the golden calf (Ex 32:30-35 NIV) relates to this discussion:[72]

> The next day Moses said to the people, "You have committed a great sin. But now I will go up to the LORD; perhaps I can make atonement for your sin." So Moses went back to the LORD and said, "Oh, what a great sin these people have committed! They have made themselves gods of gold. But now, please forgive their sin— but if not, then blot me out of the book you have written." The LORD replied to Moses, "Whoever has sinned against me I will blot out of my book. Now go, lead the people to the place I spoke of, and my angel will go before you. However, when the time comes for me to punish, I will punish them for their sin." And the LORD struck the people with a plague because of what they did with the calf Aaron had made.

Moses offered to have his name blotted out of the book of life[73] to

---

[70]Here I depart from Whybray, who asserts that in "bearing sin into the wilderness" the point is about the physical act of removing the sin far away and not about the suffering of the goat. While I agree that the action symbolizes the removal of sin to a distant place, the wilderness was never seen in OT literature as a positive place. The goat being sent there certainly symbolized its extreme suffering and probably its death as part of the process of removing sin far from Israel.

[71]It is interesting to note that Whybray deals with this passage only in passing (*Thanksgiving*, 74).

[72]Note that it is the outbreak of the wrath of God that requires atonement.

[73]I.e., to die, which is clearly self-sacrificial on the part of Moses.

atone for Israel and to spare them further wrath. Yahweh's answer was clear: the one who sinned will die, not you. As has been observed,[74] this certainly seems to state clearly that one human cannot die to make atonement for another.

The salient concerns from these four passages for the issue of "bearing guilt" are as follows: While Ezekiel may suffer, his action is symbolic and does not prevent the exile; the removal of guilt is atonement;[75] and God's response to Moses' intercession in Exodus 32:30-35 implies that he will not accept the death of one human to make atonement for another.

So What Does It Mean That the Servant "Bears Their Guilt" in Isaiah 53?

I agree with Whybray that the situations described in categories 2-4 do not represent vicarious suffering.[76] But concerning his extrapolation from this data to the situation in Isaiah 53 that the Servant does not suffer vicariously, I disagree. The uniqueness of the syntax in Isaiah 53 cannot be ignored and warrants another conclusion. However, the unique syntax of the two "bearing guilt" clauses in Isaiah 53:11-12 is not the only indicator of the unique role that the Servant "bearing guilt" plays in Isaiah 53. The Servant himself is portrayed as unique from the moment Yahweh introduces him in Isaiah 52:13. Moreover, נשׂא and סבל are *leitworts* in Isaiah 53, and Isaiah's other usage of "bearing guilt" and "bearing" in general inform the meaning of "bearing guilt" in Isaiah 53. Finally, there are clues in the immediate context that suggest a unique action in the Servant's "bearing guilt." A brief look at each of these is warranted.

The Servant of Isaiah 53 is unique from several perspectives. The unique syntax involving the verbs נשׂא and סבל mentioned earlier comports well with the uniqueness of the Servant himself. First, the language "high and lifted up" (וְנִשָּׂא רָם) applied by Yahweh to his Servant (Is 52:13) is striking. This phrasing is used four times in Isaiah

---

[74]E.g., Hofius, "Gottesknechtslied," 111-12.

[75]Leviticus 10:17 and 16:20-22. In his *Commentary on the Prophecies of Isaiah,* new and rev. (New York: Charles Scribner, 1865) 2:308, Joseph A. Alexander argues that according to the rest of the OT, the removal of sin is only accomplished by making atonement. As Oswalt says (*Isaiah*, 406, n. 63), and I agree, Alexander's argument still stands.

[76]Whybray, *Thanksgiving*, 56.

(and nowhere else in the OT).[77] Three times it refers to Yahweh, and in Isaiah 53, Yahweh applied it to his servant (Is 52:13):

> Isaiah 6:1 "I saw the Lord sitting on his throne, *exalted and lifted up* [וְנִשָּׂא רָם], and his train filled the temple."

> Isaiah 33:10 "Now I will arise, says Yahweh, *now I will be exalted; now I will be lifted up.* [עַתָּה אָרוֹמָם עַתָּה אֶנָּשֵׂא]"

> Isaiah 52:13 "Behold, my servant will prosper. *He will be exalted and lifted up* [יָרוּם וְנִשָּׂא], and highly honored."

> Isaiah 57:15 "Thus says *the one who is exalted, the one who is lifted up* [וְנִשָּׂא רָם], the one who lives forever—holy is his name: "In an exalted and holy place I live, but also with the lowly."

Yahweh's own lips declared that the Servant was to be identified with Yahweh himself. The Servant had been accorded, by honorific language spoken by the voice of Yahweh himself, a position belonging only to Yahweh. No one else in Isaiah is so honored or set apart.[78] It is most difficult to imagine, as Whybray argues, that the Servant was Second Isaiah.[79] Who would have referred to him this way?[80] It should not be overlooked that the one who has borne (נָשָׂא) the sin of others (Is 53:12) will be the one who is lifted up (נָשָׂא) by Yahweh (Is 52:13). The wordplay[81] is not accidental.

Second, what happened to the servant was so unusual that the voice that speaks as "we" in Isaiah 53:1-8 felt it essential to justify what had happened as Yahweh's doing—"Yahweh laid on him our guilt" (Is 53:6). The voice in Isaiah 53:10 is more explicit—"Yahweh desired [willed] to crush him." The point is made because something most unusual has happened. Whybray's idea that the suffering was simply

---

[77]The *Quest 1.0* (1991) search query was for either verb (נָשָׂא or רוּם) within four words of the other in either order in any tense. Isaiah 2:13 and Numbers 24:7 bear more consideration in this connection. Cf. also the similar observation by Oswalt (*Isaiah*, 378) and note the connection he draws between this word pair and the humbling of mankind/exaltation of Yahweh in Isaiah 2:6-22.

[78]While this should not be seen in its original context as claiming divinity for the Servant, it would be appropriate in light of the revelation of Christ in the NT to understand this to refer to the Servant's divinity.

[79]*Thanksgiving*, 25, 30.

[80]Oswalt, *Isaiah*, 378-79.

[81]Whybray himself notes "the predilection for word-play which is found in the poems of Deutero-Isaiah" (*Thanksgiving*, 60).

"more intense suffering" by exilic Second Isaiah does not explain why such qualifications would be necessary.

To "carry" (נשא and סבל) is a "leitwort" in Isaiah 53.[82]

The servant will be "lifted up" (נשא) (Is 52:13)

The servant carried (נשא) our infirmities and bore (סבל) our sorrows (Is 53:4)[83]

The servant will bear (סבל) their [i.e., the many] guilt (Is 53:11)

The servant carried (נשא) the sin of many (Is 53:12)

With these verbs "to carry" and the things being carried, there is an overall movement in the song from the man of sorrows and infirmities (Is 53:3), to the man who bore sorrows and infirmities (Is 53:4), to the one who bore guilt and sin (Is 53:11-12). The after-the-fact recognition by the "we" that it was not only their hurts but their *sins* that he carried came as a surprise to them. The build-up intensifies and draws a focus to these words and their unique usage.

The broader usage of נשא and סבל in Isaiah to express the "bearing of guilt." Besides the occurrences in Isaiah 53:11-12, נשא is used in the sense of "bearing sin or guilt" in only three other cases:

"Do not bear [i.e., forgive] them" (וְאַל־תִּשָּׂא לָהֶם) (Is 2:9)

"Those living in [Zion] having guilt borne " (הַיֹּשֵׁב בָּהּ נְשֻׂא עָוֹן) (Is 33:24)

"Our guilt, like the wind, has borne us away" (וַעֲוֹנֵנוּ כָּרוּחַ יִשָּׂאֻנוּ) (Is 64:5 [64:6])

In each case the usage is unusual. Isaiah 2:9 has the only occurrence of נשא in the Hebrew text to mean "forgive" *without* the use of פשע. This is

---

[82]*Leitwort* is a repeated word used in order to accent key point(s) and therefore points to the theme of a text. See Robert Alter, *The Art of Biblical Narrative* (New York: Basic Books, 1981), 95. Whybray argues in another direction, saying that "repetition does not add to the meaning of what is being repeated; and what is being repeated is not a statement about vicarious atonement" (*Thanksgiving*, 75). While Whybray is speaking about all the lexical repetitions in Isaiah 53, it is likely that his criticism of נשא and סבל as *leitworts* would be of similar kind.

[83]The syntax in Isaiah 53:5 is identical to the syntax in Isaiah 53:11-12: both lack the direct-object marker, and the back-reference of both of the pronominal suffixes is to the people and not the Servant, the subject of the verbs.

perhaps a play on the word נָשָׂא. Elsewhere in Isaiah, Yahweh "bears"
(נָשָׂא) his people. He bears (carries)[84] them, and he bears (forgives) them.
Here Isaiah is saying "don't נָשָׂא them." Does he mean "do not carry
them" or "do not forgive them"? Or both? The wordplay is ironic.

Isaiah 33:24 and Psalm 32:1 are the occasions in which a passive
form of the verb is used to express carrying guilt (in these two cases
having been forgiven by Yahweh).

The immediate context of the verbs "to carry." Each of the two
clauses, Isaiah 53:11d and 53:12d, stands in parallel with an adjacent
clause within the same verse, and in each case something surprising is
said about the Servant.

1. *Isaiah 53:11c-d.* Isaiah 53:11 has been problematic for interpreters.
Many have taken the infinitival phrase בְּדַעְתּוֹ ("in his knowledge") as
the first constituent of the following clause and have translated it "By
his knowledge, my righteous servant will justify many." Instead, I take
the phrase as the A' element in an ABB'A' structure in the first half of
the verse—"After the suffering of his soul, he will see; he will be satisfied with his knowledge" (Is 53:11a-b).[85]

מֵעֲמַל נַפְשׁוֹ • A	Isaiah 53:11a	A • After the suffering of his soul,
יִרְאֶה • B		B • he will see;
יִשְׂבָּע • B'	Isaiah 53:11b	B' • he will be satisfied
בְּדַעְתּוֹ • A'		A' • by his knowledge.

By taking the בְּדַעְתּוֹ ("in his knowledge") phrase as the A' element
in this structure, it will not be treated as part of the following clause,
therefore.

The second half of the verse also has a mirrored structure
(ABCC'B'A'),[86] which is the argument for reading these final two
clauses (Is 53:11c-d) together.

---

[84]Isaiah 40:11; esp. 46:3-4, 49:22; 63:9; 66:2.

[85]Oswalt (*Isaiah*, 404) and Childs (*Isaiah*, 419) argue for the same clause hierarchy. In grammatical terms, the structure is: prepositional phrase + verb + verb + prepositional phrase. In
each case the pronominal suffix in the prepositional phrase refers back to the Servant.

[86]In grammatical terms: verb + subject + prepositional phrase + (conjunction) + noun-phrase
+ subject + verb. The link between C and C' is by means of reference: the suffix ("their") with
the noun-phrase in C' refers back to the noun ("the many") in the prepositional phrase of C.
If adjective/noun immediately after the verb in A ("the innocent [righteous]") is treated
separately from the verb rather than idiomatically as a partner with the verb, the local structure is changed, but the overall linking of these two clauses is not overturned.

A • יַצְדִּיק צַדִּיק	Isaiah 53:11c	A • He will acquit the innocent
B • עַבְדִּי		B • my servant
C • לָרַבִּים		C • for the many
C' • וַעֲוֹנֹתָם	Isaiah 53:11d	C' • and their guilt
B' • הוּא		B' • he
A' • יִסְבֹּל		A' • will bear.

In six of the eleven other occurrences of the *hifil* of צדק in the Hebrew Bible, some form of the *hifil* of צדק is used with its cognate noun (e.g., הַצְדִּיק צַדִּיק—"acquitting the innocent [righteous]") or the inverse cognate noun (e.g., לֹא־אַצְדִּיק רָשָׁע—"I will not acquit the wicked").[87] It is arguable, then, that יַצְדִּיק צַדִּיק ("he will acquit the innocent") is idiomatic and that the combination is inseparable; a subject will not intervene between the two constituents.[88] Thus, I take עַבְדִּי ("my servant") as the subject of the predicate, and the inseparable compound יַצְדִּיק צַדִּיק ("he will acquit the innocent") as the predicate itself. The translation of the entire clause then becomes: "my Servant will acquit the innocent [righteous] for the many."[89]

We observe further that when the *hifil* form of צדק appears with its cognate noun צַדִּיק, its inverse construction—the *hifil* form of רשע, with its cognate noun (e.g., הַרְשִׁיעַ רָשָׁע, "condemning the wicked")— often appears in parallel.[90] The constituents can be swapped in order to express the negative command to forbid the condemning of the innocent and the acquittal of the wicked.[91]

In Isaiah 53:11c-d, the "bearing guilt" clause fills the slot that in other contexts is occupied by "condemning the wicked," the inverse of "acquitting the innocent." This juxtaposition creates an element of surprise. One would expect something like "My Servant will acquit the in-

---

[87]Exodus 23:7 (not acquitting the wicked); Deuteronomy 25:1; 1 Kings 8:32; Isaiah 5:23 (acquitting the wicked without a parallel); Proverbs 17:15; and 2 Chronicles 6:23 (= 1 Kings 8:32, with a minor variation). The other five occurrences stand without the inverse parallel in view: 2 Samuel 15:4; Isaiah 50:8; Psalm 82:3; Job 27:5; and Daniel 12:3.

[88]None of the other examples in the Hebrew Bible have an explicit subject with the combination, so there are no examples to prove or disprove it.

[89]Mowinkel and Westermann, according to Whybray (*Thanksgiving*, 71) have argued for a so-called internal causative *hifil* and translate it as "My Servant will show himself righteous before the many." Whybray also finds this option the most likely.

[90]E.g., 1 Kings 8:32.

[91]E.g., Proverbs 17:15.

nocent and condemn the guilty." The Servant does indeed acquit the innocent, but then, instead of condemning the wicked, he bears the guilt of the many!

One final peculiarity in Isaiah 53:11d is the use of the verb סבל, which is found only in Isaiah 53:4, 11, and Isaiah 46:4, 7.[92] The use of the more rare verb to express "bearing guilt" in Isaiah 53:11d, and the connection it might evoke to the context in Isaiah 46—where Yahweh is carrying and sustaining his people—marks this usage and calls attention to it. Once again, there is an element of the unusual in what the servant is doing. So not only is the internal syntax of the "bearing guilt" clause in Isaiah 53:11d unusual, but its content is unexpected as well.

2. *Isaiah 53:12c-d.* "And he the sins of many carried and for transgressors will intercede." The situation in Isaiah 53:12c-d is less problematic than in Isaiah 53:11c-d. The final two clauses are also mirrored, though asymmetrically (ABCB'C').[93]

וְהוּא • **A**	Isaiah 53:12c	**A** • And he
הֵטְא־רַבִּים • **B**		**B** • the sin of the many
נָשָׂא • **C**		**C** • has borne;
וְלַפֹּשְׁעִים • **B'**	Isaiah 53:12d	**B'** • and for transgressors
יַפְגִּיעַ • **C'**		**C'** • he will intercede.

I take "the many" to be the same group as "the many" in Isaiah 53:11 and in the first half of Isaiah 53:12. It is their guilt that the Servant will bear (Is 53:11), and it is their sin that he has carried (Is 53:12).[94] Here he intercedes for them. In the rest of Isaiah 53, the Servant is silent (cf. Is 53:7) and passive. This is the only case in which the Servant acts or speaks. One might expect him to protest the injustice that he, being innocent, should suffer for the guilty, but instead we find that he intercedes for them. This is surprising and unusual behavior. Its surprise

---

[92]There are two nominal uses of סבל: in Isaiah 9:3 and 10:27, where it means "burdens."

[93]Grammatically: conjunction + subject + object + verb + conjunction + prepositional phrase + verb. The subject is not repeated, giving the asymmetrical structure. The A' element would be an explicit subject in Isaiah 53:12d, coming at the beginning of the clause (not the normal syntactical position) and followed by a clause constituent that is *not* the predicate is most unusual.

[94]On identity of "the many" I agree with Clines (*I, He, We, and They*, 22), which means that "the many" in Isaiah 52:14-15 are also the same set of people (i.e., including the nations).

value is accented by its position as the final clause in the song.

Summary of the immediate context of the "bearing guilt" clauses in Isaiah 53:11-12. Each of the "bearing guilt" clauses is unexpected in light of the clause with which it is paralleled in its immediate context. Instead of condemning them for their guilt, he will bear it (Is 53:11c-d). Instead of speaking out in protest that, although innocent, he carried their guilt and sin, he will actually intercede for the transgressors (Is 53:12c-d). At every turn there are surprises in Isaiah 53.

Summary of "Bearing Guilt" in Isaiah 53

There are two primary arguments that "bearing guilt" in Isaiah 53 cannot have anything to do with atonement. First, nowhere else in the Old Testament is human suffering a possibility for making atonement;[95] and secondly, nowhere else in the Old Testament, except in the scapegoat passage, is "bearing guilt" used in a vicarious sense, and Isaiah 53 does not seem an adequate parallel in circumstances or syntax.

The primary argument that the two "bearing guilt" clauses in Isaiah 53:11-12 should be interpreted to mean that by "bearing guilt" the Servant "makes atonement" is that the internal syntax of the two clauses in 53:11-12 form a unique set over against all the other occurrences in the Hebrew Bible. The unique syntax is well suited to indicate a unique meaning, "to make atonement."

There are several other features in Isaiah 53 as well as in all of Isaiah that reinforce both the uniqueness of Isaiah 53 and of the "bearing guilt" clauses. First, the use of the verb נשׂא in constructions that mean to "bear guilt" in Isaiah is always unusual. Second, when Yahweh says the Servant will be exalted and lifted up, like Yahweh himself, he is making the Servant and the passage about the Servant unique. Hence, it is not unexpected that there will be many surprises in the content and even the syntax of Isaiah 53. Third, נשׂא and סבל as *leitworts* in Isaiah 53 move the song forward from surprise ("bearing infirmities and sorrows" in Is 53:4) to even greater surprise ("bearing guilt and sin" in Is 53:11-12). Moreover, the servant who bore guilt (נשׂא) will be the one lifted up (נשׂא) as well. Fourth, each of the other occurrences of נשׂא in Isaiah, when it means to "bear guilt," is unusual. It should be no surprise that the usage in Isaiah 53 is unusual too. Fifth, the immediate

---

[95]See Exodus 32:30-35.

context of each clause shows that they are unexpected in their immediate context—bearing the guilt of the many rather than condemning the wicked, and after having borne the sin of the many, interceding for them. Finally, Leviticus 10:17, 16:22 can be understood as showing that "bearing guilt" is part of the atoning process.

The problem in Isaiah 53 is not the absence of the language of the cult. "Bearing guilt" is itself the language of atonement, whether the cult is mentioned or not. The problem instead is the humanness of the one making atonement with his sacrifice and death. But the uniqueness of Isaiah 53 in general, and the syntax, lexical choices and context of the "bearing guilt" passages in Isaiah 53:11-12 in particular, argue that human sacrifice might indeed be what this passage is uniquely arguing. But it is not enough that the humanness of the sacrifice be unique. What point does so radical a sacrifice serve? The outline of the answer follows.

An Outline of How Isaiah 53 Sits in the Broader Framework of Isaiah

Isaiah 53, therefore, is using the language of "bearing guilt" in a unique and most unusual fashion. If the foregoing argument is correct, then for the Servant to "bear guilt" is for him to make atonement. But Isaiah 53 is not the lone voice speaking about atonement in the book of Isaiah. Indeed, it is part of a grander and more comprehensive vision of purification.[96]

In the singular vision[97] of Isaiah, a "new" and startling purification was unveiled. Isaiah 40—66 revealed a purification that secured *global*,[98] *permanent*[99] purity and that actually *changed* the object for which

---

[96]As mentioned in the introduction to this chapter, my forthcoming work deals with this issue more fully.

[97]While Isaiah's prophetic speeches were delivered in sundry settings over many years, they were collected and edited into a single coherent "vision" at the end of his life (the superscript in Isaiah 1:1 suggests the time frame) about the Holy One of Israel and his past and future dealings with his people. On the literary unity of Isaiah, cf. Marvin A. Sweeney, *Isaiah 1—39 with an Introduction to Prophetic Literature*, The Forms of the Old Testament Literature XVI (Grand Rapids: Eerdmans, 1996), 41. See Raymond B. Dillard and Tremper Longman III, *An Introduction to the Old Testament* (Grand Rapids: Zondervan, 1994), 273-74, on how arguments used by conservatives for the unity of Isaiah have been marshaled anew to demonstrate the *literary* unity of Isaiah.

[98]Not in the sense that everyone is redeemed, for the wicked will be cast out. Rather, in the sense that only the holy will remain. Yahweh will create a new heavens and a new earth (Is 65:17).

[99]I.e., for all time (Is 51:1-8).

purification had been made—removing sin, sin's effects and sin's source.[100] It was a purification that began with judgment and culminated in salvation.[101] It was a purification of Zion (Is 1:25, 27) and her inhabitants (Is 4:4) that (unthinkably) included the nations (Is 2:2-4) and even the entire heavens and earth (Is 24:1-6, 65:17)! It was a purification that meant *free* access to the mountain of God (Is 2:2-4) and no more standing at a distance. It was a purification that was synonymous with *enduring* salvation (Is 51:1-8). It was a purification that rendered judgment obsolete, because sin and its sources had been eternally eradicated from every corner of Yahweh's dwelling place with men. The wicked and all wickedness had been banished and could never corrupt again (Is 66:24); the righteous and righteousness would endure forever in a holy environment of peace and justice.

It was a purification that expected, even demanded, atonement as its basis.[102] If Yahweh was so holy as to leave Isaiah fearing for his life, if his glory was everywhere, if Israel was also so unclean that the presence of that glory meant destruction and death, if atonement spared Isaiah, how much more would Isaiah then expect and anticipate atonement for Israel.

It is precisely by means of the revelation of the *extraordinary* nature of the purification of which Isaiah spoke that the prophecy makes its most distinctive contribution to redemptive history. While the Torah spoke of atonement as the only means by which the wrath of Yahweh against sin and uncleanness could be stayed,[103] the Torah knew no atonement that produced the universal and permanent purification envisioned in Isaiah. Such extraordinary purification required an atonement of equally extraordinary and radical nature. Isaiah made clear that certain means would *not* secure this purification. It would *not* be by means of the traditional vehicle of atonement—e.g., Leviti-

---

[100]The wicked will be removed (Is 66:24), and the heart of the people will be changed (e.g., Is 59:21).

[101]In Isaiah, judgment and salvation are understood as elements in the broader purification scheme. Judgment is often expressed by the imagery of wounding, and salvation by the imagery of healing. Purification, then, is a wounding and healing process.

[102]In his view of the need for purification by atonement, Isaiah was in harmony with the Levitical regulations of the Old Testament—there were no means of purification to contain the consuming fire of the wrath that blazed out from Yahweh's holiness other than by means of atonement.

[103]I.e., arrest wrath that has already broken out as well as preventing the outbreak of wrath in advance.

cal sacrifice (Is 1:11-15). Nor would it be by means of repentance (Is 6:10) or Israel's suffering in the Babylonian exile. Rather, it would be accomplished by a *new* thing (Is 48:7), something previously unknown and not derived from human experience or wisdom[104]—the astounding suffering of one righteous Israelite (Is 52:13—53:12), who bore the sins of others. This alone would make an atonement sufficient to accomplish the global, permanent purification revealed in Isaiah's vision.

Therefore, while in terms of the Torah, human suffering and death as the means of atonement is unexpected, startling, and even appalling, it is the means toward which the glorious purification envisioned in Isaiah pressed. Only an atonement based on the Servant's sacrifice could accomplish the purification that Isaiah envisioned.

---

[104]Eep Talstra, "Second Isaiah and Qohelet: Could One Get Them on Speaking Terms?" in *The New Things: Eschatology in the Old Prophecy*, Amsterdamese Cahiers voor Exegese van de Bijbel en zijn Tradities Supplement, ed. F. Postma, K. Spronk and E. Talstra (Maastricht: Uitgeverij Shaker Publishing, 2002) 3:229, 234.

atonement in the synoptic gospels and acts

"Poured Out for the Forgiveness of Sins"

Royce Gordon Gruenler

From his earliest days as a professor of theology, my longtime friend and colleague Roger Nicole has passionately defended the classical view of Christ's atoning work. The Basis of Faith of Gordon-Conwell Theological Seminary was shaped by Professor Nicole's influence and continues to be normative in the life of the school. The classical view of atonement has not been widely accepted in modern and postmodern theological circles, as Professor Nicole was acutely aware during the 1950s, 60s and 70s when he was especially active in the Boston Theological Institute, a consortium of nine theological seminaries in the area. As a regular participant in the Boston Theological Society he stood his ground graciously but fearlessly against revisionist versions of the atonement more sympathetic to the presumptions of contemporary naturalism than to biblical authority.

Our distinguished colleague must feel continued chagrin and sadness that revisionists are no longer simply "out there" in liberal circles of critical thought where one has traditionally expected them to be, but inside evangelicalism itself, seeking inclusion within extended redefinitions of the term. This chapter is written in view of the watershed 2001 meeting of the Evangelical Theological Society—a society that has been of special interest to Professor Nicole since its founding—and its general topic, "Defining Evangelicalism's Boundaries." The debate is ongoing, and it is fitting that I have the opportunity to draw up alongside Professor Nicole and others of his persuasion in presenting a case for the biblical-classical view of the atonement against current revisions. One of the more prominent topics in the revision of classical theology at present is the proposal of a nonsacrificial view of the atonement.[1]

A troubling aspect in the methodologies of revisionism is that they are not sufficiently focused on defining words in the larger contexts of biblical sense units, but rely on philosophical predilections and/or lexical studies without sufficient grasp of an overarching biblical theology or, more immediately, without any discourse analysis of the flow of propositions within an argument. Our purpose here does not permit us to undertake a discourse analysis of Romans 3:21-26, which constitutes an integral sense unit within which ἱλαστήριον ("mercy seat/propitiation") must be defined,[2] but to inquire directly into Jesus' own view on his atoning work as represented by the Synoptic accounts of his words and work, and the proclamation of the apostolic church as described in Acts. Certain key terms in the Synoptic Gospels and Acts that define atonement in the teaching of Jesus and the apostolic mission will be explored in the remainder of our study.

---

[1]See, e.g., Daniel P. Bailey, "A Non-Sacrificial Interpretation of Hilasterion in 4 Maccabees 17:22," a paper delivered at the SBL Upper Midwest Regional Meeting at Luther Seminary, St. Paul, Minnesota (April 20-21, 2001); idem, *Jesus as the Mercy Seat: Paul's Use of Hilasterion in Romans 3:25,* Wissenschaftliche Untersuchungen zum Neuen Testament (second series) (Tübingen: Mohr Siebeck, forthcoming); idem, "Defining Evangelicalism's Boundaries: The Doctrine of the Atonement," a paper delivered at the Evangelical Theological Society national meeting, Denver, Colorado (November 2001). Bailey's revision of the atonement eliminates the classical view that God's wrath against sinners is propitiated by the substitutionary sacrifice of Christ. For him, "mercy-seat" (Rom 3:25) denotes only mercy, not God's assuaged wrath and fulfilled justice, which leads to mercy. This is not a new view on the atonement but appropriates the nonsacrificial interpretations of C. H. Dodd, *The Bible and the Greeks* (London: Hodder & Stoughton, 1935), 82-95; N. H. Young, "C. H. Dodd, 'Hilaskesthai,' and His Critics," *Evangelical Quarterly* 48 (1976): 67-78; W. G. Kümmel, "Paresis and Endeixis: A Contribution to the Understanding of the Pauline Doctrine of Justification," *Journal for Theology and the Church* 3 (1967): 1-13. Per contra, and in defense of the classical view of propitiation: L. Morris, *The Apostolic Preaching of the Cross* (Grand Rapids: Eerdmans, 1965), 136-56; idem, "The Meaning of Hilasterion in Romans 3:25," *New Testament Studies* 2 [1955-1956]): 34; R. R. Nicole, "C. H. Dodd and the Doctrine of Propitiation," *Westminster Theological Journal* 17 (1954-1955): 117-57; D. J. Moo, *The Epistle to the Romans*, NICNT (Grand Rapids: Eerdmans, 1996), 218-43; T. Schreiner, *Romans*, Baker Exegetical Commentary on the New Testament (Grand Rapids: Baker, 1998), 176-99; J. Piper, *The Justification of God: An Exegetical and Theological Study of Romans 9:1-23* (Grand Rapids: Baker, 1983), 115-30.

[2]But see chapter 6 below [ed.].

Preliminary Considerations

A word needs to be said about the so-called Synoptic Problem and the presumptions that will be made concerning the historicity of the Gospel accounts in what follows. An example of recent state-of-the-art discussion of Synoptic scholarship by evangelical scholars may be found in *Rethinking the Synoptic Problem*,[3] in which the two principal competitors, Markan priority and Matthean priority, are contrasted. What emerges from this conversation is that the debate continues to be complex and allows no absolutely assured results as to the order of the traditions. Considerable humility is accordingly called for, although each scholar will have his or her own preferences. The consensus of the authors is that while the Synoptic writers selected their materials from original sources for specific purposes, (1) there is not sufficient evidence in the Gospels to reconstruct distinctive church settings, since each evangelist writes for a wide audience;[4] and therefore, (2) it is risky to argue that church communities created sayings of Jesus out of whole cloth and projected them backward onto the lips of Jesus. Accordingly, the Synoptics represent selective history, but history nonetheless, not the genre of historical novel.[5]

My own composite view synthesizes a number of perspectives on the origins of the Gospels, including some minority opinions of

---

[3]David R. Beck and David Alan Black, eds., *Rethinking the Synoptic Problem* (Grand Rapids: Baker, 2001). Contributors include Darrell L. Bock, Scot McKnight and Grant R. Osborne, defending the Oxford Markan priority position; the late William R. Farmer, representing the Griesbach Matthean priority view; and Craig L. Blomberg, arguing basically for Markan priority but also for an early Matthean version resembling Q, later expanded by reference to Mark. See also Blomberg's *Jesus and the Gospels: An Introduction and Survey* (Nashville: Broadman & Holman; Leicester: Inter-Varsity Press, 1998) where he makes the same point. Both volumes contain extensive bibliographies on the current debate.

[4]This is also the view of Richard Bauckham, *The Gospel for All Christians: Rethinking the Gospel Audiences* (Grand Rapids and Cambridge: Eerdmans, 1998).

[5]Representing the postmodern view that the Synoptic Gospels and the Gospel of John are historical novels comprised of some actual history plus pious stories intended to convey a higher truth, see Frank Kermode, *The Genesis of Secrecy* (Cambridge: Harvard University Press, 1979) on the Gospel of Mark; and Alan Culpepper, *Anatomy of the Fourth Gospel* (Philadelphia: Fortress, 1983). Interpreters who employ this methodology assume that each evangelist or community is writing from various theological-literary perspectives and that the original as well as present-day readers will find meaning through subjective interaction with the biblical text, as one looks into a mirror at oneself rather than merely looking through a window into the past. Textual meaning and exegesis are accordingly negotiated by reader response to the multiple meanings possible in the text (polyvalence).

merit. Because of the parallel data of the Synoptics, their relationships are frustratingly complex; and in view of the fact that after a century and a half of intense scrutiny no scholar or school can claim assured results, it seems the better part of wisdom to take the inner witness of the Gospels themselves as a starting presumption and highlight a text like John 14:25-26 as normative: "All this I have spoken while still with you. But the Counselor, the Holy Spirit, whom the Father will send in my name, will teach you all things and will remind you of everything I have said to you." This saying of Jesus, which I take to be historical and indicative of his messianic intention and authority, contains all the ingredients necessary for a positive assessment of the historicity and authority of the Gospel accounts, based on the threefold and unified witness of the triune God. The Son speaks and promises that the Father will send the *Parakletos,* the Holy Spirit, who will bring to remembrance everything Jesus has said and will teach the disciples all things. In this dominical saying, accordingly, fact and interpretation function under the auspices of the Holy Spirit with approval of Father and Son. This Jesus-originating presumption allows interpreters to adopt whatever theories of Gospels formation they might favor as long as they presume the narrative data to be historical, early and reliable.

In perusing the Synoptic Gospels on the subject of atonement, I will assume that the narratives are given in an orderly and accurate manner, based on the eyewitness accounts of the original eyewitnesses and guardians (αὐτόπται καὶ ὑπηρέται) as Luke attests in the foreword to his Gospel (Lk 1:1-4), and that this will also apply to his sequel account of Acts. My critical view of the Gospels assumes an original pool of remembrances of Jesus' words and works from which the historian-evangelists drew their narratives. They fashioned their works from angles of vision guided by the Holy Spirit, who simultaneously honored the complementary perspectives of the authors as valid secondary agents in the writing of authoritative Scripture, inspiring them in their selections out of the original pool to address special needs in the mission of the church. At the same time, each of the Gospels, together with the Acts of the Apostles, is written for the instruction and edification of the whole church, both then and now. For this reason, none is really amenable to fashionable reconstructions of the original words and works of Jesus in light of hypothetical church settings supposedly drawn from the Gospels.[6]

Jesus' View of Atonement in the Synoptic Gospels

Principal texts in the Synoptics that narrate Jesus' direct teaching on his atoning work are Mark 8:31: "He then began to teach them that the Son of Man must suffer (παθεῖν) many things and be rejected by the elders, chief priests and teachers of the law, and that he must be killed (ἀποκτανθῆναι) and after three days rise again" (par. Mt 16:21; Lk 9:22); and Matthew 26:28: "This is my blood of the covenant (τὸ αἷμά μου τῆς διαθήκης), which is poured out for many for the forgiveness of sins (τὸ περὶ πολλῶν ἐκχυννόμενον εἰς ἄφεσιν ἁμαρτιῶν)" (par. Mk 14:24; Lk 22:20). These two texts disclose the continuity in Jesus' messianic understanding, with Levitical and prophetic theology as aspects of the larger Mosaic typology.[7] It is important to observe that Jesus does not stand against the law but views himself as the one who fulfills it in all its aspects (Mt 5:17-18). The atoning work of Yahweh in the Old Testament is exemplified in the shedding of blood for the remission of sin, by which he reveals that rebellion against him is deserving of death and that only by the divine principle of a life for a life is his demand for righteousness and justice satisfied. Atonement is accordingly penal, substitutionary and propitiating of divine wrath against the sinner in the sense that God himself graciously provides the means by which he propitiates and satisfies his own internal moral nature.

This OT principal of atonement by propitiation is not abrogated by Jesus through any kind of liberalizing, as though the mercy seat sprinkled with blood on the Day of Atonement could be deconstructed to signify only mercy without attending to the suffering and deathly cost of mercy. If such were the case, Jesus would not have had to suffer and die, and his shed blood would not bear any atoning efficacy. Yet Jesus speaks directly and indirectly of his impending death in a manner not only reminiscent of OT atonement theology but in such a way that the whole OT system must be personalized and embodied in him and

---

[6]For further detail on my views on the formation of the Gospels, see Royce Gordon Gruenler, *New Approaches to Jesus and the Gospels*, (Grand Rapids: Baker, 1982); idem, *The Trinity in the Gospel of John* (Grand Rapids: Baker, 1986), vii-xxi; idem, *Meaning and Understanding* (Grand Rapids: Zondervan, 1991), 129-202; idem, "Mark," in W. Elwell, ed., *Baker Commentary on the Bible,* (Grand Rapids: Baker, 2000).
[7]Cf. Matthew 26:28 and Leviticus 17:11; Mark 8:31 and Isaiah 52:13—53:12.

therefore "christified" and reified in order to be efficacious.

Herein lies the key to Jesus' view of atonement in the Synoptic Gospels. He claims to be the eschatological fulfillment of OT images and prophecy and announces at the beginning of his ministry that the OT time, the *kairos*, has come to fulfillment, that the saving reign of God has come upon his hearers, and that his hearers need to repent and believe his gospel (Mk 1:15). This unifying view of Scripture and of the doctrine of atonement is therefore couched in Jesus' sense of eschatological completion, like the flower of humble and simple beginnings that contains in seed form the whole genomic pattern of redemption and courses its way upward in stages of growth through the growing stem until finally it breaks forth into the glorious blossom intended all along by divine design. Jesus' view of atonement needs to be seen through such an image of organic unfolding in redemptive history.[8]

The unifying view of atonement disclosure in Scripture is accordingly eschatological, as God moves from first creation to new creation in Christ, who is at the beginning, the center, and the end of history, of humanity, and indeed of the whole created order. This view of Jesus Christ as the center of the eschatological unfolding of history gives proper weight to continuities between OT and NT teachings on atonement as well as differences in emphasis within the unfolding story of salvation.

One of the most debated issues in theology is the relationship of Jesus and the law, regarding which many take the view that Christ, the Spirit and faith are substituted in the New Testament for works of the law in the Old Testament, and merciful expiation in the New Testament for propitiation of wrath in the Old Testament. Thus, in modern theological discussion the "boundary markers" of acceptability (i.e., theologically correct definitions) are identified with NT faith rather than with the works of the law, as in the OT and Judaism; or, in more liberal circles, different markers identify multiple viable ways to God. While modern terms of identity markers and badges and boundary cir-

---

[8]In the organic and dynamic flow of redemptive history and the image of the unfolding flower, one may refer to the programmatic views of Geerhardus Vos, the father of modern evangelical biblical theology, which are represented in the methodology of Meredith G. Kline, *Kingdom Prologue: Genesis Foundations for a Covenantal Worldview* (Overland Park, Kan.: Two Age Press, 2000); see also Royce Gordon Gruenler, *The Word Became Flesh: The Doctrine of Christology in Biblical, Systematic, and Historical Perspective* (forthcoming).

cles are useful, the direction of this essay will develop in a somewhat different manner from the typical faith versus works or Christ versus law motifs employed by many interpreters. The discontinuities or differences between OT teaching on atonement and Jesus' teaching will be seen rather as a divinely guided eschatology that moves from the shadow images of the law and its atoning offerings to the actualization or reification of law and atonement in the person and work of Jesus, from a typology that is abstract to one that is personalized in the Son of God and Son of Man, Jesus Christ, who fulfills the period of law and cultic atonement because he is the goal of the law and of atonement. Once the goal has been achieved in the faithful life and death of Jesus and he has completed his atoning work both actively and passively, the old typologies cease to function as such and are absorbed into the superlative typology of Christ himself (so Paul's understanding of τέλος as both goal and end in Romans 10:4).

Accordingly, along with the differences in emphasis between the Testaments, there is a fundamental continuity. Christ performs a work of redemption both in his life and in his death and resurrection which fulfills the law "to the smallest letter and stroke" (Mt 5:17-18). It is a work of grace on our behalf, but it is a work of grace because it is first of all a work of fulfilling the law. We are saved by works, the works of Jesus. Jesus the Messiah thus performs a double work of redemption. First, as the new Adam (the Son of the Man [Adam], a title Jesus uses extensively in the Synoptics), he actualizes true humanity in himself by perfectly fulfilling the moral law of the Old Testament. Second, in his death and resurrection he fulfills the ceremonial law of the Old Testament as the perfect substitute who bears the penalty of death on our behalf, satisfying, vindicating and propitiating divine holiness once for all. Jesus Christ is the central figure of history, redeeming by his righteous work all believers before him and all who come after him. Viewed in this way, OT believers too were saved by prevenient faith in Christ through the presence of the Spirit in their lives, but within boundary markers that were preparatory to the Messiah's coming and therefore forward-leaning. Enoch, Noah and Abraham were justified by faith, as were the faithful in the period of the law that was in place till the death of Christ on the cross.

Believers who lived in the period of the law pursued the moral and ceremonial law as the means of grace and did not stand on claims of their own righteousness but "leaned forward" to the fulfillment of righteous atonement in the work of the Messiah to come. When Jesus came and announced the fulfillment of the OT messianic time, those who were faithfully pursuing the intent of the law recognized, accepted and followed him; those who were not did not, and they rejected him. In view of the overall continuity within the "discontinuities" of different emphases and epochs in the history of salvation, we may appreciate Jesus' teaching on atonement in the Synoptics and the apostles' proclamation of Christ in Acts.

Normally, one would do a word study on atonement at this juncture, but I will simply refer the reader to a good overview of the four word groups that define the dimensions of reconciliation between God and human beings: (1) (ἐξ)ἱλάσκομαι, which with its derivatives involves the priestly Levitical liturgy of the Torah, ordered by Yahweh for the satisfaction of divine wrath against sinful Israel (propitiation); (2) καταλλάσσω, a secular term indicating the amelioration of a negative attitude in a relationship; (3) ἀποκατάστασις, a word with political and eschatological overtones, indicating restoration either partial or universal; and (4) λύω, to set free or ransom.[9]

In this chapter, however, I will trace the dynamic of key declarations and actions on the part of Jesus that define his intention to fulfill the atoning task of reconciling God and fallen humanity. Jesus' activity of releasing, reconciliation, restoration, propitiation and atonement is best understood by way of the comprehensive picture afforded through the methodology of biblical theology. The Synoptics may be seen as dimensional portraits of the atoning person of Christ based on the format of the OT gospel genre of Exodus, the Gospel of Moses.[10] Prominent in the Gospel of Moses and the Synoptic Gospels are themes of covenant inauguration and ratification by the covenant mediator, and the deliverance of God's people from hostile, threatening forces by the ruler-deliverer-shepherd-guide, coupled with a priestly ministry of

---

[9]E.g., Colin Brown, ed., *The New International Dictionary of New Testament Theology* (Grand Rapids: Zondervan), 3:145-223.

[10]For the development of this approach, see my article, "Old Testament Gospel as Prologue to New Testament Gospel," in Howard Griffith and John R. Muether, eds., *Creator, Redeemer, Consummator: A Festschrift for Meredith G. Kline* (Jackson, Miss.: Reformed Theological Seminary, 2000), 95-103. See also Meredith G. Kline, "The Old Testament Origins of the Gospel Genre," in *The Structure of Biblical Authority*, rev. ed. (Grand Rapids: Eerdmans, 1975), 172-203; idem, *Kingdom Prologue*.

sacrifice and intercession. Also thematically significant is the construction of the tabernacle under the leadership of Moses in the later chapters of Exodus and the raising up of the temple of the new covenant by Jesus, who declares himself to be the personification of the temple.

The Gospel of Moses and the Synoptic Gospels share the common theme of the conquest of hostile space by the deliverance figures Moses and Jesus. In Jesus' conquest of demonic space the typological drama of atonement is intensified, as the typology of geopolitical space and salvation so dominant in the Mosaic motif gives way to the deeper action on the stage of redemptive history through Jesus' invasion and binding of demonic forces that hold humanity in spiritual bondage. The theme of spatial conquest in the ministry of Jesus, which continues in the apostolic mission of Acts and into the present mission of the church, is to be seen in his announcement of the inauguration of the new redemptive covenant and its ratification as he lays claim to enemy-occupied territory in the name of Father, Spirit and Son. In my brief comments the Gospel of Mark will be our primary focus, but Mark may be seen as representative of the other complementary Gospels, each functioning as a covenant witness document to the atoning activity of Jesus the Messiah. At the conclusion of Mark and the other Gospels, the person of Jesus has brought victory from apparent defeat and has embodied in himself the space of the OT land, its people, the law and the temple—indeed, the whole space and time of OT theology and soteriology.[11]

A Particular Look at the Gospel According to Mark

In selecting and arranging his material, drawing from a large pool of written and oral eyewitness reports about Jesus and from his own intimate association with Peter's recollections and proclamations, Mark dramatically highlights major episodes in Jesus' ministry that prove him to be the great servant preacher and conqueror who announces the good news of God's saving reign and sets its power to invade into action. Mark takes only fifteen verses of introduction before Jesus launches faithfully into the field of battle to grapple with the demonic forces that hold his people in captivity and formally to begin his atoning work.

---

[11]For more extensive commentary on Markan spatial motifs, see my "Mark" in *Baker Commentary on the Bible*, ed. Walter Elwell (Grand Rapids: Baker, 2000).

Jesus must pass two tests before his major invasion is inaugurated. The first is his approbation by the Father and the Spirit as faithful and righteous Son who is not only willing, but is worthy to place himself at the disposal of sinners in the baptism of water at the beginning of his ministry, as he will show himself willing and worthy to die for them in his atoning baptism of death at the end of his ministry. The divine Community unites in one accord in the redemptive mission. The Father expresses love for the Son and is well pleased with him, signifying that up to this point Jesus has faithfully lived a righteous life that is worthy of approval for the redemptive task that lies ahead.[12] The Spirit adds to the Father's vocal approval a visual anointing of divine dove-descent upon the Son. The mission of invasion-redemption is therefore social in the highest archetypal sense because it is initiated by the triune Society of Father, Son and Holy Spirit acting as one—the Father and Spirit honoring the Son as spokesman and redemptive agent on their behalf, and the Son honoring the Father and the Spirit as their faithful servant.[13] Mark's dramatic description of the heavens "torn open" portrays this salvific mission of the divine Family as an awesome theophany that causes nature to tremble.[14] The violence of hostile nature under satanic control is about to be subdued and conquered by the greater power of the God who created it, but it will take a divine act of creative violence to reclaim a lost kingdom.[15] This Jesus will proceed to do throughout his ministry as he invades the hostile powers of fallen creation and finally, on the cross, brings about the ripping of the veil of the temple in two, from top to bottom (Mk 15:38), forming an inclusio of violent tearings at the beginning and end of the Gospel that dramatically attests the removal of the wall of separation

---

[12]Cf. Isaiah 42:1; Psalm 2:7.

[13]See my *The Trinity in the Gospel of John: A Thematic Commentary on the Fourth Gospel* (Grand Rapids: Baker, 1986) for an extended study of the societal nature of the Trinity and the appropriateness of the descriptive terms "divine Family, Society, Community" in referring to the dynamic and interpersonal relationships that are characteristic of the archetypal Tri-unity.

[14]Cf. Moses and the mountain of revelation, Exodus 19:10-19; Isaiah 64:1-3.

[15]The theme of violent warfare between spiritual forces is also highlighted by Greg Boyd, *God at War: The Bible and Spiritual Conflict* (Downers Grove, Ill.: InterVarsity Press, 1997), but in a much different way. Boyd makes human and angelic freedom central in the battle, with God limited by his own choice to an open future, which is undetermined as far as individual choices are concerned. More scriptural is the presumption that God is the archetypal composer and dramatist who is glorified in cosmic and world history by bringing victory out of apparent defeat.

between God and humanity through the atoning work of Christ. His ministry signals the inauguration of the new humanity as the first fruits of the new creation.

Jesus' second test in the wilderness recapitulates the testing of the first Adam in the Garden. Jesus is both the beloved Son of the Father who has passed scrutiny as the Son of God and won approval from Father and Spirit at the baptism; now he must pass the probation of faithfulness as the Son of the man Adam[16] in order to proceed on the path of his atoning work and right the wrong of the first Adam who turned the garden of the first creation into a wilderness. The first test lay in pleasing the Father and the Spirit; the second, in vanquishing Satan the despoiler of humanity and the old creation.

As the Synoptic narrative unfolds, Jesus progressively invades both wilderness and city with his personal demonstration of redeeming power through proclamation, healing and exorcism (Mk 1:16—8:26). The reign of God, which he embodies, also brings into being a secondary realm of followers who apprentice with the master teacher in preparation for future proclamation of Christ's atoning mission following Pentecost. It should be noted, in anticipation of the apostolic proclamation in Acts, that Jesus' kerygma and the kerygma of the early church share the same three points. In Mark 1:15 Jesus announces that (1) the messianic time is fulfilled, (2) the reign of God is upon them, in light of which (3) they are to repent and believe in the gospel. In Peter's paradigmatic sermon on the day of Pentecost (Acts 2), he announces that (1) the OT messianic prophecies have been fulfilled; (2) they have been fulfilled in Christ (who personifies the reign of God); and therefore, (3) those who hear are to repent and be baptized. Jesus' work of invasion on the windward side of the cross is heavy with metaphors because his secret must be veiled until the work of atonement is accomplished, whereas on the leeward side of the cross and resurrection, all is made clear by the interpretation of the

---

[16]A growing number of scholars are beginning to appreciate the importance of the article in Jesus' messianic declaration that he is "the Son of the man" (ὁ υἱὸς τοῦ ἀνθρώπου) by which he implies that he is the Son of the man Adam, the fulfillment of the Adamic line, the second Adam (so Paul, Rom 5:12-21; 1 Cor 15:20-28, where Christ is the firstfruit [ἀπαρχή]) of the new humanity and the new creation; cf. "the one new man" in Christ, Ephesians 2:14-21, who brings peace where there was enmity between Jew and Gentile and fashions a growing holy temple incorporating believers in himself. The person of Christ exemplifies all these images and others in his many-sided work of atonement.

Holy Sprit given at Pentecost. The metaphor of the saving reign of God is now seen by the apostles to have been embodied all along in the person of Christ; hence, to preach the kingdom is to preach Christ: he is *autobasileia;* he is "himself the kingdom."

As the king of the heavenly kingdom, Jesus opposes the reign of Satan and his minions. Barely a dozen verses in Mark's abbreviated account separate Jesus' confrontation of Satan in the wilderness and an evil spirit in Capernaum (Mk 1:21-28). Other healings and exorcisms follow in rapid succession, between wilderness and town, as Mark apparently replicates the staccato-like preaching of Peter his mentor. The progressive nature of the atoning warfare of invasion is illustrated in Jesus' accompanying teaching in parables, which both reveal and mask the deep significance of what he is doing. Small beginnings have big endings, as the growing seed moving toward fruitful harvest demonstrates repeatedly in nature. So Jesus personifies the reign of God in the spiritual realm. Accordingly, moving with the dynamic power of the Creator/Redeemer requires belief and trust and fruit-bearing, not insipid doubt. This is the fault of the disciples, for whom Jesus recapitulates the deliverance of Israel in the exodus and the crossing of the Red Sea by calming the storm and subduing the hostile powers of nature (Mk 4:35-41). The disciples are teachable and malleable; however, they receive progressive empowerment to participate peripherally in the invasion ministry (Mk 6:30), although their full empowerment will not come until Pentecost, when Jesus' atoning work on the cross and in the resurrection has been accomplished.

Far more serious is the attitude of those who adamantly reject his redemptive claims, debate with him, and conspire to kill him. The Pharisees, with their subtleties and oral addenda to Mosaic law, externalize religion into legalism and remove themselves from the covenantal nomism of true believers, those who recognize Jesus' messianic claims though they do not yet fully understand his person or mission. Jesus' opponents reject any fuller definition of atonement, though they themselves have in fact lost the deep significance of atonement in the Gospel of Moses. Implicit in his exchange with the Pharisees and teachers of the law is Jesus' insistence that healing and salvation must come from an inner faith that humbly and voluntarily submits to his messianic authority (Mk 7:1-23).

To illustrate prophetically the messianic time that he is inaugurating and the requirement of faith in him, Jesus turns momentarily to an itinerant Gentile mission (Mk 7:24—8:10), where he finds many who accept his invitation that all who show faith in him, whether Jew or Gentile, will receive salvation. Once back in Jewish territory (Mk 8:11-26), Jesus is confronted by recalcitrant religious authorities who try to tempt him to produce signs to their liking (Mk 8:11-21).[17] Jesus views this request as an extension of Satan's temptation that he function as a worldly spectacular messiah. The unbelieving generation they represent will receive no more than the evidence Jesus is presenting, which is sufficient. His atoning mission is not political according to the norms of the old fallen creation, but personal and moral according to the norms of the new humanity and the new creation.

Jesus now turns his face toward the invasion of the hostile city of Jerusalem (Mk 8:27—15:47). At Caesarea Philippi he discloses revelations and prophecies to the disciples about his coming redemptive passion. Everything in this section anticipates the invasion of Jerusalem, the citadel ironically symbolizing the seat of demonic power, which in the name of religion keeps his people imprisoned and unatoned for. It is not without significance that Jesus begins his journey from Caesarea Philippi, an area that was familiar with the Greek god Pan and the lordship of Caesar and that was the residence of Herod Philip, as though symbolically he is announcing to those who have eyes to see (certainly Mark's Christian readers) that he is claiming his lordship over both pagan and Jewish powers that lay rival claim to the world and offer rival theories of atonement.

Jesus has been widely misunderstood up to this point, being generally taken by the masses to be John the Baptist brought back to life, or Elijah, or one of the prophets (or a wonder-working god-man in the Hellenistic fashion of the day), while the religious authorities consider him demonic. That Jesus is more than an ordinary prophet will be dramatically and visually substantiated in the transfiguration (Mk 9:2-9), but it is now articulated by Peter, who speaks for the disciples when he replies to Jesus' question, "You are the Christ," that is, the Messiah, the Anointed One. The disciples understand that Jesus is the Messiah in some sense, but they do not yet understand his interpretation of messiahship, which involves suffering and dying for their sins and rising

---

[17]Cf. Moses and the wilderness generation, Deuteronomy 32:5-20.

again, as Jesus' rebuke of Peter (Mk 9:33) and the disciples' lingering political misconception of messiahship (Acts 1:6-7) attest.

In his journey to Jerusalem and the final invasion of that hostile city, Jesus does indeed lay claim to the geopolitical space of the land he traverses in the sense that he claims the people who occupy that space, their land, their exodus history and former Davidic dynasty, and "christifies" the old typologies, breathing them into himself. Now, upon entering Jerusalem, he claims the space of both Sinai and Zion, of both moral law and ceremonial law, and is about to fulfill their shadowy fore-imaging in his atoning death. Within the precincts of the temple space, which he claims the right to occupy, Jesus challenges the highest court of Jewish authority. His messianic reign fulfills Moses' and David's domains on a higher level. His warfare probes deeper into the realm of dark demonic powers that occupy the space of human beings and of nations, hence his goal as Messiah to put his enemies underfoot (Mk 11:27—12:37). Jesus' prophetic Olivet discourse (Mk 13:1-37) anticipates the coming mission-invasion by his followers, who will apply his atoning work through proclamation to the world.

The irony of Jesus' space-invasion is further heightened by the setting of Passover and the Feast of Unleavened Bread, which provide the background to Jesus' atoning passion. This is the sacred time in which the urgent exodus from slavery to freedom is reenacted in the eating of unleavened bread and the sprinkling of the blood of the lamb, which saves the believer from the righteous wrath God will visit upon his enemies (Ex 12:1-14). The final meal with his disciples is the last Passover lamb Jesus will eat before he himself becomes the Lamb sacrificed once for all (Mk 14:12-26).[18] Jesus is about to take the OT time and space of Passover into himself and personify its deepest meaning on the cross. The irony of the last Passover meal is the narrowing process within the expansive setting of the feast by which the old is transposed into the new and the space of the old is absorbed by the solitary figure of Jesus, who in reality is more capacious than the extensive site of the temple with all its OT symbols. Jesus is larger on the inside than the land, the people and the temple are on the outside. He fulfills the typology of atonement to perfection and becomes the reality of the new exodus from slavery to freedom, from death to life.

---

[18]Cf. Hebrews 7:27; 9:26-28; 10:10.

Mark's account of Jesus' death (Mk 15:33-41) intimates how Jesus, at the climax of his warfare against the realm of iniquity, recapitulates and fulfills the themes of Genesis, Exodus and Passover. The plague of darkness that fell upon Egypt before the Passover (Ex 20:21-22) falls over the land of Judah when Jesus becomes the final Passover and substitutionary curse (Mk 15:33).[19] Nature participates in the prelude to Jesus' cry of dereliction as he suffers divine wrath on behalf of sinners. Because he has taken the space and the redemptive ceremony of the temple into the true temple of his own person, the physical demolition of the old temple begins at his death with the tearing of the temple curtain, a sign that the rejection of Jesus as Messiah by the religious leaders will lead inexorably to the total demolition of the old house of sacrifice.[20] Jesus has completed his formal invasion assault on the house of the strong man Satan, has bound him so that he deceives the nations no longer, and has begun the final plundering of his goods.[21]

Conclusion: A View Toward Acts

The plundering of the strong man's house continues with the Spirit-anointed mission of Jesus' followers on the day of Pentecost through the proclamation of the crucified and risen Christ. The divine attributes assigned to Jesus in his atoning work are in continuity with the self-revelation of the one God of the Old Testament. Jesus is proclaimed to be the fullest revelation of the nature and purpose of God in the apostolic kerygma and teaching, as documented in the Acts of the Apostles and the apostolic letters to the churches. Jesus is God crucified, who graciously atones for the sins of fallen humanity.[22] The atoning work of Jesus is accordingly the centerpiece of the apostolic kerygma. At the same time, there is emphasis now on the responsibility of the Spirit-empowered apostles to witness to "all that Jesus began to do and to teach until the day he was taken up to heaven" (Acts 1:1-2). Acts is therefore also the narrative of what the crucified and risen Jesus was continuing to do in applying his atoning work to Jews and Gentiles

---

[19]Cf. Galatians 3:13.

[20]Mark 15:38; 13:2; 14:58; 15:29.

[21]Mark 3:27; Matthew 12:28-29; Luke 11:20-22.

[22]For a recent and compelling study of the continuity and propriety of assigning the divine attributes to Jesus as a fuller explication of the nature of God, see Richard Bauckham, *God Crucified: Monotheism and Christology in the New Testament* (Grand Rapids: Eerdmans, 1999).

through the witness of the church. Jesus spells this out in a programmatic prophecy delivered to the disciples before his ascension, accentuating that the empowering Spirit is about to fall upon them. The baptism of the Holy Spirit (Acts 1:5) is the horizontal baptism of empowerment to mission (Acts 1:8), energizing Christian witnesses to proclaim in concentric circles of expansion a powerful Christ and a powerful cross and resurrection, beginning from the epicenter of Jerusalem at Pentecost. The book of Acts is the narrative account of how the prophecy of Jesus in Acts 1:5, 8 was being fulfilled in successive stages of missionary activity, beginning with Peter in Jerusalem and ending with Paul in Rome.

It is a striking fact that while the fundamental atoning work of Christ was accomplished once for all in his faithful keeping of the law, both moral and sacrificial, he has nonetheless called us to partnership in fulfilling what is lacking in his atoning work (to use Paul's arresting language in Colossians 1:24). Christ's atoning work continues in the world through evangelism and mission proclamation as the Holy Spirit continues to apply it to repentant sinners and to struggling and growing churches. It is fitting, therefore, to end our study by noting that the book of Acts ends with Paul faithfully proclaiming Christ and the kingdom in Rome (28:30-31), as a prisoner who continued to suffer as a witness to Christ until his execution under Nero. This reminds us that victory over apparent defeat never comes cheaply—not for the Son of God in his atoning ministry, nor for us in our responsibility to proclaim the gospel of atonement in his name.

atonement in
john's gospel and epistles
"The Lamb of God Who Takes Away the Sin of the World"

J. Ramsey Michaels

Years ago, in another life, I once had a light-hearted conversation with friend and colleague Roger Nicole about what some people call "limited atonement" but what he liked to call "definite atonement," the belief that Jesus died for elect believers only and not for the whole world.[1] Roger told me of a Puritan writer who had written several volumes on 1 John 2:2 showing how the second part of that verse ("and not only for ours but also for the sins of the whole world") was compatible with definite atonement. I said this was not surprising, because to get that doctrine out of that verse would *require* several volumes. I no longer recall who the Puritan was, nor the title of his work, but I offer this essay to Roger belatedly, not as an apology exactly (for I think he knew I was only teasing), but as a serious resumption of our conversation.

The nature and the extent of the atonement have both been major themes of Roger Nicole's distinguished career, and the two cannot be separated, least of all in the gospel and epistles of John. If 1 John 2:2 speaks to the issue of the atonement's *extent*, a glance at the NIV reveals that it has also a strong bearing on the *nature* of Jesus' saving work on

---

[1]The more common term, especially among Baptists, has been "particular redemption." See my article, "Baptism and Conversion in John: A Particular Baptist Reading," in *Baptism, the New Testament and the Church: Historical and Contemporary Studies in Honor of R.E.O. White*, *JSNTSup*, no. 171 (Sheffield: Sheffield Academic Press, 1999), 136-56.

the cross. The NIV text reads, "He is the atoning sacrifice for our sins," while the margin offers the alternative, "He is the one who turns aside God's wrath, taking away our sins." The marginal reading seeks to incorporate the idea of "propitiation" (KJV, NASB) in the sense of placating God's wrath, as well as "expiation" (RSV) in the sense of taking away sin. "Expiation" assumes that humans need to be reconciled to God, but "propitiation" adds the notion that God must be placated, or reconciled to them. "Atoning sacrifice" (NIV, NRSV) is open to either interpretation. Roger Nicole worked on the NIV, and its marginal note reflects the interpretation he so ably defended.[2]

The Atonement in John's Gospel: Benefits of the Passion

While 1 John 2:2 is crucial to the subject at hand, it is not necessarily the place to start. With the canonical order of the NT books in mind, I will begin instead with the Gospel of John.[3] Almost right away we encounter a challenge to definite atonement or particular redemption in John the Baptist's announcement, "Look, the Lamb of God, who takes away the sin of *the world!*" (Jn 1:29, italics added). "Lamb" evokes the image of sacrifice, and John's words seem to refer to Jesus' death on the cross as an atoning sacrifice for the whole world. Yet this Lamb does not "bear" the sin of the world as a passive victim, but "takes it away" (ὁ αἴρων) as an active redeemer. He is victor, not victim, and there is no explicit mention of Jesus' death. So this "taking away" is not what is usually called expiation. Rather, John's words correspond to what he says in Luke of "one more powerful than I," who will "clear his threshing floor and . . . gather the wheat into his barn, but he will burn up the chaff with unquenchable fire" (Lk 3:16-17). But if this is what he had in mind, why "Lamb of God," with all its sacrificial associations? What does the metaphor of the Lamb contribute to a message of judgment? The answer is not gentleness or silence or a willingness to be sacrificed, but purity. John could as well have said "Son of God," as he does in John 1:34, but his use of "Lamb" makes the point that the One who pu-

---

[2]His key article is "C. H. Dodd and the Doctrine of Propitiation," *WTJ* 17 (1954-1955): 117-57, written in response to C. H. Dodd, *The Bible and the Greeks* (London: Hodder & Stoughton, 1935), 82-95; see also "Hilaskesthai Revisited," *EQ* 49 (1977): 173-77.

[3]Also, for what it is worth, modern scholarship has become more and more convinced that the Gospel of John was written before the three Johannine Epistles. See, for example, Raymond E. Brown, *The Community of the Beloved Disciple* (New York: Paulist, 1979), and compare D. Moody Smith, "When Did the Gospels Become Scripture?" *JBL* 119.1 (2000): 12.

rifies the world is himself pure (like the Passover lamb of Ex 12:5). The
One who takes away sin is himself sinless. The closest parallel is in
1 John 3:5, where Jesus was revealed "so that he might take away
[αἴρω] our sins." The author immediately adds, "in him is no sin," and
three verses later he explains "taking away" sins as destroying "the
devil's work" (1 Jn 3:8). It is not a matter of bearing the guilt of sins by
an atoning death, but of judging the world's sins and quite literally doing away with them. "Lamb of God" is rather like the Lamb in the book
of Revelation who (though "slain") functions, not as victim, but as
Lord and Judge of the world, right beside "the One sitting on the
throne."[4] Unlike the Revelation,[5] however, John's gospel never speaks
of "the blood of the Lamb," and it stops well short of attributing to
John the Baptist any explicit notion of atonement or cleansing from sin
through Jesus' blood.

John 1:29 is the first of several passages in the gospel that show that
the coming of Jesus, including both his words and his works, his life
and his death, did have a profound effect on "the world" (κόσμου), not
just on believers. "The world," after all, is where sin is, especially in the
Gospel of John. Jesus is God's gift to the world because God "loved"
the world (Jn 3:16). He is God's Light "coming into the world."[6] He is
the "Savior of the world,"[7] because he came to save and not to condemn. He is the "grain of wheat" who by falling to the ground dies and
"bears much fruit," and by rising from the ground "draws everyone"
to himself (Jn 12:24, 32). He is "the bread of God . . . who comes down
from heaven and gives life to the world" (Jn 6:33), and he further defines the bread as "my flesh . . . for [ὑπέρ] the life of the world" (Jn 6:51).
Quite clearly, "my flesh" means "my death,"[8] and this is about as close
as the Gospel of John ever comes to universal (as distinct from definite)
atonement. Without question, Jesus' death benefits the world, yet

---

[4]On John 1:29, see the discussion in C. H. Dodd, *The Interpretation of the Fourth Gospel* (Cambridge: Cambridge University Press, 1958), 230-38.
[5]E.g., Revelation 5:9; 7:14; 12:11.
[6]John 3:19; 12:46. Cf. John 1:9; 8:12; 9:5.
[7]John 4:42. Cf. John 3:17; 12:47.
[8]"Flesh" means death here, just as Jesus' "blood" commonly means his death. Paul too uses
this image, although rarely. In Ephesians 2:15, after speaking of being "brought near *by the
blood of Christ,*" Paul adds that Christ has "destroyed the enmity *by his flesh,*" and in Romans
7:4 he speaks of being "put to death to the law *through the body of Christ,*" that is, through the
offering up of Christ's body in death. Cf. Hebrews 5:10.

John's Gospel never articulates a real *doctrine* of the atonement. In very general terms, we find recorded here the "benefits of his passion,"[9] but without specifying *how* Jesus' death "gives life to the world," or *on what basis* he "takes away sin."

Most references to Jesus' death in John's gospel have to do with its benefits *for believers*, or Jesus' own disciples, and are thus fully consistent with "particular redemption" as the early English Baptists understood it. Jesus lays down his life "for [ὑπέρ] the sheep," (Jn 10:11, 15), that is, for those who "hear his voice" and "follow" him (Jn 10:3-4, 27), and "for [ὑπέρ] his friends" (15:13), those who "do the things I command you" (Jn 15:14-15), not for those who do not. He dies "for [ὑπέρ] the nation" (presumably Israel) (Jn 11:51),[10] and sometimes there is a wider circle of beneficiaries as well. He has "other sheep that are not of this sheep pen" (Jn 10:16), and he intends to gather into one, not just Israel, but "the scattered children of God" (Jn 11:52). In his final prayer he "sanctifies" or "consecrates" himself as high priest "for [ὑπέρ] them," that is, for his own disciples (Jn 17:19), and he looks beyond them to "those who will believe in me through their message, that all of them may be one" (Jn 17:20-21) or "brought into complete unity" (literally, "perfected into one," Jn 17:23). Yet the "wider circle" never embraces the whole world. Jesus does not pray for the world (Jn 17:9), and his hope "that the world may believe that you have sent me" (17:21), or "know that you have . . . loved them even as you have loved me" (17:23) envisions not so much the world's salvation as the vindication of Jesus and his disciples in the world's eyes.

While Jesus clearly dies "for" or "on behalf of" (ὑπέρ) his disciples in the Gospel of John, what is missing is any statement that he dies explicitly for *sins*, whether of the world or of believers. It is no secret that the death of Jesus in John's gospel is more characteristically a

---

[9]Ironically, *Benefits of His Passion* was the title of a book on Christ's death by C. H. Dodd (London: Lutterworth, 1947), with whom Roger Nicole disagreed at a crucial point. See n. 2.

[10]This is the only intimation in John's gospel that Jesus died "for" (ὑπέρ) the Jewish people as a corporate entity. Here the gospel writer's words echo Caiaphas' pronouncement in John 11:50, that "it is better for you that one man die for [ὑπέρ] the people than that the whole nation perish." It was a purely political statement, but when repeated in John 11:51 it takes on the meaning of a sacrificial death. It is still a death for "the elect," however, and not for the whole world, even if some of those who are elect corporately turn out *not* to be elect individually. See Paul's argument in Romans 9—11.

"glorification"[11] or "exaltation"[12] or "departure"[13] than a sacrifice for sin. That Jesus "lays down his life for the sheep" or for his "friends" does not *have* to mean more than that he risks his life for their safety, or that he dies for them to show his love, as a soldier might die for his country. In this respect, John's terminology differs from that of Paul,[14] and other New Testament writers.[15] Jesus does not come to call "sinners" in the Gospel of John.[16] Those who come to him do not come as sinners in need of forgiveness. Nathaniel, for example, came not as a sinner but as a "true Israelite in whom there is nothing false" (Jn 1:47). When Jesus' disciples suggested that the blind man may have been born that way because either he or his parents were sinners, he replied, "Neither this man nor his parents sinned, but this happened so that the work of God might be displayed in his life" (Jn 9:3). The Pharisees denounced the man as one "steeped in sin at birth" (Jn 9:34), but Jesus never does.

Nicodemus, like everyone else, needed to be "born from above" (Jn 3:3, 5, 7), yet nothing is said of any sins of which he must "repent" and be "forgiven." On the contrary, the conclusion of his encounter with Jesus is that those who "come to the Light" are *not* those who do evil, but precisely those who "live by the truth" and whose works are "done through God" (Jn 3:20-21).[17] The Samaritan woman's situation is different in that we do learn something of her sinful past (Jn 4:16-18), yet only as an example of Jesus' ability to tell her (as she put it) "everything I ever did" (Jn 4:29, 39). Nowhere does Jesus either condemn or forgive the woman for her past actions. They are no more relevant to the story than are the particulars of what Nathaniel might have been doing or thinking "under the fig tree" before Jesus called him. Jesus, in fact, never explicitly "forgives" anyone in this gospel. He comes closest when he warns the sick man of Bethesda, "See, you have been made well; sin no more, so that nothing worse will happen to you" (Jn 5:14), but the man's immediate action in informing the authorities of Jesus' identity does not inspire confidence

---

[11]John 11:4; 12:16, 23; 13:31-32; 17:1, 5.
[12]John 3:14; 8:28; 12:32-34.
[13]John 7:33-34; 8:21; 13:1, 33; 14:19; 16:16.
[14]Romans 4:25; 1 Corinthians 15:3; Galatians 1:4.
[15]1 Peter 2:24, 3:18; Hebrews 9:28; Revelation 1:5.
[16]Contrast Mark 2:17 and parallels; see also Luke 5:8.
[17]See Michaels, "Baptism and Conversion in John," 145-46.

that he is truly redeemed.[18]

Only at the end of the story do we hear of anyone's sins being "forgiven," when the risen Jesus breathes on his disciples and tells them, "Receive the Holy Spirit. If you forgive anyone his sins, they are forgiven; if you do not forgive them, they are not forgiven" (Jn 20:22-23). In the course of his ministry Jesus sometimes retains sins,[19] but instead of forgiving sins he calls "true Israelites" like Nathaniel, who, if not explicitly "righteous," are at any rate "chosen,"[20] "given," and "drawn" to Jesus by the Father,[21] and therefore "greater than all" (Jn 10:29).[22] They are "not of the world,"[23] for those who are "of this world" will "die in their sins" (Jn 8:24). Sin characterizes the world, not the believer or disciple. Jesus solemnly declares that "everyone who sins is a slave of sin," and he invites the "slaves" to freedom, but they refuse (Jn 8:31-35). "Sinners" in the Gospel of John cannot "believe" and remain sinners,[24] for the very definition of sin is unbelief (Jn 16:9). By the same token, it might seem that believers cannot sin and remain believers, but the Gospel of John never addresses that issue. Because sin belongs to the world, John's gospel is relatively uninterested in believers' sins, whether before or after their conversion.[25] Its accent is on salvation positively as the giving of eternal life, not negatively as repentance or

---

[18]The account appended later to the gospel where Jesus tells the adulterous woman, "Nor do I condemn you. Go, and from now on sin no more" (Jn 8:11), comes closer to an actual forgiveness story.

[19]John 8:21, 24; 9:41; 15:22.

[20]John 6:70; 13:18; 15:16, 19.

[21]John 6:37, 39, 44, 65; 17:2, 6, 9, 24.

[22]See the NRSV, based on the Nestle Greek text and most of the better manuscripts (including Codex B): "What my Father has given me is greater than all else." In later manuscripts (followed by the RSV, NIV and REB), the Father is the one said to be "greater than all." B. M. Metzger, *A Textual Commentary on the Greek New Testament* (London/New York: United Bible Societies, 1971), 232.

[23]John 15:19; 17:14, 16.

[24]John 8:30 is only apparently an exception. Here some of those who Jesus had said would "die in your sins" seem to have turned and "believed in him," but when he invites them to "remain in my word" so as to be "truly my disciples"(Jn 8:31-32), they take offence (Jn 8:33) and try to take his life (Jn 8:37-59).

[25]The footwashing is a possible exception. Even as he assures his disciples that they are "clean" (Jn 13:10), Jesus washes their feet and commands them to do the same for each other. Mutual footwashing can be interpreted as mutual forgiveness of sins in the Christian community. See J. C. Thomas, *Footwashing in John 13 and the Johannine Community, JSNTSup,* no. 61 (Sheffield: JSOT Press, 1991), 155-72. Yet the explicit interpretation given near the chapter's end views the footwashing positively as mutual love rather than negatively as forgiveness of sins (see Jn 13:34).

the forgiveness of sins. In itself, the Gospel of John has no explicit theology of the atonement.[26]

No Christian reader today, however, reads the Gospel of John "in itself," or by itself. An academician may do so for academic or antiquar-
ian reasons, to find out how it sounded to its first readers, but today it
is part of a canon called the New Testament. Within that canon it comes
last in a smaller collection of four gospels, ending with a colophon appropriate to all four (Jn 21:25). By virtue of a common attribution to
"John," it is linked to four other canonical writings as well: a brief tract
on themes familiar from the gospel (1 John), two very short letters (2
and 3 John), and a much longer letter calling itself an "apocalypse" or
"prophecy" (Revelation).

Reading any narrative requires a certain amount of filling in gaps in
light of one's own knowledge and experience, and a Christian reader
familiar with the entire New Testament will inevitably fill in some gaps
in John's gospel. Even though Nathaniel, Nicodemus, the Samaritan
woman and the man born blind are not explicitly *called* sinners, a
Christian reader acquainted with Romans will know that they *were* in
fact sinners, and that Jesus in this gospel (as in the others) *did* come to
redeem them from their sin. I believe that Roger Nicole would say that,
and when we turn from the gospel to 1 John, we find such a reading
vindicated.

The Atonement in 1 John: "For Our Sins"

If the "message" (ἀγγελία) of 1 John is that "God is light," its immediate corollary is "The blood of Jesus, his Son, purifies us from all sin" (1
Jn 1:5, 7). The "us" is striking. The author, having begun by speaking
for an authoritative (perhaps apostolic) group ("we") to an unidenti-
fied Christian congregation ("you") somewhere in the Mediterranean
world (1 Jn 1:1-5), now includes himself with his readers as "we"
(ἡμεῖς), acknowledging both his and their sinfulness. "If *we* claim to be
without sin," he continues, "*we* deceive ourselves and the truth is not

---

[26]Vincent Taylor once commented "Many who find their spiritual home in the Fourth Gospel
pass somewhat lightly over the ideas of Romans iii. 25," adding that "the truth is we ought
never to make the Fourth Gospel our 'home'; it is the Interpreter's House in which we stay
for awhile, and to which we often return, in order to survey with new eyes the wealth of
New Testament teaching" (*The Atonement in New Testament Teaching* [London: Epworth,
1940], 228-29).

in *us*. If *we* confess *our* sins, he is faithful and just and will forgive *us our* sins, and purify *us* from all unrighteousness."[27]

As we have seen, the Gospel of John was preoccupied with its dualism: light and darkness, life and death, sinners and believers, but little or nothing about the sins of believers. 1 John, by contrast, places the sins of those *within* the Christian community front and center. If not sinners by nature, they do sin on occasion, and if they say they do not, they are liars (1 Jn 1:8). Significantly, it is in connection with "our" sins, the sins of believers, that the author first introduces an explicit theology of Christ's atoning sacrifice.

The terminology of the Gospel of John, that Jesus "laid down his life for his sheep" or for his "friends," could serve this purpose, but for the author of 1 John it does not. He uses it only to make the point that Jesus showed his love by putting his life on the line for us, as we should do for each other (1 Jn 3:16). When he wants to speak of Jesus' atoning death, he prefers the more explicit language of "propitiation" (ἱλασμός).[28] He seems to introduce the stronger terminology because of some in the congregation who had claimed, or were claiming, not to have sinned at all. Such people were deceiving themselves and making God a liar. God's truth was not in them (1 Jn 1:8, 10).

Our survey has shown that it is indeed possible to read John's gospel through perfectionist eyes, with Christian believers as "true Israelites," God's chosen and perfect gift to his Son. Such a grandiose vision may be true so far as it goes, but it does not fill in the gaps as the author had assumed they would be filled in, that is, with the recognition that God's chosen were at the same time sinners saved by grace. 1 John's intent is to provide the needed clarification. While the author of 1 John does not claim to have written the Fourth Gospel and does not even refer to the Gospel as an existing document, he does begin with the firm insistence that he was there "from the beginning," when "we heard" and "saw with our eyes" and "our hands touched" the things of which he speaks (1 Jn 1:1). Such claims are, if anything, even clearer and more explicit than those of the Gospel itself.[29] While common authorship cannot be proven, the author of 1 John shows a

---

[27]1 John 1:8-9, my italics.
[28]1 John 2:2, 4:10.
[29]See John 1:14, 19:35, 21:24.

proprietary interest in the Gospel's teaching, developing it and clari-
fying it as his own.[30] His postscript (if we may call it that) comes to us
with canonical authority, and the arrangement of the present volume
confirms this by assigning atonement in the gospel and epistles of
John to a single article.

As for the controversial ἱλασμός (1 Jn 2:2; 4:10), there is no need to
go over the lexicographical ground again.[31] "Propitiation" and "expiation" are *both* attested as possible meanings of the ἱλασμός or
ἱλάσκεσθαι word group in both the Greek OT and NT. But in deciding
between Dodd's interpretation and that of Nicole, two observations
are in order. First, there is exclusivity in Dodd's proposal that is not
present in Nicole's. When Dodd proposes "expiation" as the correct
translation of ἱλασμός, he means to exclude any idea of "propitiation,"
but Nicole's argument for "propitiation" does not similarly exclude
"expiation." It is a matter of both/and, not either-or. Second, literary
context takes precedence over linguistic background, never more so
than when the latter is inconclusive, as here. The question is not, "What
does ἱλασμός mean?" but "What does ἱλασμός mean in these two
texts?" As we have seen, 1 John 2:2 comes in a context focusing on "us"
and on "our sins," that is, on the sins of Christian believers. "My dear
children," the author writes, "I write this to you so that you will not
sin. But if anybody does sin, we have one who speaks to the Father in
our defense [παράκλητος, literally 'an Advocate']—Jesus Christ, the
Righteous One" (1 Jn 2:1). Then he adds, "He is ἱλασμός for our sins,
and not only for ours but also for the sins of the whole world" (2:2). The
image of Jesus as "Advocate" with the Father makes God the *object*, not
the subject, of the reconciliation said to be taking place, and to that extent supports "propitiation" as the meaning of ἱλασμός.[32] Jesus acts as

---

[30]For rather full discussions of the complex issue of authorship, see Raymond E. Brown, *The Epistles of John*, AB, no. 30 (Garden City, N.Y.: Doubleday, 1982), 19-35, and I. Howard Mar-shall, *The Epistles of John*, NICNT (Grand Rapids: Eerdmans, 1978), 31-42.

[31]See above, n. 2. In addition, see (in agreement with Nicole) Leon Morris, *The Apostolic Preaching of the Cross* (London: Tyndale, 1955), 125-85; D. Hill, *Greek Words and Hebrew Mean-ings* (Cambridge: At the University Press, 1967), 23-48; and T. C. G. Thornton, "Propitiation or Expiation? *Hilasterion* and *Hilasmos* in Romans and 1 John," *ExpTim* 80 (1968-69): 53-55. Also (in support of Dodd), S. Lyonnet, "The Noun *hilasmos* in the Greek Old Testament and 1 John," in *Sin, Redemption, and Sacrifice* (Rome: Biblical Institute, 1970), 148-55; H. Clavier, "Notes sur un mot-clef du johannisme et de la sotériologie biblique: *hilasmos*," *Novum Tes-tamentum* 10 (1968): 287-304, and (guardedly and with qualifications) Brown, *Community of the Beloved Disciple*, 217-22.

our "Advocate" on the basis of his sacrifice "for our sins." I. Howard
Marshall's comment clearly defines this as propitiation:

> There can be no doubt that this is the meaning. In the previous verse the
> thought was of Jesus acting as our advocate before God; the picture which
> continues into this verse is of Jesus pleading the cause of guilty sinners be-
> fore a judge who is being asked to pardon their acknowledged guilt. . . . In
> order that forgiveness may be granted, there is an action in respect of the
> sins which has the effect of rendering God favorable to the sinner.[33]

At the same time, the second occurrence of ἱλασμός in 1 John 4:10
makes God the *subject* of reconciliation, and to that extent supports
"expiation": "This is love, not that we loved God, but that he loved us
and sent his Son as ἱλασμός for our sins." The common factor is the
phrase "for *our* sins."[34] In both instances, the sins of Christian believers,
not the sins of the whole world, are what leads the author to introduce
the explicit language of atonement. But here the initiative rests with
God the Father, not with Jesus acting as Advocate in our behalf,[35] and
the accent is not on placating God so much as on removing the guilt of
"our sins."[36] The apparent standoff confirms what several commentators have said, and what Roger Nicole himself clearly implied, that
Jesus' death in 1 John is *both* "propitiation" and "expiation."[37] There is
no need or reason to pit one against the other. There is "not contradiction, but complementarity," according to one commentator.[38] More

---

[32]Even Dodd, in *The Bible and the Greeks*, 94-95, grants the force of this point, yet (with no real
counter-argument) concludes rather weakly that nevertheless "the common rendering
'propitiation' is illegitimate here as elsewhere" (95). For a more detailed and convincing response than is possible here, see Nicole, "Doctrine of Propitiation," 143-46.

[33]*The Epistles of John*, 118. Charles Wesley put it more poetically: "Five bleeding wounds he
bears, received on Calvary. They pour effectual prayers, they strongly plead for me. 'Forgive
him, O Forgive,' they cry, 'nor let that ransomed sinner die, nor let that ransomed sinner die.'"

[34]Italics added.

[35]Cf. Romans 3:25, which also stresses God's initiative: "whom God put forward as a sacrifice
of atonement [ἱλαστήριον] by his blood, effective through faith" (NRSV). Naturally, Dodd,
The Bible and the Greeks, 94, appeals to this verse in support of "expiation."

[36]Brown, *The Epistles of John*, comments that 1 John 4:10 "favors expiation" because "the Son is
sent from God—if he was propitiating God, the action would be in the other direction" (220).

[37]See Nicole's inclusive summary of redemption's varied aspects ("Doctrine of Propitiation,"
119-21). See also Stephen Smalley, *1, 2, 3 John*, WBC, no. 51 (Waco, Tex.: Word, 1984): "Possibly these two interpretations . . . one in which God is the subject of the action of sin-offer-
ing, and one in which he is the object, need not be regarded as mutually exclusive" (39).
Marshall adds, "The one action has the double effect of expiating the sin and thereby propitiating God" (*The Epistles of John*, 118). A better way of putting it might have been, "propitiating God and thereby expiating the sin."

than that, the two together point toward a mystery at the very heart of the Christian gospel, defying all our attempts at rationalization: God placates God! The Prosecutor himself sends and appoints the Defense Attorney to plead with the Prosecutor to show mercy!

And what of the *extent* of the atonement in 1 John? What about the text with which our discussion began, "and not only for ours but also for the sins of the whole world" (1 Jn 2:2)? Most efforts by defenders of limited or definite atonement to explain these words have been less than convincing. Arthur W. Pink, for example, proposed that "our" in the phrase "for our sins" (1 Jn 2:2) referred to "*Jewish believers*" and that with the additional phrase "of the whole world" (1 Jn 2:2), John "signified that Christ was the propitiation for the sins of *Gentile* believers *too*, for, as previously shown, 'the world' is a term *contrasted* from Israel."[39] Pink appealed to John 11:51, 52, which uses the same construction, "not alone . . . but also" (οὐ μόνον. . . ἀλλὰ καί) to distinguish between the "nation" of Israel and "the scattered children of God" (that is, Gentile believers scattered throughout the earth).[40] He could have appealed as well to John 17:20, where the distinction is between Jesus' immediate followers and the next generation of believers: "My prayer is not for them alone [οὐ . . . μόνον], but also [ἀλλὰ καί] for those believing in me through their word." Pink is on the right track to the extent that in each of these parallels Jesus is concerned with a wider, or different group of believers, not with undifferentiated universal humanity. But his attempt to show that 1 John is addressed to *Jewish* Christians in particular is unconvincing. 1 John is written to a Christian community without reference to its ethnic background, whether Jewish or Gentile or both. Its concern, as we have seen, is with the sins of Christian believ-

---

[38]Smalley finds the same complementarity in the Jewish sacrificial system: "Theologically it is in any case true that God is the *initiator* of the Jewish principle and pattern of sacrifice for sin. . . . But he also *receives* that sacrifice, so that atonement may be made 'for all the sins of the Israelites'" (39).

[39]*The Sovereignty of God* (Grand Rapids: Baker, 1979), 258-59. Charles Hodge is on stronger ground in stating, "He was a propitiation effectually for the sins of his people, and sufficiently for the sins of the whole world" *Systematic Theology* 2 (London and Edinburgh: Thomas Nelson, 1873), 559, but his remarks cry out for further elaboration. On the other hand, those who assume universal atonement here run the risk of opening the door unintentionally to universal salvation: see for example Marianne M. Thompson, *1-3 John*, IVP New Testament Commentary (Downers Grove, Ill.: InterVarsity Press, 1992): "The emphasis falls on the universal effectiveness [*sic*] of Christ's atoning work" (51).

[40]Pink, *Sovereignty of God*, 259.

ers after their conversion, emphasizing that "the blood of Jesus . . . purifies *us* from all sin" (1 Jn 1:7), that "if anybody sins *we have* an Advocate with the Father" and that he is a propitiation "for *our* sins" (1 Jn
2:1-2, my italics). But having introduced an explicit theology of atonement to deal with the specific problem of "our" sins now, after conversion and baptism, the author adds, almost as an afterthought, that of
course this is God's way of dealing with sin always and everywhere:
"and not only for ours but also for the sins of the whole world."[41] There
is not one "propitiation" for us and another for the rest of the world,
but Jesus (καὶ αὐτός) is the only sacrifice, and the only way of salvation
for all.[42] The point is not that Jesus died for everyone indiscriminately
so that everyone in the world is in principle forgiven, but that all those
forgiven are forgiven on the basis of Christ's sacrifice and in no other
way. Having made the point once, the author of 1 John does not bela-
bor it, but contents himself the second time with mentioning only "our
sins" (1 Jn 4:10) and not "the whole world." His emphasis throughout
is on the sins of believers, the kind of sin that because of Christ's sacrifice "does *not* lead to death" (1 Jn 5:16-17, my italics). As for "the whole
world," while Christ's atoning work is wide enough and strong
enough to cover it, the author of 1 John sees no sign of its immediate
transformation. Rather, "we know that we are children of God, and
that *the whole world* is under the control of the evil one" (1 Jn 5:19, my
italics). Even while recognizing and addressing the reality of sin
among Christian believers, the author of 1 John in no way blunts or
minimizes the fundamental dualism of John's gospel.

Conclusion

The Baptist tradition, to which Roger Nicole and I both belong, was divided from the beginning, over the extent of the atonement, between
so-called Particular and General Baptists. Most Baptists in America
now would probably hesitate to identify themselves with either group,
but Roger never showed such hesitation. I used to be more timid than
he, but my studies in John and 1 John have convinced me that, at least
with reference to these New Testament witnesses, he was right and the

---

[41]It is overly subtle to press the point that the Greek text says "for the whole world" and not
"for the *sins* of the whole world." The sentence is elliptical, and the accent is on "sins" in
any case, as the NIV recognizes.
[42]See also John 14:6, Acts 4:12.

Particular Baptists were right. On the nature of the atonement, the downplaying of creeds and the accent on soul liberty has meant that Baptists could be found all over the theological map, but here again I find myself on Roger's side, certainly from reading Paul but also from John, provided that John and 1 John are read as they should be, together. There are more important things than being right, and I have always found much to respect and admire in my friend even when we did not fully agree. On the atonement we do agree, even though our ways of getting there may be a little different, and that is cause for rejoicing.

atonement in romans 3:21-26

"God Presented Him as a Propitiation"

D. A. Carson

Romans 3:21-26 has for a long time been a focal text for debate about the atonement. With the rise of the "new perspective" on Paul, some of the parameters of these debates have shifted. Within the constraints of this essay, I cannot attempt the full-blown interaction that the subject demands. My aim is more modest. I intend to discuss ten of the turning points in the text that affect the outcome of one's exegesis and briefly indicate at least some of the reasons why I read the text as I do.

The Significance of the Preceding Passage, Romans 1:18—3:20

Disputants are unlikely to agree on the solution to a problem if they cannot agree on the nature of the problem. Today's disputes focus on whether or not the situation envisaged in Romans 2:5-16 is real or hypothetical; the extent to which Romans 2:17-28 focuses on the failure of the nation of Israel rather than on the individual; the extent to which Paul's theology, which on the face of it runs from plight to solution, betrays his own experience, which was (it is argued) from solution to plight; the nature and focus of his rhetoric; the extent to which covenant categories control this section; and much more. Each of these topics could call forth a very lengthy chapter.[1]

---

[1]Apart from the major commentaries, see the admirable treatment by Andrew T. Lincoln, "From Wrath to Justification: Tradition, Gospel, and Audience in the Theology of Romans 1:18—4:25," in *Pauline Theology*, vol. 3, *Romans*, ed. David M. Hay and E. Elizabeth Johnson (Minneapolis: Fortress, 1995), 130-59.

However such matters are resolved, the framework must not be forgotten. The section opens with the wrath of God being revealed from heaven "against all the godlessness and wickedness of men" (Rom 1:18), and ends with a catena of texts to prove that no one is righteous, not even one (Rom 3:9-20). Jews and Gentiles are alike condemned. Nor will it do to make the failure exclusively national (though it is not less than national): if it is true to say that Jews and Gentiles collectively are alike under sin, Paul carefully goes farther and specifies that they "alike are *all* under sin" (Rom 3:9, italics added). Indeed, *every* mouth is to be silenced on the last day, and there is *no one* righteous (Rom 3:19, 20).

What these observations establish, then, is the nature of the problem that Romans 3:21-26 sets out to resolve. The problem is not first and foremost the failure of Israel (national or otherwise), or inappropriate use of the law, or the urgency of linking Jews and Gentiles (all genuine themes in these chapters), but the wrath of God directed against every human being, Jew and Gentile alike—a wrath elicited by universal human wickedness. This is not saying that human beings are incapable of any good. Clearly, even those without the law may do things about which their consciences rightly defend them (Rom 2:15). But the flow of argument that takes us from Romans 1:18-32 to Romans 3:9-20 leaves us no escape: individually and collectively, Jew and Gentile alike, we stand under the just wrath of God, because of our sin.[2]

Moreover, the closing verses of this section establish two other points that support this analysis and help to prepare for Romans 3:21-26. First, the second half of Romans 3:19 paints a picture that is unavoidably forensic; and second, the slight modification of Psalm 143:2 (142:2 LXX) in Romans 3:20 by the addition of the phrase "by the works of the law" establishes (1) that although the indictment of Romans 1:18—3:20 embraces all of humanity, there is special reference to Jews, precisely because to them were given the oracles of God (as Romans 9 puts it); (2) that in the light of the forensic catastrophe summarized in

---

[2]Surprisingly, B. W. Longenecker, *Eschatology and Covenant: A Comparison of 4 Ezra and Romans 1—11* (Sheffield: JSOT Press, 1991), 175-81, argues that Paul's indictment, especially in Romans 1:18-32, is rhetorical polemic typical of the technique of ethical denunciation, but without any empirical correspondence. Not only does this argument presuppose that polemic cannot have pedagogical purpose, but it presupposes that rhetoric cannot be deployed to make points about empirical reality. That would cut the ground out from Paul's conclusion in Romans 3:9-20.

the preceding verse the expression "works of the law" cannot easily be reduced, in this context, to boundary markers such as laws relating to circumcision, kosher food and Sabbath, for in fact these "works of the law" by which one cannot be justified must be tied to the judgment according to works (Rom 2:8), to the unyielding principle of performance (Rom 2:13);[3] and (3) that therefore the law itself was not given, according to Paul, to effect righteousness, for even "if the deeds by which one hopes to be justified are deeds laid down in the law, this fails to alter the universal indictment that no one passes the judgment, no one is righteous."[4] This does not mean the law is intrinsically evil, of course (Rom 7:12); it does mean that Paul adopts a certain salvation-historical reading of the law's role, and according to that reading, the law (by which he here means the law-covenant), while it enabled human beings to become conscious of sin and doubtless performed other functions described elsewhere, could not, in the nature of the case, justify anyone (Rom 3:20).

Νυνὶ δέ ("But now"), Romans 3:21

Although this expression can signal a logical connection, here it is almost certainly temporal,[5] indeed salvation-historical. But granted the contrast between the old era of sin's dominion and the new era of salvation or between the old era of the law covenant and the new era that Jesus Christ has introduced (these most basic of contrasts in Paul's eschatology), what is the precise nature of the temporal contrast here? If Romans 3:21-26 is contrasted with all of Romans 1:18-3:20, then it is possible, with Moo, to say, "As the 'wrath of God' dominated the old era (Rom 1:18), so 'the righteousness of God' dominates the new."[6] But perhaps that is not quite Paul's focus. In general terms, the NT writers, including Paul, do not encourage us to think that God pre-

---

[3]For the narrower view that connects "works of the law" to ethnic boundary markers, see, inter alios, B. W. Longenecker, *Eschatology*, 200-202, 206-7; and James D. G. Dunn, *Romans 1— 8*, WBC no. 38a (Dallas, Tex.: Word, 1988), 153-55. For the broader view espoused here, see, e.g., Ulrich Wilckens, "Was heisst bei Paulus: 'Aus Werken des Gesetzes wird kein Mensch gerecht'?" in *Rechtfertigung als Freiheit: Paulusstudien* (Neukirchen: Neukirchener Verlag, 1974), 77-109; idem, *Der Brief an die Römer*, EKKNT vol. 6 (Zürich: Benziger Verlag, 1978), 1.130-31, 145-46, 175-76; and especially Douglas J. Moo, *The Epistle to the Romans*, NICNT (Grand Rapids: Eerdmans, 1996), 204-17.
[4]Lincoln, "From Wrath to Justification," 146.
[5]Its customary meaning, e.g. Romans 6:22; 7:6.
[6]Moo, *Romans*, 222.

sents himself in the old covenant as a God of wrath, and in the new as a God of grace (justifying grace?). Although the point cannot be defended here at length, it would be truer to say that just as the portrait of God as a God of justifying grace is ratcheted up as one moves from the old covenant to the new, so the portrait of God as a God of holy wrath is ratcheted up as one moves from the old covenant to the new. Moreover, in this very paragraph, the *earlier* period is characterized as the time of God's "forbearance."[7]

A closer contrast lies at hand, one that nevertheless presupposes the shift from the old era to the new. On this reading, Romans 3:21-26 is tied more tightly to the immediately preceding verses. If, in the nature of the case, the law covenant could not effect righteousness or ensure that anyone be declared righteous—I leave the expression open for the moment—then, granted the universality of human sin, under the new era what is needed is righteousness that is manifested apart from the law.

Χωρὶς νόμου ("apart from law"), Romans 3:21

Should this phrase be read with δικαιοσύνη θεοῦ ("But now a righteousness from God apart from law, has been made known") or with πεφανέρωται ("But now a righteousness from God has been made known apart from law")? The matter cannot be decided by mere syntactical proximity; it is not uncommon in Greek for a prepositional phrase to modify a verb from which it is somewhat removed. The question must be resolved by appealing to context. If the first interpretation were correct, "a righteousness from God apart from law," the phrase "apart from law" would most likely mean "apart from doing the law" or the like, or perhaps "apart from the works of the law," referring back to Romans 3:20. But despite the popularity of this view,[8] by itself it is not quite adequate. It is quite correct to observe that God's righteousness is attained without any contribution from the "works of the law." But to say that it is *now* obtained without any contribution from the "works of the law" would be to imply that it was *once* ob-

---

[7]Romans 3:26 in the Greek text; Romans 3:25 in the NIV.

[8]E.g., Anders Nygren, *Commentary on Romans* (Philadelphia: Muhlenberg, 1949), 148; C. E. B. Cranfield, *The Epistle to the Romans*, ICC (Edinburgh: T & T Clark, 1975-1979) 1.201 (though he finds this meaning present even while holding, rightly, that the prepositional phrase modifies the verb); Brendan Byrne, *Romans*, SP (Collegeville, Minn.: Liturgical, 1996), 129; Thomas R. Schreiner, *Romans*, BECNT (Grand Rapids: Baker, 1998), 180.

tained with (at least some) contribution from the "works of the law"—
and that is precisely what Paul has ruled out in the previous verses. So
if the temporal contrast embedded in "But now" is taken seriously,
then it is contextually inadequate to think that "apart from law" is really a shorthand for "apart from the works of the law" or "apart from
doing the law" or the like. After all, as Paul himself will point out in
Romans 4, justification has always been by faith and apart from law.

In fact, if, as most sides agree, the prepositional phrase is connected
with the verb πεφανέρωται, then another reading is possible: "a righteousness from God has been made known apart from law" focuses attention not on the *reception* of righteousness, since it is received by faith,
but on the *disclosure* of this righteousness, since it has been made known
apart from law. In that case, the expression "apart from law" most probably means something like "apart from the law-covenant." The issue is
not whether or not people can do the the law (the previous verses have
insisted that they cannot: all are sinners), but "law" as a system: this side
of the coming and death and resurrection of Jesus the Messiah, God has
acted to vindicate his people "apart from the law," apart from the law as
an entire system that played its crucial role in redemptive history.[9]

But this does not mean that what has been inaugurated in Christ is
utterly independent from what has preceded; Paul is not antinomian.
Far from it: he insists that this newly disclosed righteousness is that "to
which the Law and the Prophets testify" (Rom 3:21). In other words,
according to Paul God gave the law not only to regulate the conduct of
his people and, more importantly, to reveal their sin until the fulfillment of the promises in Christ,[10] but also because the law has a prophetic function, a witness function: it pointed in the right direction; it
bore witness to the righteousness that is *now* being revealed. It is not
simply that the national identity markers are now obsolete; there is a
sense in which the entire law-covenant is "obsolete"[11]—or, more precisely, its ongoing validity is in that to which it bears witness, which
has *now* dawned.[12] There is a dramatic shift in salvation history.

---

[9]In fact, since νόμου is anarthrous, there may be a hint not only of the Mosaic law-covenant,
but of the "law" known even to Gentiles (Rom 2:13-16): the entire demand structure could
not justify men and women in the past, and now God has acted to justify men and women
"apart from" it.

[10]Cf. Romans 4:13-15; 5:20; Galatians 3:15—4:7.

[11]To use the language of Hebrews 8:13.

[12]This is, as I have argued elsewhere, the argument of Jesus himself in Matthew 5:17-20.

δικαιοσύη θεοῦ ("righteousness from God") and Cognates, Romans 3:21

This expression clearly dominates the passage. It occurs four times,[13] the cognate adjective "just" (δίκαιος) occurs once,[14] and the cognate verb "to justify" (δικαιόω) twice.[15] Probably no NT word-group has elicited more discussion during the past century than this one. Few doubt that the noun and adjective cover a range of meanings in the NT, so that any particular usage is largely determined by context. Arguably, Paul always uses the verb in the forensic sense, "to justify."

Granted the complexity of the discussion, I shall venture only a few observations and claims, with minimal argumentation. In part, the force of the expressions in this passage must be teased out in conjunction with the delineation of the flow of the argument. (1) The preceding section (Rom 1:18—3:20) has established the need for this righteousness. That need is bound up with human sin and the inevitability of universal human guilt before God. That already constitutes some support for the view that this "righteousness from God" is God's eschatological justifying or vindicating activity. (2) Despite the extraordinary popularity of the view that the expression actually means something like "God's covenant faithfulness" or the like, recent research is making such a view harder and harder to sustain. The history of the interpretation is itself suggestive; more important yet is the fact that in the Hebrew Bible the terms בְּרִית ("covenant") and צְדָקָה ("righteousness"), despite their very high frequency, almost never occur in close proximity.[16] In general, "one does not 'act righteously or unrighteously' with respect to a covenant. Rather, one 'keeps,' 'remembers,' 'establishes' a covenant, or the like. Or, conversely, one 'breaks,' 'transgresses,' 'forsakes,' 'despises,' 'forgets,' or 'profanes' it."[17] Righteousness language is commonly found in parallel with terms for rightness

---

[13]Romans 3:21, 22, 25, 26—though the last two are "his righteousness."
[14]Romans 3:26.
[15]Romans 3:24, 26.
[16]On both points, see the excellent discussion by Mark A. Seifrid, "Righteousness Language in the Hebrew Scriptures and Early Judaism," in *Justification and Variegated Nomism*, vol. 1, *The Complexities of Second Temple Judaism*, ed. D. A. Carson, Peter T. O'Brien and Mark A. Seifrid (Tübingen: Mohr-Siebeck, 2001), 415-42. See further, Moo, *Romans*, 70-90; and, more briefly, Peter Stuhlmacher, *Paul's Letter to the Romans: A Commentary*, trans. Scott J. Hafemann (Louisville, Ky.: Westminster John Knox, 1994), 61-65.
[17]Seifrid, "Righteousness Language," 424.

or rectitude over against evil. The attempt to link "being righteous" with "being in the covenant" or with Israel's "covenant status," especially in Qumran and rabbinic literature, does not fare very well either. (3) Even at the level of philology, the δικ- words are so commonly connected with righteousness/justice that attempts to loosen the connection must be judged astonishing. (4) Not least in this paragraph, but also elsewhere, there is a dual concern that God be vindicated and that his people be vindicated.[18] So also here at the beginning of the passage: this is a righteousness "from God," that is, it is first and foremost God's righteousness (Rom 3:2), but it is precisely *this* righteousness from God which comes to all who believe (Rom 3:22).[19]

Διὰ πίστεως Ἰησοῦ Χριστοῦ ("through faith in Jesus Christ"), Romans 3:22

Traditionally, this phrase has been understood to establish Jesus Christ as the object of faith, the objective genitive reading. More recently, influential voices have argued for either a possessive genitive, "through the faith of Jesus Christ," or, more commonly, a subjective genitive, taking πίστις to mean "faithfulness," that is, "through the faithfulness of Jesus Christ."[20] Even if the subjective genitive were to prevail, the traditional interpretation of the paragraph as a whole remains plausible: after all, some NT writers, especially John and Hebrews, make much

---

[18]Romans 3:26; see below.

[19]*Pace* N. T. Wright, "Romans and the Theology of Paul," in *Pauline Theology*, vol. 3, *Romans*, ed. David M. Hay and E. Elizabeth Johnson (Minneapolis: Fortress Press, 1995), 38-39, who claims that "righteousness" means "covenant faithfulness," and therefore that this "righteousness" is "not a quality or substance that can be passed or transferred from the judge to the defendant" (39). The righteousness of the judge is simply the judge's "own character, status, and activity" (39), demonstrated in doing various things; the "righteousness" of the defendants is their status when the court has acquitted them—and obviously this righteousness must not be confused with the latter. "When we translate these forensic categories back into their theological context, that of the covenant, the point remains fundamental: the divine covenant faithfulness is not the same as human covenant membership" (39). Wright's errors here can be traced first of all to a misunderstanding of δικαιοσύνη, and second (as we shall see), to a less plausible reading of the passage at hand.

[20]E.g., Luke T. Johnson, "Rom 3:21-26 and the Faith of Jesus," *CBQ* 44 (1982): 77-90; Bruce W. Longenecker, *Eschatology*, 149-50; G. Howard, "'The Faith of Christ,'" *ExpTim* 85 (1973-1974): 212-14; D. W. B. Robinson, "'Faith of Jesus Christ'—A New Testament Debate," *RTR* 29 (1970): 71-81; Richard B. Hays, "ΠΙΣΤΙΣ and Pauline Christology: What Is at Stake," in *Society of Biblical Literature 1991 Seminar Papers*, ed. E. H. Lovering Jr. (Atlanta: Scholars Press, 1991), 714-29; idem, *The Faith of Jesus Christ: The Narrative Substructure of Galatians 3:1—4:11*, 2nd ed. (Grand Rapids: Eerdmans, 2002).

of the obedience, and thus the faithfulness, of Jesus Christ in accomplishing his Father's will, even though they *also* insist that Jesus is the object of our faith. But the subjective genitive reading can be used to support a "new perspective" interpretation of this passage in a way that the objective genitive cannot: the "covenant faithfulness" ("righteousness" on this reading) of God is revealed through the faithfulness of Jesus the Messiah for the benefit of all. Indeed, N. T. Wright goes so far as to say that "the success of this way of reading this passage is the best argument in favor of the subjective genitive (faith 'of' Christ) in some at least of the key passages."[21]

The linguistic arguments, though complex, are usually judged to be far from conclusive.[22] Perhaps the one exegetical argument that carries an initial weight against the objective genitive is something that is lost in English, the apparent tautology generated by the objective genitive in Greek: διὰ πίστεως Ἰησοῦ Χριστοῦ εἰς πάντας τοὺς πιστεύοντας ("through *trust* in Jesus Christ to all who exercise *trust*" or "through *faith* in Jesus Christ to all who have *faith*"). The apparent tautology is lost in most of our English translations because of the difference in root behind our noun "faith" and our verb "believe" ("through *faith* in Jesus Christ to all who *believe*"). Yet closer inspection discloses that there is a profound reason for this repetition, namely, the prepositional phrase "for all." The point may be demonstrated by the somewhat paraphrastic rendering, "This righteousness from God comes through faith in Jesus Christ—to *all* who have faith in him."[23] The advantages of this explanation of the repetition are many. (1) It takes the crucial expressions, including "righteousness" and "faith," in their most natural ways. For instance, πίστις almost always means "faith" in Paul; it takes strong contextual support to permit "faithfulness," and such support is lacking here. (2) Moreover, although, as we have seen, other NT writers develop the theme of Christ's obedience or

---

[21]Wright, "Romans and the Theology of Paul," 37 n.9.

[22]Among the better treatments, see Moo, *Romans*, 226-28; Schreiner, *Romans*, 181-87; Dunn, *Romans* 1.166-67; Joseph A. Fitzmyer, *Romans*, AB no. 33 (New York: Doubleday, 1993), 345-46; and the literature cited in these works. From a linguistic perspective, the most penetrating treatment is that of Moisés Silva, "Faith Versus Works of Law in Galatians" in *Justification and Variegated Nomism*, vol. 2, *The Paradoxes of Paul*, ed. D. A. Carson, Peter T. O'Brien and Mark Seifrid (Tübingen: Mohr-Siebeck, forthcoming).

[23]Similar arguments can be mounted in other passages where a charge of tautology is leveled, e.g., Galatians 2:16; Philippians 3:19.

faithfulness, this is not, demonstrably, a theme that Paul develops, even, as in Romans 4, where he might have had an excuse for doing so.[24] (3) More importantly, this reading ties the passage to the preceding section. Romans 1:18—3:20 demonstrates that *all*, Jews and Gentiles alike, are guilty before God; but now, Paul argues, a righteousness from God has appeared that is available to *all* without distinction, but on condition of faith. The connection is explicit in the text, highlighted by the repetition of the word "all" and by two logical connectors. We might continue our rendering: "This righteousness from God comes through faith in Jesus Christ—to *all* who have faith in him. For [γάρ] there is no difference, for [γάρ] *all* [πάντες] have sinned[25] and come short of the glory of God." (4) This reading also prepares us for the last clause of Romans 3:26, and for Paul's argument in Romans 3:27-31, with its massive emphasis on faith.

To summarize the argument so far: Paul has established that all are condemned, Jew and Gentile alike, apart from the cross of Christ; all stand under his judicial condemnation and face his wrath. But now, he says, a new righteousness has appeared in the history of redemption to deal with this. Paul first relates this righteousness to OT revelation (Rom 3:21). Then he establishes the availability of this righteousness to all human beings without racial distinction but solely on condition of faith. He now turns to the source of this righteousness from God. It is nothing other than the gracious provision of Jesus Christ as the propitiatory sacrifice for our sin.

διὰ τῆς ἀπολυτρώσεως ("through the redemption"), Romans 3:24

Paul says that the "all" who have faith are "justified[26] freely by his grace through the redemption that came by Jesus Christ, whom God presented as a propitiation."[27] Thus, three images are deployed, and these three correspond to the different ways that sin itself may be viewed. First, justification, grounded in the imagery of the law court, continues. Lincoln writes:

---

[24]A point shrewdly made by James D. G. Dunn, *Romans* 1.167.

[25]I would here prefer to see what traditional grammarians would call a "global aorist," i.e., "for all sin"—but that is another issue.

[26]Gk. δικαιούμενοι, the participle of the verb: there is no reason to doubt the verb's forensic force.

[27]Where the English translation departs from the NIV, it is mine.

God's righteousness is the power by which those unable to be justified on the criterion of works are set right with him and being set in a right relationship with God involves his judicial verdict of pardon. It is not that people are deemed innocent of the charges in the indictment against them. Their unrighteousness has been clearly depicted in Paul's argument. But he believes the righteous judge has acted ahead of time in history and in his grace has pronounced a pardon on those who have faith in Christ, so that their guilt can no longer be cited against them.[28]

This language, then, answers to the controlling theme of Romans 1:18—3:20: all human beings stand under God's judicial condemnation; all are guilty; all deserve his wrath. And this is God's provision for our plight.

Second, God's justification of sinners is "through the redemption that is in Christ Jesus." One might say the *origin* of this justification is God's grace, δωρεὰν τῆ αὐτοῦ χάριτι, "by his grace as a gift"; the *historical basis* of this gift is "the redemption that came by Christ Jesus." All sides recognize that this imagery is tied, both in the Greco-Roman world and in the Jewish world, if we may indulge in the distinction, to freedom from slavery. But there are also roots in Scripture beyond the world of the slave market: God liberated his people from slavery in Egypt and from exile in Assyria and Babylon.[29] So also here: sin, Paul has already said, has not only made all human beings judicially guilty before God, but it has enslaved them. It has unleashed God's "giving them over" to the chaining degradations of the human heart; all are imprisoned "under sin" (Rom 3:9). To meet this need, we must have redemption—emancipation from slavery.

The third imagery is drawn from the cultic world and will be taken up in the next section. But before turning to it, we should remind ourselves that the redemption (ἀπολύτρωσις) that is effected is accomplished by the payment of a price or a ransom (λύτρον). Leon Morris argued decades ago that "the LXX usage is such as to leave us in no doubt that λύτρον and its cognates are properly applied to redemption by payment of a price."[30] More recent writers have tended to confirm that conclusion.[31] In the passage at hand, the price in view is Jesus'

---

[28]Lincoln, "From Wrath to Justification," 148.
[29]Cf. Deuteronomy 7:8 and Isaiah 51:11.
[30]*The Apostolic Preaching of the Cross* (Leicester: Inter-Varsity Press, 1965), 27.
[31]E.g., Dunn, *Romans* 1.169, 179-80.

death,[32] which frees us from death that is nothing other than sin's penalty.[33] "With his redemptive act in Christ, God has acted to free us from the penalty he himself imposed."[34]

ἱλαστήριον ("propitiation," NIV "sacrifice of atonement"), Romans 3:25

Here the imagery is drawn from the cultus. Yet before we briefly unpack this expression, we should observe that the three images are not parallel metaphors that one may cherry-pick according to personal preference. Each is essential if the paragraph is to be understood and if a full-orbed Pauline theology of the cross is to be sustained; more importantly, they are not strictly parallel. The historical basis of the justification, we have seen, is "the redemption that came by Christ Jesus." Now Paul unfolds the *means* inherent in this redemption: this redemption comes about by the will of God the Father, who "presented" Christ—that is, he set forth or publicly displayed[35] Christ—as a ἱλαστήριον. What does this mean?[36]

There is fairly widespread recognition that the OT background is the "mercy seat," the cover of the ark of the covenant over which Yahweh appeared on the Day of Atonement and on which sacrificial blood was poured. The one other NT occurrence of the word (Heb 9:5) certainly refers to the mercy seat, and so do twenty-one of the twenty-seven occurrences in the LXX.[37] It follows, then, that Paul is presenting Jesus as the ultimate "mercy seat," the ultimate place of atonement, and, derivatively, the ultimate sacrifice. What was under the old covenant bound up with the slaughter of animals, whose most crucial moment was hidden behind a veil, and whose repetition

---

[32]Cf. Romans 3:24-25.

[33]Romans 5:12; cf. Romans 6:23.

[34]David Peterson, "Atonement in the New Testament," in *Where Wrath and Mercy Meet: Proclaiming the Atonement Today,* ed. David Peterson (Carlisle: Paternoster, 2001), 41.

[35]This is the most likely meaning of προέθετο in this context.

[36]For a good history of interpretation, see Arland Hultgren, *Paul's Gospel and Mission* (Philadelphia: Fortress Press, 1985), 47-72; and especially Daniel P. Bailey, "Jesus as the Mercy Seat: The Semantics and Theology of Paul's use of *Hilasterion* in Romans 3:25" (Ph.D. dissertation, Cambridge University, 1999).

[37]For a detailed defense of this view, see, in addition to the major commentaries, the references to Hultgren and Bailey in the previous note and such works as those by T. W. Manson, "ἱλαστήριον," *JTS* 46 (1945): 1-10; L. Sabourin and S. Lyonnet, *Sin, Redemption and Sacrifice: A Biblical and Patristic Study* AnBib no. 48 (Rome: Biblical Institute Press, 1970), 157-66.

almost invited reflection on the limitations of such a system to "cover" sin,[38] is now transcended by a human sacrifice, in public, once for all—and placarded by God himself.

Granted this background, one must still ask what Jesus' antitypical sacrifice accomplishes. As is well known, C. H. Dodd set off a lengthy debate on this subject in 1931 by arguing that "means of atonement" is an "expiatory sacrifice" or an "expiation," that its object is to cancel sin.[39] The notion of "propitiation," where the object is not sin but God, is too pagan to be appropriate: there, human beings offer sacrifices to their gods in order to make them "propitious," or favorable, and the sacrifices are propitiations. But how can one think that the God of the Bible must be made propitious, when he himself is the one who sends forth his Son and publicly displays him as the needed sacrifice? He has demonstrated his love toward us precisely in this, that while we were still enemies, Christ died for us (Rom 5:8).

Today it is widely recognized that in his central contentions Dodd was wrong. Certainly the OT commonly connects the "covering" or forgiving of sins with the setting aside of God's wrath.[40] Certainly when Josephus uses ἱλαστήριον and cognates, propitiation is bound up with his meaning.[41] None of this denies that it is simultaneously true that sin is expiated, indeed must be expiated. It simply means that ἱλαστήριον includes the notion of propitiation.

Certainly that makes sense in the context of Romans 3:25. For the preceding section, as we have seen, sets the problem up in terms of the wrath of God. Now God has taken action to turn that wrath away. To

---

[38]The reference, of course, is to the verb כָּפַר, with which כַּפֹּרֶת, "mercy seat," is cognate.

[39]Dodd, "ἱλαστήριον, Its Cognates, Derivatives and Synonyms in the Septuagint," *JTS* 32 (1931): 352-60; reprinted in idem, *The Bible and the Greeks* (London: Hodder & Stoughton, 1935), 82-95.

[40]The honoree of this volume presented much of the evidence half a century ago: see Roger R. Nicole, "C. H. Dodd and the Doctrine of Propitiation," *WTJ* 17 (1954-55): 117-57; cf. Morris, *Apostolic Preaching*, 136-56. Although the meaning of כָּפַר is disputed, a solid case can be made for the view that the notion of propitiation is bound up with the verb when the cultus is the matrix where it is used: see P. Garnet, "Atonement Constructions in the Old Testament and the Qumran Scrolls," *EQ* 46 (1974): 131-63, who argues that the verb in such contexts is tied to the removal of guilt or the punishment of sin and that this inevitably brings with it a change in God's attitude toward the sinner—or, otherwise put, propitiation. See further, Bernd Janowski, *Sühne als Heilsgeschehen: Studien zur Sühne–theologie der Priesterschrift und zur Wurzel KPR im Alten Orient und im Alten Testament*, WMANT no. 55 (Neukirchen/Vluyn: Neukirchener Verlag, 1982), 15-102.

[41]E.g., *B.J.* 5.385; *Ant.* 6.124; 8.112; 10.59.

put it this way, of course, simultaneously succeeds in doing two things. First, it distinguishes this notion of propitiation from pagan notions of propitiation. In the latter, human beings are the subject of the action, the ones who are offering the propitiating sacrifice, while the gods receive the action and are propitiated. All sides agree, however, that God is the subject of the action here. Certainly human beings are not turning aside God's wrath by something they offer. Nor is it right to imagine in this context that Christ is well-disposed toward guilty sinners, while his Father is simply at enmity with them until Christ intervenes and by his own sacrifice makes his Father favorable, or propitious. In this passage, God himself is the subject.[42] But that raises the second point: Is this manner of speaking, in which God is both the subject and the object of propitiation, coherent?

Many do not think so. How can God be simultaneously loving toward us and wrathful against us? Dodd himself put forward a solution: he depersonalized God's wrath, arguing that "wrath" terminology applied to God is merely a colorful way of speaking about the inevitable outcome of sin's nastiness. Travis argues that God's wrath must be understood in a nonretributive sense,[43] which surely makes little sense in the light of Romans 2:5-9: on the last day, the day of God's wrath, God himself personally "gives to each person according to what he has done" (Rom 2:6). One suspects that part of the problem is the failure to perceive that the Bible can speak of the love of God in diverse ways,[44] with the result that love and wrath are set over against each other improperly. If love is understood in an abstract and fairly impersonal way, then it becomes difficult to see how, in the same God, such love can co-exist with wrath. But the Scriptures treat God's love in more dynamic ways, in diverse ways that reflect the varieties of relationships into which God enters. Thus the Bible can speak of God's providential love, his yearning and inviting love, his sovereign and elective love, his love conditioned by covenant stipulations, and more. Moreover, the same Scriptures that teach us that God is love insist no less strongly that God is holy—and in Scripture, God's wrath is nothing other than his holiness when it confronts the rebellion of his crea-

---

[42]Romans 3:25: προέθετο ὁ θεός.
[43]Stephen Travis, "Christ as Bearer of Divine Judgement in Paul's Thought About the Atonement," in *Atonement Today*, ed. John Goldingay (London: SPCK, 1995), 29.
[44]Cf. D. A. Carson, *The Difficult Doctrine of the Love of God* (Wheaton, Ill.: Crossway, 2000).

tures. It is far from clear that any biblical writer thinks God's love is personal while his wrath is impersonal.

We may usefully approach this matter another way. Holding that the Hebrew law court establishes the framework of what "forensic" means, Wright points out that in such a law court

> the judge does not give, bestow, impute, or impart *his own "righteous-ness"* to the defendant. That would imply that the *defendant* was deemed to have conducted the case impartially, in accordance with the law, to have punished sin and upheld the defenseless innocent ones. "Justifica-tion," of course, means nothing like that. "Righteousness" is not a qual-ity or substance that can thus be passed or transferred from the judge to the defendant.[45]

This argument reminds me of the inappropriateness of the illustra-tion used by some zealous evangelists: the judge passes sentence, steps down from the bench, and then pays the fine or goes to prison, in the place of the criminal. But neither Wright's argument nor the evange-list's illustration is convincing, and for the same reason: in certain cru-cial ways, human law courts, whether contemporary or ancient He-brew courts, are merely analogical models and cannot highlight one or two crucial distinctions that are necessarily operative when the judge is God. In particular, both the contemporary judge and the judge of the Hebrew law court is an administrator of a system. To take the contem-porary court: in no sense has the criminal legally offended the judge. Indeed, if the crime has been against the judge, the judge must rescue him- or herself; the crime has been "against the state" or "against the people" or "against the laws of the land." In such a system, for the ad-ministrator of the system, the judge, to take the criminal's place would be profoundly unjust; it would be a perversion of the justice required by the system, of which the judge is the sworn administrator. But when God is the judge, the offense is always and necessarily against him.[46] He is never the administrator of a system external to himself; he is the offended party as well as the impartial judge. To force the categories of merely human courts onto these uniquely divine realities is bound to lead to distortion. And this, of course, is precisely why idolatry is so central in the Scriptures: it is, as it were, the root sin, the de-godding of

[45]Wright, "Romans and the Theology of Paul," 39.
[46]Recall Psalm 51:4.

God, which is, of course, Paul's point in Romans 1:18-25. This, in turn, is why God's "wrath" is personal: the offense is against him. Righteous Judge he doubtless is, but *never* a distanced or dispassionate judge serving a system greater than he is.

Precisely because God is holy, it would be no mark of moral greatness in him if he were dispassionate or distant or uncaring when his creatures rebel against him, offend him and cast slurs on his glory. Because he is holy, God does more than give sinners over[47] to their own deserts, a kind of pedagogical demonstration that the people he created, silly little things, have taken some unfortunate paths: this abandonment of them is judicial, a function of his wrath (Rom 1:18), an anticipation of the great assize (Rom 2:5-10; 3:19). But because he is love, God provides a "redemption" that simultaneously wipes out the sin of those who offend and keeps his own "justice" intact, as we shall see is the most plausible reading of Romans 3:25-26. God does not act whimsically, sometimes in holy wrath and sometimes in love. He always acts according to the perfection of his own character. As Peterson nicely puts it, "A properly formulated view of penal substitution will speak of retribution being experienced by Christ because that is our due. Moreover, the penalty inflicted by God's justice and holiness is also a penalty inflicted by God's love and mercy, for salvation and new life."[48]

Nor is this the only Pauline passage where such themes come together. Space limitations forbid even a survey of 2 Corinthians 5:14—6:2,[49] but it is important to see the place of 2 Corinthians 5:21 in the argument. Strangely, Travis writes, "But God's wrath is not mentioned in the context, and the focus is in fact on Christ's death absorbing or neutralizing the effects of sin. And that does not involve notions of retribution."[50] Yet already in Romans 5:10, Paul has established that all must appear before the judgment seat of Christ to receive recompense for what has been done in the body. Certainly in a parallel passage that treats the theme of reconciliation (cf. Rom 5:1-11), wrath is not absent. The fact of the matter is that in Christ's reconciling work, God was "not counting men's sins against them" (2 Cor 5:19). Why not? Because he

---

[47]This is mentioned five times in 1:18ff.
[48]Peterson, "Atonement," 38.
[49]On which see, in addition to the major commentaries, Peterson, "Atonement," 36-39.
[50]Travis, "Christ as Bearer of Divine Judgement," 27.

simply wiped them out, in the sense that he treated them as if they did not matter? No, far from it: "God made [Christ] who had no sin to be sin[51] for us" (Rom 5:21). It is the *unjust* punishment of the Servant in Isaiah 53 that is so remarkable. Forgiveness, restoration, salvation, reconciliation—all are possible, not because sins have somehow been cancelled as if they never were, but because another bore them *unjustly*. But by this adverb "unjustly" I mean that the person who bore them was just and did not deserve the punishment, not that some moral "system" that God was administering was thereby distorted. Rather, the God against whom the offenses were done pronounced sentence and sent his Son to bear the sentence (Rom 5:8); he made him who had no sin to be sin for us (2 Cor 5:21). And the purpose of this substitution was that "in him we might become the righteousness of God."[52] In this context, "righteousness" cannot call to mind "covenant faithfulness" or the like, for its obverse is sin.[53] "The logic of 2 Corinthians 5 is that God condemns our sin in the death of his sinless Son so that we might be justified and reconciled to him (cf. Rom. 8:1-4, 10). This 'great exchange' is a reality for all who are 'in him,' that is, united to Christ by faith."[54]

---

[51]Even if one decides to render this "sin" by the paraphrastic "sin offering," the ideal of penal substitution remains inescapable. See Richard Gaffin, "'The Scandal of the Cross': The Atonement in the Pauline Corpus," chapter 7 in this volume.

[52]δικαιοσύνη θεοῦ, 2 Corinthians 5:21b.

[53]Part of the contemporary (and frequently sterile) debate over whether or not Paul teaches "imputation," it seems to me, turns on a failure to recognize distinct domains of discourse. Strictly speaking, Paul never uses the verb λογίζομαι to say, explicitly, that Christ's righteousness is imputed to the sinner or that the sinner's righteousness is imputed to Christ. So if one remains in the domain of narrow exegesis, one can say that Paul does not explicitly teach "imputation," except to say slightly different things (e.g., that Abraham's faith was "imputed" to him for righteousness). But if one extends the discussion into the domain of constructive theology, and observes that *the Pauline texts themselves* (despite the critics' contentions) teach penal substitution, then "imputation" is merely another way of saying much the same thing. To take a related example: as Paul uses "reconciliation" terminology, the movement in reconciliation is always of the sinner to God. God is never said to be reconciled to us; we must be reconciled to him. At the level of exegesis, those are the mere facts. On the other hand, because the same exegesis also demands that we take the wrath of God seriously, and the texts insist that God takes decisive action in Christ to deal with our sin so that his wrath is averted, *in that sense* we may speak of God being "reconciled to us": Wesley was not wrong to teach us to sing "My God is reconciled," provided it is recognized that his language is drawn from the domain of constructive theology and not from the narrower domain of explicit exegesis (although, we insist equally, the constructive theology is itself grounded in themes that are exegetically mandated). On the theme of penal substitution, it is still worth reflecting at length on J. I. Packer, "What Did the Cross Achieve? The Logic of Penal Substitution," *Tyndale Bulletin* 25 (1974), 3-45.

[54]Peterson, "Atonement," 38.

In some such frame as this, then, it is entirely coherent to think of God as both the subject and the object of propitiation. Indeed, it is the glory of the gospel of God. But let Paul have the last word:

> You see, at just the right time, when we were still powerless, Christ died for the ungodly. Very rarely will anyone die for a righteous man, though for a good man someone might possibly dare to die. But God demonstrates his own love for us in this: While we were still sinners, Christ died for us. Since we have now been *justified* by his blood, how much more shall we be saved *from God's wrath* through him! For if, when we were God's enemies, we were reconciled to him through the death of his Son, how much more, having been reconciled, shall we be saved through his life! (Rom 5:6-10, emphasis mine)[55]

Or, in terms of Lincoln's summary of Romans 3:21-25 thus far:

> Corresponding to the universal situation of guilt, bondage to sin, and condemnation under the wrath of God is a gospel of the righteousness of God, which is available universally to faith and which through Christ's death offers a free and undeserved pardon, liberates into a new life where the tyranny of sin is broken and righteous behavior becomes possible, and provides satisfaction of God's righteous wrath.[56]

ἐν τῷ αὐτοῦ αἵματι ("in his blood"), Romans 3:25

Several prepositional phrases are piled up in this verse, of which two draw our attention here. The first, "through faith" (διὰ τῆς πίστεως), probably does not modify the verb "presented" or "publicly displayed" (προέθετο), since faith was certainly not the instrument through which God publicly displayed Christ as propitiation. Rather,

---

[55]Ralph P. Martin, "Reconciliation: Romans 5:1-11," in *Romans and the People of God*, ed. Sven K. Soderlund and N. T. Wright (Grand Rapids: Eerdmans, 1999), proposes, without any convincing exegetical evidence, that Paul moves from a focus on justification in Romans 1—4 to a focus on reconciliation in Romans 5 because he is dissatisfied with "the forensic-cultic idiom that limited soteriology to covenant renewal for the Jewish nation" (47). Martin thus limits and misunderstands the nature of justification in Romans 1—4 and then depreciates his misunderstanding, all in support of his preferred term "reconciliation." That sort of contrast introduces a further error of judgment: Martin is treating Paul's soteriological terms as if they are disjunctive options that one may pick and choose, or from which one might have preferences, being dissatisfied with this one in order to advance that one. In fact, even in this passage Paul interweaves several terms. As Romans 3 attests, Paul's rich and diverse atonement imagery is, in his own mind, profoundly interlocked. We cannot legitimately cherry-pick his "models" or his "images."
[56]Lincoln, "From Wrath to Justification," 149.

this phrase must modify ἱλαστήριον ("propitiation"). It signals the means by which people appropriate the benefits of the sacrifice. Moreover, the similarity between this expression and the fuller expression in Romans 3:22, "through faith in Jesus Christ," favors the reading of the objective genitive there: Paul is still talking about the faith of the believer, not the faithfulness of Jesus Christ.

What the phrase "through his blood" modifies is harder to establish. The options are three: (1) It is the object of faith, that is, "through faith in his blood" (KJV). This is possible if we understand "his blood" to refer to Christ's life violently and sacrificially ended and thus a rhetorical equivalent to Christ's death, or Christ's cross. But Paul never elsewhere makes "blood" the object of faith, so this option remains unlikely. (2) It modifies the verb "presented" or "publicly displayed": "through his blood God has publicly displayed him" or the like. But the expressions are a long way apart, and so the third option is marginally to be preferred. (3) It modifies ἱλαστήριον ("propitiation"): "God has publicly displayed Christ as a propitiation in his [Christ's] blood." Paul means to say that Christ's blood, that is, his sacrificial death, is "the means by which God's wrath is propitiated. As in several other texts where Christ's blood is the means through which salvation is secured,[57] the purpose is to designate Christ's death as a sacrifice."[58]

εἰς ἔνδειξιν κτλ. ("to demonstrate etc."), Romans 3:25b-26

All sides recognize that this phrase introduces the purpose for which Christ set forth Christ as a propitiation. But the precise meaning turns in no small measure on how one understands δικαιοσύνη ("justice"). At the risk of oversimplification, there are two principal views, with many refinements that need not be explored here.

1. If God's "justice" or "righteousness" refers to his character, in particular to his covenant faithfulness, then the meaning is something like this: "in order to demonstrate God's saving, covenant faithfulness through his forgiving of sins committed before, in the time of his forbearance." But as popular as this view is today, it falters on three exegetical obstacles. First, it finds a meaning in δικαιοσύνη, "covenant

[57]Romans 5:9; Ephesians 1:7; 2:13; Colossians 1:20.
[58]Moo, Romans, 237.

faithfulness," that we have already found to be insufficiently warranted. Second, it understands the phrase διὰ τὴν πάρεσιν τῶν προγε–
γονότων ἁμαρτημάτων to mean "through his forgiving of sins committed before," and this is an unlikely rendering. The word πάρεσις
means "overlooking" or "suspension" or "remission [of punishment]"
or "postponement [of punishment]," especially in reference to sins or
to legal charges; it does not mean "forgiveness." Third, it is difficult to
justify rendering the preposition διά plus the accusative as
"through."[59] In short, the rendering "through his forgiving of sins committed before" depends on too many philological or syntactical im-
probabilities. But if that rendering is rejected, there is little left to support "covenant faithfulness" as the appropriate translation of δικαιοσύνη
in this context.

2. If δικαιοσύνη designates God's righteousness or justice, whether
his impartiality, or his fairness, or all that is in accordance with his own
character, then the entire phrase might be paraphrased as follows: "in
order to demonstrate that God is just, [which demonstration was nec-
essary] because he had passed over sins committed before." Here the
previous disabilities are turned into strengths: δικαιοσύνη is read more
naturally, πάρεσις is now rendered "passed over," and διά plus the accusative is translated "because." The expression "sins committed before" is explained in Romans 3:26. The phrase "in his forbearance"[60]
must be connected with the "passed over": it refers to the period before
the cross.[61] In other words, the sins committed beforehand are not
those committed by an individual before his or her conversion, but
those committed by the human race before the cross. This brings us
back to the profoundly salvation-historical categories already manifest
in Romans 3:21. As Moo nicely says,

> This does not mean that God failed to punish or "overlooked" sins com-
> mitted before Christ; nor does it mean that God did not really "forgive"
> sins under the Old Covenant. Paul's meaning is rather that God "post-
> poned" the full penalty due sins in the Old Covenant, allowing sinners

---

[59]In fairness, this usage is not unknown in Hellenistic Greek. But it is very rare, and therefore
convincing reasons must be adduced for adopting this reading if a more common one is
available.
[60]Lit. "in the forbearance of God," which in the Greek text occurs in 3:26, not Romans 3:25 as
in NIV.
[61]Note Paul's other use of "forbearance" in Romans 2:4; cf. Acts 14:16; 17:30.

to stand before him without their having provided an adequate "satis-faction" of the demands of his holy justice (cf. Heb 10:4).[62]

And this, in turn, means that God's "righteousness" or "justice" must refer to some aspect of his character that, apart from the sacrifice of Christ, might have been viewed with suspicion had sinners in the past been permitted to slip by without facing the full severity of condemnation for sin. God's "righteousness" has been upheld by his provision of Christ as the propitiation in his blood.

This means, of course, that God's "righteousness" in Romans 3:25-26 does not mean exactly what it means in Romans 3:21. There, it refers to God's "justifying" of his sinful people; here, it refers to something intrinsic to God's character, whether his consistency or his determination to act in accordance with his glory or his punitive justice: these and other suggestions have been made. And this is in line with the broader observation that for Paul, justification is bound up not only with the vindication of sinners, but even more profoundly with the vindication of God.[63]

In short, Romans 3:25-26 makes a glorious contribution to Christian understanding of the "internal" mechanism of the atonement. It explains the need for Christ's propitiating sacrifice in terms of the just requirements of God's holy character. This reading not only follows the exegesis carefully, but it brings the whole of the argument from Romans 1:18 on into gentle cohesion.

The Significance of the Succeeding Passages, Romans 3:27-31; 4:1ff.
Ideally, the bearing of this treatment of Romans 3:21-26 on the rest of Paul's argument in Romans should now be teased out. But here I must restrict myself to some cursory observations on the immediately succeeding verses.

Even a superficial glance at Romans 3:27-31 shows that the emphasis now falls on faith. In other words, these verses unpack emphases already made in Romans 3:22, 26, while developing the argument further by showing that when faith is properly understood, it simultaneously reinforces grace (cf. Rom 3:24) and provides the mech-

---

[62]Moo, *Romans*, 240.
[63]See, above all, Mark A. Seifrid, *Christ Our Righteousness: Paul's Theology of Justification*, NSBT (Leicester: Inter-Varsity Press, 2000).

anism by which Jews and Gentiles alike may be justified. Several scholars have also noted that the themes Paul sketches in Romans 3:27-30 are developed in various ways in Romans 4. In particular, Paul establishes three points in Romans 3:27-30, all of them paralleled in Romans 4:1ff: (1) Faith excludes boasting (Rom 3:27), a principle already observed in the life of Abraham (Rom 4:1-2). (2) Faith is necessary, apart from the works of the law, to preserve grace (Rom 3:28), once again observed in the life of Abraham (Rom 4:3-8). (3) Such faith is necessary if Jews and Gentiles alike are to be justified (Rom 3:29-30).[64] And this point, too, finds a curious warrant in the life of Abraham, in that it is said of him that his faith was credited to him as righteousness *before* he had received the sign of circumcision (Rom 4:9ff.).

Paul's closing verse, "Do we, then, nullify the law by this faith? Not at all! Rather, we uphold the law" (Rom 3:31), should not be taken to mean that the apostle still wants to maintain the Mosaic covenant in full force after all, or to uphold νόμος ("law") as *lex*, as ongoing legal demand. Rather, Roman 3:31 is the unpacking of the last clause of Romans 3:21: the law and the prophets testify to this new "righteousness from God" that has come in Christ Jesus, and thus their valid continuity is sustained in that to which they point. If Paul's reading of the Old Testament, and of the Mosaic covenant in particular, is correct, then that ancient revelation continues in that for which it prepared the way, to which it pointed, and which fulfilled it. The law is upheld precisely because the redemptive-historical purposes and anticipations of the law are upheld.

---

[64] On these two verses, see especially Jan Lambrecht, "Paul's Logic in Romans 3:29-30," *JBL* 119 (2000): 526-28.

atonement in
the pauline corpus

"The Scandal of the Cross"

Richard Gaffin

The word *atonement* does not occur in Paul's writings.[1] But no concern is more central for him than the meaning of the death of Christ, the church's perennial concern in its doctrine of the atonement. What does Christ's death achieve? How is it effective for the salvation of sinners? This chapter considers Paul's answers to such questions with an eye to the issue of continuity between Paul's teaching and later church doctrine. How faithful to the apostle is subsequent Christian understanding of the atonement?

Contemporary Pauline scholarship is marked by a fairly widespread consensus that in its dominant and most influential expressions, traditional atonement theology departs from Paul in at least two substantial ways. First, it fails to recognize, or at least do justice to, the *Christus Victor* theme in Paul, that Christ's death destroys actual slavery to sin and its consequences in the sinner. Second, its notion of the cross as penal substitution, particularly as it has been developed beginning with the Reformation, is foreign to Paul.[2] In my view, the first of

---

[1] In Romans 3:25 ἱλαστήριον should be translated "propitiation"; see D. A. Carson's extended discussion of this passage in chapter 6 of this volume.

[2] Cf. J. T. Carroll and J. B. Green, *The Death of Jesus in Early Christianity* (Peabody, Mass.: Hendrickson, 1995), 113-32, esp. 121-25; J. E. D. Dunn, *The Theology of Paul the Apostle* (Grand Rapids: Eerdmans, 1998), 207-33, esp. 218-23; J. B. Green and M. D. Baker, *Recovering the Scandal of the Cross: Atonement in New Testament and Contemporary Contexts* (Downers Grove, Ill.: InterVarsity Press, 2000), 23-32, 46-67, 90-115, 140-52, 201-3; J. B. Green, "Death of Christ,"

these critiques contains some measure of truth; however, the second is wrong. As a fair generalization, historic Christianity, including Protestant orthodoxy, is weak in not recognizing adequately Paul's teaching that the cross destroys sin in the sinner as a corrupting and enslaving power, but modern historical-critical scholarship is defective for not dealing adequately with his teaching that the cross removes the guilt and just punishment of sin.

Following a short overview of Paul's teaching, noting along the way, albeit very briefly, the centrality of the theme of the cross as victory, I will review, at somewhat greater length, evidence that the cross is also a penal substitution. My own preference would have been to focus on the victory theme, in view of the need for its fuller appropriation within my own Reformed and other evangelical traditions. But concentrating on penal substitution has seemed more necessary because its presence in Paul is so widely depreciated or even denied today. In the space at my disposal I am able to offer little more than a sketch; key passages could not be treated in depth. But my goal is to provide the reader with an overall perspective, something of the total picture in Paul, the accuracy of which I am confident more extended exegesis substantiates.

Overview

Without becoming involved here in the question, much debated in recent decades, of whether Paul's theology has a "center," I think few, if any, will deny that Christ's death is at its heart.[3] "For what I received," he writes to the church at Corinth, likely using an already-existing con-

---

in *Dictionary of Paul and his Letters,* ed. G. Hawthorne and R. Martin (Downers Grove, Ill.: InterVarsity Press, 1993), 203-8; O. Hofius, "Sühne und Versöhnung. Zum paulinischen Verständnis des Kreuzestodes Jesu," in *Paulusstudien* (Tübingen: Mohr, 1989), 33-49; S. H. Travis, "Christ as Bearer of Divine Judgment in Paul's Thought about the Atonement," in *Jesus of Nazareth: Lord and Christ,* ed. J. B. Green and M. Turner (Grand Rapids: Eerdmans, 1994), 332-45, esp. 341-45; U. Wilkens, *Der Brief an die Römer* (Zürich: Benzinger, 1978), 1:241-43.

[3]Is Paul a "theologian" and does he have what may properly be termed a "theology"? While his thirteen letters (and sermon records in Acts) are obviously not theological treatises, much of their content is such that they force us, by deduction, to take into account the fuller, overall theology or coherent body of teaching that lies in back of them and, in turn, gives rise to each. His letters in this respect may aptly be compared to the visible portion of an iceberg; much of its total mass is below the surface. See my *Resurrection and Redemption: A Study in Paul's Soteriology,* 2nd ed. (*The Centrality of the Resurrection* [Phillipsburg, N.J.: Presbyterian and Reformed, 1987], 25-29); Dunn also adopts the iceberg analogy (*Theology of Paul,* 15).

fessional fragment,[4] "I passed on to you as of first importance: that Christ died for our sins according to the Scriptures, that he was buried, that he was raised on the third day according to the Scriptures" (1 Cor 15:3-4).[5] Earlier in this same letter he declares, "For I resolved to know nothing while I was with you except Jesus Christ and him crucified" (1 Cor 2:2) and with a similar sweep, he tells the Galatian Christians, capturing much of the substance of his letter to them, "May I never boast except in the cross of our Lord Jesus Christ" (Gal 6:14).

However, this exclusive "boast" in Christ's death, Paul found, had become the occasion for contention. He speaks categorically of "the offense of the cross" (Gal 5:11). For some, "those who are perishing," his gospel, "the message of the cross," is "foolishness" (1 Cor 1:18), and "Christ crucified," a "stumbling block" (1 Cor 1:23).[6] What causes this offense? The source and dimensions of this "scandal" (as we might also translate σκάνδαλον) will emerge as our discussion unfolds.

A further glance at 1 Corinthians 15:3-4, enables us to highlight a couple of other factors basic to Paul's theology of the cross. First, also "of first importance" in the gospel he preaches, is Christ's resurrection.[7] Historically distinct ("on the third day") from his death but inseparably connected, the one event is plainly inconceivable apart from the other. Particularly applicable to Paul is Calvin's observation about Scripture as a whole, that references to the death alone or to the resurrection alone are synecdochic.[8] To speak of the one always brings into view the other; the significance of the one invariably entails the significance of the other. Paul's theology of the cross involves his theology of the resurrection and is simply unintelligible apart from it.

Second, the death and resurrection are plainly not in view as bare, isolated facts. Their occurrence is "according to the Scriptures"; that is, they have meaning as they fulfill the Old Testament. Furthermore, the death is "for our sins" (ὑπὲρ τῶν ἁμαρτιῶν ἡμῶν). This yields the base-

---

[4]See A. C. Thiselton, *The First Epistle to the Corinthians* (Grand Rapids: Eerdmans, 2000), 1177, 1886-90 and the literature cited there.

[5]Cf. Romans 4:25.

[6]Using the same Greek word, σκάνδαλον, as in Galatians 5:11.

[7]Note especially the summary statement in 2 Timothy 2:8: "Remember Jesus Christ, raised from the dead, descended from David. This is my gospel . . ."; cf. Romans 4:25; 2 Corinthians 5:15.

[8]J. Calvin, *Institutes of the Christian Religion*, trans. F. L. Battles, ed. J. T. McNeill, Library of Christian Classics, no. 20, 21 (Philadelphia: Westminster Press, 1960), 1:521 (2:16:13).

line conclusion (leaving open for now the precise force of this prepositional phrase) that at the center of Paul's gospel, Christ's death, inseparable from his resurrection and as the fulfillment of Scripture, has its
significance in relation to human ("our") sin and its consequences.

It needs to be emphasized that the fulfillment indicated in 1 Corinthians 15:3-4 is nothing less than eschatological in its proportions. That
is perhaps most explicit for Christ's death in Galatians 1:4: Jesus Christ[9]
"gave himself for our sins to rescue us from the present evil age." The
expression "the present evil age" reflects Paul's use of the distinction
between this (the present) age and the age to come,[10] a construction
that comprehends, consecutively and antithetically, the whole of history from creation to and including its consummation.[11] The purpose
of Christ's death is to effect the deliverance of the church from the
present world order (αἰών), which is marked by sin and its consequences, and with that, by implication, to bring believers into the coming world order, which is marked by eschatological life in all its fullness.[12] The deliverance in view, certainly personal and individual, has
corporate and even cosmic, aeonic dimensions. In a similar vein, later,
in Galatians 6:14, he speaks autobiographically but surely representa-
tively for all believers[13] of "the cross of our Lord Jesus Christ, through
which the world has been crucified to me, and I to the world." Here,
more clearly than in Galatians 1:4, the eschatological deliverance effected in the cross and resurrection is an already present reality.

Elsewhere, in Ephesians 2:1ff., those who have been "raised up with
Christ and seated with him in the heavenly realms in Christ Jesus"
(Eph 2:6), and so, by implication, crucified with Christ,[14] have been delivered from their former condition of being "dead in transgressions
and sins" (Eph 1:1, 5), which consisted of a lifestyle marked by "the
ways of this world," or more precisely, "according to the age of this
world" (Eph 1:2). By being united to Christ in his death and resurrection, they have been released from the life of this world-age into the

---

[9]The one whom God the Father raised from the dead, Galatians 1:1.
[10]This is explicit in Ephesians 1:21.
[11]Among the best treatments of the basic structure of Paul's eschatology are G. Vos, *The
Pauline Eschatology* (Grand Rapids: Baker, 1979/1930), 1-41; H. Ridderbos, *Paul: An Outline
of His Theology* (Grand Rapids: Eerdmans, 1975), 44-90.
[12]Cf. Colossians 1:13.
[13]Cf. Galatians 2:20.
[14]Cf. Romans 6:6; Galatians 2:20.

resurrection-life of the eschatological world-age. Again, the salvation effected in the cross and resurrection is of sweeping cosmic and "new-aeon" proportions.

United to Christ in his death and resurrection, believers share in the eschatological triumph of God over sin and its consequences. While for them that victory has a still-future aspect, in the resurrection of the body[15] it is a present reality that has taken hold of, and renewed them at the core of their being.[16] They are no longer slaves of sin but alive to God;[17] they "no longer live for themselves but for him who died for them and was raised again" (2 Cor 5:15), a life in union with the resurrected Christ that transforms every aspect of their existence.[18]

Christ's death and resurrection inaugurates the realization of God's final, consummate purposes for the creation. As events of such cosmic and eschatological importance, they also have corporate significance. They are inclusive of others, those "in Christ," who have been crucified and resurrected "with Christ." Within this union or bond, Christ's identity and role are plainly unique and not interchangeable. That uniqueness is captured by Paul's identification of Christ as the "last Adam" or "second man."[19] Whatever else this contrasting parallelism with Adam involves, both are key figures in the sense that their actions are uniquely determinative for others—for humanity comprehended in Adam, on the one hand, and for the new humanity, the church, comprehended in Christ, on the other.[20] Specifically and repeatedly, Christ's death is "for" (ὑπέρ) others,[21] but never the reverse.[22] Christ may be said to be the representative of those in union with him, but he is more than that, particularly where the category of representation is reduced to a paradigm or understood in no more than essentially empowering or exemplary terms. Particularly in his death, his representative role has an aspect, as we shall see, that is not adequately termed other than "substitutionary."

We may say, then, that for Paul, Christ's death involves an "inclu-

---

[15]See Romans 8:23; 1 Corinthians 15:20-28, 42-57.
[16]See 2 Corinthians 4:16.
[17]Romans 6:6, 11, 13, 14; cf. Romans 6:16-22.
[18]See Ephesians 4:17ff.; Colossians 3:1ff.
[19]1 Corinthians 15:45, 47; cf. 1 Corinthians 15:21-22; Romans 5:12-19.
[20]Cf. 1 Corinthians 15:48-49.
[21]See Romans 5:8; 2 Corinthians 5:14; 1 Thessalonians 5:10.
[22]Note esp. the rhetorical question in 1 Corinthians 1:13: "Was Paul crucified for you?"

sive substitution."[23] In order not to distort his teaching, we must account for both the exclusive or strictly substitutionary and the inclusive or representative aspects, both the "for us" and the "in him" and "with him" of Christ's death. The polarization that has frequently marked the theology of the atonement in the West, particularly over the past several centuries, between Christ as substitute and Christ as empowering example, poses a dilemma that Paul (and the other NT writers) would reject. The same thing has to be said of the tendency in the modern era to polarize "juristic" and "participatory" concerns in Paul, almost always to the depreciation or effective elimination of the former.[24] For Paul the participatory or relational involves an inalienable juristic, forensic aspect, and the forensic does not function apart from the relational.

Sin

Repeatedly in Paul, as already noted, Christ's death is seen in relation to sin.[25] In broader forms of expression, though with his death at least principally in view, his person and coming into the world are associated with sin.[26] In fact, apart from sin and its consequences, Paul sees no place for the person and activity of the incarnate Christ, the one in whom, uniquely, "all the fullness of the Deity lives in bodily form" (Col 2:9).[27] Absent the sin of Adam and its universal repercussions,[28] there is no need for the last Adam. "Christ Jesus came into the world to save sinners" (1 Tim 1:15). This, likely an already existing formulation taken over by Paul,[29] encapsulates for him the agenda for Christ's ministry, and specifically, the rationale for his death.

Sin, then, is the "plight"; Christ, the "solution,"[30] particularly his being "obedient to death—even death on a cross" (Phil 2:8). Certainly

---

[23]The language, though taken over here in a different sense, of J. Becker, *Paul: Apostle to the Gentiles* (Louisville, Ky.: Westminster, 1993), 409; cited in Dunn, *Theology of Paul*, 223, n. 88.

[24]See recently and influentially, E. P. Sanders, *Paul and Palestinian Judaism* (London: SCM, 1977), 502-8.

[25]Romans 4:25; 1 Corinthians 15:3; Galatians 1:4; Ephesians 1:7.

[26]Romans 8:3; 2 Corinthians 5:21; Colossians 1:14; 1 Timothy 1:15; Titus 2:14.

[27] Cf. Romans 9:5.

[28]Romans 5:12-19.

[29]G. W. Knight, *The Pastoral Epistles* (Grand Rapids: Eerdmans, 1992), 99-100; I. H. Marshall, *A Critical and Exegetical Commentary On the Pastoral Epistles* (Edinburgh: T & T Clark, 1999), 326-30, 397-98.

[30]To put it in terms widely current since Sanders, *Paul and Palestinian Judaism*, 442ff., 474ff.

that plight is made clearer in the light of its solution, but it exists (and is even clear according to Romans 1:19-20) prior to the solution. The plight is definitive; it specifies what the solution must remedy and that apart from it the solution ceases to be a solution. So if we are to understand Paul's teaching about Christ's death, at least in any adequate way, we must first have an accurate understanding of what he teaches about sin. The following sketch seeks especially to highlight facets that tend to be downplayed or even denied in much current interpretation. Where this happens, a further tendency is to find nonexistent ambiguities and uncertainties in Paul's statements about the cross and therefore discontinuity and conflict between him and later church doctrine, particularly its notion of penal substitution. The clarity and coherence of Paul's teaching on Christ's death will never be perceived where a defective understanding of his teaching on sin is at work.

Paul's treatment of sin and its consequences is extensive and multifaceted, particularly in Romans.[31] Above all, sin is theocentric; it is primarily against God and then, derivatively, against human beings, including the self.[32] As such, sin is both relational and judicial, and it is the one only as it is the other. Sin is relational in that it is essentially rebellion against God, the image-bearing[33] creature's effective renunciation of God as creator. It is willful rejection of fellowship with God by refusing to acknowledge him as Creator and to live out of thankful creaturely dependence on him.[34] Inevitably, then, sin is idolatrous, the exchange of "the truth of God for a lie," which consists, in virtually numberless ways, in worshiping and serving "the creature rather than the Creator" (Rom 1:25 ESV). All told, sin is deeply rooted hostility, particularly toward God.[35] Thus, inevitably, it is also against others and the self, as made in God's image, again, in nearly countless ways.[36]

Sin is also illegal. It is that, not in addition or peripheral to its being relational, but as it is relational, and it is relational only as it is illegal. That is reflected in the varied vocabulary that Paul uses for sin, most of

---

[31]Pertinent literature is extensive; see for the following discussion esp. Ridderbos, *Paul*, chap. 3; L. Morris, *The Cross in the New Testament* (Grand Rapids: Eerdmans, 1965), chap. 5, and "Sin, Guilt," in *Dictionary of Paul and his Letters*, 877-81; cf. Dunn, *Theology of Paul*, chap. 3.
[32]Romans 1:18-32; Ephesians 4:17-19.
[33]1 Corinthians 11:7-9.
[34]Romans 1:19-21.
[35]Romans 8:7.
[36]See Romans 1:26-27, 29-31; Galatians 5:19-21; Ephesians 4:19.

which has in view what does not accord with God's will or law.[37] "For by the law *is* the knowledge of sin" (Rom 3:20 ESV),[38] he affirms categorically. The law, as the revealed will of God, identifies and reveals sin; it is the criterion for sin, the standard by which the likes of pride, rebellion, idolatry and hostility are sin and manifest themselves as such. Paul, unlike many of his current interpreters with humanistic and post-Enlightenment assumptions, would not share the minimizing of individual acts as specific violations of (God's) law relative to dispositional or attitudinal sin as allegedly more primal.[39] Any sort of disjunction, in identifying sin, between motive and act or between relationships as personal and law as impersonal, is simply foreign to Paul. Rather, an essential and inalienable aspect of sin is that it is "any want of conformity unto, or transgression of, the law of God."[40]

Like God himself and reflective of his person, "the law is holy, and the commandment is holy, righteous and good" (Rom 7:12). Undoubtedly, almost always when Paul refers to the law he has in view the body of legislation given by God through Moses to Israel at Sinai—that legislation, marking out the period of covenant history until Christ, which as a specific codification has been terminated in its entirety by Christ.[41] At the same time, however, it is difficult to deny that in a statement like Romans 7:12, just cited, or in Romans 13:9,[42] Paul recognizes that at its core (the "Torah in the Torah," as it has been put[43]), the Mosaic law specifies imperatives bound up with the indicative of the Creator-creature relationship from the beginning and enduring because of who God is. In its central commands, the law given at Sinai (the Decalogue) reveals God's will, inherent in his person and so incumbent on his image-bearing creature as such, regardless of time and place.[44] Sin

---

[37]See *Greek-English Lexicon of the New Testament Based on Semantic Domains*, ed. J. P. Louw and E. A. Nida (New York: United Bible Societies, 1988), § 88.118, 1:289-318 (775, 773-77).
[38]Cf. Romans 7:7-13.
[39]A clear instance of such a marginalizing of sin as individual acts of disobedience is Green and Baker, *Recovering the Scandal of the Cross*, 54, 95, 201-2. This seems bound up with their repeated and emphatic denial that Christ's death as involving penal substitution is taught in the New Testament.
[40]The language of the *Westminster Shorter Catechism*, answer 14.
[41]See Romans 6:14; 7:6; 10:4; 2 Corinthians 3:6-11; Galatians 3:17-25.
[42]Cf. "God's commandments," 1 Corinthians 7:19.
[43]*De thora in de thora*, ed. J. van den Berg (Aalten: de Graafschap, n.d.), 1:5.
[44]See, on this point, the helpful observations concerning Jesus and the NT writers in J. Douma, *Christian Morals and Ethics* (Winnipeg, Manitoba: Premier, 1983), 38-39.

as relational is inherently illegal, the violation of God's will as revealed in Scripture and the creation. This means that for Paul, sin incurs guilt. Sin, of whatever sort, renders the sinner guilty before God, and nothing is more central to the (now broken) relationship between God and the sinner than that guilt.

Sin is also universal. Jew as well as non-Jew, "all have sinned" (Rom 3:23),[45] reiterating a major conclusion of the first main segment of the argument in Romans,[46] intent as much as anything on documenting the universality of human sin. Sin is universal not only because every human being actually sins but also because everyone is a sinner by birth, because everyone enters the world with an inherited disposition to sin, which is itself sinful and therefore culpable. This is surely one of Paul's points in Romans 5:12-19. This perennially important and much disputed passage,[47] structured by a contrasting parallelism between Adam and Christ (by plain implication from 1 Corinthians 15:45, as the "last Adam"[48]) makes the following points: First, the sustained emphasis on the one side of the contrast is on the one sin of the one man (Adam), with its consequences. Second, by Adam's disobedience, "the many [= "all" in v. 18] were made sinners" (Rom 5:19); sin is universal (cf. Rom 5:12). Third, the universality of sin is documented by the universality of death. Death in the world is a consequence of Adam's sin (Rom 5:12). But death is also universal "because all sinned" (Rom 5:12).[49] All human beings are implicated in sin and death by Adam's sin, even those who, unlike Adam, do not violate an explicitly stated commandment (Rom 5:13-14); by his sin they are disposed to sin and actually sin. Fourth, Adam's sin brings judgment consisting in con-

---

[45]Cf. Romans 3:9, 19; 5:12.

[46]See Romans 1:18-3:20.

[47]Pertinent literature is voluminous, see esp. J. Murray, *The Imputation of Adam's Sin* (Grand Rapids: Eerdmans, 1959), and among the commentaries, J. Murray, *The Epistle to the Romans,* NICNT (Grand Rapids: Eerdmans, 1959), 1:178-206; D. J. Moo, *The Epistle to the Romans,* NICNT rev. ed. (Grand Rapids: Eerdmans, 1996), 314-50; T. R. Schreiner, *Romans* (Grand Rapids: Baker, 1998), 270-93.

[48]Cf. 1 Corinthians 15:21-22. Dunn's puzzling assertion (*Theology of Paul*, 242, 265) that Christ did not become the last Adam until the resurrection is hardly correct in light both of 1 Corinthians 15:45 itself (as "last Adam" and being resurrected *in*, not *to*, that identity he became "life-giving Spirit") and the sustained comparison in Romans 5:12ff., where Christ's "adamic," that is, representative and corporate, role, culminating in his death (the "one act of righteousness," Rom 5:18), is integral to the sense of the passage.

[49]The sense of ἐφ ᾧ has been disputed; the majority of commentators today and most English translation take it causally ("because").

demnation on all (Rom 5:16); "the result of one trespass was condemnation for all men" (Rom 5:18). In Adam, all human beings are sinners in the sense that they are accounted guilty for his sin.

To write, as D. E. H. Whiteley has, "St. Paul does believe in Original Sin, but not in Original Guilt,"[50] introduces a disjunction the apostle would never recognize. The same has to be said of the recent effort of James Dunn to show that Paul's varied vocabulary for sin, in Romans 5 and elsewhere, "allows a concept of guilt to be attached solely to 'transgression,' deliberate breach of divine command," and that "guilt only enters into the reckoning with the individual's own transgression. Human beings are not held responsible for the state in which they are born. That is the starting point of their personal responsibility, a starting point for which they are not liable."[51] But, Paul affirms categorically, "the wages of sin is death" (Rom 6:23), and there is no reason to think that not all sin is in view. Within the immediate context (Rom 6:15ff.) the accent here, in pointed contrast to the freeness of God's gift of eternal life in Christ, is that death is the earned or due payment for service rendered to sin, precisely as it is an enslaving power. Given the nature of this justly deserved "reward," death, while the image is pecuniary, has, as we will see more clearly, a penal edge. Paul knows of no sin, whether as imputed, inborn disposition or actual commission, that does not entail guilt and liability for its consequences.[52]

Sin is not only rebellion against God and violation of his law but also an enslaving power. Paul captures this aspect of sin most emphatically in Romans 6—7 by personifying it as a lord or master. Correlatively, the sinner is a slave, in bondage to sin.[53] Elsewhere, the unrelieved desperateness of this slavery is expressed as being "dead in . . . transgressions and sins," a deadness that manifests itself as corrupt living in submis-

---

[50]*The Theology of St. Paul* (Oxford: Blackwell, 1964), 51, quoted with approval by Dunn, *Theology of Paul*, 97, n. 81.

[51]Dunn, *Theology of Paul*, 96-97. But Romans 5:18 (cf. Rom 5:16) specifically connects the condemnation (= guilt) of "all," not with their individual sinning but with the "one trespass" (of Adam). An inevitable consequence of a view such as Dunn's, it seems, is that all human beings in their inborn depravity and disposition to sin are innocent victims, a view hardly evident in Paul.

[52]Telling is Dunn's recognition that an aspect of Paul's use of sin vocabulary "does not help" the case he believes Paul is making for limiting guilt to one's own transgressions (*Theology of Paul*, 96). Paul lets him down because he is trying to find in Paul what is not there.

[53]See Romans 6:6, 12, 14, 16ff.; Romans 7:6, 25.

sion to Satan, as "the ruler of the kingdom of the air" (Eph 2:2). Furthermore, in this deadness and corruption, sinners are as culpable as they are helpless; they are "by nature objects of wrath" (Eph 2:3).[54]

Wrath

God's wrath is his response to sin, relational and illicit, in all its expressions. This is stated in a sweeping and emphatic fashion in Romans 1:18: "The wrath of God is being revealed from heaven against all the godlessness and wickedness of men," setting the tone for the lengthy treatment of the universal sway of sin that follows in Romans 1:18—3:20. In order to be clear on Paul's understanding of sin, particularly its consequences, it is essential to be clear on his understanding of divine wrath or anger.[55]

Well over a century ago, George Smeaton wrote, "The question of divine wrath is at present the great point in debate on the subject of the atonement."[56] That observation continues true to the present, and nowhere more so than for the teaching of Paul. Influential in the current debate has been the view of C. H. Dodd that Paul speaks of God's wrath "not to describe the attitude of God to man, but to describe the inevitable process of cause and effect in a moral universe."[57] This reduces wrath to an impersonal process, "a purely immanent causal connection between guilt and retribution."[58] If for no other reason, this view is deficient because it hardly does justice to Paul's vigorously active language, "being revealed from heaven" (Rom 1:18).

Much more widespread are views that find a greater measure of God's involvement in his wrath but are essentially the same as Dodd's. Typical is the notion that his wrath is "God's allowing people to experience the intrinsic consequences of their refusal to live in relation with him," "the God-ordained consequences of human sinfulness."[59] According to another recent expression, God's wrath, both present and

---

[54]Cf. Ephesians 5:6; Colossians 3:6.

[55]For the following discussion, see esp. L. Morris, *The Cross in the New Testament*, 189-92, and *The Apostolic Preaching of the Cross* (London: Tyndale, 1955), 161-66; cf. G. L. Borchert, "Wrath, Destruction," *Dictionary of Paul and his Letters*, 991-93.

[56]Smeaton, *The Apostles' Doctrine of the Atonement* (1870; reprint, Edinburgh: Banner of Truth, 1991), 310.

[57]Dodd, *The Epistle of Paul to the Romans* (New York: Harper, 1932), 23.

[58]E. Käsemann, *Commentary on Romans* (Grand Rapids: Eerdmans, 1980), 37.

[59]Travis, "Christ as Bearer of Divine Judgment," 338, 345.

future, is his "handing people over to experience the consequences of the sin they choose."[60]

This view does capture an aspect of the truth, expressed, for instance, in Romans 1:24, 26-31, in effect the negative counterpart of "virtue is its own reward"; sin is its own punishment. This view is deficient in what it denies, often emphatically. It is intent on excluding from God's wrath any affective or emotional aspect and, with that exclusion, denying that it is punitive or retributive in any extrinsic or reactive way that goes beyond leaving sinners to the natural and inherent effects of their sin.[61]

Such views simply do not do justice to Paul.[62] "God's wrath," both present and future, "comes on those who are disobedient" (Eph 5:6), not as somehow consisting in that disobedience or being left to its various perverse expressions (Eph 5:3-6), but "because of such things" (διὰ ταῦτα).[63] Wrath here is distinct from these things; it is God's response to ("because of") them, his (surely personal) reaction against them, provoked by them. On its negative side, it involves exclusion from "any inheritance in the kingdom of Christ and of God" (Eph 5:5), an exclusion that, in view of its terms, deprivation of eschatological beatitude, is surely the punitive payback for sin. Similarly, God's wrath will result, on "the day of the Lord," in "sudden destruction" coming upon the unrepentant (1 Thess 5:2-3, 9).

Death for Paul is not simply a reflex of sin, its natural or inevitable consequence and not involving God's active recoil against sin. In the flow of the argument in Romans 5:12ff. there is a middle factor between sin and death: condemnation (κατάκριμα).[64] Death is God's judicial reaction to sin, which is to say, death is penal. It is his active punitive response to sin, "from the outside" so to speak, not simply his allowing death as the self-generating result of sin. Sinful activities

---

[60]Green and Baker, *Scandal of the Cross*, 54; see also J. B. Green, "Death of Christ," *Dictionary of Paul and his Letters*, 206; and Carroll and Green, *The Death of Jesus in Early Christianity*, 122-23.

[61]See notes 59 and 60; "*Our sinful acts do not invite God's wrath but prove that God's wrath is already active*" (Green and Baker, *Scandal of the Cross*, 55, emphasis in the original).

[62]Truly remarkable is the failure of the authors cited in notes 59 and 60, in discussing God's wrath, even to mention the passages considered in this and the next several paragraphs, much less address them; this is largely true for Dunn as well.

[63]Cf. Colossians 3:5-6.

[64]Romans 5:16, 18.

"deserve death," and that they do is because of "God's righteous decree" (Rom 1:32). Furthermore, in Romans 8:20-21, fairly seen as commentary on Genesis 3:16-19,[65] due to sin the entire creation has been
"subjected to frustration" (or "futility") and "bondage to decay." This
is so not simply as a natural outworking of sin, its inherent entropy,
but ultimately "because of him [God] who subjected it" (Rom 8:20
ESV).[66] Death, including those conditions now present in the creation
that tend toward death, is God's calculated response to sin, his retributive curse on sin.

2 Thessalonians 1:8-9 is clear, even emphatic: "He will punish
those who do not know God and do not obey the gospel of our Lord
Jesus. They will be punished with everlasting destruction and shut
out from the presence of the Lord and from the majesty of his
power."[67] The punishment in view here is plainly retributive; it consists in God's response to disobedience, not in an attendant aspect of
disobedience itself.[68] Specifically, it is "everlasting destruction,"
which, as "everlasting," is what disobedience justly deserves (1 Thess
1:6) but hardly its natural effect. Less clear perhaps, but to the same
effect, is Philippians 3:19: the "destiny" of those who are "enemies of
the cross of Christ" is "destruction."

The deepest, most decisive consideration, however, is present in the
awesome and unfathomable mystery of God's electing purpose. In his
active resolve to exercise ("choosing to show") "his wrath," those who
are "the objects of his wrath—prepared for destruction" (Rom 9:22) are
such before they "were born or had done anything good or bad" (Rom
9:11).[69] For Paul, God's judicial wrath as it terminates on the finally unrepentant, according to his sovereign predestination, is for them abso-

---

[65]Murray, *Romans*, 1:303; Moo, *Romans*, 515; Schreiner, *Romans*, 436.

[66]"by the will of the one who subjected it" (NIV) over-translates but is certainly true to the
sense.

[67]Cf. 2 Thessalonians 1:6, 2:10, 12; Romans 2:8; 1 Thessalonians 1:10.

[68]The retributive sense that attaches to the word group for punishment used here is plain
(e.g., Acts 7:24; Rom 12:19; 13:4; 1 Pet 2:14; Jude 7).

[69]Careful exegesis, I take it, shows that the predestination/election in view in Romans 9—11
is individual and pretemporal/eternal (cf. Rom 8:29-30; Eph 1:4-12), as well as corporate
and salvation-historical; for commentary defenses of this view, see, among others, J. Murray, *The Epistle to the Romans* (Grand Rapids: Eerdmans, 1965), 2:8-38, esp. 14-19; Moo, *Romans*, 571-72, 604-609; Schreiner, *Romans*, 477, 497-98, 513-24; see also J. Piper, *The Justification of God* (Grand Rapids: Baker, 1993), esp. his conclusion (217-20) and T. R. Schreiner,
"Does Romans 9 Teach Individual Election unto Salvation?" *JETS*, 36 (1993): 25-40.

lute and unmitigated. Divine wrath and justice are not merely penulti-mate (and no more than metaphorical) expressions of his ultimately all-embracing love.[70]

It is unnecessary, and it weakens the biblical concept of the wrath of God, to deprive it of its emotional and affective character. Wrath in God must not be conceived of in terms of the fitful passion with which anger is frequently associated in us. But to construe God's wrath as consisting simply in his purpose to punish sin or to secure the connec-tion between sin and misery is to equate wrath with its effects and vir-tually eliminate wrath as a movement within the mind of God. Wrath is the holy revulsion of God's being against that which is the contradic-tion of his holiness.[71]

To conclude, for Paul sin in its universality is relational and legal. It is first of all, as violation of his will made explicit in his law, an affront to God's person, and as such, it is also against others and against one's self. It elicits God's wrath, his recoil against sin arising from concerns of his person, especially his holiness and justice, and finding its ulti-mate expression, necessarily punitive and retributive in view of those concerns, in death as the eternal destruction of sinners. Sin, with its multiple ramifications and its basic twofold liability, renders sinners both inexcusably guilty and utterly helpless. This is the plight that the cross of Christ remedies. His cross is a scandal because, left to them-selves, sinners are unable to recognize or adequately acknowledge ei-ther their guilt or their corruption and bondage to sin.[72] But the efficacy of the cross is this: together with the resurrection, it destroys sin—both guilt for sin and slavery to sin—and it does so only as it eradicates them together.

Metaphors?

Having Paul's basic understanding of sin in hand is essential for con-sidering his teaching on the efficacy of Christ's death. In addressing the latter today we need to be alert to another development, the wide-spread view that sees Paul's language about the meaning of Christ's

---

[70]Contra the view widely held, e.g., by the authors cited above (notes 59 and 60) and Dunn; the view also of N. T. Wright, *What Saint Paul Really Said: Was Paul of Tarsus the Real Founder of Christianity?* (Grand Rapids: Eerdmans, 1997), 110-11.

[71]Murray, *Romans*, 1:35.

[72]1 Corinthians 2:14, in the context of 1:18ff.; cf. 2 Corinthians 2:15-16.

death to be pervasively or even entirely metaphorical.[73] Let me be clear immediately: the issue here is neither the legitimate place of metaphor in theological discourse nor the necessarily analogical nature of all human speaking about God, including that of Paul and the other biblical writers. However, there are several factors that qualify whatever use Paul makes of metaphors and imagery, particularly in speaking about Christ's death, factors often not acknowledged or even denied by his contemporary interpreters. I can only touch on them briefly here.

First, Paul is quite well aware of the "dialectic" that marks all sound theological knowledge; it is, memorably put, "to know the love of Christ that surpasses knowledge" (Eph 3:19 ESV),[74] and surely with his death primarily in view (2 Cor 5:14). Paul comprehends that God's love and wisdom displayed preeminently in the cross transcend the comprehension of those who for now, until Jesus comes, "see but a poor reflection as in a mirror" (1 Cor 13:12). Considered comprehensively, God's gift, in Christ, is "beyond words" (2 Cor 9:15 REB). But—and this especially is the point to be noted here—Paul *understands* this. He is confident that he not only comprehends, truly if not exhaustively, the incomprehensible "mystery of God" that Christ is, but is able as well to provide his readers with "the full riches of complete understanding," a "knowledge," among other things, that enables them to recognize and refute spurious though "fine-sounding arguments" (Col 2:2, 4).[75] In other words, Paul's gospel involves adequate discursive knowledge. To maintain as does Dunn, for instance, that because of the inadequacy of "rational description," metaphor is indispensable to express the reality of which Paul speaks, introduces a post-Kantian understanding of religious language with a resulting tension between "poetry" and "clinical analysis" that is foreign to Paul.[76]

Second, much is made today of the great variety of metaphors Paul

---

[73]See Dunn, *Theology*, 231-33, 328-33; cf. Green and Baker, *Scandal of the Cross*, 65-67, 93-99; Carroll and Green, *Death of Jesus*, 125-27; Green, *Dictionary of Paul and his Letters*, 203-5; Travis, "Christ as Bearer of Divine Judgment," 344; A. E. McGrath, "Cross, Theology of," *Dictionary of Paul and his Letters*, 196. The broader background here is the increasing stress in recent decades on the metaphorical status of all religious language; see C. E. Gunton, *The Actuality of the Atonement* (Grand Rapids: Eerdmans, 1989), esp. chap. 2 ("Metaphor and Theological Language").

[74]Cf. "the unsearchable riches of Christ," Eph 3:8.

[75]Cf. Col 2:8; 2 Cor 10:5; Tit 1:9.

[76]Dunn, *Theology of Paul*, 332-33; "clinical" here seems chosen for its pejorative edge. Why not rather say "careful and deliberate"?

uses for the meaning of Christ's death.[77] Based on this plurality, it is alleged that no one image is central or captures all the truth of the atonement. In response, at least three things need to be said. First, while it is surely true that Paul speaks of Christ's death in a variety of ways and it is important not to neglect any one, there is no inherent reason why one may not be more predominant than another. Reconciliation, for instance, is surely more central than, say, Christ as Passover lamb. Second, there is no inherent reason why this variety cannot be accounted for in a body of teaching, a doctrine if you will, that is unified and coherent. To say, "It is the reality rather than any specific theory of the power of God to deliver from sin through the death of Christ that dominates Paul's horizons,"[78] is no doubt true but is expressed in a way that suggests a polarizing of reality and theory Paul would not recognize. Third, it does not follow from the variety of images Paul uses that no one image is indispensable under all circumstances, that any one, say sacrifice or penal substitution, may be disposable under some circumstances.[79]

Third, the presence of metaphors in Paul's letters and preaching is widely associated with their "occasional" character, that is, as they are directed to particular persons or groups in concrete circumstances. This hardly means that the power of his metaphors is largely, in some instances entirely, limited to the culture of his day, so that to be "faithful to Paul" and "guided by apostolic testimony to the cross" interpreters today "must continuously seek out [new] metaphors that speak specifically to culture and/or circumstance."[80]

One's most basic assessment of Paul and his letters is at stake here. Briefly here, in their fully occasional character, thoroughly reflecting

---

[77]Green and Baker (*Scandal of the Cross*, 95) speak of "an almost inexhaustible series"; cf. Carroll and Green (*Death of Jesus*, 125), several dozen"! Such language is surely excessive; these authors make no effort to document such assertions and in fact identify and discuss no more than several of what they consider to be metaphors.

[78]McGrath, *Dictionary of Paul and his Letters*, 196, col. b., expressed with a view to avoiding what he deems "the selectivity and prioritization that inevitably accompany systematization of the event of redemption."

[79]Contrary to the view of the authors cited in n. 73; on Dunn, see further my "Paul the Theologian," *WTJ* 62 (2000): 136-37.

[80]Green, *Dictionary of Paul and his Letters*, 204, col. a. Specifically, with sacrifice as a metaphor for Christ's death in view, Dunn (*Theology of Paul*, 233) speaks of "the outdated metaphor [that] has to be remetaphored rather than simply discarded if the potency of its message for Paul and the first Christians is not to be lost." As far as I can see, what this "remetaphored potency" entails is spelled out vaguely at best.

his personality and the culture of his day, they are nonetheless to be received today, as his preaching was originally, "not as the word of men, but as it actually is, the word of God" (1 Thess 2:13). Written, as he is an apostle of Christ, they have a "God-breathed" character (2 Tim 3:16), along with "the other Scriptures" (2 Pet 3:16), that gives them enduring divine authority.[81] Furthermore, while addressing readers in his own time, Paul also knows himself to be writing, with revelatory and apostolic authority, for all times until Jesus returns, for that entire redemptive-historical epoch.[82] Whatever metaphorical elements there may be in his speaking about the cross, they retain their validity and applicability, as metaphors, until then. And while it may be appropriate for the church in generations subsequent to Paul to search for other cultural-specific images for the atonement, such images, with their limited applicability, are valid only as they can be shown to be consonant with his metaphors retaining their status as universal and abiding norms.

Fourth, and perhaps most important, sin, while it may be spoken of metaphorically, is not a metaphor. Nor is the guilt of sin or living in the corruption of sin and being under its absolute control; nor, however awesome and ultimately incomprehensible, is the wrath of God or eternal destruction. Whatever metaphorical elements there may be in the message of the cross, that message, as the remedy for sin, must be decisively nonmetaphorical. "But where sin increased, grace increased all the more" (Rom 5:20). As sin is not a metaphor, so neither, however unfathomable and inexpressible in human language (of whatever sort) their ultimate dimensions, are God's love and grace effective in the death of Christ.

The Efficacy of the Cross

Only now are we in a position, finally, to address more specifically how Paul unfolds the efficacy of Christ's death. He does so using a number of themes or motifs that reinforce each other, and at points overlap. Prominent among these are sacrifice, or expiation; propitiation; reconciliation; redemption; and justification. As we have already

---

[81]See H. Ridderbos, *Redemptive History and the New Testament Scriptures* (Phillipsburg, N.J.: Presbyterian and Reformed, 1988), 1-52.
[82]See 1 Corinthians 1:7; 1 Thessalonians 1:10; cf. 1 Timothy 6:14; Titus 2:13.

seen, Christ's death, together with his resurrection, is God's eschato-logical answer to sin as rebellion against God, specifically his revealed will. In the cross and resurrection, God addresses sin in its essential and irreducible twofold aspect. He removes the sinner's sin both as in-curring guilt and as corrupting and enslaving power, and in so doing, he effects the removal of his just wrath, terminating in eternal destruc-tion, which that guilt and corruption deserve. If this is a fair reprise, then we should anticipate that the themes just noted would concern one or both of these facets of sin with its manifold repercussions. Here I can only touch on them briefly and, in keeping with the overall pur-pose of this chapter, will do so in order to point out how each contem-plates Christ's death as a penal substitution.

From the modern period to the present no notion has been more vig-orously opposed than that for Paul, Christ's death was a propitiation.[83] The key text, Romans 3:25, is treated in depth elsewhere in this vol-ume.[84] Here I note the broader implication of this issue for his teaching as a whole. Assuming its coherence, we may say that the cross is bound to be propitiatory; it removes God's just wrath, with its punitive con-sequences, and renders him merciful. Those who reject this conclusion do so, it seems, primarily for two reasons. They deny or tone down Paul's teaching that God's wrath is such that concerns of his person, his holy and just aversion to sin, require that to be true to himself he punish sinners. Also, they point out what is undeniably and emphati-cally true, that for Paul the cross is the initiative of God's love.[85] Such objections, unlike Paul, fail to acknowledge and wrestle with the ulti-mately impenetrable mystery that, in dealing with sin and sinners, God's mercy and his just wrath are equally ultimate concerns, as Ro-mans 9:22-23 shows. Certainly Paul does not teach a divine *Umstim-mung*, as if on the cross a loving Christ interposes himself on behalf of sinners to pacify an angry and remote God. Particularly applicable to Paul is the following comment:

> It is one thing to say that the wrathful God is made loving. That would
> be entirely false. It is another thing to say the wrathful God is loving.
> That is profoundly true. But it is also true that the wrath by which he is

---

[83]See, e.g., the authors cited in n. 2.
[84]See the essay by D. A. Carson.
[85]Romans 5:8; cf. Ephesians 2:7; Titus 3:4.

wrathful is propitiated through the cross. This propitiation is the fruit of
the divine love that provided it . . . . The propitiation is the ground upon
which the divine love operates and the channel through which it flows
in achieving its end.[86]

Given the truly propitiatory effect of the cross, it is plain in what
sense Paul also speaks of it as an expiatory sacrifice. Taken together, his
numerous "for our sins" and "for us" statements include a sacrificial
meaning that is strictly substitutionary. Christ's death does for sinners
what they cannot do for themselves; it clears them from the just punishment of death issuing in eternal destruction.[87]

Dunn's view is fairly representative of much contemporary interpretation. Though he deems it "unwise" to think of Christ's death as
"literally a sacrifice provided by God," he recognizes that "sacrifice"
is "a central metaphor" in Paul. But it is "a difficult metaphor for contemporary commentators." As he notes earlier, the idea of bloody
sacrifice is "one of the most repellant features of Paul's (and early
Christian) theology for modern readers . . . generally abhorrent to
post-Enlightenment culture, something to be consigned to a more
primitive and cruder period of conceptualization of divine-human
relationships."[88] Dunn, it seems, is of a divided mind here. On the
one hand, sound exegetical instincts do not allow him to follow those
who marginalize the idea of sacrifice as secondary in Paul. On the
other hand, he also seems to share something of the modern antipathy he notes and is hesitant about fully approving Paul's teaching on
sacrifice, even as a metaphor. One must choose at this point between
modern sensibilities and Paul's clear teaching.

As the cross propitiates and expiates, it is not difficult to see how for
Paul it also reconciles God and sinners. The longstanding issue here is
whether the alienation and enmity that mar the relationship between
God and sinners are mutual, whether in the cross not only the sinner
but God as well is reconciled. The primary exegetical reason for denying the latter, akin to rejecting propitiation in Paul, is that God plainly
takes the initiative in reconciliation, in removing the alienation be-

---

[86]J. Murray, *Redemption—Accomplished and Applied* (Grand Rapids: Eerdmans, 1955), 37-38.
[87]Dunn states, "But Paul's teaching is *not* that Christ dies 'in the place of' others so that they
escape death (as the logic of 'substitution' implies)" (*Theology of Paul*, 221, his italics). What
Dunn rejects is precisely Paul's "logic."
[88]*Theology of Paul*, 231, 233, 212.

tween himself and sinners, and that he does so in love.[89] But from the vantage point of Paul's understanding of sin and God's wrath, it is apparent that reconciliation is mutual.[90]

Key passages on reconciliation confirm this. In 2 Corinthians 5:19 reconciliation involves, or is effected by, God's "not counting men's sins against them." This nonimputation of sin[91] does not describe a change of attitude, a pacification, produced within the sinner, but it points to peace as stemming from the justification[92] entailed in the removal of the guilt for sin that from God's side is a barrier to his fellowship with sinners. Second Corinthians 5:21 confirms this. Whatever may be its full dimensions, "the righteousness of God" that believers have become in Christ surely includes the forensic and imputative component just mentioned in verse 19 and apart from which God himself is not reconciled to sinners. That is so as Christ is not simply a representative but a true substitute, "him who knew no sin to be sin for us" (2 Cor 5:21). Similarly, in Romans 5:9-10, "we were reconciled to him through the death of his Son" is closely correlative with "we have now been justified by his blood," both with a view to being "saved from God's wrath."

As to the theme of redemption, the key pronouncement is Galatians 3:13, where the deliverance in view is "from the curse of the law." As the law, when violated, establishes guilt and consequent liability to punishment, so redemption is effected by Christ on the cross "becoming a curse for us"; that is, as our substitute, he bears the guilt of our sin and the consequent punishment from God it deserves.[93] Colossians 2:13-15 is particularly instructive for showing how the themes of penal substitution and Christ as victor are inseparable and mutually conditioning. Only as God, in order to forgive sins, has "canceled the written code, with its regulations, that was against us and that stood opposed to us; . . . nailing it to the cross," has he "disarmed the powers and authorities . . . triumphing over

---

[89]See Romans 5:8; 2 Corinthians 5:18-19.

[90]Hofius's flat assertion that Paul nowhere speaks of God's enmity against sinners ("Sühne und Versöhnung," 36) can only be made by ignoring, as he does, the passages considered above in discussing God's wrath.

[91]Cf. Romans 4:8.

[92]See Romans 5:1.

[93]See Galatians 4:5; in Ephesians 1:7, redemption equals the forgiveness of sins; see also Colossians 1:13.

them by the cross." Elsewhere, in 1 Timothy 2:5-6, Christ "gave himself as a ransom for all," not as he mediates God's dealing with sinners for their reformation in an entirely unidirectional fashion, but as he is the "one mediator between God and men," that is, as he satisfies the respective needs and concerns of both. For Paul what God effects in Christ's death has reference, first of all, not to the needs of sinners, but to the concerns of his own person, specifically his justice and holiness.

Earlier we noted the unbreakable bond between the cross and resurrection. Here, finally, it is worth noting that the resurrection, seen by Paul as being not primarily evidentiary but fully soteriological, is essential for the efficacy of penal substitution as he understands it. When he writes, for instance, "And if Christ has not been raised, your faith is futile; you are still in your sins" (1 Cor 15:17), there is no reason, contextual or otherwise, to suppose that he has in view slavery to sin but not guilt for sin (any more than that would be the case for "died for our sins" in 1 Corinthians 15:3). In other words, as our substitute, a crucified but unresurrected Christ still bears the guilt of our sins; as long as he remains in a state of death, its penal force continues and he (and believers) are unjustified. The resurrection is his de facto justification and so secures the believer's justification. This is the likely sense in Romans 4:25 of the formula, whether or not taken over by Paul, "He was delivered over to death for our sins and was raised to life for our justification."[94]

This survey of the efficacy of the cross in Paul, though in itself brief, is adequate, especially when kept firmly tethered to what he teaches about sin and God's wrath, to show that Christ's death is a penal substitution. To conclude otherwise, short of also rejecting or ignoring what we have seen as essential aspects of his clear teaching about sin and God's wrath, would mean that those aspects remain unaddressed by Christ's death. In that case the cross as his "solution" would not be adequate, by his own analysis, to the sinner's "plight," exegetically a hardly satisfying or even plausible conclusion.

---

[94]Cf. 1 Timothy 3:16. See further my *Resurrection and Redemption*, 119-24; on the pre-Pauline origin of v. 25, J. D. G. Dunn, *Romans*, WBC (Dallas, Tex.: Word, 1988), 224, 240-41; Moo, *Romans*, 288; Schreiner, *Romans*, 243 are all tentative.

Conclusion

> To conceive of Jesus as primarily the victim of divine punitive justice is
> to commit three sins: to treat one metaphor of atonement, the legal, in
> isolation from the others; to read that metaphor literally and merely per-
> sonalistically; and to create a dualism between the action of God and that
> of Jesus.[95]

This would be news to Paul, who leads the church in showing, as we
have seen, that giving a primary place to Jesus' death as the substitutionary bearing of God's just punishment on sinners need not entail
committing the above three "sins." Paul does not treat the legal aspect
of the atonement in isolation from others. Though he does take that aspect literally, he does not do so "merely personalistically" but also addresses its interpersonal and cosmic implications. And he maintains in
all of its ultimately mysterious fullness the unity of God's action manifested in Christ's self-giving, propitiatory and mutually reconciling
sacrifice on the cross.

The above quotation is in a paragraph bracketed by the following
statements: "There is required a concept of substitution, albeit one controlled not by the necessity of punishment so much as by the gracious
initiative of God in re-creation," and "At issue is the actuality of the
atonement: whether the real evil of the world is faced and healed *ontologically* in the life, death and resurrection of Jesus."[96] Expressed here,
mutedly but unmistakably, is the regrettable polarizing that, especially
in the modern era, has impaired access to Paul and other biblical writers: a supposed tension between "the necessity of punishment" and
"the gracious initiative of God in re-creation," or, more elementally, between punishment and grace, and so a blurring of the irreducible distinction between the forensic and renovative aspects in Paul's gospel.
For Paul there is no new creation in Christ that does not also involve
and presuppose the gracious justification of the ungodly by faith resting in Christ, who bore the wrath of eternal destruction they deserve.
Justification may not be sublimated or otherwise shaded into another
metaphor for the new creation.

---

[95]Gunton, *The Actuality of the Atonement*, 165. I leave to the side in this statement how adequately (and fairly) Jesus as "victim" represents the penal substitution view, as well as the
semantics of "primarily."

[96]Ibid., 164, 165 (italics in the original).

Certainly for Paul the atonement is concerned with "the real evil of the world" and its elimination, but for him sin as illegality is a component of evil's *reality*, a component so intrinsic that unless that illegality is removed by the penal substitution of the cross, any hope of real and ultimate ontological healing is illusory, and the atonement lacking in actuality. That, as much as anything, in Paul's day as in ours, remains the scandal of the cross.

8

atonement in Hebrews

"A Merciful and Faithful High Priest"

Simon J. Kistemaker

Hebrews is an epistle in which Christ's priesthood is mentioned explicitly and implicitly in all thirteen chapters. It is an epistle that speaks decisively about the priestly sacrifice Jesus made once for all.[1] Although the author mentions the word *cross* only once (Heb 12:2), he nonetheless teaches the doctrine of atonement. Throughout the letter, he describes Christ's atoning work directly and indirectly in relation to his high priestly office. A vivid example is Hebrews 2:17: "For this reason he had to be made like his brothers in every way, in order that he might become a merciful and faithful high priest in service to God, and that he might make atonement (ἱλάσκεσθαι) for the sins of the people."

Translators of this Greek term have resorted to a choice of words that range from atonement (NRSV, NIV) to expiation (RSV, NEB, NJB, REB, NLT) and propitiation (NKJV, NASB). Of these three, atonement is a general term; expiation appears more frequently; and propitiation less frequently. *Atonement* is commonly defined as the reparation of a broken relationship that exists between God and his people but that is restored through the death and resurrection of his Son Jesus Christ. *Expiation* means that the vicarious blood of Christ covers sin, which is a failure to keep one's obligations to God. *Propitiation* refers to sin that arouses

---

[1]See Hebrews 9:12, 26, 28; 10:12.

God's anger, which Christ through his death on the cross has removed. It reveals that Christ, by taking sin upon himself, has averted God's wrath from his people, but it does not specify how God's favor was gained. Critics often object to the term *propitiation* because it implies divine wrath; they argue instead that God is a God of love.

C. H. Dodd wrote a relatively brief study on the atonement and concluded that even though in classical Greek the term ἱλάσκεσθαι means "propitiate," in the Septuagint and the New Testament it signifies expiation, not propitiation.[2] With respect to Hebrews 2:17, he writes, "Christ is represented as performing an act whereby men are delivered from the guilt of their sin, not whereby (the wrath of) God is propitiated."[3] He implies that in Luke 18:13, Romans 3:25, Hebrews 2:17 and 1 John 2:2; 4:10 where ἱλάσκεσθαι and its cognates occur the accent should fall on God's love and mercy and not on his wrath.

Both Roger R. Nicole and Leon Morris have effectively refuted Dodd's study by pointing out numerous inadequacies in his examination of the Hebrew and Greek texts.[4] They prove that Dodd, citing OT and NT passages, fails to examine these passages in their respective contexts that prove the presence of God's wrath. Indeed, they point out that his conclusion fails to gain support, for instance, in the general context of the epistle to the Hebrews, which repeatedly speaks about God's wrath against sin.[5] The verb ἱλάσκεσθαι indicates the removal of divine wrath directed against sin. This is implied in Hebrews 2:17, where the author reveals that Christ, being made like his brothers and sisters, is a merciful high priest. The term *merciful* points to grievous sins committed by his people, who consequently have to face the wrath of God. Also, the words "faithful high priest in service to God" point to God. Morris remarks, "A Godward aspect expressed by ἱλάσκομαι is likely to include propitiation, to put it mildly."[6]

---

[2]C. H. Dodd, *The Bible and the Greeks* (London: Hodder & Stoughton, 1935), 82-95. He published the chapter first as "ΙΛΑΣΚΕΣΘΑΙ, Its Cognates, Derivatives, and synonyms, in the Septuagint," *JTS* 32 (1931): 352-60.

[3]Dodd, *Bible and the Greeks*, 94.

[4]Roger R. Nicole, "C. H. Dodd and the Doctrine of Propitiation," *WTJ* 17 (1955): 117-57. Leon Morris, *The Apostolic Preaching of the Cross* (Grand Rapids: Eerdmans, 1956), 174-80. See also his *The Cross in the New Testament* (Grand Rapids: Eerdmans, 1965), 349.

[5]Hebrews 2:2, 3; 3:11, 18; 4:3, 5; 6:8; 8:9; 9:22; 10:27, 30-31, 39; 12:25, 29.

[6]Morris, *Apostolic Preaching*, 175.

Expiation and Propitiation in Hebrews 2:17

Many modern theologians have adopted Dodd's study as a definitive word on translating and explaining the atonement. Thus, they stress the love of God but not his wrath. They extol God's love and kindness but minimize and even deny his anger. These scholars choose the noun *expiation* in place of *propitiation* because they understand that Christ's sacrifice recounted in the epistle to the Hebrews is aimed at expiating sin but not at propitiating God. In fact, commenting on Hebrews 2:17, Harold W. Attridge writes, "In Hebrews, Christ's sacrifice is always directed at removing sin and its effects, not at propitiating God."[7] Similarly, Hugh Montefiore summarily states, "Propitiation is not a biblical concept, but expiation is the motive underlying atonement sacrifice. Expiation is what the high priest was believed to achieve on the Day of Atonement, when he expiated the sins of the people."[8] R. McL. Wilson notes that in the Septuagint and the New Testament, "the primary meaning is not that of placating or propitiating an angry deity but of the removal or wiping out of the sins which stand between God and man."[9] And finally, Paul Ellingworth, who discusses propitiation, notes that "the most natural sense" in Hebrews 2:17 is "expiation."[10] He finds no justification for the version "to make atonement for" and its marginal note "turn aside God's wrath, taking away."

Certainly, by his death Christ removed the sins of his people. And by expiating sin, he restored the divine and the human relationship that sin had severed. But ignoring the meaning of the concept *propitiation* is unwarranted. God is the offended party whose anger against sin is evident throughout Scripture. In the Apocalypse, John even mentions "the wrath of the Lamb" (Rev 6:16). In other words, there is no division in the Godhead on the matter of wrath against sin. Yet Jesus, through his vicarious death on the cross, eliminates this wrath. C. K. Barrett remarks, "It would be wrong to neglect the fact that expiation has, as it

---

[7]Harold W. Attridge, *The Epistle to the Hebrews*, Hermeneia (Philadelphia: Fortress, 1989), 96 n. 192.

[8]Hugh Montefiore, *The Epistle to the Hebrews*, HNTC (New York: Harper & Row, 1964), 68.

[9]R. McL. Wilson, *Hebrews*, NCBC (Grand Rapids: Eerdmans, and Basingstoke: Marshall Morgan & Scott, 1987), 63. See also Friedrich Büchsel, "ἱλάσκομαι," *Theological Dictionary of the New Testament*, ed. Gerhard Kittel and Gerhard Friedrich (Grand Rapids: Eerdmans, 1964-76), 3:314-17.

[10]Paul Ellingworth, *The Epistle to the Hebrews: A Commentary on the Greek Text*, NIGTC (Grand Rapids: Eerdmans, 1993), 189. He overlooks the studies of Roger R. Nicole and Leon Morris, who prefer the translation "propitiation" to "expiation."

were, the effect of propitiation: the sin that might have excited God's wrath is expiated (at God's will) and therefore no longer does so."[11]

The dispute centers on the translation "to make propitiation for the sins of the people" (Heb 2:17 NASB), for the Greek text demands that the noun *sin* is the object of the verb ἱλάσκεσθαι. This means that the Greek verb should be translated "to make expiation for the sins of the people" (NEB). It conveys the idea that expiation is made toward sin, not toward God. But scholars who replace the word *propitiation* with *expiation* still have to account for God's wrath. Says Leon Morris, "[expiation] is an impersonal word (one expiates a thing, a sin or a crime), whereas a personal word is needed to describe what Christ has done for His people."[12] And that word is propitiation, even though it is inadequate. To find a way out of this difficulty, we suggest that the verb ἱλάσκεσθαι can communicate the sense of both propitiation and expiation and thus express a double meaning: first, "to make atonement and reconciliation for sin, appeasing the anger of God against it"; and second, "to remove and take away sin, either by the cleansing and sanctifying of the sinner, or by any means prevailing with him not to continue in sin."[13] This denotes that sin is an affront to God, who is rightly offended by it. The removal of sin calls for a sacrifice or similar means to make atonement, for appeasing God, and for pardoning the sinner.[14]

In a lengthy footnote, F. F. Bruce justifies the translation "to make expiation for" and "to expiate" (RSV, NEB) because the direct object of the verb ἱλάσκεσθαι is "sins." He notes that in the Greek Bible this verb "is not found with the person propitiated as its object."[15] But in the Septuagint "there are four or five places where the construction is accusative of person with the plain meaning 'appease, propitiate.'"[16] In addition, the accusative of the word ἁμαρτίας (sins) may be taken as an accusative of reference and translated "with respect to the sins of the people."

---

[11]C. K. Barrett, *The Epistle to the Romans*, BNTC (New York: Harper, 1957), 78.

[12]Leon Morris, "Propitiation," *International Standard Bible Encyclopedia* (Grand Rapids: Eerdmans, 1979-88), 3:1005.

[13]John Owen, *An Exposition of Hebrews* (Evansville, Ind.: Sovereign Grace, 1960), 2:475.

[14]Ibid., 476. See also Morris, *Apostolic Preaching*, 177.

[15]F. F. Bruce, *The Epistle to the Hebrews*, rev. ed. (Grand Rapids: Eerdmans, 1990), 78, n. 57.

[16]Morris, *Apostolic Preaching*, 175. The Greek manuscripts A, Ψ, and 33 feature the dative plural ταῖς ἁμαρτίαις instead of the accusative. Copyists understood the dative to be a dative of reference. Owen, on the other hand, supposes that an ellipsis has occurred but that the sentence should read "to make reconciliation with God for sins" (*Hebrews*, 2:477).

The use of the accusative of reference or respect even occurs in the immediately preceding clause, "in respect of things pertaining to God."

The objection that scholars level against the word *propitiation* is that the writer of Hebrews would incorporate a pagan idea of placating an angry god. He would then turn a loving God into a spiteful and whimsical deity who expresses his wrath to people that fail to bring him the required offerings. But Scripture reveals, not a God who can be appeased by gifts people offer to him, but a holy God who expresses his anger against those who sin and persist in sinning. Both the OT and NT teach that God expresses his wrath from heaven.[17] And yet it is God himself who initiates propitiation by having Jesus Christ turn aside divine wrath and take away sin out of love for lost humanity.[18]

Paul K. Jewett discusses the matter of expiation and propitiation by asking a few penetrating questions:

> If one reduces the language of Scripture from "propitiation" to "expiation" in all instances, he still must answer the question, "Why should sins be expiated? What would happen if no expiation were provided? Can one deny that, according to the teaching of Scripture, men will die in their sins?" The logical implication of the denial of propitiation as unworthy of God is the teaching that God will ultimately manifest His forgiving love to everyone, regardless of how one is related to Christ—a point of view that is increasingly the vogue, but one that is contrary to Scripture.[19]

There is no conflict between love and wrath, for it is God who in his love for the human race initiated the process of reconciling us to himself, even while we were still sinners (Rom 5:8). We are the ones who offended him, and we should have to make reparations to God, but it was "God who reconciled us to himself through Christ" (2 Cor 5:18). Jesus became the propitiation for us by undergoing God's utter displeasure against sin that he suffered both in Gethsemane and at Calvary.

Hebrews 5:7
The writer of the epistle to the Hebrews gradually unfolds the high

---

[17]See Deuteronomy 4:24; 9:3; Hebrews 10:31; 12:29.
[18]See Romans 3:25; 5:8. Donald Guthrie, *The Letter to the Hebrews: An Introduction and Commentary*, TNTC (Leicester: Inter-Varsity; and Grand Rapids: Eerdmans, 1983), 95.
[19]Paul K. Jewett, "Propitiation," in *The Zondervan Pictorial Encyclopedia of the Bible*, ed. Merrill C. Tenney (Grand Rapids: Zondervan, 1975), 4:904-5.

priesthood of Christ. First, he mentions that this merciful and faithful high priest might make atonement for the sins of the people (Heb 2:17). This is followed by an exhortation to contemplate the significance of this high priest (Heb 3:1). Then the author calls Jesus a great high priest who has gone through the heavens but who also is able to sympathize with human weakness (Heb 4:14-15). That is, he refers to the Aaronic high priest who sprinkled the blood of a bull for his own sins and after that the blood of a goat for the sins of the people (Heb 5:3). Then he depicts Christ as king and high priest according to the order of Melchizedek (Heb 5:5-6).

At this point the author of Hebrews pens his one and only reference to Jesus' earthly life by saying, "During the days of Jesus' life on earth, he offered up prayers and petitions with loud cries and tears to the one who could save him from death, and he was heard because of his reverent submission" (Heb 5:7). Every part of this verse is significant and meaningful. Does the first clause allude to Jesus' entire life, the period of his three-year ministry, or the last day of his life? As the sinless one, Jesus suffered all the days of his earthly life. And we know from the gospel accounts that during his ministry he was always subject to verbal abuse. But it was during the last twenty-four hours of his life that he especially endured spiritual and physical torture. Hence, I suggest that it is prudent to take the third option as the correct one. I do so by noticing that the author of Hebrews draws a parallel and a contrast between the Aaronic high priest and Jesus. The Aaronic high priest entered the most holy place of either tabernacle or temple on the Day of Atonement to atone for his own sins and then for those of the people (Heb 5:3). Likewise, Jesus atoned for the sins of his people during the last night and day of his earthly life. Hence, out of the high priest's life, the writer lifts the most telling event: the atonement. And this holds true not only for any Aaronic high priest but also for Jesus. The highlight in the life of a high priest was that day of the year when he alone of all humanity might enter the very presence of God to offer the blood of animal sacrifices to atone for sin. Similarly, the author of Hebrews focuses attention on Jesus' last day when he offered himself to God in the garden of Gethsemane and at Calvary as a sacrifice for sin.

A few days before his death, Jesus met some Greeks who were among those that had come for worship at the Passover feast. He intimated that the hour of his agony was fast approaching when he said,

"Now my heart is troubled, and what shall I say? 'Father, save me from this hour'? No, it was for this very reason I came to this hour" (Jn 12:27). This passage is usually called "little Gethsemane," for it points forward to Jesus' suffering in the garden of Gethsemane.[20] There in the garden he told Peter and the two sons of Zebedee, "My soul is overwhelmed with sorrow to the point of death"; and when he went away from them he prayed, "My Father, if it is possible, may this cup be taken from me" (Mt 26:38-39). The cup refers to God's anger with human sin that became reality at Gethsemane when Christ, bearing the sins of his people, faced divine wrath. "God made him who had no sin to be sin for us, so that we might become the righteousness of God" (2 Cor 5:21). "The LORD has laid on him the iniquity of us all" (Is 53:6). As the sin-bearer, Jesus was separated from his God, so Isaiah writes prophetically, "But your iniquities have separated you from your God; your sins have hidden his face from you, so that he will not hear" (Is 59:2). Consequently, Jesus experienced God's holy wrath directed against him because of sin, for this wrath caused a severance between God and the bearer of human sin.

Already in the garden, Jesus' suffering was so acute that he feared he might die. Luke reports that God sent an angel to strengthen him, but after the arrival of the angel Jesus' spiritual and physical agony became increasingly severe to the degree that his subcutaneous capillaries oozed blood, which mingled with his perspiration (Lk 22:44). And this happened during a night that was so chilly that the soldiers had lit a fire in the high priest's courtyard to keep themselves warm (Mk 14:54; Lk 22:55). At Gethsemane Jesus prayed to God by addressing him as Abba, Father, and Matthew specifies that he prayed twice as he called upon his God as Father (Mt 27:39, 42). The bond between Father and Son remained intact even though God did not remove the cup. This cup may be interpreted as the cup of wrath. Jesus knew that he had to face the cross where he would suffer both spiritually and physically.

Jesus' prayers and petitions did not end at Gethsemane; he continued to address his Father from the cross. The garden is actually the prelude to the suffering that Jesus had to endure at Calvary. Of the seven words he spoke from the cross, the first and the last were prayers ad-

---

[20]Cf. Matthew 26:38-46; Mark 14:32-42; Luke 22:40-46.

dressed to his Father: "Father, forgive them, for they do not know what they are doing," and "Father, into your hands I commit my spirit" (Lk 23:34, 46). Three evangelists record that Jesus cried out with a loud voice just before he gave up his spirit,[21] and two of them also note his calling out in a loud voice, "My God, my God, why have you forsaken me?"[22] Although the evangelists do not mention tears, they are clear about Jesus' loud cries from the cross. And the author of Hebrews alludes to these loud cries, for he had in mind Jesus' suffering in the garden of Gethsemane and on Calvary's cross. Yet there is more. He writes that Jesus prayed to the one who could save him from death. Jesus addressed his first and his last words from the cross to his Father, but the fourth one he addressed to God. He quoted Psalm 22:1, "My God, my God, why have you forsaken me?" Note that the address is not to his Father, but to God who had turned his face away from the suffering Servant. Jesus faced God's anger and displeasure directed against him because he bore the burden of sin and accepted his people's penalty.

What did the writer of Hebrews mean when he wrote that Jesus asked God to save him from death? For Jesus, physical death was an unavoidable certainty when the crowd called for his crucifixion and Pilate handed him over to the soldiers (Jn 19:15-16). But he had told his disciples more than once that he would rise from the dead on the third day.[23] If Jesus' death on the cross were limited to his physical suffering, he would be like many others who had undergone similar punishment. The criminals to the left and right of him suffered the same torture. Jesus, however, suffered a spiritual as well as a physical death, for this becomes evident when God abandons him. If Jesus had only died a physical death, nothing would have been accomplished. But on Calvary's cross he died a spiritual death when he experienced the full measure of divine anger against sin. He died spiritually to appease God and to satisfy the divine demand for justice.[24]

We will never to be able to understand Jesus' cry, "Why have you forsaken me?" Although Jesus' faith in God remained strong, he knew

---

[21]Matthew 27:50; Mark 15:37; Luke 19:30.
[22]Matthew 27:46; Mark 15:34.
[23]E.g., Matthew 16:21; 17:23; Luke 18:33.
[24]John Calvin, *Institutes of the Christian Religion*, ed. John T. McNeill, trans. Ford Lewis Battles (Philadelphia: Westminster Press, 1960), 3.4.4, 1:627. Cf. Philip Edgcumbe Hughes, *A Commentary on the Epistle to the Hebrews* (Grand Rapids: Eerdmans, 1977), 183.

that he had been abandoned for being the one who bore the sins of his people. The fourth word from the cross ("My God, my God, why have you forsaken me?") is indeed a "hard saying," for it touches on the person of Christ and the Trinity. Can the Father forsake his Son? Leon Morris admits that he "would find the situation much more tolerable if these words did not stand in the record."[25] But the gospel writers have recorded them, and the author of Hebrews hints at them. On the cross Jesus bore for us the penalty of our sin, namely, our spiritual separation from God.

German theologian Zacharias Ursinus asked the question, "What do you understand by the word 'suffered'?" He answered:

That during his whole life on earth,
but especially at the end, Christ sustained
in body and soul the anger of God
against the sin of the whole human race.
This he did in order that,
by his suffering as the atoning sacrifice,
he might set us free, body and soul,
from eternal damnation,
and gain for us God's grace, righteousness, and eternal life.[26]

Forsaken by God because of our sin, Jesus suffered a spiritual death when he had no help from God or mankind. The demand of the crowd directed to Pontius Pilate to crucify him was being fulfilled (Lk 23:21). The people, assembled in front of the Roman governor, called on God to curse his Son, because "anyone who is hung on a tree (cross) is under God's curse."[27] Thus, when Jesus experienced the curse of God during which every trace of divine grace was removed, he actually "descended into hell." Consequently, on the cross his spiritual death preceded his physical death.[28] Jesus suffered what John in his Apocalypse calls "the second death."[29] This second death means to be spiritually cut off from God. Christ died this death for his people so that they would not be hurt by the second death and would never be forsaken

---

[25]Morris, *The Cross in the New Testament*, 44.
[26]Heidelberg Catechism, Question and Answer 37.
[27]Deuteronomy 21:23; Galatians 3:13.
[28]F. W. Grosheide, *Het Heilig Evangelie volgens Mattheus.* Commentaar op het Nieuwe Testament. 2nd rev. ed. (Kampen, Netherlands: Kok, 1954), 436.
[29]Revelation 2:11; 20:6, 14; 21:8.

by God. Satan and his followers are consigned to suffer this second death, but all of Christ's followers are exempt because he himself suffered abandonment for the sake of his people.

Why did Christ have to suffer death? The answer is, "God's justice and truth demand it: only the death of God's Son could pay for our sin."[30] Surely, God is a God of love and grace who could have set sinners free from the consequences of their sin. In the parable of the wedding banquet, the king demonstrates his love toward his guests by inviting them to the feast. But he also shows his wrath toward those guests who spurn him, and that includes the one who refused to wear the wedding clothes. Jesus concludes the parable with the words, "For many are invited, but few are chosen" (Matt 22:14). If God should only show love and not wrath, his justice would never be served. God's grace and justice go hand in hand in the epistle to the Hebrews. For instance, believers are urged to come boldly to the throne of grace to receive mercy and find grace in time of need (Heb 4:16). And in that same epistle the references to the judge and judgment are these: eternal judgment awaits those who reject God and continue to practice sin (Heb 6:1-2); the sequence of death and judgment is spelled out (Heb 9:27); and finally, God is the judge of all people (Heb 12:23). Both the love of God and the justice of God are the two scales that are kept in perfect equilibrium. In the one scale is God's love to the world by giving it his one and only Son (Jn 3:16) and in the other is God's justice with the demand that his Son bear the full penalty for his people's sin. Philip Edgcumbe Hughes writes, "In Christ, the Son of man and only lawkeeper, dying in the place of man the law-breaker, the justice and the love of God prevail together."[31]

If this exegesis of the word *death* is correct, the clause "the one who could save him from death" takes on a more profound meaning (Heb 5:7). Having suffered both a spiritual death and a physical death on the cross, Jesus sets his people free from the fear of death. Indeed, the writer of Hebrews notes that Jesus by his death destroyed Satan, who holds the power of death, and freed "those who all their lives were held in slavery by their fear of death" (Heb 2:15). The death that human beings face is both physical and spiritual. Spiritual death is eternal for

---

[30]Heidelberg Catechism, Question and Answer 40.
[31]Hughes, *Hebrews*, 113.

those who are apart from Christ and face God's judgment (Heb 9:27). For them nothing is left but "a fearful expectation of judgment and of raging fire that will consume the enemies of God" (Heb 10:27). Believers, however, are acquitted because Christ has borne God's judgment to set them free from the fear of eternal death.

The Greek term θάνατος (death) occurs nine times in Hebrews, most of which refer to physical death.[32] But the words "held in slavery by their fear of death" (Heb 2:15) allude to the spiritual death of Christ. Hughes notes, "The death that man fears, moreover, is not just the physical death that he faces; it is the 'second death,' the fact that after death there is judgment (Revelation 2:11; 20:6; 21:6; Hebrews 9:27)."[33] That is, because of sin we were condemned to die a spiritual death and be eternally separated from God. But Christ took our place and died an eternal death for us on the cross when God abandoned him. He underwent death to destroy Satan, who held the power of death, first to liberate those enslaved by the devil (Heb 2:14-15), and second to nullify their spiritual death sentence. In the Apocalypse, John points out that as the saints bask in God's eternal light and that of the Lamb,[34] they will never experience the eternal darkness that those who die a second death suffer and are forever cut off from the living God. Christ died this second death for his people and set them free.

The author of Hebrews writes that Jesus appealed "to the one who could save him from death" (Heb 5:7). The emphasis is on the verb *to save*, which conveys the meaning of divine deliverance. At the cross, bystanders ridiculing Jesus used this word by taunting him three different times: (1) "You who are going to destroy the temple and build it in three days, save yourself! Come down from the cross, if you are the Son of God!" (2) "He saved others but he can't save himself"; and (3) "Let's see if Elijah comes to save him."[35] In the same way, one of the crucified criminals said, "Save yourself and us!"(Lk 23:39). The concept *save*, however, has a deeper meaning than sparing someone's physical life. Jesus saved the other criminal who repented, not physi-

---

[32]Hebrews 2:9 (twice), 14; 7:23; 9:15, 16; 11:5.
[33]Hughes, *Hebrews*, 113. See also Simon J. Kistemaker, *Exposition of the Epistle to the Hebrews* (Grand Rapids: Baker, 1984), 137.
[34]Revelation 21:23; 22:5.
[35]Matthew 27:40, 42, 49.

cally, but spiritually. Jesus' cry, "Father, save me from this hour" (Jn 12:27), pointed to the agony of dying a spiritual and physical death on the cross to set his people free. The words "from death," therefore, refer not to deliverance from his imminent death on the cross, but rather that God brings to an end both the spiritual and physical death of Jesus. "The prayers and supplications which He is said to have offered up were not that He might be saved from death, but that He might saved out of it."[36]

The author completes Hebrews 5:7 with the clause, "and he was heard because of his reverent submission." The use of the passive voice implies that Jesus addressed God, who heard him and responded positively to his request. This response was based on, and was the result of, his reverence demonstrated in his complete surrender to God when he obediently fulfilled his role of mediator. The writer of Hebrews adds that Jesus was heard and that he received what he asked for, namely, not to escape from death but to gain salvation for his people through and out of spiritual and physical death. An older interpretation that understands Christ's being heard "in that he feared" (AV/ KJV) with respect to his death goes against the author's intent. The Greek word εὐλαβείας means, not a state of being afraid, but an attitude of devout reverence, which the Vulgate translates as *pro sua reverentia* (in consideration of his veneration). Because of Christ's reverent regard for God's honor, justice and rule, God responded to him.

Jesus directed his prayers and petitions to his Father in heaven, and they were granted him because he was fulfilling God's will by obediently accomplishing the work entrusted to him. God answers prayer when it is offered in obedience to his commands and in accordance with his will.[37] But how do we understand the positive statement "he was heard" when Jesus had to suffer death? The answer is that God forsook him briefly during the three hours of darkness when Jesus was separated from God (Mt 27:45). But he rescued Jesus from spiritual death when he restored the relation between Father and Son. And he saved him from physical death when Jesus rose from the dead on the third day.

---

[36]Geerhardus Vos, "The Priesthood of Christ in Hebrews," in *Redemptive History and Biblical Interpretation: The Shorter Writings of Geerhardus Vos*, ed. Richard B. Gaffin Jr. (Phillipsburg, N.J.: Presbyterian and Reformed, 1980), 147.
[37]1 John 3:22; 5:14.

Conclusion

We still face the question of how the person of Christ and the Trinity fit into the exegesis of Hebrews 5:7. How do we explain the two natures of Christ in respect to his suffering in the garden and on the cross? With our sin-darkened minds we are unable to understand where the human and divine natures meet in Christ. This aspect will always remain a mystery to God's people here on earth. The same is true when we try to understand how within the Trinity the Father forsakes the Son and yet loves him. John Calvin asserts,

> We do not admit that God was ever hostile with him, or angry with him. For how could he be angry with his beloved Son, "in whom his soul delighted?" or how could Christ, by his intercession, appease the Father for others, if the Father were incensed against him? But we affirm, that he sustained the weight of the Divine severity; since, being "smitten and afflicted of God" (Is 53:4), he experienced from God all the tokens of wrath and vengeance.[38]

The difference between an Aaronic high priest and Jesus the Great High Priest is unique and insuperable. Aaron and his successors offered animal sacrifices as substitutes for humans, but as the God-man Jesus offered himself. All these high priests died a natural death, but Jesus died a physical and spiritual death as a substitute for his people. None of them were ever able to remove the fear of death, but Jesus removed the fear of death once for all. Also, Jesus as the high priest in the order of Melchizedek, fulfilled the Aaronic priesthood by bringing it to an end. And finally, Aaron and those who followed him in the high priestly office performed their duties in the inner room of the tabernacle or temple, but Jesus performed his high priestly duty in full view of the people by hanging on the cross. "But now he has appeared once for all at the end of the ages to do away with sin by the sacrifice of himself" (Heb 9:26). Jesus is, indeed, our atoning sacrifice. As the Lamb of God, he took away the sin of the world (Jn 1:29). And he took upon himself the wrath of God against sin by dying spiritually and physically for his people.

---

[38]Calvin *Institutes* 1:565.

atonement in james, peter and jude

"Because Christ Suffered for You"

Dan G. McCartney

It is well known that 1 Peter develops more clearly than any other book of the New Testament the Suffering Servant of the Lord theme, quoting explicitly from Isaiah 53 and applying it to the suffering of Christ. It does so because its author over and over finds the solution to the problem of Christian suffering in identification with Christ's atoning suffering. On the other hand, James, 2 Peter, and Jude have very little to say about the atoning death of Christ. This has given rise either to the neglect of these letters or, for the contentious, to an overly vigorous stress on their alleged lack of interest in redemption. It is therefore necessary to say something about these letters before delving into the treasury of 1 Peter.

Jude
Jude is almost exclusively concerned with the problem of false teachers (probably antinomians) and licentiousness in the church, and it simply assumes the knowledge of the content of the "faith once delivered to the saints" on the part of his audience. Since the writer's concern is not with Christian doctrine per se, we have only a fragmentary indication of Jude's understanding of atonement, but the fragments are there, most notably in the opening verses, and these are compatible with other NT teaching on redemption.

First, the opening of Jude refers to his audience as "beloved (ἠγαπημένοις) in God, kept for Jesus Christ." The perfect participle presumes some finished work of God in loving his people. Though not spelled out here, this indicates that Jude does have some understanding of redemption. And "kept for" Jesus Christ presumes a christological teleology, which is hardly conceivable without a recognition that Christ has fulfilled the redemptive purpose of God. R. Bauckham suggests that the three verbs of the opening, *called, loved* and *kept,* may all derive from the Servant Songs of Isaiah that use these terms of Israel.[1] If so, it reinforces Jude's concurrence with Christian tradition in applying Isaiah 40—55 to the church through the particular Servant, Jesus, and is certainly compatible with Jude's acceptance of the atoning work of the Savior.

Second, the implicit paralleling of Christian experience with the exodus in Jude 5 presumes a common thread with 1 Peter, or at least an awareness that his audience has experienced a redemption similar to, indeed greater than, the redemption of Israel from Egypt. Again, we see no explicit reference to how the Christian "exodus" was accomplished, but the christological emphasis of the opening and closing leads naturally to the conclusion that Jude identified the Christ as the vehicle of that redemption.

Finally, the phrase "through Jesus Christ" in the benediction (Jude 25) presumes the mediatorship of Christ, again comporting well with the rest of the New Testament, though offering no specifics regarding the nature of Christ's redemptive work.

Hence Jude, while offering no details on the atoning work of Christ as the means of redemption, says nothing that conflicts with other NT teaching on atonement and does say a few things that support it. We can also say that it is clear that Jude is not unconcerned about redemption; he rather presupposes it, though his primary concern in the letter is focused elsewhere.

2 Peter
Second Peter has two passing references to the atoning work of Christ. In 2 Peter 1:8-9 the author connects "cleansing from old sins" with the knowledge of Christ. In 2 Peter 2:1 he refers to false teachers as "denying the Lord who bought them." Hence, two images of Christ's atoning

[1] R. Bauckham, *Jude; 2 Peter,* WBC (Waco, Tex.: Word, 1983), 25.

work, cleansing and purchasing, are noted in passing as items that he
assumes are known by his audience and therefore do not need exposition. In both cases, of course, the author's concern, like that of Jude, is
with the problem of false teaching and immorality in the church, and he
therefore leaves the subject of the atonement undeveloped.

Of these two passages, only 2 Peter 2:1 makes any explicit mention
of Christ's atoning work.[2] The false teachers in chapter 2 are described
as those who are "denying the Master (δεσπότην) who bought them,
bringing upon themselves swift destruction." Δεσπότης is rare in the
NT (found only six times) and is usually used in specific reference to
masters of slaves. Here, in combination with the notion of "buying," it
conveys the idea of believers as Christ's slaves by virtue of his purchasing them.[3] Although this is the only explicit reference to atonement in
2 Peter, as with Jude there is a strong undercurrent of assumed knowledge of atonement as background throughout the letter. Its explicit appearance here reinforces the assertion that in both 2 Peter and in Jude,
the lack of explicit reference to redemption does not imply its unim-
portance to the authors of these letters.

Second Peter 2:1 also presents a difficulty, however. How can believers who were purchased by Christ be capable of denying their
Master? Does this verse call into question the biblical teaching that
Christ's redemptive death was truly efficacious, being undertaken
specifically for the sake of his elect people and actually securing
their eternal redemption?

To answer this requires that we locate the situation of the audience.
Writing to a church that is threatened not so much by external threats
(as in 1 Peter) as by internal ones (false teachers especially), he speaks
to people who have named the name of Christ as their Savior. Furthermore, the concern appears to be not with people who have simply
apostatized or denied their Christianity outright, but with those
whose licentiousness and immoral teaching act as a denial of their
ownership. They know the way of righteousness but turn from it and
back to their old immoral ways like a dog returning to its vomit (2 Pet
2:21-22). The passage thus shares the standpoint of Hebrews 6:4-6;
10:26-27 in spelling out the horror and inconceivable blasphemy of

---

[2]In 2 Peter 1:8-9 no indication is given as to how the cleansing was accomplished.
[3]The word also occurs in a parallel passage in Jude 4, but Jude makes no reference to buying.

people (or angels[4]) actually turning their back on God after they have tasted his goodness.

Hence, the reference to "the Master who purchased them" calls to mind the fact that, as members of the community (i.e., the purchased people of God), they have been branded as Christ's, and denying him is therefore analogous to a slave in the Roman Empire denying his master. There is no question that many who have had Christ's seal of ownership placed upon them have nevertheless by word or life denied that ownership, to their own destruction. Even hypocrites, by virtue of their sometime identification with the people of God, are under Christ's seal of ownership and hence are doubly condemned when they deny their Master who warranted ownership of his people by his redemptive death. This passage cannot therefore be used to disprove the notion that Christ's redemption was intended for the benefit of specific people.[5] Quite the contrary, since Peter gives no indication whatever that all people without distinction are the slaves of Christ, the reference to Christ's purchasing of "them" as his slaves supports rather than denies the definiteness of the atonement.

James
It must be acknowledged at the outset that James says virtually nothing directly about the redemptive atoning work of Christ. His concern is with the practical application of Christian ethics and the wisdom of Jesus. However, the letter presupposes a Christian audience (whom he refers to as "brothers"), and a Christian eschatology.[6] James also preserves some aspects of Christian soteriology, particularly the fact that believers are "produced" or brought forth by the word of truth, which is according to God's purpose (βουληθείς) so that they may be a kind of firstfruits of God's created order (Jas 1:18). This word of truth is elsewhere equated with the gospel,[7] and although James may not necessar-

---

[4]Second Peter's comparison to angels is significant. If even angels were not spared, neither shall be those who have been part of the people of God. Faith should not be confused with presumptuousness.

[5]Although some may understand this passage as referring to individuals whose sins have actually been atoned for, such an exegesis would call into question not so much the definiteness of the atonement but rather the guarantee of their perseverance. However, the passage is not really intended to address the issue of the believer's true internal regeneration and cleansing by the atoning redemptive work of Christ.

[6]They are awaiting the parousia of "the Lord" (Jas 5:7), that Lord being Jesus (Jas 2:1).

[7]Colossians 1:5.

ily be using the phrase in exactly the same way as Paul, it is clear that
James attributes to this word, not just creative but also saving power
(Jas 1:21). It is also worth noting that the setting aside of believers as
"firstfruits" (Jas 1:18) is an action that Revelation 14:4 specifically refers
to as a redemption: "they have been redeemed from humankind as
first fruits for God and the Lamb" (NRSV). This redeeming is attributed
in Revelation 5:9 to the blood of the lamb. James is therefore not in any
way divergent from Christian doctrine of redemption and may be presumed to have known of it.

1 Peter

First Peter is dense with allusions to, and applications of, the atonement
wrought by Jesus Christ. In fact, there are few books in the New Testament that are more intensely concerned with the atonement than 1 Peter.
Yet the comments in this letter on the redemptive work of Christ in his
suffering and death all take place in the context of ethical discussions
about the behavior of servants, or the Christian response to undeserved
suffering, or general exhortations regarding the Christian life. It is because the atonement has practical force in the believer's life that 1 Peter
returns to this matter so frequently. The matter is summarized in 1 Peter
4:1-2: Since Christ has suffered and dealt with sin, so the believer in suffering must have done with sin.[8] The key to the Christian life and to dealing with the problem of suffering is covenant identification with Christ.

To accomplish the goal of helping the believer identify with the
Lord, 1 Peter develops at least five different types of metaphor or imagery to depict and elaborate on the atoning work of Christ, a work
that both makes that identification possible and real, and motivates the
believer to live accordingly. These are:

1. Servant imagery, especially the notion of representative or substitutionary obedience.

2. Cultic imagery, which uses the language of ritual cleansing, sacrifice
   and the sacrificial system of the OT.

3. Marketplace imagery, or the idea of purchasing or buying back out
   of hock and particularly the notion of purchase out of slavery.

---

[8]This is true whether one takes the "one who suffers" of the second half of 1 Peter 4:1 as the
believer or as another reference to Christ's suffering, since 1 Peter 4:2-3 certainly applies the
principle to believers.

4. Conflict resolution imagery, which speaks of reconciling of enemies or propitiating the anger of an offended party.

5. Military imagery, the notion of monomachy or representative single combat as warfare.

What links all of these is the idea of *substitution* or *representation*, where one party or thing stands in place of, or works on behalf of, another.

Servant imagery—representative obedience. The Servant image is the controlling metaphor.[9] The Servant of the Lord of Isaiah 40—55 is undoubtedly the source, not just of Peter's, but also of the early church's idea of Jesus' death as a representational substitution. The Servant Song has its culmination in Isaiah 53, which is both quoted and applied by 1 Peter 2:21-25 as that which explains the suffering and death of Christ on behalf of his people.[10] It is because Christ is the obedient Servant of the Lord that he fulfils the covenant obligations on behalf of his people and is qualified to suffer in place of others. We may see at least two principles at work in the application of Isaiah 53 here in 1 Peter 2: representation and example.

The principle of *representation* is operative in the phrase "Christ suffered *for* you" (ἔπαθεν ὑπὲρ ὑμῶν). That particular phrase of "suffering for" is rather unique to 1 Peter,[11] but the notion of Christ's death being on behalf of others is found throughout the New Testament.[12] But in what way is Christ's suffering "for you" (1 Pet 2:21)? Does it mean simply "for the benefit of" or does it include "as a substitute for"? The immediate context would certainly include the former; but the latter is made evident in 1 Peter 2:24: Christ "bore our sins in his body on the

---

[9]As John Murray pointed out in his little study on *Atonement* (International Library of Philosophy and Theology; Biblical and Theological Studies) ed. Marcellus J. Kik (Philadelphia: Presbyterian and Reformed, 1962), 12, Christ's obedience is the most basic and inclusive of the categories defining Christ's vicarious work. Murray's other categories are sacrifice, propitiation, reconciliation and redemption.

[10]Isaiah 53 is also quoted in connection with Christ in Matthew 8:17, Luke 22:37, Acts 8:32 and Revelation 14:5, and is alluded to in numerous places in the NT. It thus surely lies behind much of the earliest church's reflection on the meaning of the Messiah's death, though it remains rather undeveloped except for here in 1 Peter (cf. O. Cullmann, *Christology of the New Testament*, rev. ed. [Philadelphia: Westminster Press, 1963], chap. 3).

[11]1 Peter 2:21 and 3:18. Several manuscripts at both 2:21 and 3:18 read "died" instead of "suffered," probably because of the dominant influence of Paul's use of the former. See note 14.

[12]Luke 22:19-20; Romans 5:8; 8:32; 1 Corinthians 15:3; 2 Corinthians 5:20; Ephesians 5:2; 1 Thessalonians 5:10; Titus 2:14; Hebrews 9:24; 1 John 3:16.

tree." Especially given its roots in Isaiah 53,[13] this clearly means he endured the appropriate punishment for those sins in place of us. In 1 Peter 3:18 the notion of substitution is also clear: "The Christ suffered
once for (περί, "concerning") sins, the righteous one *for* (ὑπέρ, "on behalf of") the unrighteous ones, in order that he might bring you to
God" (author's translation). Bringing unrighteous people (i.e., those
who deserved suffering) to God first required the righteous bringer to
suffer in their stead.

The second principle of servant imagery is that of *example*. Christ is
not just an example, though; he is a representing example. Here we
have not just the notion of imitating on the part of the followers but
also the notion of leading on the part of the exemplar.[14] It was as a forerunner, as the one to blaze the trail, the one who laid down the footsteps to be followed (1 Pet 2:21), that Christ serves as an example.[15] But
of course the point here is that believers are to *follow* Christ. Following
is the term for discipleship. The purpose of the vicarious suffering of
Christ was not just so believers could be free of condemnation, but so
they could become connected to Christ and conformed to his likeness.[16] We see this particularly in the application part of 1 Peter 2:24.
The purpose of the substitutionary carrying of sins was "so that we
might live to righteousness, having put away sins." As Christ was an
obedient servant on behalf of Christians, Christians are to be obedient
servants as his followers. Thus are believers rightly called "children of
obedience" (1 Pet 1:14).

The reference to Isaiah 53 in chapter 2 comes in the context of an exhortation to slaves to endure unjust suffering, which is something a
slave is faced with constantly. Peter makes a special point of referring to
Isaiah 53:5, "With his stripes we are healed." Stripes would have been
intimately familiar to slaves. Few people today could claim to have experienced as much unjust suffering as slaves frequently did, but there
is still plenty of injustice around, and Peter's application of the example

---

[13]I think it not unlikely that Isaiah 53:4-6 is itself building upon the figure of the Levitical goat
for Azazel or "scapegoat" that made atonement by symbolically carrying the sins of the
people into the wilderness (Lev 16:21-22).
[14]Altogether absent is the Grotian idea of Christ's death being an "example" to show the
world what a terrible thing sin is, sometimes termed the "governmental" view of atonement.
[15]Cf. Hebrews 6:20.
[16]Cf. Romans 8:29.

of Christ's suffering is still relevant. The suffering of injustice is opportunity for the Christian to identify with the Christ's suffering in reality, not just in theory.[17] The calling of God is to suffer the way Christ did—without reviling—and to live the way he did—without sin.

Both representation and example are operative in the exhortation to trust. Christ "entrusted himself to him who judges justly" (1 Pet 2:23). In the context of not reviling or threatening while being unjustly abused, this must refer to his eschatological trust. He knew he would be vindicated by God in the future. As this eschatological trust is presented as part of his representative activity, it becomes clear that even the requirement of trust is something in which Jesus acts as vicarious forerunner as well as example. Not that he trusted and therefore we do not need to, but he trusted and therefore we trust. This is explicitly applied in 1 Peter 4:19—"so then, those who suffer according to God's will should commit themselves to their faithful creator and continue to do good."

In my judgment, the connection between Christ as representative sufferer (he suffers in our place) and Christ as exemplary sufferer (we suffer like him) provides the best way to approach the problem of 1 Peter 4:1: "Since therefore Christ suffered in flesh, arm yourselves with the same thought, for whoever has suffered in the flesh has ceased from sin" (RSV). The text at first sounds strange. It hardly seems right to say that everyone who has suffered has stopped sinning. Hence, many exegetes follow the lead of A. Strobel in arguing that "the one who has suffered" in the second half of the verse is also a reference to Christ, understanding "has ceased from sin" not as "has stopped sinning" but "has finished with sin," that is, put an end to it.[18] But this is an oddly redundant way of reading the verse, since it doubles the opening clause, "Christ suffered in the flesh." More importantly, the context rather expects a preparation for the exhortation of 4:2-4 not to live any longer by human passions but by the will of God. Moreover, the word παύομαι with genitive, which ordinarily means "cease from,"

---

[17]Although the word *Christ* in 1 Peter 2:21 does not have an article, for a Jew like Peter the term would retain its character as a title rather than simply be a proper name. Hence Peter's comment: "because even the Messiah suffered on your behalf" serves to awaken the reader to the fact that even the most favored chosen one of God had to endure unjust suffering.

[18]A. Strobel, "Macht Leiden von Sunde frei? Zur Problematik von 1 Petr, 4:1f.", TZ 19 (1963): 412-25.

is difficult to push toward the semantic value of "finished with," a
meaning for which the lexical evidence is sparse and ambiguous.

The verse is much better taken as expounding on how Christ's suffering entails the suffering of those whom he represents,[19] and how
that actual suffering functions in the believer's life. Christ's representation calls forth a "re-presentation" by believers. The point of the
verse, then, is not that the believers' own suffering redeems them from
their sins or of itself enables them to stop sinning, but that those who
suffer *in Christ* are partaking in the suffering *of* Christ.[20] This *in-Christ*
suffering actually does ultimately result in the cessation of their sinning, and indeed, this cessation from sin should already be a reality according to 1 Peter 4:2-4.[21] The atonement, which Christ brings, is not
simply passively received but actively realized.

One other passage in 1 Peter also shows this kind of obedient representation at work. In 1 Peter 2:4 Christ is identified as a living stone rejected by men but chosen and precious to God, picking up on passages
from Psalm 118, Isaiah 8 and Isaiah 28, as the quotations in 1 Peter 2:6-8
make clear. First Peter 2:5 refers to the believers as living stones. Again,
as Christ is *the* chosen stone who is honored (ἔντιμον), believers are chosen stones who receive honor (τιμή), according to 1 Peter 2:7.[22]

Cultic imagery—sacrifice. The second category of atonement im-

---

[19]H. Millauer, *Leiden als Gnade: Ein traditionsgeschichtliche Untersuchung zur Leidenstheologie des
erste Petrusbriefes* (Bern: Lang, 1976), 32-53. Another possible exegesis is to take "the one
who has suffered" of 4:1b as referring to the Christian who has died, but then the clause has
little relevance to the exhortation of the context.
[20]Cf. 1 Peter 4:13.
[21]1 Peter regularly refers to Christ's *suffering* where Paul would refer to Christ's *death*. Compare 1 Peter 2:21, and 3:18 with Romans 5:6-8. 1 Peter 4:1 may then be seen as analogous to
Romans 6:10-11:

The death he died he died to sin, once for all, but the life he lives he lives to God. So
you also must consider yourselves dead to sin and alive to God in Christ Jesus. Let not
sin therefore reign in your mortal bodies, to make you obey their passions. (Rom 6:10-
11 RSV)

Since therefore Christ suffered in the flesh, arm yourselves with the same thought, for
whoever has suffered in the flesh has ceased from sin, so as to live for the rest of the
time in the flesh no longer by human passions but by the will of God. (1 Pet 4:1-2 RSV)

[22]Although almost all translations render 1 Peter 2:7 making "honor" refer to Christ ("to you
who believe [he] is honored"), almost all commentaries recognize that the noun "honor"
must be here applied to "you who believe" (i.e., "to you who believe, there is honor"). Cf.
P. Achtemeier, *1 Peter: A Commentary on First Peter*, Hermeneia (Minneapolis: Fortress, 1996),
160-61.

agery active in 1 Peter is cultic. Christ is presented as accomplishing that which sacrifices accomplished, and his death is described in cultic terms in three places in 1 Peter: 1:2; 1:19; and 2:5. The first of these emphasizes the *covenantal* character of Jesus' sacrifice. In the context of his trinitarian opening greeting[23] Peter already introduces this cultic imagery when he refers to his hearers as chosen for obedience and "sprinkling" of Christ's blood. This is clearly an allusion to the covenant-satisfactory sacrifice, and the people's pledge to obedience implied thereby, described in Exodus 24:4-8.[24] There Moses builds an altar with twelve pillars to represent the whole of Israel, sacrifices are made, half the blood is sprinkled on the altar, the people pledge obedience, and then the other half of the blood is sprinkled on the people, whereupon Moses declares: "Behold the blood of the covenant which the Lord has made with you" (Ex 24:8 RSV). "Chosen for obedience and sprinkling" therefore introduces forcefully the notion that Peter's hearers are the people of the covenant ratified, not by animal blood, but by Jesus' blood. His blood, that is, his death, is efficacious in making people the people of the covenant.

1 Peter 1:19 occurs in the context of a "marketplace" image of the atonement (see below), but is clearly alluding to cultic sacrifice as well, combining the notions of redemption as an economic transaction with the notion of a prophylactic sacrifice that "guards" or covers and protects. It has been observed that 1 Peter makes many allusions to Passover and the exodus,[25] and this is clearly one such allusion. Exodus 12:5-7 requires a lamb without blemish whose blood is smeared on the doorframes as a guard against the destroying angel. Peter's point would seem to be that the redemptive death of Christ protects and marks the people of God.[26]

---

[23]The opening identifies the readers as chosen, according to the foreknowledge of God the Father, by the sanctification of the Spirit, and unto obedience and sprinkling of the blood of Jesus Christ.

[24]Some commentators, in their enthusiasm for seeing baptismal allusions in 1 Peter, find one here too, but this is not a sprinkling with water but with blood. In the one place in 1 Peter where baptism is actually mentioned (1 Pet 3:21), it is the antitype, not of blood-sprinkling, but of water-deluge.

[25]E.g., Paul Deterding, "Exodus Motifs in First Peter," *Concordia Journal* 7:2 (1981): 58-65.

[26]The reference to the spotless lamb's blood is seen by some also to have affinity with the cultus described in Numbers 28—29, where the lamb's blood is a means of maintaining Israel's relationship with a holy God. If this is in view in 1 Peter, it suggests that the blood of Christ serves not only to initiate the relationship but also to maintain the relationship of the Christian with God. The context in 1 Peter 1:18-19, however, seems more focused on the initiatory redemption than on the continuing cultic cleansing.

The third cultic aspect of the atonement is hinted at in 1 Peter 2:5. Through Jesus Christ, believers are like "living stones, being built as a spiritual house to be a holy priesthood, offering spiritual sacrifices acceptable to God." Though only implicit, the words "through Jesus Christ" and the move from unique stone of 1 Peter 2:4 to stones of 1 Peter 2:5 once again show the inherent connection between the atoning work of Christ and the work of the ones atoned for, this time with reference to their activities of worship and intercession. It is because Jesus offered an acceptable sacrifice that his people now can and must do so. But this image, so prominent in Hebrews, is here left undeveloped.

Cultic redemption also involves cultic cleansing or washing. Cleansing is mentioned briefly in 1 Peter 3:21, where baptism is described not as a putting off of filth from flesh, but as a pledge[27] of good conscience toward God through Christ's resurrection. The atoning work of Christ as a cleansing presumably lies behind this, but is undeveloped in 1 Peter.

Marketplace imagery—redemption. 1 Peter 1:18-19 declares that believers were *ransomed* (ἐλυτρώθητε, "redeemed"), not with corruptible things, silver and gold, but with the precious blood of Christ. The depiction of God's rescue of his people in the language of an economic transaction, namely ransom or redemption, is very common in both Old and New Testaments.[28] It is beyond the scope of this article to explore this extensive background, but the specific background of 1 Peter 1:18-19 is clearly Isaiah 52:3: "This is what the LORD says: 'You were sold for nothing, and without money you shall be redeemed.'" The redemption price is spelled out in the following chapter of Isaiah—the suffering of the Lord's Servant.

The primary notion is one of retrieval from bondage. Israel in Egypt was in bondage, and the Lord ransomed them.[29] Although a transaction may be difficult to see here, the Hebrew word for "ransom" is in

---

[27]The Greek word for pledge, ἐπερώτημα, is rare, occurring just once in the NT (here) and once in the Greek OT (Dan 4:17). Its meaning in older Greek ("petition") does not seem to work well here; in later Hellenistic Greek it appears to be semantically close to the Latin *stipulatio* which means "covenant" (G. C. Richards, "I Pet. iii.21," *JTS* 32 [1931]: 77). If this notion was implicit in the Greek word, the meaning here would be that baptism is a "covenanting" of a good conscience, the basis for the ethical *having* a good conscience in 1 Peter 3:16. For a thorough discussion of the phrase's difficulties, see Achtemeier, *1 Peter*, 270-72.

[28]E.g., Exodus 6:6.

[29]Deuteronomy 7:8. The LXX consistently, though not exclusively, uses λυτρόω and cognates to translate the Hebrew גאל.

fact the word used where transactions are involved, as when a kinsman "redeems" the land on behalf of his destitute relative.[30] The bondage in view here in 1 Peter is thralldom to futile ancestral traditions.[31] By designating Christ's precious blood as the means of redemption, the author shows just how radical the redemption price was,[32] and thus how radical the departure from former servitude should be. Atonement involves not just being brought to God but also being brought out of an old way of life.

Conflict resolution imagery—reconciliation. The fourth category of atonement imagery is its depiction as the reconciling of enemies or resolution of conflict. Though Peter does not use the vocabulary of reconciliation per se (καταλλαγή and cognates), there is in 1 Peter 3:18, nonetheless, an implicit assumption of the need for, and accomplishment of, reconciliation. The purpose of Jesus' suffering for sins, righteous for unrighteous, was to "bring you to God." We may infer from this that sinners could not be brought to God without such vicarious suffering. Presumably the prepositional phrase "for sins" that defines the focus of the sufferings explains why such substitutionary suffering is requisite. 1 Peter is written in a milieu that well understands that sin causes a breaking of fellowship with God and must be dealt with before restoration is possible.

The notion of reconciliation is also under the surface of 1 Peter 2:10. First Peter is almost certainly written to Gentiles, who were once "no people" but now have become the people of God, who had once been shown no mercy but now have received mercy. A former enmity has been turned to friendship.

Military imagery—monomachy. In the early church, one of the more popular understandings of the atonement was that of a "victory over Satan," which Christ accomplished by the cross and resurrection.

---

[30]Leviticus 25:25.

[31]1 Peter 1:18: τῆς ματαίας ὑμῶν ἀναστροφῆς πατροπαραδότου. The reference is to the empty rituals of (pagan) religion that the recipients received from their ancestors and that they had slavishly followed until they believed in Christ. Cf. W. C. van Unnik, "The Critique of Paganism in I Peter 1:28" in E. E. Ellis and M. Wilcox, eds., *Neotestamentica et Semitica; Studies in Honor of Matthew Black* (Edinburgh: T & T Clark, 1969), 132, 137.

[32]"Precious blood" is in the instrumental (dative) case rather than in the genitive that ordinarily is used to indicate price (cf. 1 Cor 6:20). The focus is not so much on a particular quantitative value or kind of coin used for the redemption but on the fact that the redeeming of one life requires another.

The church later rightly saw the notion of propitiatory dealing with the wrath of God as more basic, but it ought not to have neglected the fact that Christ's death was indeed a victory over Satan. Though 1 Peter 3:19-22 is a heavily debated passage, most commentators now see it as reflecting the victory aspect of Christ's death and resurrection.[33] Even if this is not the case, 1 Peter 3:22 at least depicts the exaltation of Christ as somehow related to the rescue of his baptized people (1 Pet 3:21), especially when taken with the following verse, 1 Peter 4:1, which uses military imagery.[34] Just as the battle between Philistines and Israel was on one occasion decided by a representative combat (Goliath and David), so the defeat of the powers of 1 Peter 3:22 is decisive for those whom Christ so represents. Furthermore, as we have seen with regard to the other types of atonement imagery, the representative activity of Christ in spiritual warfare is exemplary and thus entails the active warriorship of those he represents. As already noted, both 1 Peter 1:13 and 1 Peter 4:1 exhort believers in the language of a warrior preparing for battle.

Summary

Several NT images for the meaning of Christ's death are thus presented in 1 Peter. In each case, the atoning work of Christ is applied to the believer's life because the believer is by virtue of that work covenantally identified with the Suffering Servant. Because of that identification, Christ's representative acts not only deal with the sin of those who are so identified but also provide a pattern or template for the believer. As Christ was an obedient servant, so must his people be. As

---

[33]The difficulty of the passage has given birth to several different interpretations, but only two are viable in my judgment: the view that the "preaching" referred to is Christ's preincarnate spirit proclaiming the coming judgment through the lips of Noah (the view of Augustine of Hippo, recently defended by John Feinberg, "1 Peter 3:18-20, Ancient Mythology, and the Intermediate State," *WTJ* 48 [1986]: 303-36), and the view that the "preaching" is not an offer of salvation but the declaration of doom that Christ declared to the "spirits in prison," i.e., evil spirits, as an aspect of his death and resurrection envisaged in 1 Peter 3:18 (see esp. W. J. Dalton, *Christ's Proclamation to the Spirits: A Study of 1 Peter 3:18—4:6*, 2nd ed. [Rome: Pontifical Biblical Institute, 1989]). Though L. Goppelt, *Der Erste Petrusbrief* (Göttingen: Vandenhoeck & Ruprecht, 1978); J. Alsup, *A Commentary on 1 Peter* (Grand Rapids: Eerdmans, 1993), and a few others have tried to resuscitate the old *descensus ad inferos* reading of the passage (Christ descended to hell to preach the gospel to those who died without faith in him), their exegesis is not convincing, and it is difficult to relate such a meaning to the context in 1 Peter.

[34]"*Arm* yourselves also with the same attitude"; cf. 1 Peter 1:13, "gird up your mental loins."

Christ did not retaliate, so his people must not. As Christ by suffering did away with sin, so his suffering people are done with sin. As Christ was a precious stone, so his people are stones honored by God. As Christ offered the truly acceptable sacrifice, so his people offer spiritual sacrifices acceptable to God.

Christ's suffering, the righteous for the unrighteous, enacted a unique covenantal union between him and his people, enabling him to bring them to God and delivering them from bondage. That suffering now sets a pattern and utters a call to a similar obedient suffering that must apply to his people, who now too are righteous by virtue of that union.

atonement in the apocalypse of john

"A Lamb Standing As If Slain"

Charles E. Hill

In the Johannine gospel, the Baptist heralds the coming of Jesus with the words, "Look, the Lamb of God, who takes away the sin of the world" (Jn 1:29, 36). In the Johannine apocalypse, the imagery of Jesus as the sacrificial Lamb not only becomes a leading aspect of its portrayal of Jesus but also plays a dominant role in the book as a whole. As we open the book of Revelation, we find a rich tapestry of conceptions and images taken both from the Old Testament and from the New that teach us about Christ's atoning work. We find many of the theological truths familiar from other portions of Scripture and expounded elsewhere in this volume pictured in John's visions, explained in angelic interpretations, sung in the praises of heavenly choirs, and contemplated in John's own reflections on the revelations he received. Despite the variety of these modes of expression, it is significant that the prevailing context or framework for the atonement theology of Revelation is doxology; that is, it occurs in expressions of praise to Christ.

Revelation 1:5-6: Liberation Through Jesus' Blood
Though the central motif and vehicle for atonement theology in Revelation is the image of the slain Lamb, atonement language in Revelation precedes the appearance of the Lamb in the visions. Already in the fifth verse of the book, John addresses a doxology "To him who loves

us and has freed (λύσαντι)[1] us from our sins by (ἐν) his blood, and made us to be a kingdom and priests to serve his God and Father" (Rev 1:5-6). In terms of the literary process reflected in the book, this doxology in the book's prologue was written *after* John had received the visions he later describes, particularly the initial vision of the Lamb in the heavenly throne room in Revelation 5. The doxology of Revelation 1:5-6 thus has a kind of summarizing quality when seen in the light of the revelations in the remainder of the book and may be regarded as a product of John's own reflection on those revelations.[2] From the point of view of the reader, however, this is the first thing he or she encounters of the atonement language in the book. What John says here, therefore, becomes foundational for understanding the teaching of the rest of the book.

To him who loves us (Rev 1:5). The verb "loves" is paired with the next verb, "freed" in such a way that the first may be seen as the basis for the second. Texts such as John 3:16, 1 John 4:10 and Ephesians 2:4 speak of *God's* love as his motive for sending his Son to die for us. Here the love of *Christ himself* for his people is named as his own motive, much as in Paul's personalizing statement in Galatians 2:20, "the Son of God, who loved me and gave himself for me," and in his analogy in Ephesians 5:25, "Husbands, love your wives, just as Christ loved the church and gave himself up for her." It is his love for us that led Jesus Christ to shed his own blood to free us from our sins. As Jesus himself said, "I lay down my life for the sheep . . . I lay it down of my own accord" (Jn 10:15-18). It is significant that here in Revelation 1:5 John uses the present tense, "loves."[3] Christ's love for us is exemplified in, but not exhausted by, his shedding of his blood for us.[4]

And has freed us from our sins by his blood (Rev 1:5). John's doxology connects the blood/death of Jesus directly with the severing of the

---

[1]The variant λούσαντι, "to him who washed," probably arose from the similarity of the sounds. It would cohere well with Revelation 7:14, etc., but λύσαντι has by far the better textual support and fits the Exodus symbolism of the next verse better.

[2]This offers a different perspective than the one taken by Elisabeth Schüssler Fiorenza, *The Book of Revelation: Justice and Judgment*, 2nd ed. (Minneapolis: Fortress, 1998), 68-81, who believes that in Revelation 1:5-6 John merely repeats a traditional baptismal formula, which he then deliberately modifies in a decidedly sociopolitical direction in Revelation 5:9-10.

[3]Simon J. Kistemaker, *Exposition of the Book of Revelation*, NTC (Grand Rapids: Baker, 2001), 84.

[4]"This love encompasses the act of redemption, but is not limited to it alone," Pierre Prigent, *Commentary on the Apocalypse of St. John*, trans. Wendy Pradels (Tübingen: Mohr Siebeck, 2001), 119.

hold that our *sins* have over us. This declaration, the product of John's contemplation of his visions, assures us that the purchase mentioned in similar terms in Revelation 5:9-10 does indeed have to do with sin and is not chiefly a sociopolitical liberation. This liberation from our sins is obviously of crucial importance, though John does not specify in precisely what sense Christ's blood frees us from them. Is it by expiation or by propitiation? Or does it invoke a metaphorical conception of bondage to "sin" from which Christ's death redeems us? Or is some other conception in mind? Already the exodus associations of Revelation 1:6 seem to favor the idea of "redemption" or deliverance from bondage.[5] Redemption from sin as slavery may have roots in Jesus' teaching in John's gospel, where he says to his antagonists, "I tell you the truth, everyone who sins is a slave to sin" (Jn 8:34-36).[6] We know the idea also from Romans 6:16-23, which also speaks of being enslaved to sin; from Titus 2:14, which speaks of redemption from iniquity; and from 1 Peter 1:18-19, which mentions redemption from the futile ways inherited from pagan forebears. All of these use the image of sin as slavery or as a slaveholder from which the sinner must be freed, and all find the basis for that liberation in the death of Jesus.[7]

On the other hand, in Revelation, this idea of sin as bondage is probably combined with that of sin as a "debt" owed to God. Sin may be conceived of as a charge taken out against God's holiness or justice, each of our misdeeds placing us further and further in God's debt. The debt must be repaid or the "borrower" will be "paid back" with judgment. The idea is close to that of propitiation in that it conceives of God, or his justice, as the offended party who must be compensated. Yet it is not the "cultic" language of propitiation but financial language that is employed. We get this explicitly in texts such as Revelation 5:9; 14:3-4 (to be considered below) and from a glimpse at what it means *not* to be loosed from one's sins, as with Babylon, whose sins "are piled up to heaven, and God has remembered her crimes" (Rev 18:5). The pronouncement against her is to "give back to her as she has given; pay her back double for what she has done. Mix her a double portion from her own cup" (Rev 18:6). This conception is found elsewhere in Reve-

---

[5]Cf. Exodus 19:6.
[6]On the connection of this verse to its context, see F. F. Bruce, *The Gospel of John: Introduction, Exposition and Notes* (Grand Rapids: Eerdmans, 1983), 197-98.
[7]First Peter 1:18-19 also speaks of him as a spotless lamb.

lation, where judgment is couched in terms of repayment for one's unrighteous works: "and I will repay each of you according to your deeds" (Rev 2:23); "Behold, I am coming soon! My reward is with me, and I will give to everyone according to what he has done" (Rev 22:12). It has a strong background both in the Old[8] and in the New Testament.[9] The idea of sin as debt is fixed in Christian devotion and liturgy in the Lord's Prayer in Matthew 6:12, "Forgive us our debts, as we forgive our debtors." Whereas sin as bondage has more to do with the brute power of sin to hold us in its thrall, sin as debt brings constantly to mind that we owe God our lives and our obedience and that our accounts must eventually be settled with him.

We have suggested that sin as bondage is the dominant idea in Revelation 1:5, and yet sin as debt, which we see elsewhere in Revelation, may be involved here as well. How are they combined? Isaiah 40:2 in the Septuagint offers a close parallel to the language John uses and may in fact play a role in his thought.[10] Here the words used for sin and release are the same as in Revelation 1:5: "Speak tenderly to Jerusalem, and proclaim to her that her hard service has been completed, that her sin has been paid for (λέλυται αὐτῆς ἡ ἁμαρτία),[11] that she has received (ἐδέξατο) from the LORD's hand double for all her sins."[12] We have already seen the same idea in Revelation, except that there it is not Jerusalem but her adversary, Babylon, who is paid back double for her sins![13] Isaiah 40:2 combines the notion of Israel's corporate sin as a debt that has to be paid off and sin as "hard service," here the service of captivity. It is helpful to note that selling one's debtors into slavery[14] or handing them over to imprisonment[15] were both known and accepted means of dealing with debtors who could not pay. God had in fact de-

---

[8]E.g., Psalms 49:7-9, 15; 62:12; Proverbs 24:12; Isaiah 40:10; 62:11; Jeremiah 16:18; 17:10.
[9]Matthew 16:27; 18:21-35; Romans 2:6; Colossians 3:25; 2 Thessalonians 1:5-10.
[10]Pace, Büchsel, "λύω, κτλ," *TDNT* 4:328-56, esp. 336 n. 8. Though ἁμαρτία is the object of the verb λύω in Isaiah 40:2, the words are the same, and the conception too is the same, though viewed from a different angle. See also Psalm 129 (Engl. 130):8, which uses the related verb λυτρόω and speaks of God redeeming Israel from (ἐκ) all her iniquities.
[11]The KJV, ASV and RSV translate "her iniquity is pardoned." This is certainly lexically legitimate, but the next phrase makes it plain that λέλυται cannot mean "pardoned" but must mean "paid for."
[12]Cf. Jeremiah 16:18.
[13]Revelation 18:6, whose repayment is with fire, Revelation 18:8.
[14]Leviticus 25:47; 2 Kings. 4:1; Matthew 18:25.
[15]Matthew 18:30, 34.

livered Israel into captivity in Babylon for her sins. In this OT typical enactment of redemption, corporate Israel was taken into captivity until the Lord had exacted from her a double retribution. In the NT antitypical reality, no longer is the captivity a national, literal one in Babylon or Egypt. When Jesus told his antagonists that the Son could set them free (Jn 8:32, 36), they did not at first understand that he was talking about enslavement to sin (Jn 8:34). The assumption in Revelation and elsewhere is that all sinners are, as Paul says, "sold [πεπραμένος] under sin," (Rom 7:14),[16] and their debt cannot be satisfied by serving a sentence in captivity; rather, their temporary bondage to sin leads ultimately only to death.[17] Nor is redemption achieved through an arbitrary cancellation of the debt: a price was paid.[18] In Revelation 1:5 John tells us what that price was when he offers praise "to him who loves us and has freed us from our sins by his blood." Jesus alone, by the price of his blood, has rendered to God the acceptable payment which has liberated us from our bondage to sin and death.[19]

And made us to be a kingdom and priests to serve his God and Father (Rev 1:6). This great blessing of honor and privilege before God is also credited to the blood of Jesus. Here again it is evident that John is repeating what he had heard the heavenly voices proclaim in Revelation 5:10. This means that John's "us" here is an application of what was said there to be a host from every tribe, language, people and nation. These Asian Christians—and we no less today—drawn from Jewish and Gentile stock, a collection of diverse people, are the object of his redeeming work and are elevated to the dignity of priesthood and members of God's kingdom. The background for this is God's proclamation at Sinai in Exodus 19:5-6, and like many other NT texts,[20] these two in Revelation[21] display the early Christian conception of the church as the new or true Israel, defined, not by race, but by the faith of Abraham.[22]

---

[16]Cf. Rom 1:24, where God gave people over (παρέδωκεν) to the lust of their hearts; Ephesians 4:19.
[17]See Romans 6:20-21, 23.
[18]1 Corinthians 6:19-20; 7:23.
[19]By the same token, he is also God's agent who will recompense with judgment those sinners who do not have him as their representative debt-payer (Rev 2:23; 22:12).
[20]E.g., 1 Peter 2:9.
[21]Revelation 1:6, 5:10.
[22]Galatians 3:6-7, 29.

Notions of kingdom and priesthood with respect to believers abound throughout the book, and these must always be seen in the light of the work Christ has accomplished for them. Believers are now participants in Christ's kingdom, and they now possess priestly honor, even before Christ's return, both in their present lives[23] and in their lives in heaven;[24] and when he comes, they will reign with him for eternity.[25] All this is only because Christ, who is now reigning,[26] has won for them these privileges by his blood.

Revelation 5:6-14 (14:3, 4): Behold the Lamb
Thus, John's doxology in Revelation 1:5-6 helps prepare the reader for the striking introduction of the image of the Lamb in Revelation 5. In a vision of the heavenly throne room, we find the prophet weeping because a scroll sealed with seven seals lay unopened in God's right hand, for there was no one in heaven or on earth or under the earth worthy to open it or look inside it. Then he is told by one of the heavenly elders, "Do not weep. See, the Lion of the tribe of Judah, the Root of David, has triumphed. He is able to open the scroll and its seven seals" (Rev 5:5). Immediately, John saw a Lamb, "looking as if it had been slain, standing in the center of the throne" (Rev 5:6). This Lamb came and "took the scroll from the right hand of him who sat on the throne," causing the attendants in the heavenly court to fall down before the Lamb and to sing to him a song of praise:

> You are worthy to take the scroll
> > and to open its seals,
> because you were slain,
> > and with your blood you purchased men for God
> > from every tribe and language and people and nation.
> You have made them to be a kingdom and priests to serve our God,
> > and they will reign on the earth. (Rev 5:9-10)

There are many points about this portion of the vision that draw our attention.

---

[23]Revelation 1:6, 9; 8:4.
[24]Revelation 3:5, 21; 7:15; 20:4-6. See C. E. Hill, *Regnum Caelorum: Patterns of Millennial Thought in Early Christianity*, 2nd ed. (Grand Rapids/Cambridge: Eerdmans, 2001), 220-42.
[25]Revelation 5:10; 22:5.
[26]Revelation 1:5; 2:27; 3:21; 12.10, etc.

A Lamb, looking as though it had been slain (Rev 5:6). First is the paradoxical juxtaposition in Revelation 5:5-6 of the Lion of the tribe of Judah, and the Lamb of God.[27] After being told about the triumphant Lion,[28] the Root of David,[29] it must have been a shock for John to look and see a Lamb, looking as though slain! From here to the end of the book, the Lamb becomes the predominant title for Christ, used a total of twenty-eight times. Because the Lamb is presented as having all heavenly power and authority to judge,[30] the Lamb figure in Revelation is often said to be a symbol denoting military strength, triumph and judgment.[31] Examples of such a conception have been hard sought in Jewish apocalyptic literature, but the results have really been quite meager.[32] And even if the background in Jewish apocalyptic thought for a "conquering militaristic lamb" (or ram) were stronger, this would still not fit the character of Revelation very well. Even the word John uses for Lamb, ἀρνίον, has been interpreted in this light, for it is a different word from that found on the Baptist's lips in John 1:29, 36 (ἀμνός).[33] The word used by John the Baptist may well have been based

---

[27]David E. Aune, *Revelation 1—5*, WBC 52A (Dallas, Tex.: Word, 1997), 1:373: "The striking contrast between the two images suggests the contrast between the type of warrior messiah expected by first-century Judaism and the earthly ministry of Jesus as a suffering servant of God (see Matt 11:2-6 = Luke 7:18-23)."

[28]Genesis 49:9.

[29]Isaiah 11:1-5.

[30]See Revelation 6:16-17; 17:14.

[31]E. g., N. Hillyer, "'The Lamb' in the Apocalypse," *EQ* 39 (1967): 228-36. "The Lamb of Revelation, however, is not a figure of weakness . . . The Lamb is indeed the Lion of the tribe of Judah" (229, 231).

[32] C. K. Barrett, *The Gospel according to St. John: An Introduction with Commentary and Notes on the Greek Text*, 2nd ed. (Philadelphia: Westminster John Knox, 1978), 176, commenting on their relevance to John 1:29, 34, says they are "very shaky." As Aune (*Revelation*, 1:368) says, "there is only a single disputed instance in which the figure of the lamb is used of the Messiah in early Jewish literature (*T. Jos.* 9:3 . . .)." And later (369), Aune says that the title "Lamb of God" in T. Jos. 19:6 and T. Benj. 3:8, is probably a Christian interpolation based on John. In the so-called Animal Apocalypse in *1 Enoch* 85-90, the patriarch Jacob is represented as a white sheep "who in turn sires twelve sheep. . . . God is frequently called 'the Lord of the sheep' (ὁ κύριος τῶν προβάτων; 89:16, 22, 26, 29, etc.)" (369-70). The Lord delivers his sheep from the wolves (Egyptians) and finally brings kings, Saul and David, in the form of sheep who become rams (κρίοι). It is the Lord himself who will deliver his sheep, finally giving them a sword with which they scare off the other animals (90:19). The speaking lambs in Egyptian lore, referred to by Aune (370) seem quite unrelated.

[33]Hillyer, "Lamb," 229. See also Aune, *Revelation*, 368. Some have also argued for the translation "ram," as befitting its "wrath (Rev 6:16ff.), warfare and triumph (Rev 17:14)," though, according to J. Jeremias, "ἀμνός, ἀρήν, ἀρνίον," *TDNT*, 1:338-41, there are no good philological grounds for doing so (341).

on the LXX of Isaiah 53:7:[34] "like a sheep [πρόβατον] he was led to slaughter and like a lamb [ἀμνός] mute before its shearer, so he did not open his mouth" (author's translation).[35] Not only is ἀμνός used in Isaiah 53:7, but it is also the term used for the Passover lamb as well as for the lamb offered in the daily sacrifices and the sacrifices connected with the feasts (in all, about a hundred times in the OT). The Baptist's proclamations about the ἀμνός of God in John 1:29, 36 are certainly drawing on these aspects of Israel's ritual, yet all twenty-eight references to the Lamb and the one reference to his counterfeit (Rev 13:11) in Revelation, use the term ἀρνίον instead of ἀμνός. Norman Hillyer proposed that this was because ἀρνίον would "include the idea of authority and triumph" on the basis of "the horned Messianic, triumphant lamb of the intertestamental literature," that is, of 1 *Enoch* 89 and 90.[36] But the word in *Enoch* is ἄρνας, of which ἀρνίον is the diminutive.[37] Though many deny that the diminutive form has any real diminutive force, the change in form makes it harder to identify the figure with 1 *Enoch*. On the other hand, the diminutive form would be appropriate for laying the emphasis on the Lamb's smallness, apparent weakness and lack of power.

While there does not seem to be any theological point in John's choice of ἀρνίον instead of ἀμνός in Revelation, it seems to indicate a background in Jeremiah 11:19, "I had been like a gentle lamb led to the slaughter." Though the context is somewhat different, this verse sounds like a close parallel to Isaiah 53:7 and may well have been associated with it in the minds of early Jewish believers. We know from Justin Martyr that these two "lamb" texts were explicitly associated with each other and interpreted christologically in the second century.[38] They were even related to Revelation 5:6 by Origen in his com-

---

[34]Peter Whale, "The Lamb of John: Some Myths about the Vocabulary of the Johannine Literature," *JBL* 106 (1987): 289-95.

[35]Cf. the NT uses of these verses in Acts 8:32 and 1 Peter 1:19.

[36]Hillyer, "Lamb," 229.

[37]Cf. also ἄρνας in Luke 10:3 (πρόβατα in Matt 10:16), where Jesus sends out his disciples as lambs in the midst of wolves (see also Ps. Sol. 8:28; 2 *Clem.* 5.2, 4). Here the word can hardly bear the suggestion of power (Jeremias, "ἀμνός, ἀρήν, ἀρνίον," 340.)

[38]Justin *Dialogue with Trypho* 72. Justin even charges that some Jews had cut Jeremiah 11:19 out of their copies of the Scriptures, "since from these words it is demonstrated that the Jews deliberated about the Christ himself, to crucify and put him to death, he himself is both declared to be led as a sheep to the slaughter, as was predicted by Isaiah, and is here represented as a harmless lamb."

ments on John 1:29.[39] In Jeremiah 11:19 the prophet is speaking osten-
sibly of his own situation (not of a Servant of the Lord, as in Isaiah),
and he uses a different Hebrew word for lamb כֶּבֶשׂ, which the LXX
renders with ἀρνίον. Jeremiah's tormenters are the men of Anathoth
who betrayed him and plotted behind his back to kill him. This experience of the prophet would be reminiscent of that of Jesus,[40] as is explicitly recognized by Justin. The prophet goes on to pray that the
Lord would execute his own vengeance on them: "But, O LORD Al-
mighty, you who judge righteously [LXX, κρίνων δίκαια] and test the
heart and the mind, let me see your vengeance upon them, for to you
I have committed my cause" (Jer 11:20). It is the Lord and not the
lamb (Jeremiah) himself who executes this vengeance,[41] so the figure
of the lamb itself carries no connotations of power or triumph in this
text. But perhaps because this text describes a righteous sufferer betrayed by his countrymen and led as a gentle lamb to the slaughter,
and because (unlike Is 53) the notion of the Lord's vengeance was
close at hand, the word used in this text commended itself to John.
Supporting this is the description of the Lord as the one who judges
righteously (κρίνων δίκαια) in Jeremiah 11:20, a theme that is prominent in Revelation. The wording of Jeremiah 11:20 is possibly echoed
in Revelation 16:7; 19:2 (ἀληθιναὶ καὶ δίκαιαι αἱ κρίσεις σου).[42] This
is also corroborated by the virtual repetition of Jeremiah 11:20 in 1 Peter 2:23 (τῷ κρίνοντι δικαίως), where it is in fact blended in with allusions to Isaiah 53:4, 9, 12. Thus, 1 Peter 2:23, Justin, and Origen
show the suitability of combining of Isaiah 53:6-7 and Jeremiah 11:19-
20 in early Christian reflection on Christ's sacrificial death. It is likely
that this exegetical tradition was known to John and is reflected in his
choice of the word ἀρνίον.

   To define the Lamb in Revelation with reference to an alleged militaristic lamb figure in Jewish apocalyptic, or even chiefly on the basis of
his subsequent acts of judgment in the book of Revelation, is to miss the
compelling paradox of the image, which throughout the OT has strong
associations, not with power, but with weakness,[43] even the weakness

---

[39]*Commentary on John* 6:35.
[40]Cf. John 1:11; 13:2, 11, 21; 19:11, etc.
[41]Jeremiah 11:22-23.
[42]Cf. Revelation 16:5; 19:11.
[43]E.g., Jeremiah 11:19.

of a sacrificial victim.[44] This is in the forefront in Revelation 5 by the introduction of the Lamb as slain[45] and by the reference here and elsewhere to his blood.[46] Yes, his subsequent acts will prove that he is awesomely powerful, but not only does the exercise of his power come as a result of his self-sacrificial suffering for his people, but he still executes these acts of justice, power and authority *as the Lamb slain.*[47] If a symbol of power were wanted, the more "fitting" Lion of the tribe of Judah lay close at hand, as is proved by Revelation 5:5. But strikingly, this title does not reappear in the book! The incongruity of the earth dwellers fearing the "wrath of the Lamb" (Rev 1:16) is what gives the image much of its power, and we lose something if it is obscured.

It was important for the Christians in Asia Minor, as a marginalized and often-persecuted group, to know that their Savior was King of kings and that he would one day return, his recompense with him. But it was just as important for them not to forget that the one who returns to judge is the same one who shed his blood to free them from their sins and to purchase them for God! The paradox remains. Here, and throughout the book, he is both victor and victim—and he is the former because he was first the latter.

Later in the book it will be by becoming like the Lamb of God himself, in allowing themselves to be "overcome" by the powers of this world, even unto death, that his followers too will overcome.[48] So the image of "the Lamb, looking as if it had been slain," retains its relevance and power for the ongoing life of the church in a hostile world.

---

[44] As Richard Bauckham well says, "The juxtaposition of the contrasting images of the Lion and the Lamb expresses John's Jewish Christian reinterpretation of current Jewish eschatological hopes" (*The Climax of Prophecy: Studies on the Book of Revelation* [Edinburgh: T & T Clark, 1993], 214). In fact, the uniqueness of Revelation among other so-called apocalyptic works is perhaps nowhere more graphically seen than in Jesus' role as Lamb of God. The two roughly contemporary Jewish apocalypses, *2 Baruch* and *4 Ezra* have messiahs, but they are strictly militaristic and do not serve any atoning function.

[45] Revelation 5:6; cf. 13:8.

[46] Revelation 5:9; 7:14; 12:11.

[47] As George Smeaton observed long ago, "Christ's official power is throughout [the book of Revelation] exhibited as a dominion based on the atonement. It is as the Lamb that He prevails to open the book, and to loose the seven seals thereof (Rev. v.-vii.). The perpetual allusion indeed to the Lamb has no other object in view than to show that He was invested with this dominion as the reward of His abasement, and that the cross is the foundation of His throne" (*The Doctrine of the Atonement According to the Apostles* [Peabody, Mass.: Hendrickson, 1988 repr. of 1870 ed.], 468).

[48] Revelation 12:11.

You are worthy to take the scroll and to open its seals (Rev 5:9). This is the first strain of the "new song" sung by the four living creatures and the twenty-four elders. "Worthy is the Lamb, who was slain," is also sung by the full chorus of the heavenly hosts in Revelation 5:12. The immediate cause for praising the Lamb as worthy is that his death has entitled him to break the seals of the scroll (Rev 5:5, 9). There is disagreement among interpreters as to both the contents of the scroll and the exact significance of the Lamb's opening it. The scroll is often seen as the "book of human destiny," the eschatological judgments to come on the world, or the remaining contents of the prophecy given to John. There is a good case to be made, I believe, for understanding the scroll to be what Revelation elsewhere calls the book of life.[49] This book, which is said to belong to the Lamb,[50] contains the names of all of the redeemed. If this is the same scroll, it is easy to see that the revelation of its contents should be withheld until the Lamb had conquered, for until then the redemption of the elect had not been accomplished. The good news proclaimed in these verses is that the Lamb has now been slain and has risen; the opening of the book of life is now inevitable, and the saints are now assured of the fullness of their salvation.

You were slain, and with your blood you purchased [ἠγόρασας] *men for God*. The idea of redemption as purchase was only implied in Revelation 1:5-6; here it is specified. The connection between the shedding of the Lamb's blood and redemption from sin, however, has been seen as somewhat problematic. First, while the associations with the exodus and with the Passover lamb are unmistakable and well recognized,[51] "the blood of the Paschal lamb," as Hillyer says, "was not primarily expiatory or redemptive; it was sprinkled on the doorposts that the destroying angel might 'pass over' the house (Ex 12:13)."[52] And yet, it was the sacrifice of the lamb and the application of its blood to the

---

[49]Revelation 3:5; 13:8; 17:8; 20:12; 21:27.

[50]Revelation 13:8; 21:27.

[51]Jesus as the Passover lamb, after all, is found in 1 Corinthians 5:7, "for Christ our Passover lamb (τὸ πάσχα) has been sacrificed" (cf. Lk 22:7 for πάσχα as Passover lamb), and John 1:29, 36 refer to Jesus as "the lamb of God who takes away the sin of the world." Also in 1 Peter 1:18-19 Christ's redeeming blood is compared to the blood of a pure and spotless lamb.

[52]Hillyer, "Lamb," 230. Aune, *Revelation*, 1:371: "a title taken by most scholars to refer to the paschal lamb, even though the expiation of sins was not linked to the Passover sacrifice." Barrett, *St. John*, 176, writing of the declaration of John the Baptist in John 1:29, 36: "It is certain that this phrase has an Old Testament background, less certain what that background is."

doorposts that turned God's judgment on the firstborn of Egypt away from the households of the Israelites.[53] In this sense it was both substitutionary and redemptive, and it approaches notions of propitiation, though it was not, strictly speaking, an expiation for sin.

Second, the logic of the metaphor is sometimes criticized by posing the question of just who might have been compensated in the purchase of men for God. There is no thought of a ransom paid to Satan or to sin. But as we have observed above, one may say that the "payment" was made to God himself or to his justice.[54] Sin incurs a debt against God's holiness and justice, which has resulted in our being sold into slavery or captivity. Therefore, that the Lamb "purchased" us means that he bought us out of our captivity, paid the debt that had bound us over to sin and death. This he did with the price of his blood.

The purchase of people (οἱ ἠγορασμένοι) for God and the Lamb is mentioned twice again in Revelation: 14:3, 4, where John sees 144,000 standing with the Lamb on the heavenly Mount Zion.[55] Their new ownership is signaled by the names they bear on their foreheads, the names of the Lamb and his Father (Rev 14:1). This new mark of ownership sets them off as the antithesis of the beast-worshipers,[56] who are marked with "the name of the beast or the number of its name" (Rev 13:7). Their purchase "from the earth" or "from mankind" identifies them as among those whom the Lamb purchased "from every tribe and tongue and people and nation," whom he made "a kingdom and priests to serve our God" in Revelation 5:9-10. Just as in Revelation 5:9-10, there is mention here of the singing of a new song.[57] In Revelation 5:9-10 the new song was sung by the heavenly multitude, praising the Lamb for redeeming humans. But here in Revelation 14:3, it is the redeemed themselves who have now learned the new song of praise, which only they are entitled to sing.

---

[53]See Hebrews 11:28.

[54]Roger Nicole: "If the question be pressed, 'to whom was the ransom paid?' the answer should not be: 'to Satan,' but rather, 'to the Triune God in satisfaction of the full claims of divine justice against the sinner'" ("The Nature of Redemption," originally published in Carl F. H. Henry, ed., *Contemporary Evangelical Thought: Christian Faith and Modern Theology* [New York: Channel Press, 1964], cited from *Standing Forth: Collected Writings of Roger Nicole* (Fearn: Christian Focus Publications, 2002), 256. So also Kistemaker, *Revelation*, 210.

[55]Galatians 4:26; Hebrews 12:22.

[56]Revelation 13:16-18; 14:9; 15:2, etc.

[57]Prigent, *Commentary on the Apocalypse*, 257.

For God. Christ's purchase set us free but did not set us adrift. Rather, he purchased us wholly and solely "for God." This is reminiscent of Paul's words in 1 Corinthians 6:20, "You were bought at a price. Therefore honor God with your body."[58] John uses the phrase "for God" in several of the contexts in which the Lamb's redemptive death is mentioned (Rev 1:6, made us a kingdom, priests *for his God and Father*; Rev 5:9, purchased people *for God*; Rev 5:10, made them a kingdom and priests *for God*; Rev 14:4, purchased from men as first fruits *for God and the Lamb*).

From every tribe and language and people and nation. This expresses the glorious universality of the effects of Jesus' redemptive work; the Lamb's redemption is by no means confined to Israel according to the flesh. Jesus told his listeners, "I have other sheep that are not of this sheep pen. I must bring them also. They too will listen to my voice, and there shall be one flock and one shepherd" (Jn 10:16). And yet this verse also clearly expresses the particularity of his redemptive work. For those purchased were "from" (ἐκ) every tribe, tongue, people and nation and do not comprise the entirety of those human designations. This corresponds to words of Jesus in the Johannine gospel when he said to some, "But you do not believe because you are not my sheep. My sheep listen to my voice; I know them, and they follow me" (Jn 10:26-27).[59] It forms no incongruity with 1 John 2:2, which says that Jesus is the propitiation for the sins of the whole world. For there it is what Jesus is, rather than what he has done, that is in view.[60] Here in Revelation 5:9, what is emphasized is that which Jesus has accomplished: he has purchased people for God from every natural division of humanity and has made them a kingdom and priests for God,[61] who shall reign on the new earth (Rev 22:5).

Revelation 7:14-17: The Blood That Whitens
In Revelation 5:9 we heard the declaration that the Lamb had bought people for God out of every tribe and tongue and people and nation and had made them a kingdom and priests to God. In a new vision in Revelation 7, John sees this very multitude of purchased people, a

---

[58]Also 1 Corinthians 7:23.
[59]John 10:26-27; cf. 6:44, 65; 17:6, those "whom you gave me out of (ἐκ) the world"; 17:9.
[60]See Ramsey Michaels's exposition of this passage earlier in this volume.
[61]See above on Revelation 1:6.

group "that no one could count, from every nation, tribe, people and language, standing before the throne and in front of the Lamb. They were wearing white robes and were holding palm branches in their hands" (Rev 7:9). John even hears the collective voice of this vast multitude, crying out, "Salvation belongs to our God, who sits on the throne, and to the Lamb" (Rev 7:10). In Revelation 7:14-17 these saints clothed in white are described by the heavenly elder as those who have: "come out of the great tribulation, and they have washed their robes and made them white in the blood of the Lamb. For this reason, they are before the throne of God; and they serve him day and night in His temple . . . for the Lamb in the center of the throne shall be their shepherd; and shall guide them to springs of the water of life" (NASB).

Here again we meet wonderful paradoxes. Combined in this passage are the notions of Christ as Lamb and Christ as Shepherd who guides his sheep to springs of living water. Perhaps the more jarring paradox is the whitening of the robes of the saints in the blood of the Lamb in Revelation 7:14. In the same passage in which the Israelites were told that they would be "a kingdom of priests and a holy nation" (Ex 19:6-7), they were also told to wash their garments, before God would meet with Moses on Mt. Sinai (Ex 19:10). Here in John's vision it is not only the single mediator but also the entire innumerable multitude that come into the presence of the Lord with praise on the heavenly mountain (Rev 14:1). This multitude is not restricted from touching the mountain.[62] Instead, the Lord even spreads his tabernacle over them; they are before his very throne and serve him (as priests) day and night in his temple (Rev 7:15). And how is it that each member of this great host can serve in the place once reserved to Moses or the high priest? It is because ("for this reason," 7:15) their garments have been washed in the blood of the Lamb, because the effects of the Lamb's slaughter have been applied to them to sanctify them for this privilege.

Here we are dealing with the idea of sin, not as debt or bondage, but as defilement, rendering sinners impure and unfit for the presence of a holy God. And here John sees in visionary form the truth proclaimed in 1 John 1:7, "If we walk in the light, as he is in the light, we have fellowship with one another, and the blood of Jesus, his Son, purifies us

---

[62]Cf. Exodus 12—14; Hebrews 12:18.

from all sin."[63] The clothing metaphor (here "robes"), in which one's
garment represents his life or deeds, good or evil, was introduced earlier in the soiled garments of those in Sardis (Rev 3:4-5). It appears
again in the fine linen, bright and pure, in which the Lamb's Bride is
clothed in Revelation 19:7-8,[64] where we are told that it represents the
righteous deeds of the saints. And according to Revelation, the deeds
are righteous because they are like garments washed and made white
in the blood of the Lamb (Rev 7:14; 22:14). The image appears again in
the final benediction of the book in Revelation 22:14, "Blessed are those
who wash their robes, that they may have the right to the tree of life
and may go through the gates into the city."

That ransomed sinners should be sanctified to serve in unmediated
worship of God for eternity is another benefit won for them by nothing
other than the shedding of Christ's blood.

Revelation 12:11: Overcoming the Accuser
A new scene in Revelation 12 parallels that of Revelation 5 in that both
portray a decisive change effected by the death, resurrection and ascension of Christ, a change not only on earth but in the heavenly realm
as well. In Revelation 12:1-5 John sees a woman, representing "the covenant community of both the Old Testament and the New Testament
eras,"[65] adorned with the heavenly glory, who gives birth to a male
child, "who will rule all the nations with an iron scepter" (Rev 12:5).
This child is then "snatched up to God and to his throne," thereby
eluding the grasp of the dragon who sought to devour him (Rev 12:4).
A great war immediately ensues in heaven, resulting in the defeat and
casting down of the dragon and his host. Clearly, the martial defeat of
the dragon is directly related to the ascension of the nation-ruling male
child to the throne of God. It depicts the situation Jesus predicted, referring to his impending crucifixion and resurrection: "Now is the time
for judgment on this world; now the prince of this world will be driven

---

[63]Cf. Hebrews 9:14, "How much more, then, will the blood of Christ, who through the eternal
Spirit offered himself unblemished to God, cleanse our consciences from acts that lead to
death, so that we may serve the living God!" (cf. also Heb 9:6-10).
[64]Here the mere fact that the Bride is represented, not as "the Christ's," but as "the Lamb's,"
keeps before our minds that the Bride's purification has been accomplished through the
shed blood of her Husband. The fact that it was "given" her to be clothed in this bright and
pure linen also stresses this.
[65]Kistemaker, *Revelation*, 355.

out" (Jn 12:31). And at the point of Satan's casting down to earth, a loud voice is heard in heaven saying,

> Now have come the salvation and the power and the kingdom of
> our God,
> and the authority of his Christ.
> For the accuser of our brothers,
> who accuses them before our God day and night,
> has been hurled down.
> They overcame him
> by[66] the blood of the Lamb
> and by the word of their testimony;
> they did not love their lives so much
> as to shrink from death. (Rev 12:10-11)

This is another way of depicting what was said in Revelation 1:6; 5:10: the Lamb has made his people a kingdom. Here the coming of "the kingdom of our God and the authority of his Christ" is not restricted to a future geopolitical embodiment but is bound up with the past defeat of Satan and his expulsion from heaven—the direct result of Christ's ascension to God and to his throne. This is also seen in that the brethren too have achieved their victory over him (Rev 15:2-3), and not as the result of an eschatological battle on earth in which they overcame with sword or spear. This victory is attained because the Lamb has already shed his own blood, and as a result, also because the redeemed who confess him on earth follow his example in giving up their lives rather than their confession.[67]

The vision depicts Satan's defeat in terms of a battle in heaven in Revelation 12:7-8. Martial imagery is used elsewhere in the New Testament for what Christ accomplished in his cross and resurrection,[68] often where legal[69] or cultic[70] aspects of sin and atonement are also present. The key for understanding the idea of redemption in Revelation 12:7-12 as well is to recognize that the serpent is defeated here explicitly in his role as *accuser*, reiterated in the listing of his names, Devil and Satan (Rev 12:9), each of which has the connotation of accuser or

---

[66]Or, because of; $\delta\iota\acute{\alpha}$ + the accusative.
[67]Cf. Revelation 2:10.
[68]E.g., John 12:31; Colossians 2:15; Hebrews 2:14-15.
[69]Colossians 2:13-14.
[70]Hebrews 2:17.

adversary. Accusations have to do with guilt, and thus we are dealing with the idea of sin as legal transgression. This language of the law court is more usually associated with Paul.[71] But it is also present elsewhere in Johannine thought in 1 John 2:1,[72] where Jesus is called our Paraclete, or Advocate, before God, to defend us from the condemnation of our sin.

In Revelation 12:11 the accuser, the one who would bring a charge against God's elect, has been decisively defeated; his claims in God's court have been stricken down through the blood of the Lamb. This means that in Revelation as well as in Galatians and Romans Christ's death is regarded as having justifying power on behalf of the sinner. But another aspect of this legal triumph is revealed here in that the dragon's defeat resounds again each time one of Christ's followers faithfully brings forth his or her own testimony—most especially when that testimony is given before a human tribunal.[73] Though this may result in an apparent victory for the dragon, the slain and martyred Christian is the true victor.

Satan's violent removal from the heavenly courtroom, where he formerly had a place,[74] is a distinctively Christian conception.[75] This is because it is the direct result of the shedding of the Lamb's blood, the unique redemptive act of Jesus Christ that brought the entire sacrificial system of Judaism to a conclusion.[76]

Revelation 13:8: The Lamb and the Book of Life

"And all who dwell on earth will worship it, every one whose name has not been written before the foundation of the world in the book of life of the Lamb that was slain" (RSV).

In this section of the prophecy, the beast rising from the sea (Rev 13:1) has been given authority on earth to compel worship and to conquer the saints (Rev 13:7). But paradoxically, this "conquering" of the saints appears to take place in the very act by which they themselves conquer the beast and the dragon as we have just seen in Rev-

---

[71]E.g., Romans 8:1, 33-35.
[72]Cf. John 14:16.
[73]Matthew 10:17-21, 32-33; 24:9; 1 Peter 3:15; Revelation 2:13.
[74]See Job 1—2; Zechariah 3:1-2.
[75]E.g., John 12:31; Romans 8:1.
[76]Daniel 9:27; Romans 5:18; Hebrews 7:27; 9:12, 25-28.

elation 12:11—the act of giving up their lives for their confession of Christ. To the world, they, like the Lamb they follow, appear weak, helpless and defeated. But in dying they live. Being faithful unto death, they are given the crown of life (Rev 2:10). And on the last day, it is those who would not worship the beast, who steadfastly confessed the slain Lamb and were themselves willing for to be slain for his sake, whose names will be found written in the Lamb's book of life (Rev 20:15).

There is a question about whether the phrase "from the foundation of the world" (RSV) goes with the names written or with the Lamb slain. In Revelation 17:8 it is clear that the names of the elect were written in the book from before the foundation of the world.[77] Yet 1 Peter 1:20 also says that Christ, who shed his blood to ransom us, like a lamb without blemish or spot, was "chosen before the creation of the world." And many scholars think that in Revelation 13:8 it is most natural to take the phrase to refer to the Lamb (as in KJV, NIV), despite the same being said of the writing of the names in Revelation 17:8. And even on the reading taken here (RSV), the book of life written from the foundation of the world is expressly said to belong, not merely to the Lamb but to the *slain* Lamb, which all but affirms the same thing, that the Lamb was predestined to be slain for those whose names are written in the book. In either case, we recognize that the death of Jesus was no unforeseen tragedy, nor was it a makeshift or surrogate maneuver. "Yet it was the LORD's will to crush him and cause him to suffer" (Is 53:10); and this was the eternal, gracious purpose of God by which he would accomplish salvation for all of his elect.

In the imagery of John's Revelation, sin is portrayed in several of its horrible effects: as bondage or captivity, as incalculable debt, as defilement and as incurring legal guilt. Yet all of these aspects of sin's vicious craft are resolved for the sinner by the blood of the Lamb! Defiled, condemned, indebted and sold into captivity, those whose names are written in the Lamb's book of life have, by his blood, been purchased for God and installed by Christ as pure and holy, acquitted, priests in his kingdom. They have become the Lamb's spotless bride (Rev 19:7-8). Their praise is as everlasting as their redemption.

Well suited to express the doxological character of Revelation's pre-

---

[77]Cf. Ephesians 1:14.

sentation of Christ's atoning work, and the gratitude it inspires in the
redeemed, are Anne Cousins's words:

> The bride eyes not her garment,
>
> But her dear Bridegroom's face.
>
> I will not gaze at glory
>
> But on my King of grace;
>
> Not at the crown he gifteth,
>
> But on his pierced hand;
>
> The Lamb is all the glory
>
> Of Immanuel's land![78]

---

[78] Anne R. Cousins, 1857, based on Samuel Rutherford, 1600-1661.

PART II

THE ATONEMENT IN
CHURCH HISTORY

Frank A. James III

The cross has found its own unique symbolic place in Christian history. According to Eusebius of Caesarea, when the Emperor Constantine surveyed the skies just before the famous battle of Milvian Bridge (A.D. 312), it was the burning cross that he saw accompanied by these famous words: *in hoc signo vinces* ("in this sign conquer").[1] For the early Christians, the sign of the cross was bittersweet. On the one hand, it reminded them of centuries of suffering at the hands of Imperial Rome. On the other, it was a sign of triumph over adversity. After centuries of persecution, the empty cross represented not only victory over death and forgiveness of sins but also triumph over Caesar.

It may surprise modern Christians to learn that there is no single prevailing Christian view of the atonement. While orthodox Christians have, over the course of time, settled on a general consensus on the Trinity, on the deity of Christ and his two natures, and on salvation by grace, convergence on the atonement has been more elusive. To be sure many doctrinal divergences and nuances plague Christianity, but it is somewhat surprising that no single theory of the atonement predominates, given the fact that so many in church history have dubbed it the central doctrine of Christianity. The concept has been important, even if the term did not really emerge as a theological category until the sixteenth century. This is evident in Calvin and Luther, neither of whom

---

[1]Eusebius of Caesarea *Vita Constantini* 1.27-30. English translation in *A Select Library of Nicene and Post-Nicene Fathers of the Christian Church*, ed. Philip Schaff and Henry Wace, second series, 14 vols. (New York: The Christian Literature Company, 1890-1900), 1:489-90.

advocated a single theory of the atonement.[2] Later Christian theologians either were uncomfortable with existing theories or, like Calvin, they constructed the doctrine in their own way.

Theories of Atonement

As the first part of this volume has demonstrated, the notion that sins against God must be atoned for has had a very long history. The disclosing of God's approved means of atonement, from its shadows and types to its fulfillment in the work of Jesus Christ, forms a central strand of the biblical revelation. Steeped in the conceptions of the Old Testament, the apostles and other first-century Christians saw in Jesus the ultimate fulfillment and completion of the repeated sacrifices of the Mosaic code. But as we have seen, no single "theory" of the atonement emerges from the New Testament writings. Rather, they display a rich and multifaceted, yet interrelated, expression of truths about the redemption Christ has accomplished, set in language drawn from the experience of God's people under the old covenant. In the first centuries of the church's expansion, most Christian theologians seemed content to repeat biblical phrases without much systematic development. Even so, certain elements tended to receive more attention than others, and it was not long before writers spoke of "theories" of atonement, attempts at encapsulating the biblical teaching, usually in terms of one or a few main images.

As one surveys the theological landscape of the church, the various theories fall into three main categories. First, there are the *ransom theories* of the atonement. This view was particularly dominant in the early church. In its simplest form, this theory understands the cross as a ransom paid to the devil in order to free sinful humans from their sinful bondage. Some advocates of the ransom theory reasoned that Satan was within his rights to imprison sinners, but he overreached himself when he sought to imprison the sinless Christ. Some saw in Christ's death an effectual deception and hence victory of Christ over Satan. But why would a sovereign God grant the devil the right to imprison sinners so that God must resort to deception on the cross? Whether this theory is viable depends on how one answers this question.

A second way of approaching Christ's death on the cross is linked to various viewpoints that come under the broad umbrella called *satis-*

---

[2]Ronald Wallace, *The Atoning Death of Christ* (Westchester, Ill.: Crossway, 1981), pp. 76-77.

faction theories. The grandfather of this theory is Anselm, and it was first expressed in his *Cur Deus Homo* (1098). There is a significant shift in Anselm's approach, for he is principally concerned with the relationship of God and humankind, whereas the ransom theories tend to concentrate attention on God and the devil. Anselm rejected the ransom theory in favor of a theory that reconstructs the dynamic interplay between God, humanity and the devil. Because sin offends the divine dignity, the sinner must render compensation or satisfy the dishonor. But the disgrace to God's honor is an infinite insult, while the sinner is a finite being whose greatest compensations are still finite and finally unworthy of the infinite injury to God's honor. Therein lies the problem. How is a finite creature to satisfy an eternal offense? The death of the God-man on the cross is the only valid way that divine dishonor can be satisfied. Indeed, only the eternal divine One can satisfy the dishonor—hence the incarnation.

As the Middle Ages progressed into the sixteenth-century Reformation, Anselm's theory of the atonement underwent development and refinement. The Reformers tended to view the debt of sin no longer in terms of dishonor but in the sense of punishment. This understanding laid stress on divine justice and the legal principle that violations must be punished, hence the emergence of the idea of penal substitution. According to this reformational refinement of Anselm's satisfaction theory, Christ pays the debt of punishment owed by sinners by means of self-substitution. In other words, Christ offers himself as a substitute to suffer the penalty deserved by sinners. However, one is immediately struck by the apparent injustice of this theory. How is it that God directs his wrath against deserving sinners to the perfectly righteous and innocent Jesus? What kind of God punishes the innocent and not the guilty?

The Reformers did devote considerable attention to penal substitution, but they nuanced their particular formulations in different ways. A favorite theme in Luther's concept of the atonement was the idea of the "wonderful exchange," that is, Christ's righteousness exchanged for the sinner's sin. In Calvin, one of the more significant motifs in his understanding of Christ's death is the mysterious encounter between God's love and justice on the cross. For Calvin, the cross is where "he loved us even when he hated us."[3] Despite different emphases, the Re-

---

[3]Calvin *Institutes of the Christian Religion* 2.16.4.

formers defended the love and justice of God, arguing that what appears to be unjust in the human realm is, in the heavenly realm, a dynamic act in which love, justice and compassion fuse in a singular moment on the old rugged cross. Christ voluntarily takes the guilt of sin upon himself because of his love, and the Father accepts Christ's sacrifice because he loves the Son and has compassion on sinners, all the while preserving the eternal integrity of divine justice. What is impossible with man is possible with God.

Since the Enlightenment, a third theory has gained considerable support. The *exemplar theory* of the atonement claims that the death of Christ was essentially an inspiring example of love and faithfulness. In contrast to the other "objective" theories of the atonement, the exemplar theory is described as "subjective" because its power lies exclusively in the subjective influence on the minds and behaviors of sinners to live lives more fully in accord with Christ's example. Exemplar theories generally comport well with Enlightenment views of Christ as a mere human, although an extraordinary human. Advocates of the objective theories acknowledge that Christ's death was indeed inspiring, but without an objective transaction the real significance of the cross is diluted in the mist of subjectivism.

Two contemporary theologians have entered into the theological fray with their own contributions to the doctrine of the atonement. In recent years Richard Swinburne's *Responsibility and Atonement* and the late Colin Gunton's *The Actuality of the Atonement* have offered their own take on the doctrine of the atonement. In significant ways, both employ traditional motifs in new ways. Swinburne, for example, speaks of the atonement in terms of reparation, repentance and sacrifice. Gunton, in like manner, views the atonement as the divine restoration of the broken relationship with sinful humanity. Neither is adverse to traditional themes such as sacrifice and payment of legal debt. Both scholars reject the role of the devil in the ransom theories and see, as well, that Christ's death is more than an inspiring example. However, both are uneasy with the transference of the sinner's guilt and the punishment it deserves to Christ.

The Priestly Work of Christ
That Christianity has to do with Christ is a truism. This is nowhere more evident than in the systematic development of the doctrine of the

atonement, where the significance of Christ's death on the cross is especially in focus. Historically, Christians, beginning with the Reformation, have tended to divide the doctrine of Christ into two broad categories—distinguishing between the person and the work of Christ. The early church gave concentrated attention to the matter of Christ's person, reaching a definitive climax at the great fourth ecumenical church council at Chalcedon (A.D. 451). Over the centuries, the work of Christ has also received considerable attention from theologians. As the doctrine of the atonement has developed historically, the work of Christ has been particularly in view. Although the early church fathers spoke of the various "offices" of Christ, John Calvin was first to codify the three offices of Christ as "prophet, priest and king" and introduced this threefold distinction into the theological parlance of Christian theology.[4] Christ's work, especially his death on the cross, is mediatorial; that is, it has to do with interceding and reconciling the broken relationship between the holy God and sinful humans. In his role as mediator, Christ the prophet represents God with humankind; as priest he represents humanity in the presence of God; and as king he exercises his authority and restores the original dominion of humanity. The doctrine of the atonement, from the perspective of systematic theology, is more narrowly focused on Christ's priestly work on the cross. The OT priest provides the basic image for understanding the cross. Just as the high priest acted as a representative of the nation of Israel, so also Christ represents the elect people of God. The OT priest offered sacrifices for the sins of the nation; in like manner, Christ offers a sacrifice for the elect. The difference is that Christ the Great High Priest offers himself as a sacrifice for his people to satisfy the holy God.

To address the fundamental question of why Christ died on the cross, theologians have typically pointed to two ultimate causes: the love and the justice of God. That the cross is an expression of God's love for his people is perhaps most evident in the most beloved biblical text of all in the Gospel of John: "for God so loved the world, that he gave his only begotten Son" (Jn 3:16 KJV). But love is not the only cause for the cross; in a profound juxtaposition, love is joined with divine justice. One of the crucial theological ingredients to an historical understanding of the cross is that sin is a violation and offense against the

---

[4]Calvin *Institutes* 2.15.

holy character of God, and as such, it must be punished. To allow sin
to go unpunished would be unjust in a world created by a holy and
righteous God. Therefore, Christ's death on the cross is seen as a "propitiation" whereby the just wrath of God is turned away and satisfied
by the sacrificial offering of Christ's death.[5]

In order to better understand Christ's death on the cross, theologians have distinguished further between his *active obedience* and his
passive obedience. By active obedience is meant Christ's perfect lifelong
obedience to the divine law on behalf of his people. His life of perfect
obedience earned a perfect righteousness that is graciously imputed to
his elect. In addition to perfect obedience to the law of God, Christ endured terrible suffering and a painful death as a penalty for our sins.
Not only was there physical suffering, but there was also unimaginable
spiritual suffering. Christ bore the full weight of human sins and the
agony of divine rejection, but he also endured the eternal wrath of God
against sin. Evangelicals especially have come to view the priestly
work of Christ on the cross as a *penal substitutionary* atonement. It is penal in that it understands Christ's death as a penalty for sin, and it is
substitutionary, or vicarious, because Christ is seen to have served as a
substitute sacrifice on behalf of sinners. It is the priestly work of Christ
on the cross that displays divine justice, and it is also where God's love
finds the ultimate expression in the active and passive obedience of
Christ on behalf of sinners.

In all of this, as in much of Christ's teaching, the cross retains a paradoxical quality. Followers are told that "the first shall be last" and that
we ought to "love our enemies." This theological trajectory underscores the richness and depth of the cross. On the one hand, the cross
is the point of greatest defeat (Jesus was killed, crucified and buried);
yet at the same time, it is the point of greatest triumph, for it was precisely in his death that his followers have life eternal. His was a death
with eternal significance. In a redemptive-historical sense, the death of
Christ on the cross is directly related to the fall of Adam. By disobedi-

---

[5]C. H. Dodd in his book, *The Bible and the Greeks* (Hodder & Stoughton, 1935), 82-95, argued
that the idea of propitiation was alien to the Bible. Two of Dodd's leading detractors were
Leon Morris, *The Apostolic Preaching of the Cross* (London: Tyndale, 1965), 144-213, and Roger
Nicole, "C. H. Dodd and the Doctrine of Propitiation," *Westminster Theological Journal* 17
(May 1955): 117-57. The *locus classicus* for propitiation is Romans 3:25. The paradox is that
God provides the means of removing his own wrath. It is God's love that "sent his Son to
be the propitiation for our sins" (1 Jn 4:10 NASB).

ence in the Garden, death became a reality for himself and all humanity. But by Christ's obedience, eternal life becomes a reality for true believers.

The Messiness of Multiple Metaphors

One of the difficulties inherent in any discussion of the atonement is the
variety of images the New Testament employs to unfold its understanding of the atonement. This "messiness of multiple metaphors" as Vanhoozer describes it in chapter eighteen in this volume,[6] is part of our historical legacy. Some have identified the primary metaphors as
justification, redemption, reconciliation, sacrifice and victory—or, in a
more traditional configuration, sacrifice, punishment, ransom, victory
and Passover.[7] John Stott recognizes four motifs: propitiation, redemption,
justification and reconciliation but insists that the substitutionary principle is "the essence of each image and at the heart of the atonement itself."[8]

Paradoxically, Christ's death on the cross was the triumph over
Adam's disobedience and the consequent pall of death that fell over all
humanity. The relationship between God and humanity was horribly
disrupted, and what had been a good relationship became a bad relationship. What had been a relationship of love became a relationship of
wrath. But the death of Christ was the one unique death that brought
ultimate victory over death itself. It was the "death of death," as John
Owen described it.[9] Because Christ died on the cross, he brought about
a new relationship. Instead of wrath, there was grace and love. Before,
we were far off; now we are brought near.

The Historical Essays in This Book

The essays in this section provide a rich array of historical and theological insight into the development of the doctrine of the atonement. As
with any grouping of scholars, there is no necessary unanimity of un-

---

[6]For further discussion, see P. S. Fiddes, *Past Event and Present Salvation: The Christian Idea of
the Atonement* (Oxford: Oxford University Press, 1989); Colin Gunton, *The Actuality of the
Atonement: A Study of Metaphor, Rationality and the Christian Tradition* (Edinburgh: T & T
Clark, 1988); and R. G. Swinburne, *Responsibility and Atonement* (Oxford: Oxford University
Press, 1989).

[7]See Vanhoozer, chapter 18 in this volume.

[8]John R. W. Stott, *The Cross of Christ* (Downers Grove, Ill.: InterVarsity Press, 1986), p. 203.

[9]John Owen, *The Death of Christ*, in *The Works of John Owen*, ed. William Goold (1850-1853; reprint, Edinburgh: Banner of Truth Trust, 1965-1968), 10:157ff.

derstanding. The editors wanted to ensure that representative expressions of this doctrine were treated, touching down in the patristic and medieval foundations, Reformation and post-Reformation refinements, as well as contemporary analysis of the doctrine. This way, the student of the atonement gets a broader perspective on how this doctrine has evolved throughout church history.

Stanley Rosenberg provides a masterful reassessment of Augustine's understanding of the atonement. What makes his essay especially important is that he approaches Augustine through the genre of his sermons rather than his dogmatic treatises, that is to say, from the perspective of the pulpit instead of the isolated study. This new perspective yields interesting results. Rosenberg finds evidence of a ransom theory in Augustine but with a cosmic and personal restoration in view. Augustine preaches that Christ rescues his people from Satan's captivity, but the rescue is for the purpose of moral and ontological renewal. For him, the atonement is the healing of the deformity resulting from original sin and a restoration to original beauty.

Gwenfair Walters concentrates her attention on the Middle Ages—one of the most historically significant periods in the history of this doctrine. Her work is significant because she rightly concentrates on the two medieval theologians at the center of the maelstrom over the atonement—Anselm and Abelard—and isolates the key differences at issue between them. The doctrine of the atonement underwent perhaps its greatest development during this time. Three of the most important theories in the history of Christianity (the ransom theory, the satisfaction theory and the exemplar theory) were much in evidence and much debated throughout the Middle Ages. Eventually the satisfaction theory of Anselm prevailed. Walters is especially keen to identify the ways in which the atonement affected the sacramental life of the church. She expertly considers the impact of the atonement with regard to three of the pillars of medieval church: the mass, purgatory and the sacrament of penance.

Timothy George takes the reader into the fascinating world of Martin Luther with all Luther's boldness and audacity. For the German monk, justification was the guiding theological principle, and his doctrine of the atonement was driven in large part by his understanding of justification. Dr. George suggests that what captivates Luther is not the reality and efficacy of Christ's death on the cross, about which there was no debate with Rome, but how the individual believer appropriated the reality of Christ's death. George engages two leading interpretations of Luther—Walther von Loenwich's *Luther's Theology of the Cross,* and Gustaf Aulen's *Christus Victor*—and then delves carefully into Luther's instructive commentary on the subject in Galatians. This essay will surely stimulate further discussion.

Henri Blocher, one of Europe's leading Calvin scholars, considers the Genevan's view of the atonement from a slightly unusual perspective. Blocher endorses Stauffer's insight that "in order to understand Calvin the reformer, one must know Calvin the preacher." One cannot properly understand Calvin unless one fully appreciates the fact that he was a preacher first—a notion that prompts Blocher to go primarily to the sermons and commentaries for Calvin's view of the atonement. This is not an attempt to sidestep the *Institutes,* but it is to appreciate that Calvin always intended the *Institutes* to be read in conjunction with his commentaries and, in a sense, his sermons as well. Blocher finds in Calvin the atonement themes of expiation and victory as well as the sacrificial, penal and polemical aspects. Calvin, Blocher notes, had the ability to conjoin various aspects of the atonement into a unified comprehensive whole.

Blocher notes the paradox in Calvin, namely, that God "loved us and hated us at the same time." Calvin has the ability to nuance his view of the atonement. As others have noted, there is an integrative approach in Calvin—he embraces no single view of the atonement but conjoins penal sacrifice and substitution into his view. Blocher bravely wades into a longstanding scholarly debate over whether Calvin's thought owes a significant debt to the medieval theologian Duns Scotus. Scholars such as Ritschl and Dilthy have argued that Calvin's theology manifests a Scotist stress on the absolute power of God *(potentia absoluta).* Blocher's analysis places this debate in proper perspective.

Raymond Blacketer brings his historical and theological expertise to one of the nagging questions that has beset competing theories of the atonement: For whom did Christ die? Or, asked another way, what was the design of the atonement—was it for the elect only or for all humanity? Blacketer comes at this question from a broad historical perspective—considering whether Augustine, Aquinas or Calvin taught such a doctrine as definite atonement. Having laid the groundwork, he then turns to the historical ground zero when this doctrine was given center stage at the famous Synod of Dort, where Reformed representatives from all over Europe dealt with the teachings of Jacob Arminius. One of the central issues centered on what later came to be known as the extent of the atonement. This is a fascinating look into one of the major theological developments of the seventeenth century.

The editors have sought to ensure a contemporary relevance by giving special attention to some of the most important nineteenth- and twentieth-century traditions, thoughts and theologians worldwide on the atonement. *Joel Beeke* introduces the reader to the Dutch theologian Herman Bavinck. Not only was Bavinck one of the greatest Dutch theologians in history, he was also an influential cultural critic. When it comes to his understanding of the atonement, his central focus is on the expiatory sacrifice of Christ, who is both sacrificing priest on behalf of the people and the sacrifice itself. One of the characteristic features of Bavinck is his confessionalism. In his writings in general, and particularly those on the atonement, he relies self-consciously on the Reformed confessions, the Heidelberg Catechism and the Belgic Confession. In this regard, Bavick is a representative of the confessional theological outlook, yet he is uncomfortable with "theories" of the atonement. On the one hand, Bavinck views Anselm's satisfaction theory as foundational; to it he added a consideration of divine wrath and the necessity of a divine-human Messiah who would serve as the substitute. On the other hand, Bavinck speaks of the conjunction of Christ's active and passive obedience in his atoning work on the cross. This essay offers a close-up look at one of the more intriguing theologians of the modern period.

Bruce McCormack, professor of systematic theology at Princeton Theological Seminary and one of the leading authorities on the theology of Karl Barth, presents readers with a Barth-inspired refinement of the doctrine of penal substitution. He observes that the evangelical doctrine of penal substitution has in recent years faced pointed feminist and liberation challenges. Traditional arguments, McCormack states, inevitably have failed to deal with such challenges because of the tendency to abstract the person of Christ from his work. He argues that the only satisfactory response to these challenges is pressing for an integrated understanding of the person and work of Christ within a trinitarian context. He considers how the christology of Karl Barth integrates the person and work of Christ and therefore provides the best defense for an evangelical doctrine of penal substitution. McCormack offers evangelicals a new insight into Barth.

Kevin Vanhoozer is one of the most highly respected evangelical theologians working today. In his thought-provoking and insightful essay he navigates the postmodern theological terrain and discusses how evangelicals can address the serious issues related to constitutive elements of the historic doctrines of the atonement raised by postmodern thinkers. He begins by reviewing the most important postmodern critics of the traditional theories of the atonement—those by Paul Ricoeur, Jacques Derrida, René Girard, John Milbank and Jean-Luc Marion—then offers his reflections on how postmodernity both challenges and contributes to a recovery of some neglected biblical themes.

Each of these essays makes a vital contribution not only to a full-orbed understanding of the doctrine of the atonement but also to how it developed in church history. It is our hope that these scholars will provide insight and stimulation for further discussion on this crucial doctrine.

11

INterpretINg atonement IN augustine's preaching

Stanley P. Rosenberg

When one approaches an author whose corpus of writings is both extensive and significant, good practice would seem to indicate that one's focus should begin with the "classic" texts that are both fundamental to, and representative of, his or her thought. Not unnaturally, we allow that author's major works to act as a focus for our lens. This is particularly true for an author like Augustine. Isidore of Seville's comments on the near impossibility of reading the whole corpus may provide both solace and apology for our own limits.[1] But then, having set and found satisfaction with such limits, we encounter surprises and may find ourselves offering summaries of Augustine's thought that, like Isidore's, misrepresent him if only by missing vital materials through the shear bulk of his corpus. For example, would we expect the following comment on the atonement from one such as Augustine: "God Himself, the blessed God, who is the giver of blessedness, became partaker of our human nature, and thus offered us a short cut to participation in His own divine nature"?[2] Likely this expression of participation does not fit the picture of Augustine generated by most studies.

---

[1] *Etymologiae* 6.7.3
[2] *De Civitate Dei* (hereafter cited as *DCD*), trans. Henry Bettenson (New York: Penguin, 1972), 9.15. Text in *De Civitate Dei Libri* XXII, ed. B. Dombart and A. Kalb, Corpus Christianorum Series Latina, 47 and 48 (Turnholt: Brepols, 1955), trans. rev., 361.

Approaches and Misapprehensions

It is not unusual to find it suggested that the doctrine of atonement in the early church was rather unformed and lacked the greater sophistication of the period initiated by Anselm, advanced by the analysis of the Scholastics, and offered renewed coherence by the Reformers. This rather novel period of reflection, some would suggest, primarily offered a position predicated on the idea of cultic sacrifice and emphasized the concept of "ransom." Cursory review of general literature on the subject will suggest to the reader that the position of the early church on the matter amounts to emphasizing that the death of Christ on the cross paid the price of redemption. Jesus' triumph denied Satan some of his captives and led to the pillage of hell in which Christ reclaimed the faithful of old who were temporarily held by the enemy. But is this understanding wholly realistic?

Much has been written about the history of this doctrine, and some very informed works provide valuable and thoughtful insights on the period of the Fathers.[3] Gustaf Aulén famously set out the modern terms of discussion of patristic sources in his work *Christus Victor*.[4] His history of the doctrine offers a thoughtful study of Irenaeus and the relationship between his treatment of recapitulation and the notion of redemption. Aulén helpfully focuses our attention on the role of redemption in Irenaeus (and other Greek Fathers) as a means of restoring fellowship with God.[5] Often we find that the emphasis is placed on the act of redemption saving humans from God's just punitive action: ransom. But this is not the whole approach. Witness Irenaeus' famous words, "He became what we are so that we may become what He is."[6] It is the combination of considering the healing of guilt and the restoration of relationship that laid the foundation in which the concept of "ransom" was enunciated. Yet this approach also presents a problem. One is easily tempted to interpret the historical development of the doctrine of atonement as inevitably leading toward Anselm's views on satisfaction. Falling prey to this temptation results in both interpreting

---

[3]Among these is that of H. E. W. Turner, *The Patristic Doctrine of Redemption: A Study of the Development of Doctrine During the First Five Centuries* (London: Mowbray, 1952).
[4]G. Aulén, *Christus Victor: A Historical Study of the Three Main Types of the Idea of the Atonement*, trans. A. G. Herbert (London: SPCK, 1931).
[5]Ibid., 25.
[6]Irenaeus *Adversus Haereses* 4.33.4

and presenting earlier views as intellectual forebears that are judged in light of the evolutions of the idea. Assessments that follow this approach find it more difficult to look at the earlier positions in their own right and, by looking for foundations of later thought, risk missing the genius of earlier positions.

Substantial study has been given to Augustine's doctrine of grace and particularly his understanding of the atonement. There are viable studies to which one would want to turn in order to better understand Augustine's handling of the doctrine.[7] This present offering is not written in response to these but as a supplement and extension.[8] Not only are there additional layers to emphasize—layers that can give us a more complete understanding of Augustine's view on the subject, but also there is a new opportunity to be grasped. Studies generally, and textbooks particularly, often focus primarily on Augustine's dogmatic works without making recourse to the large body of other works he produced: pastoral communications that include his many sermons, letters and exegetical commentaries. These works are not just other writings to be cited in a long list to supplement what is found in the dogmatic works. They form a unique genre of writing requiring special attention, interest and interpretation. Partly these other writings have not been readily available, as many of the works have been translated into English for the first time only in the last twenty years. The lack of complete translations of these items is itself telling; they were largely placed at the bottom of the priority list. This lacuna has perhaps skewed the understanding of Augustine among those who do not read Latin. It also indicates which works receive (or do not receive) both popular and critical attention, since publishers and editors must set priorities, and texts are assigned for which there is sufficient interest.

Nonetheless, this state of affairs, whether symptom, signal or cause, leads to misapprehension. Study of Augustine's thought without recourse to the pastoral writings treated in their own right necessarily

---

[7] Among these, see Gerald Bonner, "The Doctrine of Sacrifice: Augustine and the Latin Patristic Tradition," in *Sacrifice and Redemption: Durham Essays in Theology*. ed. S. W. Sykes (Cambridge: Cambridge University Press, 1991), 101-17; idem, "Augustine's Doctrine of Man: Image of God and Sinner," *Augustinianum* 24 (1984): 495-514; and J. Patout Burns, "The Economy of Salvation: Two Patristic Traditions," *TS* 37 (1976): 598-619.

[8] E.g., Gerald Bonner has previously demonstrated the significance of notions of participation and deification in the thought of Augustine in his "Augustine's Conception of Deification," *JTS* 37 (1986): 369-86.

omits the fuller context. To focus too quickly and extensively on Augustine's specifically dogmatic writings (such as those on predestination) also, then, risks blinding the casual reader and specialist alike to the depths of devotion and delight to be found in his writings. A study of Augustine's views in the sermons provides both material and context for further reflection. For in his pastoral communications, as in those of other preachers of his period, we find the musings of an individual who was wholly captured by the sheer awe that God has drawn near to his creation. Augustine was transfixed by the notion that the Creator would take on the form of that which he made *ex nihilo*, in order that the very creation marred by rebellion and sin, deprived of its original purity and integrity, might be renewed in the image and likeness, and thus remade, increasingly, like unto God. Such a creature, then, is able once again to draw near and enjoy the Creator, the source of life and blessing. Nor was he alone among the early church, for the emphasis among them was both profound and sustained.

Though the notion of "ransom" does describe the process by which the Latin church contemplated the mechanism, it is an incomplete description of their theological vision.[9] We must beware of reading back into the early church concerns and foci particular to later periods or merely as precursors to later developments. Looking for a detailed discussion of the atonement in terms of the particulars of the mechanism for reconciliation is nigh impossible in the Fathers. First, they were far more concerned with the foundational matters related to the definition of God as triune and the intricacies of forming a coherent Christology. There is no conciliar attention to definitions of atonement mounting to something on the level of a Nicaea, Chalcedon or the like. Yet one cannot also understand these debates without acknowledging how integral concepts of salvation were to the definitions of the great councils. Second, the word *atonement* itself is of much later derivation (the first secular use of its root form was in the thirteenth century, and the first theological use was in the sixteenth century[10]). Near Latin

---

[9]Eugene Teselle makes a strong argument for the validity of ransom theory over against those who want to thoroughly discount it in favor of later approaches ("The Cross as Ransom," *JECS* 4 [1996]: 147-70; repr. in E. Ferguson, ed. *Doctrinal Diversity: Varieties of Early Christianity*, vol. 4, *Forms of Devotion: Conversion, Worship, Spirituality and Asceticism* [New York: Garland, 1999]).

[10]*Oxford English Dictionary* (Oxford: Clarendon, 1933), s.v. "At one," "Atone," "Atonement."

terms include *liberator, expiatior, salvator, redemptor, mundator, mercator* and *sacrificator.*

Does the lack of a focused discussion or debate such as was held over the nature of the Trinity during most of the fourth century (bounded largely by the Councils of Nicaea and Constantinople) or the relationship between the divine and human in Jesus Christ during the fifth century (leading up to the Council of Chalcedon with further debates following) leave the Fathers wanting on this issue? Far from it—for in the doctrine of the atonement, we approach the question of reconciliation. When one examines the question of how we are reconciled in the writings of the Fathers, we find a vision that is far more integrated, dynamic and substantive than is sometimes allowed—particularly of the Latin Fathers. Witness the richness and vibrancy of this extract from the *City of God* (quoted briefly in the introduction) in which the language of participation in the divine life expresses the purpose of Christ's mediatory role:

> That Mediator in whom we can participate, and by participation reach our happiness, is the uncreated Word of God, by whom all things were created. And yet He is not the Mediator in that He is the Word, for the Word, being pre-eminently immortal and blessed, is far removed from wretched mortals. He is the Mediator in that He is man, by His very manhood making it plain that for the attainment of that good, which is not only blessed but beatific also, we have not to look for other mediators, through whom, as we may think, we can achieve the approach to happiness. God Himself, the blessed God, who is the giver of blessedness, became partaker of our human nature, and thus offered us a short cut to participation in His own divine nature.[11]

Phrases such as this might be surprising because they do not fit our expectations and impressions. However, the issue is far more nuanced, interesting and integrated in one who has written as extensively and dramatically as Augustine than attention to ransom theory alone would suggest. Two factors, I would suggest, have limited the ability to comprehend earlier positions: the approach taken, and the evidence used.

One approach to studying the development of doctrine is to treat earlier positions as somehow serving as intellectual predecessors to later ideas. When ransom theory is viewed primarily as the necessary step toward Anselm's satisfaction theory, then the approach to these

---

[11]*DCD* 9.15.

earlier texts becomes somewhat contrived. One easily limits inspection of the texts to those statements that might have influenced later theologians. Hence, vital evidence is missed. This then leads to a second reason for misunderstanding earlier views. Investigations of doctrinal positions in the fourth century have largely limited themselves to a study of dogmatic works, ignoring vital and significant materials and thereby missing critical data.

A methodological assumption stands in the way. Nondogmatic works—including sermons, catechetical works, epistles and exegetical writings—have been largely ignored and have only begun to garner interest in recent years. With regard to the place of the sermons, their exclusion evolves partly out of a debate in Late Antique studies over the extent of the gulf separating the literate and the illiterate, the intellectual elite and the commoners, the bishops and the congregations. Some take the view that these works are not serious forms of communication and could not represent a significant source of information either about the preacher or his audience. Thus, it is to the dogmatic treatises that one should turn for the full elucidation of their thought. What one finds in the sermons is largely incidental. The validity of such opinions is not the issue here, but the dubious byproduct: some regularly ignore the more popular materials—namely, sermons and other forms of popular communication—offered by the theologians who were, after all, active pastors and ecclesiastical leaders. In essence, we favor works that are occasional and controversial by nature rather than paying close attention to the works that represent more normative pastoral communication. Even when not ignored outright, such materials tend to be used merely as a means to correlate ideas, as a (minor) supplement to our understanding of the writer, or as a means of gathering data about the social fabric, such as the presence of slavery in the society.

This neglect of pastoral communications arguably influences our understanding substantially. Interpretation of the major figures of Late Antiquity focuses on their writings, which were primarily occasional works written in response to a question or an issue and which thus cannot really be said to be either normative or regular forms of communication (even if they are extensive). Developing our understanding of the individual primarily through these materials—occasional communications that are often controversial by nature—not surprisingly leads to a perception that the individual was a controversialist. It also focuses on their concerns more narrowly than the person actually did, so there is a danger of misconstruing their notions by lack of proper emphasis. These individuals were preachers in a society largely defined by oral pedagogy. It is to such pedagogy, then, that one must turn to better understand their notions.

For example, Augustine's debate with Pelagius (and his followers) on freedom and predestination has profoundly shaped his reception and formed a perception that emphasizes the controversialist. The impression received is of a stern patriarch arguing to the end of his days for a God who is immutable and must take any and all actions on matters of reconciliation. There is no doubt that this was a significant debate that preoccupied Augustine's attention and was of such gravity that it has profoundly shaped theology in the West. This Augustine, near the end of a long and difficult episcopal ministry, was embroiled in a bitter struggle with one of his most difficult and equally intractable challenges from Julian of Eclanum.

This debate was so significant and has so captured the interest of theologians, historians and more popular writers that the reader might well expect that this chapter will focus on his view of predestination vis-à-vis atonement. It will not. Though a valid point for discussion, it is one that has been studied at great length. This aspect of Augustine, though true, is not wholly true. It represents only one part of his work. It is well to remember that Augustine authored ninety-three books (all but one of which are extent), was an extensive correspondent (299 letters are extant), and was foremost a preacher. It has been estimated that he delivered between 8,000 and 10,000 sermons, many of which were recorded at the time by *notarii,* or stenographers, and some of which he dictated for distribution.[12] Preaching occurred on Saturdays as well as Sundays and even daily during Lent and the week following Easter. Of these sermons we have over a thousand still available. The amount of space devoted to predestination per se is a relatively small part of his corpus. At the same time that he was debating with Pelagians, he was offering regular homilies and writing pedagogical works such as the

---

[12]Cf. his comment in *Enarrationes in Psalmos* (hereafter cited as *Psal*), 51.1. Text in *Enarrationes in Psalmos*, ed. D. Eligius Dekkers, O.S.B., and Johannes Fraipont, Corpus Christianorum Series Latina, 38, 39 and 40 (Turnholt: Brepols, 1956).

Enchiridion on Faith, Hope and Charity. For a balanced and coherent understanding of Augustine's emphases, it is to works like these that we must turn.

Pedagogy and Preaching

It is well to remember that Augustine was not an academic theologian but a pastor and bishop and that much of his important work was carried out in the context of his duties as a bishop.[13] There is a conscious attempt to form and inform an audience that was still largely influenced by paganism and for whom participation in pagan festivals, if not pagan cultic practice, was still an option.[14] The church had grown extensively during the fourth century, and there was a need to more fully immerse the congregations in the foundations of a Christian worldview.

Augustine considered the sermon to be an appropriate venue for both pastoral exhortation and doctrinal teaching. Manichaeans, Donatists, Pelagians and pagan philosophers all received his focus at various times. In the *Retractationes* he offers a particularly telling comment. Regarding his replies to Adimantus, a disciple of Mani, he says, "I replied to certain questions [in writing], not once, but a second time. . . . Actually, I solved some of these questions in sermons delivered to the people in church. And, up to the present time, I have not yet replied to some."[15] Augustine clearly considered the congregation to be capa-

---

[13]This has been a subject of recent attention. On the role of bishops and priests in the formation of theology in the early church, see Rowan Greer, *Broken Lights and Mended Lives: Theology and Common Life in the Early Church* (University Park: Pennsylvania State University Press, 1986).

[14]See *Sermones ad Populum* (hereafter cited as *Sermo*) 198 (also cited as Dolbeau 198) in which Augustine delivers a sermon that would have been over three hours long in the attempt to keep his parishioners from going out and joining a pagan festival on the streets outside the basilica. Unless noted otherwise, the translations of particular *Sermones ad Populum* are taken from the translations of Edmund Hill in *The Works of Augustine for the Twenty-first Century*, Part 3, vols. 1-11 (New York: New City Press, 1990-98). Texts are found in *Sermones ad Populum*, ed. J.-P. Migne. *Sancti Aurelii Augustini, Hipponensis Episcopi, Opera Omnia*. PL 34.173-220. PL 38-39. The newly found sermons have been compiled and are found in *Vingt-Six Sermons au Peuple D'Afrique*, ed. F. Dolbeau (Paris: Institut d'Études Augustiniennes, 1996).

[15]*Retractationum libri duo* (hereafter cited as *Retr*) 1.21; Aliquas sane earundem quaestionum popularibus ecclesiasticis sermonibus solui. *Retractations*, trans M. Bogan, Fathers of the Church 60 (Washington: Catholic University of America Press, 1968). Text in *Retractationum Libri II*, ed. Almut Mutzenbecher, Corpus Christianorum Series Latina 57 (Turnholt: Brepols, 1984). Also see Peter Brown, *Augustine of Hippo: A Biography*, 2nd ed. (Berkeley: University of California Press, 2000), 457, 458.

ble of understanding him and thought the church service an appropriate forum for spirited persuasion. He considered the basilica, cathedra
and homily to be a venue, platform and means wholly appropriate for
responding to heretical writings.

For Augustine at least, this clearly places the sermon *and its recipients* on a level equivalent to his dogmatic, exegetical and apologetic
works and their respective audience(s). This is not surprising and
seems to be almost a truism if not facile to repeat. Yet its significance
for shaping our view of the sermons is easily forgotten. His many sermons preached against various heterodox positions indicates the significance Augustine attached to the sermon as a venue for substantial
discourse. Noteworthy among these are the sermons preached
against the Platonists (*Sermones ad Populum* 240-42). Furthermore, at
the end of his career Augustine intended to review the sermons along
with his ninety-three works. He concludes his *Retractions,* a brief
compendium and review of all his works, by saying that he intends
to go on to "re-examine my letters and my sermons to the people, the
former dictated, the latter spoken."[16] He treated these as a substantial
part of his legacy.

Augustine and his peers considered their homilies to be a serious forum for enquiry. Not only did they contend with substantial moral issues dealing with the practice of the Christian life, but they also used
the homily as a means to convey critical concepts—both the basic tenets of the faith and more substantial doctrinal issues. This would be
no surprise to a contemporary pastor or even scholar. Yet it is easily
overlooked when it comes to studying ancient authors. One reason
may be the assumptions we bring to our study of ancient people. Public pedagogy is often treated in a rather cursory and desultory fashion,
for we have thought that the audiences were themselves insubstantial,
based on assessments of the degree of literacy found among the
broader populace.[17] These have generally run counter to Auerbach,
who argued for the creation of a Christian literary culture able to reach

---

[16]*Retr* 2.93. Unfortunately, he never accomplished this review.

[17]For example, see W. H. C. Frend, "Heresy and Schism as Social and National Movements,"
    Studies in Church History 9 (1972): 37-56; repr. in *Religion Popular and Unpopular in the Early
    Christian Centuries* (London: Variorum Reprints, 1976) and *The Donatist Church: A Movement
    of Protest in Roman North Africa,* 2nd ed. (Oxford: Clarendon, 1985). Particularly influential
    for this interpretation is the work of Ramsay MacMullen, "The Preacher's Audience (AD
    350-400)," *JTS* 40 (1989): 503-11.

a diverse social and educational spectrum.[18]

Yet one must ask if the degree of literacy—both the ability and the inclination to read—was found in equal proportions among pagans and Christians. As has been noted variously by other writers, literacy was highly prized among the Christian communities. Averil Cameron in *Christianity and the Rhetoric of Empire* states that "the Christian communities had an impulse toward literacy and reading that was generally lacking in pagan culture, and thus . . . the growth of Christianity as a system brought with it a changed attitude toward texts. Christianity early became a religion of books."[19]

Since Christianity is a religion of the Book and of books, education proliferated in the church as it did in the synagogue to a degree far greater than was found among the pagan society. Hence, "popular" thought among the Christians cannot be so easily and uniformly compared to "popular" thought in paganism. Christianity's use of, and attachment to, written texts was in a sense countercultural. Profoundly unlike any attitude or practice found in pagan culture at the end of the fourth century, written texts—especially the Scriptures—were available to all.[20] They were not the possession of an elite group.

While the rate of illiteracy was surely high, this assessment does not necessarily lead to the conclusion that the audience could barely understand their rhetor's eloquent words.[21] Rather, we should understand their illiteracy as a condition for how they learned. Though it is true that one's level of understanding can be tied to one's ability to

---

[18]Erich Auerbach, *Literatursprache und Publikum in der lateinischen Spätantike und im Mittelalter* (Bern: Franke Verlag, 1958). It is translated by R. Manheim as *Literary Language and its Public in Late Latin Antiquity and in the Middle Ages* (Princeton: Princeton University Press, 1965). See particularly chap. 2, *Sermo Humilis.* Also see Phillip Rousseau, "'The Preacher's Audience': A More Optimistic View," in *Ancient History in a Modern University*, vol. 2, ed. T. W. Hillard et al. (Grand Rapids: Eerdmans, 1998): 391-400. Recent focus on John Chrysostom adds valuable details to the picture as well. See W. Mayer, "Female Participation and the Late Fourth-Century Preacher's Audience," *Augustinianum* 39 (1999): 139-47, and "John Chrysostom: Extraordinary Preacher, Ordinary Audience," in M. Cunningham and P. Allen, eds., *Preacher and Audience: Studies in Early Christian and Byzantine Homiletics* (Leiden: Brill, 1998).

[19]Averil Cameron, *Christianity and the Rhetoric of Empire: The Development of Christian Discourse* (Berkeley: University of California Press, 1991), 109. Of course, one must also acknowledge that Judaism was a religion of the book.

[20]On this matter, see Cameron's discussion in *Christianity and the Rhetoric of Empire*, chap. 3 and especially 109-11.

[21]One also has the problem of defining literacy. Where does one set the standard? See William Harris, *Ancient Literacy* (Cambridge, Mass.: Harvard University Press, 1989), chap. 1.

read, there is no necessary connection. The fact of illiteracy offers us in this case relatively little information. It tells us *how* they learned, not *what* they learned.

The Roman world certainly adopted and used writing extensively, yet it largely retained the features of an oral society—including the significant place given to memorization.[22] Moreover, discussions of education focus largely on the formal and neglect the informal. Surely, the weekly and even daily training the individuals in the congregation received in the homily, combined with the more extensive information inculcated in catechesis should not be ignored?[23] The Christian populace had access to books in a form wholly extraordinary to pagan experience. In addition to the concentrated teaching, the practice of reading aloud provided access to the texts. Certainly, the readings of the text by the lector should not be considered insignificant. Nor should we neglect other forms of information and teaching. In Epistle 28* we learn that Augustine directed that the minutes from the Council of Carthage be read to the congregation in Hippo. This practice argues for an extensive commitment to pedagogy of the populace. Not only did this mirror the practice in Carthage, but Augustine had his own analysis of the Council read as well.[24] Public teaching, particularly homilies, was thus a critical form of pedagogy, and we must refer to this material to assess Late Antique theology.

Moreover, this form of access was not unconscious and tenuous, but it was contemplated and commented upon. In *Enarrationes in Psalmos* 121 Augustine says, "Who indeed is Israel? The meaning of this name has already been stated, and let it be recited often; for perhaps, though it has been stated even recently, it has escaped you. By reciting it, let us make it so that it may not escape from those who have been unable or unwilling to read. Let us be their book."[25] Less direct, yet affirming the same attitude is the statement found in *Enarrationes in Psalmos* 103 (ser-

---

[22]Cf. Harris, *Ancient Literacy*, chap. 7.

[23]Cf. William Harmless, *Augustine and the Catechumenate* (Collegeville, Minn.: Liturgical Press, 1995).

[24]Robert Eno, in his introduction to Letter 28* (Augustine's letters recently discovered by Divjak), suggests that the *Breviculus collationis*, Augustine's summary, was read rather than the actual minutes due to the length, and that a reading of his *Ad Donatistas post collationem* would then follow. *Letters 1*-29**, trans. R. Eno, Fathers of the Church 81 (Washington, D.C.: Catholic University of America Press, 1989), 187.

[25]*Psal* 121.8; "Quid est enim Israel? Interpretatio nominis eius dicta est iam, et saepe dicatur; forte enim etsi recens dicta est, excidit. Dicendo nos faciamus ut non escidat etiam eis qui legere non nouerunt aut noluerunt; nos simus codex ipsorum." Translation mine. Readers

mon 3), where he comments on life in the heavenly Jerusalem: "There we shall have a book to read, or speech to be explained as it is now explained to you. Therefore is it now treated, that there it may be held fast: therefore is it now divided by syllables, that there it may be contemplated whole and entire. The Word of God will not be wanting there: but yet not by letters, not by sounds, not by books, not by a reader, not by an expositor. [But rather by the presence of the divine Word]."[26] Books, lectors and expositors—here we find Augustine's understanding of the primary forms of access to the written word (more particularly, the Bible) for the ordinary populace. This was tantamount to pedagogy in Late Antiquity, and Augustine recognized it as such; he likened these forms of access to the educational structures elsewhere, calling the churches the "sacred lecture halls for the people."[27] We should not be surprised, then, to find that Augustine's preaching reflected both his theological concerns and a substantial amount of speculative enquiry.[28]

Atonement in Sermons

The ideas incorporated or implied in the doctrine of atonement are of course addressed in many of his works. However, the sermons provide us a particularly vibrant and important set of texts worthy of focus in their own right.[29] The sermons, divided into three sets, represent a prodigious output over the whole of Augustine's career. His Sermons to the

---

should note that the Latin translations of the Psalms (including the old North African translation Augustine depended upon as well as the Vulgate translated by Augustine's older contemporary, Jerome) depended on the structure of the Septuagint. It uses a different system of enumerating the psalms in which Psalms 9 and 10 are conflated and Psalm 147 is split in two.

[26]*Psal* 103 (sermo 3).3; "quod codex ibi nobis legendus est, aut tractandus sermo, quemadmodum uobis modo tractatur. Ideo modo tractatur, ut ibi teneatur; ideo modo per syllabas diuiditur, ut ibi totus atque integer contempletur. Non ibi deerit uerbum Dei; sed tamen non per litteras, non per sonos, non per codices, non per lectorem, non per tractatorem."

[27]*Epistulae* (hereafter cited as *Ep*) 91.3; "hi autem mores in ecclesiis toto orbe crescentibus tamquam in sanctis auditoriis populorum." In addition to the Divjak letters cited above, translations of Augustine's epistles are found in St. Augustine, *Letters*, trans. W. Parsons, Fathers of the Church 12, 18, 20, 30 and 32 (Washington, D.C.: Catholic University of America Press, 1951-1956). Text in *Epistulae*, ed. Boldbacher, Corpus Scriptorum Ecclesiasticorum Latinorum 34.1, 34.2, 44, 57 and 58 (Vienna: F. Tempsky, 1895-1923). Cf. similar comments in *Sermo* 340A, 4 and *de Disciplina Christiana (Christian Discipline)*, 1.1.

[28]Christine Mohrmann, "Saint Augustin Prédicateur," in *Études sur le Latin des Chretiens* (Rome, 1958): 391-402. Originally in *La Maison-Dieu* 39 (1954): 83-96.

[29]Dogmatic and apologetic works of Augustine to which one might turn to see the doctrine of atonement include: *DCD*, 10; *Diverse Question* 68; *Trinity*, 4, 12, 13; *Nature and Grace*; *Admonition and Grace*; *Grace and Free Will*; *Predestination of the Saints*; and *Gift of Perseverance*.

People (*Sermones ad Populum*) are a diverse set of sermons delivered to his congregation in Hippo, the basilica in Carthage, and various other churches. The 576 extant sermons reflect a small portion of the actual number Augustine delivered.[30] Included are the recent discovery by F. Dolbeau of thirty additional sermons either known heretofore in fragmentary form or wholly unknown. Many of these are extremely difficult to date, but they span the range of his career.

The Tractates on the Gospel of John (*Tractatus in euangelium Ioannis*) and the First Epistle of John (*Tractatus in epistolam Iohannis ad Parthos*) are a composition of 124 and 10 sermons respectively. Most scholars date these to a period between 411 and 420. Some of these sermons were delivered orally, while others were particularly dictated for dissemination to priests in his diocese. Augustine began the third major set, the Enarrations on the Psalms (*Enarrationes in Psalmos*) ca. 392. This series on the Psalms took some twenty-six years to complete. Like the Tractates on John, some of these he wrote out ahead; others he preached extemporaneously. Augustine's use of scribes insured that many of the sermons delivered extemporaneously were transcribed, distributed and preserved. In both instances, whether prepared and written ahead or delivered extemporaneously, he appears to have intended these sermons for wider dissemination by providing them to priests in his diocese to preach themselves. In addition to these sets, there are important sermons that stand separate from a set, such as his Sermon on the Destruction of Rome (*Sermo de Urbis excidio*)[31] delivered in 410 or 411, and his On the Creed to Catechumens (*De symbolo ad catechumenos*).[32] The rest of this chapter will rely on the three major sets of sermons.

Deformation and Reformation

Though comments from the pulpit include the notion of ransom,[33] a further, critical component of Augustine's understanding of the atone-

---

[30]We are all indebted to Edmund Hill for his fine translations and to the New City Press for the recent publications of these sermons en masse for the first time in *The Works of Augustine for the Twenty-first Century*, Part 3, vols. 1-11 (New York: New City Press, 1990-1998).

[31]Translation available in E. M. Atkins and R. J. Dodaro, eds., *Augustine: Political Writings*, trans. E. M. Atkins, Cambridge Texts in the History of Political Thought (Cambridge: Cambridge University Press, 2001), pp. 205-214.

[32]Text in Corpus Christianorum Latinorum 46.1-85-199; translation in Fathers of the Church 27, trans. M. Ligouri (Washington, D.C.: Catholic University of America Press, 1955).

[33]E.g., *Sermo* 27.2 and 86.7. Also note *Tractatus in euangelium Ioannis* (hereafter cited as *Io*) 41.4.

ment is also present: the refashioning of our nature. This further component is a regular focus in his comments on Christ's act of ransoming humans. In many cases his discussion of ransom serves as a steppingstone to achieve this end. Witness his comments in *Sermo* 86: "He must have held you very dear, since he bought you so dearly. You acknowledge the one who bought you; observe what he bought you back from."[34] Ransom theory stands out in many sermons but, again, it is not the whole of his concern. *Sermo* 27, which perhaps dates to ca. 418 and so comes amid his debate with the Pelagians, is a particularly apt example: "From the first transgression of the first man, the whole human race, being born in the shackles of sin, was the property of the devil who had conquered it. After all, if we hadn't been held in captivity, we wouldn't have needed a redeemer. . . . So he came to the captives not having been captured himself. He came to redeem the captives, having in himself not a trace of the captivity, that is to say, of iniquity, but bringing the price for us in his moral flesh."[35] On the face of it, this is a classic example in patristic literature of ransom theory. And in fact it is, but not in the way we have come to expect. It would be a mistake to treat these words in isolation. The point of these reflections is found just a bit further on in the sermon where he turns to the question of the reason behind the Savior's actions. Citing Isaiah 53, Augustine says, "Christ's deformity is what gives form to you. If he had been unwilling to be deformed, you would never have got back the form you lost. So he hung on the cross, deformed; but his deformity was our beauty."[36] In another sermon we find Augustine commenting that "the law of charity is the law of Christ. He came because he loved us; not that he may be loved, but by his love he might make us loveable."[37]

By defining the doctrine by a narrow study of the dogmatic formulation, we place ourselves in the unenviable but common position of misreading the texts. Augustine was, after all, a rhetorician of particular note and merit. Fluidity and literary craftsmanship were staples of his preaching. Augustine attempted to move his audience toward a

---

[34]*Sermo* 86.7.
[35]*Sermo* 27.2.
[36]*Sermo* 27.6; "deformitas Christi te format. Ille enim si deformis esse noluisset, tu formam quam perdidisti non recepisses. Pendebat ergo in cruce deformis: deformitas illius pulchritude nostra erat."
[37]*Sermo* 163B; "Ipsa est enim lex Christi; lex caritatis est lex Christi. Ideo uenit, quia nos amauit; et non erat quod amaret, sed amando amabiles fecit."

particular vision and goal. To take too close an examination of a particular section of the text leading up to the goal is tantamount to misrepresentation. Ransom theory was a tool for Augustine, important as an explanation of the means, but rather limited, since he was primarily concerned with the ends.

In doing this, Augustine attempted to lead his listener to a fuller vision of God and practice of life as one renewed by God. Like Irenaeus and Athanasius before him, he argued that there is a profound and necessary connection between the means of renewal, the origins of the cosmos, and its fulfillment.[38] The gift of renewal comes only from the Creator of life. In a Tractate on John's Gospel he says, "Christ is the former and reformer of humans, the creator and recreator, the maker and remaker."[39] His is a work of restoration. It is a work that Christ is uniquely able to perform because the Son is the agent of creation.

Augustine regularly emphasizes that Christ's deformity on the cross is the means by which the creation is restored, recovering the form lost by sin. This assessment follows from Augustine's use of privation theory to explain the origin and nature of evil. In his rejection of Manichaean thought, Augustine had turned to privation theory to answer his most pressing questions on the problem of evil. In this theory he found a means to maintain God's goodness in the face of horrific evil by positing real, structural change in the ontological and moral structure of the creation through the free choice of the will. Augustine's use of privation theory has led some to believe that he thought evil to be illusory. This is a complete misunderstanding of his position, however. For Augustine, privation theory meant that creatures are twisted away from their pure, original structure, purpose and practice. Hence, evil, though specifically thought of as a privation of goodness, is both expressed and experienced by real, concrete individuals. Far from illusory, it is profoundly present in creation afflicting all creatures.[40]

The atonement provides for the resolution and the healing of origi-

---

[38]Irenaeus *Adversus Haereses* 4.33.4; Athanasius *de Incarnatio* 54.3. This is not to argue that Augustine knew their works directly, but the implication is suggestive.

[39]*Io* 38.8; "hominis formator et reformatore, creator et recreator, factor et refactor." Text in *Tractatus In Iohannis euangelium*, ed. Willems, Corpus Christianorum Series Latina 36 (Turnholt: Brepols, 1984). It is worth noting that Augustine demonstrates a similar notion to that found in Athanasius's *de Incarnatione* 20-22, wherein Christ is called *autozoe*—self-existing life.

[40]Cf. *Io* 10.13; 13.10; 102.5; *Psal* 44.3.

nal sin. In light of later formulations of the doctrine of original sin, it is
critical to be clear here that Augustine treats the original sin as causing
an actual defect or privation in the actual nature of humans. Humans
are not in Adam and Eve in some representative fashion. There is no
notion of federal headship. Rather, original sin indicates that the choice
in the Garden led to a marring and a profound alteration of human nature.[41] The nature given to the children of the first parents is a mutated
corruption of the original. Hence, humans require healing and restoration to the original design (or actually something even better, Augustine thought, since the cross offers a superior form of grace that was
neither known nor experienced by Adam and Eve). Even more, reconciliation is a work of wonder and delight. In one place he suggests that
the penitent who has sold himself out for the sake of a brief pleasure
says: "[I] have been twisted under the weight of iniquity, but your
word is the set-square of truth. So straighten me out, twists and all, as
though in line with a set-square, that is to say with your straight word.
So *direct my steps according to your word, and let no iniquity master me.* I
have sold myself; you, please redeem me. I have sold myself by my
own choice; redeem me by your own blood."[42] This neatly captures the
imagery of corruption and redemption as restoration.

His wonder at the work of reconciliation is an oft-repeated theme. In
Enarrationes in Psalmos 32, Augustine states that the soul is the highest
thing next to God. Yet it is defiled by sin. Hence, Christ, who first of all
fashioned the soul, came to refashion it.[43] He often uses the analogy of
the minting and refashioning of coinage to explain this process.[44] This
is a telling analogy recalling its basis in imperial politics and rhetoric:
a new emperor would reclaim coins (of course, it could not be all the
coins) minted under previous rulers and have them restruck with his
image. Similarly, Augustine believes that the work of the Savior leads

---

[41]For studies on privation theory, see J. Patout Burns, "Augustine on the Origin and Progress
of Evil," in *The Ethics of St. Augustine* , ed. William S. Babcock, Journal of Religious Ethics:
Studies in Religion 3 (Atlanta: Scholar's Press, 1991); Donald Cress, "Augustine's Privation
Account of Evil: a Defence," *Augustinian Studies* 20 (1989): 109-28. Among Augustine's
works that particularly reflect his understanding of privation theory are the *Confessiones*
(*Confessions*) and *de natura boni* (*The Nature of the Good*).

[42]*Sermo* 30.2; "ego, inquit, distortus sum sub pondere iniquitatis, sed verbum tuum est regula
veritatis: me ergo a me distortum corrige tanquam ad regulam, hoc est, ad verbum rectum."

[43]*Psal* 32 (sermo 3).16, on verse 12.

[44]See for example *Io* 40.9.2

to a profound refashioning of human nature that begins the eradication of corruption.[45] "Let the good soul be praised in the Lord, since it is his possessing it that makes it good, his breathing life into it that makes it flourish, his enlightening it that makes it shine, his forming and shaping it that makes it beautiful, his filling that makes it fruitful. It was through his abandoning it to its own devices, you see, that it was once tossing about dead, dark, deformed, and barren, before it had come to believe in Christ."[46]

Formation, deformation and reformation—these three terms set in apposition encapsulate his understanding of the process.[47] This, then, is a hallmark of his thinking and would be a driving force in much of his preaching. It would also be one of the touchstones in the doctrinal battles with both the Donatists, who held to a sacramental perfectionism, and the Pelagians with their emphasis on individual perfection.

Conclusion: Participation and Invitation

Augustine's focus on participation in the divine life stands as a centerpiece of this pastoral agenda. Though it can be found in a few critical texts among his dogmatic writings (such as in book 4 of *On the Trinity*), it is not always so apparent. By narrowing our focus and ignoring critical sources of his thought, we miss vital aspects of his theology, misrepresent him and marginalize our understanding of him. As a result, some have marginalized Augustine. If we tread this path, we miss the great vision of holiness that he presents.

In a tractate on John 2:12-21, probably dating from the second decade of fifth century, Augustine begins: "This Lord, our God, the Word of God, the Word made flesh, the Son of the Father, the Son of God, the Son of man, exalted that he might create us, humbled that he might re-create us, walking among men, suffering what is human, concealing what is divine."[48] Herein is a profound vision of the nature of atonement. It is a vision that leads further on, though, for at the end of the sermon he concludes: "Let every sigh be a panting after Christ. Let that

---

[45]*de natura et gratia* (Nature and Grace), 40(47).

[46]*Sermo* 312.2; "quo possidente fit bona, quo inspirante uiget, quo illuminante fulget, quo formante pulchra, quo implente fecunda est."

[47]The classic study of this is found in Gerhart Ladner, *The Idea of Reform: Its Impact on Christian Thought and Action in the Age of the Fathers* (New York: Harper Torchbooks, 1967).

[48]*Io* 10.1; "Filius hominis, excelsus ut nos faceret, humilis ut nos reficeret, ambulans inter homines, patiens humana, abscondens divina."

most beautiful one, who loved even the ugly that he might make them beautiful, let him be longed for. Hurry to him alone, sigh for him."[49] We saw above his profound reflection that Christ became deformed that we might become beautiful.[50] Elsewhere he says that God's love aims at creating beauty in place of deformity.[51]

Ultimately, Augustine held that this reformation and the formation of beauty by a beautiful Creator would refashion the creature both ontologically and morally. Reshaping these would renew the deep connection between God and his creation. He comments on this in a manner reminiscent of the notion of deification usually associated with the Greek Fathers: "In order to make gods of those who were merely human, one who was God made himself human; without forfeiting what he was, he wished to become what he himself had made. He himself made what he would become, because what he did was add man to God, not lose God in man."[52] Though Augustine certainly would not hold that humans become God in their nature, he did believe that the renewal of created nature would enable humans to become like unto God morally. Elsewhere he describes it as an invitation to participate in the divine life: "The Teacher of humility became a sharer in our infirmity to enable us to share in his divinity; he came down to us both to teach us the way to become the way, and he graciously willed to make his own humility above all a lesson to us."[53]

"To share in his divinity"—though not a theological comment one would necessarily expect to find in Augustine's works, it is there to be found. And when one takes into account his sermons, the mention of it in the *City of God* is not so surprising. The availability of Augustine's sermons and other pastoral works are an invitation, opportunity and challenge to reassess our understanding of this theologian who crafted his most noteworthy works during the time that he was the Bishop of Hippo.

---

[49]*Io* 10.13; "ille unus pulcherrimus, qui et foedos dilexit ut pulchros faceret, desideretur."
[50]*Sermo* 27.6.6; "deformitas illius pulchritude nostra erat."
[51]*Io* 9.9
[52]*Sermo* 192.1.1; "Deos facturus qui homines erant, homo factus est qui Deus erat: nec amittens quod erat, fieri voluit ipse quod fecerat. Ipse fecit quod esset, quia hominem Deo addidit, non Deum in homine perdidit." I am indebted to Gerald Bonner's work in his aforementioned article, "Augustine's Conception of Deification."
[53]*Psal* 58 (sermo 1).7; "Doctor autem humilitatis, particeps nostrae infirmitatis, donans participationem suae divinitatis, ad hoc descendens ut viam doceret et vis fieret, maxime suam humilitatem nobis commendare dignatus est." Cf. *Psal* 32 (sermo 3).18; *Ep* 91; and *de Trinitate* (*On the Trinity*) 3.2.

tHe atonement in medieval tHeology

Gwenfair M. Walters

The late medieval world devoted itself to eternity. Cloistered monks in tonsured silence contemplated God through the daily rhythm of the Psalter in the oratory. Butchers, coopers and candlemakers in guilds produced pageants with hell-mouths and angels in the streets of York. Priests lifted thin wafer hosts in golden, bejeweled pyxes before delicately painted triptychs and elaborately carved altars that carried the enduring images and crumbling bones of the saints. Soaring cathedrals with flying buttresses and birds nesting in the pilasters encompassed the stained glass scenes of crucifixion suffering. It was an era of passionate spirituality and deep speculation about the divine, a time when the heroes of the day were those who were holy, self-sacrificing, God-focused. It was a culture that encouraged people to go to extremes in their attempts to please God, to strive diligently in earnest anticipation of the afterlife.

From what did this late medieval preoccupation with the other world arise? What caused the medieval parishioner to exert great energy in preparing for life after death? Why did so much of the worship and the practice of the medieval church revolve around paying penalties for sin? Why did so much of the art and architecture focus on the crucifixion? The critical factor in all of this was the reigning view of the atonement at the time: the theory of the atonement as satisfaction.

In broad terms, the Middle Ages was a time in which there was a shift from the ransom theory to the satisfaction theory, in which the satisfaction theory triumphed over the moral influence theory, and in which the satisfaction theory emerged from, and then strengthened, the core of medieval spirituality, liturgy and piety. The ransom theory did not vanish completely, for it played an important role for some of the medieval theologians, but the two medieval theologians best known for their views on the atonement, Anselm of Canterbury (c. 1033-1109) and Peter Abelard (1079-1142), eschewed it. They proposed two new theories to replace it, one of which became the one that most reflected and informed the soteriology of the era, particularly at its close.

This chapter will examine the two key medieval theories and their impact on late medieval spirituality. The first part will explore six aspects of the theories. First, Anselm and Abelard shared a similar methodology in formulating their theories, and second, they both rejected the ransom theory. However, third, they differed in their key questions. Fourth, as a result, their atonement theories diverged from each other, and fifth, the two theories reflected or resonated with two separate models for relationships found in the culture of their day. Sixth, their views varied, consequently, in the relationship of the atonement to the sacraments. The second part of the essay will explore how—with its implications made explicit by Thomas Aquinas (1224-1274)—the satisfaction theory bolstered the Mass, the cults of the passion and the saints, the penitential system and the doctrine of purgatory. In the end it was Anselm's theory, the theory of satisfaction, that would undergird late medieval spirituality and piety.

Anselm's and Abelard's Methodology
Anselm and Abelard shared a similar methodology in approaching the atonement, namely, scholasticism. Anselm of Canterbury was the Archbishop of Canterbury from 1093. His *Cur Deus Homo*[1] was the "first serious attempt to set forth a doctrine of atonement in positive and precise

---

[1]Historians and theologians have debated the precise meaning of the title. The Latin is most often interpreted as "Why God Became Man." John McIntyre argues for "Why the God-Man" in *St. Anselm and His Critics: A Re-Interpretation of the Cur Deus Homo* (Edinburgh: Oliver and Boyd, 1954), 117, 198. Burnell Eckardt Jr. argues that it means "Why God Became Man" rather than "Why God Became a Man" in *Anselm and Luther on the Atonement: Was It "Necessary"?* (San Francisco: Mellen Research University Press, 1992), 36-39.

form."[2] Early in the development of scholasticism, Anselm raised one of the key themes of the movement, the relation of faith and reason. He said of those that had asked him to write about the atonement:

> They make their request not in order to approach faith by way of reason but in order to delight in the comprehension and contemplation of the doctrines which they believe, as well as in order to be ready, as best they can, always to give a satisfactory answer to everyone who asks of them a reason for the hope which is in us.[3]

Anselm set out to argue rationally for the necessity of the atonement involving a God-Man, but he recognized that his argument would not exhaust the truth on the matter.[4]

Peter Abelard was the first to formally state the moral influence theory of the atonement. His views on the atonement, formulated at least partly in response to Anselm's theory, can be found in his *Exposition of the Epistle to the Romans, The Epitome of Christian Doctrine* and in the articles that Bernard of Clairvaux charged against him at the Council of Sens in 1141.[5] Like Anselm, he was a scholastic. For him, although faith was preeminent, reason played a very important role in theological thought. Abelard argued in favor of this on the basis of Christ being called the *logos*, from which the word *logic* was derived; philosophers were lovers of wisdom, and God was the supreme Wisdom; and when God promised the disciples in Luke 21:15, "'For I myself will give you wisdom and utterance that your adversaries will not be able to resist', he [gave them...] that armour of reason by which they would be made supreme logicians in disputations."[6]

Rejection of the ransom theory. Both Anselm and Abelard rejected the ransom theory. For Anselm, there was only one allegiance, the alle-

---

[2]H. D. McDonald, *The Atonement of the Death of Christ: In Faith, Revelation, and History* (Grand Rapids: Baker, 1985), 168. Views similar to Anselm's were expressed by Bruno of Segni in *On the Incarnation of the Lord and His Burial;* by Gilbert of Crispin, Anselm's disciple; by Guibert of Nogent; and by Odo of Cambrai. See Jaroslav Pelikan, *The Christian Tradition: A History of the Development of Doctrine: The Growth of Medieval Theology* (600-1300) (Chicago: University of Chicago Press, 1978), 107.

[3]Anselm *Cur Deus Homo* 1.1, in *Anselm of Canterbury,* ed. and trans. Jasper Hopkins and Herbert Richardson (Toronto: Edwin Mellen Press, 1976), 3:49.

[4]Ibid., 1.2:52.

[5]McDonald, *The Atonement of the Death of Christ,* 174.

[6]Abelard quoted in Richard E. Weingart, *The Logic of Divine Love: A Critical Analysis of the Soteriology of Peter Abailard* (Oxford: Clarendon, 1970), 21.

giance to God. He believed that under the ransom theory, mankind had a double allegiance, to God and to the devil. Unlike the ransom theory's teaching that the devil had a legal right to hold mankind, Anselm taught that the devil had no rights over humanity. Anselm did not eliminate the devil from the atonement story; however, he did redefine his role and the focus of the atonement. The atonement was no longer a transaction between God and the devil; rather, it was a restoration of honor due to God. By giving in to the devil's temptation in Eden, humanity had not upheld God's honor. Humanity was therefore responsible to restore God's honor, but was incapable of doing so.[7] This would serve as part of Anselm's argument for the necessity of the atonement's being made by a God-Man. It was important to Anselm's theory that satisfaction be made to God, not to the devil.

Abelard questioned the ransom theory on five grounds. First, he explored the possible impact of the concept of "the elect" on the dominion of the devil. Then he suggested that the devil could not have tortured humanity without God's permission. Third, the devil used seduction to capture humanity, and a seducer does not gain any rights by his seduction. Fourth, the devil promised immortality to humans in order to get them to sin, but he was not able to fulfill that promise, so any rights he hoped to get via that promise were moot. Fifth, humanity sinned only against God, not against the devil, so the devil did not have any rights.[8]

Anselm's and Abelard's key questions. Although Anselm and Abelard both rejected the ransom theory, they went in separate directions as they formed their new theories, partly because they were interested in different questions. The key question that *Cur Deus Homo* addressed was set forth in the book's title. This God-Man question was expanded by Anselm in the early part of the book:

> For what reason and on the basis of what necessity did God become a man and by His death restore life to the world (as we believe and confess), seeing that He could have accomplished this restoration either by means of some other person (whether angelic or human) or else by merely willing it?[9]

---

[7]*Cur Deus Homo* 1.22:90-91.
[8]Peter Abelard, "Exposition of the Epistle to the Romans (An Excerpt from the Second Book)," in *A Scholastic Miscellany, Anselm to Ockham,* ed. Eugene Fairweather, Library of Christian Classics, vol. 10 (Philadelphia: Westminster Press, 1956), 280-82.
[9]*Cur Deus Homo* 1.2:49.

McIntyre explains that Anselm's purpose was, "to offer justification for faith in two ways: on the one hand, by demonstrating that it is logically inferrible from general principles of reason, and, on the other, by exhibiting the logical self-contradiction involved in the denial of the faith."[10]

Abelard's key questions, on the other hand, arose from his rejection of the ransom theory itself. Since God, simply by appearing, could have taken humanity from the devil's grasp, why did the Son of God need to endure the punishment of the cross and all the pain that entailed? Second, how could humanity be justified through the crucifixion if, by crucifying Christ, humanity committed a worse crime than the one Adam and Eve committed in the first place? Third, how could God release humanity from captivity if he was the one who had set the ransom price himself? And fourth, how could killing an innocent person result in the reconciliation of God to humanity?[11]

Anselm and Abelard on the nature of the atonement. Following on from their starting points, Anselm and Abelard continued to take very different approaches in formulating their replacement theories. Anselm focused first on sin's resulting in the need for satisfaction and then on the necessity of a God-Man to make that satisfaction. Abelard emphasized Christ's act as a demonstration of love for humanity.

Anselm began to answer his own key question with a definition of sin as failure to give to God what was due to him. That which was due to God was the complete subordination of one's will to his. To withhold this honor that was owed to God was to dishonor him and, in essence, to steal honor from God. In order for God's honor to be kept intact, either the honor had to be repaid voluntarily or the one who had

---

[10]McIntyre, *St. Anselm and His Critics*, 15. In addition, Anselm believed that by proving the necessity for God to become a human, he was also going so far as to prove that everything in the Old and New Testaments was true (*Cur Deus Homo* 2.22:137).

[11]Abelard, "Exposition of the Epistle to the Romans," 282-83. The nominalists would ask similar questions: "The Nominalist criticism [of Anselm's theory] is that in the last resort all depends on the arbitrary act of God in accepting the satisfaction. The work of Christ has no value necessarily belonging to it, but only such value as God is pleased to recognize in it. It could not be called necessary that mankind should make the satisfaction which Anselm had laid down, for the sin committed by finite men could not involve an infinite guilt. Nor, again, could the merit of Christ be infinite, since He only suffered in His human nature. Finally, no such infinite merit could be necessary, since God can assess any meritorious act precisely as He pleases" (Gustaf Aulén, *Christus Victor: An Historical Study of the Three Main Types of the Idea of the Atonement* (London: SPCK, 1950), 110.

withheld the honor had to be punished.[12] Sin marred the beauty of the universe by its disruption of the perfect hierarchy of subjection. Just as the owner of a pearl dropped in the mud needed to clean it before placing it into its beautiful treasure box, so God could forgive only those who had made satisfaction for their sins (and, as it turned out, those for whom satisfaction had been made). Any sin, no matter how small, was serious because it was an act against God's will.[13] Sin had upset God's purposes for humanity. God created humans as rational beings so that they could be happy for eternity, enjoying and loving him. He needed to complete what he had begun, bringing them to a glorified state. But because of sin, there was a need to make satisfaction before that could be possible. The question, therefore, was how this satisfaction for sin could be achieved.

This brings us to the heart of Anselm's argument. The only way that atonement could be accomplished was by something that was greater than everything other than God, and by someone who was greater than everything other than God. That someone, of course, could be none other than God.[14] But that someone had also to be a human being, since it was humans who had to make satisfaction for their own sins. Therefore, the only one who could make satisfaction was a God-Man, and the only way he could make that satisfaction was through death.[15]

Anselm wrote a parable that illustrated how the God-Man's actions functioned. He told of a city in which the subjects sinned against their king so severely that death was the necessary judgment. Only one of the inhabitants was innocent, and he chose to perform, out of love, an act that would please the king. As a result,

> because of the magnitude of this service, the king grants absolution from all past guilt to all those who either before or after that day acknowledge

[12]*Cur Deus Homo* 1.6:67; 1.8:71.
[13]Ibid., 1.14:85; 1.21:88-91; 2.1:98-99; 2.4:100.
[14]Ibid., 2.6:102. Of the members of the Trinity, it was only the Son who could become the God-Man. First, if any other than the Son became the God-Man, then there would be two "sons" in the Trinity, and the one begotten of God would have a higher status than the one begotten of a virgin, so there would be an unacceptable inequality within the Trinity. And if the Father became the God-Man, there would be two grandsons in the Trinity. Also, it seems more appropriate for the Son to be the supplicant to the Father than for either of the other two. And also, because the Son is the true likeness of the Father, he was the one who was most sinned against by man taking on a false likeness by his sin. So he is the one most appropriate to make satisfaction for the sin (*Cur Deus Homo* 2.9:107).
[15]Ibid., 2.4:102; 2.9:113.

their desire both to obtain pardon on the basis of the work done on that day and to assent to the agreement then contracted. And [the king grants that] if they sin again after this pardon, they will be pardoned anew through the efficacy of this agreement, *provided they are willing to make an acceptable satisfaction* and thereafter to mend their ways. Nevertheless, [all of this occurs] in such way that no one may enter his palace until after the execution of the service on the basis of which his guilt is pardoned.[16]

Christ, as the "sole inhabitant" deserved a reward from God for the deed he performed on the cross, but there was nothing that God could give him that Christ did not already have, since he was God. So the only way that the Father could reward the Son was by allowing the Son to bestow what his death had earned onto his brothers and sisters so that they would be able to have their sins forgiven. God would not reject anyone who came to this grace in the way that the Scriptures indicated.

For Abelard, the necessity for the atonement did not arise from issues of honor and satisfaction, but rather from God's essence, which was love:

Now it seems to us that we have been justified by the blood of Christ and reconciled to God in this way: through this unique act of grace manifested to us—in that his Son has taken upon himself our nature and preserved therein in teaching us by word and example even unto death—he has more fully bound us to himself by love; with the result that our hearts should be enkindled by such a gift of divine grace, and true charity should not now shrink from enduring anything for him.[17]

Thus, for Abelard the atonement was primarily an act of love that inspired love for him in humans: "Wherefore, our redemption through Christ's suffering is that deeper affection in us which not only frees us from slavery to sin, but also wins for us the true liberty of sons of God, so that we do all things out of love rather than fear-love to him who has shown us such grace that no greater can be found."[18]

For Anselm the goal was to preserve God's honor; for Abelard it was to propound God's love. Anselm focused on the objective; Abelard, on the subjective. Anselm emphasized the effects of the atonement on God, and Abelard the effects of the atonement on humanity.

---

[16]Ibid., 2.18:120. Italics added.
[17]Abelard, "Exposition of the Epistle to the Romans," 283.
[18]Ibid., 284.

Models of relationship: Feudalism and courtly love. Abelard and Anselm's central themes were consonant with two different medieval models of relationship. There were a variety of relationship models in the Middle Ages, from families to monasteries to the Crusades. They involved a number of written and unwritten codes of behavior. Anselm's emphasis on the preservation of God's honor echoed aspects of one such model: feudalism. And Abelard's focus on the transforming power of love paralleled a central characteristic of another: courtly love.

Feudalism was starting to wane during Anselm's lifetime, but it had already had an impact on the church. Grensted argues that part of the reason there was a shift in the view of the atonement with Anselm is that there had been a political shift since the early church: "Anselm [regards] God no longer as a Judge, but rather as a feudal Overlord, bound above all things to safeguard His honor and to demand an adequate satisfaction for any infringement of it."[19] One could argue that Adam's not having upheld God's honor in Eden paralleled a failure of a vassal to live up to his obligations to defend his lord's interests from attack.

Abelard's views, on the other hand, would resonate more with the courtly love that was developing during his lifetime. The theme of love's transforming role appeared first in his own life and then in his theology. One needs to be tentative in drawing causal connections between theologians' views and their personal lives, but there is probably some truth in A. V. Murray's assessment of Abelard:

> As a human being the most outstanding thing in his experience was the unselfish, passionate, disinterested love shown to him by Heloise. The characteristic thing in his theology was his emphasis on the unselfish love of God inflaming the soul with passionate disinterested love in return. The two cannot be unconnected. . . . Abelard found God through his own human life story.[20]

The transforming power of love was present not only in his life and his theology; it would become part of the courtly love movement.

---

[19]L. W. Grensted, *A Short History of the Doctrine of the Atonement* (Manchester: University of Manchester Press, 1920), 123. For the relationship between feudalism and courtly love, cf. C. S. Lewis, *Allegory of Love* (Oxford: Oxford University Press, 1936), 2, and C. Stephen Jaeger, *Ennobling Love: In Search of a Lost Sensibility* (Philadelphia: University of Pennsylvania Press, 1999).

[20]A. Victor Murray, *Abelard and St Bernard: A Study in Twelfth Century "Modernism"* (Manchester: Manchester University Press, 1967), 13.

Many of the characteristics of courtly love would have been rejected by Abelard, but one of the central tenets is one he might have extolled. It is described by Larry Benson: "What distinguishes this style of love [i.e., courtly love] from the styles of other times and places is . . . the conviction that this sort of love is admirable—that love is not only virtuous in itself but is the very source and cause of all the other virtues, that indeed one cannot be virtuous unless he is a lover."[21]

By the late Middle Ages, courtly love was seen as a civilizing, ennobling love. Castiglione, in his *Book of the Courtier*, wrote that it was love that made men valiant in battle against the Moors, "[They] marched on to encounter with the enemies, with that fierceness of courage that Love, and the desire to show their ladies that they were served with valiant men, gave them." A poem attributed to Edward III as advice to his son, the Black Prince, states, "For we hardly ever see a valiant man / Who does not or has not loved." And a fourteenth-century biographer wrote, "Thus one reads of Lancelot, of Tristan, and of many others whom Love made good and famous . . . and whom love has made valiant and virtuous."[22] More work would need to be done to show a causal connection between Abelard's views and courtly love, of course, but the parallels are nevertheless interesting.[23]

Appropriation of the atonement. Although Anselm and Abelard explored in some detail the inner workings of the atonement, neither wrote extensively about how the atonement was appropriated by the believer. In the little that they wrote, however, they remained consistent with their theories. Abelard spoke in general terms of the appropriation of the grace of the atonement as occurring through the Holy Spirit's applying faith, hope and love to the believer.[24]

---

[21]Larry D. Benson, "Courtly Love and Chivalry in the Later Middle Ages" in Robert F. Yeager, ed. *Fifteenth-Century Studies: Recent Essays* (Hamden, Conn.: Archon Books, 1984), 240. Cf. Irving Singer, *The Nature of Love: Courtly and Romantic* (Chicago: University of Chicago Press, 1984), 25-27.

[22]*The Book of the Courtier, from the Italian of Count Baldassare Castiglione: Done into English by Sir Thomas Hoby, anno* 1561, introduction by Walter Raleigh (London: D. Nutt, 1900), 265; *Oevres de Froissart*, ed. Kervyn de Lettenhove (Brussels: Devaux, 1867-77), 1:546, and *Livre des faits du Mareschal de Boucicault*, in *Collection complete des memoirs relatifs a l'histoire de France*, ed. Claude B. Petitot (Paris: Foucault, 1825), 6:393 quoted by Benson, "Courtly Love and Chivalry ," 253, 241.

[23]For a discussion of parallels between Abelard's and courtly love's ideals of disinterested love, cf. Etienne Gilson, *The Mystical Theology of Saint Bernard* (London: Sheed & Ward, 1940), 158-66.

[24]Cf. Weingart, *Logic of Divine Love*, 166-76.

But now, in this dispensation of grace, a righteousness of God—something which God approves and by which we are justified in God's sight, namely love—has been manifested, through the teaching of the gospel, of course, apart from the law with its external and particular requirements. . . . By the faith which we hold concerning Christ love is increased in us, by virtue of the conviction that God in Christ has united our human nature to himself and, by suffering in that same nature, has demonstrated to us that perfection of love of which he himself says: "Greater love than this no man hath," etc. So we, through his grace, are joined to him. As closely as to our neighbor by an indissoluble bond of affection. . . . A righteousness, I say, imparted to all the faithful in the higher part of their being—in the soul, where alone love can exist—and not a matter of the display of outward works.[25]

Abelard taught that baptism removed original sin's punishment of eternal death,[26] that penance was "necessary for the forgiveness of sins,"[27] and that the Eucharist was

rightly called great where the food of the soul is taken in the sacrament of the Lord. The Lord erected this table when he immolated himself on the cross for us. We approach it when we take the sacrament of his body and blood from the altar. When taking this sacrament, we should remember that Christ warned those who partook, "Do this in memory of me" [Lk 22:19], as if he had openly said "So celebrate this sacrament in memory of my passion that this memory prepares you to suffer together with me." For as the Apostle reminds us, "If we suffer together with him, we shall reign with him" [2 Tim 2:12].[28]

Baptism launched the Christian into a life of being infused with Christ's transforming love and of imitating Christ; penance was repentance out of love for God; and the Eucharist prepared one to suffer with Christ, in love. Abelard emphasized the believer's role, examining the impact of love on the believer and the believer's imitation of Christ.[29]

---

[25]Abelard, "Exposition of the Epistle to the Romans," 278.
[26]Weingart, *Logic of Divine Love*, 191-92.
[27]Peter Abelard, *A Dialogue of a Philosopher with a Jew, and a Christian*, trans. Pierre J. Payer (Toronto: Pontifical Institute of Mediaeval Studies, 1979), 160. Abelard did not consider penance a sacrament (Weingart, *Logic of Divine Love*, 190).
[28]Anselm *Sermo* 32:75ab, quoted in Weingart, *Logic of Divine Love*, 193.
[29]Weingart, *Logic of Divine Love*, 188-94.

Remaining consistent with his emphasis on God's role, Anselm did not dwell on humans' responsibility in appropriating what Christ had done on their behalf. In fact, his relative silence on the subject was perhaps an expression of this very emphasis. Nevertheless, although he did not focus on the issue of whether humans needed to perform additional work to make the satisfaction complete, he did seem to allow an opening for the necessity of humans' involvement by his phrase "provided they are willing to make an acceptable satisfaction and thereafter to mend their ways," in the above story of the king.[30]

It remained for Thomas Aquinas (1224-1274), the most well known of the scholastic theologians, to make more explicit the connections between the atonement and the sacraments[31] and to work out the implications of the theory of satisfaction for the life of the church. He brought together Anselm's and Abelard's atonement theories in his sermon on the clause, "Suffered under Pontius Pilate, Was Crucified, Was Dead, and Was Buried" in his series on the Apostles' Creed:

> But, what was the necessity that the Son of God should suffer for us? Great need. And it can be reduced to necessity that is twofold. (1) A remedy against sin, and (2) an example for behavior. As for the "remedy," through the passion of Christ we find a remedy against all the evils that we undergo because of sin.[32]

Although Aquinas combined Abelard and Anselm's views somewhat, it was Anselm's idea of satisfaction that had the greatest impact on his views on the appropriation of the atonement via the sacraments. According to Aquinas, confession and absolution delivered the sinner from eternal punishment, that is, from hell, and from guilt. But temporal punishment remained and either had to be suffered in purgatory or, through the power of the keys exercised in the sacrament of penance,

---

[30]Even this reference needs to be weighed lightly, however, for it is uncertain whether Anselm wrote this line or whether it was a later interpolation.

[31]George Williams attempts to find direct connections in Anselm's writings between his theory of atonement and his attitude toward the sacraments, but the ties are somewhat fragile (*Anselm: Communion and Atonement* [Saint Louis, Mo.: Concordia Publishing House, 1960], 26-67).

[32]Nicholas Ayo, ed. *The Sermon-Conferences of St. Thomas Aquinas on the Apostles' Creed* (Notre Dame: University of Notre Dame Press, 1988), 69. For a discussion of the doctrine of atonement in this sermon, cf. Hughes Oliphant Old, *The Reading and Preaching of the Scriptures in the Worship of the Christian Church* (Grand Rapids: Eerdmans, 1999), 417-23.

could be reduced to the point where it could be met through satisfaction made in this life.[33]

In the late Middle Ages penance became one of the most important avenues of the appropriation of the atonement. There had been vigorous debates amongst the scholastic theologians as to what role contrition (true repentance) played versus attrition (fear of punishment) in the sacrament; how much responsibility was on the penitent, the priest and on God; and on the exact relationship of the sacrament of penance to issues of forgiveness, remission of sin, absolution and so forth. Contritionists such as Peter Lombard argued that forgiveness came in response to true sorrow for sins on the part of the penitent person. But the trend toward the later Middle Ages put more power in the hands of the sacrament and the priest. In the thirteenth century there was a change in the priest's absolution phrase from "May God forgive you" to "I absolve you."[34] Guido de Monte Rocherii, a fourteenth-century curate, in *Manipulus curatorum*, reflected this trend: "Thus I believe that a single Our Father imposed in penance by a priest is more efficacious than one hundred thousand said on one's own, because it has the merit of the passion of Christ."[35]

It was not only the sacrament of penance that was important in the late medieval church. In the *Summa Theologica*, Aquinas had stated that sacraments in general were critical:

> Christ's Passion is a sufficient cause of man's salvation. But it does not follow that the sacraments are not also necessary for that purpose: because they obtain their effect through the power of Christ's Passion; and Christ's Passion is, so to say, applied to man through the sacraments according to the Apostle (Rom. vi. 3): *All we who are baptized in Christ Jesus, are baptized in His death.*[36]

For Aquinas, the sacraments were essential to salvation because it was through them that Christ's atonement was applied. And the grace that was conferred by the sacraments helped human beings not only to

[33]Fathers of the English Dominican Province, trans., *St. Thomas Aquinas: Summa Theologica* (New York: Thomas More Publishing, 1948), Suppl.Q. 10 Art. 2; 5:2593.
[34]Thomas N. Tentler, *Sin and Confession on the Eve of the Reformation* (Princeton, N.J.: Princeton University Press, 1977), 281.
[35]Guido de Monte Rocherii in *Manipulus curatorum* 2, 3, 10, fol. 95b-96a, quoted by Tentler, *Sin and Confession*, 283.
[36]Thomas Aquinas *Summa Theologica* Q. 61 Art. 1, 4:2347.

remedy previous sins but to better resist future sin.[37] It was this connection between atonement and sacrament that became critical for the cohesion of late medieval piety. It was expressed, for example, in the *Angelica*, a highly popular fifteenth-century confessors' *summa*, which
stated that "the sacraments are the immediate application of the passion of Christ to us."[38]

   The results of Abelard's and Anselm's views. Finally, it was in this
atonement-sacrament nexus that Anselm's and Abelard's atonement
theories found their dramatically different responses. Abelard's, running counter to the prevailing views of his day, resulted in personal
tragedy; whereas Anselm's, drawing from and then reinforcing the
contemporary sacramental piety, was triumphant.

   Abelard's views resulted in controversy. William of St. Thierry
(ca.1055-1145) stopped writing a commentary on the Song of Songs because he could no longer pursue "a task of such pleasant leisure within
while Abelard without was so cruelly laying waste the regions of the
faith with unsheathed sword."[39] In his letter to Pope Innocent arguing
against Abelard, Bernard of Clairvaux (1090-1153), who held to a version of the ransom theory, wrote:

> I see three chief virtues in this work of our salvation: the form of humil-
> ity in which God emptied himself; the measure of charity which He
> stretched out even to death, and that the death of the Cross; the sacra-
> ment of redemption by which He bore that death which He underwent.
> The former two of these without the last are as if you were to paint on
> the air. A very great and most necessary example of humility; a great ex-
> ample of charity, and one worthy of all acceptation hath He set us; but
> they have no foundation, and, therefore, no stability, if redemption be
> wanting. I wish to follow with my strength the lowly Jesus; I wish Him,
> who loved me and gave Himself for me, to embrace me with the arms
> of His love, which suffered in my stead; but I must also feed on the Pas-
> chal Lamb, for unless I eat His Flesh and drink His Blood I have no life
> in me. It is one thing to follow Jesus, another to hold Him, another to
> feed on Him.[40]

---

[37]Ayo, ed. *The Sermon-Conferences of St. Thomas Aquinas*, 71.
[38]Angelus de Clavasio, *Angelica*, quoted by Tentler, *Sin and Confession*, 298.
[39]*Epistola ad Fratres de Monte Dei, Prologus*, ed., A. Wilmart, 239, quoted by D. E. Luscombe,
    The School of Peter Abelard (Cambridge: Cambridge University Press, 1969), 106.
[40]Quoted in S. Cave, *The Doctrine of the Work of Christ* (London: University of London Press,
    1937), 139-40.

In addition, Bernard insisted that the atonement was not merely about mercy but also about justice and stated that Christ came for the liberation, not just the instruction, of humanity.[41] Most of the nineteen propositions attributed (some erroneously) to Abelard and officially condemned by Pope Innocent II dealt with issues other than the atonement, but one *capitulum* condemns Abelard for teaching that Christ's death was not intended to deliver humanity from the devil.[42] Abelard would die in a monastery after traveling toward Rome to try to defend himself from the accusations, and his ideas would have only a limited impact on medieval theology.

Anselm's views on the atonement, on the other hand, became foundational to medieval atonement theory as well as to medieval worship and piety. A strong emphasis on the theme of satisfaction came to be a driving force in medieval piety, and the necessity of additional satisfaction to be made by Christians became a central part of medieval spirituality. While Anselm most likely did not intend such a large role to be played by human beings in activating and completing the work of the atonement,[43] his emphasis on the idea of satisfaction was certainly echoed in the piety of the late Middle Ages.

The ransom theory did not vanish from the worldview of the laity, but it was not the driving force of medieval piety. In *Mirk's Festial*, a fifteenth-century preachers' handbook, for example, the author argued that one of the important reasons to observe the Mass was

> for love, that man shall for the sight thereof think, how the Father of Heaven had but one son that he loved passing all things. And yet for to buy man out of the devil's thraldom, he sent him into this world, and with his own heartblood wrote him a charter of freedom, and made him free for ever.[44]

---

[41]Murray, *Abelard and St Bernard*, 81-88.

[42]Luscombe, *The School of Peter Abelard*, 137-38.

[43]Writing to a dying man, for example, Anselm advised: "If the Lord God will judge thee say, 'Lord, I place the death of your Lord Jesus Christ between me and Thy judgment: in no other way do I contend with Thee.' If he says to thee that thou art a sinner, say, 'Lord, I place the death of our Lord Jesus Christ between Thee and my sins'. . . . If he shall say that he is angry with thee, say, 'Lord, I place the death of our Lord Jesus Christ between me and Thy anger.'" Quoted by McDonald, *The Atonement of the Death of Christ*, 173.

[44]Theodor Erbe, ed., *Mirk's Festial: A Collection of Homilies by Johannes Mirk*, Early English Text Society Series (London: Kegan Paul, Trench, Trubner & Co., 1905), 172. I have modernized the English.

C. W. Marx argues that "medieval theology after Anselm constructed a new understanding of the defeat of the Devil in which the Devil's right to possess humanity continued to be an important question; and the revised formulation of the place of the Devil in the redemption produced the convention of the debate between Christ and the Devil, and in vernacular writing a new version of the harrowing of hell episode."[45] But although there were still hints of the ransom theory in literature and drama, what was at the core of the late medieval system, in its very structure, was the concept of satisfaction, of the payment of ongoing debts.

At first glance it may seem ironic that Anselm's theory, although based on ideas from a system (feudalism) that was waning, was the one that prevailed, while Abelard's, having at its core a concept similar to one at the heart of courtly love (which was just being born and would become an important aspect of medieval aristocratic life) should be the minority position. The irony, however, is mitigated when one looks at a set of shifts that is far more central to medieval piety. George Williams argues that the shift from the ransom theory to the satisfaction theory arose historically from a liturgical shift from the early church's emphasis on baptism to the medieval focus on the Eucharist and the sacrament of penance.[46] The second part of this essay will show how this liturgical-theological shift during the high Middle Ages transformed four key aspects of late medieval piety: the sacrament of the Mass, the cults of devotion to the passion and the saints, the doctrine of purgatory and the sacrament of penance.

---

[45]C. W. Marx, *The Devil's Rights and the Redemption in the Literature of Medieval England* (Woodbridge, Suffolk: D. S. Brewer, 1995), 4.

[46]Williams summarizes studies that link "Judaeo-Christian demonology and the primacy of Baptism in the ancient church as the sacramental means whereby the catechumens appropriated the redemptive work of Christ by submitting to elaborate and repeated exorcisms, by renouncing Satan and the would-be triumphal pomp of all the demonic host of the dethroned deities of paganism, by swearing in the presence of the good angels sacramental allegiance to Christ in the struggle with Satan, by going down with Christ into the waters of Baptism to overcome the dragon of the deep, by dying to this world to rise with Him in a new birth and thus cheating Satan of his right to inflict a *definitive* death. Christ's own descent into Hades between his expiration on the cross and the resurrection, a descent which was in a sense re-enacted symbolically in the plunge into the waters of the baptistery, was understood by many as the deliverance of the captive from the clutches of the devil" (*Anselm: Communion and Atonement*), 14-15.

The Mass

The relationship between the Mass and the appropriation of the atonement to the medieval believer was a complex one. Transubstantiation, Mass as sacrifice, the real presence of Christ in the Eucharist, the relationship between substance and accidents before and after the moment of consecration, the implications of Aristotelian philosophy, the Platonic elevation of spirit over matter, realist versus nominalist approaches, the intentions and morality of the priest, the faith of the recipient, the frequency of communion by the laity, even practical issues of how to treat the spilled wine or accidentally scattered crumbs, and the efficacy of masses for the dead all were debated at length by medieval theologians. By the late Middle Ages, however, the church agreed as a whole that at the moment of consecration, the moment when the priest elevated the host before the altar and said "Hoc est corpus meum," transubstantiation occurred. That meant that Christ's body and blood were present in the elements, and this had implications for the salvation of the believer.

The emergence of a new festival, Corpus Christi, reflected the growing importance of the Mass. Developing in the early to mid-thirteenth century, the feast of Corpus Christi was universally celebrated by the early fourteenth century and was officially incorporated into canon law in 1317.[47] The Corpus Christi sermon in *Mirk's Festial* began with the invitation, "Christian men and women, you shall know well that this is a high feast in the holy church of Christ's body, the which is each day offered up in holy church in the altar to the Father of Heaven in remission of sin to all that live here in perfect charity and in great succor and release of their pain that be in purgatory."[48] It was an exhortation to honor the host, believed to be the body of Christ. The Mass being offered up was effective in bringing about remission of sins for the living and in reducing the time of suffering for those in purgatory. Not only that, but simply participating fully in the Corpus Christi festival events would bring certain numbers of days of pardon, cutting additional time off of purgatorial sentences.

Christ was offered up again in each Mass, and belief in transubstan-

---

[47]Miri Rubin, *Corpus Christi: The Eucharist in Late Medieval Culture* (Cambridge: Cambridge University Press, 1991), 181.
[48]Erbe, ed., *Mirk's Festial*, 168. I have modernized the English.

tiation was important for the appropriation of the merit of his shed blood. Mirk's Corpus Christi day sermon continued, "Then as Christ that day shed his blood on the cross in help of all mankind, so yet each day in the mass he sheds his blood in high merit to all that this believe; for without this belief there may no man be saved."[49] The *Speculm Sacerdotale* expressed a similar idea, "'Though Christ suffered the Passion and was sacrificed upon the cross for us in one time, yet for that we each day do sin as our infirmity will not allow anything else, therefore he is each day for us sacrificed figuratively.' And that is a needful point to our belief and to be trusted both for remission of venial sins and also for increasing of perfection and of virtues."[50] Scholastic theologians differed on whether the offering up of Christ each day was literal or figurative. What they agreed upon was that it effected an ongoing remission of sins.

It was in the Eucharistic prayers that developed after Anselm, addressed to Christ at the moment of elevation, that one found the God-Man language and the idea of appropriation of salvation through the Mass being expressed by the laity. One example was the following prayer from the early fifteenth century:

> Welcome be thou, soul food,
> Both who, Jesu, God and Man,
> For me thou hung upon the cross
> Thy body pale and wan.
> The water and the blood out of thy side ran,
> Of my sins, Lord, do me remedy,
> Jesu, God and Man,
> Grant me that I thee might love . . .
> I am sinful, as thou well knowest
> Jesu, thou have mercy on me,
> Nor suffer never that I be lost,
> For whom thou diest upon a tree.[51]

---

[49]Ibid., 170. I have modernized the English.

[50]Edward H. Weatherly, ed., *Speculum Sacerdotale*, Early English Text Society Series (London: Oxford University Press, 1936), 162. I have modernized the English.

[51]BM Addit. 37787, quoted in R. H. Robbins, "Levation prayers in Middle English verse," *Modern Philology* 40 (1942-43): 138. I have modernized the English. For additional discussion of the impact of medieval atonement theories on the Mass, cf. P. J. Fitzpatrick, "On Eucharistic Sacrifice in the Middle Ages," in S. W. Sykes, ed., *Sacrifice and Redemption: Durham Essays in Theology* (Cambridge: Cambridge University Press, 1991), 142-46.

Another popular prayer addressed the host as well:

> Welcome Lord in form of bread!
> For me thou suffered painful death.
> Blissful body sacred before me,
> Have mercy on me [that] I be not lost
> Hail! Iesu Christ, Saviour of this world,
> The father's Son of Heaven,
> Holy, oft sacred, corporeal in flesh
> Truly god and very man:
> Thee, the precious body of Iesu Crist
> With all my heart I worship.[52]

Each time people observed the elevation of the host and said these prayers, they would be reminded of the God-Man's dying on the cross for them and of the role of the Mass in transmitting the grace of redemption to believers.

The cults of devotion to the Passion and of the saints. The centrality of the Mass was part of late medieval spirituality's focus on the passion of Christ, which found expression in many contexts.[53] Mystics such as Margery Kempe and Julian of Norwich had visions of Christ's death. One of the best-selling books was Pseudo-Bonaventura's *Meditationes Vitae Christi,* which was translated into many European languages and which taught the laity how to meditate on the final week of Christ's life. Dying parishioners were instructed to look at the crucifix in the hands of the priest at their bedside. The most popular presentation of Christ in art, other than as a child in depictions of the Madonna and child, was of Christ on the cross.[54] In stained glass, in devotional triptychs, on altarpieces, in sculptured crucifixes, Christ appeared, suffering perpetually on the cross. A thirteenth-century religious lyric from England provides an example of how Christ's death was linked devotionally with the doctrine of the atonement:

> Whan I thenke on the rode [cross]
> Wher-upon thou stood,

---

[52]R. H. Robbins, "Popular Prayers in Middle English Verse," *Modem Philology* 39 (1939): 373-74, as quoted in Rubin, *Corpus Christi,* 161. I have modernized the English.

[53]Cf. Eamon Duffy, *The Stripping of the Altars: Traditional Religion in England* 1400-1580 (New Haven, Conn.: Yale University Press, 1992), 234-56.

[54]Cf. Henk van Os, *The Art of Devotion in the Late Middle Ages in Europe,* 1300-1500 (London: Merrell Holberton Publishers Ltd., 1994), 87.

Swete Jhesu my lemman [beloved];
How by thee was stondyng
Thy moder wepyng
And thy disciple Seint Iohan;
How thy rigge [back] was i-swongen,
And thy side thurgh-stongen [pierced]
For the gilt [guilt] of man;
How thy feet y-bledden...
No sely [wonder] thogh I wepe
And my synnes bete [make amends for]
If I of love can.[55]

Ironically, however, even as people were drawing nearer to the suffering Christ, the relationship between the believer and the Christ who was now in heaven was growing more distant. The most common post-ascension presentation of Christ in art was that of the Last Judgment.[56] This often took the form of dramatic, quite frightening murals that loomed large as one departed from the cathedral or parish church. Christ was seen as a judge and therefore as unapproachable.

This, in turn, contributed to the ongoing development of the cult of the saints. Although people initiated contact with saints most often to request aid during times of illness or crisis, one can also find connections between the cult of the saints and the remission of sins. The fourteenth-century preacher's handbook *Fasciculus Morum* teaches:

> Further, if our offense against our father Christ should be so great that we are afraid to pray for his mercy, let us do as he does who causes the king of his land such great indignation that he does not dare come before him in order to ask for his grace in whatever form. Such a person goes secretly to the queen and sends her some gift so that she may pray and intercede with the king. . . . Indeed, thus should we do when we have offended Christ our father and are afraid to pray for his mercy. First let us go to the Mother of Mercy, the Queen of Heaven and Earth, and send her as a gift something special, such as waking, fasting, prayer, or almsgiving. At this she will certainly, like a loving mother, hasten to come between you and Christ your father who wants to chastise you for your failing, and she will stretch her mantle between you and his rod. And he

---

[55]MS Ashmole 360, quoted by Robert D. Stevick, ed., *One Hundred Middle English Lyrics*, rev. ed. (Urbana: University of Illinois Press, 1994), 24.
[56]Cf. Philippe Aries, *The Hour of Our Death* (Oxford: Oxford University Press, 1981), 99ff.

will surely relinquish all punishment or at least soften it to a large extent, so that we will go free without grief.[57]

Penitential acts offered as "gifts" to the saints, whether to the Virgin Mary or to lower saints, would cause her to intercede on the sinner's behalf and result in a softening of the sentence of punishment. This was still, of course, a variation on the satisfaction theory, for something was offered by the sinner in exchange for forgiveness. But here mediators had entered between God and humanity.

The doctrine of purgatory. A third aspect of medieval piety strengthened by the satisfaction theory was the doctrine of purgatory. It is noteworthy that at the same time that Satan's role in the atonement story was being downplayed by the shift away from the ransom theory, the flames of purgatory were being stoked. By 1254 the doctrine had advanced to the point where a pontifical letter spelled out the following:

> The souls of those who die after receiving penance but without having had the time to complete it, or who die without mortal sin but guilty of venial (sins) or minor faults, are purged [in purgatory] after death and may be helped by the suffrages of the Church.[58]

The letter described purgatory as "this temporary fire." The doctrine of purgatory was officially defined as an article of faith at the Council of Florence in 1439.[59] For those who had not paid their full penalty, that is, had not made full satisfaction before their deaths, purgatory was the place for making up the balance. It was believed that one would go to purgatory for a length of time that matched the amount of penalty one still had to pay and that this length of time could be measured in years, sometimes hundreds or thousands of years. Thus prayers and indulgences and penitential acts had certain numbers of years of remission attached to them.

There were many stories circulating across Europe, translated into various languages, detailing near-death experiences in which individuals visited purgatory and returned with vivid reports. One popular place where people went on pilgrimage intentionally to receive visions

[57]Siegfried Wenzel, ed. and trans., *Fasciculus Morum: A Fourteenth-Century Preacher's Handbook* (University Park: Pennsylvania State University Press, 1989), 73.
[58]Jacques Le Goff, *The Birth of Purgatory,* trans. Arthur Goldhammer (Aldershot: Scolar Press, 1990), 283.
[59]Ibid., 357.

of purgatory was St. Patrick's Purgatory in Lough Derg, Ireland. An excerpt from an account of one of those pilgrims, William of Stranton, illustrated a common aspect of purgatorial visions, and that was the matching of torment to sin:

> Then St. John showed me other diverse souls, and some were enclosed in plates of iron all burning, and on the plates were letters and words well written, and through the words were nails of iron all burning, smitten into their heads and so into their hearts and into their bodies. And among these souls I saw one that his tongue and his heart were taken out and shorn small, and fiends cast them on his face again. . . . And St. John said to me, "These are the souls of vicars and parsons and other priests also, and the letters that are written on the plates which are smitten on their heads betoken divine services, that they should have said and done every day with great devotion. But they have more false devotion and lust in hawking and hunting and other lewd places and idle occupations and worldly mirths, than in the service of God, and therefore are they thus pained with horrible pains."[60]

Whatever the sins one had committed and had not already done penance for, one would pay for through various carefully matched tortures in Purgatory.

The sacrament of penance. Such stories helped to motivate the laity to take the sacrament of penance seriously, and many ways of paying penance became popular in the high to late Middle Ages. Fasting, prayer and giving alms to the poor remained the most common. Pilgrimages, masses and indulgences became very important as well.

The first indulgence coincided with the first Crusade in 1095, which in many senses was itself a pilgrimage. Pope Urban II, in calling for this Crusade, declared, "Know, then, that anyone who sets out on that journey, not out of lust for worldly advantage but only for the salvation of his soul and for the liberation of the Church, is remitted in entirety all penance for his sins, if he has made a true and perfect act of confession."[61] The indulgences seemed to become more valuable with each Crusade. By the third Crusade, Pope Celestine in 1195 granted "For they who have undertaken the labour of this journey with contrite

[60]Robert Easting, ed., *St. Patrick's Purgatory,* Early English Text Society Series (Oxford: Oxford University Press, 1991), 101, 103. I have modernized the English.
[61]Elizabeth Hallam, ed., *Chronicles of the Crusades: Eye-Witness Accounts of the Wars Between Christianity and Islam* (Godalming, U.K.: CLB International, 1989), 63.

heart and humble spirit are to obtain a plenary indulgence for their sins, and eternal life thereafter."[62] Other kinds of indulgences emerged, attached to pilgrimages to saints' shrines and holy sites in Rome and the Holy Land, to prayers to the Blessed Virgin and other saints, and even to raising funds for cathedral building.

According to Aquinas, it was possible for one person to make satisfaction for another person's sin.[63] People, especially the wealthy, took steps during life to provide, after their deaths, for their own souls and those of their families to get out of purgatory. Chantries were set up so that prayers and masses could be said for the dead long after their death. A rich wool merchant could build a chantry chapel onto the side of a cathedral, for example, where the chantry priest that he hired would say daily masses for the souls of everyone in his family who had died. Entire monastic orders were formed by rich patrons who wanted the monks to say prayers for their souls in perpetuity. Perhaps the best example of this was the Cluniac Order. The Duke of Cluny, in the foundation charter, after listing all the property he was giving to the order, gave the reasons for his large donation:

> I give . . . all these things to the aforesaid apostles—I, William, and my wife Ingelberga—first for the love of God; then for the soul of my lord king Odo, of my father and my mother; for myself and my wife—for the salvation namely, of our souls and bodies;—and not least for that of Ava who left me these things in her will; for the souls also of our brothers and sisters and nephews, and of all our relatives of both sexes; for our faithful ones who adhere to our service; for the advancement, also and integrity of the catholic religion. Finally, since all of us Christians are held together by one bond of love and faith, let this donation be for all,—for the orthodox, namely, of past, present or future times.[64]

People left money and instructions in their wills for a variety of purgatory-shortening activities to be performed on their behalf after their death. William Hanyngfield of Essex's will in 1426 specified the following:

> First, I will that the Manors of "Chardacre and Valans" in the shire of

---

[62]Ibid., 196.

[63]Thomas Aquinas *Summa* Suppl Q. 13 Art. 2, 5:2604.

[64]"The Foundation Charter of Cluny," in Patrick Geary, ed., *Readings in Medieval History* (Ontario: Broadview, 1989), 340.

Suffolk that they be sold by my executors to as high a price as it may, without fraud . . . and the money thereof received, be dispensed for my soul after the discretion of my executors. Moreover I will that [three manors] be sold by the same executors, and with the money thereof received, and more, if need be, be founded two priests, singing continually during the term of 40 winters in the Prior of "Bykenacre" in the Chapel of St. Nicholas, for the souls of men, the foresaid William, Agnes, John, Cisily my wife, William Nicholas Martyn, Eleanor, Elisabeth, Roger, and Margery, and for all the souls that I am bound to do for, after the discretion of my executors.[65]

Other wills included the detailing of specific dates for masses to be performed, gifts to be left for the poor (as alms), chapels to be built, colleges to be founded and objects to be given to priests and to churches, all so that prayers and/or masses would be said for the deceased.

Those who participated in the sacramental system would go to purgatory when death came and then eventually to heaven. The thought of that time in purgatory was kept continually before the laity in art, in sermon illustrations, in instructional books and in the sacraments. Doing the right things in order to keep the time in purgatory as short as possible was quite possibly the primary spiritual drive in many people's lives in the Middle Ages. And it was in turn powered by the belief in the necessity of making satisfaction for sins, making satisfaction for one's sins here on earth so that one could avoid having to make satisfaction for them in purgatory.

Conclusion

Although each focused on a number of important points, both Anselm and Abelard's theories were inadequate to capture the full import of Christ's atonement. Bernard of Clairvaux may not have accurately understood all the nuances of Abelard's theory, but he captured the poverty of the exemplarist stance when he noted that the lack of emphasis on the objective nature of the atonement leaves humanity trying in vain to live up to the example of love that Christ presented on the cross. Anselm's rejection of the ransom theory in favor of stating that the primary transaction of the atonement took place between God and him-

---

[65]Frederick J. Furnivall, ed., *The Fifty Earliest English Wills*, Early English Text Society Series (London: Oxford University Press, 1882), 69-70. I have modernized the English.

self rather than between God and the devil was a step in the right direction. By leaving an opening, however, for the necessary appropriation of the atonement through the sacraments, Anselm's satisfaction theory—especially as it was elaborated by Aquinas and integrated into medieval piety—left people in a similar position of believing that they were required to add to the work of Christ.[66]

As a result, in contrast to much of the Western culture of today, the medieval world possessed a sober God-focus, a passionate intention to deal with the afterlife that is laudable and worthy of imitation. But in contrast to the implications of the atonement views that would come with the Reformation, the medieval world was lacking in the peace, the security and the joy that come from believing that the atonement was not merely satisfaction but was sufficient satisfaction. The medieval worldview lacked a satisfaction made fully by Another, taking care not only of the guilt but also of the penalty, one where the work was truly finished on the cross and thereby completely guaranteed satisfaction. It would take the Reformation to bring a transformation in the prevailing medieval theory of the atonement and its culture-deep impact.

---

[66]For a helpful critique of Anselm and Abelard's views of the atonement, cf. McDonald, *The Atonement of the Death of Christ*, 168-73; 179-80.

tHe atoNemeNt IN martIN LutHeR's tHeoLoGy

Timothy George

There is no article on "atonement" in the *Oxford Encyclopedia of the Reformation,* although there are various entries that deal with the saving work of Jesus Christ, including topics such as justification, grace, original sin, salvation, Christology and so forth. Perhaps this is because atonement, understood as a distinctive locus in systematic theology, was not a matter of great debate between the Protestant Reformers and their Roman Catholic adversaries. With the exception of the Socinians and a few other radicals, theologians on both sides of the Reformation divide believed that the death of Christ on the cross had secured an objective satisfaction for sin, one that was of infinite value, and without which no salvation was possible for lost human beings.

In the sixteenth century, the real issue at stake was not the reality and efficacy of the atoning work of Christ on the cross, but rather how that achievement was to be appropriated. Was it by faith formed by love, or by faith alone? Was salvation received through the sacraments of the church, or by grasping the word of promise in the preaching of the gospel? To know Christ is to know his benefits, as Melanchthon famously said. But the obverse also held: to misconstrue the benefits was to remain ignorant of Christ and his salvific work on our behalf.

But the matter is not quite so simple as this, especially for Martin Luther, who once described the belief that Jesus Christ, the Son of God, had suffered and died for us as "the most joyous of all doctrines and the

one that contains the most comfort."[1] One cannot so easily separate
Luther's understanding of Christ's work on the cross from his doctrine
of justification by faith. Put another way, Luther's christological teaching is soteriologically driven. Much debate has also centered on how
Luther's view of the work of Christ is related to earlier models of atonement in the Christian tradition. Does Luther really have a distinctive
"theory" of atonement at all? We shall explore these questions first by
looking briefly at two landmark interpretations of Luther's theology,
and then by considering several themes in Luther's exposition of Galatians 3:13, a key passage in his most important biblical commentary.

Theology of the Cross

The publication of two books, one by a German historian in 1929,
Walther von Loewenich's *Luther's Theology of the Cross,* and the other,
Christus Victor, by a Swedish theologian, Gustaf Aulén, in 1931,
spurred a new appraisal of Luther's understanding of the work of
Christ. The immediate context for both of these books was the liberal
Enlightenment ideal of Luther that had prevailed for more than a hundred years—from Hegel to Harnack. Hegel interpreted Luther as "the
all-illuminating sun, which followed that day-break at the end of the
Middle Ages," the hero and champion of freedom, progress and the
liberated conscience.[2] This idea was carried forward by Albrecht
Ritschl and given classic expression by Adolf von Harnack who concluded his massive *History of Dogma* with this verdict: "In Luther's Reformation the old dogmatic Christianity was discarded and a new
evangelical view substituted for it."[3]

Against the reductionist readings of Luther that prevailed in the tradition of liberal Protestantism, both von Loewenich and Aulén presented a Luther who was deeply concerned about the dogmatic heart
of the Christian faith, a Luther for whom true theology and recognition
of God were to be found only in the crucified Christ. This was the

---

[1]*Lectures on Galatians (1535), Chapters 1-4,* in *Luther's Works,* ed. Jaroslav Pelikan and Walter A.
Hansen (St. Louis and Philadelphia: Concordia and Fortress, 1958-1986), 26:28. (Volumes in
this series are hereafter abbreviated *LW.*)

[2]Georg Wilhelm Friedrich Hegel, *Sämtliche Werke,* ed. Hermann Glockner (Stuttgart, Germany: F. Frommann, 1927-1957), 11:519.

[3]Adolf von Harnack, *History of Dogma* (1900; reprint, New York: Dover Publications, 1961)
7:227. On Hegel, see Timothy George, *Theology of the Reformers* (Nashville: Broadman and
Holman, 1988), 13-14.

Luther who said *"CRUX sola est nostra theologia"* (the cross alone is our theology).[4] In his vain attempts to satisfy God by his prayers, fastings, vigils and good works, Luther had been directed by his confessor Johannes von Staupitz to turn to "the wounds of the most sweet Savior" as a way out of his despair.[5] By pointing Luther to the cross, Staupitz had "started the doctrine," as Luther put it, that would eventually lead to his Reformation breakthrough. Scholars are still divided as to when precisely this breakthrough occurred, but it is clear that a new and deeper understanding of the cross was at the heart of Luther's developing theology. Von Loewenich traced the emergence of a distinctive *theologia crucis*, which came to articulate expression in Luther's Heidelberg Disputation in April 1518. This was a pivotal moment in Luther's career, midway between his posting of the Ninety-five Theses on the door of the castle church at Wittenberg in 1517 and his famous debate with Johannes Eck over Scripture and tradition at Leipzig in 1519.

Staupitz encouraged Luther to present his emerging evangelical theology to his fellow Augustinian monks at Heidelberg, and he did so in forty memorable theses. Luther reveals his radical Augustinian bias by declaring that the human free will, in its fallen state, is incapable of turning toward God. In fact, he holds that the will is enslaved to evil forces outside its control—a position he will later elaborate in his famous debate with Erasmus in *The Bondage of the Will* (1525). Luther also breaks with the nominalist concepts of merit and grace. The nominalists taught that doing one's best could serve as a predisposition for the reception of grace; Luther declares that such behavior simply "adds sin to sin" and thereby makes one doubly guilty before God.

In 1518 Luther's theology was still in flux. Many of his later ideas about the atonement were still inchoate at this point in his development. However, von Loewenich argues (correctly, I think) that *theologia crucis* remained a guiding principle for Luther's theology as a whole. Luther's understanding of the atonement, and indeed all of his theology, was shaped by the basic contrast he developed between the theologian of glory and the theologian of the cross. This distinction is set forth in Theses 19-21 of the Heidelberg Disputation:

---

[4]*D. Martin Luthers Werke. Kritische Gesamtausgabe* (Weimar: Hermann Böhlau, 1833), 5:176. (Hereafter cited as *WA*.)
[5]*LW* 48:66: "The commandments of God become sweet when they are read not only in books but also in the wounds of the sweetest Savior."

19. That person does not deserve to be called a theologian who looks upon the invisible things of God as though they were clearly perceptible in those things which have actually happened [Rom 1:20].

20. He deserves to be called a theologian, however, who comprehends the visible and manifest things of God seen through suffering and the Cross.

21. A theologian of glory calls evil good and good evil. A theologian of the Cross calls the thing what it actually is.[6]

Luther claims here that a proper approach to the cross will have a decisive impact not only on what one believes about sin and salvation but also on how one does theology. The theologian of glory has no place for suffering or surrender but seeks instead to "explain" God and the world in terms of human assertiveness, natural theology and evidentialist apologetics. By contrast, the theologian of the cross knows that all efforts to understand God and achieve a standing before him by such efforts are doomed to fail. The cross puts a question mark around all of our theodicies and requires us to confess that "it depends not upon man's will or exertion, but upon God's mercy" (Rom 9:16).

Luther faces the world and the human condition with a radical realism. This is what he means by "calling the thing what it actually is." What a thing "actually is," of course, may well be something other than what it seems to be. Indeed, the cross reveals to us the God who is "hidden under the opposite" (*absconditus sub contrario*). God's revelation in Christ is indirect, concealed, paradoxical. "When God brings to life," Luther says, "he does so by killing; when he justifies, then he does so by accusing us; when he brings us into heaven, he does so by leading us to hell."[7] The cross shatters all of our illusions about God even as it confronts all our pretentions about ourselves. The cross, Luther says, puts everything to the test (*crux probat omnia*).

As we shall see when we survey Luther's exposition of Galatians 3:13, Luther's teaching on the atonement was, in effect, an attack on the theology of glory in epistemology, soteriology and ecclesiology. Alister McGrath has aptly characterized Luther's cross-centeredness as "one of the most powerful and radical understandings of the nature of Christian theology which the Church has ever known."[8]

---

[6]*LW* 31:40.
[7]*WA* 18:633.
[8]Alister E. McGrath, *Luther's Theology of the Cross* (Oxford: Blackwell, 1980), 1.

Christus Victor

The subtitle of Gustaf Aulén's *Christus Victor* is "An Historical Study of the Three Main Types of the Idea of the Atonement." Whereas von Loewenich had illuminated Luther's appeal to the cross as a major motif in his theological methodology, Aulén painted on a much broader canvas, relating Luther's concept of the atonement to the entire history of Christian thought. Aulén finds three basic models of atonement theology in the history of doctrine: the "classic," the "Latin" and the "ethical" types.

The title of Aulén's book is a shorthand description of the classic idea of atonement. Its central metaphor is that of struggle and battle: the good news of the gospel is that Jesus Christ has defeated Satan and his pomp and by doing so has liberated their prey, lost humanity, from their clutches. The scene of Christ's triumphant victory is the cross. Aulén also refers to the classic theory as "dualistic" and "dramatic." It is dualistic because it takes seriously the role of the devil in the history of salvation; it is dramatic in that its dominant story line is the narrative of Jesus' struggle with the evil powers.

Aulén claims that the classic type of atonement theology prevailed in the early church and was later rediscovered by Luther. However, the Latin idea came to prominence in the Middle Ages through the influence of Anselm and his influential treatise *Cur Deus Homo?* Anselm did not emphasize Christ's victory over Satan but rather the vindication of divine justice through the work of Christ, who, in his capacity as a human being, offered the Father a surplus of merit, thereby making possible the redemption of his fellow human beings. Aulén depicted the Anselmian doctrine of atonement as "legalistic" and found its roots in the medieval concept of penance, which required human beings to make an offering or payment for sin in order to satisfy the justice of God.

Aulén's third type, the ethical idea of atonement, surfaced in Abelard's construal of God's reconciling love but came to prominence only in the post-Reformation liberal Protestant tradition. This ethical or subjective view of atonement denies both the dramatic motif of God struggling with the devil and defeating him at the cross, and also the concepts of satisfaction, propitiation and substitution so central to the Latin view. Aulén criticized the subjective understanding of Christ's work as anthropocentric and ineffectual: its central weakness is that "the forgiving and atoning work of God is *made dependent upon* the ethical effects in human lives; consequently, the Divine Love is not clearly set forth as a free, spontaneous love. . . . The active hostility of the Divine Love towards evil has faded away and the dualistic outlook has been banished by the monism which dominates the view."[9]

The publication of *Christus Victor* in 1931 elicited an enormous literature of response. It still remains the single most influential book about the atonement since Ritschl's *The Christian Doctrine of Justification and Reconciliation* in the nineteenth century. Liberal theologians were quick to denigrate Aulén's attempt to revive the classic idea of atonement with its "grotesque" imagery of divine chicanery: Jesus as the worm whom the Father dangles on the hook in order to snare Satan, the sea monster. Anselmian scholars also protested that Aulén had misunderstood and misrepresented the thought of the great "father of scholasticism." Many Luther scholars also found unconvincing Aulén's attempt to impose a rigid typology on the Reformer's unsystematic theology.

We shall return to some of these objections shortly, but at this point it is well to note the importance of Aulén's study for our theme in general. Both von Loewenich and Aulén published their influential books at the midpoint between the First and Second World Wars. The carnage of Verdun and the Somme lay just behind them, and the flames of the Holocaust were being kindled around them even as they wrote. Both of their books put the cross front and center on the theological agenda. They were tracts for the times as well as essays in historical theology. True enough, the "liberal Luther" did not immediately vanish from sight, and soon enough the Nazis would create a new Luther made in their own image. But the folly of all theologies of glory had been effectively unmasked. The nature of an evil so demonic and so radically destructive that only the decisive intervention of God could overcome it was shown for all the world to see. Once again, Christians began to read Martin Luther.

Luther on Galatians 3:13

Martin Luther was not a systematic theologian but a *lectura in Biblia*, that is, a professor of biblical exegesis at the University of Wittenberg, where he had received the doctorate in theology in 1512. During his long career he lectured several times on Paul's letter to the Galatians.

---

[9]Gustaf Aulén, *Christus Victor* (New York: Macmillan, 1969), 137, 139.

The American edition of *Luther's Works* translates both his short commentary of 1519 and his definitive revision of 1535. Luther always considered his commentary on Galatians one of his finest achievements. He frequently referred to it as "my Katie von Bora," after his beloved wife.

Galatians 3:13 is a key verse in this important book: "Christ redeemed us from the curse of the law by becoming a curse for us—for it is written: Cursed be everyone who hangs on a tree" (NRSV). Many of Luther's central ideas about the atoning work of Christ come together in his extensive exposition of this verse. Several of these themes are treated more extensively elsewhere in Luther's writings, but the fact that he brings these different elements together here is an indication of the complexity and depth of his teaching on the atonement.

Christ Accursed
The immediate context of Galatians 3:13 is the very grim picture of the human situation painted by Paul. The law requires a life of perfect obedience in order to be right with God. Yet no person can meet such a high standard. Consequently, everyone in the world has become "a prisoner of sin" (Gal 3:22), suffering the just condemnation of the curse of the law. For the first time in Galatians, Paul here used the word "redeemed," declaring that Christ has become a curse for us through his death on the cross. Luther opens his discussion of this theme by considering an objection raised by "Jerome and the sophists," namely, that Paul could not possibly have meant what this text seems to declare, for in no way would it have been "fitting" for Christ to have been cursed by God. Luther sneers at their dissimulation: "Thus they evade this statement this way: 'Paul was not speaking in earnest here.'"[10] Theologians of glory come to the atonement with a preconceived idea of what it is appropriate for God to do, and thus they miss the good news of what he has actually done in Christ.

"The proper subject of theology is the man accursed for his sin and lost, and the God who justifies and saves the sinner," Luther once wrote. "In theology, whatever outside of this subject is researched or disputed is error and poison."[11] To speculate about what was "fitting" for God to do, as was common in scholastic theology, was already to

---

[10]*LW* 26:276.
[11]*WA* 40/2:328.

lose sight of the real God we encounter in the crucified Christ, the God who saves us and damns us. Luther's way of theologizing about the atonement is very different from that of Anselm, who sought to prove the necessity of the incarnation by reason alone, apart from the data of revelation—*remoto Christo,* as he put it, without any prior knowledge of the cross and its consequences.[12] Kenneth Hagen draws a helpful contrast between Anselm and Luther on the basis of the accepted rule for doctrinal development in medieval theology:

> Concerning a doctrinal matter, the medieval theologian asks, (1) Is it possible (*potuit*)? If yes, then (2) Is it becoming of God (*decuit*)? If yes, the conclusion is (3) it happened (*fecit*). Anselm worked out his view of atonement on the level of *deceo,* what is fitting or becoming of God, all in the framework of faith seeking understanding. Luther, however, worked on the level of *fecit,* what happened.[13]

Although Luther was trained in the late medieval scholastic theology of the nominalist tradition, he broke decisively with his teachers in favor of a Christ-centered biblical theology. When he spoke derisively of the philosopher Aristotle and castigated reason as a "whore," he did not of course mean to reduce theology to a nonrational, mystical exercise. Instead, he intended to set the knowledge of God within the limits of divine revelation. The human intellect is limited both by finitude and fallenness. The suffering of the Son of God on the cross—his being made a curse for us—makes no sense by the canons of human logic. This is why the "sophists" cannot entertain the very thought of it. But—*reducto Christo*—it is a window into the heart of God and the only means by which we see God's eternal purpose fulfilled in history.

Jesus—God and Man

While the "sophists" want to speculate about what God could or should do, as opposed to what he has in fact done, other "fanatics" obscure the reality of redemption by denying the deity of "the one and only Person of Christ":

> Here you see how necessary it is to believe and confess the doctrine of the divinity of Christ. When Arius denied this, it was necessary also for

---

[12]Cf. Ted Peters, "The Atonement in Anselm and Luther, Second Thoughts about Gustav Aulén's *Christus Victor,*" *LQ* 24 (1972): 301-14.

[13]Kenneth Hagen, "Luther on Atonement—Reconfigured," *CTQ* 61 (1997): 256.

him to deny the doctrine of redemption. For to conquer the sin of the world, death, the curse, and the wrath of God in Himself—this is the work, not of any creature but of the divine power.[14]

Luther is the great theologian of Christmas and Good Friday. Whoever would encounter God must encounter him, not in the majesty of his eternal essence, but rather in the lowliness of the incarnation: asleep on his mother's lap, writhing on a bloody cross. Luther's Christology is well expressed in this hymn by H. R. Bramley:

> A Babe on the breast of a Maiden He lies
> Yet sits with the Father on high in the skies;
> Before Him their faces the Seraphim hide
> While Joseph stands waiting, unscared, by His side.
> O wonder of wonders, which none can unfold;
> The Ancient of Days, is an hour or two old.[15]

While Luther emphasizes the full deity of Jesus Christ even to the point of using monophysite language about the incarnated Christ, he accepts without reservation the full unity of the deity and the humanity in keeping with the Chalcedonian formula: one person in two natures. The redeemer in the flesh is one with the eternal Son of God. In the incarnation, Christ did not, of course, renounce his deity; but rather, he concealed it under the "veil" or "mask" (*larva*) of his flesh.

While Luther clearly affirms the christological consensus of the early church, he never loses sight of the insoluble link between the person and the work of Christ:

> Through the Gospel we are told who Christ is, in order that we may learn to know that He is our Savior, that He delivers us from sin and death, helps us out of all our misfortune, reconciles us to the Father, and makes us pious and saves us without our works. He who does not learn to know Christ in this way must go wrong. For even though you know that He is God's Son, that He died and rose again, and that He sits at the right hand of the Father, you have not yet learned to know Christ aright, and this knowledge still does not help you. You must also know and believe that He did all of this for your sake, in order to help you.[16]

---

[14]*LW* 26:282.
[15]H. R. Bramley, *English Hymnal* (no. 29), quoted in John G. Strelan, "Theologia Crucis, Theologia Gloriae: A Study in Opposing Theologies," *Lutheran Theological Journal* 23 (1989): 102.
[16]*LW* 30:29-30.

Love: The Divine Motive

In explaining how, according to Paul in Galatians 3:13, Christ had borne the sin of the world and the curse of the law, Luther observes: "Therefore Christ was not only crucified and died, but *by divine love* sin was laid upon Him."[17] The question of how the love of God is related to the death of Christ raises two theological issues. First, why did God make the world in the first place, and having made it, why did he take such extraordinary measures to redeem it? At the level of popular piety one persistent answer declares that the ultimate motive for God's creating and redeeming work was the desire for him to have a partner on whom he could display his love—for love, by definition, requires an object for its fulfillment. Luther was aware of this kind of thinking but had no sympathy for it. The one God who has forever known himself as the Father, the Son and the Holy Spirit does not "need" anything external to himself—the world or humanity—in order to supply some inner deficiency in his own being. No, the love of God that sent Jesus to the cross is the ultimate motive behind which there is no other. *Ne plus ultra!*

In discussions about the atonement, another issue is often raised: How are God's love and justice related? According to Aulén's interpretation of the Latin theory of the atonement, divine love and divine justice are pitted against one another so that "the love of God is regulated by His justice, and is only free to act within the limits that justice marks out."[18] This construal of the issue is foreign to Luther's world of thought. What J. I. Packer has said of Calvin is also true of Luther: "Calvin shows no interest in the reconciling of God's love and justice as a theoretical problem; his only interest is in the mysterious but blessed fact that at the Cross God did act in both love and justice to save us from our sins."[19]

Satisfaction

In seeking to distance Luther from the Latin view of the atonement, Aulén played down the concept of satisfaction in Luther's understanding of the cross. It is too "legalistic" to fit into Luther's dramatic reading of Christ's triumphant victory over the Evil One. Now it is true that

---

[17]*LW* 26:279, emphasis mine.
[18]*Christus Victor*, 173.
[19]J. I. Packer, "What Did the Cross Achieve?" *Tyndale Bulletin* 25 (1974): 5.

Luther on several occasions criticized the word *satisfaction*, largely because of its association with the medieval sacrament of penance. For example, he once threatened to send this word home to the judges, lawyers and hangmen, from whom the pope had stolen it![20] Again, Luther can say that satisfaction alone is "too weak" a description for what Christ has accomplished on the cross, for "He not only made satisfaction for sin but also redeemed us from the power of death, the Devil and hell, and establishes an eternal kingdom of grace and a daily forgiveness even of the remainder of sin that is in us."[21] But in his comment on Galatians 3:13, Luther does not hesitate to refer to Christ's becoming a curse for us as the real judgment of God against sin: "He has and bears all the sins of all men in His body—not in the sense that He has committed them but in the sense that He took these sins, committed by us, upon His own body, in order to make satisfaction for them with His own blood."[22] Luther makes clear that there was no remedy for sin except for God's only Son to become man and to take upon himself the load of eternal wrath thus making his own body and blood a sacrifice for sin.

Aulén and others who would minimize satisfaction language in Luther confuse legalistic with legal. They have failed to understand Luther's own dialectic of law and gospel. For sure, no one can be saved by the works of the law, but equally sure, no one can be saved apart from Christ's having borne the brunt of the law's demands and the law's curse. This is to say that the death of Christ has a Godward dimension—"by undergoing the cross Jesus expiated our sins, propitiated our Maker, turned God's 'no' to us into a 'yes,' and so saved us."[23] Jesus did not need to get himself "strung up on a tree like a damned fool," to quote Clarence Jordan's jarring but accurate translation of Galatians 3:13, in order to pass on pious platitudes about how human beings should get along with one another and make the world a better place in which to live. No, "God was reconciling the world to himself in Christ" (2 Cor 5:19).

At several points, however, Luther does not follow Anselm's satisfac-

---

[20]WA 34/1:301. This citation is given by Phillip S. Watson, who defends Aulén's interpretation of Luther. See his *Let God be God* (Philadelphia: Fortress, 1947), 120.
[21]WA 21:264.
[22]LW 26:277.
[23]Packer, "What Did the Cross Achieve?" 21.

tion theory of the atonement. Perhaps the major divergence is Luther's rejection of Anselm's formulation of *either* punishment *or* satisfaction as a remedy for sin. Luther, following Paul rather than Aristotle, rejects this false alternative: the satisfaction Christ offered to the Father on the cross was not in lieu of the penalty owed because of sin. No, it was precisely the penalty (*poena*) itself due to us from God the Judge because of our transgression of his holiness, justice and goodness. Wolfhart Pannenberg has summarized Luther's distinctive contribution to the doctrine of atonement in this way: "Luther was probably the first since Paul and his school to have seen with full clarity that Jesus' death in its genuine sense is to be understood as vicarious penal suffering."[24]

Substitution

One of Luther's favorite metaphors for the relationship between Christ and the forgiven sinner is the joyous exchange (*fröühlicher Wechsel*). In his treatise *The Freedom of the Christian* (1520), Luther draws on the imagery of the bride and bridegroom to express this idea:

> So Christ has all the blessings and the salvation which are the soul's. And so the soul has upon it all the vice and sin which become Christ's own. Here now begins the happy exchange and conflict. Because Christ is God and man who never yet sinned, and his piety is inconquerable, eternal and almighty. So, then, as he makes his own the believing soul's sin through the wedding ring of its faith, and does nothing else than as if he had committed it, just so must sin be swallowed up and drowned.[25]

The idea of substitution—that Christ has literally taken our place—is central to Luther's gospel of the joyful exchange. Perhaps Luther's most graphic expression of the substitutionary motif comes in this comment on Galatians 3:13:

> When the merciful Father saw that we were being oppressed through the Law, that we were being held under a curse, and that we could not be liberated from it by anything, he sent his Son into the world, heaped all the sins of all men upon him, and said to him: "Be Peter the denier; Paul the persecutor, blasphemer, and assaulter; David the adulterer; the sinner who ate the apple in Paradise; the thief on the cross. In short, be the person of all men, the one who has committed the sins of all men. And see

---

[24]Wolfhart Pannenberg, *Jesus—God and Man* (Philadelphia: Westminster Press, 1974), 279.
[25]*LW* 31:351-52.

to it that you pay and make satisfaction for them." Now the Law comes and says: "I find him a sinner, who takes upon himself the sins of all men. I do not see any other sins than those in him. Therefore let him die on the cross!" And so it attacks him and kills him. By this deed the whole world is purged and expiated from all sins, and thus it is set free from death and from every evil.[26]

Christ the Victor

Aulén cites numerous examples from Luther's writings that depict the work of Christ as a battle with the demonic powers. Drawing on his christological exegesis of Psalm 22:6 where Christ is made to say "I am a worm and no man," Luther depicts the crucified Christ as the bait God uses to "hook" the devil and so destroy his power over lost humanity. "For Christ sticks in his gills, and he must spew him out again, as the whale the prophet Jonah, and even as he chews him the Devil chokes himself and is slain, and is taken captive by Christ."[27]

This motif also occurs in Luther's comment on Galatians 3:13. Here the "duel" between Christ and the devil is extended to include a battle with "those monsters": sin, death and the curse. Elsewhere, Luther does not hesitate to include also the law and the wrath of God among the "enemies" with which Christ must grapple.

Many scholars have criticized Aulén for drawing too sharp a dichotomy between the idea of penal substitution and the motif of victory over the evil powers. We need not accuse Luther of being inconsistent for having seen the truth—that is to say, the biblical basis—for both views of the atonement. Indeed, this may well be Luther's major contribution to atonement theology: just as he brought together the ideas of satisfaction and punishment in the doctrine of penal substitution, so too he saw that the cross of Christ was at once the scene of Satan's definitive defeat and the objective basis of justification by faith alone. What one scholar has called the "near organic relationship between the notions of Christ's victory and satisfaction rendered to God" is clearly seen in Luther's *Larger Catechism*:

> He has snatched us, poor lost creatures, from the jaws of hell, won us, made us free, and restored us to the Father's favor in grace. . . . Christ

---

[26]LW 26:280.
[27]Aulén, *Christus Victor*, 104.

suffered, died, and was buried that he might make satisfaction for me and pay for what I owed, not with silver and gold, but with his own precious blood.[28]

In discussing the victory of Christ over Satan, it is important to note that Luther includes both the harrowing of hell and the resurrection as crucial moments in Christ's triumph over sin and the devil.[29]

A Cruciform Church

Luther concludes his discussion of the work of Christ in Galatians 3:13 by relating the finished work of Christ on the cross to the holiness of the church confessed by all Christians in the Apostles' Creed. Already in his own day, Luther faced the charge that his univocal insistence on justification by faith alone left no room for sanctification, good works or growth in grace and holiness. The Catholic prince Duke George of Saxony thought so: "Luther's doctrine is good for the dying, but it is no good for the living." Erasmus was less kind: "Lutherans seek only two things—wealth and wives . . . to them the gospel means the right to live as they please."[30]

Luther refuted these false charges by showing how the atoning work of Christ on the cross, appropriated through justification by faith, issued in a life of obedient and holy living: "Hence it is evident that faith alone justifies. But once we have been justified by faith, we enter the active life . . . which exercises itself in works of love toward one's neighbor."[31] At the same time, Luther insisted that the holiness of the church on earth was entirely derived, emergent and incomplete. In this life the true church is always *ecclesia in via*, the church in a state of becoming, buffeted by struggles, made up always of justified sinners who are at once *simul iusti et peccatores*. In this way a true theology of

---

[28]*Book of Concord*, ed. Theodore G. Tappert (Philadelphia: Fortress, 1959), 414.

[29]This point is well made by Gerhard O. Forde: "It is important to include resurrection and exaltation because there is considerable confusion abroad about their place in a theology of the Cross. It is often claimed, for instance, that a theology of glory is a theology of resurrection while a theology of the Cross is 'only' concerned with crucifixion. Nothing could be further from the truth. As a matter of fact, a theology of the Cross is impossible without resurrection. It is impossible to plumb the depths of the crucifixion without the resurrection" (*On Being a Theologian of the Cross: Reflections on Luther's Heidelberg Disputation, 1518* [Grand Rapids: Eerdmans, 1997], 1).

[30]P. S. Allen and H. M. Allen, eds., *Opus Epistolarum Des Erasmi Roterodami* (Oxford: Oxford University Press, 1928), 7:366.

[31]*LW* 26:287.

the cross implies an ecclesiology of the cross as well.

Many evangelicals are happy to claim Luther's theology when it comes to personal salvation, but their understanding of the church has all the marks of an ecclesiology of glory—robust, self-sufficient and proud of itself. To counter this notion, Luther insisted that suffering was a mark of the true church. In this world, he said, the true church is not a glorious princess to be decked with jewels, but rather a lowly maid, an ashen Cinderella before the ball:

> If, then, a person desires to draw the church as he sees her, he will picture her as a deformed and poor girl sitting in an unsafe forest in the midst of hungry lions, bears, wolves, and boars, nay, deadly serpents; in the midst of infuriated men who set sword, fire, and water in motion in order to kill her and wipe her from the face of the earth.[32]

In God's sight the church is pure, holy, unspotted, the dove of God; but in the eyes of the world, it bears the form of a servant. It is like its Bridegroom: "Hacked to pieces, marked with scratches, despised, crucified, mocked" (Is 53:2-3).[33]

In the Reformation era, Luther's image of the church "under the cross" was perhaps better lived out among many of the despised Anabaptists than with the later Lutherans, Calvinists and other established Protestants. Today it is more evident perhaps among Christians who face hostility in persecution in the developing world than among many of us more privileged believers who cozily practice the faith at ease in Zion.

Conclusion

From this brief survey of Luther on theology and the atonement, we may draw the following conclusions: (1) Luther's thought does not lend itself to any one "theory" of atonement but encompasses the biblical truths found in both the classic and Latin types. (2) For Luther, there is a direct correlation between the doctrine of atonement and theological methodology. In other words, the cross challenges the desire of all humans to explain God and control God through human ingenuity, speculation and philosophy. The cross unmasks every human presumption and pretension. The mind, no less than the will, is radi-

---

[32]*WA* 40/3:315.
[33]*LW* 54:262.

cally affected by sin. We must receive the true knowledge of God, no less than salvation itself, as an unmerited gift of grace. (3) Despite its one-sided emphasis, Aulén's famous typology of the atonement reminds us that at the heart of the Christian gospel there is a titanic struggle between diabolical evil and the God of love. Through his cross and resurrection, Jesus Christ has emerged victorious over all the monsters and tyrants whose mission is to destroy and dehumanize all persons made in the image of God. In the wounds of Jesus we too share a victory over sin, hell and the grave. Luther puts it this way in his great Easter hymn of 1524, "Death Held Our Lord in Prison":

> Death held our Lord in prison,
> For sin that did undo us;
> But He hath up arisen,
> And brought our life back to us.
> Therefore we must gladsome be,
> Exalt God and thankful be
> And sing aloud: Allelujah.
>
> That was a right wondrous strife
> When Death in Life's grip wallowed:
> Off victorious came Life,
> Death he was quite upswallowed.
> The Scripture has published that—
> How one Death the other ate.
> Thus Death is become a laughter. Allelujah![34]

---

[34]*LW* 53:257. Cf. this appraisal by Bernhard Lohse: "With regard to Luther, rejection of the Anselmian tradition might be too subtle. On the other hand, the importance of the victory motif should not be ignored. Not only in the context of atonement doctrine but also in ethics and in general observation of the world, the idea of victory has considerable significance" (*Martin Luther's Theology* [Minneapolis: Fortress, 1999], 228).

the atonement in john calvin's theology

Henri Blocher

The main part of our salvation," so could John Calvin describe the truth of the atonement as he understood it in the light of Isaiah 53, is "the expiation of human sins by Christ's death," which Michel Servet had denied.[1] If justification by faith stands out as the heart of the Reformers' gospel, its foundation or presupposition is found in the objective work of atonement for Calvin no less than for the others; such a heavy-weight witness as Albrecht Ritschl had to acknowledge the fact,[2] which James I. Packer powerfully expounded.[3]

In view of such a central role, it is somewhat surprising that the doctrine has been granted comparatively short shrift from historical theo-

---

[1] *Refutatio errorum Michaelis Serveti*, in *Calvini opera* (henceforth *CO*), ed. G. Baum, E. Cunitz, E. Reuss (Brunswick & Berlin: Schwetschke, 1863-1900), 8:498 (497 on Isaiah 53 and Servet's ascription to Cyrus of the Servant's prophecies). Calvin's phrases are "praecipuum salutis nostrae caput, de expiatis Christi morte hominum peccatis..." *Nota Bene*: since we had no easy access to English translations, we draw our quotations from Calvin's French and/or Latin original text and make our own translations, unless otherwise specified. Apart from some exact quotations, references to the *Institutes* and the *Commentaries* will simply indicate paragraph or verse.

[2] A. Ritschl, *Die christliche Lehre von der Rechtfertigung und Versöhnung*, 3rd ed. (Bonn: Adolph Marcus, 1889), 1.217: "haben sie [die Reformatoren] alles, was man zur objektiven Versöhnungslehre zu rechnen pflegt, immer nur als Voraussetzung jener Wahrheit behandelt. Auch Calvin . . . hat . . . nicht die unmittelbar religiöse Conception der Vorstellung, dass 'wir' durch Christi Genugthuung versöhnt sind, überwinden."

[3] J. I. Packer, "Sola Fide: the Reformed Doctrine of Justification," in *Soli Deo Gloria—Essays in Reformed Theology*, Festschrift for John H. Gerstner, ed. R. C. Sproul (Philadelphia: Presbyterian & Reformed, 1976), 11-25.

logians. David F. Wright can observe that standard works devote little space to the topic,[4] and Robert A. Peterson Sr., when he undertook to compose a panoramic account of Calvin's views, avowedly wrote "to fill a gap in the Calvin literature."[5]

One question, however, *has* attracted considerable interest and aroused controversies still unabated: that of the precise reference of Christ's atoning substitution. Did Calvin hold to the so-called "limited atonement," or was Moïse Amyraut right in claiming him on his side? "Of the twenty-two Calvin sources that I added to the bibliography for this edition," Peterson writes, "half deal with this issue."[6] Since Professor Roger Nicole himself, in his scrupulous and thoroughgoing manner, surveyed whatever evidence from Calvin's works may be relevant to the discussion,[7] we see no real need for any supplement. Apart from the fact that Calvin gives no hint of hypothetical universalism when commenting on Amyraldian proof-texts (such as 1 Jn 2:2), the convincing force of two arguments, among many, overcomes our hesitations: the close and organic connection of Christ's atonement (expiation) and intercession for Calvin, intercession being undoubtedly *particular* (cf. Jn 17:9); and the uncontroversial historical datum that Calvin's most intimate disciples, assistants, co-laborers—the first of these his successor, Théodore de Bèze—taught a redemptive substitution for the elect, the Body of Christ.[8] Counterarguments usually fail to perceive the

---

[4]D. F. Wright, "The Atonement in Reformation Theology," *EuroJTh* 8 (1999): 39. Wright mentions W. Niesel and T. George; the same would hold true for William Cunningham or François Wendel. In a way, Wright observes, it was already the case in the sixteenth century (38ff.), as the Reformers' writings and the Confessions did not dwell systematically on the doctrine: "The atonement was not an issue in Reformation controversy, unlike justification. Its theological treatment is dispersed, appearing under other heads, such as sacrifice and the mass or Christology, if at all" (47).

[5]R. A. Peterson Sr., *Calvin and the Atonement*, rev. ed. (Fearn, Ross-shire: Mentor, 1999), 10.

[6]Ibid., 115.

[7]R. Nicole, "John Calvin's View of the Extent of the Atonement," *WTJ* 47 (1985): 197-225.

[8]Roger Nicole, ibid., marshals these arguments to full effect. He also notes (p. 197) that the matter had been discussed earlier than Calvin, at least since Gottschalk. According to Peterson, Jonathan Rainbow in his doctoral dissertation (University of California, 1986) canvassed this antecedent evidence in the light of which Peterson was led to some degree of *retractatio* (op. cit., 115, 118ff.). Regarding the famous sentence in Calvin's treatise against Heshusius (Tilemann Hesshusen): "Et quando tam mordicus verbis adhaeret, scire velim quomodo Christi carnem edant impii, pro quibus non est crucifixa, et quomodo sanguinem bibant, qui expiandis eorum peccatis non est effuses" (*Dilucida explicatio . . .*, CO 9.484), which W. Cunningham adduced and which reads as a formidable rebuttal of Amyraldism, we still confess a small measure of uncertainty: could Calvin be thinking more of application, of the salvific eating and drinking according to John 6, than of the cross event itself?

logic of "definite atonement" and what it consistently allows, that is, sufficiency for all, universal offer, salvation accomplished for the "race" as an organic whole, and the like. After Dr. Nicole's magisterial contribution, this should have been clear to all; it is enough that we express our gratitude—and move on to comment on other aspects of Calvin's doctrine of the atonement.[9]

A full-scale treatment would require an exposition of the threefold office of our Mediator and of the christological presupposition of his work, the Chalcedonian dogma that Calvin defended with dominantly soteriological interests.[10] But the scope of this study precludes such a wide-ranging inquiry, and we may feel excused from the task when we consider that it has been done, and so well, by Robert A. Peterson Sr. We shall concentrate on the atonement in the narrower sense which, he claims, Calvin expounded with six biblical themes, also Peterson's chapter titles: "Christ the Obedient Second Adam," "Christ the Victor," "Christ our Legal Substitute," "Christ our Sacrifice," "Christ our Merit" and "Christ our Example."[11] Timothy George, in a thought-provoking summary, has highlighted five original features of Calvin's view compared with Anselm's: the denial of simple or absolute necessity; the primary reference to divine wrath and love; the inclusion of the "whole course" of Christ's obedience; the presence of the "other" theme, that of *Christus Victor*; and interest

---

The question arises since he is wont to speak of both together—hence the reader's frustration in so many passages where Calvin had such a wonderful opportunity of taking sides (on the extent of Christ's substitution) and does not; for example, in the fourth sermon on Christ's Passion, CO 45.881, when he stresses that the Passion does not *bear its fruit* in all people. We may also adduce a passage that seems to have been left aside in the debate in spite of its remarkable phrases, in the fourth sermon on the Epistle to the Ephesians: "Whether all participate in the good which our Lord Jesus Christ secured for us? No: for unbelievers have neither part in it nor portion. It is, therefore, a special privilege for those whom God draws to himself. And also St. Paul shows that faith is required, or else Christ will bring us no benefit. Though, therefore, Christ be in general the Redeemer of the world [*en général Rédempteur du monde*], his death and passion brings no fruit but to those who receive what St. Paul here demonstrates" (CO 51.287ff.).

[9]Still on the preceding point, we may mention a fine article that often goes unnoticed, the refutation of Kendall's thesis by Amar Djaballah (now the "doyen" of the *Faculté de Théologie Evangélique*, Montreal): "Calvin and the Calvinists: An Examination of Some Recent Views," *Reformation Canada* 5/1 (Spring 1982): 7-20, esp. 8-15.

[10]So strongly, Otto Weber, "Calvin, II. Theologie," in *Die Religion in Geschichte und Gegenwart*, 3rd ed., ed. Hans von Campenhausen et al. (Tübingen: J.C.B. Mohr, 1986), 1.1595. Robert S. Paul, *The Atonement and the Sacraments: The Relation of the Atonement to the Sacraments of Baptism and the Lord's Supper* (New York: Abingdon, 1960), 100ff.

[11]Peterson, *Calvin and the Atonement*, chaps. 4-9.

in the believer's response, entailing radical obedience.[12] Our aim will not be to cover the same ground but, in the field where "other men labored" and "entering into their labors," further to examine some features that call for a nuanced treatment.

Our investigation has led us into diverse sections of Calvin's extant works, but we cannot claim that it has been exhaustive. Yet, though we shall not disregard his *Institutes,* we shall bring to the fore references to less known writings of his, the *Commentaries* (from which Peterson was able to quote extensively) and, especially, the *Sermons,* which have seldom been used. This is not to suggest any substantial difference in doctrine across that diversity: on the contrary, we have been struck by the stability, constancy and consistency—sometimes even the repetitious character—of Calvin's teaching on the atonement.[13] We hope to verify our growing feeling that Calvin was first and foremost a *preacher.* Richard Stauffer concluded that "in order to understand Calvin the Reformer, one must know Calvin the preacher,"[14] and he buttressed his claim (also that Calvin created a new civilization "essentially through his preaching") by Calvin's own words on his death-bed—Calvin mentioned his sermons *first* as the vehicle of his scriptural ministry.[15]

We shall start from the "core," it seems, of Calvin's doctrine and then consider the place of the polemic or "victory" scheme; admire Calvin's eye for solidarities and clear-cut distinctions; revisit the issue of his stance toward necessity and allegedly Scotist ideas; and end with a few remarks on the cognitive import, for him, of the "God-talk" and "Christ-talk" he used in his teaching and preaching.

---

[12]Timothy George, *The Theology of the Reformers* (Nashville: Broadman, 1988), 221-23. We would avoid calling St. Anselm's "the theory of penal, substitutionary atonement" (220): to Anselm, penalty and satisfaction were alternatives (*satisfactio aut poena,* in mutual exclusion, cf. *Cur Deus Homo,* book I, chap. 15) and Christ's death atones as a work of supererogation, which is compared to the choice of virginity (book 2, chap. 18b), not as vicarious punishment.

[13]Richard Stauffer, *Dieu, la création et la providence dans la prédication de Calvin* (Las Vegas: Peter Lang, 1978), 304, observes that Calvin's theology remained invariant (*invariance théologique*) over a long period of time, at any rate on the topics he studied.

[14]"Quelques aspects insolites de la théologie du premier article dans la prédication de Calvin," in Richard Stauffer, *Interprètes de la Bible: Etudes sur les Réformateurs du XVIᵉ siècle* (Paris: Beauchesne, 1980), 248 (n. 120 supporting Emile Doumergue and Rodolphe Peter). The chapter was first published in *Calvinus ecclesia doctor* (Kampen, 1980).

[15]Richard Stauffer, "Un Calvin méconnu: Le prédicateur de Genève," *Bulletin de la Société d'Histoire du Protestantisme Francais,* 123rd year (1977): 187. Cf. Albert-Marie Schmidt, "Avant-Propos: Calvin prédicateur: Introduction à sa méthode," in his edition of several sermons, *Œuvres de Jean Calvin III* (Paris: Je Sers; Geneva: Labor, 1936), 36.

Central Emphases: Expiating Crime

If anyone engages in reading Calvin's exposition of atonement doctrine, they will soon meet synthetic statements of his understanding: the way they are introduced and the sheer repetition suggest that they were central in his theology. These statements interlace two main language-sets: the religious, cultic language of *sacrifice*, with such terms as expiation (*expiatio, piaculum*), curse, propitiation, uncleanness and purification by means of shed blood; and the forensic or judicial language of *condemnation*, with guilt, imputation, judgment, penalty, remission and so forth. Other elements may be added or included in one of these, such as the metaphor of debts and repayment.

A few sample quotations should suffice. In his fifth sermon on Christ's Passion, Calvin explains the title the *Lamb*. It implies being offered as a sacrifice, and

> this is why it is said that our Lord Jesus was made a curse for us, which means that he received the curse that was due to our sins. In this quality and in this condition he was condemned: because God had established him as the lamb that was to be offered in sacrifice.[16]

In the *Commentaries*, the clause *to introduce everlasting righteousness* in Daniel 9:24 is explained in the following words:

> This righteousness depends on expiation. How does it happen that God should consider believers as righteous or reckon to them righteousness, as Paul says (Rom 4:11), if it is not by burying and covering their sins or because they are purged by Christ's blood? And because God is propitiated [*placatus*] by the sacrifice of his Son? / Through his death he has achieved the satisfaction, so that we no longer stand under guilt nor be liable to the verdict [*iudicio*] of eternal death.[17]

---

[16]*CO* 46.900. From the same series of sermons, one could quote also 858: the apostles' main emphasis was to show "that by the shedding of our Redeemer's blood we are washed and purged of all our stains; that he made the full payment to God his Father of all the debts to which we were obligated; that he obtained for us perfect righteousness." A similar association of the theme of sacrifice and of God as judge would be found in the Sermons on Isaiah 53, *CO* 35.599.

[17]*CO* 41.181. For a NT example, see the *Commentary* on 2 Corinthians 5:19: "Here is the sum of this passage: where sin is, there is God's wrath; therefore, God is not propitious to us in any other way, and before, he effaces our sins by not imputing them. Since our consciences cannot apprehend this benefit [the French text adds "and participate in it"] without Christ's sacrifice intervening, Paul, with good reason, locates the principle and the cause of reconciliation in respect to us in this sacrifice," *CO* 50.72; the French text (which, in the case of

Of the *Institutes* (in the final 1559-60 form), one could quote almost the whole chapter sixteen and most of seventeen in book two. One passage in 2.16.2 sums "what Scripture teaches" about man:

> He was estranged from God by sin, heir of wrath, liable to the curse of eternal death, excluded from every hope of salvation, banished [*extraneum;* French: *banny*] from all divine blessing, slave of Satan, captive under the yoke of sin, and, at last, destined to a horrible exit [*exitio*] and already involved in that fate; here Christ intervened as an intercessor [*deprecatorem*], he received and underwent the penalty in himself which was ready [*imminebat*] for all sinners, by God's just verdict; he expiated by his blood the misdeeds [*mala;* French: *vices*] that rendered sinners hateful to God; by this atonement [*piaculo,* expiatory sacrifice; French: *payement*] God the Father was satisfied and suitably appeased; by this intercessor his wrath was placated; on this foundation the peace of God with men was established [French: *l'amour que Dieu nous porte*]; by this bond his goodwill towards them was made firm [*contineri*].[18]

A reason for the interlacing of languages surfaces when one considers Calvin's account of the sacrificial system.[19] In a sermon on Isaiah 53, he explains why sacrifices for sin were called "sins" in Hebrew: "because the curse which men had deserved [*meritée*] and under which they would have been totally engulfed was, so to say, unloaded and transferred on a calf or a sheep."[20] The concept of deserts belongs to judicial logic. In the *Institutes* 4.18.13, Calvin gathers in two classes only the various offerings of the Mosaic law, and the first one related to sin "by way [*specie;* French: *par une manière*] of satisfaction" is more precisely defined:

> Propitiatory, or of expiation. A sacrifice of expiation is one the purpose of which is to appease God's wrath, to satisfy his judgment, and thus to wash and wipe away sins; thus does the sinner, having been purged

---

2 Corinthians was published before the Latin one), *Commentaires sur le Nouveau Testament* (Paris: Ch. Meyrueis, 1854), 3.577.

[18]CO 2.369.

[19]Robert S. Paul writes: "I suggest that not sufficient attention has been given to the things Calvin said about the Old Testament sacrifices and the significant light they throw upon his idea of the Atonement" (*Atonement and the Sacraments*, 101). Whether he was able to fulfill the task is another matter.

[20]CO 35.655. Cf. a sermon on Daniel 9:23, CO 41.589ff., and on Christ's Passion, CO 46.934, where he says that the blood of the sacrifices represented "the reward [*recompense*] of iniquities."

from his uncleanness and restored into the purity of righteousness, come back into God's favor.[21]

The satisfaction of justice lies near the heart of sacrificial atonement!

Furthermore, it appears that the notion of divine wrath and that of satisfaction, both of which Calvin puts forward with high frequency, may be connected with either language-set. It is already the case in Scripture itself: wrath expresses the divine reaction against cultic offences (2 Chron 29:8, 10) and unbelief (Jn 3:36), but also when widows and orphans are ill-treated in society (Ex 22:23ff.) and in the form of human justice (Rom 13:4, 5); similarly, the verb *rāṣāh*, which best corresponds in Hebrew to the idea of satisfaction, is found for sacrifices (Lev 1:4) and for punishment (Is 40:2), considered as the payment of debts (Lev 26:41, 43). The very cultic word *kipper* (*piel* inf.), "to atone or expiate," is used for the capital punishment of crime (Num 35:31-33). The two languages coalesce in key scriptural texts: Isaiah 53 mentions punishment (*mûsar*, and the idiomatic phrase "bear sin") and sacrifice (*ʾāšām*, and even "making aspersion," *yazzeh*, in Is 52:15); Romans 3:25-26 mixes sacrificial propitiation by means of blood and the concern for justice in view of sins left unpunished. One surmises that one main factor for Calvin's "interlacing" of languages was simply the biblical precedent. How, after all, could they be separated if the Holy One of Israel *is* the Righteous Judge of all the earth? One language translates the other if it is recognized that the object of worship is no amoral numen, but the Good in Personal Existence.

Robert A. Peterson Sr. notices that Calvin "joins the images of Christ our merit, Christ our legal substitute, and Christ our sacrifice" and "blends" the various "pictures."[22] One wonders, however, whether this admission and complement fully compensates for his presentation of the "themes of the Atonement" under separate heads, in separate chapters. Clearly to disentangle the one from the other brings pedagogical advantages; it sharpens our intelligence of the concepts used. But there is a disadvantage also: it may obscure the organization of Calvin's thought, the central presence of one theological logic that governs both

---

[21]*CO* 2.1060. Cf. also *Institutes* 2.16.6.

[22]Robert A. Peterson Sr., *Calvin and the Atonement*, 126, adding: "This phenomenon of allowing the themes of the atonement to overlap is evident in Calvin's commentaries and treatises too." He quotes 2.12.3 and 2.17.4 from the *Institutes*.

the sacrificial and the judicial expressions—and possibly others.

In this light one may assess the comments made by scholars of various stripes. Robert S. Paul perceives that the "sacrificial images—propitiation, victim" in Calvin "are often being used with a meaning that is close to penal substitution," and that many "passages could be abstracted from Calvin and woven in a very strict penal theory of Atonement."[23] Yet he argues from the presence of a second "way of thinking," the sacrificial one, that "the penal theory was modified in the *Institutes*."[24] He underscores three main modifications: (1) the initiative of God's love: "It was God the Father's mercy which alone made Christ's action possible"; (2) the essential role of Christ's obedience; and (3) the "teaching that the love of God calls us to be not merely partakers in the benefits of our Lord's atoning work but sharers in his sacrifice."[25]

We first respond by rejoicing over the clear recognition that Calvin preached God's love as the great motive of our redemption. Through a strange misreading of the texts (at times, one wonders about non-reading), some scholars have missed this primary datum.[26] Yet is it a *modification* of penal substitution theory? It can only be that of an unfortunate caricature of that doctrine! Substitution under the curse we had deserved, so that divine justice is satisfied and we go free, marks the culmination of God's love for us, the ultimate point on the road of self-denial and self-giving, farther than which none can be conceived. When Calvin preaches Christ our pledge that suffered our punishment in our stead—yes, he insisted, who suffered the torments of hell in his

---

[23]Paul, *Atonement and the Sacraments*, 98ff. The "very strict theory" is described: "in which our Lord voluntarily (or at the command of the Father?) became the victim of God's wrath against sin, so that the atonement he offered is seen wholly in terms of the satisfaction rendered to Divine Justice by his substitutionary Passion and Death"; he comments on his quotation from the *Institutes* 2.12.3: "The penal element is there—very much to the fore—and Calvin puts an accent upon our Lord's human flesh as 'the price of satisfaction to the just judgment of God' and tells us that in the same flesh Christ paid 'the penalty which we had incurred,'" 99.

[24]Ibid., 103.

[25]Ibid., 105-8.

[26]Among the most prestigious, Emile G. Léonard, *Histoire générale du protestantisme: I/ la Réformation* (Paris: Presses Universitaires de France, 1961), 269, could write: "If for Luther Love is God's essential attribute, and for Zwingli, Wisdom, for Calvin it is Order." Note Léonard's obvious personal antipathy for Calvin (cf. 261, n. 3; 267; 305ff.). On Calvin's preaching of God's love, especially when he spoke of his own experience, cf. Richard Stauffer, "Les Discours à la première personne dans les sermons de Calvin," in *Interprètes de la Bible*, 219ff.; the chapter was first published in the symposium *Regards contemporains sur Jean Calvin* (Paris: Presses Universitaires de France, 1965), 206-38.

anguish of soul[27]—he does so in praise of the goodness and compassion and mercy and loving kindness and grace and love of God.[28] Any antithesis between forensic logic and "grace and gentleness towards unworthy sinners" stems from the romanticist deception and is alien to Scripture.[29]

Regarding Paul's second feature, Calvin's emphasis on Christ's total obedience, we do agree that it was exceptionally strong (and we shall add a few comments on this topic below). But again, the obedient, voluntary character of Christ's sacrifice is strictly required by penal substitution from several angles. Since the substitute victim must be spotless (the Lamb could not, otherwise, bear the sins of others), perfect obedience is required, not only to the general precepts of the law but to personal calling and commission from God. Since the main part of punishment is *spiritual* death, the substitute must undergo the same in his spirit, with his will being involved. And since God himself (God the Son) had to bear that punishment, the freedom of his sacrifice shines forth indeed. It is misleading, therefore, to suggest that "had [Calvin] held closely to this insight," the importance of Christ's obedience, "he would . . . have avoided overconcentration upon punitive ideas which did not honor the God he wanted to honor."[30] Rather, Calvin was consistent when he stressed both the transfer of the penalty *and*, because of the conditions of substitution, the fact that Christ's death was a sweet-smelling sacrifice of devotion to his God and Father.[31]

On the third element of alleged modification, we are not entirely sure of R. S. Paul's intended meaning: if he wishes to refer to our following Christ (*Nachfolge Christi*) in self-denial and self-giving, it is a different theme than penal substitution, but it involves nothing incompatible with it; if he means something else by his phrase "sharers in its sacri-

---

[27]This is a striking feature of Calvin's doctrine, bound to his interpretation of the clause in the Creed *descendit ad inferos*. See, e.g., the first sermon on the Passion, *CO* 46.840f and the *Institutes* 2.16.10-12.

[28]A moving sentence from the *Institutes* 2.16.5 states that "it was a greater testimony of the incomparable love he had for us that he sustained so horrible assaults against the torments of death," Christ's love being one with the Father's for humankind.

[29]Paul, *Atonement and the Sacraments*, 105ff., yields too much to that antithesis; at the same time, he reaches the precious insight that it was the sense of God's fullness of mercy "that brought the theory of penal substitution to the center of evangelical religion and kept it there for three hundred years," 106.

[30]Ibid., 108.

[31]Seventh sermon on the Passion, *CO* 46.917.

fice," it would be hard to substantiate from the Reformer's writings.

François Wendel also appeals to the emphasis on free obedience (especially as it is found in the *Institutes* 2.16.5) to justify his comment, after he has noted the teaching that Christ brought the required satisfaction by bearing the penalty: "However, this is not a sort of settlement of accounts in the juridical sense."[32] Since free obedience does not weaken in any way settlements of accounts, and in view of Calvin's massive use of a juridical vocabulary and of the phrase "payment of debts,"[33] Wendel's opinion does not seem to rest on very solid ground.[34] Olivier Fatio offers a fine summary of Calvin's doctrine, but he introduces a special nuance: "The Reformer, however, moderates the juristic cast [*juridisme*] of this doctrine as he makes it a testimony of the gratuitous character of salvation. He states that the Father is satisfied by his own mercy as it is manifested in the passion of his Christ,"[35] and he refers to the *Institutes* 3.20.45. The phrase is indeed accurately quoted (*en se satisfaisant de sa propre miséricorde en Jésus-Christ*), but Calvin does not express the "weak" idea of "manifestation": his sentence ends with the clause "who gave himself once for all for us as the compensation [or reward, *recompense*] of our crimes." God's satisfaction by his own mercy does not appear to mean that the payment was somehow indifferent to him, but rather "mercy" stands metonymically for the payment the merciful God made at his own cost, in Jesus Christ, and that he freely accepts to settle all accounts. As Calvin tackles the same theme in his fifteenth sermon on the First Epistle to Timothy, he says that God "by his pure and gratuitous mercy accepts the payment that was made in the person of his Son."[36] The nuances of the Reformer's theology do not sap the strength of the main message: in Professor Nicole's words, "Calvin functions clearly with the concept of penal substitution."[37]

---

[32]F. Wendel, *Calvin: The Origins and Development of his Religious Thought*, trans. Philip Mairet (London: William Collins, 1963, Fontana Lib., 1965), 226.

[33]E.g., the 2nd sermon on the Passion, *CO* 46.858 (quoted above, n. 16).

[34]We also doubt the right of his claim (p. 231) that the dependence of Christ's work on God's eternal decree, as with Scotus, lessens the import of that work. Calvin proceeds much less deductively then Wendel's comments suggest.

[35]O. Fatio, "La Conception du salut chez Calvin," in *Le Salut chrétien: Unité et diversité des conceptions à travers l'histoire*, ed. Jean-Louis Leuba (Académie internationale des sciences religieuses; Paris: Desclée, 1995), 170.

[36]"Par sa pure miséricorde et gratuite il accepte le payement qu'en a esté fait en la personne de son Fils." *CO* 53.171.

[37]Nicole, "John Calvin's View," 224.

The Proclamation of Effects: Disarming Tyranny

"One of Calvin's favorite themes of the atonement is Christ as victor, who conquers the foes of his people."[38] The presence of unmistakable elements of what Gustaf Aulén called "the classic theory"—a misnomer indeed—is conspicuous in all the categories of Calvin's extant works, with a special emphasis on the conquest of death[39] and of the devil, now defeated tyrants. The chief question relates to the articulation of that scheme with the central doctrines of Calvin's teaching: Was the polemic (from *polemos*, fight[40]) theme independent, in his view, from that of sacrifice and punishment, or was it connected with it, and how?

In most passages the French Reformer would proclaim victory won and freedom gained without giving clues on that connection.[41] At times, at least, he celebrates the superior resources of deity: only the One who was life could swallow death, who was righteousness could overcome sin, who was power above all highness could defeat the powers of the world and the air.[42] One notices, however, his stress on *paradox:* when he writes against "the Scandals," he is acutely aware that many scoffers (already) deride the foolishness of the victorious cross and mock us because we "seek our life in the death of Jesus Christ, . . . we take gallows as our refuge, as our only anchor [*anchoram*; French: *port*] of eternal salvation."[43] "There is nothing stranger to human reason," he writes, "than to hear that God became mortal, life was subjected to death, righteousness was covered by the appearance of sin, blessing was subjected to the curse: so that through this means men be redeemed from death, that, being made partakers of blessed immortality, they obtain life, that, sin having been abolished, righteousness reign, so that death and the curse be engulfed."[44] No ordinary

---

[38]Peterson, *Calvin and the Atonement*, 69.
[39]As R. S. Paul, *Atonement and the Sacraments*, 104, perceives.
[40]The 7th sermon on the Passion, CO 46.926, says: "the Son of God wrestled for us" (*a bataillé*).
[41]See quotations in Peterson, *Calvin and the Atonement*, 70ff.
[42]*Institutes* 2.12.2.
[43]CO 8.17.
[44]*Commentary* on 1 Corinthians 1:21, *Commentaires sur le N.T.*, 3.295 (CO 49). Cf. in the sermons on Isaiah 53, with the polemic scheme less markedly on the fore: "How is Jesus Christ our life if not because, dying, he engulfed death? And how are we raised by him if not because he entered the very abysses of hell, i.e., he sustained the horrors that were upon us in consequence of our sin and which would have crushed us? For we always had to meet God as our judge, and there is nothing more frightening than having God against us. Jesus Christ had to enter there as our pledge, as the one who was to pay for us, and bear our condemnation to absolve us."

logic of quantitative superiority, of the stronger protagonist overcoming the weaker one, can apply here.

The metaphor of redemption, as it implies deliverance from tyranny, lies very close to the theme of victory, and so it is in Calvin's text. He often mentions the ransom of our deliverance: "Why did [our Lord Jesus] endure so bitter and shameful a death if not because it was necessary [*il faloit*] that we be delivered by such a ransom?"[45] To whom was the ransom paid? It is clearly identical, for Calvin, with the payment made for our debts. Satan is once mentioned alongside with God, in a rather surprising way: "If we are deep in debts, not only towards God but towards Satan, as our foe, the payment was made in the death and passion of the Son of God."[46] Even here, the payment is not said to have been made *to* Satan.[47] There is a constant equivalence in Calvin's teaching between the satisfaction offered to God, the payment of debts, that of the "price of our redemption," and Christ's vicarious suffering.[48] A likely interpretation thus emerges: Satan and death, as they draw their power from the administration of divine justice, were disarmed by the satisfaction of that justice. It agrees with the presence, usually, of the penal-sacrificial theme in context when the *Christus Victor* is proclaimed. Charles A. M. Hall captures the heart of the matter: "The central answer lies in the fact that there man's sin has been dealt with, atoned for, washed away, forgiven; and thus, to put the whole in terms of the spiritual warfare, the power of sin over men's lives has been broken."[49]

A few more explicit passages confirm this reading. As he preaches on Isaiah 53:12, Calvin explains that "the devil holds no right nor property over us [*n'ha nul droict ni appartenance sur nous*], when we

---

[45]Sixth sermon on the Passion, *CO* 46.905.

[46]"Si nous sommes plongez en dettes, non seulement à Dieu mais à Satan, comme à nostre adversaire, le payement a esté fait en la mort et passion du Fils de Dieu," Sermons on Isaiah 53, *CO* 35.670. This is the only occurrence that we have found (but we lay no claim to exhaustivity).

[47]We wonder about a possible influence of Thomas Aquinas *Summa Theologiae* III^a, Q.48, art. 4, who writes that "regarding the penalty, man was mainly obligated to God, as the supreme judge, but also to the devil as the executioner [*diabolo autem tanquam tortori*]," but adds that "the price was not to be paid to the demon, but to God" (*non erat pretium solvendum diabolo, sed Deo*).

[48]E.g., *Institutes* 2.17.5.

[49]C. A. M. Hall, *With the Spirit's Sword: The Drama of Spiritual Warfare in the Theology of John Calvin* (Richmond, Va.: John Knox, 1970), 105, as quoted by Peterson, *Calvin and the Atonement*, 76.

are made partakers of the death and passion of the Son of God."[50]
This suggests the effect of a legal transaction. In his *Commentary* on
Romans 3:24, he explains that Christ, vicariously, "delivered us from
the tyranny of death . . . for [*nam;* French: *car*) by the expiation of the
sacrifice he offered, our condemnation was lifted and abolished."[51]
On Hebrews 2:15, he comments that Christ freed us from the fear of
death, which is the chain of the devil's tyranny according to the context, "when, by sustaining our curse, he took out what was dreadful
in death."[52] Most precisely, commenting on Colossians 2:15 and the
archai and *exousiai* that Christ spoiled at the cross, he writes that the
apostle "undoubtedly means the devils, to whom Scripture ascribes
the role of accusing us before God. But Paul says that they are disarmed, so that they can bring nothing against us, since the certificate
of our guilt [the legal *cheirographon* of Col 2:14] was itself cancelled."[53]
If the devil's weapon is essentially accusation, his ruin follows from
the satisfaction of justice.

The evidence of such statements demonstrates that the *Christus Victor*
scheme depends on the more central understanding of the atonement
in a lucid and consistent way. Yet one may be surprised by the paucity
of very explicit statements articulating it. One reason may be that
Calvin did not insist on Satan the Accuser (Rev 12:10 did not catch or
grip his attention). Satan appears (often) as the dreadful foe, the roar-
ing lion, the cunning tempter, the sower of lies and the instigator of
persecution. The last feature, of course, had a great historical and existential relevance. Perhaps Calvin's sense of God's wrath was so
overwhelming that he did not need the thought of the Accuser. The
second cause of the rarity of explanations may be, we suggest, that
Calvin *the preacher*—and he goes on preaching in the *Institutes*—

---

[50]*CO* 35.676.

[51]*Commentaires sur le N.T.*, 3.61 and *CO* 49.61 (the last clause is a little shorter in Latin: *sublatus est noster reatus*). Similar association in the 17th sermon on Titus, *CO* 54.578. Also, *Commentaires sur le N.T.*, 3.757, on Ephesians 1:7: "We are redeemed in that our sins are not imputed to us. From this comes the gratuitous righteousness by which we are accepted by God and freed from the tyranny of the Devil and of death."

[52]Ibid., 386, and *CO* 55.33.

[53]Ibid., 4.86, and *CO* 52.109. Cf. *Institutes* 2.17.5: this cancellation was made by adequate sat-isfaction and payment, and a clear statement in the 7th sermon on the Passion, *CO* 46.918: "Jesus Christ triumphed on the cross. It is true that [St. Paul] applies this to the fact that he tore up the obligation that was against us, and that he acquitted us towards God, and that by that means Satan was vanquished [*par ce moyen Sathan a esté vaincu*]."

preaches the truth that will move his audience, either rebuke and humble, or comfort and "compel" into grateful obedience, and elicit a definite response.

The Broader Perspective: Conjoining and Distinguishing

The coalescence of the sacrificial, the penal and the polemic themes reflects a remarkable inclination and ability of Calvin's thought: broad comprehension that majors on solidarities and does not stumble over artificial separations between topics. His paschal interpretation of the atonement is closely bound to the penal-sacrificial one.[54] The whole chapter 2.17 of the *Institutes* justifies the affirmation of "Christ our Merit" and expounds its significance in terms of the expiatory and forensic doctrine.[55] It is typical of the breadth of Calvin's perspectives that the atonement finds its proper place in the structure of the threefold office of Christ—as R. A. Peterson Sr. has shown in a way that excuses us from attempting the same. Suffice it to quote here Calvin's definition of the contents of Christ's priestly work: "Sacerdotal dignity belongs to Jesus Christ only on that count: that he cancelled, by the sacrifice of his death, the obligation that made of us criminals before God and satisfied for our sins."[56] Again, the same synthesis, which also conjoins satisfaction and intercession!

The same intellectual and spiritual tendency manifests itself in the way the atonement and its application are closely bound together, though Calvin does not confuse the one with the other. A. Ritschl already observed "the identity of the remission of sins, justification, atonement [*Versöhnung*] and allowing into communion with God finds its classical expression with Calvin."[57] In a sermon on Isaiah 53, Calvin can speak of a "twofold (*double*) reconciliation,"

---

[54]Eighth sermon on the Passion, CO 46, 833ff.

[55]Almost the entire chapter was added in the final edition (1559) after the rather nervous discussion Calvin had with Lelio Socinus (Sozzini) in 1555, who had been preceded in 1545 by another Italian, Camillus Renatus from Chiavenna, according to Albrecht Ritschl, *Die christliche Lehre*, 1, 228.

[56]*Institutes* 2.15.6 (from the French). In 1536 Calvin started with a twofold office only (the teaching ministry was included in the priesthood), and there has been some debate on his doctrine of the *munus triplex*, though he is considered "classically," as *the* theologian of that topic; see Peterson, *Calvin and the Atonement*, 45ff., and Wendel, *Calvin*, 225, who suggests that the inspiration may have come from Bucer in his *Enarrationes in Evangelia*, 1536.

[57]*Die christliche Lehre*, 3.71.

when Christ offered himself in sacrifice and every day, now, by faith.[58] This ties in with the preacher's concern for appropriation and response.

Among the expressions of Calvin's talent for comprehension, one may select the matter of Christ's obedience. Since Piscator (1546-1625) maintained that the so-called "passive" obedience of the cross is the *exclusive* ground of our salvation and thus aroused a famous controversy, Calvin's position has been scrutinized with heightened interest. He is claimed as the great witness for the broader, more inclusive choice; and indeed, when he broached the issue, as in the *Institutes* 2.16.5, he took sides and referred to "the whole course of [Christ's] obedience"—a contrast with Melanchthon's only consideration of the "passive" work.[59] He did not fail to preach that message: "It is true that our Lord Jesus constituted himself as the ransom through his whole life: for he rendered obedience in this world to God the Father to make a reparation for Adam's offence and for all the iniquities of which we were guilty."[60] Yet the next sentence adds that "we must go [*il nous faut adresser*] to his death and passion, as to the sacrifice that has the power of blotting out all iniquities," and this is typical of Calvin's other passages—not to mention the countless number of those which only focus on Christ's passion. Otto Weber complains that the Geneva Catechism omits the life Christ lived: "It would be difficult to agree with Calvin that only in the statements of the Creed about the One who suffered, was crucified, dead, buried, and rose again from the dead, are we speaking 'properly about the substance of our redemption'."[61] In Calvin's comprehensive scheme, there is no "even" division of emphasis: the cross is central.

The second nuance relates to the *way* of Calvin's stress on obedience. When he refers to the life of Jesus, he seems to be interested mostly in our Lord's *submission*, his servant status, under the law, in the light of

---

[58]*CO* 35.671. David F. Wright, "Atonement in Reformation Theology," 46, expresses his surprise that the *Commentary* on 2 Corinthians 5:20 should use "expiate" for daily forgiveness; the French version, *Commentaires sur le N.T.*, 3.578, uses "to efface, blot out" (*n'effaceast*). The real target in that paragraph is the "Romish" idea that baptism grants remission from antecedent sins only, with the need for other means afterwards.

[59]A. Ritschl, *Die christliche Lehre*, 1.234ff.

[60]Fourth sermon on Ephesians, *CO* 51.286.

[61]O. Weber, *Foundations of Dogmatics*, trans. Darrell L. Guder (Grand Rapids: Eerdmans, 1983), 2:185.

Galatians 4:4-5 and Philippians 2:7-8;[62] whereas, as we already noted, he underscores the *voluntary* character of his self-giving in death. One could say that his emphasis falls on the *passive* dimension of Christ's "active" obedience and on the *active* dimension of the "passive" one! This binds the two together more strongly. As regards the active willing in the passion itself, we have argued that there is nothing incompatible with penal substitution, but we acknowledge that Calvin stressed it much more heavily than most advocates of this doctrine have. May we imagine some influence of his beloved St. Bernard of Clairvaux, who, in his 190th letter had written: "What pleased [God] was not the death but the will of the one dying"?[63] The main factor may have been the desire to show the full and real humanity of our Lord: Calvin went far beyond tradition in his realistic, biblical account of Jesus' emotions, anguish, inner struggle—and also trust and faith.[64] He could then preach the Lord's example, especially to those persecuted and assaulted by Satan.

The unitive or synthetic bent does not preclude the use of the sharpest *analytical* razor. In Calvin's treatment a remarkable role is played by key distinctions, very neat and assured. Though admittedly they thrust their roots deep into mystery, he brings them into play with sovereign ease; failure to follow him causes many to stumble over his doctrine. The first of these is the distinction between God's eternal love for his elect, the origin of the Son's mission to redeem them, and God's wrath against sinners that only Christ's obedience appeases. Calvin is not embarrassed to take up the Augustinian paradox: "He loved us and he hated us at the same time."[65] The duality, though marvelous and mysterious as God's love must always remain in our eyes, does not involve a real difficulty for understanding, as he immediately explains: "He hated in each of us what we had done, and loved what He had done." And this is constant: "God does not detest in us his work . . . but our uncleanness";[66] "though all are hateful in Adam, his love

---

[62]Apart from the *Institutes*, one can quote the sermons on Isaiah 53, CO 35.647; more briefly, on the Passion, CO 46.835.

[63]"*Non mors sed voluntas placuit ipsius morientis,*" Migne's Patrologia Latina 182.1053, as quoted by M. Mellet in the collective work *Initiation théologique, tome IV/l'économie du salut,* rev. ed. (Paris: Cerf, 1961), 196.

[64]E.g., in the sermons on the Passion, CO 46.186, 209ff.

[65]*Institutes* 2.16.4.

[66]*Commentaires sur le N.T.,* 3:62 of CO 49.62.

shines forth in creation."[67] Calvin's conclusion is firm: "I admit that the love of God is prior in time and also in order as regards God (*quantum ad Deum*), but from our point of view (*respectu nostri*) the beginning of love is placed in Christ's sacrifice."[68] D. F. Wright comments: "Not the least interesting feature of this sentence is that Calvin uses two words for love, *dilectio* and *amor*";[69] the French original, however, uses the same word twice, *amour*.[70] The distinction answers basically to the duality of created being and sinful corruption, finiteness and guilt, which was axiomatic for Calvin—meaning the *alien*, nonmetaphysical, character of evil that is entailed by radical monotheism and bound up with a historical Fall.

The other distinction, not altogether independent from the first one, is central in penal substitution. Calvin clearly teaches that Jesus Christ on the cross was both "the spotless Lamb, full of blessing and grace [*plenus benedictione et gratia*]" and "the sinner, guilty of the curse," that "he could not be outside the grace of God [*neque extra Dei gratiam*]" and, at the same time, suffered under his wrath (*et tamen sustinuit iram eius*).[71] Our sins entail God's withdrawal from us, a kind of rejection; Jesus Christ "had to bear those pains"; yet "he never was rejected by God his Father, this is certain."[72] This distinction is none other than the distinction between Christ in himself (*in se, en soy*) and Christ *in our person*. Calvin the jurist[73] is wont to use that phrase with its juridical connotations.[74] He can also say "in our name," in our stead, and develop the same thought: "The true man appeared, our Lord, and clothed him-

---

[67]"*Responsio . . . de occulta Dei providentia*," CO 9.290.

[68]*Commentary* on 2 Corinthians 5:19, CO 50.71, in translation used by D. F. Wright, "Atonement in Reformation Theology," 45.

[69]Ibid.

[70]*Commentaires sur le N.T.*, 3.577. The phrase corresponding to *respectu nostri* is *au regard de nous*, which is less open to a subjective interpretation. Cf. the sermon on Galatians 3:13ff., CO 50.511ff.

[71]*Commentary* on Galatians 3:13, CO 50.210 (*Commentaires sur le N.T.*, 3.64); parallel statement in the sermon on Galatians 3:13f, CO 50.511ff.

[72]Seventh sermon on the Passion, CO 46.920.

[73]Another sign of the importance of juridical categories is Calvin's insistence that Jesus had to be condemned by an earthly judge, e.g., fourth sermon on the Passion, CO 56.886, and *Institutes* 2.16.5, where he goes so far as to say that God would not have been satisfied had Jesus been killed by bandits.

[74]In the sermons on the Passion only, we have met it several times, CO 46.834, "in the name or person of all sinners"; 847, "in our person"; 870, "in the person of all those cursed and transgressors"; 888 and 920, "in our person."

self [*induit*] of Adam's person, took up [*assumpsit*] his name, and came in his stead to obey the Father, in order to offer our flesh as the price of satisfaction to the just judgment of God."[75] The frequent title of "pledge," the thought of guilt-transference and, finally, of substitution are tools to elucidate the same distinction, ultimately based on the solidarity into which the Son of God entered through his incarnation[76] and the special "headship structure" that prevails, the Head carrying the burden of his members, the Second Adam for the race.

The Speculative Edge: Questioning the Necessity

Several scholars, in the wake of Albrecht Ritschl (in 1868) and Wilhelm Dilthey (1833-1911), have detected a Scotist strain in Calvin's thought, with the theme of God's "absolute power,"[77] and it is possible to interpret elements of the doctrine of atonement accordingly: on the satisfactory value of Christ's obedience (freely conferred upon it by God)[78] and on the necessity of the atonement.

In general terms, we should not deny some affinities between Calvin and Duns Scotus: the emphasis on the divine *will*; the distinction between the sacramental *opus operatum* and the causation of grace (only God's); reservations concerning philosophical reason (though Scotus was such an abstract thinker!); offered points of comparison; maybe also a dose of sympathy for Plato versus Aristotle. On the other hand, Scotus's semi-Pelagian leanings, his Mariology—he was, against St. Thomas, the champion of the immaculate conception—and his famous thesis that the incarnation would have taken place even if Adam had not sinned, a view that Calvin fiercely combated in Osiander's version, and must have been strongly repulsive to the Reformer. As to *potentia absoluta*, Calvin never tires of *attacking* the concept, as Warfield underlined.[79] "What the scholastic theologians trifle with, of absolute power,

---

[75]*Institutes* 2.12.3, *CO* 2.341.

[76]Ibid., 342.

[77]See Emile Doumergue, *Jean Calvin. Les hommes et les choses de son temps. T. IV La pensée religieuse de Calvin* (Lausanne: Georges Bridel, 1910), 232, n. 5, and 431ff. Also Benjamin B. Warfield, "Calvin's Doctrine of God" (1909) as reprinted in *Calvin and Augustine*, ed. Samuel G. Craig (Philadelphia: Presbyterian & Reformed, 1971), 155ff. (with n. 46), no. 623 in the *Bibliography of Benjamin Breckinridge Warfield, 1851-1921*, by John E. Meeter and Roger Nicole (Presbyterian & Reformed, 1974).

[78]So Wendel, *Calvin*, 228.

[79]Warfield, "Calvin's Doctrine of God."

not only I repudiate, but I loathe, because they separate (God's) justice from his rule."[80] This is a familiar tune, which we hear in the *Institutes* (1.16.3) and in the sermons.[81] Duns Scotus is not named, and he seems to have argued for a milder version of the *potentia absoluta*,[82] but still, he explicitly started the process of divorcing God's freedom from his righteousness as defined by his law that was so hateful to Calvin.[83] On the whole, Calvin may have been nearer to Aquinas than to Scotus,[84] and we must beware of opposing excessively the two major Scholastics.[85]

Regarding the intrinsic value of Christ's satisfaction, the lack of a clear analysis of the concepts involved has too often clouded the debates of scholars. It will be helpful, therefore, if we listen to Warfield's magisterial elucidation (in his review of Mozley, who tended to confuse *acceptatio* and *acceptilatio* and the relationship to satisfaction):

> The Constitutive fact of doctrine of "satisfaction" is that the reparation "accepted" by God is held to be *per se* equivalent to the obligation resting on the sinner. The characteristic feature of Scotist theory, on the other hand, is that the reparation provided is declared to possess no intrinsic equivalence to the obligation, but to be "accepted" by God in its place by an act of gracious will . . .. A "satisfaction," *ex vi verbi*, is the rendering of an equivalent; not the very thing in obligation (that would be *solutio* in the strict sense) nor something merely "accepted" in lieu or the obligation (that would be *acceptatio* in the Scotist sense) but, in distinction from both, a real *equivalent*.[86]

Acceptilatio would be acceptance of the person *without* any payment, which would be nearer to Faustus Socinus's, not Scotus's, doctrine. If

---

[80]"Quod de absoluta potestate nugantur Scholastici non solum repudio, sed etiam detestor, quia iustitiam eius ab imperio separant," in his *Responsio . . . de occulta Dei providentia, CO* 9.288.

[81]Richard Stauffer, *Dieu, la providence*, 114-15, quotes from several sermons on Job, especially the 21st which denounces the distinction of the "absolute" and the "ordinary" power, the 64th and the 88th.

[82]Ibid., 113-16.

[83]Cf. the account of Scotus' theses in T. George, *Theology of the Reformers*, 42ff.

[84]Cf. Arvin Vos, *Aquinas, Calvin and Contemporary Protestant Thought* (Exeter: Paternoster, 1985), to which we had no access except through a review. We remember Richard Stauffer telling us personally his feeling that Calvin depends on Thomas Aquinas much more than most people think.

[85]See Etienne Gilson's warning in *L'Esprit de la Philosophie médiévale*, Gifford Lectures, Second Series (Paris: J. Vrin, 1932), 266ff.

[86]B. B. Warfield, review of *The Doctrine of the Atonement* by J. K. Mozley, *Critical Reviews, Works 10* (reprint, Grand Rapids: Baker, 1981).

Scotus's position is clearly seen, Calvin's seems to be far from it: in his response to L. Socinus, he strenuously refuses to set the value of Christ's sacrifice *over against* the divine decree; he affirms the priority of the latter; but the whole effort of his argument is to show and celebrate the proper value of Christ's historical work as realization of the decree. Far be it from him to deny its intrinsic worth and virtue! He extols the extraordinary price of our redemption (*Institutes* 2.17.5), and since the divine nature was required for our liberation and that liberation obtained by satisfaction, we may understand that the *deity* of Christ conferred value to his sacrifice (*Institutes* 2.12.2-3). The *Commentaries* stress that "the whole world and all the things that men hold dear are nothing compared with the excellence of that price."[87] A daring metaphor of lasting and (it seems) intrinsic virtue occurs at least twice: the blood shed by Christ remains ever *fresh* to avail for sinners.[88] One may not assimilate Calvin's strict *satisfactio*, based on the Decree, and the mere *acceptatio* of Scotists.

On the necessity of the atonement (satisfaction) for reconciliation, the evidence may be more complex. In contrast with Anselm, Timothy George writes, "Calvin denied any simple of [sic] absolute necessity for the incarnation" and the atonement "has no necessity outside of God's gracious will toward us."[89] To buttress the claim, he refers to the *Institutes* 2.12.1 (as most scholars do) and to an important sentence in the first sermon on the Passion: "God was well able to rescue us from the unfathomable depths of death in another fashion, but he willed to display the treasures of his infinite goodness when he spared not his only son."[90] Such a quotation does seem to settle the issue. Nevertheless, we suggest that interesting nuances may be introduced.

The first consideration relates to the intriguing disproportion between the very few passages that speak against the idea of necessity and the massive use by Calvin of words that sound like the expressions of that very idea! "It was necessary [*il faloit*]," "there was no other

---

[87]*Commentaires sur le N.T.*, on 1 Peter 1:18, 4.560. On the next verse (4.561), the sacrifice "has been legitimate and approved of God because it was whole and immaculate." On Hebrews 9:14 (4.456), the perfection and efficacy of the "work more than human" is ascribed to the agency of the Spirit.

[88]Ibid., 3.757, on Ephesians 1:7, *comme si le sang de Christ séchoit et perdoit sa vigueur* (denied); and the sermons on Isaiah 53, *CO*, 35.635.

[89]George, *Theology of the Reformers*, 221.

[90]*CO* 46.833, in George's (excellent) translation.

means," "it was impossible, but . . ." A few paragraphs after the sentence quoted from the first sermon on Christ's Passion, we read that "he came to give himself over to death since we could not be reconciled though other means, nor appease God's wrath."[91] Had Pilate been successful in his attempt to release Jesus, we would have been lost; Calvin even fancies that the devil inspired that attempt to prevent redemption and, since the devil was also driving the high priest to demand Christ's death, that the devil behaves as a mad man (*forcené*).[92] In the context of such utterances, there is no suggestion that the necessity expressed is hypothetical just because God willed it. On the contrary, the necessity is often related to the attributes of God, especially his holiness and justice: "God must be our mortal foe . . . since God, being the fount of all righteousness [*iustice*] and uprightness, must hate the evil he sees in us."[93] Similarly, in the sermons on Isaiah 53,[94] and in the *Institutes* 2.17.3, he says: "Since God is the fount of all justice, it is necessary that we have him as our foe and our judge, as long as we are sinners." The fullest statement of that thought occurs in the sixth sermon on the Passion: "We cannot get grace without justice. God must hate and reject us, until we be just and cleansed of all impurities and offences before him. That it be so, can God deny himself? Can he divest himself of his holiness, justice and integrity?"[95] Only through Christ's condemnation as a criminal can we escape. This evidence does not square easily with a "Scotist" Calvin.

The second consideration focuses on the multiplicity of levels at which one can talk of "necessity." One is not restricted to the two alternatives of absolute necessity and pure contingency, or indeterminate freedom. St. Anselm himself wrestled with the theme because he did not wish to surrender divine freedom (see *Cur Deus Homo*, bk. II, chaps. 5 and 18). St. Thomas Aquinas, for whom Anselm was too much of a necessitarian, worked out a finer analysis: there is absolute necessity (*simpliciter*) when it proceeds from the nature (formal cause) of the being involved, without any other possibility; there is necessity of violence (*coactionis*) when it is imposed by an external cause (efficient

[91]Ibid., 835. Cf. 905, "it was necessary [*il faloit*] that we be delivered by such a ransom."
[92]Ibid., 894ff.
[93]Fourth sermon on Ephesians, *CO* 51.283.
[94]*CO* 35.622, 625, 648 (*il n'y a eu moyen d'appaiser son ire, sinon*).
[95]*CO* 56.910.

cause); there is hypothetical necessity (*suppositionis*) when it depends on the goal of the action (final cause), but either strict, *sine quo non*, when the means is indispensable, or looser, *propter melius*, if the means is better than others; the necessity of the atonement belongs to the last named category, which implies a greater *congruence*.[96] One realizes that congruence may know various degrees and be assessed by various criteria; if the means is much better than any other than can be conceived and fits the *nature* of the agent, the necessity will not be so light! In a Leibnizian perspective, one could (arrogantly, we think) consider that God is *obligated* by his own goodness and wisdom to choose the means that best fits his nature!

The evidence from Calvin's writings suggests that the congruence of the atonement was very strong in his eyes. The statement in the *Institutes* 2.12.1 only rules out absolute necessity and is concerned to affirm the priority of God's decree, not even the freedom of God's choice; Calvin hastens immediately to add that God ordained the best means (*quod nobis optimum erat*; French: *le plus utile*). A. Ritschl himself was able to discern that the passage does not reduce the necessity of the satisfaction.[97] The most impressive statement comes from the sermon on Isaiah 53:10: "It is true that God was well able to rescue us from death by another means: but he did not want it, and also *that would not have been good*."[98] May God choose what is not good without denying himself?

With all due deference, the last-quoted statement sounds so awkward that we may take it as the symptom of embarrassment. It betrays an inner tension in Calvin's thought. As he teaches and preaches ordinarily, he follows the logic of penal-sacrificial substitution, and he sounds strongly neccessitarian; it is also a theme that leads his hearers to the realization of their guilt and plight. But then he is afraid of infringing on the holy rights of Transcendence. God is higher. We may not set bounds to his freedom.

As he mitigates that affirmation of necessity, Calvin may be moved by his respect for St. Thomas Aquinas, and for St. Augustine, who wrote

---

[96] *Summa Theologiae* III[a], Q.46, art. 1-3, and the comments in P. Synave's appendix on the topic in the "édition de la Revue des Jeunes" (Paris, Tournai, Rome: Desclée, 1931), 211-16.

[97] Ritschl, *Die christliche Lehre*, I:228 (*Die . . . Nothwendigkeit . . . wird auch nicht verkurzt*).

[98] *CO* 35.659: "Il est vray que Dieu par un autre moyen nous pouvoit bien retirer de la mort: mais il ne l'a pas voulu, *et n'estoit pas bon aussi*" (italics added). We have found only one other passage, ibid., 666: "For God was well able to save us without any means, but we always presuppose that life had to be gotten for us by Jesus Christ."

that God did not lack another means "but there had not been another mode *more convenient* to cure our miseries."[99] More deeply, the tension we spot corresponds to the duality of God's ordinary justice and God's "secret justice," to us incomprehensible.[100] A few times, in the interest of transcendence, one can feel the fleeting shadow of dualism: in his sixteenth sermon on Job, Calvin speaks of the guilt of the angels (the faithful ones), who satisfy ordinary, legal justice but not infinite justice;[101] humans, he can say, were *created* weak (*infirmus*) and susceptible to defection, though he clams that this "debility" was still "very good"[102]— not the most convincing of paradoxes. In view of the infinite distance between the Creator and his creature, Calvin feels it would be unseemly audacity to speak of necessity for God. And this also "preaches well": to crush to the ground all human pride and presumption, to foster the sense of utter unworthiness and dependence on God's mercy.

Concluding Comments: The Import of Doctrinal Language

Other facets of Calvin's doctrine of the atonement would deserve further study: his powerful emphasis that all the benefits Christ obtained for us are found in his person,[103] and the links with his theology of the Lord's Supper. But we should devote our final remarks to a more general question: What is, in Calvin's own estimate, the cognitive import of all his discourses, arguments, explanations? Do we grasp, through their mediation, beyond language and subjective effects, a *reality* of God and for God?

---

[99]*De Trinitate*, 8.10.13. We have been led to that passage by Francois Turretini, *Institutio theologiae elencticae*, Pars secunda (New York and Pittsburgh: Robert Carter, 1847), locus 14, Q.10, 386. Turretini has Calvin in view, without naming him, when he speaks of "several of us, most of them wrote before [Faustus] Socinus," who settle for the "necessity of congruence."

[100]Cf. R. Stauffer, *Dieu, la création*, 118ff., 108ff.

[101]As quoted by R. Stauffer, 191ff (referring to *CO* 33.207ff.). The biblical basis in Eliphaz's words (Job 4:18; 15:15) is precarious: these words (apart from a possible hyperbole) receive scant praise from the Lord at the end of the book (Job 42:7)!

[102]*Responsio . . . de occulta Dei providentia*, CO 9.291: "Quamvis infirmus, et ad defectionem flexibilis creatus fuerit homo, hanc debilitatem fuisse valde bonum, quia paulo post docuit eius ruina, extra Deum nihil firmum esse, vel stabile." *Infirmus* may have the meaning of "not firm."

[103]*Institutes* 2.16.19. This trait is also clear in the sermons, as Wilhelm Niesel perceives, "Der theologische Gehalt der jüngst veroffentlichen Predigten Calvins" (*Regards contemporains sur Jean Calvin,*. Actes du colloque Calvin, Strasbourg, 1964 [Paris Presses Universitaires de France, 1965], 10).

A crude and unthinking literalism seems to be ruled out by Calvin's stress on *accommodation*. It is an important theme of his doctrine of revelation,[104] with the famous image of God "lisping" with us as a nurse does with small children (*Institutes* 2.12.1). It entails that God does not reveal himself "in his essence," though Calvin falls into inconsistencies at this point.[105] Is this another symptom of the "inner tension"? At any rate, the tension is there. When, in his teaching on the atonement, especially on propitiation, he writes: "Though God, as he uses such manner of speech, accommodates himself to our crudity," he adds, "nevertheless, it is the truth" (*Institutes* 2.16.3).

When Calvin expounds the doctrine of the atonement, he gives very few hints, if any, that his language should be interpreted along the "as if" line, or as offering sets of inadequate images with an essentially regulative function. The only data that could point in that direction is the occasional reference to our consciences in sentences that deal with the necessity of Christ's death: "Consciences that are fearful and thunderstruck by God's judgment can only find rest if there is a sacrifice and a washing to wipe away sins" (*Institutes* 2.16.5, cf. 17 and comfort for the consciences of God's servants); "our consciences cannot apprehend the benefits [of God's favor] except through the intervention of Christ' sacrifice."[106] But this implies no *reduction* to subjective effects: it is objective satisfaction that appeases conscience. On the other hand, Calvin speaks forcefully against the doctrine, inspired by the devil, that concentrates on Christ as the model (*patron de toute vertu*),[107] and he rebukes the libertines who interpret the events of the passion as a passion play.[108] Those who deny the saving substitution lack a "true feeling of conscience." Calvin's diagnosis is clear: "As Satan has made them drunk, they are in no way touched by the fear of God's judgment, nor by the thought of their sin."[109]

---

[104]Cf. J. I. Packer, "Calvin's View of Scripture," in *God's Inerrant Word: An International Symposium on the Trustworthiness of Scripture*, ed. John W. Montgomery (Minneapolis: Bethany Fellowship, 1974), 102ff; T. George, *Theology of the Reformers*, 192ff; R. Stauffer, *Dieu, la création*, 21ff. who notes (p. 36, n. 31) that Calvin rendered his two Latin words *accommodare* and *attemperare* by *accommoder* in French but in 1560 tended to shift to *se conformer*.

[105]R. Stauffer, *Dieu, la création*, 21-26, with statements that contradict the usual thesis quoted in p. 36, n. 34, and p. 41, n. 90.

[106]*Commentary* on 2 Corinthians 5:19, *CO* 50.72, see n. 17. *Commentaires sur le N.T.*, 4.456, on Hebrews 9:13: cleansing is a gift to consciences.

[107]First sermon on the Passion, *CO* 46.844.

[108]*CO* 7.199. We could say: they read the Passion Narrative as story rather than history.

[109]*De scandalis, CO* 8.17.

Such utterances confirm the impression one gains from Calvin's constant reliance on the logic of penal-sacrificial substitution and the high degree of "integration" he achieved with the various biblical languages of atonement. He believed he was preaching God's truth and not merely playing a church language-game. His mind reached so vibrantly to the meaning of the biblical writers, he felt so sure about it (especially in Isaiah 53), and was so convinced that it was God-given, that he had great assurance. Yet the inner tension was there—his respect for the unthinkable transcendence of the Most High—though, apart from a few statements, it had only light *doctrinal* consequences. Both factors in that tension were born of humility, born of a radical fear of God: submission to Scripture as the word of God to be humbly received and applied, and humble recognition that God is greater. Calvin's doctrine of the atonement is that of a God-fearing servant of the Word.

15

Definite atonement in historical perspective

Raymond A. Blacketer

Did God the Father, in sending his Son into the world to make atonement for sinners, intend to make salvation available to every individual person, or was his purpose that his Son's death should provide satisfaction for the sins of the elect alone? Did Christ go to the cross in order to make salvation possible for whoever might believe, or did he have in mind those whom the Father had foreknown, elected and given to him? The question of whether Christ's satisfaction on the cross was universal and indiscriminate or specific and definite was the most contentious issue at the great Synod of Dort (Dordrecht) in 1618-19, and it continues to be one of the most controversial teachings in Reformed soteriology.[1]

The Synod of Dort affirmed what has come to be called the doctrine

---

[1]For a general introduction to the history of the Synod, including the personalities and theological issues involved, see P. Y. De Jong, ed., *Crisis in the Reformed Churches: Essays in Commemoration of the Great Synod of Dort, 1618-1619* (Grand Rapids: Reformed Fellowship, 1968). On the debate over limited atonement at Dort, see W. Robert Godfrey, "Tensions Within International Calvinism: The Debate on the Atonement at the Synod of Dort, 1618-1619" (Ph.D. diss., Stanford University, 1974), hereafter cited as *Tensions*. An important chapter from Godfrey's study was also published as "Reformed Thought on the Extent of the Atonement to 1618," *WTJ* 37 (1975-76): 133-71, hereafter cited as "Reformed Thought." There is also a study by Stephen Strehle, "The Extent of the Atonement and the Synod of Dort," *WRJ* 59 (1989): 1-23, but Strehle depends heavily on extremely biased secondary sources, especially Gerard Brandt's *History of the Reformation and Other Ecclesiastical Transactions in and about the Low-Countries* (New York: AMS Press, 1979) and is somewhat lacking in objective analysis.

of *limited atonement*, although *definite atonement* or *particular redemption* would be more apt descriptions of this teaching.[2] In brief, this is the belief that the satisfaction rendered by Christ on the cross was of infinite value and worth by virtue of Christ's incarnation but that its intended object was not sinners in general, or every individual, but rather those whom God had elected from eternity. Furthermore, this specific, or definite efficacy is not the result of human free choice with respect to the call of the gospel. In other words, the limitation in Christ's satisfaction is not the result of human failure to believe. Rather, it is the divine decree of election that is the limiting factor. The Father sent his Son to the cross to pay the price of the sins of the elect.

Over the past century and a half, this doctrine has been the object of attacks not only from Lutherans and Arminians, who never accepted it in the first place, but also from scholars *within* the Reformed tradition. This opposition from within was spearheaded by an 1856 treatise on the subject by John McLeod Campbell, in which he blamed the doctrine of definite atonement for robbing Presbyterians of their comfort and assurance of salvation.[3] If God did not die for all, McLeod Campbell argued, how can one know that he died for him? McLeod Campbell was reacting to a distorted form of Scottish Reformed piety characterized by legalistic preaching and agonizing self-examination and questioning of one's salvation.[4]

Rejection of definite atonement is also common among Reformed theologians influenced by the theology of Karl Barth. Barth's doctrines of incarnation and election excluded a priori any restriction of Christ's satisfaction. These developments, in turn, motivated Barthian historians to attempt to demonstrate that this doctrine was not to be found in John Calvin and thus did not belong to the pristine spirit of Reformed theology. Moreover, these scholars frequently charged that the rise of the doctrine of limited atonement was the result of a rapid decline in Reformed theology after Calvin. It was argued that while the Genevan

---

[2]See Richard A. Muller, *Dictionary of Latin and Greek Theological Terms* (Grand Rapids: Baker, 1985), s.v. *satisfactio vicaria*, esp. p. 273; and Roger Nicole, "Particular Redemption," in *Our Savior God: Man, Christ, and the Atonement*, ed. J. M. Boice (Grand Rapids: Baker, 1980), 165-78.
[3]John McLeod Campbell, *The Nature of the Atonement and its Relation to Remission of Sins and Eternal Life*, 3rd ed. (London: Macmillan, 1869).
[4]The origins of this tortured piety are likely found in the Marrow Controversy of the early eighteenth century. See David C. Lachman, *The Marrow Controversy* (Edinburgh: Rutherford House, 1988).

Reformer's teachings were biblically based and conducive to a warm, balanced piety, those who came after Calvin quickly turned to a dry, speculative form of theologizing that took human reason as its starting point. Post-Reformation Reformed theology was thus a deviation from, and distortion of, Calvin's original views. Scholars frequently identified Theodore Beza, Calvin's successor in Geneva, as the chief culprit in this move away from the scriptural roots of the Reformation. Beza supposedly transformed Reformed theology into a rational system that deduced all of its tenets from an abstract notion of the divine decree of predestination,[5] and the doctrine of limited atonement was a direct result of this regrettable development. This characterization of Protestant orthodoxy was backed up by the general consensus of nineteenth- and early-twentieth-century church historians and theologians.[6]

Beginning in the 1970s, however, scholars began to question these long-held stereotypes and assumptions about the theological tradition after Calvin. What began with a few voices of dissent quickly grew into a large chorus, so that today there is a substantial body of revisionist scholarship that offers a vigorous challenge to the old caricatures of Protestant orthodoxy and provides a more historically accurate picture of the assumptions, methods and aims of Reformed theologians after Calvin. A radical reappraisal of post-Reformation and Puritan theology has taken place that leaves little supports for the older perspective.[7] The

---

[5]Proponents of the radical discontinuity between Reformation and post-Reformation theology include Basil Hall, "Calvin against the Calvinists," in *John Calvin*, ed. G. E. Duffield (Grand Rapids: Eerdmans, 1966): 19-37; Brian G. Armstrong, *Calvinism and the Amyraut Heresy* (Madison: University of Wisconsin Press, 1969); Holmes Rolston III, *John Calvin versus the Westminster Confession* (Richmond, Va.: John Knox, 1972); R. T. Kendall, *Calvin and English Calvinism to 1649* (New York: Oxford University Press, 1979); J. B. Torrance, "The Incarnation and 'Limited Atonement,'" *EQ* 55 (1983): 83-94.

[6]Including, e.g., Alexander Schweitzer, Heinrich Heppe, Hans Emil Weber and Paul Althaus. For detailed bibliography, see Richard A. Muller, *Christ and the Decree: Christology and Predestination in Reformed Theology from Calvin to Perkins* (Durham: Labyrinth, 1986), and his *Post-Reformation Reformed Dogmatics*, 4 volumes, on theological prolegomena and Scripture (Grand Rapids: Baker, 1987-2003), hereafter *PRRD*; idem, "Calvin and the 'Calvinists': Assessing Continuities and Discontinuities Between the Reformation and Orthodoxy," parts I and II, in *CTJ* 30/2 (1995): 345-75 and 31/1 (1996): 125-60; idem, "The Myth of 'Decretal Theology,'" *CTJ* 30/1 (1995): 159-67; idem, "Found (No Thanks to Theodore Beza): One 'Decretal' Theology," *CTJ* 32/1 (1997): 145-51.

[7]See the groundbreaking study of Richard A. Muller, *Christ and the* Decree; idem *PRRD*; idem, "Calvin and the 'Calvinists'"; idem, "The Myth of 'Decretal Theology' "; idem, "Found (No Thanks to Theodore Beza)." Paul Helm's *Calvin and the Calvinists* (Edinburgh: Banner of Truth, 1982) provides a compelling refutation of Kendall's thesis and includes valuable

long-held myth that Beza was the chief distorter of Calvin's theology has been laid to rest by scholars who have carefully studied his life and works.[8] Moreover, the fiction that Reformed theology was the brainchild of a single man, John Calvin, is also being dispelled. New scholarship is shedding light on Calvin's Reformed contemporaries, such as Wolfgang Musculus, Peter Martyr Vermigli and Jerome Zanchi.[9] Numerous studies are accumulating evidence and documentation that demonstrate a high degree of continuity between Reformation and post-Reformation thought, even as later generations of Reformed scholars put the insights of the earlier Reformers into orderly forms suitable for teaching, defended them against external and internal attacks, and constructed confessional documents for the Reformed churches.[10]

If the doctrine of definite atonement, then, was not the result of a speculative, rationalistic tendency in theology, what were its origins, and how did it come to its mature formulation in the canons of the Synod of Dort?

Patristic and Medieval Precedents

While the issue of the extent of Christ's satisfaction on the cross and the divine intentions in that satisfaction did not become a major mat-

---

reflections on the doctrine of limited atonement. See also the revisionist introduction to Reformed scholasticism: *Inleiding in de Gereformeerde Scholastiek*, ed. Willem J. van Asselt *et al.* (Zoetermeer: Boekencentrum, 1998).

[8]See Jill Raitt, *The Eucharistic Theology of Theodore Beza: Development of the Reformed Doctrine* (Chambersburg, Penn.: American Academy of Religion, 1972); Tadataka Maruyama, *The Ecclesiology of Theodore Beza: The Reform of the True Church* (Geneva: Librarie Droz, 1978); and especially Ian McPhee, "Conserver or Transformer of Calvin's Theology? A Study of the Origins and Development of Theodore Beza's Thought, 1550-1570" (Ph.D. diss., University of Cambridge, 1979).

[9]Notable studies on Calvin's Reformed contemporaries include Craig S. Farmer, *The Gospel of John in the Sixteenth Century: The Johannine Exegesis of Wolfgang Musculus*, Oxford Studies in Historical Theology (New York: Oxford, 1997); Frank A. James III, *Peter Martyr Vermigli and Predestination: The Augustinian Inheritance of an Italian Reformer* (Oxford/New York, Oxford, 1998); John Patrick Donnelly, *Calvinism and Scholasticism in Vermigli's Doctrine of Man and Grace* (Leiden, E.J. Brill, 1976); John L. Farthing, "*De coniugio spirituali:* Jerome Zanchi on Ephesians 5:22-33," *Sixteenth Century Journal* 24/3 (1993): 621-52; idem, "*Foedus Evangelicum:* Jerome Zanchi on the Covenant" *CTJ* 29/1 (1994): 149-67.

[10]See the collection of essays, including the viewpoint of the older scholarship as well as that of the more recent revisionist perspective: *Later Calvinism: International Perspectives*, ed. W. Fred Graham (Kirksville, Mo.: Sixteenth Century Journal Publishers, 1994). See also *Protestant Scholasticism: Essays in Reassessment*, ed. Carl R. Trueman and R. S. Clark (Carlisle: Paternoster, 1999), and *Reformation and Scholasticism: An Ecumenical Enterprise*, ed. Willem J. van Asselt and Eef Dekker (Grand Rapids: Baker, 2001).

ter of dispute until the late sixteenth century, the issue goes back to debates in the early centuries of the church. Francis Turretin's extensive treatment of the object of Christ's satisfaction in his *Institutio Theologiae Elencticae* is imposing in terms of his accumulation of the exegetical evidence for definite atonement;[11] he also cites patristic and medieval authorities to back up the claim that the teachings of the Reformed churches are by no means novel. The earliest of these authorities is St. Jerome, who, commenting on Matthew 20:28, asserts that Jesus "does not say that he gave his life for all, but for many, that is, for all those who would believe." Turretin adds his own explanatory gloss: "who are none other than the elect." While there may be some ambiguity in Jerome's statement, there is certainly none in the medieval *Glossa Ordinaria's* comments on that same text, which Turretin proceeds to cite: Jesus gave his life "for many, not for all, but for those who were predestined to life."[12] In addition, Turretin cites evidence to the effect that one of the differences between Augustine and his opponents, the Pelagians, was that the latter affirmed that Christ died for every individual sinner.[13]

Sixteenth-century combatants on both sides of the issue attempted to claim the support of St. Augustine for their positions; however, there is no single statement from the bishop of Hippo that explicitly declares that God's intention in the satisfaction of Christ was to procure redemption for the elect alone. Nonetheless, there are numerous indications that this was precisely the view that Augustine held.[14] This fact is even recognized by J. Pohle in his 1913 *Catholic Encyclopedia* article on grace, in which he claims that after 421 Augustine believed that "the divine will regarding human salvation was no longer universal, but particular."[15]

Commenting on John 10:26, Augustine explains that Jesus viewed

---

[11]Francis Turretin, *Institutio Theologiae Elencticae*, locus 14, quest. 14, in *Francisci Turrettini Opera* (Edinburgh: J. D. Lowe, 1847-1848), 2:400-423; ET: *Institutes of Elenctic Theology*, trans. G. M. Giger, ed. James T. Dennison Jr. (Phillipsburg, N.J.: P&R Publishing, 1992-97), 2:455-82.
[12]Turretin, *Opera*, 2:406; *Institutes* 2:462. The reference is to Jerome's *Commentariorum in Evangelium Matthaei*, in *PL* 26:150; and to the interlinear gloss.
[13]Turretin, *Opera*, 2:400; *Institutes* 2:455.
[14]The evidence for this contention is probably stronger than Godfrey's work indicates. Cf. Godfrey, *Tensions*, 72-74; "Reformed Thought," 133-34.
[15]*The Catholic Encyclopedia* (New York: Encyclopedia Press, 1913), s.v. *grace*. Pohle, of course, thinks this is a bad development, resulting from "torturous and violent interpretations of the clear, unmistakable text." See vol. 6:700a.

the Pharisees as "predestined to everlasting destruction, not won to eternal life by the price of His own blood."[16] It is no stretch to conclude that the implication of this statement is that the price of Christ's blood was paid for those who are predestined to eternal life. Later in the same work, Augustine refers to the "many mansions" of John 14:2 and says that at the last day "those whom he [Christ] has redeemed by his blood, he shall then have delivered up to stand before his Father's face."[17] Here Augustine draws a direct connection between being redeemed by the blood of Christ and being delivered to the Father at the last day as Christ's possession. Those who are redeemed on the cross are the same ones who are saved.

Augustine connects Christ's sacrifice on the cross directly with those whom the Father had given to the Son, namely, the elect. Referring to John 17:11-12, Augustine writes, "Those, therefore, are understood to be given to Christ who are ordained to eternal life. These are they who are predestinated and called according to the purpose, of whom not one perishes."[18] The Father sent the Son to propitiate, that is, to offer sacrifice, for *our* sins, says Augustine, commenting on 1 John 4:10. Augustine seems to imply that Christ's propitiation and sacrifice were directed *pro nobis* (to us)—that is, to the elect.[19]

Moreover, as Godfrey points out, Augustine interprets 1 John 2:2—a key passage in the post-Reformation debates—in the same manner as those who would later defend the doctrine of definite atonement. According to Augustine's interpretation, Christ is the atoning sacrifice for the "whole world" in the sense that he atones for the sins of the "church in all nations" and "the church throughout the whole world."[20] In addition, he rejects the Pelagians' interpretation of 1 Timothy 2:4 (God "wants all men to be saved and to come to a knowledge of the truth"). Augustine rejects the idea that God desires the salvation of every individual but that this divine will is frustrated by the free choice of the sin-

---

[16]Augustine, *Tractatus in Ioannis Evangelium* 48.4 (erroneously cited as 68.4 in Godfrey, *Tensions*, 73, and "Reformed Thought," 134), Migne, *PL* 35:1742; ET in *Nicene and Post-Nicene Fathers*, series 1, ed. P. Schaff (1886-89; repr. Peabody, Mass.: Hendrickson, 1994), 7:267, hereafter *NPNF*[1].

[17]*Tractatus* 68.2; *NPNF*[1] 7:323.

[18]*De Correptione et Gratia* (*On Rebuke and Grace*), cap. 21; *NPNF*[1] 5:480.

[19]*In Epsitolam Iannis Tractatus decem*, 7.9, *NPNF*[1] 7:504.

[20]*In Epsitolam Iannis Tractatus decem*, 1.8, *NPNF*[1] 7:465; see Godfrey, *Tensions*, 74, "Reformed Thought," 134.

ner.[21] For Augustine, the cross is mere foolishness to those who are perishing, but it is the power of God to those who are saved (1 Cor 1:18), and it is only to the latter, the elect, that Paul refers in 1 Timothy 2:4. It is all of *these* whom God teaches to come to Christ; he wills all of them to be saved and come to the knowledge of the truth.[22] Thus, we ought to understand Paul to mean "that no man is saved unless God wills his salvation: not that there is no man whose salvation he does not will, but that no man is saved apart from his will."[23]

Augustine's defender and younger contemporary, Prosper of Aquitaine, is even more explicit on the extent of Christ's redemption. Prosper admits that Christ can be said to have died for all in the sense that he takes on the human nature common to all because all humanity shares the same fallen condition and because of the "greatness and value" of the price he paid on the cross. But at the same time, Prosper maintains that Christ "was crucified only for those who were to profit by his death,"[24] who are none other than the elect. Moreover, in his letter to Augustine, Prosper reports that one of the teachings that the so-called semi-Pelagians champion in opposition to the teachings of Augustine is the contention that "the propitiation which is found in the mystery of the blood of Christ was offered for all men without exception," and thus anyone who is willing has the potential for being saved.[25] It is clear that Prosper does not concur with this perspective, nor does he think that Augustine would agree with this universal view of propitiation, and Augustine offers no evidence to the contrary in his reply to Prosper.

The ninth-century monk Gottschalk of Orbais explicitly taught the doctrine of limited redemption. He was probably not alone in his views on the matter, but by this time the Augustinian doctrines of grace had been pushed to the margins of mainstream theology; and this perspec-

---

[21]*Contra Julianum*, 4.8.42; *PL* 44:759-60.
[22]*De Praed. Sanct.* 14; *PL* 44:971.
[23]*Enchiridion*, cap. 103; cf. *De Corrept. et Gratia*, 47, in which Augustine argues that Christians should preach the gospel to all persons without distinction and that believers should desire the salvation of all to whom they preach the gospel. In this sense, God wills the salvation of all because believers ought to will this.
[24]Cited in Godfrey, *Tensions*, 75; "Reformed Thought," 135.
[25]Letter 225, cap. 1, translated in *Saint Augustine: Four Anti-Pelagian Writings*, trans. John A. Mourant and William J. Collinge (Washington, D.C.: Catholic University of America, 1992): 201; cf. also cap. 6, 205-6.

tive was considered by most to be extreme, if not heretical.[26]

In the twelfth century, Peter Lombard formulated the distinction that would become standard for centuries as well as the starting point for the debates in the era of early Reformed orthodoxy. According to Lombard, Christ is both the priest and the sacrificial victim for our reconciliation, who offers himself "for all, with respect to the sufficiency of the ransom, but for the elect alone with regard to its efficiency, because it effects salvation for the predestined alone."[27] Considered abstractly, the death of Christ has more than enough inherent value to cover the sins of every individual; but Lombard limits its efficacy to the elect. This distinction, while a significant move toward the concept of definite atonement and particular redemption, still leaves room for ambiguity. In fact, an Arminian could accept this formula. If the elect are those whom God foresees will believe in Christ by their own free choice, as defined by Arminius, then the satisfaction of Christ, though offered for all, only becomes effective when applied to the believer. It is doubtful that this interpretation would be true to the Master of the Sentences, given his Augustinian leanings. But what is lacking in Lombard is a clear indication of God's intentions in the cross and the specific object and end of Christ's propitiatory sacrifice.

The case of Thomas Aquinas is not so clear. It is certain that Thomas, who has a very Augustinian view of election, would have had little sympathy for the position of the Remonstrants; he denies that foreknowledge of a person's merits is the cause of election, and he would certainly say the same thing about the Arminians' foreseen faith.[28] In fact, according to Thomas, predestination is not based on anything in the person; rather, it is based solely in God's will.[29] Moreover, Thomas can even say that there is a sense in which God does not will that all persons be saved. Referring to 1 Timothy 2:4, Thomas ex-

---

[26]See the study by Jonathan H. Rainbow, *The Will of God and the Cross: An Historical and Theological Study of John Calvin's Doctrine of Limited Redemption* (Allison Park, Penn.: Pickwick, 1990), 25-32.

[27]"Christus ergo est sacerdos, idemque et hostia pretium nostrae reconciliationis; qui se in ara cruces non diabolo, sed Trinitati obtulit pro omnibus, quantum ad pretii sufficientiam; sed pro electis tantum quantum ad efficaciam, quia praedestinatis tantum salutem effecit." Peter Lombard *Sententiae in IV Libris Distinctae* 3.20.5 (Grottaferrata: Collegii S. Bonaventurae ad Claras Aquas, 1981), 2:128; in the *PL* the reference is 3.20.3, *PL* 192:799.

[28]*Summa Theologiae* 1, Q23, art. 5. Latin texts of the *Summa Theologiae* are from the Leonine edition (Rome, 1886-87).

[29]*Summa Theologiae* 1, Q23, art. 2.

plains that these words "can be understood as applying to every class of individuals, not to every individual of each class; in which case they mean that God wills some men of every class and condition to be saved, males and females, Jews and Gentiles, great and small, but not all of every condition."[30] Similarly, Thomas explains the words of institution in the Last Supper as applying to the elect of various classes: "The blood of Christ's Passion has its efficacy not merely in the elect among the Jews, to whom the blood of the Old Testament was exhibited, but also in the Gentiles."[31] Elsewhere Thomas speaks of the union of Christ with the elect in a manner that might add weight to the concept of definite atonement: "The head and members are as one mystic person; and therefore Christ's satisfaction belongs to all the faithful as being his members."[32]

On the other hand, Thomas speaks of God's willing the salvation of all according to his antecedent will and willing the salvation of the elect according to his consequent will.[33] The validity of this distinction was a matter of debate among orthodox Reformed theologians, most of whom rejected it because it was used to defend universal atonement and because it seems to make God's will contingent on human actions.[34] Thomas affirms Lombard's distinction: "Christ's Passion sufficed for all; while as to its efficacy it was profitable for many."[35] Like Lombard, he restricts the efficacy of Christ's satisfaction to the elect, but the cause of this restriction is some unspecified "impediment."[36] Is this impediment the unwillingness of some people to accept the redemption purchased for them by Christ on the cross? This seems unlikely, given Thomas's emphasis on the God's love as the sole cause of election as well as his emphasis on the immutability of God's will, which is not affected or altered by contingent events such as human

---

[30]*Summa Theologiae* 1, Q19, art. 6, ad 1. English text by Fathers of the English Dominican Province, 5 vols. (New York : Benziger Bros., 1947-48).

[31]*Summa Theologiae* 3, Q78, art. 8, ad. 8.

[32]"caput et membra sunt quasi una persona mystica. et ideo satisfactio christi ad omnes fideles pertinet sicut ad sua membra" (*Summa Theologiae* 3, Q48, art. 2, ad. 1).

[33]See *Summa Theologiae* 1, Q19, art. 6, obj. 1, and *In ad Thim. I*, at 1 Tim 4:10.

[34]See Turretin, *Institutes* 3, Q16 (1:226ff.).

[35]"passio christi non solum sufficiens, sed etiam superabundans satisfactio fuit pro peccatis humani generis" (*Summa Theologiae* 3, Q78, art. 8, obj. 8).

[36]"ipse est propitiatio pro peccatis nostris, pro aliquibus efficaciter, sed pro omnibus sufficienter, quia pretium sanguinis eius est sufficiens ad salutem omnium: sed non habet efficaciam nisi in electis propter impedimentum" (*In ad Thim. I*, at 1 Tim 4:10).

choices.[37] Nonetheless, his comments about God's salvific will in the cross remain ambiguous.[38]

There is a trajectory of thought in the Christian tradition running from the patristic era through the Middle Ages that stresses a specific, particular and defined purpose of God in salvation; but it is a minority position and is frequently ambiguous. In the sixteenth century, this Augustinian tradition becomes more clearly defined with respect to identifying the objects of God's saving work in Christ as the elect.

In fact, while the Lutheran confessional tradition would ultimately endorse universal atonement, Luther himself reflects the tradition of Augustinian particularism. Refuting arguments against predestination in his lectures on Romans, Luther rejects the universalistic interpretation of 2 Timothy 2:4:

> For these verses must always be understood as pertaining to the elect only, as the apostle says in 2 Tim. 2:10 "everything for the sake of the elect." For in an absolute sense Christ did not die for all, because He says: "This is My blood which is poured out for you" and "for many"—He does not say: for all—"for the forgiveness of sins."[39]

The Reformation Era

Scholars from within the Reformed tradition who oppose the doctrine of definite atonement frequently attempt to bolster their position by appealing to John Calvin, who, they argue, never taught such a thing.[40] There is a very small grain of truth to that assertion. Calvin never explicitly teaches a doctrine that limits the saving intention of God in the

---

[37]On Aquinas's view of predestination, see Jill Raitt, "St. Thomas Aquinas on Free Will and Predestination," *Duke Divinity School Review* 43 (1978): 188-95; Lee H. Yearly, "St. Thomas Aquinas on Providence and Predestination," *AThR* 49 (1967): 409-23.

[38]Rainbow argues that in fact Thomas teaches universal atonement, *The Will of God and the Cross*, 34-38; but cf. the discussion in Carl Trueman, "Puritan Theology as Historical Event: A Linguistic Approach to the Ecumenical Context," in *Reformation and Scholasticism*, 253-75, esp. 269-71. Trueman points out how Aquinas's discussion of the human will, originally employed to battle semi-Pelagianism, were employed by Arminius and thus rejected by John Owen. See also Trueman's thorough and illuminating discussion of Owen on the extent of the atonement in *The Claims of Truth: John Owen's Trinitarian Theology* (Carlisle: Paternoster, 1998), 199-26.

[39]*Luther's Works*, American edition, ed. H. T. Lehmann et al., vol. 25 (St. Louis: Concordia, 1955-1986), scholia in Romans 8, II.

[40]See, e.g., M. Charles Bell, "Calvin and the Extent of the Atonement," *EQ* 55 (1983): 115-23, and the works cited above, n. 5.

cross to the elect, but he comes quite close. The argument that Calvin really advocated universal atonement is quite dubious. The work of Roger Nicole and others on this subject is compelling,[41] and for the purposes of this section, two frequently cited examples from Calvin's writings will be sufficient to illustrate the point.

First, in his comments on 1 John 2:2, Calvin dismisses the arguments of those who would use this passage to extend salvation to the reprobate. In this context, Calvin refers to the famous distinction of Lombard—sufficient for all, efficient for the elect—and remarks that this is the common solution in the schools. While he accepts this distinction, he does not think that it applies to the present passage; rather, the intention of John was to make this benefit "common to the whole Church." The whole world (*totius mundi*) here "does not include the reprobate, but indicates those who would believe as well as those who were scattered throughout various regions of the world."[42] Calvin concludes that the grace of Christ is the only true salvation of the world; in other words, Christ is the Savior of all in the sense that all who are saved are saved by Christ. It is quite clear from this passage that Calvin restricts the propitiation of Christ to the elect.

The second passage is even more striking, and it is the closest Calvin comes to explicitly stating the idea of a defined, specifically directed intention in Christ's satisfaction. In his treatise against the sacramental theology of Heshusius, who taught that Christ is bodily present in the elements, Calvin declares: "I should like to know how the wicked can eat the flesh of Christ which was not crucified for them? And how can they drink the blood which was not shed to expiate their sins?"[43] It seems quite clear that Calvin sees the work of Christ on the cross and the expiation of sins accomplished on the cross as not only ultimately

---

[41]In addition to Rainbow, see Roger Nicole, "John Calvin's View of the Extent of the Atonement," *WTJ* 47 (1985): 197-25; Frederick S. Leahy, "Calvin and the Extent of the Atonement," *Reformed Theological Journal* 8 (1992): 54-64; John Murray, "Calvin on the Extent of the Atonement," *Banner of Truth* 234 (1983): 20-22.

[42]"Ergo sub omnibus, reprobos non comprehendit: sed eos designat, qui simul credituri erant, et qui per varias mundi plagas dispersi erant" (*CO* 55:310).

[43]"Et quando tam mordicus verbis adhaeret, scire velim quomodo Christi carnem edant impii, pro quibis non est crucifixa, et quomodo sanguinem bibant, qui expiandis eorum peccatis non est effusus." CO 9:484; ET in *Tracts and Treatises*, trans. Henry Beveridge (Edinburgh, 1849), 2:527.

efficient for the elect but also solely intended for the elect.[44]

It should be clear that from the evidence cited above and from Calvin's strong Augustinian emphases in matters of grace and predestination that it is extremely doubtful that he would have advocated the doctrine of universal atonement. But since the issue had not yet become a matter of debate, he does not explicitly address the matter in the way the Reformed pastors and theologians were forced to do in response to Arminius and the Remonstrants. Moreover, the Reformed tradition is not defined by what John Calvin did or did not teach. It is a common but fallacious assumption that Calvin's thought should be the sole criterion of what is genuinely Reformed. In fact, the Reformed theological tradition is not the brainchild of one individual. Many thinkers, representing diverse backgrounds and theological training, contributed to this tradition. Most notable among these was Martin Bucer, who, it is agreed, taught a very clear doctrine of definite atonement.[45]

Some of Calvin's contemporaries are not as clear on the issue. The writings of Wolfgang Musculus, the Benedictine-trained reformer of Augsburg, could be interpreted to support either side in the debate. In his *Loci Communes*, Musculus takes pains to emphasize that Christ is the Savior of the world and that his redemption is universal in scope. But immediately he is faced with the problem of particularity. How can Christ be the Savior of the whole human race when "we know that not all are made participants in this redemption"?[46] Musculus proceeds to define this universality in terms that would later be used by proponents of definite atonement. First, Christ's redemption is universal in that it is not limited to one nation, as was Israel's election. Second, it is universal in the sense that it is the sole mode of salvation, so that all who are saved are so by Christ (an argument that goes back to Augustine). This is connected with the idea that Christ's redemption is the sole remedy to the common lot of fallen humanity, and thus his re-

---

[44]Bell's argument that neither of these passages is relevant to the debate is extremely strained. Bell argues that in 1 John 2:2 Calvin is only talking about limitation of the gift of faith, not the extent of the atonement (119) and that Calvin's language in the treatise against Heshusius is an unfortunate use of hyperbole (120). Bell is committed to the belief that the Scriptures "clearly teach universal atonement" (121) and thus Calvin must have as well.

[45]See Rainbow's discussion in *The Will of God in the Cross*, 49-63.

[46]"Scimus non omnes redemptionis huius fieri participles" (*Loci Communes Sacrae Theologiae* [Basel: Ioannes Hervagius, 1564], 151). See also the English text: *Commonplaces of the Christian Religion*, trans. John Man (London: Henry Bynneman, 1578), 305.

demption is universal in that sense as well. But while Musculus constantly stresses this *universalis redemptio,* its universality really pertains to all of the elect: "For God forbid that our Redeemer should deliver us in such a way as to give back to Satan any of those whom he had bound to himself, who gave himself to death for all, in order to redeem all."[47]

The *redemptio* effected by Christ is also a permanent, irrevocable binding of the redeemed to himself, something that cannot be said of the reprobate. Any remaining ambiguity is cleared up when Musculus comes to the locus of predestination and interprets 1 Timothy 2:4 to mean that God desires, not the salvation of every individual, but all types and classes of persons.[48] It is a manifestly wicked (*plane impius*) idea that God desires the salvation of all and yet his will can be frustrated by the free choice of human beings.

One of Calvin's students and a Heidelberg theologian, Caspar Olevianus, clearly taught that Christ was sent into the world for the sake of the elect, that the price of atonement was paid for the sins of believers throughout the whole world, and that the Christ came to atone for the sins of believers of all ages.[49] It is also very likely that Zacharius Ursinus, another Heidelberg theologian, also viewed Christ's sacrifice as directed toward the elect, despite the fact that he was a student of the synergist Melanchthon.[50]

Two Protestant theologians from Italy also merit our attention. The first is Peter Martyr Vermigli, who, like Martin Luther, was an Augustinian monk turned Reformer. Vermigli, however, found his place among Martin Bucer and others who would come to be known under the rubric of "Reformed," as opposed to Lutheran, Protestants. Vermigli has a very clear statement in his *Loci Communes* in which he says, "God decreed to give his own Son up to death, and indeed a shameful death, in order to rid his elect of sin."[51]

---

[47]"Absit enim ut redemptor noster sic nos liberarit, ut quos ipsi sibi habet obstrictos, Satanae vicissim restituat, qui ut omnes redimat, pro omnes sese neci dedit." *Loci Communes,* 153.

[48]*Loci Communes,* 253; Musculus refers to Augustine's argument in the *Enchiridion,* cap. 102, but he certainly means cap. 103, where Augustine deals with the interpretation of 1 Timothy 2:4.

[49]Roger Nicole, "The Doctrine of Definite Atonement in the Heidelberg Catechism," *Gordon Review* 3 (1964): 138-45.

[50]See ibid., 143-44.

[51]". . . decreverit Filium suum dare in mortem, et quidem ignominiosam, ut a suis electis peccatum depelleret." Peter Martyr Vermigli, *Loci Communes* (London: Thomas Vautrollerius, 1583), 607.

Jerome Zanchi was another Augustinian monk who, under the tutelage of Vermigli, threw his lot in with the Reformers. Like Vermigli, Zanchi was well trained in the theological tradition, and, like the Reformers before him, he identified the Augustinian trajectory of thought in that tradition as the most authentic expression of the doctrine of divine grace. Zanchi was one of those biblical commentators who discussed the theological topics that arose out of the biblical text immediately after his exposition of the text; and in his commentary on Ephesians, he considers the subject of the sacrifice of Christ after his exposition of Ephesians 5. Among the several questions that he poses with respect to this sacrifice is: For whom did Christ offer himself? For Zanchi the answer is clear: "For us, the elect, who are nonetheless sinners." He then adds that the sacrifice is efficacious for the salvation of the elect, although it would be completely sufficient for the redemption of the whole world.[52] Here we have a clear statement of definite atonement that interprets and clarifies Lombard's sufficient/efficient distinction so that the intended recipients of the benefits of Christ's sacrifice are clearly indicated.

It is well known that Theodore Beza argued for the doctrine of definite atonement.[53] His reflections on the issue were deepened and clarified in contrast to the views of the Lutheran Jacob Andreae. Beza rightly saw that the traditional distinction from Lombard's *Sentences* was inherently vague, although it is probably too much to say that he rejected this formula.[54] Beza developed the doctrine of definite atonement in detail in several publications. One of Beza's students, a certain James Arminius, would later come to reject not only limited atonement but the whole Augustinian conception of grace and predestination.

The Extent of the Atonement and the Synod of Dort

It is sometimes argued that James Arminius represented a slightly dif-

---

[52]"Pro quibus obtulerit: Pro nobis, electis, scilicit, sed peccatoribus. Efficaciter enim pro Electorum tantum salute oblatum esse hoc sacrificium: quanquam ad totius mundi redemptionem sufficientissimum sit" (*Commentarius in Epistolam Sancti Pauli ad Ephesios*, ed. A. H. De Hartog [Amsterdam: J. A. Wormser, 1888], 2:266).

[53]See, e.g. Godfrey, *Tensions*, 80-89.

[54]Cf. Godfrey, *Tensions*, 86ff. Godfrey makes much of the use or nonuse of Lombard's distinction; but it seems to have little consequence in the ensuing debate over the extent of the atonement. Nor is it correct to say that those who use this distinction are somehow more "moderate," 88.

ferent take on the Reformed faith rather than a serious deviation from the Reformed theological tradition.[55] He has also been represented as less scholastic and speculative and more biblical in his thinking than the pastors and theologians who would later oppose his views at the Synod of Dort. Both of these contentions are extremely difficult to substantiate and maintain. The great majority of Arminius's colleagues in the ministry and at the universities judged his views to be a substantial deviation from the Reformed conception of grace and predestination. This was no minor variation within Reformed thought, but an alternative to it.

Moreover, the method Arminius employed in working out his theological views was just as scholastic as that of his theological opponents and, as some of his contemporaries concluded, quite speculative. This is particularly evident in his complex multiplication and ordering of the divine decrees. Arminius divided predestination into four distinct decrees: a decree to appoint Christ as Savior and mediator; a second decree to save believers and reject unbelievers; a third decree to provide sufficient means for faith and repentance; and the fourth decree to save or reject particular individuals based on God's foreknowledge of who would, and who would not, believe and persevere in faith.[56]

This speculative multiplication of decrees was one of the major criticisms of Arminius's theology by the French Reformed pastor Pierre DuMoulin, who, had he not been prevented by King Louis XIII, would have been one of the French delegates to the Synod of Dort.[57] Arminius's ideas were not entirely new; they had precursors in the medieval theological tradition as well as in sixteenth-century Jesuit thought.[58]

---

[55]E.g., Carl Bangs, *Arminius: A Study in the Dutch Reformation*, 2nd ed. (Grand Rapids: Zondervan, 1985); and see the survey of Arminius scholarship in Richard A. Muller, *God, Creation, and Providence in the Thought of Jacob Arminius: Sources and Directions of Scholastic Protestantism in the Era of Early Orthodoxy* (Grand Rapids: Baker, 1991), 3-14.

[56]*Certain Articles* (*Articuli nonnulli*) 15.1-4, in *The Works of Jacob Arminius*, trans. James Nichols and William Nichols (Grand Rapids: Baker, 1991; orig. 1825-75), 2:718-19; cf. Muller, *God, Creation, and Providence*, 162-63.

[57]DuMoulin published his *Anatomia Arminianismi* in 1619; it appeared in English the next year as *The Anatomie of Arminianisme* (London, 1620). In chapter 12 he critiques Arminius's division of the decree of predestination into four distinct decrees, see esp. pp. 85-91. In chapters 28-30 DuMoulin deals with the extent of the atonement. On DuMoulin, see Godfrey, *Tensions*, 237-52.

[58]See Eef Dekker, *Rijker dan Midas: Vrijheid, genade en predestinatie in de theologie van Jacobus Arminius (1559-1609)* (Zoetermeer: Boekencentrum, 1993); and Muller, *God, Creation, and Providence*.

His contemporaries knew exactly where he was coming from, and they did not want the Reformed churches to take that theological path.

For Arminius the work of Christ on the cross does not effect salvation (understood as propitiation, satisfaction or redemption) for any person or group; instead, it only makes salvation *possible*. The cross brings about a new legal situation in which God consequently has the right to enter into a new relationship to humanity, under new conditions that God is free to prescribe. The condition that he prescribes is faith; and it is up to the individual sinner to use the universal grace provided by God to take that step of faith. The determinative factor in salvation is the free choice of humanity, albeit assisted by cooperating grace. Predestination is simply God's determination, based on his foreknowledge that persons will make the decision of faith, to predestine believers as a class to eternal life. Faith is not the fruit of election, but its cause.

Arminius himself did not live to see the theological battle at Dordrecht that grew out of his alternative to Reformed soteriology. His followers, known as the Remonstrants because of their protest against certain doctrines in the Dutch Reformed Church, espoused a latitudinarian view of doctrine that would accommodate significant theological diversity. But to the majority of ministers in the church, this perspective compromised an essential component of what it was to be Reformed, namely, the Augustinian perspective on grace and predestination.[59]

The issue of the extent of the atonement was certainly the most difficult and contentious matter the Synod faced. Formulating the final statement on this issue took a great deal of debate and compromise. But it is also important to note that the vast majority of delegates were agreed that the position of the Remonstrants was completely unacceptable. There may not have been immediate consensus about how exactly the doctrine ought to be stated, but the consensus was that the Remonstrant position was not an option. That view, as stated in the Remonstrant articles, was that "Jesus Christ, the Savior of the world, died for all men and for every man, so that he has obtained for them all, by his death on the cross, redemption and the forgiveness of sins; yet that no one actually enjoys this forgiveness of sins except the be-

---

[59]Note DuMoulin's use of Augustine in *Anatomie,* chaps. 23 and 47.

liever,"[60] and as proof the Remonstrants cited John 3:16 and 1 John 2:2.

After much debate, and considerable compromise, the delegates formulated their response to the Remonstrant position:

> For it was the entirely free plan and very gracious will and intention of
> God the Father that the enlivening and saving effectiveness of his Son's
> costly death should work itself out in all his chosen ones, in order that he
> might grant justifying faith to them only and thereby lead them without
> fail to salvation. In other words, it was God's will that Christ through the
> blood of the cross (by which he confirmed the new covenant) should effec-
> tively redeem from every people, tribe, nation, and language all those and
> only those who were chosen from eternity to salvation and given to him
> by the Father; that he should grant them faith (which, like the Holy Spirit's
> other saving gifts, he acquired for them by his death); that he should
> cleanse them by his blood from all their sins, both original and actual,
> whether committed before or after their coming to faith; that he should
> faithfully preserve them to the very end; and that he should finally present
> them to himself, a glorious people, without spot or wrinkle.[61]

With this statement, the delegates of the Synod of Dort clarified what had been implicit in the Augustinian understanding of salvation. Moreover, they rejected the idea that the death of Christ merely makes salvation possible or merely lays the groundwork for God to enter into a new covenant with humanity. Instead, the death of Christ actually effects salvation for the elect and establishes a new covenant with his people.

The synod decisively rejected the charge that this definite and specific view of Christ's atonement had negative implications for the preaching of the gospel or for the individual's assurance of faith. The church is called to preach the gospel indiscriminately to all persons (3/4.8). Moreover, it should not be presumed that the number of the elect is small or that the majority of persons in the world are reprobate, as the *Second Helvetic Confession* had already warned a half-century earlier.[62]

With regard to assurance of salvation, such assurance is not depen-

---

[60]The five Remonstrant articles, in Latin, Dutch, and English, can be found in P. Schaff, *Creeds of Christendom* (Grand Rapids: Baker, 1993; orig. 1931), 3:546.

[61]Canons of Dort, II.8. For the Latin text, see Schaff, *Creeds of Christendom*, 3:562; the English text is from *Ecumenical Creeds and Reformed Confessions* (Grand Rapids: CRC Publications, 1988), 130-31.

[62]See the Second Helvetic Confession, cap. 10: "We must hope well of all, and not rashly judge any man to be a reprobate" (Schaff, *Creeds of Christendom*, 3:848); cf. Canons of Dort, Conclusion, Rejection of False Accusations, in *Ecumenical Creeds and Reformed Confessions*, 144.

dent upon the question of whether Christ died for every individual. The theory of universal atonement simply postpones the question of assurance, contrary to the assumption of McLeod Campbell. Assuming that Christ died for every individual, how do I know that I have adequately appropriated that universally available salvation? For those who claim that Christ died for all but only intercedes for the elect, the question simply becomes: How do I know that Christ intercedes for me?[63] The pastors at Dort would respond that the very concern over one's salvation is a sign of the Holy Spirit's activity in one's life. Only the elect tend to ask such questions. The Canons of Dort include a number of encouraging statements about the assurance that believers can and should enjoy.[64]

In formulating their statement on the extent of the atonement, the various delegations did not simply make rational deductions from the doctrine of election, nor did they simply speculate about the implications of the divine decree, regardless of their specific conclusions on the matter of the extent of the atonement. An examination of the *judicia* (advisory reports) of the various delegations to the Synod reveals that, while the various delegations differed significantly in method and style, they have in common a biblical, exegetical foundation for their arguments.[65] The Genevan delegation, for example, amasses a great deal of exegetical evidence to support the doctrine of definite atonement.[66] While delegates drew upon many passages from the Pauline epistles and OT texts such as Isaiah 53:10, the Gospel of John provided many of the most effective passages for bolstering the perspective that would ultimately prevail at the Synod. Such Johannine themes include the idea that those who come to Christ are all those who are given to Christ by the Father; the assertion that Jesus the Good Shepherd definitely knows his sheep, rather than simply laying down the conditions for becoming one of his sheep; and the fact that Jesus explicitly prays for those whom the Father has given him, and not for "the world."[67]

Nor did the accumulation of numerous biblical passages imply a crude and simplistic method of "proof-texting." These *dicta probantia*

---

[63]See Helm, *Calvin and the Calvinists*, 48ff.
[64]See Canons 5.8-13.
[65]This point is overlooked in Strehle, "The Extent of the Atonement and the Synod of Dort."
[66]*Acta Synodi Nationali . . . Dordrechti habitae* (Dordrecht, 1620), 2:130-33.
[67]John 6:37; 10:14-15; 17:6, 9.

assumed, and referred back to, an established exegetical tradition that lies behind them; and many of the delegates were accomplished and sophisticated biblical interpreters.[68] Even when biblical references are not present in the *judicia*, as is the case with the Swiss delegation, their arguments presuppose a common exegetical background and allude to specific biblical texts.[69] Thus, while one may challenge the results and conclusions of their exegetical work, there is little evidence to support the accusation that the doctrine of definite atonement was the product of mere rational deduction rather than the result of careful, sound exegesis.

The principle of rational coherence, on the other hand, did play a role in the formulation of this doctrine, just as it did in the formulation of the Remonstrant theses. Common among Remonstrants and Calvinists alike was the assumption that there exists in the Scriptures a unified, rationally coherent message that can be put into rational, coherent form. The task of theology, according to this view, is to put the various teachings of Scripture into a coherent form and to make sense out of them. Thus to claim, for example, that God the Father intends the salvation of the elect, while the Son intends the salvation of every individual, would be considered absurd, since there cannot be two contradictory wills in the godhead. This is not rationalistic theology, but rather the avoidance of irrational theology.

Conclusion

The specific and definite divine intention in the death of Christ was latent in the more strictly Augustinian trajectory of theological thought on the atonement, and it came to explicit expression as a result of the controversies of the late sixteenth and early seventeenth centuries, just as trinitarian and christological formulations were sharpened through controversies in the early centuries of the church. The formulation of this doctrine was not the result of rationalism or immoderate speculation, nor did it disregard biblical exegesis or the pastoral considerations of the believer's assurance of salvation or the indiscriminate preaching of the gospel. Rather, the leading Reformed thinkers

---

[68]See Muller, *PRRD* 2:525-40. Muller notes that the bulk of Gomarus's work was exegetical (526).
[69]See *Acta Synodi Nationalis*, 2:121-23.

from the period of early Protestant orthodoxy formulated and defended this doctrine as a legitimate development of the Christian intellectual tradition, with ample scriptural warrant, just as their theological heirs do today.[70]

---

[70]Most notably in the previously cited works of Roger Nicole and Paul Helm; cf. also J. I. Packer, "The Love of God: Universal and Particular," in *The Grace of God and the Bondage of the Will*, ed. Thomas R. Schreiner and Bruce A. Ware (Grand Rapids: Baker, 1995), 2:413-27.

the atonement in herman bavinck's theology

Joel R. Beeke

Roger Nicole, a leading theologian on the doctrine of the atonement, has deep respect for Abraham Kuyper (1837-1920), Herman Bavinck (1854-1921), and the Dutch neo-Calvinist revival of the late nineteenth century. Nicole shows particular interest in the writings of Bavinck, the premier theologian of this movement. Studies in English of Bavinck's theology have been sparse, partly because Bavinck's four-volume magnum opus, *Gereformeerde Dogmatiek*,[1] is only now being translated, and partly because Bavinck has often been perceived more as Kuyper's follower than as a groundbreaking theologian.

---

[1] *Gereformeerde Dogmatiek,* 4th ed. (Kampen: Kok, 1928-1930). Two paperback volumes, translated by John Vriend and edited by John Bolt, have recently been published by Baker under the auspices of the Dutch Reformed Translation Society: *The Last Things: Hope for This World and the Next* (1996) and *In the Beginning: Foundations of Creation Theology* (1999). The society hopes to publish volume 1 of *Gereformeerde Dogmatiek* in hardback in late 2003 and complete the entire project in 2006, D.V. This will include a fresh translation of the theology proper, first translated by William Hendriksen and published by Eerdmans in 1951 as *The Doctrine of God* (reprint, Grand Rapids: Baker, 1977).

Bavinck's one-volume survey of Christian doctrine, *Magnalia Dei* (Kampen: J. H. Kok, 1909), was translated by Henry Zylstra and published in 1956 by Eerdmans as *Our Reasonable Faith* (reprint, Grand Rapids: Baker, 1977). Other books by Bavinck translated into English include *Biblical and Religious Psychology,* trans. Herman Hanko (Grandville, Mich.: Protestant Reformed Theological School, 1974); *The Certainty of Faith,* trans. Harry der Nederlanden (St. Catharines, Ontario: Paideia, 1980); *Mental, Religious and Social Forces in the Netherlands,* vol. 18 of *A General View of the Netherlands* (The Hague: P.P.I.E., 1915); *The Philosophy of Revelation* (Grand Rapids: Eerdmans, 1953; reprint, Grand Rapids: Baker, 1977); and *Sacrifice of Praise,* trans. John Dolfin, 2nd ed. (Grand Rapids: Kregel, 1922).

James Hutton MacKay refers to Bavinck as "Dr. Kuyper's loyal and learned henchman."[2] Likewise, Bastian Kruithof writes, "In their maturity, the fundamental convictions of the two men were the same."[3] And R. H. Bremmer, whose two volumes on Bavinck as theologian and Bavinck's relation to his contemporaries provide a wealth of information on Bavinck's life and thought, concludes that Bavinck and Kuyper can be spoken of in the same breath. Bremmer does acknowledge a threefold development in their relationship, however. He says that initially Bavinck worked independently of Kuyper, then worked so closely with him that they became devoted friends. After 1905 that friendship cooled as Bavinck became increasingly critical of Kuyper and his school.[4]

Eugene P. Heideman was the first to sharply criticize the subordination of Bavinck to Kuyper and the virtual merging of their thought. Heideman viewed the doctrine of common grace as the key to understanding differences between Kuyper and Bavinck.[5] John Bolt concurs with Heideman. In further development of Heideman's ideas, Bolt shows how Bavinck relied more on the notion of imitating Christ in his cultural-ethical ideal than Kuyper did.[6]

For forty years after Bavinck's death, scholars centered on his pedagogy and educational philosophy rather than on his theology.[7] The first

---

[2]J. H. MacKay, *Religious Thought in Holland During the Nineteenth Century* (London: Hodder & Stoughton, 1981), x-xi.

[3]B. Kruithof, "The Relation of Christianity and Culture in the Teaching of Herman Bavinck" (Ph.D. diss., University of Edinburgh, 1955), 12.

[4]R. H. Bremmer, *Herman Bavinck als Dogmaticus* (Kampen: Kok, 1961), 13-64; and *Herman Bavinck en Zijn Tijdgenoten* (Kampen: Kok, 1966), which include considerable correspondence between Bavinck and Kuyper. Bremmer, however, still reads Bavinck too much through Kuyperian glasses, particularly in the area of regeneration, as Anthony Hoekema has pointed out in *Reformed Journal* 12 (February 1962): 20.

[5]E. P. Heideman, *The Relation of Revelation and Reason in E. Brunner and H. Bavinck* (Assen: Van Gorcum, 1959), 6, 178, 196-97.

[6]Bolt defines the term *cultural-ethical ideal* as a "comprehensive social, political, ethical, cultural vision, rooted in a philosophical-theological system of thought" in "The Imitation of Christ Theme in the Cultural-Ethical Ideal of Herman Bavinck" (Ph.D. diss., St. Michael's College, Toronto School of Theology, 1982), 1.

[7]Five major works on Bavinck's educational philosophy and pedagogy were published within sixteen years of his death: Fr. S. Rombouts, *Prof. Dr. H. Bavinck, Gids Bij de Studie van Zijn Paedagogische Werken* ('s-Hertogenbosch, Antwerpen: Malmberg, 1922); J. Brederveld, *Hoofdlijnen der Paedagogiek van Dr. Herman Bavinck, met Critische Beschouwing* (Amsterdam: De Standaard, 1927); L. van der Zweep, *De Paedagogiek van Bavinck* (Kampen: Kok, 1935); Cornelius Jaarsma, *The Educational Philosophy of Herman Bavinck* (Grand Rapids: Eerdmans, 1936); and L. van Klinken, *Bavincks Paedagogische Beginselen* (Meppel: Boom, 1937).

major study of Bavinck's theology was Anthony A. Hoekema's dissertation, "Herman Bavinck's Doctrine of the Covenant" (1953).[8] That same year S. P. van der Walt completed a study of Bavinck's philosophy.[9] In 1961 Bremmer published his 450-page doctoral dissertation, *Herman Bavinck als Dogmaticus*. Anthony Hoekema describes that work as "the first full-dress evaluation of Bavinck's theology."[10] That was followed in 1968 by Jan Veenhof's massive dissertation on Bavinck's views concerning revelation and inspiration.[11]

Bavinck was a profound Christian and a superb Reformed theologian. His life and theology deserve to be better known than they are. It is hoped that the publication of his dogmatics in English will generate a number of studies and that Bavinck scholarship will markedly improve. The following chapter will describe a bit of Bavinck's life and influence, then focus on his theology of the atonement.

Early Life and Education

Herman Bavinck was born December 13, 1854, at Hoogeveen in the Netherlands, in the province of Drenthe, where his father, Jan Bavinck, was a pastor and leader in the *Christelijke Gereformeerde Kerk* (Dutch Christian Reformed Church).[12] That denomination seceded in 1834

---

[8]Princeton Theological Seminary. Jerome DeJong completed a short Th.M. thesis in 1947 for Union Theological Seminary entitled "The *Ordo Salutis* as Developed by the Dutch Theologian Herman Bavinck."

[9]S. P. van der Walt, *Die Wysbegeerte van Dr. Herman Bavinck* (Potchefstron: Pro-Rege Pers, 1953).

[10]"Herman Bavinck as Dogmatician: A Review," *Reformed Journal* 12 (February 1962): 18.

[11]J. Veenhof, *Revelatie en Inspiratie* (Amsterdam: Buijten en Schipperheijn, 1968).

[12]The best source for Bavinck's life is Valentijn Hepp, *Dr. Herman Bavinck* (Amsterdam: W. Ten Have, 1921). Unfortunately, Hepp's projected second volume on the significance of Bavinck's thought in various fields was never completed. A definitive biography on Bavinck has yet to be written. In addition to Bolt, Hoekema, Jaarsma and the two volumes of Bremmer already noted, biographical sources include J. H. Landwehr, *In Memoriam: Prof. Dr. H. Bavinck* (Kampen: Kok, 1921); Henry Elias Dosker, "Herman Bavinck," *Princeton Theological Review* 20 (1922): 448-64; G. E. Meuleman, "Bavinck, Herman," in *Christelijke Encyclopaedie*, ed. J. C. Rullmann (Kampen: Kok, 1925); A. B. W. M. Kok, *Dr. Herman Bavinck* (Amsterdam: S.J.P. Bakker, 1945); Henry Zylstra, preface to Bavinck's *Our Reasonable Faith*, 5-11; J. Geelhoed, *Dr. Herman Bavinck* (Goes: Oosterbaan & Le Cointre, 1958); R. H. Bremmer, "Bavinck, Herman," in *Encyclopedia of Christianity*, ed. Edwin H. Palmer (Wilmington, Del.: National Foundation for Christian Education, 1964), 1:597-99; Jarry Fernhout, "Man, Faith, and Religion in Bavinck, Kuyper, and Dooyeweerd" (M. Phil. diss., Institute for Christian Studies, Toronto, 1974); R. H. Bremmer, "Bavinck, Herman," in *Biografisch Lexicon voor de Geschiedenis van het Nederlandse Protestantisme*, ed. D. Nauta (Kampen: Kok, 1978), 1:42-45.

from the *Hervormde Kerk,* the state church of the Netherlands, because of theological liberalism. The protest movement, led by Hendrik de Cock and Hendrik Scholte, became known as the *Afscheiding* (Secession) of 1834.[13] Herman's father was of a modest disposition; his mother was more outspoken. Both were godly people who cherished the strong pietistic emphases of the secession church that were rooted in the *Nadere Reformatie* (Dutch Second Reformation), an influential seventeenth- and eighteenth-century movement of experiential Reformed theology, and in an early-nineteenth-century international, evangelical revival movement known as the *Réveil.*[14]

When Herman Bavinck was a year old, his father accepted a call to Bunschoten. From there the Bavincks went to Almskerk, in the province of Noord-Brabant. From age seven to sixteen Bavinck studied at the Hasselman Institute, a private school of excellent reputation at Almskerk. He then left home to enroll at the gymnasium in Zwolle, where he completed a four-year degree in three years.

After that he went to Kampen to study for one year at the Theological School of the *Christelijke Gereformeerde Kerk.* To thoroughly understand the theological-scientific method of study, Bavinck then went to the University of Leiden. There he studied under professors Johannes Henricus Scholten (1811-1885), Abraham Kuenen (1828-1891) and Jan Pieter Nicolaas Land (1834-1897), all leading exponents of modernism in nineteenth-century Netherlands. Bavinck later wrote that God's grace preserved him in the faith despite these liberal teachers. Nevertheless, he suffered spiritual impoverishment at Leiden. "I have learned much, but also unlearned much," he said of his Leiden years.[15]

At Leiden, Bavinck majored in Semitic languages and systematic theology. Though his theology differed radically from his professors, he admired their scholarly aptitude and learned to adapt their theo-

---

[13]For historical details on the background of the Secession of 1834, see Bolt, "The Imitation of Christ Theme," 39-57, and *The Reformation of 1834* (Orange City, Iowa: Pluim Publications, 1984). For a sociological analysis of the Secession of 1834, see L. H. Mulder, *Revolte der Fijnen* (Meppel: Boom, 1973).

[14]For further details on Bavinck's parents, see Dosker, "Herman Bavinck," 450. For the Dutch Second Reformation, see Joel R. Beeke, *The Quest for Full Assurance: The Legacy of Calvin and His Successors* (Edinburgh: Banner of Truth Trust, 1999), 286-309. For the *Réveil,* see M. Elizabeth Kluit, *Het Protestantse Réveil in Nederland en Daarbuiten, 1815-1865* (Amsterdam: Paris, 1970).

[15]Hepp, *Dr. Herman Bavinck,* 84-87.

logical method to his own beliefs. From Scholten, Bavinck learned to
appreciate the history of Reformed dogmatics; from Kuenen (who
with Wellhausen had reconstructed OT history along Hegelian
lines), to reproduce the thoughts of others with accuracy and com-
pleteness; and from Land, to appreciate philosophy. Bavinck completed his study at Leiden in 1880 with a doctoral thesis on the ethics
of Ulrich Zwingli.[16]

Professor at Kampen

Bavinck's first and only pastoral charge was at Franeker in the province of Friesland. People there deeply appreciated his scholarly
preaching and diligent pastoral work. After eighteen months in the
pastorate, he was appointed by the Synod of Zwolle as professor of
systematic theology and ethics at the Theological School in Kampen,
where he labored with great distinction from 1883 to 1902.

Bavinck's inaugural address, "De Wetenschap der Heilige Godgeleerdheid" (The Science of Sacred Theology), laid the foundation for his
later dogmatics and helped stake his position as a Calvinistic theologian in the landscape of Dutch theology. Bavinck asserted that God in
Christ is the object of theology, the *principium cognoscendi* (principle of
knowledge). Our knowledge of God is ectypical, conformed to God's
archetypal self-knowledge. The Scriptures contain a system of the
knowledge of God. The task of theology is to discover and expound
this system for the building up of the church and for the glory of God.[17]

Bavinck helped to raise the seminary academically from mediocrity
to excellence. His encyclopedic mind compensated for the under-
staffed seminary. In addition to dogmatics, he lectured in ethics, philosophical history, logic, rhetoric and aesthetics. His lectures were instructive, inspiring and erudite. His work at Kampen, which included
the publication of the first edition of his *Dogmatiek* (1895-1901), established his reputation as a first-rate Reformed theologian.

While at Kampen, Bavinck married Johanna Schippers (1891). They

---

[16]For an overview of the major schools of Dutch Reformed theology in the nineteenth century,
see MacKay, *Religious Thought in Holland*. For more detail on the modernist school, see Eldred C. Vanderlaan, *Protestant Modernism in Holland* (New York: Oxford University Press,
1924). For Bavinck's experience at the Leiden school, see Bolt, "The Imitation of Christ
Theme," 57-73.

[17]Bremmer, "Bavinck, Herman," in *Biografisch Lexicon*, 1:42.

had one daughter. He also made the first of two trips to America. He was invited to Toronto in 1892 to address the Alliance of Reformed Churches. He went first to Grand Rapids, Michigan, where he stayed with Geerhardus Vos, then a professor at Calvin Seminary. In Holland, Michigan, Bavinck stayed with Henry Dosker, professor at Hope College who accompanied him on trips to Chicago and to Orange City, Iowa. In Toronto, Bavinck gave a talk titled "The Influence of the Protestant Reformation on the Moral and Religious Conditions of Communities and Peoples." He concluded his trip with visits to Princeton, New Jersey, where he was accompanied by Benjamin B. Warfield, and New York City, where he met Charles Briggs.[18]

Professor at Amsterdam
One year after Abraham Kuyper became prime minister of the Netherlands, Bavinck took Kuyper's place in the chair of systematic theology at the Free University of Amsterdam. He delivered his inaugural address on "Godsdienst en Godgeleerdheid" (Religion and Theology). The Free University was an independent institution founded largely through the influence of Abraham Kuyper to counteract the liberalism of Leiden and similar schools. Although the Free University was much larger than Kampen's Theological School, where Bavinck had towered above the rest of the faculty, his work at Amsterdam was also deeply appreciated. He held this position from 1902 until his death in 1921.

In Amsterdam, Bavinck built on the groundwork laid in Kampen and came to full development of his thought. He completed his second, revised edition of the *Gereformeerde Dogmatiek* in 1911 and then sold most of his books on dogmatics so as to concentrate on his growing interest in philosophy, psychology, pedagogy, politics and ethics.[19] He also became directly involved in Dutch political life when he was appointed to the Second Chamber of the Dutch Parliament.[20]

Through his writings and scholarly addresses, Bavinck's influence spread far beyond the Netherlands. In 1908 the professor was invited to deliver the Stone Lectures at Princeton Seminary, which gave birth to his *Philosophy of Revelation*. He then visited Grand Rapids, Holland and

---

[18]Hepp, *Dr. Herman Bavinck,* 211-22.
[19]Ibid., 317-18. The unaltered third and fourth editions of the *Dogmatiek,* also published by Kok, appeared in 1918 and 1928-30 respectively.
[20]See chapter 11, "In de Politiek," in Bremmer, *Tijdgenoten,* 219ff.

Chicago again. In Washington, D.C., he met with President Theodore Roosevelt. Bavinck went on to New Brunswick, Paterson, Boston and New York before returning to the Netherlands. On this second trip to America, Bavinck preached eighteen times and gave twenty lectures.[21]

Throughout his scholarly career, Bavinck remained close to his separatist origins in piety and lifestyle. In a preface to a Dutch reprint of the sermons of the Scottish preachers, Ebenezer and Ralph Erskine, he wrote that their sermons contained a biblical, "spiritual psychology lacking in our day." He then added perhaps the harshest words he ever wrote: "It seems that we no longer know what sin and grace, guilt and forgiveness, regeneration and conversion are."[22]

After delivering a report at the Synod of Leeuwarden in 1920, Bavinck suffered a heart attack. At first he seemed to rally, but soon he suffered a second attack. He was ill for several months before passing away on July 29, 1921. When he was dying, he was asked if he was afraid. "My dogmatics avails me nothing, nor my knowledge, but I have my faith, and in this I have all," he responded.[23]

Influence and Writings
Bavinck was influential throughout his life, through both the way he lived and the writings he produced. It is possible, however, to look at his influence in four different areas: as a dogmatician, as a practical church theologian, as a biblical philosopher and finally, as a pedagogue.

As an able dogmatician. Bavinck was recognized both inside and outside of Reformed circles as a competent and exhaustive theologian. Comparing him to such contemporaries as Kuyper, Warfield and James Orr, Henry Dosker viewed Bavinck as "the broadest and technically the most perfect" systematician of his day.[24]

Bavinck supplemented his *Gereformeerde Dogmatiek* with a 650-page compendium, *Magnalia Dei* (1909; *Our Reasonable Faith*, 1956), intended for the common people. The subtitle indicates its purpose: "Instruction in the Christian Religion in Accord with the Reformed Confession." This volume covers the same ground as the *Dogmatiek*, but is more pop-

[21]Hepp, *Dr. Herman Bavinck*, 300-310.
[22]*Levensgeschiedenis en Werken van Ralph en Ebenezer Erskine* (Doesburg: J. C. van Schenk Brill, 1906), p. 5.
[23]Dosker, "Herman Bavinck," p. 459.
[24]Ibid., p. 448.

ular and practical, less technical and historical, and contains copious scripture proofs.

At both the academic and popular levels, Bavinck's dogmatics are marked by fidelity to Scripture, clarity of expression, erudition and absolute honesty. His method in dogmatics is, first, to provide a thorough exposition of the relevant scripture passages dealing with the doctrine being considered. Second, he offers a careful historical-theological survey of what other theologians, including ones from non-Reformed traditions, have to say. Though he remained faithful throughout his life to the Reformed point of view, Bavinck was a broadminded scholar who appreciated the good in other points of view. His standard approach was to present his opponent's viewpoint objectively, stressing its strong points before revealing its inadequacies. Finally, he concluded with his own position, which was often a synthesis of other viewpoints arrived at through painstaking scriptural exegesis and reasoning. In this Bavinck differed from Kuyper, who was more antithetical and less careful exegetically in his approach to problems.[25] Bavinck habitually sought to incorporate elements of truth that he found in other theological systems. That is evident in his views on supra- and infra-lapsarianism, creationism and traducianism as well as on questions related to the covenant of grace and the *ordo salutis*.[26]

Bavinck's theology was exhaustive and contemporary. His knowledge of Hebrew, Greek and Latin was a great asset for exegetical and historical theology. That he also read widely in French, German and English sources is evident in his bibliographical and footnote references. He stayed current with the theological literature of his day: every successive volume of his dogmatics includes references to the articles and books published in that particular year. A scrupulous, inductive theologian with an instinctive feel for problems, Bavinck of-

---

[25]Bavinck's first biographer, J. H. Landwehr, contrasted Bavinck and Kuyper as follows: "Bavinck was an Aristotelian, Kuyper a Platonic spirit. Bavinck was the man of the clear concept, Kuyper the man of the fecund idea. Bavinck worked with the historically given; Kuyper proceeded speculatively by way of intuition. Bavinck's was primarily an inductive mind; Kuyper's primarily deductive" (cited by Henry Zylstra in Bavinck, *Our Reasonable Faith*, 5).

[26]E.g., Bavinck's "The Catholicity of Christianity and the Church," *CTJ* 27, 2 (1992): 220-51, translated by John Bolt from *De Katholiciteit van Christendom en Kerk* (Kampen: Zalsman, 1888), shows both his broadmindedness and his theological method. This article is divided into three sections: scriptural teaching on catholicity, the idea of catholicity in the history of the church, and the obligation catholicity places on us today.

fered no answers without thoroughly studying an issue. He considered all angles of a problem and addressed every pro and con before arriving at a definite conviction, which he then powerfully stated and ably defended.

As a practical church theologian. Bavinck's practical influence on the *Gereformeerde Kerken,* established under the leadership of Abraham Kuyper in 1892, was invaluable. Though thousands of people followed Kuyper's leadership through his writings and his weekly paper, *De Heraut,* a substantial number of people in the churches of the 1892 union, led by Kampen professors Lucas Lindeboom (1845-1933) and Maarten Noordtzij (1840-1915), felt that Kuyper's theology was not sufficiently scriptural. They believed it was often too deductive and speculative, particularly his views of baptism as a basis of presumptive regeneration, of justification from eternity and of the scientific character of theology.

In several debates, Bavinck played a mediating role in modifying some of Kuyper's viewpoints. In effect, he became the leader of a third group that stood between dissidents on both fringes. The Conclusions of Utrecht of 1905, which brought into closer proximity the *Afscheiding* and the *Doleantie,* groups that had joined together in 1892, reflected Bavinck's approach.[27] Without Bavinck, there may well have been a split in the young denomination during those critical years.

In later years, due in part to Kuyper's declining health, Bavinck became the man of the hour, particularly for the younger generation of Reformed adherents. He provided leadership in addressing the pressing problems of women suffrage, war and education, all of which became important issues in ecclesiastical, social and political life after World War I. He also gave advice on these issues when they were discussed in the Dutch Parliament.

As a biblical philosopher. In his *Christelijke Wereldbeschouwing* (Christian Worldview), Bavinck wrestles with the problem of the relationship between faith and science, and develops his philosophy of critical realism. In this, Bavinck followed Augustine, who had "Christianized" Plato's doctrine of ideas.[28] Bavinck viewed creation as the

---

[27]Herman Huber Kuyper, an advisor of the Synodical Committee that drafted these Conclusions, said that Bavinck should be recognized as the spiritual father of the Conclusions (E. Smilde, *Een Eeuw van Strijd over Verbond en Doop* [Kampen: Kok, 1946], 251).

[28]Bremmer, *Bavinck als Dogmaticus,* 370.

embodiment of divine ideas and norms that the human spirit accepts as axiomatic. By reason, believers are able to grasp the world of ideas and learn the reality behind the visible world, thus drawing out of the universe the divine ideas built into it. The task of philosophy and science is to arrange these ideas systematically into an ordered whole so as to satisfy both humanity's minds and its hearts. Humanity's reasoning capacity, however, is limited, for it is bound to reality; it cannot, as Kant taught, produce that reality. The heart of an individual can find rest only in God's revelation through the cross. Without divine revelation, science and philosophy cannot fulfill their own vocation.

Bavinck's philosophy was strongly apologetic. He zealously combated modern, post-Kantian autonomous thought in his *Wijsbegeerte der Openbaring* (*Philosophy of Revelation*, 1909), where he asserts that the Christian faith ought to oppose the rejection of supernaturalism in modern culture rather than oppose the culture itself. Later Dutch philosophers, such as Dooyeweerd and Vollenhoven, built upon Bavinck's philosophical insights.

As a pedagogue. During Bavinck's time, Christian grade schools were given equal status with the public schools. This created a great need for leadership among the teachers. Bavinck filled this need in several ways. In 1906 he founded the Gereformeerde Schoolverband (Association of Reformed Schools), which he chaired for many years. His *Paedagogische Beginselen* (1904; *Pedagogical Principles*) propagated pedagogy as a normative science and dealt with education's objectives and methods as well as the nature of the student. It greatly influenced Dutch teachers and the nature of the Christian school movement in the Netherlands. He also published *De Opvoeding der Rijpere Jeugd* (1916; *The Education of the Adolescent*) and *De Nieuwe Opvoeding* (1917; *The New Education*), in which he discussed the problems of secondary education and the new German method of empirical education. These books were used and appreciated even in Roman Catholic circles. He was an outspoken advocate of Christian education and offered recommendations and advice to the government.

Finally, Bavinck's interest in education spilled over into psychology as well. His *Beginselen der Psychologie* (1897; *Principles of Psychology*) and *Bijbelsche en Religieuse Psychologie* (1920; *Biblical and Religious Psychology*) broke new ground in the Netherlands.

Throughout the Netherlands—in schools, churches, auditoriums and the halls of government—Bavinck promoted and defended a Calvinistic worldview that strove to do justice to the spiritual, intellectual and emotional needs of man. Calvinistic thinking in all spheres of life remained for him "Christianity of first choice."[29] That was also true of his doctrine of atonement.

Bavinck on the Atonement

Characteristic of Bavinck was his desire to engage fully with the thought of his times while remaining true to Scripture and the Reformed faith. Both his intellectual engagement and his biblical and confessional faithfulness shine in his treatment of the doctrine of the atonement in *Gereformeerde Dogmatiek*, Section 7, Part 46, titled "The Work of Christ in His Humiliation."[30]

Bavinck opens the discussion by making this observation on human experience: "Among all the people of the world we encounter a sense of sin and misery and all feel a need and a hope for redemption."[31] Two lines of thought are clearly at work here. First, Bavinck appeals to the growing awareness of the world at large on the part of his fellow scholars in nineteenth-century Europe and North America. The general study of humankind in all its richness of human history, culture and experience had passed through its infancy in the eighteenth century and had arrived at a stage of robust adolescence by Bavinck's time. Accordingly, Bavinck begins with anthropology and psychology, asking: What are the felt needs and cherished hopes of men and women around the world?

Second, Bavinck's choice of a twofold starting point, "the sense of sin and misery" and "a need and a hope for redemption," is authentically Reformed. It is the very same starting point taken by the Heidelberg Catechism in its exposition of the Christian faith, when it asks: "How many things are necessary for thee to know, that thou, enjoying this comfort, mayest live and die happily? Answer: Three; the first, how great my sins and miseries are; the second, how I may be delivered from all my sins and miseries."[32] In a simple and direct way

---

[29]G. E. Meuleman, "Bavinck, Herman," in *Christelijke Encyclopaedie*, 1:488.

[30]3:349ff. Quotations to follow are cited according to pagination in the Dutch *Dogmatiek* (e.g., 3:350) but are taken from the unpaginated English translation (in preparation) with permission of the translator, John Vriend.

[31]Ibid., 3:350.

[32]*Doctrinal Standards, Liturgy, and Church Order*, ed. Joel R. Beeke (Grand Rapids: Reformation Heritage Books, 1999), Q. 2, p. 27.

Bavinck shows how the fundamentals of the Christian faith, identified from Scripture in the Reformed confessions, answer the burdens, needs and hopes of the human race. Polemically and apologetically, Bavinck displays the skill of an accomplished surgeon.

Throughout his introduction Bavinck turns the tables on many scholars of his day. Comparative studies of human religions commonly were contrived to show that historic Christianity was just one primitive religion among others. Crassly racist notions of the superiority of European civilization and its progress were common themes. Bavinck's approach is quite different. He works with an attractive kind of Christian humanism, taking interest in all that is truly and universally human with no smug assertion of the superiority of his own particular kind of humanity. His biblical and confessional training opens his eyes to these human universals.

An advanced material civilization simply does not deliver all it promises, Bavinck says. "However much people may have achieved culturally, they were never satisfied with it and did not attain the redemption for which they are thirsting," he writes. This thirst is "for a redemption which saves them physically as well as spiritually, for time but also for eternity. . . . The redemption which humans seek and need is one in which they are lifted up above the whole world into communion with God."[33] This distinctly Reformed analysis asserts that humans are creatures made in God's image and are therefore capable of having communion with God. At the same time we are estranged from God because of our sin against God. However great this estrangement, the human heart still longs for redemption and reconciliation.

In various methods of understanding the approach to God among the world's peoples, Bavinck notes the common theme of sacrifice. Reviewing the chaotic state of scholarly opinion regarding this subject, Bavinck comments, "However this may be, remarkable in any case is the universal, profound, and powerful urge which at all times and places drives people to offer sacrifices." He adds, "That urge arises from the ineradicable sense that humans are related in some fashion to an invisible divine power, whether reconciled or unreconciled, and that by their sacrifice they can exert some influence on the deity. Sacrifice is so central and prominent in worship that Vedic reli-

---

[33]Ibid., 3:351-52.

gion can speak of it as the navel of the world."[34]

What Bavinck explains here was stated earlier in a terse summary by Charles Hodge. In his *Systematic Theology*, Hodge argues for the connection between sacrifice and expiation. Appealing to "the general sentiment of the ancient world," Hodge writes:

> Even those who repudiate the doctrine of expiation as belonging to the religion of the Bible admit that it was the doctrine of the ancient world. But if it was the doctrine of the ancient world, two things naturally follow: first, that it has a foundation in the nature of man and in the intuitive knowledge of the relation which he as a sinner bears to God; and, second, that when we find exactly the same rites and ceremonies, the same forms of expression, and the same significant actions in the Scriptures, they cannot fairly be understood in a sense diametrically opposite to that in which all the rest of the world understood them.[35]

Hodge's words are a natural lead to Bavinck's remarks on sacrifice. Turning to Scripture, Bavinck offers a compelling argument for the antiquity of sacrifice as something that "originally belonged to the religion of humankind—religion which cannot in essence be different before and after the fall." In other words, Adam offered sacrifices to God in the state of original righteousness. This explains "why soon after the fall there is mention of Cain's and Abel's sacrifice without any reference to God expressly instituting sacrificial worship."[36]

With the fall of humanity, expiation must be added to the concept of sacrifice. As Bavinck says, "Not reverence and gratitude alone but especially fear and dread impel [fallen human beings] to bring sacrifices as they also impel them to pray." Indeed, redemption is so wedded to reconciliation that we cannot clearly distinguish between ordinary and expiatory sacrifices. Every sacrifice includes a certain amount of expiatory power. As a sense of guilt and misery increases, the expiatory sacrifice becomes central.[37]

In the final part of his introduction, Bavinck describes a special class of priests. He notes that "it is only as the sense of sin among peoples grows stronger and the consciousness of separation from God deepens

---

[34]Ibid., 3:355.
[35]C. Hodge, *Systematic Theology* (New York: Scribner, Armstrong, 1877), 2:500.
[36]*Dogmatiek*, 3:356.
[37]Ibid.

that everywhere the idea of a mediatorship arises." He concludes, "All human priesthood and sacrifice points—directly in Israel, indirectly also among the peoples—to the one perfect sacrifice which was brought in the fullness of time by Christ, the mediator between God and humankind, on Golgotha."[38]

This is Bavinck's central idea, which he will then substantiate on the basis of Scripture and Christian doctrine and defend against the alternatives offered by recent and current theologians. Christ's work in his humiliation centers in his death on the cross. In this expiatory sacrifice, he is both priest and sacrifice who redeems his people and reconciles them to God. No other religion can compete with the witness of Scripture; no other can match the power of Christ's death to bring peace to the sinner.

After this introduction, Bavinck turns to the "testimonies of the law and the prophets" that culminate in Christ.[39] Here again, Bavinck is strongly influenced by the Reformed confessions. His very words are taken from the Belgic Confession, Article 25, "The Abolishing of the Ceremonial Law," in which the churches confess: "In the meantime we still use the testimonies taken out of the law and the prophets to confirm us in the doctrine of the gospel."[40] A similar statement appears in the Heidelberg Catechism, Questions 18 and 19, significantly, at the conclusion of the section devoted to a review of Anselm's argument from *Cur Deus Homo:*

> *Question 18: Who then is that Mediator, who is in one person both very God, and a real righteous man?*
> Answer: Our Lord Jesus Christ, "who of God is made unto us wisdom, and righteousness, and sanctification, and redemption."
>
> *Question 19: Whence knowest thou this?*
> Answer: From the holy gospel, which God Himself first revealed in Paradise; and afterwards published by the patriarchs and prophets, and represented by the sacrifices and other ceremonies of the law; and lastly, has fulfilled it by His only begotten Son.[41]

The next section, on the witness of Scripture, is the strongest, most

[38]Ibid., 3:357-58.
[39]Ibid., 3:363.
[40]*Doctrinal Standards*, 17.
[41]Ibid., 33.

compelling part of Bavinck's argument. The master exegete reads
Scripture with an eye for detail, giving full justice to contextual and
historical concerns and preparing the reader for what follows. The
reader will find the church fathers alternately satisfying and disappointing as Bavinck measures them against the witness of Scripture.
He will appreciate the remarkable achievement of the Reformers as
they recover the fullness of biblical teaching. He will grow restless as
he reviews the shifting shadows of rationalist theology in the eighteenth and nineteenth centuries and wonder, *Did these men ever read
the Bible?*

Bavinck concludes his detailed summary of OT teaching on sacrifice by saying that as an agency of reconciliation, the system of sacrifices provided in the law was limited. He notes, "It needs to be said,
however, that the sacrifices for atonement do not atone for all but only
for a few specific unintentional sins. . . . Even though the sins of aber-
ration were taken very broadly (Lev 5, 6), the atonement effected by
the sacrifices for atonement remained highly restricted." He adds:
"Countless sins remained, therefore, for which the law did not indicate any atonement by sacrifices: not only a few sins committed 'with
a high hand' (sins of defiance) which were punished with death but
also a wide range of spiritual and carnal sins, sins by thoughts and
words, sins of pride and self-seeking. For all these sins no prescribed
sacrifices existed."[42]

The saints of the Old Testament were also aware of this. As Bavinck
writes, "They knew that sacrifice for atonement opened a way of
atonement in only a very few cases; and for that reason they repeatedly
reached behind those sacrifices and appealed to the mercy of God." He
goes on, "The few sacrifices prescribed in the law did not cover the
whole of life; they did not bring about the true atonement; they served
only to arouse a sense of sin and were types which pointed to another
and better sacrifice."[43]

Bavinck next focuses on the prophets, who spoke of another covenant administered by a mediator who is prophet, priest and king as
well as of another, better sacrifice. He says, "That sacrifice will be
brought by the Servant of the Lord who will take Israel's place, do its

---

[42]*Dogmatiek*, 3:359-60.
[43]Ibid., 3:360.

work, be a covenant to the people and a light to the Gentiles (Is 42:6; 49:6), and make himself an offering for the sins of his people (Is 53:10)."[44]

The section on the New Testament, which expounds Christ as the fulfillment of the law and the content of the gospel, becomes critically important as Bavinck discusses the way theologians in the nineteenth and early twentieth centuries handled the atonement. First, Bavinck seemingly calls Christ and the apostles to the witness stand and asks, How did Christ interpret his life and ministry? How did the apostles understand and explain his death on the cross?

Bavinck then barrages the reader with text upon text and point after point until the reader can only conclude that the New Testament offers a clear, consistent and thorough understanding of Christ's death as "the true covenant sacrifice."[45] This is sound preparation for seeing through the notion perpetrated in the nineteenth century and still maintained by many Protestants today that there are many possible theories of atonement. The New Testament presents but one view, which cannot be called a theory unless one regards NT teaching as mere speculation.

The remainder of this section deals with the doctrine of Christ's work and the historical development of this doctrine in Christian thought. Here Bavinck recognizes the lack of any clear-cut formulation. On the one hand, no great controversy was evident in early church history that might have produced such a formulation. On the other, as Bavinck says, "Scripture is so many-sided in its description of that work that in the history of theology there has emerged an array of views on the word of Christ, all of which contain a core of truth."[46]

Bavinck then offers guidance on the doctrine of atonement through the turbulent waters of medieval church history. He traces the church's understanding of Christ's suffering back to the work of Anselm. "The ideas on Christ's suffering we encounter in the church fathers return in scholasticism. But it is especially Anselm's work *Cur Deus Homo* that gave the 'satisfaction' view predominance over all others," he says.[47] Bavinck notes elements of Anselm's thought that were later rejected but declares: "Anselm was the first to understand, and to understand

---

[44]Ibid., 3:361.
[45]Ibid., 3:365.
[46]Ibid., 3:368.
[47]Ibid., 3:371.

most clearly, that the redemption accomplished by Christ was a deliverance, not primarily from the consequences of sin, from death and Satan's power, but above all from sin itself and sin's guilt. Christ's redemption, according to Anselm, consists mainly in reconciliation between God and humankind." Bavinck adds, "Yet in scholastic and Roman Catholic theology, this truth has much less come into its own than in Protestant theology."[48]

Anselm provided a foundation that the Reformers later built upon. With Anselm's view of Christ's work as a starting point, Reformed theology added this perspective: sin aroused God's wrath, and the only one who could appease that wrath and satisfy God's justice was the "God-man," Jesus Christ, who put himself "in our place as the guarantor of the Covenant, taking upon himself the full guilt and punishment of sin and submitting to the total demand of God's law."[49] Thus, the foundation for salvation is the once-for-all atonement accomplished by Christ and applied by his Spirit. Of course, there were alternate views to this in earlier times as well as during the Reformation. In noting these, Bavinck regards the views of the Socinians as "the most serious and substantial opposition to the doctrine of vicarious satisfaction."[50]

Faustus Socinus (1539-1604) was something of a Renaissance prophet whose rationalism eventually led him to deny almost every cardinal Christian doctrine, including the deity of Christ, predestination, original sin, total depravity, vicarious atonement and justification by faith. Socinianism, which had its roots in older heresies such as Arianism and Pelagianism, struck a responsive chord in a generation influenced by Renaissance humanism's optimistic view of humanity. Like the Remonstrants, Socinians tried to interpret Christianity to accommodate the views of the Renaissance.

In the eighteenth century, Socinianism influenced English Baptists and Presbyterians and, in New England, Congregationalists, eventually culminating in Unitarianism on both sides of the Atlantic. In the nineteenth century, Socinianism gained adherents among Quakers in the United States. In form and content Socinianism can hardly be distinguished from

[48]Ibid., 3:372.
[49]Ibid., 3:373-74.
[50]Ibid., 3:377.

the modernism of the late nineteenth and early twentieth centuries.

Bavinck recognized the danger in this movement. In tracing Socinianism from its roots into the nineteenth century, Bavinck writes, "The criticism by Faustus Socinus was so sharp and complete that later dissenters could do little else than repeat his arguments."[51] Indeed, it is striking that, like this Socinian attack, so many others have been levied against Reformed theology and its soteriology, specifically explained in the five Canons of Dort. Surely the Reformed faith must be a giant to attract such a host of challengers!

Bavinck goes on to stress that atonement is initiated by God's love and serves his glory. The incarnation was an act of divine love even as it was a divine imperative, "not as a compulsion laid upon God external to him and from which he cannot escape, but as an act that is in harmony with his attributes and displays them most gloriously."[52] Satisfaction of God's justice by means of the incarnate Son of God glorifies God. "Sin was a denial of God and all his virtues, a turning to and adoration of the creature," Bavinck writes. "In Christ, however, God has again revealed himself, redemonstrated his sovereignty, vindicated all his virtues and attributes, and maintained his deity. God's purpose, also in the work of atonement, was that his glory should be exalted."[53]

Christ responded to his Father's initiative of love by accomplishing a double mediatorial obedience, best termed as active and passive obedience. The entire person of Christ was active in being surety, and his entire humanity was involved in suffering passively to pay for sin. These two aspects of obedience form one inseparable whole. Bavinck summarizes much of his viewpoint here in *Our Reasonable Faith* when he writes,

> In former times, the passive obedience was put into the foreground so far that the active obedience virtually disappeared behind it. But lately so much emphasis is put upon the active obedience that the first does not get its just due. According to Scripture, however, both go together, and they are to be viewed as the two sides of one and the same matter. Christ has at all times, from His conception and birth on, been obedient to the Father. His whole life is to be viewed as a fulfilling of God's justice, His law, and His commandment.[54]

---

[51]Ibid., 3:379.
[52]Ibid., 3:407-8.
[53]Ibid., 3:411.
[54]*Our Reasonable Faith*, 354.

The vicarious, satisfying obedience of Christ as mediator cannot be explained from any other phenomena, Bavinck asserts. It is "a concrete fact, entirely unique in human history, explained by nothing and yet entirely self-explanatory, resting upon a special provision of God." That provision bears a covenantal character, for it is rooted in the eternal council of the triune God, in "the most perfect and complete love" of God.[55] Bavinck asserts that the covenant of grace provides the context for Scripture's "many-sided description" of Christ's work. It offered Reformed theology a foundation from which to view Christ's work comprehensively and at long last to formulate it in a way that does justice to the total witness of Scripture.[56]

To appreciate what Bavinck achieves in the rest of his material on the work on Christ, one should understand how different was the time in which he wrote. It was a time when the church was the center of every village, town or city. Preachers and theologians were respected leaders in society. Sermons, lectures and books were the news of the day. In that context, when Bavinck, well known and widely admired in the Netherlands, decided to leave Kampen's Theological School for the Free University of Amsterdam, it created a national sensation.

Bavinck knew much was at stake in his discussion of the atonement. Whether by rationalism's devalued "historical Jesus" or romanticism's vague, elusive "Christ idea," the gospel that had won a hearing among Europe's pagans and had secured for the churches a place of influence in European and American life, was at risk. The Christianity of Christ and the apostles was not simply being reinterpreted; it was being co-opted altogether. In the process, the churches would eventually lose all influence and be pushed to the margins of society. Who could have foreseen the scope and speed of the great falling away that occurred between the wars and after World War II?

While identifying and critiquing a wide range of erroneous views, Bavinck treats the reader to a rich array of biblical teaching. However one may stumble over the names of obscure theologians of a bygone era, much can be gleaned from a careful reading of this material. Bavinck's expositional and preaching gifts are richly evident throughout. Along the way, Bavinck introduces the reader to well-known Reformation

---

[55]*Dogmatiek*, 3:454.
[56]Ibid., 3:455.

leaders such as Martin Luther and a host of his understudies, as well as to Cardinal Bellarmine (1542-1621), the great theologian of the Counter-Reformation. In all of this discussion, Bavinck displays a profound grasp of the theologians whom he opposes in the name of the Reformed faith.

As his many references and footnotes suggest, Bavinck was intimately acquainted with a great number of Reformed theologians, many of whom are not familiar even to orthodox Reformed believers today. He was deeply interested in the views of Old Princetonians such as Charles and A. A. Hodge and B. B. Warfield. In fact, it seems there was no one or nothing in the field of Christian thought that did not interest Bavinck.

Bavinck concludes his treatment of Christ's work with an extensive discussion of the words added to the fourth article of the Apostles' Creed: "He descended into hell." At issue is that the interpretation of this article by Reformed confessions differs radically from that of pre-Reformation churches of the West. The Reformation itself offered no unanimous alternative to the pre-Reformation view. As Bavinck says, "Luther put forward various interpretations and ended by saying: 'the matter is not clear.'"[57] The problem is complicated by an apparent difference in the view of Calvin and the Heidelberg Catechism versus the views of later Calvinists such as the Westminster divines. The older view, expressed in the Heidelberg Catechism, explains Christ's descent into hell as the hellish sufferings that Christ experienced on the cross (Q. 44). The later view, explained in the Larger Catechism of the Westminster divines (Q. 50), says: "Christ's humiliation after his death consisted in his being buried, and continuing in the state of the dead, and under the power of death till the third day; which hath otherwise been expressed in these words, He descended into hell."[58]

Bavinck presents these various views, exegetically sorts through them, logically examines them, and then arrives at the conclusion that there is no "contradiction or antithesis" in the two views identified with Reformed theology:

> The state of death into which Christ entered when he died was as essentially a part of his humiliation as his spiritual suffering on the cross. In

---

[57] Ibid., 3:465.
[58] *Reformed Confessions Harmonized*, ed. Joel R. Beeke and Sinclair B. Ferguson (Grand Rapids: Baker, 1999), 77-78.

both together he completed his perfect obedience. He drank the cup of suffering to the last drop and tasted death in all its bitterness, in order to completely deliver us from the fear of death and death itself. Thus he destroyed him who had the power of death and by a single offering perfected for all time those who are sanctified (Heb. 10:14).[59]

Some may regard this issue as a minor point, but Bavinck sees a greater issue at stake—that of the *terminus ad quem* for Christ's sufferings in his humiliation. He feels deeply obligated to maintain and defend the teaching of the Reformed confessions. Yet he does so with a gracious spirit as he clearly but gently identifies problems in other viewpoints.

Conclusion

Herman Bavinck vindicates the Reformed doctrine of atonement in a way most consistent with Reformed tenets, by sound exegesis of the Scriptures. Significantly for today's Reformed Christians, where he sees views that deviate from his own, Bavinck takes care to show how these views complement each other.

Bavinck's evangelicalism, expressed particularly in his concluding section, reveals his deep commitment to the authentic gospel of the New Testament. Here one sees the driving force behind his vast arsenal of learning, argument and eloquence. As Henry Dosker wrote, "All his teaching, all his preaching, all his writing was shot through and through with the richness of divine grace as revealed in Christ."[60] Cornelius Van Til put it this way: "Humble before God and courteous to his fellow-man, Bavinck always refused to compromise his Savior whose voice he heard in the Scriptures."[61]

Bavinck is *against* many things, but supremely he is *for* the gospel for two reasons: first, because it is the word of God, and God's word is truth (Jn 17:17); and second, because "it is the power of God for the salvation of everyone who believes" (Rom 1:16). This passion for the gospel accounts for the power of Bavinck's writings—a power that has not diminished after nearly one hundred years. "He being dead, yet speaketh."

Roger Nicole reminds me of Bavinck in several ways. He too is an able exegete and inductive dogmatician, well versed in many lan-

---

[59]*Dogmatiek*, 3:469.
[60]Dosker, "Herman Bavinck," 454.
[61]C. Van Til, "Bavinck the Theologian," *WTJ* 24 (1961): 48.

guages, an avid book collector and reader, broad-minded and pains-takingly thorough, irenic in harmonizing Reformed doctrinal options, and influential as a practical church theologian. I well remember Nicole's defense of a paper I presented at the Evangelical Theological Society. When I was challenged about my assertion that a backsliding Christian can lose his consciousness of assurance, Nicole rose and said in his booming voice, "The Christian who backslides had better lose his assurance!"

Nicole also reminds me of Bavinck in his kindness. Many of us have been encouraged at one time or another by a note from Nicole affirming some book we have written or some address we had given. Nicole is the kind of mentor to us that Bavinck was to him.

tHe ontoLoGicaL PResUPPOSItIONS of BaRtH's DOCtRINe of tHe atoNemeNt

Bruce L. McCormack

In the mid-1970s it was my privilege to spend two years in the master of divinity program at Covenant Theological Seminary—then and now one of the finest Reformed and evangelical seminaries in this country. The education I received there was "classical"—by which I mean, there was a heavy emphasis on biblical languages and exegesis and a steady diet of rigorous courses in systematic theology. The goal was to make each student into the quintessentially Reformed "pastor-theologian." And it was a goal that was reached more often than not. Every day of my working life as a professor of systematic theology at Princeton Seminary, I have reason to be grateful that my seminary education began at Covenant. Certainly, it provided me with solid theological foundations that have continued to serve me well.

And yet I cannot help but think that there was a weakness in the approach taken to teaching systematic theology at that time, which I have come to see since then as a weakness of Protestant theology generally, going all the way back to the sixteenth century. There was a decided lack of interest in "ontological" questions within the realm of dogmatics. "Systematic Theology II" was a course devoted to the doctrines of God, creation and humanity. The method employed in that particular course was oriented more to biblical theology than to systematics. The focus of the treatment of the doctrine of God, for example, had more to do with the attributes of God than with the doctrine of the Trinity—which was thoroughly understandable, given the desire to stay strictly within the bounds of biblical theology. Where the doctrine of the Trinity was concerned, we filled in the gaps in lectures by reading the appropriate chapter on the subject in Louis Berkhof's *Systematic Theology*. But it wasn't discussed much in class. We then moved on in the following semester to "Systematic Theology III," a course on soteriology. Here the most surprising discovery for me, even as a green seminarian, was that the syllabus for the course called for us to plunge immediately into a consideration of the work of Christ. The lion's share of the semester would then be devoted to the topics found in the Reformed *ordo salutis*. I remember asking my professor, "Don't we study the doctrine of the *person* of Christ at some point?" He responded with a counterquestion: "Didn't you already get that in Systematic Theology II?" When I answered in the negative, he looked a bit chagrined and announced that he would add a lecture on the subject to his syllabus. The content of that lecture, as it turned out, consisted in a brief look at the Chalcedonian formula.

The impression I took away with me at the time was that the doctrines of the Trinity and Christology were regarded by my professors as questions that had long been settled by the Great Church in a satisfactory way and that our task was simply to commit the results to memory. What I have learned since is that, if we don't have a thorough understanding of the problems with which theologians at Nicaea and Chalcedon wrestled, then we will only have a superficial grasp of their solution. Our problem—and now I am speaking of traditional Protestant theologians generally and not just of my teachers—is that, for most of us, the questions and problems that led to the formulation of the Nicene and Chalcedonian creeds are no longer *living* questions and problems. And they cannot be when we simply regard these issues as settled and do not enter into them as fully and with as much love and attention as did the Fathers. Even more important, I have learned that the doctrine of the *work* of Christ must not be allowed to gain even a small measure of independence from that of the *person* of Christ. Where that happens, both doctrines suffer. Where the person of Christ is abstracted from his work, our treatment of the Chalcedonian formula becomes all too "metaphysical." That is to say, we tend to flesh out the meaning of the chief terms—"hypostasis" and "natures"—along the lines of a priori definitions of general classes of things, rather than attending to the historical particularity of Jesus Christ, the incarnate God, whose "person" was actualized in and through his work. And where the work of Christ is abstracted from his person, our understanding of that work is severely attenuated and we are left without adequate answers in the face of the challenges that are today being brought against traditional evangelical teaching on the subject. It is the latter problem that is my central concern in this essay.

The penal substitution theory of the atonement has long been a favorite target of "liberal" criticism. But the signs are growing in number that evangelicals, too, are being swayed by the new line of criticism being brought against it, particularly by feminists and liberationists.[1] The critique runs something like this: a God who engages in violence as a means to attaining even the most worthy of ends (namely, the redemption of the human race) is a God who legitimizes violence; a God who, whether he wills to or not, grants to the creature permission to behave as he does. Such a critique is made to seem all the more compelling, on the emotive level, by the ethics of nonviolence and pacifism, which has been growing in strength throughout the Christian subculture since the 1960s. Certainly, sensitive evangelicals have felt the pinch of such arguments.[2] But the response given thus far has fallen short of demonstrating the firm grasp of the importance of an integrated understanding of the person and work of Christ that is needed for addressing the challenge. Indeed, an adequate response would require that penal substitution be integrated not only into a well-ordered Christology, but into a well-ordered doctrine of the Trinity as well. And this means entering into questions of theological ontology with the same degree of rigor that the early church leaders displayed.

It is precisely here that I think Karl Barth offers a great deal of help. I do not mean to suggest that he is the only possible resource that evangelicals could turn to when confronted by the current moral challenge to penal substitution. But I do think that he is the best. I would like to offer here a *Barthian* answer to current criticisms of the penal substitution theory. This will not be a piece of detailed research in Barth's writings that

---

[1]I do not know whether it was this argument or some other that moved Philip Yancey to interpret Jesus' death, in a recent *Christianity Today* editorial, as a death in solidarity with "victims." What is certainly true is that the view he outlines in his essay comes to conclusions similar to those drawn by the advocates of the moral critique of penal substitution that I have in mind here. See Yancey, "Why I Can Feel Your Pain," *Christianity Today* 43 (1999): 136.
[2]See Richard J. Mouw, "Violence and the Atonement," *Books and Culture: A Christian Review* 7 (2001): 12-17.

only specialists in the field of Barth studies would fully appreciate. Instead, I will allow myself the freedom to speak in Barth's voice, to respond to the critique as I think he would have done had he lived to see it.

The Christological Background to the Penal Suffering of Christ

The significance of the Chalcedonian formula. The Chalcedonian formula is one of the greatest achievements in the history of Christian theology. Though its sources and its significance have often been debated, this much is clear: the formula does not simply split the difference between Cyril of Alexandria and Nestorius; though it qualified Cyril's position in significant ways, it ultimately gave the nod to him where the truly decisive issues were concerned. And that already suggests that the formula was not simply a negative statement, an exercise in setting the boundaries of orthodox opinion where the christological problem was concerned so as to rule out certain options as heretical. That is also true, but the formula accomplished much more than that.

The formula begins with a formulation that takes up the valid concern in Nestorius's position. It affirmed "one and the same Son, our Lord Jesus Christ; the same perfect in divinity and perfect in humanity, the same truly God and truly man, of a rational soul and body; consubstantial [*homoousion*] with the Father as regards his divinity, and the same consubstantial [*homoousion*] with us as regards his humanity; like us in all respects except for sin; begotten before the ages from the Father as regards his divinity, and in the last days the same for us and for our salvation from Mary, the virgin God-bearer [*theotokou*], as regards his humanity."[3] But having affirmed that Jesus Christ was both God and human, the Chalcedonian formula then sought to bring some degree of positive expression to the *kind* of unity that resulted from the coming together of complete deity and complete humanity. It said of the two "natures" that they "come together into a single person and a single subsistent being" and that, as such, "he is not parted or divided into two persons, but is one and the same only-begotten Son, God, Word, Lord Jesus Christ."[4] In other words, the unity of divine and human in Jesus Christ is wrongly thought of where it is conceived along

---

[3]Norman P. Tanner, S.J., ed., *Decrees of the Ecumenical Councils* (Washington, D.C.: Georgetown University Press, 1990), 1:86.
[4]Ibid.

the lines of the union of two distinct persons. The unity is rather explained in terms of the singularity of the "person" (or, as we might say today, "subject") in whom are grounded two distinct "natures." Most significantly of all, that "Person" was identified as the only-begotten Son who was equated with God the Word.

So Nestorius's concerns are acknowledged to the extent the formula affirms that each "nature" is preserved in its integrity *after* being united in a single Person. But the affirmation of a singularity of "Person" meant that ultimately the victory belonged to Cyril's party.[5] The door to adoptionism had been closed decisively. Not God *in* a human (as One who indwells an already existing human being) but God *as* a human[6]—that was the positive significance of the formula. We may depict the results of the Chalcedonian formula diagrammatically in the following way:[7]

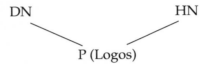

DN   HN

P (Logos)

Unattended issues. Notwithstanding this great achievement, the Chalcedonian formula did leave at least two very significant christological issues unattended that continue to haunt theology in both West and East right up through the present day. This is not surprising since these issues were not controverted at the time. But the open-endedness of the formula where these issues are concerned did have the effect of leaving the formula itself exposed to interpretations that would continue to lead the churches into error.

The first of these "unattended issues" has to do with the relation between the "natures" that resulted from their hypostatic union and the question of a possible "communication of attributes" (*communicatio idiomatum*) between them. Certainly, the Chalcedonian fathers could have taken a stance on the questions that arise in this connection had they wished to do so. The reigning paradigm for understanding

---

[5]That the Council was finally giving a nod to Cyril is also shown in its affirmation that Mary the Virgin is the "God-bearer" (*theotokos*). For it was Nestorius's rejection of that term as an apt description of Mary that set off the controversy that led to the calling of the Council.

[6]This excellent phrase is taken from T. F. Torrance, *The Trinitarian Faith* (Edinburgh: T & T Clark, 1988), 150.

[7]In this diagram, DN = divine nature; HN = human nature; and P = Person, or, more expansively, the Person of the Union.

Christ's work at that time had embedded within it the beginnings of a response to the problem of a *communicatio idiomatum*. The reigning soteriological paradigm was centered in the concept of *theosis*, or "divinization." The fundamental problem confronting the human race was not conceived of in this soteriology as primarily moral (i.e., the need for forgiveness) but as ontic (i.e., the need to overcome that corruption of being which leads to death). The solution to this problem was explained in terms of the Logos infusing life into human nature, restoring and recreating it, and thereby overcoming the threat of non-being. Had the Chalcedonian fathers sought to explain the ontological conditions that would make possible this kind of direct influence of the Logos on his human nature, they would doubtless have done it the way Cyril of Alexandria did.[8] They would have affirmed a "communication" of the divine life to the human nature. Whether any would have understood this communication of divine life to have entailed a concomitant communication of the divine attributes (e.g., omnipotence, omniscience and omnipresence) to the human nature of Christ is doubtful. Certainly, the later Lutheran explication of the *communicatio idiomatum* did take this step. In an effort to explain the bodily presence of Christ "in, with and under" the elements of the Lord's Supper, the Lutherans interpreted the "communication" in terms of several subclasses, the chief of which was the *genus majestaticum* (the "genus of majesty") in accordance with which the human "nature" was granted a share in all the divine attributes as a consequence of the hypostatic union. But as I say, the ancient church would not have taken "divinization" quite this far. Still, this much is clear: the logic of the communication of the "life" of God to the human "nature" certainly opened the door to the later Lutheran development. After all, it is difficult to conceive of the life of God

---

[8]Though Cyril did not use the language of a "communication of attributes" (language which did not exist in his time), he certainly had a well-developed understanding of the subject matter to which the later language refers. "What he was searching for was a concept of natural interpenetration where the two realities (e.g., deity and humanity) both subsided perfectly intact, but not in any parallel association, rather in a dynamic interpenetration and mutuality that effected new conditions and possibilities by virtue of that intimate union" (John Anthony McGuckin, "Introduction" to St. Cyril of Alexandria, *On the Unity of Christ* [Crestwood, N.Y.: St. Vladmir's Seminary Press, 1995], 38). Cyril's ultimate goal in his struggle for the acceptance of such a dynamic interpenetration of the natures is one that was shared by the majority of his contemporaries in the East at that time, that is, to render intelligible the idea of *theosis* (the transformation of that which is mortal into that which is immortal). See ibid., 34.

as present to and in a creaturely reality in the absence of the presence
of God himself (together with all his attributes).

Equally clear is the fact that the supposition that the Logos exercised
a direct influence on his human nature gives evidence of an Apollinarian tendency. Though the Councils of Constantinople in 381 and Chalcedon in 451 strove mightily to distance themselves from Apollinarianism (through the insistence that the human nature assumed by the
Logos was full and complete), the elimination of Apollinarian tendencies did not prove to be so easily purchased. For the heart of Apollinarian Christology lay not so much in the truncated humanity that it ascribed to Christ. The heart of the matter lay rather in the motive that
led to that truncation, the drive to understand the Logos as the ruling
principle of Christ's human nature. Apollinarius's own way of achieving that end—through the notion that the Logos simply takes the place
of the human mind (*nous*)—was rather crude. A more sophisticated
way of achieving the same goal would be through the affirmation of a
"communication" between the divine nature and the human nature
such that it becomes reasonable to think of the Logos as acting upon his
human nature. In both cases, the human nature is reduced to the status
of a passive instrument in the hands of the Logos; it is the object upon
which the Logos acts.[9] Against this tendency it has to be said that if the

---

[9]No one has made more of the soteriological axiom "the unassumed is the unhealed" in recent theology than has T. F. Torrance. In doing so, he has rightly pointed to the fact that the
mind of the human, too, is fallen and is in need of redemption. But in spite of the opposition
to Apollinarius implied in this emphasis, Torrance has not been able to free himself completely from Apollinarian tendencies. It is quite typical for him to speak of "Christ" acting
upon the assumed humanity, doing something to that human nature. So, for example, the
work of redemption is said to consist in this: that "the Lord transferred to Himself fallen
Adamic humanity which He took from the Virgin Mary, that is our perverted, corrupt, de-
generate, diseased human nature enslaved to sin and subject to death under the condemnation of God. However, far from sinning himself or being contaminated by what he appropriated from us, Christ triumphed over the forces of evil entrenched in our human existence,
bringing his own holiness, his own perfect obedience to bear upon it in such a way as to condemn sin in the flesh and deliver us from its power" (*Trinitarian Faith,* 161). Here, the grammatical subject "Christ" is equated, not with the God-human in his divine-human unity, but
with the deity in him alone. "Christ" has taken on human flesh in order to act upon it, to heal
it from its disease through his own obedience. God the Son is seen as doing something in
and to his human nature. "Through his penetration of the perverted structures of human existence, he reversed the process of corruption and more than made good what had been destroyed, for he has now anchored human nature in His own crucified and risen being" (ibid.,
182-83). Here again, the human nature is regarded as the passive instrument in the hands of
a subject who, in the absence of willed activity from the side of the human nature, can only
be regarded as the eternal Son, the Logos.

mind and will that are proper to Christ's human nature do not cooperate fully and freely in every work of the God-human, then Christ's humanity was not full and complete after all. The only adequate safeguard against this tendency is to understand the humanity of Jesus as doing the work it does *humanly*, that is, doing it as we would have to do it were we in a position to do so. And that means doing his miraculous works and living his life of sinless obedience, not as a consequence of the direct influence of the Logos within, but in unbroken dependence on the power of the Holy Spirit.

The second unattended issue has to do with the identity of the Logos. Just who is the Logos? Though the answer to that question might seem obvious, it is not. We only need to look back for a moment at our diagrammatic presentation of the Chalcedonian formula to realize just how complex the answer to this question is. If we were to ask: who, finally, is the subject who performs the work of reconciliation and redemption, three logical possibilities immediately present themselves. The first is that the Redeemer is a human being, period— a human being indwelt by the Holy Spirit, perhaps, and even maximally so, but a human being for all that. This answer, which we would today associate with "liberal" theologies, is excluded by the two-natures Christology of Chalcedon. But that still leaves two possibilities, both of which can be construed as consistent with the Chalcedonian formula. The second possible answer is that the subject who performs the work of reconciliation and redemption is the Logos *simpliciter*. We have already noted that the Chalcedonian formula does not suppress the Apollinarian tendency to make the Logos the operative agent in all that is done in and through the human nature of Christ; indeed, the formula as written—two natures in one Person— lends itself quite well to that tendency. And that is not at all surprising, given the soteriological commitments of the majority of the Chalcedonian fathers. The third logical possibility is to say that the subject who performs the work of reconciliation and redemption is the God-human *in his divine-human unity*.

Now on the face of it, it might seem that the Sixth Ecumenical Council (in A.D. 681), decided this question once and for all in favor of the third alternative. That Council affirmed "two *natural* volitions or wills in Him and two *natural* principles of action which undergo no division, no change, no partition, no confusion" as a result of the union.[10] But it has proven to be a lot easier to say that than it is to really mean it. The problem does not lie so much on the side of "no change" and "no confusion"; the problem lies on the side of "no division" and "no partition." The tendency of the overwhelming majority of theologians from the ancient church right on through the Reformation was to parcel out the work of Christ to the "natures" in such a way that some actions were assigned to the divine nature and some to the human nature alone.[11] Where this occurred, the "natures" were made "subjects" in their own right. The singularity of the subject of these natures was lost to view—and with that, the unity of the work.[12] What was left was two distinct works, which, it was argued, succeeded in complementing each other well enough that they could be regarded

---

[10]Tanner, ed., *Decrees of the Ecumenical Councils,* 128.

[11]Calvin provides a good (if subtle) example of this in *Institutes of the Christian Religion,* ed. John T. McNeill, trans. Ford Lewis Battles (Philadelphia: Westminster Press, 1960), 2.14.1. He claims that "the Scriptures . . . sometimes attribute to him [Christ] what must be referred solely to the humanity, sometimes what belongs uniquely to his divinity; and sometimes what embraces both natures but fits neither alone." He offers as evidence the following sorts of considerations. "Before Abraham was, I am" (Jn 8:58) is a statement which cannot be applied meaningfully to the humanity of Christ; therefore, it pertains to the divinity only. Likewise, Paul's description of Christ as the "first-born of all creation . . . who was before all things and in whom all things hold together" (Col 1:15, 17) is applied "exclusively to his divinity." And when it is said of Jesus Christ that he "increased in age and wisdom" (Lk 2:52), did not "seek his own glory" (Jn 8:50), did not know "the Last Day" (Mk 13:32; Mt 24:36), willed not to "do his own will" (Jn 6:38)—all of these "refer solely to Christ's humanity." In none of these examples, Calvin says, do we have evidence of a "communication" of properties. In each, there is simply a straightforward assignment of a divine work or quality to the divine nature only or a human work or quality to the human nature only. A "communication of properties" only appears in the Scriptures where something is said that, on the surface, is an impossibility. To this category belong the following: "God purchased the church with His blood" (Acts 20:28) and "the Lord of glory was crucified" (1 Cor 2:8) and "The Word of life was handled" (1 Jn 1:1). Calvin comments, "Surely God does not have blood, does not suffer, cannot be touched with hands. But since Christ, who was true God and also true man, was crucified and shed His blood for us, the things that he carried out in his human nature are transferred improperly, although not without reason, to his divinity" (*Institutes* 2.14.2). Calvin is certainly right that the capacity for suffering is a quality of the human. But if this human nature is not a subject in its own right, then how can we fail to assign such acts and experiences to the one subject in whom this nature is given its existence? The Logos clothed in his human nature is the subject who performs all aspects of the reconciling and redemptive work; there is no other subject.

[12]Many would appeal at this point to the so-called *communicatio apotelesmatum* in order to guarantee the unity of the work of Christ. A "communication of the works of each nature" would indeed guarantee the unity of the work of Christ *so long as* the singularity of subject is maintained. Where it is not, we clearly have crossed the line into Nestorianism. And the *communicatio apotelesmatum* offers us no deliverance from that error.

as being empirically indistinguishable as to their origin and as unified; but "unified" only in the sense of conducing to a single end. But it is no longer the case, on this view, that the work of Christ is the work of a single, unitary subject. Now the question becomes: Why do so many theologians have this tendency? The answer has to do with the hold that a particular concept of divine immutability has had on the minds of theologians since ancient times. It was unthinkable for the ancients that God could suffer and die. Only a human was believed able to do that. Confronted by *theopaschitism*, even the most Cyriline theologian often turns into a Nestorian.[13]

However contrary they are with respect to their results, both of the tendencies we have examined—the tendency toward Apollinarianism resident in the thought that the Logos is the operative agent who achieves redemption in and through his human nature, as well as the tendency toward Nestorianism generated by the flight from a mutable God—have the same source. Their source is a process of thought that abstracts the Logos from his human nature in order, by turns, now to make of the human nature something to be acted upon by the Logos and now to make of that nature a subject in its own right in order to seal the Logos off hermetically from all that befalls that human nature from without. In both cases, the Logos is abstracted from the human nature he assumed, and the Chalcedonian formula is read in terms of the second of our possibilities rather than the third.

So if all of this be true, then we would do well to revise the Chalcedonian formula just a bit so that the elaboration of an "abstract" doctrine of the Logos as the redeeming subject is rendered impossible. I would suggest a revised picture, which would look like this:

S

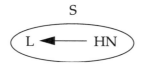

---

[13]The grand exception, so far as I know, is Cyril himself. Cyril seems to have been unique in the ancient church in affirming that the dynamic interpenetration of natures results in a two-way "communication." What is surprising about Cyril, when seen in context, is not, of course, the affirmation of *theosis* as a consequence of the influence of Christ's deity upon his humanity; what is surprising is his willingness to affirm that "the person of the Logos is the sole personal subject of all the conditions of his existence, divine or human." The deity of Christ was "enhanced" by the addition of the human nature in such a way that it became possible for God to experience humanly the conditions of human life, including suffering. See McGuckin, "Introduction," 40, 43.

In this diagram, the arrow serves to indicate that there is a real "communication" of all that belongs to the human nature (including both acts and experiences) to the Logos. The absence of an arrow pointing in the opposite direction indicates that there is no corresponding "communication" of that which belongs to the divine nature to the human nature. The divine nature has been collapsed into the Logos (represented by L), it being understood that the Logos is never without his divine nature. And the S stands for "subject." Insofar as the S stands outside of the entire complex, we are alerted to the fact that the "subject" who accomplishes reconciliation and redemption on our behalf is the God-human in his divine-human unity, and not the Logos alone (as the Chalcedonian language could easily imply).

This still leaves open the question of the divine immutability. What this diagram wants to suggest is that, even though the human cannot be "divinized" without ceasing to be human, God can indeed become human—can take on human nature and in it suffer and die—*without ceasing to be God.* But the question is, how is this possible? How can the Logos do all of this in time without ceasing to be identical with himself as he was/is/will be in eternity? How are we to understand the divine "immutability"? The stage is now set for a consideration of Barth's Christology.

Barth's "historicized" Chalcedonianism.[14] The unseen guest presiding over virtually the whole of the christological developments we have just traced is the attachment to a particular understanding of divine immutability. At its root, this understanding of immutability is itself a consequence of an even deeper-lying commitment to the substantialist ontologies of the ancient Greeks. "Substantialism," as I am employing the term here,[15] is one possible answer to the question: In

---

[14]I put the word *historicized* in quotation marks to indicate that while Barth is not himself a historicist, and was deeply opposed to those who were (like Ernst Troeltsch), still it remains true to say that the historicizing tendencies of over a century of theology before him found in his theology their relative justification and their proper limit. See on this point, my essay "Grace and Being: The Role of God's Gracious Election in Karl Barth's Theological Ontology," in *The Cambridge Companion to Karl Barth,* ed. John Webster (Cambridge: Cambridge University Press, 2000), 92-110.

[15]It should be noted that the definitions offered here are intended to be broad enough to encompass a variety of ancient Greek philosophies and not be limited in its reference to any particular one of them. It is the tendency, the direction, of "substantialist" thinking that I am interested in here.

what does the "essence" of a person/thing consist? The language of "essence" is certainly innocent enough. It refers merely to the thought of a self-identical element that perdures through all the changes that take place in a person/thing through time. It is that which makes a person/thing to be what it is, all other qualities being understood as nonessential. The Greek category of "substance" (in all of its various forms) makes the self-identical element in "persons" (which is our interest here) to be complete in itself apart from, and prior to the decisions, acts and relations by means of which the *life* of the person in question is constituted. "Substance," then, is a timeless idea; a concept whose content is complete in abstraction from an individual's lived history. So it follows that to define the "essence" of God in terms of "substance" is to make the essence of God to be complete apart from, and prior to, all of his decisions and acts. At most, what God does (whether in eternity or in time) *manifests*, or *gives expression to*, what he is, but what God does is in no sense *constitutive* of what God is.

Such an understanding of God's "being" seems to work well enough for all divine activities but one: the incarnation. A concept of divine "immutability" controlled by "substantialist" thinking would make unchangeability in God to be a function of a mode of being and existence that was complete in itself above and prior to even the eternal act of God in which God decides to create and to redeem human beings. But if the definition of "immutability" is controlled by a notion of "substance" in the way described, then it becomes impossible to understand the human nature of Jesus Christ as the human nature of the eternal Logos. Any attribution of human qualities or activities or experiences to the Logos would set aside the "immutability" of the Logos. On this view, the concepts of "Logos" and "human nature" fall apart; the unity of the two in a single "person" cannot be maintained; and the Christology that emerges is doomed to constant vacillation between Apollinarianism and Nestorianism (depending on whether the human nature is conceived of as purely passive and receptive in the act of redemption or fully operative). The unity of the Logos and his human nature can only be achieved through the abandonment of substantialist thinking and the "abstract" theological epistemology that makes it possible.

Barth's procedure in Christology constitutes a complete reversal of the trend of thought we have just reviewed. Rather than approaching the task of interpreting the ontological significance of the incarnation armed with a concept of the "divine" and a concept of the "human" whose content has been determined in advance, Barth would like to learn from the incarnation itself what it means to be God and what it means to be human.[16] What God is and what he can do is not to be learned through speculation or through an employment of the three classical "ways" (i.e., the *via negativa*, the *via eminentiae* and the *via causalitatis*). What God is and what he can do is to be learned through an attentive "following-after" of the movement of God into history in all of its concreteness. If God has done something, it must lie far from us to tell him that he is incapable of doing it (based on some a priori conception of God that we have formed for ourselves). Likewise, what it means to be "human" is not to be learned in advance from philosophy, the social sciences and so forth. What it means to be human is to be learned from the history of the man in whom human nature is restored, exalted and made to be what God intended it to be.[17] Only then will we have a *theological* anthropology worthy of the name. What is learned from other disciplines must be assimilated to a theological understanding of the "human" rather than controlling it.

So Barth begins with the historical facticity of what God has done and then asks (in effect): How must the being of God be constituted in eternity if he can do what we have seen him to do in time? What are the conditions in God for the possibility of the incarnation in time (and, we might well add, the outpouring of the Holy Spirit in time)? Barth's answer to this question involves an appeal to the doctrines of the Trinity and election. First, the doctrine of the Trinity: the condition of the

---

[16]The method employed by Barth in the realm of Christology is already set forth in some detail in the prolegomena volume, *CD* 1/1, pp. 1-44. But on this point in particular, see *CD* 3/1, p. 17, "The meaning of His deity . . . cannot be gathered from any notion of supreme, absolute, non-worldly being. It can be learned only from what took place in Christ. . . . Who the one true God is, and what He is, what is His being as God, and therefore His deity, His "divine nature," which is also the divine nature of Jesus Christ if He is very God—all this we have to discover from the fact that as such He is very man and a partaker of human nature, from His becoming man, from His incarnation and from what He has done and suffered in the flesh."

[17]See Barth *CD* 3/2, pp. 154-264, but especially 166-92 (in which Barth treats the life of the human Jesus as a life lived in correspondence to the divine Logos in whom he is given existence).

possibility of incarnation in time is to be found in the eternal generation of the Son. The condition of the possibility of the outpouring of the
Holy Spirit in time is to be found in the eternal procession of the Holy
Spirit from the Father and the Son. To the movement (the lived history)
of the Son in time, there corresponds a movement in eternity. And so
also with the Spirit.

What Barth's doctrine of election adds to this is the explanation for
why these movements correspond to each other—and therefore why
God is not changed by the incarnation and the outpouring of the Holy
Spirit. The most basic content of the doctrine of election is a choice God
makes with respect to himself. God chooses to be God only in the covenant of grace. Contained in this decision is the determination for incarnation and outpouring. Now notice, this is an *eternal* decision. There
was never a time when this decision had not already been made. To put
it this way is to suggest that the being of God in eternity is a being-in-
act; a "being" that is realized in the *act* of self-determination for incarnation, and so forth. There is no state, no mode of being or existence
above and prior to this eternal act of self-determination as substantialistic thinking would lead us to believe.[18] God's being in eternity is a being-in-act. And when, in time, he does that which he determined for
himself in eternity, no change is brought about in him on an ontological
level. To God's being-in-act in eternity there corresponds a being-in-act
in time; the two are identical in content (or, as we might also say, the
"immanent Trinity" and the "economic Trinity" are identical in content). Clearly, immutability has been preserved here. But it has been
newly defined. No longer is the meaning of divine immutability controlled by substantialistic thinking. The latter has been replaced by a
historical mode of thinking in accordance with which the "essence" of
God is constituted through his sovereign and free act of Self-determi-

---

[18]Barth *CD* 2/2, pp. 6, 7: "We cannot go back on this decision if we would know God and
speak accurately of God. If we did, we should be betrayed into a false abstraction, which
sought to speak only of God, not recognising that, when we speak of God, then in consideration of His freedom, and of His free decision, we must also speak of this relationship.
... That we know God and have God only in Jesus Christ means that we can know Him and
have Him only with the man Jesus of Nazareth and with the people which He represents.
Apart from this man and apart from this people God would be a different, an alien God.
According to Christian perception He would not be God at all. According to Christian perception the true God is what He is only in this movement, in the movement towards this
man, and in Him and through Him towards other men in their unity as His people."

nation in eternity so that "immutability" now means, quite simply, that in all that God does, he is fully himself.[19]

The most significant implication of Barth's divine ontology for the problem that concerns us in this essay is this: the second person of the Trinity did not first "become" the "Logos as human" at the point at which he assumed a human nature in the womb of the Virgin; that was his identity all along. For Barth, the second person of the Trinity is not and never was the Logos *simpliciter*.[20] To speak of an "eternal Son" in abstraction from the human nature to be assumed is to engage in illegitimate metaphysical speculation. It is, in fact, to mythologize. The second person of the Trinity has—already in eternity—a name, and his name is Jesus Christ.

It should be clear that Barth has not departed from the Chalcedonian formula. What he has done is to reinterpret the significance of its central categories in terms of a "historicized" ontology (i.e., an understanding of God's being as a being-in-act). In doing so, he has also overcome the tendency of substantialist thinking to abstract the Logos from his human nature and the human nature from the Logos. That the Subject of our redemption is neither the Logos *simplicter* nor a mere human being but the Logos as human means, among other things, that what happens to the God-human in and through his human nature happens to the God-human in his divine-human *unity*. Even that which we might, with justification, ordinarily think of as a

---

[19]We have already observed that Cyril of Alexandria could speak of the Logos as living under the conditions of the human life-form he assumed and as, therefore, suffering humanly. On that point, he and Barth agree. But Cyril was operating with a substantialist ontology, which inclined him to conclude that the suffering endured by the Logos was true of him only in the "economy"; it was not true of the Logos immanently. Such a view is certainly problematic; Cyril's opponents were not wrong to see very negative implications where the divine immutability was concerned. Barth differs from Cyril in that he does not limit "suffering" in God to the "economy." Therefore, he does not have Cyril's difficulties with immutability. Barth's "historicized" ontology has another advantage as well. For he is able to explain how it is that the redemptive sufferings of Christ, which occur only at a specific point in time, are *already effective* for believers who lived prior to their occurrence. Jesus Christ is, from eternity, the Redeemer.

[20]Among the very significant consequences of this conception is the fact that it helps to explain how it is possible for the redemption wrought by Jesus Christ to be effective for people who lived prior to his appearance in history. If his being in eternity is a being-in-act, which looks forward to and anticipates his being-in-act in time, then it is a being that looks forward to and anticipates a being in the act of accomplishing redemption. Hence, what he does in the incarnate state is already effective because he is in himself what he is in time: the Redeemer.

human experience (for example, death) is something that happens to the *Logos* as human. That also means, then, that death is a human experience that is taken into the divine life and does not remain sealed off from it.

Would we be right, then, to say that God suffers death in the death of Jesus Christ? The answer must be a cautious "yes"; cautious, because there is a right way to say this and a wrong way to say it. The wrong way would be to say that the Logos *simpliciter* dies; that the death of Jesus Christ is the death of the eternal Son. If that were the case, then the death of Jesus Christ would be an event "between God and God" as Hegel put it, an event between the eternal Father and the eternal Son. Such a way of conceiving of "death in God" would necessarily result in a rupture of the eternal relation between the Father and the Son, a rift in the very being of God. And if that relation in which the deity of the Son has been grounded and maintained from eternity were severed, the Son would not be God in the one event in which we most need him to be God, that is, in the event of the cross. Barth is absolutely right to describe this understanding of "death in God" as "supreme blasphemy." "God gives Himself, but He does not give Himself away. He does not give up being God in becoming a creature, in becoming man. He does not cease to be God. . . . And when He dies in unity with this man, death does not gain any power over Him."[21] We have already seen that we make ourselves guilty of a christological error when we conceive of the subject who performs the work of redemption as the Logos *simpliciter.* So we quite naturally also make a mistake when we think of the subject who dies as the Logos *simpliciter.* The subject who dies is the God-human, in his divine-human unity. And what is happening in this event is that the Logos as human is taking a human experience into the unity of his person. He submits himself to this experience. He "tastes" death; he experiences it in its full weight as a curse, but he is not overcome by it.

The Trinitarian Background of the Penal Suffering of Christ

There is one more piece that we need to put in place before turning directly to recent moral challenges to penal substitution. Here we can be much more brief. Barth's preferred formula for describing triunity in God

---

[21]Barth *CD* 3/1, p. 185.

is one subject "in three modes of being."[22] He sets forth this formula in studied opposition to the classical formula "one substance in three persons." As we might expect, his reservations with regard to the classical formula have something to do with the category of "substance," but they do not end there. The term "person" suggests "individuation"; in Boethius's highly influential definition, a "person" is "an *individual* substance of a rational nature."[23] It is the note of "individuation" that makes the term "person" inappropriate for speaking of triunity in God, in Barth's view. To see the members of the Godhead as "individuated" would give rise to tritheism, so he prefers the language of "modes of being."

Barth anticipates that the charge of modalism will be brought against him as a consequence of this phrase, so he explains why he is not a modalist. "Modalism" referred, historically, to the view that the three members of the Godhead are "modes of appearing" of a hidden, unknown subject standing in back of these modes.[24] This conclusion was strengthened by the use of the term *persona*, which originally referred to the masks that ancient actors wore on stage in order to play roles. Against this, Barth says that he is not speaking of mere modes of appearance; he is speaking of "modes of being." And since these are "modes of *being*," there is no hidden subject standing in back of the modes. Rather, the being of the one subject is Self-constituted in these "modes." Looked at from another point of view, it is precisely the fact that the immanent Trinity and the economic Trinity are identical in content that makes the charge of modalism impossible.

Now the importance of Barth's doctrine of the Trinity lies in the twofold fact (1) that it is thoroughly coordinated with his Christology (which guarantees that the identity of the second person of the Trinity both *a sarkos* and *en sarkos* is the God-human in his divine-human unity); and (2) that he is able to treat the trinitarian axiom *opera trinitatis ad extra sunt indivisa* as a realistic description of the operations of the triune God. The force of the axiom is to say that if one member of the Trinity does something, they all do it.

In sum, the significance of Barth's Christology and his doctrine of the Trinity for understanding what is happening in the event of the

---

[22]Barth *CD* 1/1, p. 355.
[23]Ibid., 356.
[24]Ibid., 353.

cross (or in any other event in which an economic relationship between the Son and the Father is at stake) is as follows. First, an economic relation is never merely economic. If the economic Trinity corresponds perfectly to the immanent Trinity, then the relation of the first "person" of the Trinity to the second "person" must be structured in the same way in both. An action by the first person upon the second, then, is not an action of the Father upon the "eternal Son" (conceived along the lines of a Logos *simpliciter*); nor is it an action of the Father upon a mere human being. It is an action directed toward the Logos as human (the God-human in his divine-human unity). That much is guaranteed by Barth's Christology. But secondly, the trinitarian axiom *opera trinitatis ad extra sunt indivisa* adds to this the thought that if the Father does anything, then all members of the Trinity do it. We are now in a position to think through the logic of penal substitution with a degree of care not usually found in the doctrine.

Penal Substitution

Recent moral challenges to the penal substitutionary theory are best addressed through an analysis of the logic of the "object" and the "subject" of the action in question. First, on the side of the object of the action: we wrongly conceive of the outpouring of the wrath of God the Father upon the Son (as the penalty due to human sin) if we conceive of it as an action of God directed toward an innocent human being. That much should be fairly obvious by now (though the Nestorian tendencies of even a Calvin tended to make it anything but obvious). But we also make a mistake if we conceive of it as an action of God the Father toward an "eternal Son" (conceived of as the Logos *simpliciter*, in abstraction from the human nature he assumed). The problem is that death, however it is conceived, is a *human* experience. How then could the death of Jesus Christ be an event between God and God, between, that is, an eternal Father and an eternal Son who is understood along the lines of a Logos *simpliciter*? So the logic of penal substitution is not that the Father does something to his "eternal Son" (as the charge of "cosmic" child abuse would suggest). An action of the eternal Father upon the eternal Son (seen in abstraction from the assumed humanity) would require a degree of individuation between the two such that the "separation" needed for an action of the one upon the other becomes thinkable. One could purchase this degree of individuation by taking the step of the "social trinitarians" (i.e., by fitting each member of the eternal Trinity out with his own mind, will and energy of operation). In that way, we would have made it possible to explain how the eternal Father could act upon the eternal Son. But such an explanation would have no obvious relevance to the situation before us. This is a *human* experience of the Logos. Therefore, it is an event between the eternal Father and the Logos *as human.* The "object" of the action is, therefore, the Logos as human.[25] What happens in the outpouring of the wrath of God by the Father upon Jesus Christ is that the human experience of the "penalty of death" that humans have merited through their sinfulness is taken into the very life of God himself.

But then we still have to consider the logic of the "subject." The subject who delivers Jesus Christ up to death is not the Father alone. For the trinitarian axiom *opera trinitatis ad extra sunt indivisa* means that if one does it, they all do it. So it is the triune God (Father, Son and Holy Spirit) who gives himself over to this experience. And that also means, then, that the Father is not doing something to someone other than himself. The triune God pours his wrath out upon himself in and through the human nature that he has made his own in his second mode of his being—that is the ontological significance of penal substitution. The triune God takes this human experience into his own life; he "drinks it to the dregs." And in doing so, he vanquishes its power over us. That, I would submit, is the meaning of penal substitution when seen against the background of a well-ordered Christology and a well-ordered doctrine of the Trinity.

God's action in punishing sin on the cross offers no example to be emulated for the following reason. It is not an action of one individual upon a distinct individual. One might (logically) wish to characterize it as masochism, but one could never characterize it as sadism. But, then, it is not masochism either. Masochism arises out of a desire to experience pain because some kind of perverse pleasure is had in such experiences. And God's motives have nothing to do with the pursuit of perverse pleasures; his motives throughout are the completely selfless motives of unconditional love for the creature. But the crucial point is that a well-ordered penal substitution theory (one that gets its ontological presuppositions right) does not portray this event in terms of a violent action of God (conceived of as one individual) upon his Son (conceived of as a second distinct individual). Therefore, the event in question is inimitable in the absolute degree.[26] It justifies nothing on the plane of human-to-human relations, and the moral charge against penal substitution cannot finally be sustained.

Conclusion

I have tried to make it clear in this essay that the moral charge against penal substitution cannot be sustained so long as we operate with a well-ordered Christology and an equally well-ordered doctrine of the Trinity. We must know who it is that judges here, and who it is that is judged, if we are not to fall into error. But when these things are in place, not only is the current moral challenge to penal substitution successfully answered, but a more classical objection is answered as well. By way of conclusion, we may look briefly at why this is the case and what that implies for the way we hold to "penal substitution."[27]

In its more traditional forms, the penal substitution theory all too easily suggested that God the Father's relationship to the human race is altered by what Christ did in dying on behalf of the human race. The objection such a form of the theory aroused was that it made no sense. If the Father were not mercifully inclined toward the human race all along, why would he have sent his only Son into this world in the first

---

[26]Barth *CD* 3/1, pp. 246-47. "It is not simply the humiliation and dishonouring of a creature, of a noble and relatively innocent man that we find here. The problem posed is not that of a theodicy: How can God will this or permit this in the world which He has created good? It is a matter of the humiliation and dishonouring of God Himself, of the question which makes any question of theodicy a complete anticlimax; the question of whether in willing to let this happen to Him He has not renounced and lost Himself as God . . . whether He can really die and be dead? And it is a matter of the answer to this question: that in this humiliation God is supremely God, that in this death He is supremely alive. . . . Because it is a matter of this person and His mission, the suffering, crucifixion and death of this one man is a unique occurrence."

[27]Since this essay has concerned itself more with the ontological presuppositions of Barth's doctrine of the atonement rather than with the doctrine itself, I have not here entered into the question of the meaning of "penal substitution"—how it was conceived in traditional Reformed theology and how it was modified in the theology of Barth. For my views on these questions, the reader may wish to consult my essay, "For Us and Our Salvation: Incarnation and Atonement in the Reformed Tradition" in *Studies in Reformed Theology and History* 1, no. 2 (Princeton, N.J.: Princeton Theological Seminary, 1993), 25-34.

place? Surely, a determination to be merciful and forgiving must precede and ground the sending of the Son into this world to die in our place. Surely forgiveness is not *elicited* from the Father (grudgingly?) by what Christ did on our behalf; it is rather *effected* by the Father in and through Christ's passion and death. So the picture of an angry God the Father and a gentle and self-sacrificial Son who pays the ultimate price to effect an alteration in the Father's "attitude" fails to hit the mark.

Here again we have to think through the situation of penal substitution in a more integrated way that abandons the logic of an action of the eternal Father upon the eternal Son. Jesus Christ is both the subject and the object of what happens in his passion and death. He is the subject because the outpouring of wrath in the event of the cross is not the unilateral act of God the Father (as though such a thing were even possible). It is the act of the triune God and therefore the act of the God-human as well. He is the subject even as he makes himself to be the object upon whose body and in whose soul a sentence is carried out. He is the subject of his own passion, not just in the sense that all that happened in Jerusalem on that final weekend was received by him willingly (which might still leave him passive), but in the sense that his earthly trial and execution was the medium in and through which he himself was actively judging a sinful human race and executing a just judgment.[28] So the proper meaning of "penal substitution" is that the penalty that God as Judge willed to be the consequence of human sin is a penalty that God himself (the triune God in the person of the Son) takes upon himself.

The penal substitution theory of the atonement has been one of the central elements in evangelical theology since the Reformation. If it is to survive in evangelical circles today, however, it must be subjected to close scrutiny with the goal of ensuring that it really says what must be said and does not say what cannot be said. In our efforts to refine this great legacy of the Reformation, we can find no finer guide than Karl Barth.

---

[28]Barth *CD* 3/1, p. 235. "He is the subject and not the object of what happens—the subject even when He is the object. He is the Lord as He fulfills the work which He has undertaken for us, the work of His own deepest humiliation. He has the omnipotence in the power of this work to bear our sins, to bear them away from us, to suffer the consequences of our sins. . . . It is in this omnipotence that He confronts Israel, goes to Jerusalem, enters the city of the kings as a King, shows and promises and gives His body and blood to His disciples with the bread and wine of the Lord's Supper, allows Himself to be kissed by Judas and delivers Himself up into the hands of soldiers. This is all a sovereign action. It is completed and its meaning is revealed in the passion of Christ on the cross. Even on the cross it is a divine act."

tHe atonement in postmodernity

Guilt, Goats and Gifts

Kevin J. Vanhoozer

"For Jews demand signs and Greeks seek wisdom, but we preach Christ crucified, a stumbling block to Jews and folly to Gentiles."
1 CORINTHIANS 1:22-23 RSV

A̲t the heart of the gospel is the announcement that the death of Jesus was "for us." The church's attempt to think through this "for us" results in the doctrine of the atonement. The message of the cross is still a stumbling block even after two millennia. However, what is new in our current situation is that many postmoderns consider the *doctrine* of the atonement to be just as scandalous.

An Aporia to Postmoderns
The aporia of atonement. The apostle Paul's contrast between Jew and Greek has been brought up to date by the Jewish philosopher Emmanuel Lévinas, a figure who, along with Jacques Derrida, is commonly regarded as one of the seminal postmodern thinkers. "Greek-think" is Lévinasian shorthand for the tendency, apparent throughout Western intellectual history but especially transparent in modernity, to "theorize": to "see" (*theoria* = to behold) with the mind's eye. What modern philosophy—and theology—prize above all else is theory: *knowing* as a kind of seeing.

Lévinas accuses theoretical reason of taking thought captive with a "totalizing" method that acknowledges only what conforms to its con-

ceptual schemes. To "see" is to grasp—an essentially aggressive gesture. If we "grasp" or "apprehend" something, then it does not remain
"other." For the other (an important category not only for Lévinas but
for postmoderns in general) is precisely what escapes our conceptual
reach. Yet this is precisely the temptation to which modernity has suc-
cumbed: to reduce the real to what we can "see," the "other" to the
"same" (that is, what we already know). In Lévinas's words: "The labor of thought wins out over the otherness of things and men."[1] For
Lévinas, theoretical thinking, by appropriating events and entities into
a given conceptual scheme, is ultimately both reductionist and *violent*.

Lévinas renounces the violent pretension of theoretical thought. He
and other postmoderns contrast what can be seen or explained within
the limits of reason with what cannot be thought or conceptually mas-
tered. Whereas epistemology represses the other by absorbing it into
explanatory schemes, ethics does justice to "others" precisely by let-
ting the other be.[2] Ethics resists the tendency of systems of language
and systems of thought to swallow things up (to "totalize"). For much
of European history, of course, the Jew was the principal "other." In
contrast to modern "Greek" thought, "Jew" stands for Lévinas's way
of responding as a philosopher to the command not to make any
graven images (theories), and for his decision to make respect for the
other the first principle of his philosophy ("Thou shalt not kill"). In its
concern to respect the integrity of the other, then, postmodernity is
more "Jew" than "Greek."

Through a twist of postmodern irony, the "Greeks"—modern theologians who develop systems and theories—are precisely those who
now seek to *lessen* the folly of the cross. Such is the function of atonement "theories." Again, what is "Greek" about theory is "the desire
to reconcile oppositions and differences through a movement of
thought that would finally reduce them to aspects of a single, comprehensive vision."[3] As we shall see, this is precisely what its critics say

---

[1]Emmanuel Lévinas, "Ethics as First Philosophy," in *A Lévinas Reader*, ed. Seán Hand (Oxford:
Blackwell, 1989), 79.
[2]For Lévinas himself, the "other" is a human being whose irreducibility is symbolized by the
face, but his point about respecting others can be extended to include texts and ideas as well.
In *Is There a Meaning in This Text? The Bible, the Reader, and the Morality of Literary Knowledge*
(Grand Rapids: Zondervan, 1998), for instance, I argued that interpreters need to respect the
voice of the author as an "other."
[3]Christopher Norris, *Derrida* (London: Fontana, 1987), 230.

about the penal substitution theory of the atonement. *The scandal of the cross, for postmoderns, is that theory reduces otherness precisely by explaining it.* Postmoderns might say that we need to recover the scandal— the paradox, the "aporia"—of the cross through a "sacrifice" of the intellect, acknowledging that conceptual thinking has here reached its limit, its death.

Does theory—in this case, the doctrine of atonement—really do violence to the cross? For many postmoderns the "systematic" qualification of theology is evidence of its totalizing ambition. Exegetes have often expressed a similar concern. *The challenge for theology is to "theorize" the cross (i.e., in a doctrinal formulation) while simultaneously respecting it (i.e., as an "other" that eludes our conceptual grasp).* The problem is that theologies of the atonement seem unable to articulate a theory that explains the saving significance of Jesus' death without betraying the rich testimonies to the event of his death. This, in a nutshell, is the aporia of the atonement in postmodernity.

Deconstructing the logic of penal substitution. While it is fairly easy to identify the leading medieval, Reformation and modern theories of the atonement, one is hard-pressed to identify a "postmodern" atonement theory. It is far easier to think of ways in which postmodern thinkers seek to "deconstruct" atonement theories.

Deconstruction is a strategy for viewing the world, not in terms of substances or essences, but rather in terms of linguistic, intellectual, social and political constructions. The mission of deconstruction is to show that things—texts, institutions, traditions, belief systems—are not as solid or as natural as they appear. Deconstructive postmoderns share Nietzsche's interest in genealogy—an interest not in family trees but in uncovering the historical, social and political conditions under which various belief systems of social structures were set up. Like Lévinas, Derrida wants to release the "other" from its captivity to systems. The postmodern hermeneutics of suspicion assumes that the systems we live by were constructed by whatever group had the power to do so. Deconstructors typically want to know *whose interest* a particular theory or practice serves.

This postmodern attention to theory's genealogy leads to the suggestion that every doctrinal formulation that purports to explain the significance of Jesus' death actually tells us more about the history and culture of the people who devised it than it does about the cross.

For example, the very first developed doctrine of the atonement, Anselm's satisfaction theory, bears all the marks of the social and political system of his day. Closer to home, Joel Green and Mark Baker have recently suggested that the penal substitution model of the atonement betrays the telltale hallmarks of modernity: an anthropocentric tendency to see the significance of Jesus' death as limited to human beings; an individualistic tendency to see Jesus' death as benefiting isolated persons; a moralist tendency to see Jesus' death as a punishment for the acts of sinful individuals.[4] To understand the atonement in postmodernity, then, one has to come to grips with the deconstruction (that is, the exposure of its constructedness) of the penal substitution theory. Doing so requires us to distinguish three separate problems.

1. *The methodological or "formal" problem: models and metaphors.* The first problem that postmodern thinkers point out with the penal substitution model of atonement is its tendency to reduce the many NT metaphors of speaking about the cross to one: penalty. This elevation of the law court metaphor over other NT metaphors drawn from other spheres of public life (e.g., "redemption" from the realm of commerce; "reconciliation" from the realm of personal relationships; "victory" from the battlefield) is a flagrant example of what worries Lévinas about "Greek think": its tendency to reduce the *other* (in this case, other metaphors) to the *same* (e.g., the concept of penal substitution).[5]

   The Swiss Roman Catholic theologian Hans Urs von Balthasar rightly warns us of the danger of reducing the full content of the NT language concerning Christ's death for us to "some alleged equivalent that is more 'intelligible' to the spirit of a different epoch."[6] No one metaphor should be allowed to dominate the others. Whatever tension we feel between the various images for

---

[4]Joel B. Green and Mark D. Baker, *Recovering the Scandal of the Cross: Atonement in New Testament and Contemporary Contexts* (Downers Grove, Ill.: InterVarsity Press, 2000), 25-29.
[5]Green and Baker posit five constellations of images (*Recovering the Scandal*, 23): the courts of law (justification), the world of commerce (redemption), personal relationships (reconciliation), worship (sacrifice) and the battleground (victory). Henri Blocher also sees five sets of metaphors: sacrifice, punishment, ransom, victory and Passover ("The Sacrifice of Jesus Christ: The Current Theological Situation," in *EuroJTh* 8 [1999]: 30).
[6]Hans Urs von Balthasar, *Theo-Drama: Theological Dramatic Theory*, vol. 4, *The Action* (San Francisco: Ignatius, 1994), 243.

thinking about the atonement must not be relaxed, but rather *endured.*

Some postmoderns make a further point about metaphors. It is not only that there are many of them but also that each one is irreducible. Each metaphor, one might say, remains *other*. Metaphors resist being "translated" into literal speech or being reduced to concepts. In contrast to skeptical postmoderns, Colin Gunton combines an appreciation of the power of metaphor with a healthy belief in their ability to depict reality truly, albeit only indirectly and incompletely.[7] Atonement metaphors would therefore represent indispensable cognitive instruments that enable us to begin to understand how Jesus' death has saving significance. Perhaps some divine acts—in particular, what God was doing in Jesus Christ—can only be described by means of metaphors.

Theologians need to think hard about the merits of the postmodern protest. *The formal challenge for atonement theory in postmodernity consists in justifying the move from many metaphors to one, and from the one metaphor to a single concept.* Does being biblical in one's thinking about Jesus' death require us to embrace one model of the atonement, or many? The main issue concerns how to move from Scripture to theology, metaphor to concept *nonviolently*, as it were.

2. *The soteriological or "material" problem: violence and vengeance.* "Violence" is the operative concept in the postmodern criticism not only of the conceptual form of the penal substitution view but also of its very content. Postmoderns criticize any theory that tries to make sense of the cross in terms that might legitimate violence, or in terms of retribution, or in terms of economic exchange.

An "economy" is a system of exchanges, a way of administering or managing resources. Paul uses the Greek term *oikonomia* (from *oikos* "house" and *nemo* "manage") in Ephesians 1:10; 3:9 to refer to the "administration" of the plan of salvation. We speak of the "eco-

---

[7]Gunton intriguingly suggests that some of the biblical atonement metaphors—such as "sacrifice" or "victory"—become the standard for the "real" meaning of these ideas (*The Actuality of Atonement: A Study of Metaphor, Rationality and the Christian Tradition* [Grand Rapids: Eerdmans, 1989], 50, 79). See also John McIntyre's discussion of metaphor in *The Shape of Soteriology* (Edinburgh: T&T Clark, 1992), 72-78.

nomic" Trinity to refer to the way in which God operates in history, in contrast to God's eternal essence. The penal substitutionary model of atonement presupposes a divine "economy" in which God distributes a particular resource (forgiveness) only after the appropriate payment (Jesus' death). Postmoderns are quick to point out how such thinking is both "Greek" and modern insofar as it is an example of instrumental rationality. Furthermore, such a divine economy sounds to many like the *lex talionis:* "an eye for an eye." Contra Luther, such an exchange is anything but "wonderful."[8] For to suggest that Jesus died to pay the penalty for our sins is to suggest that God only forgives after first seeking retaliation for sin. Postmoderns are apt to view this as a *murderous* exchange.

To interpret Jesus' death within the framework of such an exchange economy is, in the eyes of postmodern critics, to legitimate a violent cycle of retaliation and retribution, all in the name of "justice." Hence, the scandal of the cross is not metaphysical (how could God suffer and die?) but *moral:* Does God need to be placated before he can love and forgive? Is God party to an economy of retaliatory exchange?

3. *The pastoral or "political" problem: preaching and practice.* The suggestion that penal substitution relies on the notion of divine retribution leads to a third problem: How can we preach and, more importantly, *practice* the atonement? To what understanding of forgiveness does the penal substitution model give rise? This is no idle query, for postmodern theologians tend to focus as much, if not more, on church practices as on church doctrines. Indeed, a number of postmodern theologians have argued that the very meaning of Christian language is tied up with the shape of the church's corporate life. Christians are not disembodied souls but embodied persons who relate to one another in concrete ways. We come to understand what Christians are talking about only by participating in their "form of life."[9] If this is true, then the meaning of the doctrine of atonement

---

[8]The allusion is to Luther's description of the crucifixion as a "wonderful exchange": Christ takes the punishment of sinners; sinners take the sonship of Christ.

[9]The philosopher Wittgenstein's suggestion that language is only understood in the context of the form of life or practice in which it is used has been taken up, most notably, by George Lindbeck in his *The Nature of Doctrine: Religion and Theology in a Postliberal Age* (Philadelphia: Westminster Press, 1984).

will best be seen in conjunction with certain church practices.

Feminist theologians in particular complain that the penal substitution model fosters unhealthy social practices. Joanne Carlson Brown sees Jesus' death on the cross as a glaring instance of what she calls "divine child abuse."[10] For Brown, the idea that the Father punished the Son for the sins of the world is tragically mistaken on two counts: first, it makes God out to be a vindictive deity; second, it encourages humans to think that suffering is "redemptive." In her opinion, atonement theory must not commend practices that perpetuate suffering and abuse. Those who wish to commend the doctrine of atonement to postmoderns must henceforth demonstrate how it leads to healthy rather than abusive practices. One such constructive offering in this direction is L. Gregory Jones's *Embodying Forgiveness*, which argues that the church is a distinctive community precisely because it renounces the economy of violent retaliation.[11]

The historical question: why did Jesus die? In addition to these three problems stands the historical question: How did Jesus himself view his death? One portrait of Jesus favored by an increasing number of NT scholars is that of Jesus the deconstructor: a teacher of subversive wisdom aimed at exposing the illegitimacy of the social, political and religious hierarchies of his day. In particular, Jesus in his words and actions subverted the centrality of the Jerusalem temple. The temple represented a number of entrenched distinctions: clean and unclean, Jew and Gentile, priest and non-priest. Jesus overturned not only the tables in the temple but also these distinctions as well as a number of practices administered by the Jewish religious leaders who were the custodians, as it were, of God's presence and forgiveness.[12]

N. T. Wright suggests that Jesus' own preferred "great metaphor" for interpreting the saving significance of his death, which he employed at the Last Supper, was not the Day of Atonement, but the Passover.[13] The point raised by these historical reconstructions is whether

---

[10]J. C. Brown, "Divine Child Abuse," *Daughters of Sarah* 18, no. 3 (1992): 28.

[11]L. G. Jones, *Embodying Forgiveness: A Theological Analysis* (Grand Rapids: Eerdmans, 1995).

[12]See Joel B. Green, "The Death of Jesus and the Ways of God: Jesus and the Gospels on Messianic Status and Shameful Suffering," *Interpretation* 52 (1998): 30.

[13]N. T. Wright, *Jesus and the Victory of God* (Minneapolis: Fortress Press, 1996), 605. We will return to the significance of the Passover below. Suffice it to say for the moment that the question is whether Jesus as the lamb of God should be associated more with Exodus than Leviticus.

Jesus may have thought about his own death in terms other than penal substitution.

In a paper of this size I cannot hope to respond to each of the above challenges.[14] Instead, I propose first to examine two postmodern critiques of the economy of law, those by Paul Ricoeur and Jacques Derrida. I will then consider two postmodern alternatives to thinking about the saving significance of Jesus' death: René Girard's analysis of the scapegoat mechanism; and John Milbank's and Jean-Luc Marion's analysis of the gift. In each case, I will compare and contrast the logic of an *economy of exchange*, characteristic of the traditional view, with what I shall call the postmodern *economy of excess*. This contrast appears in each of the three parts:

Guilt: justice as satisfaction or payment of debt versus justice as what is in excess of the law

Goat: averting violence by sacrificial killing versus denouncing violence by exposing the violence inherent in sacrifice

Gift: giving to get something back versus giving without hope of return

I shall conclude with some reflections on how postmodernity both challenges traditional understandings and contributes to a recovery of certain neglected biblical themes.

Guilt: The Force of the Law

According to Adolf Harnack, it was the Latin fathers who, perhaps under the influence of Roman law, were the first to carry religion into the legal sphere.[15] Jesus' death is necessary, on this view, because God must preserve the order and integrity of the universe, which is structured according to moral as well as physical laws. According to Anselm, when sin threatens the moral order, there are two possibilities: either retributive punishment, a balancing of the scales of justice; or satisfaction, a way of remitting the penalty other than by punishment. It fell to Martin Luther to link these two ideas by suggesting that Jesus'

---

[14]See John Goldingay, ed., *Atonement Today* (London: SPCK, 1995). For a critical appraisal of this book, see Blocher, "The Sacrifice of Jesus Christ," 23-36.
[15]See further in Gunton, *The Actuality of Atonement*, 86.

punishment by death is itself the satisfaction that God's justice requires. Specifically, Christ fulfills the law by enduring the wrath of God, the proper punishment for sin, in our place. This, according to Luther, is how he has "paid God."[16]

The wrath of God and retributive justice: sacralizing the economy of law. Is God reconciled to sinners only after exercising his retributive justice? If sin is not punished, can it be justly forgiven? Penal substitution is one of thirteen models of the atonement examined by John McIntyre.[17] However, a number of scholars have questioned not only whether it is an appropriate model but also whether "penalty" is one of the biblical metaphors for interpreting the saving significance of Jesus' death. To be sure, the apostle Paul speaks of death as the wages of sin. Yet, according to Paul Fiddes, Joel Green and Stephen Travis, the concept of "penal substitution" is an example of a distinctively un-Pauline mixing of metaphors.[18] Fiddes, for example, denies that Paul ever explicitly taught that salvation is won by transferring the penalty for sin onto Jesus: "Such a theory requires the addition of an Anselmian view of debt repayment and a Roman view of criminal law."[19] This is an excellent example of how genealogical analysis of atonement theory leads to its deconstruction.

On the traditional view, Jesus' death on the cross saves because it propitiates the wrath of God kindled against sin.[20] The standard objection to this view is that a vicarious punishment in which Jesus serves as a "whipping boy" makes no moral sense.[21] Here it is impor-

---

[16]The nineteenth-century theologian Edward Irving spoke derogatorily of the "Stock-Exchange divinity" presupposed by the penal substitution view.

[17]John McIntyre, *The Shape of Soteriology* (Edinburgh: T & T Clark, 1992), 44-48.

[18]See Paul Fiddes, *Past Event and Present Salvation: The Christian Idea of Atonement* (Louisville, Ky.: Westminster John Knox, 1989), 98; Green and Baker, *Recovering the Scandal*, 95; Stephen H. Travis, "Christ as Bearer of Divine Judgment in Paul's Thought about the Atonement," in *Jesus of Nazareth: Lord and Christ, Essays on the Historical Jesus and New Testament Christology*, ed. Joel B. Green and Max Turner (Grand Rapids: Eerdmans, 1994), 332. McIntyre agrees, but goes on to observe how one might easily extrapolate from a number of texts that when taken together do seem to interpret Jesus' death in terms of penal substitution (*Shape of Soteriology*, 44).

[19]Fiddes, *Past Event*, 98.

[20]Ellen Charry argues that the idea of a wrathful God came to the fore in the medieval era, with fateful consequences for subsequent atonement theology. See her *By the Renewing of Your Minds* (Oxford: Oxford University Press, 1997), especially chapter 8 on Aquinas.

[21]William C. Placher, "Christ Takes Our Place: Rethinking Atonement," *Interpretation* 53 (1999): 7.

tant not to assume that punishment presupposes an emotionally un-
stable deity who flies into fits of rage. Penal substitution does not require such caricatures, contra Baker and Green, who argue that the
penal substitution view is built on a picture of God as "emotion-
laden . . . ever on the verge of striking out."[22] Some scholars suggest
that God's wrath refers to his handing people over to the (natural)
consequences of their unfaithfulness.[23] Others interpret God's wrath
as God's holy opposition to sin. The issue is whether God's wrath
needs to be propitiated or whether it is itself the force that expiates
and destroys sin.[24]

In spite of clear biblical testimony—for example, Paul's reference to
Deuteronomy 32:35 in Romans 12:19, "for it is written, 'Vengeance is
mine, I will repay, says the Lord'"—many contemporary theologians
dismiss as mythical the notion that God demands retribution. Gunton,
following a suggestion of George Caird, says that it is Satan rather
than God who, at least in the prologue of Job, takes on the role of prosecutor, thus personifying the economy of law, order and punishment.[25] Paul Ricoeur concurs; the book of Job is a polemic *against* the
law of retribution, for the point of the story is that Job suffers while *innocent*. Ricoeur proposes to "demythologize" the biblical rendering of
a vengeful God, not by denying the truth of the stories themselves, but
only "the secondary rationalization that holds [them] captive."[26] *What
Ricoeur ultimately questions is the adequacy of what we might call the
"moral" picture of God, that is, the idea that God operates, and operates
within, a moral economy.*

"For every action there is an equal and opposite reaction." This could

---

[22]*Recovering the Scandal*, 53.

[23]For example, C. H. Dodd, *The Epistle of Paul to the Romans* (New York: Harper & Row, 1932).
On this view, a verse like Galatians 6:7, "God is not mocked, for whatever a man sows, that
he will also reap," is a kind of wisdom statement about the consequences that naturally flow
from human acts in a morally structured created order, not a promise (or threat) that God
will personally intervene to reward or punish human acts. On the other hand, as Henri
Blocher points out, the creator God is not simply working "outside" the processes of nature,
for they execute his sovereign decree ("Sacrifice of Jesus Christ," 32).

[24]For a fuller discussion of these interpretive possibilities, see J. M. Gundry-Volf, "Expiation,
Propitiation, Mercy Seat," in *Dictionary of Paul and His Letters*, ed. Gerald F. Hawthorne,
Ralph P. Martin and Daniel G. Reid (Downers Grove, Ill.: InterVarsity Press, 1993), 279-84.

[25]Gunton, *Actuality of Atonement*, 83. Cf. George Caird, *Principalities and Powers* (Oxford: Clarendon, 1956), 37.

[26]Paul Ricoeur, "The Demythization of Accusation," in *The Conflict of Interpretations* (Evanston, Ill.: Northwestern University Press, 1974), 336.

serve equally well as a principle not only for motion, but also for *morality*. Nothing is more rational, says Ricoeur, than the exchange of guilt and punishment. Ricoeur notes that religion often underwrites the judiciary; we trace our most important laws back to the laws of God. More important for our purposes than this sacralizing of the judicial is the equivalent juridicizing of the sacred. The penal interpretation of Jesus' death is, on Ricoeur's view, a moralistic rationalization of the biblical images that express the saving significance of the cross. Ricoeur is well aware of Pauline texts about justification, but he contends that their point is to acknowledge the sinner's inability to escape condemnation by doing works of law. Ricoeur resists any interpretation that makes it difficult to imagine forgiving grace except in relation to the economy of the law with its core practice of punishment. He wants to know how a physical evil (punishment) can cancel out or compensate for a moral evil. In Ricoeur's view, punishment is "only a manner of perpetuating violence in an infinite chain of crimes."[27] Thus, crime *and* punishment both represent a wrong; and two wrongs, even when conjoined within strict penal logic, cannot make something "right."

Green and Baker link the penal substitution view with Western thinking of sin in terms of individual guilt—what they call "autobiographical justice."[28] This view locates responsibility for sin at the level of the individual rather than at the social level. Like modern thinking in general, it is atomistic rather than holistic. Moreover, the penal substitution theory is of little help if shame, rather than guilt, is the problem. Green and Baker note that in Japan criminals are imprisoned, not in order to "pay their debt to society," but "as a shameful act of exclusion from society."[29] Restoration cannot be had merely by "doing time" but only by a loving acceptance of the offender back into the community. This framework provides a very different interpretation of how Jesus' death saves: God willingly experiences shame—the ignominy of death on a cross—out of his love for us. The doctrine of the atonement looks quite different in modern-day Japan than it does, say, in Reformation-era Germany.

---

[27]Ricoeur, "Interpretation of the Myth of Punishment," in *Conflict of Interpretations*, 363. We will return to Ricoeur's own interpretation of the "myth of punishment" in our discussion of "gift" below.

[28]Green and Baker, *Recovering the Scandal*, 24.

[29]Ibid., 155.

Its postmodern critics say that the judicial system does not renounce violence but merely limits public vengeance to a single act of
reprisal. Here, of course, we may think of Michel Foucault's work
Discipline and Punishment.[30] To this way of thinking, the judicial system institutionalizes revenge; violence comes by force of the law.
"Taking the law into one's own hands" refers to individuals who exact their own vengeance, but the principle—retributive justice—is
the same. The law, like sacrifice, serves both to limit and to legitimate
acts of violent reprisal that might otherwise spiral out of control. The
significant difference between private and public retribution is that
in the judicial system the act of vengeance is not itself avenged. The
state-imposed punishment terminates the process, thus averting an
endless cycle of violence.

Postmoderns seek to escape the whole economy of legal exchange,
what Ricoeur calls "the infernal circle of law, transgression, guilt, and
rebellion."[31] Interestingly, the broader context of Paul's citation of Deuteronomy 32:35 is a teaching about loving one's enemies. The notion
that vengeance is the Lord's is part of the apostle's argument that believers must live peaceably with one another. We may also note in passing that Deuteronomy 32:36 goes on to speak of the *vindication* of the
oppressed. It is therefore possible to interpret passages that speak of
God's vengeance as affirming *God's hyper-judicial concern for the victim-
ized other.*

The main problem with exacting punishment is that it is not clear
how it saves sinners; retribution alone is not transformative. This is
commonly perceived as one of the main weaknesses of Anselm's view,
or indeed of any "objective" theory of atonement where what the cross
accomplishes is something "external" to sinners (e.g., a propitiation of
God's wrath, a satisfaction of God's honor). The biblical images for salvation suggest something more than a mere remission of a penalty. The
latter changes one's objective status or legal standing before God. It
does not, however, affect one's very being or heart. Critics of the penal
substitution view insist that forgiveness and justice, like salvation itself, must be restorative, bringing people back into right relationship:
"People are mistaken if they think of Christian forgiveness primarily

[30]New York: Vintage Books, 1979.
[31]Ricoeur, "Religion, Atheism, and Faith," in *Conflict of Interpretations*, 448.

as absolution from guilt; the purpose of forgiveness is the restoration of communion, the reconciliation of brokenness."[32] The aim of forgiveness and justice alike, then, is not to balance the books, as in a system of exchange that distributes punishment in accordance with the measure of guilt. On the contrary, their aim is personal communion. God's justice is "covenantal-relational" and is "almost synonymous with faithfulness."[33] Interestingly, this comes close to what Derrida is now saying about justice.

Deconstruction and justice: undoing the economy of law. Legal explanations of the saving significance of Jesus' death are, as our brief review has just shown, nothing new. The penal substitution view has always had the advantage of being intelligible to Europeans and Americans familiar with the justice system. The postmodern critique of penal substitution is more radical than its modern "humanitarian" counterpart inasmuch as Derrida questions the very *system* of justice itself.[34]

Derrida's more recent writings belie the common caricature of an "anything-goes-because-it's-language-all-the-way-down" relativist. It now turns out that all that philosophical play had a serious political purpose. In "The Force of Law," a 1989 lecture for a symposium on deconstruction and justice, Derrida startled his listeners by announcing that deconstruction *is* justice.[35] Derrida's claim depends on his distinction between "law" and "justice." What deconstruction calls into question is not justice itself, but the system of laws that pretends to represent justice. By justice, Derrida means our infinite duty to recognize and respect the other.[36] Justice, Derrida believes, always outruns particular legal systems. Justice cannot be fully *written*, cannot be encoded in a system of statutes and sanctions. Laws, says Derrida, are historically instituted, or *constructed*. It therefore follows that they can be *deconstructed*; they can always be taken apart and improved. Justice, we might say, always *exceeds* the law. So, while laws can be deconstructed,

---

[32]Jones, *Embodying Forgiveness*, 5.

[33]Green and Baker, *Recovering the Scandal*, 147.

[34]Whole conferences, journals and books have sprouted up whose focus is on postmodern legal theory. For a helpful survey of this literature, see Douglas E. Litowitz, *Postmodern Philosophy and Law* (Lawrence: University Press of Kansas, 1997).

[35]See Derrida, "The Force of Law: 'The Mystical Foundation of Authority,'" in *Deconstruction and the Possibility of Justice*, ed. Drucilla Cornell et al. (New York: Routledge, 1992), 68-91.

[36]Derrida acknowledges his debt to Lévinas on this point.

justice cannot be, for justice is precisely what the deconstruction of the law seeks to bring about.[37]

What are the implications of Derrida's reinterpretation of justice in terms of excess for our view of the justice of God, for our understanding of atonement, and for the model of penal substitution in particular? To date, Derrida himself has not drawn out the implications. Yet it seems clear that the basic thrust of his argument is to dispute the notion that justice can be done in any one economy of law. Economies of law (e.g., Roman, English) typically deal with guilt by means of an appropriately calculated penalty. Is justice merely distributive and retributive? One suspects that Derrida would denounce "an eye for an eye" as *unjust*. "An eye for an eye" is a law, a determinate rule whereby a wrong is righted by sanctioned violence (another wrong). Derrida contends that such laws are ultimately based on arbitrary social conventions. The founding law of the state (a constitution, for example) is itself a social construct, a forceful fiction.

Does divine justice oblige God to enter into an economy of exchange whereby sin is inevitably met with punishment? Gunton argues that this vision of God as cosmic law-enforcer corresponds more to what the ancient Greek historian Hugh Lloyd-Jones called "the justice of Zeus" than it does to Yahweh.[38] Consider Ezekiel 18:23: "Have I any pleasure in the death of the wicked, says the Lord GOD, and not rather that they should turn from their evil ways and live?" (NRSV). We may here wonder whether justice can ever be retributive.

The first point I wish to make in reply is that the biblical framework for interpreting the saving significance of Jesus' death is *covenantal* rather than merely legal. The difference is important, for neither the Abrahamic, nor the Sinaitic, nor the new covenant was founded on an originary act of violence.[39] In the context of God's covenant with Israel,

---

[37]Derrida's view of justice as something which is always "to come" (*à-venir*) resembles his new emphasis on the messianic. Deconstruction is a "messianic" faith insofar as it insists on staying open to a future that is "wholly other" and hence has the power to unsettle all our present arrangements. For a fuller discussion of this point, see John D. Caputo, *Deconstruction in a Nutshell: A Conversation with Jacques Derrida* (New York: Fordham University Press, 1997), chap. 6.

[38]See Gunton, *Actuality of Atonement*, 97.

[39]It could be argued that circumcision, the exodus and the death of Jesus are all violent acts. We shall return to this theme below. Suffice it to say that they are acts that take their meaning from a covenantal rather than a strictly legal framework.

the law served the purpose of regulating relationships, both within the cove-nant community and between the covenant community and God. Let me therefore suggest that, from a biblical perspective, God's justice is a matter of his preserving *right covenantal relationships,* and of doing so with integrity (i.e., as a holy, just and loving God).

The postmodern critique of retributive justice raises the possibility of a *restorative* sense of justice. But can it ever be just to restore a guilty person to her former state without some course of punishment?[40] How can God restore right covenantal relationships without imposing cov-enant sanctions? Is it possible *justly* to forgive an infraction of the law? Just what is forgiveness, and under what conditions can forgiveness break out of the strict economy of "an eye for an eye"? In much post-modern thinking the change that leads to "right relationship" takes place exclusively in human beings. Theories of atonement habitually emphasize only one aspect or the other. We need some such phrase as *"making right covenantal relationship"* to catch both the objective and the subjective outcomes of Christ's atoning work.[41] The atonement makes things "right," to be sure, but this rightness is legal *and* interpersonal, objective *and* subjective.

It should now be clear how the penal substitution view falls short, from a postmodern perspective, both methodologically and materially. With regard to method, it privileges one metaphor over the others; with regard to matter, it processes the metaphor according to the economy of law that leads to the notion of God's retributive justice and Jesus' puni-tive death. Yet a further problem for postmoderns is the *practice* to which this theory gives rise. John Milbank argues that the church as a distinct *polis* (the city of God) must adopt distinct social polices. In par-ticular, it must renounce the use of force, even in support of the law of God. One thinks immediately of Augustine's defense of the church's co-ercion of the Donatists. While acknowledging that force belongs to the realm of the secular, Augustine made a fateful decision to defend eccle-sial coercion by stipulating its end: peace. Subsequent emperors and popes would later use the same logic to justify "holy war." According

---

[40]C. S. Lewis's critique of the "humanitarian" theory of punishment is of some relevance here, see *God in the Dock: Essays of Theology and Ethics* (Grand Rapids: Eerdmans, 1970), 287-300.
[41]The phrase is my attempt to expand on the notion of *justus* + *facere* "to make righteous" and so to include what is normally discussed under the rubrics of both justification and sancti-fication.

to Milbank, Augustine failed to see how easily this "pedagogic" coercion could be used to justify other punishments as "positive."

There is clearly a need for a state-enforced system of justice that restrains chaos by maintaining the rule of law. Yet as we have seen, these laws are only provisional expressions of justice, and their enforcement carries the risk of inciting even more violence. Milbank believes that the church's attitude and practice concerning law, guilt and punishment ought to proceed from the ontological order of trinitarian peace, not the Darwinian order where creatures fight to survive. The church must strive to be "a social space where a different, forgiving, and restitutionary practice is pursued. This practice should also be 'atoning,' in that we acknowledge that an individual's sin is never his alone, that its endurance harms us all, and therefore its cancellation is also the responsibility of all."[42] Placher goes even further: the cross brings an end to retribution itself, and hence to the whole economy of law: "The conviction that in Christ guilt has come to an end ought to be at the heart of any authentic Christian politics."[43] So while we need to protect the innocent and rehabilitate those who have "gone down wrong paths," Placher concludes that we should stop punishing the guilty. For a Christian who lives in the shadow of the cross, forgiveness should be a way of life. Justice—in the postmodern sense of respecting others' rights and of restoring right relationships—should be the Christian way of life.

Goats: Sacrifice as "Sacred Violence"

A second biblical metaphor that has received considerable attention in postmodernity is that of sacrifice: "Without the shedding of blood there is no forgiveness" (Heb 9:22). On the all-important Day of Atonement, two goats play the crucial roles: the sacrificed goat and the scapegoat together constitute a single sin offering, "the one exhibiting the means, and the other the results of the atonement."[44] Hebrews 9—10 point to the shed blood of Christ as *effecting* what animal sacrifices only represent, namely, the removal or cancellation of sin from God's sight, and hence the purification of the sinner.

---

[42]John Milbank, *Theology and Social Theory: Beyond Secular Reasons* (Oxford: Blackwell, 1990), 422.

[43]Placher, "Christ Takes Our Place," 15.

[44]T. J. Crawford, as cited in David Edwards and John Stott, *Evangelical Essentials: A Liberal-Evangelical Dialogue* (Downers Grove, Ill., InterVarsity Press, 1988), 164.

"Look, the Lamb of God, who takes away the sin of the world!" (Jn 1:29). Is Jesus' death a literal sacrifice? On the one hand, sacrifice, even in the Old Testament, does not always refer to the slaughtering of an animal; for instance, Psalm 51:17 identifies sacrifice with "a humble heart." Moreover, Jesus did not die on an altar. Yet both Gunton and Sykes suggest that the metaphor is describing something *real*.[45] After all, Jesus himself suggested a sacrificial interpretation for his death at the Last Supper when he passed the cup: "This is my blood of the covenant, which is poured out for many." (Mk 14:24). It is hard not to hear echoes of Leviticus 17:11 in these words.

The traditional view is that Jesus' death is a sacrifice that cancels sin and therefore makes forgiveness possible. The matter is not as straightforward as that. First, does sacrificial imagery really explain the saving significance of Jesus' death? According to Green and Baker, the rationale for Israel's sacrificial system "is not worked out fully in the OT and may forever elude our full comprehension."[46] Second, postmoderns worry that the image of sacrifice sanctions violence and encourages a victim mentality. Here we would do well to recall Sykes' salient remainder: "The answer to distortions is careful analysis."[47]

Religion, society and the scapegoat mechanism. Perhaps no postmodern theorist has more thoroughly analyzed the phenomenon of sacrifice than the literary critic René Girard.[48] According to Girard, all human interaction is characterized by "mimetic rivalry": we want what we see other people striving for, and by imitating them we become rivals (e.g., Cain wanted God's approval and imitated Abel's sacrifice). Rivalry leads inexorably to competition, conflict and eventually to violence.[49] Rivalries threaten the social order, for violence begets vi-

---

[45]See Colin Gunton, "The Sacrifice and the Sacrifices: From Metaphor to Transcendental," in *Trinity, Incarnation and Atonement*, Ronald J. Feestra and Cornelius Plantinga, eds. (Notre Dame, Ind.: University of Notre Dame Press, 1989), 214; Stephen Sykes, *The Story of Atonement* (London: Darton, Longman & Todd, 1997), 18.

[46]Green and Baker, *Recovering the Scandal*, 64.

[47]Sykes, *Story of Atonement*, 124.

[48]For a brief introduction to Girard's thought, see Gerard Loughlin, "René Girard: Introduction'" in *The Postmodern God: A Theological Reader*, ed. Graham Ward (Oxford: Blackwell, 1997), 96-104; Richard J. Mouw, "Violence and the Atonement," *Books and Culture* (Jan./Feb. 2001): 12-17. For a book-length study, see Raymund Schwager, *Must there be Scapegoats? Violence and Redemption in the Bible* (San Francisco: Harper & Row, 1989).

[49]"Violence is not originary; it is a by-product of mimetic rivalry" ("Mimesis and Violence," in *The Girard Reader*, ed. James G. Williams [New York: Crossroad, 1996], 12).

olence. Girard's thesis is that the purpose of sacrifice is to restore peace and harmony to the community. This happens only when the group transfers its mutual hostility to a third party—scapegoats, individuals or a class of individuals "outside" the group. Directing violence at the scapegoat saves the community from tearing itself apart. The scapegoat is "sacrificed" (killed, exiled, punished, etc.) for the sake of social peace: "The purpose of the sacrifice is to restore harmony to the community, to reinforce the social fabric."[50] For Girard, sacrifice is the "solution" to social conflict and violence, and may be found at the origin of every culture and every religion. The dark secret of civilization is that society and religion alike are founded on collective violence.[51]

Girard's theory is typically postmodern in its genealogical thrust, namely, in its intent to expose the scapegoat mechanism "hidden since the foundation of the world." Like Freud, Girard works with a hermeneutics of suspicion, distrustful of society's "official" account of its origin. Society is "delusional"; the scapegoat mechanism cannot be acknowledged but must be denied: "Its vitality as an institution depends on its ability to conceal the displacement upon which the rite is based."[52] Second, like Lévinas, he is concerned for the "other," in this case, the innocent victim of sacrificial violence. The scapegoat is usually a marginal figure, one who can be exposed to violence without fear of reprisal by some segment of the community. The perfect victim is the one whose death "does not automatically entail an act of vengeance."[53] It is all too easy to think of historical examples of the scapegoat mechanism. Medieval Europe and the Germany of the 1920s and 30s found in Jews a convenient race of scapegoats.[54]

In Girard's view, it is Satan—the accuser—who pulls the levers of the scapegoat mechanism. It is Satan who is behind the idea that "good" violence is the answer to "bad" violence. It is Satan who oils

---

[50]*The Girard Reader*, 78.
[51]Girard's claim that an actual murder lies at the origin of society is controversial, but this has not stopped Girard from positing it. Ironically, the scapegoat is later revered by societies that ascribe their peace to its death. Rituals of sacrifice remind the community that social peace was achieved only through death. The *locus classicus*, of course, is Leviticus 16, which provides instruction for what to do with the scapegoat on the Day of Atonement.
[52]*The Girard Reader*, 75.
[53]Ibid., 82.
[54]For the church's complicity in anti-Semitism, see James Carroll, *Constantine's Sword: The Church and the Jews* (New York: Houghton Mifflin, 2001).

the wheels of the cyclical mechanisms of vengeance, thus preserving "the reciprocity of violence and of carefully calculated counter-violence."[55] What better justification for violence is there than to commit it in the name of retributive justice? The goat is guilty: crucify him! Girard acknowledges that the sacrificial character of developed democratic societies such as those in Europe and America is far from obvious. Yet these societies have an "official" or institutional system of violent retribution: the penal system. Social order continues to rely on an economy of sacrifice. Girard notes that the stories both of Job and of Jesus depict the "authorities" as finding each man guilty in order to justify his punitive suffering.[56]

In Girard's view, Christian theology too has often collaborated in the delusion: in a classic act of misdirection, theological theories invoke the notion of an angry God that needs to be placated. By focusing on God, the community is oblivious to the true nature of the scapegoat mechanism, namely, as a vent for pent-up human violence. The purpose of the scapegoat mechanism, and hence of religion as a whole, is to deal with the problem of human violence by perpetuating one of the arbitrary "binary oppositions" that Derrida sees as structuring language and life, namely, the difference between a good and a bad violence. The purpose of Girard's analysis is to expose the violence that lives at the origin and at the heart of every "ethical" religion, of every religion that adheres to the economy of sacrifice.

The phenomenon of substitutionary sacrifices appears in a very different light when viewed in a Girardian framework. Though he acknowledges a principle of substitution, he denies that it has anything to do with an "innocent" creature paying the debt for a "guilty" party. For Girard sacrifice has nothing to do with "expiation." Rather, society "is seeking to deflect upon a relatively indifferent victim, a 'sacrificeable' victim, the violence that would otherwise be vented on its own members, the people it most desires to protect."[57] In sum, *sacrifice is a sacred violence*. As we have already noted, one of the main functions of sacrifice is to maintain the distinction between good and bad violence.

---

[55]Schwager, *Must There be Scapegoats?* 30; see also "Satan," in *The Girard Reader*, 194-210. "My thesis is really that the Gospels view Satan as the principle—if not the entire reality—of human culture since the foundation of the world" (203).
[56]See Girard, *Job the Victim of His People* (Stanford, Calif.: Stanford University Press, 1987).
[57]Ibid., 73.

This is precisely the aspect to which Girard objects. Religion must not condone violence by concealing it under the guise of religious ritual. Religion must not make even a limited amount of violence acceptable. If and when it does so, says Girard, religion becomes complicit with the "God of persecutors."[58]

The nonsacrificial death of Christ. To this point, Girard appears to be a postmodern master of suspicion, unmasking the violent, though hidden, workings of powerful institutions. Yet Girard has a positive message—a gospel—to proclaim as well. It is a message that concerns a new, nonviolent basis for peace.

Girard believes that the Bible is unique among the works of world literature in *exposing* the scapegoat mechanism and, by so doing, rendering that mechanism ineffective. The Bible consistently declares the scapegoat innocent.[59] The gospel narratives in particular depict Jesus as an innocent victim. They expose the scapegoat mechanism and, by bringing it to light, render it powerless. For the scapegoat mechanism only works when we forget that the scapegoat is innocent. The hiddenness of the scapegoat mechanism is a condition of its successful operation. The Gospels are revelatory precisely in their *demythologizing* function; they remove the aura of sacred mystery from the scapegoat mechanism and show it for what it is: a pathetic cover-up for human violence. In short, Jesus' nonviolent lifestyle and forgiving attitude exposes Satan's lie (i.e., that the guilty deserve to be violently punished); hence, Jesus becomes the victim of the same satanic forces that are everywhere hidden yet at work. *Jesus had to die because his rejection of violence threatened to expose the basis of every cultural, political and religious institution that exists.*

Girard denies that Jesus had to die as a sacrifice, preferring rather to see his shed blood as continuous with "the blood of all the prophets, shed since the beginning of the world, from the blood of Abel to the

---

[58]Von Balthasar notes the conspicuous absence of the word *justice* in Girard and asks: "Can it be proved scientifically that the justice for which men long is nothing but power in disguise?" (*Theo-Drama*, 4:309). Note that "justice" in Derrida's view does not refer to the scapegoat mechanism, which he undoubtedly would categorize as part of the "economy of law."

[59]Girard is particularly impressed by the averted sacrifice of Isaac, the prophets' condemnation of the sacrifices of bulls and goats, and the story of Job, which, like the story of Jesus, clearly affirms the innocence of the suffering victim. See "The Bible's Distinctiveness and the Gospel," in *The Girard Reader*, 145-76.

blood of Zechariah" (Lk 11:50-51). It is this bloodletting or scapegoat-ing that Jesus reveals: "I will utter things hidden since the creation of the world" (Matt 13:35). However, the scapegoating delusion is so powerful that even Christians have mistakenly read the Gospels as *af-firming* the idea of sacrifice. Girard rejects any notion that depicts God as requiring sacrifice (e.g., sacred violence). On the contrary, Jesus' suf-fering and death were necessary because of the world's inability to free itself from the cycle of rivalry and violence, not because God's justice demanded death. Girard is fond of quoting Jesus' words to the Phari-sees: "Go and learn what this means, 'I desire mercy, and not sacrifice'" (Mt 9:13).

Girard hopes that Jesus' exposure of the scapegoat mechanism will change the world "[T]he violence of the cultural order is revealed in the Gospels . . . and the cultural order cannot survive such a revela-tion."[60] Girard is encouraged by evidence that more and more of soci-ety's hidden victims are being brought to light: slaves, lower classes, people of different ethnic backgrounds, the handicapped. The death of Christ is thus a unique breakthrough, a decisive event in the history of human consciousness. The purpose of his death is to end all scapegoat-ings, all sacrifices. "To be rid of violence we must refuse the illusion that there can be a legitimate, safe violence, the violence of just retribu-tion."[61] The penal substitution model, when viewed against this back-drop, represents in Girard's eyes an ironic misunderstanding, a "re-vealing indication of mankind's radical incapacity to understand its own violence."[62]

The God of Jesus Christ is not a violent God who practices retribu-tive justice, writes Girard, but "a non-violent one whose demand is for non-violence rather than sacrifice."[63] Jones writes: "Jesus' sinlessness consists in his ability to suffer human evil, particularly the human ten-dency toward destructive judgment, and to absorb it without passing it on."[64] Girard notes that Jesus forgives his enemies because "they know not what they do," and he does so *without sacrifice*. Jesus' death shows that God is with the victims; God returns forgiveness for vio-

[60]Girard, *The Scapegoat* (Baltimore: John Hopkins University Press, 1984), 189.
[61]Loughlin, "Girard: Introduction," 102.
[62]*The Girard Reader*, 178.
[63]Ibid., 18.
[64]Jones, *Embodying Forgiveness*, 122.

lence. Why did Jesus have to die? First, to expose the scapegoat mechanism. But Girard adds a second reason as well: "because continuing to live would mean a compromise with violence."[65] Jesus overthrows the violent powers by his refusal to engage the satanic powers on their own terms. As Girard observes, the first thing the risen Jesus says to his disciples who had deserted him was "Peace be with you!" (Jn 20:19). Instead of seeking vengeance, Jesus proclaims forgiveness.

Nonviolent atonement: the Passion's pacific outcome. A number of theologians have enthusiastically taken up Girard's alternative understanding of the saving significance of Jesus' death. Raymund Schwager goes to great lengths to show that the Bible never depicts God as advocating retributive justice or even violence. The prophets explicitly speak against the notion of divine vengeance: "Do I take any pleasure in the death of the wicked? declares the Sovereign LORD. Rather, am I not pleased when they turn from their ways and live?" (Ezek 18:23). The theme of Jesus' kingdom preaching was that God loves sinners. In the Sermon on the Mount, Jesus goes out of his way to contrast a kingdom way of living with the economy of the law ("You have heard it said, 'an eye for an eye', but I say to you . . ."). Furthermore, the parable of the prodigal son shows that "God forgives without demanding satisfaction and payments in return."[66]

So why the cross if God forgives without requiring something in return (e.g., satisfaction, sacrifice)? According to Schwager, Jesus' death was necessary in part because there was no other way to penetrate the hard hearts of those who rejected his kingdom preaching. *The cross demonstrates that God continues to love even when faced with a violent rejection.* In submitting to human violence, Jesus shows how far he is willing to go to identify with sinners *and with the consequences of their sin.* Does God will Jesus' death on the cross? Schwager thinks not, at least not in the sense that Jesus' death is God's precondition for forgiveness, but only in the sense of God's agreeing to surrender to the scapegoating process.

---

[65]*The Girard Reader,* 187. In his more recent writings, Girard had come to acknowledge a more positive (e.g., nonviolent) sense of "sacrificial," which has to do with one's willingness to give of oneself to others and to God. See the epilogue to *The Girard Reader,* 262-88, esp. 272, 280. See also Milbank's criticism of Girard for too quickly identifying sacrificing with scapegoating in "Stories of Sacrifice," *Modern Theology* 12 (1996): 27-56.
[66]Schwager, *Must There be Scapegoats?* 206.

In a new twist on Irenaeus's soteriological principle—"the unassumed is the unhealed"—the cross marks the spot where *violence* is assumed, absorbed and taken up into God's own being. Girard believes that only Christ, the God-man, can save us from the economy of sacrifice, for only God is able to subject himself to violence, overcome it, and enable a new nonviolent way of life.[67] The "wonderful exchange" is not about God's killing Jesus in our place, but about God's reacting to violence *nonviolently*.

This postmodern view of the cross rejects the very logic of exchange (eye for an eye, tooth for a tooth) for another logic, a hyper-logic: "The victim . . . is more than victim: when God receives and approves the condemned Jesus and returns him to his judges through the preaching of the Church, he transcends the world of oppressor-oppressed relations to create a new humanity, capable of other kinds of relations."[68] The cross saves because through it God delivers us from the cycle of violence and victimization from which we could not save ourselves. More traditional theologians, like Henri Blocher, would presumably reply: "Wondrous indeed, for it is far from clear how Jesus' death can 'absorb' sin!"[69]

Not even every postmodern theologian is convinced. According to Milbank, Girard's theory is lacking, for it makes what is essentially only a negative gesture. Girard "does not really seem to think in terms of a positive, alternative practice, but only a negative refusal."[70] It is difficult to imagine what the kingdom of God could amount to other than the renunciation of violence. However, one can partially redeem Girard by linking his idea that Jesus is divine because he exposes the scapegoat mechanism to the more positive notion that the narratives of his life display the shape of a nonviolent practice.

We must also ask whether Girard's theory passes the acid test of any doctrine of atonement: Does it explain the *necessity* of Jesus' sufferings on the cross? It is not entirely clear why only God incarnate could expose the scapegoat mechanism (Girard does a good job at this him-

---

[67]Jesus is divine because only God could reveal the truth about the human condition: "The authentic knowledge about violence and all its works to be found in the Gospels cannot be the result of human action alone" (*The Girard Reader*, 193).

[68]Rowan Williams, *Resurrection* (New York: Pilgrim, 1982), 89.

[69]Blocher's incredulous response ("The Sacrifice of Jesus Christ," 31) is actually directed against the authors of *Atonement Today*, but it applies just as well here too.

[70]Milbank, *Theology and Social Theory*, 395.

self!). Girard's answer appears to be that only God, who made human beings, can free them from what would otherwise be a necessary, vicious cycle of vengeance and violence. According to Schwager, Jesus literally bears away the violence sinners direct to God and to one another: "Jesus *had* to die because only in that way could human beings transfer their hatred of God to the Son of God and their hatred of their fellow human beings to the Son of Man."[71] The cross enables a kind of community catharsis—and, more importantly, a new kind of community. Still, Placher rightly wonders whether Girard's account provides sinners with the forgiveness they really need. Is salvation simply a matter of the cessation of scapegoating? Will the problem of guilt (not to mention the problem of bondage) really go away once the scapegoat mechanism has been exposed?[72] I think not.

Gifts: Redemption Within the Bounds of Reason Alone?

Paul's thought that God "did not spare his own Son but gave him up for us all" (Rom 8:31) points to a certain convergence between sacrificing and giving. The gospel is all about God's giving. The drama of redemption begins when God gives his word to Abraham in the form an unconditional promise: "I will make of you a great nation and I will bless you; and I will make your name great . . . and all the peoples on earth will be blessed through you" (Gen 11:2-3). The covenant of grace begins with God *giving* his word. And it reaches its apex with God giving his Word, his only begotten Son, in fulfillment of his earlier word. The atonement ultimately concerns God's self-giving. But can a gift be given, or is there an "economy" of giving whereby one gives in order to receive something back?

Milbank: ecclesiology as first theology. John Milbank contends that a postmodern theology is a matter of "explicating Christian practice."[73] Theology articulates the "logic" inherent in the new communal way of life, the church. Milbank argues that the logic that undergirds church practices is wholly "other" than the morality that undergirds modern secular societies. Morality is a matter of managing and con-

---

[71]Schwager, *Must There be Scapegoats?* 242, n. 28.
[72]See Placher, "Christ Takes Our Place," 9.
[73]Milbank, "Postmodern Critical Augustinianism: A Short *Summa* in Forty-Two Responses to Unasked Questions," in *The Postmodern God: A Theological Reader*, ed. Graham Ward (Oxford: Blackwell, 1997), 267.

straining the violence that accompanies the struggle for survival in a world where goods are scarce. Christianity, on the other hand, emphasizes the charitable giving that flows from the plenitude of God's good creation. Whereas morality is a matter of duty, gifts that are duties are not genuine gifts at all. Morality works with a logic of equivalence; the true gift is always extravagant, in the sense of exceeding what is strictly required.

In Milbank's postmodern variation on Augustinianism, Christianity is unique—and true—because of the place it accords the practices of giving and forgiving. Jesus' death is foundational, in Milbank's view, because it enables the practice of forgiveness, a practice that is ineffably beautiful. The crucified Jesus who says, "Father forgive them," is a perfect and powerful metaphor for this new nonviolent practice. The beauty of this practice forms part of Milbank's apology for its truth.

Milbank suggests that the gospel narratives may be read, not as the story of Jesus, "but as the story of the (re)foundation of a new city," of a new politics and new communal practices befitting the city of God.[74] Jesus is the founder of this new city, the first of many citizens. Jesus enables his disciples to do everything he did: cast out demons, heal the sick, suffer, and, most distinctly, forgive sins. Milbank identifies this latter empowerment to forgive with "a continuing ability to make atonement."[75] Atonement *is* "the radical newness of the practice of the gospel, as over against the tolerated violence of all other human practices."[76]

Who do we say that Jesus is? Milbank argues that one's personal identity, who one "really" is, resides in the effect an individual has on others.[77] Jesus' effect on his followers was to found a new practice. Jesus' death is efficacious, not because it satisfies God (which Milbank thinks unnecessary), but "because it is the *inauguration* of the 'political' practice of forgiveness. . . . The practice is *itself* continuing atonement."[78] However, as Frederick Christian Bauerschmidt has recently maintained, Milbank's emphasis on ecclesial practices risks losing the particularity and uniqueness of the person and work of Jesus Christ. Milbank's gospel is not about the ascriptive subject Jesus of Nazareth,

---

[74]Milbank, "The Name of Jesus," *The Word Made Strange*, 150.
[75]Ibid., 151.
[76]Ibid., 162.
[77]This is the thesis of Milbank's "The Force of Identity," in *The Word Made Strange*, 164-218.
[78]Milbank, "The Name of Jesus," 161.

but about the origin and shape of a community form of life.[79] In Witt-
gensteinian terms: the name "Jesus" is simply part of the language
game associated with the form of life called "church." Jesus has no content for Milbank except that of a norm for the Christian practice of forgiveness. As Bauerschmidt trenchantly observes, this shift of subject
matter of the gospel away from Jesus onto the church "burdens the
church with a load it cannot bear."[80]

Derrida: the aporia of the gift. Derrida is well aware of the theological importance of the idea of the gift, linked as it is to forgiveness, salvation and grace.[81] Yet he is unsure that such a thing exists. Can a gift
be truly given? It would seem not, for the moment a gift, however generous, is given, its gift-like character is nullified. The conditions that
make the gift possible also make it impossible. Gifts enter a circle of exchange; it is difficult to expunge the expectation of getting something
in return, or the sense of obligation to someone in return: "It is reintro-
duced into the circle of an exchange and destroyed as a gift."[82] As soon
as we give something to someone, we put that person in our debt, thus
taking, not giving. The gift disappears in a web of calculation, interest
and measure. Such is the aporia of the gift, according to Derrida. It cannot be given without creating an economy of *debt.*

An "economy"—a system of calculation and exchange—denotes
the regulations that govern commercial, social, even theological exchanges, exchanges that destroy the gift. Derrida confesses that he
cannot believe in a God who insists that humans have to pay off an
infinite debt with an infinitely valuable gift of blood. A true gift does
not incur a further debt but forgives it. Derrida forces us to ask the
question: Is an economy of *grace* a contradiction in terms? Can God
ever make a gracious provision? Derrida finds the story of Abraham's
sacrifice of Isaac both fascinating and disturbing in this regard. Abraham, says Derrida, was willing to sacrifice economy; he was willing
to give death to his own son without any hope of return. In the end,
of course, it is God who provides the sacrificial lamb (Gen 22:13-14).

---

[79]Frederick Christian Bauerschmidt, "The Word Made Speculative?" *Modern Theology* (1999):
424.

[80]Ibid., 162.

[81]See Derrida, *On Cosmoplitanism and Forgiveness* (London: Routledge, 2001).

[82]Derrida, "On the Gift: A Discussion between Jacques Derrida and Jean-Luc Marion," in *God,
the Gift, and Postmodernism,* ed. John D. Caputo and Michael J. Scanlon (Bloomington: Indiana University Press, 1999), 59.

Yet even God's gracious provision is not exempt from the stubborn logic of exchange: in return for his grace, God expects Abraham's obedience.

Derrida concludes that the gift as such cannot appear without losing its character as a gift. Only an "expenditure without reserve," a giving that expects no reciprocity, a giving that forgets a gift has been given, would seem to measure up to Derrida's requirements for a true giving. Like Girard, Derrida would doubtless point to the ways in which Christian theology has inscribed the cross into an economy of exchange. However, he allows for the possibility that we can *think* what we cannot know. The atonement thus becomes one more piece of apophatic theology, about which the only thing that can be said is what it is *not*.[83]

Marion: the appearance of the gift. Jean-Luc Marion is perhaps the leading postmodern theologian of the gift. He wishes to think God outside both the economy of being (ontology) and the economy of exchange and to focus instead on God's self-giving in revelation and in reconciliation. The discussion between Marion, a Roman Catholic, and Derrida, a lapsed Jew, has produced one of the most interesting dialogues on the nature of postmodern theology.[84] Marion finds an exception to Derrida's analysis, where the gift is never given, in the notion of *a gift that gives itself.*

Marion (along with many postmoderns) views modernity as the epoch of the knowing subject. In modernity, the focus is on determining the limits of the knowable: the possible, what may appear in consciousness—"presence."[85] Marion, by contrast, wants to let things themselves determine what is or is not possible. He therefore contrasts "intention," that is, the mind's ability to take aim and grasp, with "intuition," where the emphasis is on what is *given* to thought. Marion is unwilling to accord to reason (subjectivity) the privilege of determin-

---

[83]Caputo rightly notes that in deconstruction, justice and gift have the same "impossible" structure. See *Deconstruction in a Nutshell*, 140. According to Caputo, Derrida's affirmation of the impossibility of justice, or the gift of forgiveness, is a gesture, not of nihilistic despair, but of faith: the desire for something *other* than what obtains in the present world order. Derrida's faith is messianic in structure—he is waiting for something that is always "to come" but never here.

[84]Derrida and Marion, "On the Gift," in *God, the Gift, and Postmodernism*, 54-78.

[85]Marion distinguishes presence—what metaphysics studies with human reason—from givenness—what appears in consciousness whether we intended it or not.

ing the boundaries of what is or is not possible.[86] In particular, we must not let the knowledge of God be determined by the limits of what is possible for human reason to know.

In order fully to account for what is in human experience, Marion believes that we must attend not only to the phenomena that our subjectivity lets in, but also to how certain phenomena *give* themselves to us. Some phenomena cannot be fully intended: one cannot exhaust the phenomenon that is Paris even after many visits. Similarly, we cannot exhaust the phenomenon of God even after many systematic theologies. In brief, we must abandon the attempt to comprehend, much less to master, the divine. In the first place, God can only be known if he *gives* himself to be known.[87] But second, what he gives is a *saturated* phenomenon, so overflowing in meaning as to be in excess of any intention. "Impossibility" for Marion carries connotations, not of emptiness, but of fullness.

For Marion, the gift is a saturated or "excessive" phenomenon that must not be forced to fit into human conceptual economies. It is possible to think about the gift in terms other than a system of exchange. The goal is to describe pure givenness without having to refer to its constituent elements: the giver, the objectivity of the gift and the recipient. For example, we can suspend the giver by thinking of an anonymous gift. We can resist identifying the gift with a material object by thinking of phenomena such as marriage, where the gift is not the ring, but the promise it signifies. Finally, we can think about the gift without thinking about the recipient; we can think about someone's giving an unconditional gift.

It follows that we can describe gifts as such, and not simply the causes that lead to them or the consequences that follow. We can, therefore, speak of gifts outside of an economy of exchange. They are outside in the sense that they can neither be *deduced* nor *explained* in terms of some system of exchange. *Duty and debt may indeed be rational, but giving gifts without reserve exceeds the limits of reason alone.* We lack the appropriate concepts for fully comprehending a gift. For we give gen-

---

[86]The background to this discussion lies in the technical field of phenomenology. Marion is a hyper-phenomenologist: where philosophers associate "givenness" with the passivity of intuition (what appears to consciousness), Marion goes further and speaks of *gift*.

[87]This was the thesis of Marion's *God Without Being* (Chicago: University of Chicago Press, 1991), in which he characterizes divine revelation by its *excess of intuition*.

uine gifts, not out of a sense of indebtedness, which can be calculated, but out of love, which admits of no calculation. There is conceptual excess in the phenomenon of the gift that prevents it from being fully caught in our theoretical nets: "The incomprehensible, the excess, the impossible, are part and parcel of our experience."[88] We fail to comprehend the gift of Jesus' death, not because it has not been given, but because it exceeds our expectations, conceptual and otherwise. The atonement is the name, not of a logical aporia, but of the mystery of divine grace.

Ricoeur: an economy of gift? For Ricoeur, the real nature of God's gift only appears when one gets past the Bible's mythical elements and recovers its symbolic meaning. Ricoeur especially wants us to get beyond the "moral vision," together with its economy of retribution and logic of equivalence, in order to perceive the "eschatological vision," with its economy of restoration and its logic of extravagant excess. The moral vision is guilty, Ricoeur thinks, of an overly literalistic reading. The false meaning must die in order for the true meaning to live. It is only by interpreting within the old economy of law, where the loss of an eye demands exact compensation (another eye), that we arrive at the notion of penal substitution theory of atonement. Ricoeur challenges us to preserve the dynamism of Scripture's symbolic images instead of reducing them all to a single (legal or moral) concept.

God's covenant with Israel is not merely an abstract code; it is a concrete promise of love and faithfulness. The marriage metaphor for God's relationship to Israel exceeds the less personal image of the magistrate: "The juridical conceptual system has never exhausted the meaning of the Covenant."[89] The covenant, one might say, is *gift* before it is *law*. Ricoeur places great emphasis on the covenant context of the wrath of God. In the context of the covenant, the death of Christ satisfies, not merely an impersonal demand for justice, but the very personal demand for restoration of *right covenant relation*.[90] Ricoeur sug-

---

[88]Marion, "On the Gift," 75.

[89]Ricoeur, *Conflict of Interpretations*, 369.

[90]It is important not to exaggerate the disjunction between the "legal" and the "personal." Indeed, as Blocher rightly points out, the marriage metaphor itself conveys both aspects: "There is nothing more personal than in-law relationships" ("Sacrifice of Jesus," 32). In the case of marriage, it is hard to say which has priority: gift (the personal) or law (the formal ratification). In short, a nonreductive orthodoxy will resist investing too heavily in antinomies such as the legal versus the relational.

gests that sin, insofar as it entails one's alienation from the community
and the covenant alike, is its own punishment.

The symbolic richness of the narratives that recount Jesus' death exceeds the ability of concepts to explain the cross in a single explanatory
logic without remainder. What we know is that Jesus' death reconciles
sinners to God *in spite of* what sinners do to Jesus. To consider what
God does for us in Jesus' death is thus to break out of the strict logic of
equivalence in order to confess *how much more* (Rom 5:17). This Pauline
thought marks for Ricoeur the decisive break with the economy of law,
together with its system of exchange, where guilt generates equivalent
punishment. "For the wages of sin is death, but the gift of God is eternal life in Christ Jesus our Lord" (Rom 6:23). There is now a justification apart from the economy of law, a gift (righteousness) that exceeds—*explodes*—the old economy of law. "The logic of punishment
was a logic of equivalence (the wages of sin is death); the logic of grace
is a logic of surplus and excess."[91] In Ricoeur's view, the doctrine of
atonement belongs, not in an economy of crime and punishment, but
in a hyper-economy of gift and grace.

Could it be that, given the eschatological nature of God's act in Jesus
Christ, the reconciling effect of the cross might not be intelligible in *any*
explanatory economy? Doctrines of the atonement must be careful not
to explain the logic of salvation too exhaustively, for nothing forced
God to enter human history; there is no causal explanation for grace. It
is a gift—something that did not have to be, something than which
nothing better can be thought.[92] It nevertheless remains legitimate to
ask: Why just *this* gift? Though God did not have to give his Son, he
did, and we can fully appreciate what God has done only when we
know why the gift was necessary and how the gift is "for us."

God's Gift of Jesus' Death "for" Us: A Constructive Proposal
The operative concept in postmodern theological understandings of
the atonement is *excess*, not exchange. The death of Jesus *exceeds* our attempts to explain it. Postmodern treatments of the cross are thus "*hy-*

[91]Ricoeur, *Conflict of Interpretations*, 375.
[92]Derrida's commentary of Jesus' teaching in Matthew 5:44-46 is revealing. He notes that the
    exhortation to "love your enemies" is accompanied by a reference to two types of wages:
    one of retribution of equal exchange, the other which is excessive in relation to the original
    outlay, a *love* without reserve. See *The Gift of Death*, 150-56.

per-economic." They seek to articulate the saving significance of Jesus' death in a way that goes beyond explanatory economies and propositional truths.[93] *Prepositions* are another matter. Interestingly, the one NT word used more than any other to express the significance of Christ's death is *hyper*, the Greek word for "on behalf of," or simply "for." The term occurs in Paul's epistles,[94] John's Gospel and epistles,[95] 1 Peter 2:21, and the book of Hebrews.[96]

"Christ died for us" (Rom 5:8). John Calvin once remarked that if there is anything in religion worth knowing, it is the conditions under which sinners may obtain forgiveness.[97] We need a way to think nonreductively about the cross. I therefore propose to reflect on Jesus' death in terms of guilt, goats and gifts *together*. I take my lead from Jesus' own thinking about his impending death. Jesus too explained his death by means of the preposition *hyper*. He did it at the table, during supper: "This is my body given for *(hyper)* you" (Lk 22:19). Jesus was a master of excessive metaphors long before postmodernity.

Jesus gave his disciples the bread and wine in the context of the Passover feast. His reference to a "covenant" (Mk 14:24) recalls God's earlier deliverance of Israel from the bondage of Egypt. N. T. Wright has recently suggested that Jesus' message of forgiveness, in the context of first-century Palestine, carried the connotation "return from exile," an idea that included the hope of covenant renewal.[98] The exile, of course, was Israel's punishment for covenant disobedience. As such it had both penal and interpersonal implications: Israel's exile was a humiliating obstacle to the fulfillment of the covenant promise of life in God's presence.

There is another metaphor, and hence another layer of theological significance, that we must now add to the notion that Jesus' body has been broken "for us." It pertains to Jesus' claim that his body is a "temple" (Jn 2:19-22). Jesus understood his own person and work to be a re-

---

[93]A number of its critics associate propositionalist theology—that is, the attempt to reduce the truths of biblical revelation to universally true propositions—with modernity. See Henry J. Knight III, *A Future for Truth: Evangelical Theology in a Postmodern World* (Nashville: Abingdon, 1997), chap. 5, "The Inadequacies of Propositionalism."
[94]Romans 5:8; 14:15; 1 Corinthians 11:24; 15:3; Galatians 2:20; 1 Thessalonians 5:10.
[95]John 10:11, 15; 11:50-51; 15:13; 18:14; 1 John 3:16.
[96]Hebrews 2:9; 9:24; 10:12.
[97]Calvin, *Institutes* 3.4.2.
[98]Wright, *Jesus and the Victory of God*, 268-70, 577.

placement—or rather, fulfillment—of everything that Israel's temple had been and done.[99] Jesus' words during the Last Supper suggest that he substituted his own person and work for the temple and its sacrificial system: "This is my blood of the covenant, which is poured out for many" (Mk 14:24). Conversely, his cleansing of the temple was a judgment on the futility of ritual sacrifices.[100] What Jesus is claiming in the Last Supper is that his broken body and shed blood are the place where sin is dealt with (as it was in the temple on the Day of Atonement), making possible life in the presence of God. Both Paul and John allude to the mercy seat when they refer to Jesus' death as a *hilasterion* for our sins (Roms 3:25; 1 Jn 2:2; 4:10).

The shed blood is a sign that God has proved this covenant faithfulness precisely by undergoing the sanctions, legal and relational, for covenant disobedience.[101] Furthermore, Jesus' death laid the foundation for the people of God to become God's temple themselves. The stone that the builders rejected (Jesus on the cross) has become the cornerstone for a "spiritual house" (1 Pet 2:5). Jesus' death thus exceeds the levitical provisions for atonement. Not only does Jesus' death make possible a return from exile (the forgiveness of sins), but the cross of Christ somehow becomes the cornerstone for a new, living temple in which the Spirit of God dwells "bodily" (in the church as the body of Christ).

Jesus employs yet another OT metaphor when he refers to his death in terms of the great saving event of Israel's history: the exodus. In Luke 9:31 Jesus speaks of his death as his "departure" (*exodus*) which was to be accomplished in Jerusalem.[102] This exodus, like the earlier one, is God's mighty saving work. But what does Jesus' exodus accomplish? To what new Promised Land does it lead us? It leads, I submit, to the kingdom of God: to the reign of God in human hearts. Hence my thesis: the saving significance of Christ's death consists in

---

[99]Bruce D. Chilton, *The Temple of Jesus: His Sacrificial Program Within a Cultural History of Sacrifice* (University Park: Pennsylvania State University Press, 1992).

[100]Wright, *Jesus and the Victory of God*, 416-17.

[101]Again, the point is that the experience of exile was both penal (a punishment) and relational (a separation).

[102]Wright claims that the eschatological thrust of Jesus' teaching concerned the "new exodus" that was being fulfilled in Jesus' person and work (*Jesus and the Victory of God*, 243). However, Wright does not think that Jesus had a worked-out atonement theory (592). Green and Baker note the significance of exodus images in 1 Peter 1:14-20, where Jesus' blood is said to "deliver" from the bondage of sin (*Recovering the Scandal*, 84).

making possible God's gift of the Holy Spirit. The "wonderful exchange" is thus not economic but thoroughly eschatological: *Jesus gives his body and blood for us, and in return we receive his Spirit, the operative principle of the new covenant and of the new age.* Jesus says as much at the Last Supper: "It is for your good that I am going away. Unless I go away, the Counselor will not come to you" (Jn 16:7). Jesus' death both creates and cleanses a new temple, the people of God: "Don't you know that you yourselves are God's temple and that God's Spirit lives in you?" (1 Cor 3:16).

Jesus' seminal interpretation of his own death enables us to understand its saving significance as the inaugurating event of a newer and more wonderful covenant. Jesus' death on the cross is a new exodus, a new Passover supper, a new return from exile, an entry into a new kind of promised land, a building of a new and better temple. God reconciles the world to himself by providing his own Son as a substitute for the exile that should be ours. Jesus is God's gift, the goat that bears our guilt—the covenant curse, separation from the promises of God—who in doing so enables our covenant restoration. *Jesus' death on the cross is at once an exodus and an exile, the condition of the possibility of our entry to the promised land of the Holy Spirit.* The narrator of the Fourth Gospel hints at the benefits of Jesus' death when he observes the flow of blood and water from Jesus' pierced side. The sacrificial shedding of blood makes possible the forgiveness of sins; the flow of water, read in conjunction with John 4:10; 7:37-39, is a clear reference to the vivifying effects of the gift of the Spirit, which makes possible new life.[103]

Augustine believed that the Christian life would be an impossibility if it were not for the Gift, his favorite name of the Holy Spirit as God's self-donation.[104] Here the postmodern critique of "economic exchange" hits the mark. For as we learn from Acts 8:20, when Simon offered Peter and John money in order to receive the Holy Spirit, one can-

---

[103]For a fuller development of this point, see my "Body-piercing, the Natural Sense, and the Task of Theological Interpretation: A Hermeneutical Homily on John 19:34," *Ex Auditu* (2001): 1-29.

[104]*The Trinity*, 15.19.33-36. Like Augustine, though building on the work of Douglas Meeks, Stephen Webb combines the two analyses of the gift—as exchange and as excess—in a trinitarian manner in order to speak of "God the Giver," "God the Given," and "God the Giving." See Douglas Meeks, *God the Economist* (Philadelphia: Fortress, 1989) and Stephen Webb, *The Gifting God: A Trinitarian Theology of Excess* (Oxford: Oxford University Press, 1996).

not obtain the gift of God with money. No, the gift is made possible only by Jesus' death: Jesus gave up his spirit (Matt 2:50) in order to give us the Spirit. Yet the gift of the Spirit is of such a nature that those who receive it do not feel themselves to be under an obligation. Those who have received the Spirit give back to God, not because they have to, but because they want to.

Jesus' death on the cross "for us" is the means by which God gives and forgives. Nicholas Lash is right to speak of God's "laborious dona-tion of the Spirit of the Crucified through human hearts and prac-tices."[105] Yet the cross itself is God's gift too; "God has provided" for the children of Abraham as he had for Abraham (Gen 22:13-14). *Must* a gift be given? No. The cross is the expression of God's free love. The church commemorates this gift of Jesus' death by celebrating a metaphorical meal, the Lord's Supper: "the gifts of God for the people of God."

Jesus' death is ultimately the result of a divinely initiated reconciling act that deals with sin by forgiving it (thus setting aside the old econ-omy of moral law) and by establishing a new *hyper-economy* of cove-nant love. In this triune economy, Father, Son and Spirit give without reserve out of the abundance of their trinitarian life and love. Perhaps this is the lesson of the atonement in postmodernity: that the triune God is *excessive,* so much so that God shares his overflowing love with creatures who are not God: "God has poured out his love into our hearts by the Holy Spirit, whom he has given us" (Rom 5:5).

The gift of the promised Spirit, made possible by Jesus' horrific exo-dus, is in turn the indispensable condition for the inauguration of the practices of forgiving and peace-keeping that are to be distinctive of the church. We are now in a position to see what was lacking in Gi-rard's, and to some extent in Milbank's, account of the cross. What those accounts lack is an explicit acknowledgment of how the death of Jesus inaugurates these practices by providing the condition for the new coming of the Holy Spirit, and hence the condition for the forming of a new covenant people. Jesus' death saves because it enables a new *objective* situation, namely, the end of exile and the construction of a new kind of temple, indwelt by God's own Spirit. The cross saves, not by bequeathing an example, but by bequeathing to the church the same

---

[105]Nicholas Lash, *Believing Three Ways in One God* (Notre Dame: University of Notre Dame, 1992), p. 116.

power that enabled Jesus to lay down his own life for others: the Spirit of self-giving love.

Conclusion: "Fragments" of the Cross

The postmodern challenge requires us to develop a nonreductive doctrine of atonement that perceives the saving significance of Jesus' death in terms other than this-worldly economies of exchange. The gift of Jesus' death—his goat-like exile into the wilderness of the grave where he bore the covenant curse on our behalf—is itself excessive. No economic or external constraint coerced God to give himself for us. No economy mandates that God return our evil with a greater good.

David Tracy's metaphor for the spiritual and intellectual situation of our time is apt: fragments. We cannot even speak of postmodernism in the singular, only of postmodernities. Tracy sees the cross as a nonreductive, saturated phenomenon that refuses to be assimilated by medieval or modern theories alike. With other postmoderns, Tracy rejects all totalizing systems that, in their pride, claim to explain exhaustively without remainder; instead, we must content ourselves with "fragments." These fragments are so "saturated" with infinity, however, that they bear our hope simply by being "excessive."[106] To the extent that postmodernity reminds us to do justice to diverse biblical metaphors, it makes a contribution.

What *can* we ultimately affirm about the atonement in the light of postmodernity? Does God renounce or fulfill his righteous indignation on the cross of Christ? And what practical implications follow from one's decision as to how to view (*theoria*) the cross? Let me make three concluding observations:

1. *The cross is simultaneously the definitive critique of religion and the enabling condition of true spirituality.* One lesson we can take from postmodernity is not to think too highly of theory. A doctrine of atonement that pretends to explain fully the saving significance of Jesus' death is probably guilty of preferring the clarity of unifying concepts to the messiness of multiple metaphors. Furthermore, some atonement theories may, ironically, partake more of what Luther called the "theology of glory"—a trust in human reason to find out

---

[106]David Tracy, "Fragments: the Spiritual Situation of Our Times" in *God, the Gift, and Postmodernism*, 171.

the ways of God—than they do the "theology of the cross." The cross represents a powerful critique of attempts to "explain" God as well as attempts to make oneself right before God.

The cross makes possible right covenantal relations by removing the covenant sanction and by rendering the eschatological gift of the Holy Spirit. If the gift God gives in the atonement is ultimately himself (the Spirit), then the ensuing practice will be that in which the Spirit, through us, gives back gratitude, praise and obedience to God. To practice the doctrine of atonement is to offer oneself back to the Creator and Redeemer, to the glory of God.[107] According to Richard Mouw, the cross is the condition for a new kind of power, "the power of reconciling love: 'you will receive power,' [Jesus] says to his disciples . . .'when the Holy Spirit has come upon you' (Acts 1:8)."[108] Finally, practicing atonement means learning to cultivate the "craft" of forgiving others as we have been forgiven.[109]

2. *The cross is the power of God's love to salvation.* The cross stands at the center of the mystery of salvation. The atonement refers to the event where God's self-giving and forgiving on behalf of sinners is taken to the limit and beyond. *For through the death of Jesus, God gives himself—Father, Son and Spirit—to sinners.* To give oneself—to pour oneself out for others, to forgive—is the epitome of self-sacrificial love.[110] This total pouring out does not exhaust God's life, but is rather the means by which human sinners come to *share* it. In this one case, at least, we must say that a gift can and *has* been given. The proclamation of the gospel demands no less.

God's love leads, not to a bland tolerance of sin and evil, but to his triumph over them.[111] It is precisely because God is love that he op-

---

[107]So Gunton: "Sacrifice *means* the offering of the perfected creation back in praise to God" ("The Sacrifice and the Sacrifices," 226).

[108]Mouw, "Violence and the Atonement", 17.

[109]See Jones, *Embodying Forgiveness*, chap. 7, on the "craft" of forgiveness.

[110]Jesus' sacrificial death "is the expression and outworking of the inner-Trinitarian relations of giving and receiving" (Gunton, "The Sacrifice and the Sacrifices," 221).

[111]Jesus' suffering and shed blood are redemptive because they represent the total God-forsakenness (divine wrath, death, perhaps even hell) that he bore in our place. Jesus bore it all: human hatred, the accusations of the Satan, forsakenness by God. As Mouw helpfully observes, this understanding of atonement has nothing to do with commending suffering, for Jesus' suffering—the experience of being totally abandoned by God—cannot be imitated ("Violence and Atonement," 16). The gift of Jesus' death is that he actively bore the guilt—endured it, and like the scapegoat in Leviticus, bore it away.

poses sin and evil, for these are ultimately diseases that corrupt a good creation. In the final analysis, what exceeds the confines of theory is nothing less than the searing white heat of God's holy love: "The pain that God endures on the cross is the price love pays for taking sin seriously but refusing to stop loving."[112] John Stott rightly observes that this was the only way that God could both save us and satisfy himself simultaneously, hence the key phrase "divine self-satisfaction through divine self-substitution."[113] Substitution is the principle that best corresponds to the preposition (*hyper*) God pours himself out for us, not in an economic exchange, but in an excess of justice and love.[114]

3. *The cross is the condition of an exceedingly great covenantal blessing.* The supreme covenant blessing made to Israel was life with God. Sin is the complication that disqualifies and prevents us from enjoying this covenant blessing. How then can God realize his covenant promise? The cross marks the spot where this dramatic tension plays, or rather pours, itself out. What the doctrine of the atonement attempts haltingly to articulate is the equal ultimacy of God's love and God's light (justice, holiness). On the cross neither mercy nor justice loses out; the cross is rather their mutual fulfillment. It is precisely for this reason that theories of atonement must resist explanations that reduce the significance of Jesus' death *either* to unconditional mercy *or* to uncompromising justice.

The death of Jesus represents both the excess that is constitutive of the gift (love), and the excess that is constitutive of one's ethical duty toward another (justice, as understood by postmoderns). God's reconciling act in the death of Christ was "excessive." In loving his enemies (Rom 5:10), God brings his covenant partner to *justice*, not simply retribution. The apostle Paul, though no postmodern, rightly grasped the excessive nature of the new covenant: "how much more" (Rom 5:9). God did not merely compensate for human sin; he did more. He did not simply make up sin's deficit; he de-

---

[112]Placher, "Christ Takes Our Place," 17.
[113]Stott, *Essentials of Evangelical Theology,* 166.
[114]According to Stott, "the substitutionary principle is the reality at the heart of all four models" (*Cross of Christ*, 202-3). This is not to reduce atonement to substitution, but it is to make substitution a necessary, if not sufficient, condition for understanding the saving significance of Jesus' death.

stroyed it. The New Testament, of course, knows this "excess" by its proper covenantal name: *grace*. The atonement is about an exchange, but one that is not strictly economic. Like the laborers in the parable of the vineyard, we receive more—how much more!—than we are due (Lk 20:1-16). The economy of covenantal grace is not exhausted by the logic of penal substitution even though the latter has a legitimate place.

We struggle to understand adequately, yet we are fed the answer every Lord's Day when we take Communion. Postmoderns or not, we gather around the Lord's Table as we have been instructed ("Do this in remembrance of me"), awaiting the elements that signify more than our starving theories. Then, like the five thousand, we discover that after our centuries-long banquet of atonement theology, there are still more fragments of the cross left over. As we seek to understand the atonement in postmodernity or at any other time, let us fill our baskets and keep the feast.

PART III

THE ATONEMENT IN THE LIFE OF THE CHRISTIAN AND THE CHURCH

Frank A. James III

I f the atoning death of Christ is merely an intellectual proposition, if it thrives in heads and not hearts, if it is merely a part of one's theological ancestry but bears no direct relationship to the living of life, then what good is it really? The atonement, if it is as vital as Christians say, must touch the everyday lives of Christians. This is the infamous and important "so what?" question—a question that has sometimes proved elusive for theologians.

At its core, the atonement is profoundly practical. Indeed, theological reflection on the cross was born originally from the existential and practical attempt to understand what Christ's death means *pro nobis* (for us). The cross was not a mere theoretical construct, nor was it ever intended to be. In answer to the "so what?" question, Christians believe that at the cross Christ fulfilled the two greatest commandments given to his people for the living of their lives—to love God, and to love their neighbors. In so doing, Christ fulfilled the law and brought together heaven and earth, bridging the chasm between the holy God and sinful man. This is a life-transforming truth.

The substitutionary atoning death of Christ is a concept that has certainly trickled down to the church pews. Evangelicals, if they understand little else, do understand that Jesus died on the cross in the place of sinners. The spiritual, emotional and practical repercussions of Christ's substitution on the cross for undeserving sinners are manifold. This cosmic self-sacrifice satisfies something very deep within the souls of the redeemed. It is a powerful declaration that sin and death have been defeated once and for all; it generates an exultant joy that one's salvation has been secured; and finally, it excites in the believer a zest for a new kind of life—a life imbued with grace and selflessness. The reality of knowing one's sins have been forgiven is so profoundly significant that anyone who has even a glimmer of understanding of the cross will never be the same again.

The Practical Theology Essays

Because previous treatments of the atonement have tended to ignore the practical implications, it is important to develop this side of the doctrine. Broadly, the atonement, if it is as important as we assert, should have something to say to the individual Christian and to the whole of the Christian life. And if the atonement is key to a vital Christianity, it should be reflected in the preaching and ministry of the church. In this section, two of the best-known evangelical theologians today, J. I. Packer and Sinclair Ferguson, address the practical outworking of the atonement in both the Christian life and worship.

J. I. Packer stresses the "cross-centeredness" of the Christian life and turns to Paul's letter to the Galatians as a model. This letter, says Packer, reminds us that the atonement is foundational for the radically new life in Christ. At its most basic level, Christ's atoning death frees one *from* a life dominated by the power of sin and *for* a life of holiness. Without the atonement, argues Packer, there is no Christian life at all. As he reflects on this "breathtakingly wonderful" doctrine, he at the same time warns against defining the atonement in terms of a single theory, yet he underscores penal substitution as the "fundamental category" for a proper understanding of the cross. But there is more. For Packer, the taproot of salvation is our union with Christ wherein there is both forgiveness and justification but also transformation through the regeneration and indwelling of the Holy Spirit. Finally, Packer explores the relationship between the atonement and the Christian virtues of faith, hope and love. In his essay, Packer manifests his own virtuous triad of winsomeness, theological acumen and biblical fidelity.

If the cross has real value in the realm of time and space, it must have significance for the pulpit and the pastor who stands in it. The preacher of God's Word bears an awesome, even fearful responsibility to declare and explain the atoning work of Christ on the cross. But is it enough merely to declare it and explain it? Does the cross affect not only "what" but "how" the pastor is to preach? And what difference does the atonement make for the people in the pews? If one knows oneself to have been forgiven because Christ took their sins upon himself, does it make a difference in how one listens to the sermon? Following the lead of the apostle Paul, *Sinclair Ferguson* argues there is, indeed, "power" in preaching "Christ crucified" (1 Cor 1:18, 23-24).

Regarding what he calls the "central theme in all evangelical preaching," Ferguson asserts that the "scandal of the late-twentieth- and early-twenty-first-century pulpit [is] the veiling of the cross." Ferguson turns to 2 Corinthians as a model for preaching "Christ and him crucified" (2 Cor 2:14—7:4). This Pauline model avoids the pitfall, all too common among evangelical preachers, of preaching a wrathful Father who is persuaded to have mercy by a loving Son. Properly preached, the atonement, says Ferguson, is the "ultimate demonstration of the Father's love."

Ferguson not only examines the Pauline model but also engages in a piercing criticism of modern evangelical preaching. He fears that Schleiermachian subjectivism has seduced modern evangelicals so that they think they have preached the gospel when they invite sinners to be "born again." "Being 'born again' is not the gospel," Ferguson thunders. "It is the fruit of the gospel!" After reading these two essays, it is difficult to imagine that anyone would then say: "So what?"

The editors have taken the slightly unorthodox step of inviting our very orthodox honoree, Dr. Roger Nicole himself, to speak his mind on a topic that has been very close to his heart throughout his life and ministry. In a sense, we had no choice in the matter. Once the secret project had been sniffed out, it only made sense to solicit his words on this vital Christian doctrine. As the reader will see, Dr. Nicole has seized the opportunity to declare in no uncertain terms that substitution is "the linchpin of the doctrine of the atonement." When all is said and done, it is somehow fitting that Dr. Nicole have the last word.

the atonement in the Life of the christian

J. I. Packer

When we speak, as we do, of the professional life, or the academic life, the adjective is pinpointing one slice of human existence within the larger whole. But when we speak of the Christian life, the noun covers all of our existence—rational and relational, active, reactive, and passive—with all its aims, hopes, fears, joys, dreams, plans, powers, bonds and problems; and the adjective is saying that each part of it, always and everywhere, morning, noon and night, should be shaped by the realities of Christianity.

What are these realities? First come the facts set out in the Bible and in the mainstream creeds and confessions of Christian history: the holy, eternal and ubiquitous Trinity; the created nature of the world and of the human race within it; our need of salvation because of sin; the mediation of Jesus Christ, God incarnate, crucified Savior, risen, reigning and returning Lord; the action of the life-giving Holy Spirit, who illuminates and regenerates, who evokes and sustains responsive faith, hope and love, all directed Christward, who teaches, sanctifies, renews and transforms, who generates ministry and glorifies Christ to us and through us; the sovereignty of the Creator in providence and grace; the centrality for God and the godly of the church, universal and local, militant and triumphant; and endless glory as the Christian's personal prospect. Second comes the behavior that these beliefs call for: love, gratitude, adoration and obedience

410   THE GLORY OF THE ATONEMENT

to God; love, goodwill, care and service to others; self-denial and self-discipline in vivifying virtues, mortifying vices and cultivating Christlikeness; maintaining joy in God's gift of freedom, fulfillment, peace and hope while humbling oneself with the thought that this great and as yet only foretasted salvation is quite undeserved; and laboring to understand, evaluate and manage all life activities by the light of God's revealed word, within a frame of personal discipleship to the living Christ himself, whom one trusts as one's Savior, Lord and God, and before whom one lays everything in submission. In this all-embracing pattern of wisdom and worship, however, the central reference point must ever be the event that Roman Catholics call the redemption and Protestants call the atonement, and that the New Testament depicts as Christ's self-offering, blood-shedding, ransom, peacemaking, propitiation and penal substitution, on behalf of us sinners. This cross-centeredness, with its resultant cruciform perception of everything else, is modeled for us in Scripture and then confirmed to us by centuries of Christian life. It pervades the New Testament, but it is particularly clear in Paul's letter to the Galatians. On this for the moment we shall concentrate.

The Atonement and Galatians
Galatians is a very frank letter, the outflow of a very hot heart; and the pained passion that prompts Paul to let his hair down, so to speak, is precisely not piqued pride, as some have thought, but pastoral distress. Most students of Galatians see that Paul's argument expresses three evangelical concerns, all of which have been highlighted in recent years: (1) justification by faith apart from works as the heart of the gospel; (2) the union with and in Christ of believers of all racial and social stripes and of both genders as heirs together of God's covenant promise to Abraham and so as partakers of the Spirit, thus constituting God's new humanity; and (3) keeping in step with the Holy Spirit in terms of character as the test of one's Christian life. In systematic theological categories the first concern is soteriology, the second is ecclesiology and the third is pneumatology. But overarching, undergirding, triggering and enfolding all three is Paul's incessant anxiety lest his converts fail fully to grasp, enter or enjoy the new existence that is real for those who truly see and know the risen Christ of the cross. This is not always so clearly seen or so strongly stressed. It becomes evident, however, when Paul's

statements involving Christ's work of atonement are set out as a series.[1]

The atonement and the liberation Paul knew. "Grace to you and peace from God our Father and the Lord Jesus Christ, who gave himself for our sins to deliver us from the present evil age, according to the will of our God and Father, to whom be the glory forever and ever. Amen" (Gal 1:3-5).[2] Right at the start, having affirmed Jesus' resurrection, Paul describes the effect of his divinely planned death as rescuing us from our bondage and lostness in this sin-dominated, demon-ridden world[3] for that fellowship with God through adoption and the gift of the Spirit that is essential and integral to life in the world to come (call it heaven, if you wish) and to the freedom from slavery to sin that Christ bestows (Gal 5:1, 16). Atonement, says Paul, is thus foundational for entry into the new order.

The atonement and the new life Paul lived. "Through the law I died to the law, so that I might live to God. I have been crucified with Christ. It is no longer I who live, but Christ who lives in me. And the life I now live in the flesh I live by faith in the Son of God, who loved me and gave himself for me" (Gal 2:19-20). The measure ("gave himself") and the personal particularity ("for me") of the love of the atonement-maker for Paul, and by parity of reasoning for every other believer, is here made plain, and so is God's way of freeing us from the dominion of the death-dealing law that by nature all denizens of this fallen, evil world are under. What does God do? He exchanges our sin-serving existence for a Spirit-led existence by incorporating us, invisibly and intangibly, yet really and truly, into the space-time, trans-historical death and resurrection of our Savior, who now through his indwelling Spirit can truly be said to live in us and shape us as we live our new life in faith-fellowship with him. Atonement—Christ's dying for us—is thus foundational, says Paul, for entry upon the new life—Christ living in us—which is a life totally free from sin's penalty and significantly free from sin's power and ruling over us also.

Atonement and the proclamation Paul made. "O foolish Galatians! Who has bewitched you? It was before your eyes that Jesus Christ was

---

[1] I am following the order of their appearance in the letter. I gratefully acknowledge that John Stott (*The Cross of Christ* [Downers Grove, Ill.: InterVarsity Press, 1986], 339-50) suggested to me some of what follows.

[2] All citations are from the English Standard Version.

[3] See Galatians 4:3, 8, and commentaries.

publicly portrayed as crucified. Let me ask you only this: Did you receive the Spirit by works of the law or by hearing with faith?" (Gal 3:1-2). Theologically explained word-pictures parading the crucifixion of Christ and what it meant were central to Paul's preaching everywhere (cf. 1 Cor 1:23; 2:2), for Paul's aim was always to lead his hearers into the faith—the clear-headed, whole-hearted, full-scale commitment to the risen Lord—that would make new life in the Spirit a reality for them through their union with the Christ whom they were now trusting. The focus of that sort of faith, for Paul, was Christ's sin-bearing death, undergone at the Father's will and out of love, as we have seen. This is why the cross, "with all its shame, with all its grace" as the hymn puts it, was ever at the heart of Paul's message in Galatia as everywhere else. Atonement is thus fundamental, says Paul, for the faith that is the desired outcome of all properly presented gospel preaching.

Atonement and the blessing Paul announced. "Christ redeemed us from the curse of the law by becoming a curse for us—for it is written, 'Cursed is everyone who is hanged on a tree'—so that in Christ Jesus the blessing of Abraham might come to the Gentiles, so that we might receive the promised Spirit through faith" (Gal 3:13-14). Here Paul states that in our receiving through faith God's gifts of justification (Gal 3:6-9) and the Spirit (Gal 3:14; 4:6), on the basis of Christ's having received as our stand-in at the cross God's sentence of rejection and death (the curse of the law), God fulfills his gracious promise to Abraham (Gen 12:2-3). This promise of blessing now comes true for both Jewish believers (Abraham's lineal seed) and non-Jewish believers (Abraham's spiritual seed). Paul sees God's covenant promises to Abraham and Abraham's faith in the God of that promise as the biblical key to understanding the economy of grace in Christ, and we are at the heart of that understanding here. Atonement, says Paul, is foundational for the bestowing of the covenant benefits that directly structure our existence by faith and our eternal life.

Atonement and the opposition Paul faced. "If I, brothers, still preach circumcision, why am I still being persecuted? In that case the offense of the cross has been removed" (Gal 5:11). "It is those who want to make a good showing in the flesh who would force you to be circumcised, and only in order that they may not be persecuted for the cross of Christ" (Gal 6:12). Paul's reference to preaching (i.e., requiring) circumcision evidently covered two things together: insisting, first, that Gentiles who wished to become Christians must also be circumcised and so become proselytes to Judaism (of which Christianity would then be simply one form); and, second, that keeping some or all of the OT ritual law would contribute something to believers' final acceptance, so that their salvation, which began with receiving pardon for past sins through Christ's death, would end up as partly their own achievement through their own meritorious obedience. This was what Paul's Judaizing opponents seem to have taught. It is a variant on the theme of justification by works, which is the natural religion of fallen humanity.

The reason that Paul's theology of the cross was an "offense" (σκάνδαλον, "stumbling-block") was that it left no room for such thoughts. Salvation for Paul was by God's grace alone, through Christ's atoning death alone, and it becomes ours through faith in Christ alone. The offense of the cross to Judaizers and others sprang less from the shame of it, great though that was, than from the pride of the human heart, which always longs to vindicate its power of religious performance and its present religious predilections, with all the outward trappings that accompany them, whatever these are. Anti-Paul Judaizing is now dead, but religious pride remains very much alive, and a sovereign-grace understanding of Christianity is still felt as a stumbling block by many religious people. The atonement, says Paul, is foundational to the true gospel of Christ, which totally excludes self-reliant self-effort in all its forms.

Atonement and the holiness Paul taught. "Those who belong to Christ Jesus have crucified the flesh with its passions and desires" (Gal 5:24). This "astonishing metaphor," writes John Stott, "illustrates graphically what our attitude to our fallen nature is to be. We are not to coddle or cuddle it, not to pamper or spoil it, not to give it any encouragement or even toleration. Instead we are to be ruthlessly fierce in rejecting it, together with its desires."[4] That is what Paul means, and clearly he chooses the metaphor in order to link the crucifying of our "flesh" with the crucifixion suffered for us by our Savior. He is telling his readers that being Christ's by faith through the atonement entails repudiating all forms and fancies of future sinning. The idea that since Christ's sacrifice covers all sins, including future sins, as indeed it does, we may now sin freely is out: it is a monstrous mistake (cf. Rom 6).

---

[4]Stott, *Cross of Christ*, 348-49.

Knowing that Christ was crucified as sin-bearer for us, we crucify sin in our personal moral system for him. Atonement, says Paul, is thus foundational to Christian holiness.

Atonement for the pride Paul felt. "Far be it from me to boast except in the cross of our Lord Jesus Christ, by which the world has been crucified to me, and I to the world" (Gal 6:14). Thus, Paul rounds off his witness in this letter to the significance of the atonement—of Christ's cross, as he puts it. His verb "boast" (καυχᾶσθαι) carries a broader, deeper and less pejorative meaning than the English word ordinarily implies; it emphasizes enthusiasm rather than egoism. What it expresses is becoming articulate about one's rejoicing, reveling and delighting in something wonderful that has come one's way. When Paul boasts in the cross, he is being reverently euphoric about the atonement, showing himself proud of it, as we might say. (The hymn line, "In the cross of Christ I glory," catches the tone.) When he says that by Christ's cross he and the world (meaning, the Godless human community) are crucified to each other, he means that because of Christ and the atonement he now repudiates the world's value system as a delusive cheat, while the world repudiates him as a deluded freak. Atonement, he says, has thus changed his life, and, he implies, should change others' lives in the same way.

The dynamics of Paul's statement still operate. James Denney, a professorial would-be evangelist to the intellectual elite of a century ago, spelled them out well, and I pause to quote him:

> It will be admitted by most Christians that if the Atonement . . . is anything to the mind, it is everything. It is the most profound of all truths, and the most recreative. It determines more than anything else our conceptions of God, of man, of history, and even of nature. . . . It is the inspiration of all thought, the impulse and the law of all action, the key, in the last resort, to all suffering. . . . It is that in which the differentia of Christianity, its peculiar and exclusive character, is specifically shown; it is the focus of revelation, the point at which we see deepest into the truth of God, and come most completely under its power. For those who recognize it at all it is Christianity in brief; it concentrates in itself, as a germ of infinite potency, all that the wisdom, love and power of God mean in relation to sinful men. . . . The Atonement is a reality of such a sort that it can make no compromise. The man who fights it knows that he is fighting for his life, and puts all his strength into the battle. To surrender is

literally to give up himself, to cease to be the man he is, and to become another man. . . . The cross of Christ is man's own glory, or it is his final stumbling block.[5]

Surely, Denney's restatement of Paul's thrust in Galatians 6:14 is a word for our time. No one goes deeper than Denney in discerning the impact on thought and life of knowing that Christ on the cross died for my sins, so that I am everlastingly in his debt, and of realizing that the Father's love to me centers precisely on his having sent his Son to save me at the cost of the shame and public contempt, the cruelty and the agony, and the hellish sense of divine abandonment and God-forsakenness that was Christ's crucifixion experience. Nor is any writer stronger than Denney in insisting that life without this knowledge, even among church people, is not Christian life at all. So the atonement—which as we have already seen is for the believer the foundation of faith, the source of freedom, the ground of justification, the spur for sanctification, the theme of witness, the trigger for worship, the warrant for hope and the model for love—is also the litmus test for reality: should we lose sight of the atonement, our Christianity would reduce to hollow externalism, a mere copy of the real thing. This is perhaps the first truth to establish in any systematic reflection on the Christian life.

Systematic Reflection on the Atonement

Systematic reflection, based on Paul's convictions about the atonement as our exegesis has unearthed them, will now occupy us; and I begin with three caveats against undue narrowness in it.

First, we must not isolate the atonement from God's larger plan and strategy for his world. Evangelists may sometimes seem to do this through their own strategy of starting with people's need for forgiveness and new life and then presenting Christ and his cross as opening the door to both. But when the NT writers—especially in Paul's letters, in Hebrews, and in Revelation—explain Christ to Christians, they anchor his death and resurrection/enthronement in the Father's eternal purpose. That purpose produced a plan of history unfolding through promise and fulfillment, through type and antitype, to establish the Son as mediator—that is, here and now, as our teacher by his word and

---

[5]James Denney, *The Death of Christ,* enlarged ed. (London: Hodder & Stoughton, 1911), 243ff.

Spirit (prophet and apostle), our Lord, champion and final judge (king), and our great high priest who once for all offered himself in sacrifice for us, and now from his throne intercedes for us. The writers see all this as paving the way, not just to the completing of our salvation, but also, and even primarily, to the future renewing of this whole cosmos in, through and under Christ, so as to bring everything into the full glory of the already inaugurated age to come. The ransoming and reconciling transaction carried out at Calvary is seen as a step—to be sure, the decisive step—in this larger enterprise leading to God's ultimate goal.

Second, we must not define atonement in single-category terms. Exegetically, it is clear that penal substitution (Christ bearing in our place the curse, that is, the retribution that hung over us) is Paul's final and fundamental category for understanding the cross. To confirm this, see again Galatians 3:13 and with it Colossians 2:13-14, where the notice nailed to the cross is, as we would say, the charge sheet stating for what crime(s) the sufferer is being executed (cf. Mt 27:37; Lk 23:38; Jn 19:19-20). Theologically, it is evident that this category explains all the others, as the following sequence shows: What did Christ's death accomplish? It *redeemed* us to God—purchased us at a price, that is, from captivity to sin for the freedom of life with God (Tit 2:14; Rev 5:9). How did it do that? By being a *blood-sacrifice* for our sins (Eph 1:7; Heb 9:11-15). How did that sacrifice have its redemptive effect? By making *peace*, achieving *reconciliation*, and so ending *enmity* between God and ourselves (Rom 5:10; 2 Cor 5:18-20; Eph 2:13-16; Col 1:19-20). How did Christ's death make peace? By being a *propitiation*, an offering appointed by God himself to dissolve his judicial wrath against us by removing our sins from his sight (Rom 3:25; Heb 2:17; 1 Jn 2:2; 4:10). How did the Savior's self-sacrifice have this propitiatory effect? By being a vicarious enduring of the retribution declared due to us by God's own law (Gal 3:13; Col 2:13-14)—in other words, by *penal substitution*. But each of these conceptual categories, items already in the technical language of the apostolic age, covers its own distinct area of thought and meaning—its own semantic field, as we say nowadays—and the full range and glory of the atonement only appears when each is delineated in its own terms.

Third, we must not treat the atonement as if its direct benefits to believers are the whole of our salvation, for they are not. Benefits that the atonement brings us directly are forgiveness and justification, that is, full cancellation of our demerit and present acceptance of our sinful persons into the covenant fellowship of our holy God; permanent peace with this God and adoption into his family, establishing us as his heirs. This is indeed breathtakingly wonderful, so that if, as it seems, these positional blessings preoccupied Martin Luther, their sixteenth-century re-discoverer, all his days, so that other aspects of salvation took a subordinate place in his thinking, we can hardly be surprised. But the taproot of our entire salvation, and the true NT frame for cataloging its ingredients, is our union with Christ himself by the Holy Spirit. That is, to be more precise, our implantation, symbolized by the under-and-up-from-under of water baptism, into the twin realities of Christ's own dying and rising (see Rom 6:1-11; Col 2:9-12). In this union we have a salvation that is not only positional through the cross in the terms just stated, and relational through our sustained faith-communion with our Lord, but is also transformational through the regenerating and indwelling Spirit, who stirs and motivates and empowers us to express our new hearts' desires in new habits of action and reaction constituting Christlike character ("the fruit of the Spirit" in Gal 5:22-23). Indirectly, to be sure, all of this derives from the atonement, for only in the seedbed of peace with God can this fellowship with Christ and these Christlike habits grow. Directly, however, the transformation springs from the new creation of the heart through union with Christ, as well as the believer's crucifying of the flesh in true repentance and thereafter "keeping in step" with the Spirit (the image embodied in "walk" in Gal 5:25). When we discuss salvation, all the aspects of it as we have now stated them, plus all three of its tenses (past, present and future) must ever be kept in view.

The Atonement and Christian Virtues

What I wish to do now is analyze in three key areas—faith, hope and love—how inadequacy regarding the atonement skews and weakens Christian lives.

The atonement and faith. What is faith? In the New Testament, where both the noun πίστις and the verb πιστεύω occur more than 240 times, faith is the full reality of self-abandoning trust in the God and the Christ and the promises of the gospel—the many-sided, wholehearted, comprehensive trust by which Christians live. Being essentially a response, the nature and shape of faith are determined by its object of attention, and the object here is threefold. First, there is the truth—God's revealed truth; the truth of the Bible in general, and of the gospel in particular; the sacrosanct message from God about sin and salvation that Christ and his apostles delivered, that is now to be told, known, believed, loved, lived out and maintained against its detractors and corrupters; the truth in which the diagnosis of sin and sins and the declaration of atonement are central, as appears from Paul's reminder to the Corinthians: "I delivered to you as of first importance what I also received: that Christ died for our sins in accordance with the Scriptures" (1 Cor 15:3). Second, there is the Christ of the gospel, the crucified Savior and risen Lord, the divine Son, who through incarnation came to us to be part of space-time world history and to die for us, who through resurrection and ascension was then taken home to rule over all, who through the Holy Spirit is now, as we may fitly say, trans-historical in his accessibility to us and power to impact our lives, and who will one day be back in this world for judgment. Third, there is the God of the gospel, the Father of our Lord Jesus Christ and the Father also of all with faith in Christ; he is the Creator-God who planned redemption, who sent his Son to accomplish it and sends his Spirit to apply it, the God from whom everything came and comes and to whom all things must return, one way or another, to render him homage and give him praise. "From him and through him and to him are all things. To him be glory for ever. Amen" (Rom 11:36). To this threefold object of revelation faith is the due response of acceptance, adherence, dependence and reliance—in short, of total and unqualified trust.

Generically, the response of faith, which is in every case a work and gift of God and thus essentially the same, can and should be viewed from three complementary standpoints: intellectual, attitudinal and volitional. Between them, these cover the whole of what a human being consciously is, and they yield an analysis of faith matching the familiar seventeenth-century account of it as *notitia* plus *assensus* plus *fiducia*—knowledge, assent and trust. First and basic is *cognitive comprehension*, whereby the reality of God is grasped (cf. Heb 11:6), the story of redemption through Christ's cross is believed, and God's promises to mankind extended out of that story are acknowledged as authentic and trustworthy. Second and consequential is *convictional consent*, the heartfelt "yes!" of sinners who now know that this mercy of God in Christ is what they need and must have, for without it they are eternally lost. Third and finally definitive is *committed confidence*, involving actual trust and reliance on God, Christ and the promises as well as some measure, much or little, of assurance and hope, joy and peace. Assurance becomes spontaneously present as the Holy Spirit witnesses to one's new relationship with the Father through the Son and to the reality of God's redeeming love toward oneself in particular. Hope in God for the future arises spontaneously from this witness. Joy and peace spring spontaneously from the realizing of one's pardon and security in and through Christ. The variety of Christian experience due to temperament, disposition, circumstances, age and health is endless, and any of these factors may damp down, perhaps drastically, the certainty, hope, peace and joy of personal faith in individual cases. But the essential components and facets of faith as such, the faith into which God leads all his people, are always as described.

The full glory of faith, thus understood, dawned brightly on the minds and hearts of the Reformers as they battled the false religion and irreligion of their times, and naturally their definitions of faith put the spotlight on Christ-centered confidence and commitment as shaped objectively by the gospel and responsively by the Spirit: a fully biblical focus that evangelicalism maintains with emphasis to this day. Calvin, for instance, with his genius for organic statement, defined faith as "a firm and sure knowledge of God's goodwill toward us, founded on the truth of the freely given promise in Christ that is revealed to our minds and sealed on or hearts by the Holy Spirit."[6] Luther had constantly insisted that faith is not *fides* (credence, as he glossed it) alone, but *fiducia* (actual trust in the work, promise and Son of God). In the next century the Westminster Confession of Faith set forth a comprehensive definition, emphasizing commitment in a way that complements Calvin's cognitive concept:

> The grace of faith . . . is the work of the Spirit of Christ in . . . hearts, and is ordinarily wrought by the ministry of the word, by which also, and by the administration of the sacraments, and prayer, it is increased and strengthened. By this faith, a Christian believeth to be true whatsoever is revealed in the word, for the authority of God himself speaking therein,

---

[6]John Calvin *Institutes of the Christian Religion* 3.2.7, trans. Ford Lewis Battles (Philadelphia: Westminster Press, 1960), 1:551.

and acteth differently upon that which each particular passage thereof containeth; yielding obedience to the commands, trembling at the threatenings, and embracing the promises of God for this life, and that which is to come. But the principal acts of saving faith are accepting, receiving, and resting upon Christ alone for justification, sanctification, and eternal life, by virtue of the covenant of grace. This faith is different in degrees, weak or strong; may be often and many ways assailed, and weakened, but gets the victory: growing up in many to the attainment of a full assurance, through Christ, who is both the author and finisher of our faith.[7]

So far, so good. But what happens to faith if the atonement is denied—if, that is, it is no longer insisted that by offering himself as a blood sacrifice to the Father, Christ did something for us that we could not do for ourselves, and without which we would have no hope of eternal life? The English word *atonement,* as is often pointed out, means amends for wrongdoing and pacification thereby, and so adumbrates the "at-one-ment" idea that its etymology suggests—the idea that Paul approaches when he uses the word καταλλαγή ("reconciliation") to signify a status of peace with God that Christ's death achieved on our behalf for us to enter into (see Rom 5:11; 2 Cor 5:18-20). Denney writes,

> The work of reconciliation . . . is a work which is *finished,* and which we must conceive to be finished, *before the gospel is preached.* . . . The summons of the evangelist is—"*Receive* the reconciliation; consent that it become effective in your case." . . . Reconciliation, in the New Testament sense, is not something which is doing; it is something which is done. . . . A finished work of Christ and an objective atonement—a κατταλαγή . . . —are synonymous terms.[8]

The Roman legal word *satisfactio* (satisfaction), used by Anselm and most Western theology until recently to express the thought of amends for sin (with differences of specific conception, which we bypass here), points to the same thing. Our question now is, what happens to faith if this notion of Christ's achievement on the cross be denied—as it has been by liberal theologians for two centuries and as it was by Socinus two hundred years before that? Socinus's denial of the atonement was bound up with his anti-Trinitarianism, which liberals have often

---

[7]*Westminster Confession of Faith,* chap. XIV, "Of Saving Faith;" followed by chap. XV, "Of Repentance unto Life."
[8]Denney, *Death of Christ,* 103ff.

shared with him, but that too we bypass here. Focusing narrowly on our question, then, we discern that in general terms the answer to it is as follows.

The correlation between the object of a Christian's faith and the natural sense of canonical Scripture is disrupted. Whatever is believed about the cross is no longer the story of atonement that the Bible straightforwardly tells, but it expresses confidence that, with the heritage of Western culture and present-day intellectual life to guide us, modern (or postmodern) Christians can reconstruct the faith to their advantage, rendering it truer and more profound than it was.

The direct link between the Christian's exercise of faith and the ministry of the Holy Spirit as teacher through the biblical text and enlightener of our minds through the renovation of our hearts is also broken. Belief in the natural inability of fallen human beings to understand the divine realities of the gospel and appreciate them as life-giving for ourselves (cf. 1 Cor 2:12-16; 2 Cor 4:3-6; 1 Jn 2:20-27; 5:20) gives way to notions of faith as *either* a natural capacity for realizing the divine in creation, a capacity on which all religions as such and all forms of natural theology are based (indeed, all theologies are natural theology on this view); *or* faith is the verbalizing of a noncognitive self-awareness triggered by some Christian item impacting the soul; *or* faith is a rational judgment on a par with our other reflection-wrought, critically determined, probability-based beliefs. On any of these views it is clearly inappropriate to speak of faith as the gift and work of God the Holy Spirit through the Bible or the gospel.

Furthermore, God's love is now no longer framed by a holiness that maintains a moral order of retribution and requires a sacrificial offering to make amends for past wrongdoing. Sorrow for, and abandonment of, sin makes all the amends God requires in order to forgive us for the past and fellowship with us for the future. Horror at sin for its ugliness, its deadliness and its opposition to, and provocation of, God's holiness no longer haunts Christian hearts. The problem of sin, it seems, is not as grievous as we thought, for God is not as awesome as we supposed. Religious sentimentality thus replaces moral and theological sensitivity regarding sin.

Again, deleting vicarious atonement from one's gospel entails deletion of the correlative truth of justification by faith, the apostolic doctrine that bases our pardon and acceptance on Christ's obedience and propitiatory suffering for our sins. If the language of justification is still retained, as for Protestant credentialing seems often to be done, then its Pauline meaning as the second part of what Luther called the "wonderful exchange," whereby Christ took to himself our sins and guilt and gives us his righteousness in its place, drops out of sight. Perhaps we should not be surprised that those who take this line often argue the popular revisionist thesis that justification by faith, far from being the centerpiece of Paul's gospel, was for him a doctrine important only for evangelistic and polemical encounter with Jews, and thus it is a subordinate theme in Romans and Galatians, where the main matter under discussion (so it is urged) is not personal salvation from sin, death and hell but the parity of Jew and Gentile in the church.

Finally, where objective atonement is denied, Christ becomes more an exemplary model of godliness than a divine Savior, and compassion becomes the motivational mainspring of the Christian life rather than the constraint of being infinitely indebted to Christ for his dying love. Mainstream Christians sing understandingly the words of Philip Bliss:

Bearing shame and scoffing rude
In my place condemned he stood;
Sealed my pardon with his blood:
Hallelujah! What a Savior!

Understandingly too they sing with Isaac Watts:

Alas! And did my Savior bleed
And did my Sovereign die?
Would he devote that sacred head
For such a worm as I?
Was it for crimes that I had done,
He groaned upon the tree?
Amazing pity! Grace unknown!
And love beyond degree!
But drops of grief can ne'er repay
The debt of love I owe:
Here, Lord, I give myself away;
'Tis all that I can do.

Those whose thought-systems downplay or exclude substitutionary atonement, who see the death of Jesus simply as a compelling, victorious model of self-denial or penitence or fidelity or victimhood, can hardly share in such singing. By any standards of reckoning, their theologies obscure, reduce and disembowel the apostolic account of the cross. And that, by NT standards, makes fuzzy, indeed falsifies, faith. What results may be thoughtful and serious, high-minded and well-meant, but it is something less than Christianity. Just as there can be no *Hamlet* without the prince driving the plot, at whatever cost to himself, so there can be no Christianity without Christ making atonement by his blood-shedding on the cross.

The following sections, about hope and love, are direct corollaries of what has just been said, so they can be brief.

The atonement and hope. It is generally acknowledged that one mark of humanness is to live very much in one's own future and that one aspect of maturity is to do this thoughtfully—foreseeing, perfecting and planning with realistic wisdom. So one of the glories of the gospel is the fullness with which it focuses our future as believers, proclaiming Christ as our hope and spelling out the various tasks, disciplines and forms of hardship, along with deliverances from evil, that loom as we travel to what Ecclesiastes, in his dry but vivid way, calls our eternal home, where in Paul's words "we will always be with the Lord" (1 Thess 4:17). We are thus given a theological frame for understanding our journey. The Christian life is going to be a constantly deepening experience of the baptismal pattern, whereby first we feel God is bringing us down into death—darkness, pain, a blank wall, the end of everything—and then we find God is bringing us up again into a new phase of resurrection life, with our hope in him made stronger than before (cf. 2 Cor 1:8-10). We are also given a theological concept to help us "forefancy" (Alexander Whyte's word) the life that awaits us in our homeland: seeing, being accompanied by and accompanying, being served by and serving, being dazzled by and adoring, the slain and living Lamb by whose atoning blood we were redeemed (1 Jn 3:2; Rev 5:6-14; 7:9-17; 21:9-22:5).

After the Second World War the theme of hope became a major concern among theologians, as it still is; but treatments of it have regularly been this-worldly rather than that-worldly and oriented to sociological ideas of God's eschatological kingdom coming here rather than to biblical ideas of God's perfected people worshiping hereafter. It is the absence of this focus, rather than the ingenuity, sophistication and dialectical wizardry of these political-theological constructions that obtrudes.

The thought that praise to Christ for the atonement is heaven's main agenda gets missed. That is my only point at the moment.

The atonement and love. It is a matter of undisputed history that the declaration that God is love (ἀγαπή) came new to the world with Christianity, and it should be a matter of undisputed theology that what this means is only known through the atonement. For ἀγαπή is well defined as a purpose of making the loved one great, and the measure of it is how much one is prepared to do, give and suffer as the means to that end. John explains what he means when he says that God is love by continuing: "In this the love of God was made manifest among us, that God sent his only Son into the world, that we might live through him. In this is love, not that we have loved God but that he loved us and sent his Son to be the propitiation for our sins" (1 Jn 4:8-10; cf. Jn 3:16; Rom 5:8).

We learn to love, says John, by taking the redeeming love of God as our object lesson. "By this we know love, that he laid down his life for us, and we ought to lay down our lives for the brothers. . . . Beloved, if God so loved us, we also ought to love one another" (1 Jn 3:16; 4:11). By keeping the atonement before our eyes, we shall avoid the danger that nonmoral sentimentality (itself a form of worldliness) will corrupt our understanding of Christian neighbor-love, for as Denney says, "Love in the Atonement is inseparable from law. The universal moral elements in the relations of God and man are unreservedly acknowledged, and it is in the cost at which justice is done to them in the work of redemption that the love of God is revealed and assured."[9] We must always be clear that neighbor-love aims to give people, not necessarily what at this moment they want, but what they actually need. A clear view of the atonement will keep us from forgetting that. Lapses here open the door to sentimental shallowness, however, blurring the purposes of neighbor-love, demolishing its standards and weakening its motivation. The world, the flesh, and the devil conspire to make us fail here, and unhappy examples of such failure surround us today.

Here I close. Let Isaac Watts speak the last word for me:

When I survey the wondrous cross
Where the young prince of glory died,
My richest gain I count but loss,

---

[9]Denney, *Death of Christ*, 239.

And pour contempt on all my pride.

Forbid it, Lord, that I should boast
Save in the death of Christ my God;
All the vain things that charm me most,
I sacrifice them to his blood.

Were the whole realm of nature mine,
That were a present far too small;
Love so amazing, so divine,
Demands my soul, my life, my all.

My dear friend Roger Nicole knows well how weakness on the atonement undermines the Christian life, and he has labored over the years to keep it at bay where it has not yet crept in and to drive it out where it has. I offer him this essay in hope that he will see it as reinforcing what he himself has been doing with such distinction for so long.

pReachinG
tHe atonement

Sinclair B. Ferguson

In the apostolic church, the doctrine of the atonement always led to the preaching of the atonement. "The message of the cross is . . . the power of God . . . we preach Christ crucified . . . the power of God and the wisdom of God" (1 Cor 1:18, 23-24). And so it should be today as well. In this area of theology particularly, there is much to be said for sharing James Denney's sentiment, "I have no interest in a theology that cannot be preached." Thus, clarity of thinking about the biblical teaching on the atonement is not only an intellectual desideratum; it is vital for the integrity of the Christian faith, for the proclamation of the gospel and for the health of the church.

Critics regularly remind us that we are justified not by any interpretation or "theory" of the atonement but by Christ himself. But even to say that "Christ died for our sins" (1 Cor 15:3) is already to provide an interpretation of his death (a "theory"). And if the biblical interpretation of the cross becomes muted or transmuted, the result is a view of Christ's death that renders it non-atoning and empties the cross of its power (cf. 1 Cor 1:17). At least part of the church's malady today must surely be traced to this poisoned spring. Too concerned lest we commit the twenty-first-century sin of dogmatism, we nullify the concrete claims of biblical teaching that stress that Christ saves us by sacrificial atonement, victory and reconciliation. These so-called models eliminate what the atonement is. And without atonement we have no gospel.

A right understanding of the doctrine of the atonement, therefore, is as essential for the pastor-teacher as it is for the academic theologian—perhaps even more essential since the pastor-teacher ordinarily deals directly in his calling with the proclamation of the gospel. The message of the cross is the power of God, and preaching the gospel *is* preaching the cross: preaching Christ crucified (1 Cor 1:17; 2:2). Of first importance in the gospel, and therefore in our preaching, is that "Christ died *for our sins* [i.e., as an atonement for sin] according to the Scriptures" (1 Cor 15:3).

Two questions arise in thinking about the doctrine of the atonement and the preaching of the cross, one contemporary and the other perennial. The (briefer) answer to the first sets the context for, and provides the motivation to discover, the (longer) answer to the second.

Question 1: Do We Preach the Cross?
Do we *what*? Surely the cross is the undergirding, frequently emerging, central theme in all evangelical preaching, as it was for Paul. The question may seem absurd in the light of the force of Paul's description of his own focus. For evangelicals, gospel and Bible people, the answer is surely self-evident. At least until one critically (and, if need be, self-critically) analyzes the output of the evangelical world in terms of books, magazine and journal articles, sermons, seminars and conferences.

During the past decades evangelicals (by far the major purveyors of Christian resources) have inundated the market with literature and teaching opportunities on a wide variety of themes from the creational to the eschatological. But when did you last go to a Christian conference that had the cross of Christ as its theme and focused your attention on the meaning and significance of Jesus' death? Many (perhaps even most) pastor-teacher's bookshelves groan with works answering the question "How can I?" but are light on works which answer the question "How did he?"

This question becomes even more pointed when we ask it in connection with preaching. Most evangelical ministers preach or speak somewhere between one and two hundred times during the course of a year. Most committed church members are likely to hear a half or more of these messages. But how confidently could we say of contemporary evangelical preaching, that "they were determined to know nothing among us except Jesus Christ and him crucified" (1 Cor 2:2)?

To ask the question is, sadly in many cases, to answer it. The cross may be assumed and presupposed, but it is hidden. There is a scandal in the late-twentieth- and early-twenty-first-century pulpit: the veiling of the cross. And perhaps the most important contribution an essay with practical-pastoral-homiletic orientation could make to a symposium like this is simply to ask the question: Is this true—do we explore and defend the orthodox understanding of the atonement theologically but rarely preach the cross? How essential is it then, to encourage preaching that is Christ-centered and cross-centered? Here we can, perhaps, begin to do that by reflecting on Paul's seminal statement in 2 Corinthians of what is involved in preaching the cross.

Question 2: How Should We Preach the Cross?

The Corinthian church had, it seems, fallen prey to teachers with a different spirit and motive from that of Paul—"super-apostles" who demeaned him (2 Cor 12:11). Weighty as a correspondent he might seem to be, but in fact as a preacher he was—so they claimed—unimpressive (2 Cor 10:10). Thus in 2 Corinthians 2:14—7:4, in what Paul Barnett well describes as his "defensive excursus,"[1] Paul gives an openhearted insight into both the message and the experience of an apostolic minister. This is a section of Scripture of which every preacher of the gospel should have a working knowledge.

Preaching grid. Paul hints in this context at a multidimensional preaching grid with which he seems to have operated. One ought not to think of such things as slick inventions of twentieth-century professors of homiletics! In embryonic form they can be traced back through William Perkins to John Calvin, and behind them to Jesus and Paul.[2] In any and every age, the preacher must be self-consciously aware of the spiritual condition of the audience in order to address the gospel to them pointedly and relevantly.

Paul presents us with his own basic analysis of those to whom he preaches. They are (1) spiritually blind, (2) under the influence of the god of this age, (3) summoned to stand before the judgment seat of

---

[1]Paul Barnett, *The Second Epistle to the Corinthians* (Grand Rapids: Eerdmans, 1997), 210. Cf. 2 Corinthians 6:11.

[2]William Perkins, *The Art of Prophesying* (Edinburg: Banner of Truth, 1996; orig. Eng., 1606); John Calvin, *Sermons on 1 and 2 Timothy and Titus* (London, 1579), 933-45 (sermon 24 on 2 Timothy); Jesus in his Parable of the Sower; Paul in 2 Timothy 3:16—4:5.

Christ, and (4) destined to perish (2 Cor 4:3-4; 5:10). In a word, those to whom we preach the gospel are spiritually alienated from God and need to be reconciled to him. According to Paul, this is the situation whether people recognize it or not—indeed, whether they recognize God himself or not. For even in the professing atheist that alienation, rebellion and hatred cannot be forever drowned out of the conscience, as the following instance vividly demonstrates.

On October 22, 1996, in St. Martins-in-the Fields Church in central London, a congregation of some two hundred people, described the next day by the quality British newspaper *The Daily Telegraph* as "admirers," gathered to celebrate the life of the famous twentieth-century English novelist Sir Kingsley Amis. The paper described it as "a secular service: no hymns or prayers, just a lot of laughter."[3] During the service, the late Sir Kingsley's son, the novelist Martin Amis, told the following story, recalling a conversation his father had with the Russian poet and novelist Yevgeni Yevtushenko. Yevtushenko, perhaps having mistakenly assumed all Englishmen are Christians, asked Amis if it was true that he was an atheist. "Well, yes," said Sir Kingsley, and then added, "But it's more than that. *I hate him.*"[4] Here, then, was a quintessential atheist, displaying such remarkable blindness that he could shoot his own atheism in the foot without even feeling the pain. What clearer testimony could one hope to find to Scripture's claim that those who are by nature enemies of God, seek to suppress and deny the truth they know (Rom 1:18-25)? This is the blindness into which we are called to preach the gospel.

But why is Paul's "preaching grid" relevant to our thinking about the proclamation of the atonement? Because it underscores why our preaching must involve "setting forth the truth plainly" (2 Cor 4:2)—expounding it in the power of the Spirit in such a way that it exposes both the spiritual condition of the hearer and the divinely given remedy for it in the work of Christ. And if we see this as our task in preaching, then we are less likely to "lose heart" in our preaching (2 Cor 4:1, 16). When our gaze is focused on the real goal of our preaching—opening the eyes of the blind so that they see, understand and respond to the message of the cross—and when we are clear about the opposition

---

[3]*The Daily Telegraph*, October 23, 1996.
[4]Ibid., emphasis mine.

that the preaching of Christ crucified will encounter, we are less likely to cave in to the pressures.

But what are we to preach about Jesus Christ and him crucified? Paul answers at length in 2 Corinthians 5, a passage noteworthy for the fact that while addressing Christians, he does so in the language in which he preached the gospel to unbelievers in Corinth. As B. B. Warfield puts it, "We have here the phrases in which Paul was accustomed to give expression to the heart of his Gospel."[5] To a world alienated from God, the gospel comes as the message of reconciliation. In outlining his message, Paul also gives us a basic education in what is involved in preaching it.

The source of the gospel. God the Father himself is the fountain from which the gospel flows. It is God who reconciles us to himself. He is the architect of the work of Christ and of the reconciliation he accomplished (2 Cor 5:19), the source of the evangelists' commission (2 Cor 5:19), the voice issuing the evangelistic appeal (2 Cor 5:19-20). Implied here is the perfect harmony within the Trinity, sustained precisely in connection with the death of Christ, which effects our reconciliation. Jesus did not die in order to persuade the Father to love those for whom he died. On the contrary, the Father himself in love planned and enabled the death of Christ for us: "God so loved . . . that he gave his only Son" (Jn 3:16).

This may seem to be a truism, but it is often overlooked that it has important implications for the ethos and spirit of our preaching. Evangelical preaching too often falls into the trap of suggesting that the Father loves sinners only because Jesus has died for them. A wrathful Father is persuaded to have mercy by a loving Son. This in turn has a tendency to breed a deep-down suspicion of God. Thus, the great Puritan John Owen could be heard lamenting in his own seventeenth century that many Christians tend to have a distorted view of the Father:

> How few of the saints are experimentally acquainted with this privilege of holding immediate communion with the Father in love! With what anxious, doubtful thoughts do they look upon him! What fears, what questionings are there, of his good will and kindness! At the best, many think that there is no sweetness at all in him towards us, but what is pur-

---

[5]B. B. Warfield, *The Saviour of the World* (1916; reprint, Edinburgh: Banner of Truth Trust, 1991), 136.

chased at the high price of the blood of Jesus. It is true, that alone is the way of communication; but the free fountain and spring of all is in the bosom of the Father.[6]

Doubtless this is due partly to a natural fallen instinct that makes us suspicious of God. Injecting such a spirit seems to be partly in view in the original temptation.[7] But it is also due to a failure to understand the harmony of the Trinity and the nature of the atonement as the ultimate demonstration of the Father's love (Rom 5:8) and therefore of the divine unity. This failure emerges in different ways, not least when the cross of Christ and his atoning death are preached in such a manner that the God who is presented in our preaching appears to be reluctant to save, while Jesus seems eager to do so. Such a dichotomy between the motivation of the Father and the Son destroys a basic element in the gospel. For it suggests that God the Father is not truly revealed in Jesus Christ. Behind the Savior stands—it is feared—an ogre God, who is other than love. That doctrinal error leads to deep psychological-spiritual mistrust. This in turn begins to poison the Christian's sense of pardon, stability and joy, which are grounded in the knowledge that Christ is truly and fully the revelation of the Father.

The nature of the gospel message. Paul speaks about the gospel as a message or word of reconciliation.[8] This reconciliation has both an objective and a subjective side to it. In the grammar of the gospel, all subjective experience of reconciliation depends on, and is shaped by, the objective accomplishment of that reconciliation in Christ. The importance of this for preaching can scarcely be overstressed. Sadly, however, evangelical preaching can sometimes (perhaps often) either ignore it or appear to be ignorant of it.

This last statement may appear reactionary and even hypercritical. Yet it is commonplace for evangelical preaching to give the impression that the gospel is a message of salvation and justification by regeneration or by the indwelling of Christ. But the basis for our justification is not Christ *indwelling us* or our *being born again*. Rather it is that Christ

---

[6]*Of Communion with God the Father, Son. and Holy Ghost* (1657), in *The Works of John Owen*, ed. W. H. Goold (Edinburgh: Johnstone and Hunter, 1850-53), 2:32.

[7]"Did God really say, 'You must not eat from any tree in the garden'?" (Gen 3:1) casts doubt not only on God's word, but also on his character (Did he set this abundance before you and then so sullenly restrict you?).

[8]τῆς καταλλαγῆς (2 Cor 5:19).

has died for us. In Martin Luther's apt statement: The gospel is entirely outside of us.

Our time is not alone in falling into this confusion of the *subjective effects* with the *objective foundation* of the gospel. Preachers like George Whitefield in the eighteenth century and D. Martyn Lloyd-Jones in the twentieth century shared a similar misunderstanding of the gospel in their early ministries. They had to learn the lesson that we are not justified by regeneration, or by Christ indwelling, but by the objective work of Christ on the cross and in his resurrection. We must learn that lesson too.

The failure to grasp this gospel grammar: *Christ for us* the foundation, *Christ in us* the realization of the gospel, has reached epidemic proportions in some segments of contemporary evangelicalism. We see that the gospel-enervating entail of Schleiermacher's attempt to rescue the Christian faith from the Enlightenment has now come home to roost in—of all places—evangelicalism. Although assuming that they are preaching the gospel, many are in danger of preaching little more than personal subjective experience, bypassing the gospel's foundation in the cross. If anything, this has increased since the halcyon days of the "born-again" movement of the late twentieth century. But being "born again" is not the gospel. It is the fruit of the gospel. To confuse it with the gospel is to turn the gospel on its head, and to do so in such a way that the cross of Christ is no longer central and essential; it is emptied of its significance and marginalized in preaching. What is the remedy for such a malady? Paul provides us with the answer.

The Great Exchange, Dimension 1: The Finished Work of Christ— Reconciliation Accomplished

How does Paul preach the gospel as a message of reconciliation? He does so by stressing the finished work of Christ: "In Christ God was reconciling the world to himself" (2 Cor 5:19 ESV). Reconciliation is not first and foremost a subjective condition in us, but it is an objective provision made by God for us in his Son. But how is this so?

At the root of the language used for reconciliation (καταλλαγή) is the idea of a change or an exchange taking place;[9] one set of circum-

---

[9]See *Theological Dictionary of the New Testament*, ed. G. Kittel, trans. G. W. Bromiley (Grand Rapids: Eerdmans, 1964), 1:258.

stances giving way to, and being exchanged for, another. The point is expressed perfectly in Paul's great statement about Christ: "God made him who had no sin to be sin for us so that we might become in him the righteousness of God" (2 Cor 5:21). Despite attempts to show the contrary,[10] the apostle is speaking here about what lies at the heart of the gospel, namely a double exchange: our sin was imputed to Christ; Christ's righteousness is imputed to us.

Finished work. Our sin is not imputed: "God was reconciling the world to himself . . . not counting men's trespasses against them" (2 Cor 5:19). "Exactly" says John Doe—"I have always believed in a God who doesn't count our sins!" In fact, however, God *does* count our sins. *But not against us!* Rather, he counts them *against Christ.* In the exchange described in 2 Corinthians 5:21, he has taken what is ours in our fallen human nature (he was made sin) in order that we might become by grace what is his in his human nature (we become the righteousness of God).

This is what a former generation referred to as "Christ's finished work." It does not take place *because* we believe or *after* we believe; it took place on the cross. There my sins were imputed to him; there God dealt with the objective grounds for his alienation from me. He has done the reconciling. The task of the preacher now is to publish this message of reconciliation accomplished for us by Christ, offered to us by God through the preacher, and made ours by faith.

Effectual work. This aspect of the work of Christ is thus completed already; moreover, it is efficacious—God was reconciling the world to himself in Christ, not counting humans' sins against them—this has happened. That is the good news—it has already happened at the cross—and this is the message we are to preach. But this carries a biblical and logical implication: those for whom Christ died will be saved by his atoning work. There is no double jeopardy. In A. M. Toplady's words:

If Thou hast my discharge procured,
And freely in my room endured
The whole of wrath divine;
Payment God cannot twice demand,

---

[10]Cf. the recent attempt by N. T. Wright to refer these words, not to justification/reconciliation, but to Paul's own ministry ("That we might become the righteousness of God: Reflections on 2 Corinthians 5:21," in *Pauline Theology,* ed. D. M. Hay [Minneapolis: Augsburg Fortress, 1993], 2:200-208.

First at my bleeding Surety's hand,
And then again at mine.[11]

This is the doctrine of *effectual atonement*, sometimes described in terms of its most controversial implication, *limited* or *definite atonement*.[12] It bears mentioning that it is an aspect of what Paul is teaching in 2 Corinthians 5:14. Here, in a passage frequently assumed to be the clearest description of gospel preaching in Paul's letters, he makes a universal statement that has long puzzled exegetes: "We are convinced that one died for all, and therefore all died."

Paul does not say what he is sometimes misunderstood to say, either: One died for all, *therefore all do not need to die*, or that one died for all, *therefore all must learn to die* (to self). But rather he says one died for all, *therefore all died*. He uses the aorist tense in the indicative mood (ἀπέ θανεν). The death has been completed. This is not a continuing activity or a command to activity (which would have required either the present tense or the imperative mood).

But in what sense have "all died"? In the same sense as Paul teaches in Colossians 2:11-12 and 3:3, with Christ in his death, emblematized in our baptism; to sin, in Christ's death to sin (Rom 6:2, 6-8). We died with Christ, in the death of Christ, because he died that death as our representative-substitute. If Christ died for us, we died in Christ. Those of whom the former is true are those of whom the latter is also true. But not all can be said to have "died with Christ" in his death. The implication is that he therefore died effectually for those who may be said to have died with him in his death.[13]

Consequently, as those who have died in and with Christ to the old Adamic order, the implication follows that we should no longer live for ourselves but live for Christ (2 Cor 5:15). Thus, the work of Christ is (1) objective, (2) finished, (3) efficacious and (4) life-transforming. Each of these aspects presents the preacher with rich veins of gospel gold waiting to be mined in the ministry of the Word.

---

[11]From his hymn, "From whence this fear and unbelief?" verse 3.

[12]A doctrine long and ably defended and expounded by Roger Nicole. See *Standing Forth, Collected Writings of Roger Nicole* (Ross-shire, Scotland: Christian Focus Publications, 2002), 283-318.

[13]See the classic treatment in J. Owen, *The Death of Death in the Death of Christ* (1647) in *The Works of John Owen*, ed. W. H. Goold, 10:350-52; G. Smeaton, *The Apostles' Doctrine of the Atonement* (Edinburgh: Banner of Truth Trust, 1870), 210-14.

Real suffering. But the atonement is not to be preached as a merely symmetrical mathematical arrangement, as though the pardon of sin were akin to some great divine problem solved by God's perfect algebra or by a commercial transaction. Paul would hardly have become passionate about divine arithmetic, as he evidently was about the gospel (2 Cor 5:20).

In preaching, then, the question must be asked and answered: Why this passion? Because the exchange Christ made has a terrible element in it: *the Father* counted humanity's sins against his Son. The transaction in the atonement is personal; it involves the persons of the Godhead and their interpersonal relationships. If we miss this, we miss the power and also the attraction of the gospel.

The exchange adumbrated in Isaiah's fourth Servant Song was realized in the personal experience of Jesus. He "was pierced . . . crushed . . . punishment . . . was upon him . . . the LORD has laid on him the iniquity of us all" (Is 53:5-6). On the cross he became the scapegoat of the Day of Atonement (Lev 16:6-10, 20-22), bearing our guilt out into the uninhabited desert space between heaven and earth, God and humanity—isolated from the latter and feeling abandoned by the former (Mt 27:45-46). The price of our reconciliation was Christ's alienation.

Exchange lies at the heart of the action of the Passion Narrative. In the Upper Room Jesus gives his disciples the cup of blessing.[14] In Gethsemane he takes from his Father the cup of judgment (Mk 14:36), which he drinks to the bitter dregs on the cross. The OT prophets described that cup as containing the most appalling potion. It is "the cup of his wrath . . . the goblet that makes men stagger" (Is 51:17); the "cup filled with the wine of my wrath . . . When they drink it they will stagger and go mad . . . So I took the cup from the Lord's hand . . . to make them a ruin and an object of horror and scorn and cursing" (Jer 25:15, 17). It is "a cup large and deep; it will bring scorn and derision . . . You will be filled with drunkenness and sorrow, the cup of ruin and desolation" (Ezek 23:32-33). So, according to Habakkuk 2:16, "You will be filled with shame instead of glory. . . . Drink and be exposed! The cup from the LORD's right hand is coming around to you, and disgrace will cover your glory."

No wonder, then, as these prophecies unfold almost literally in the

---

[14]Cf. 1 Corinthians 10:16, τὸ ποτήριον τῆς εὐλογίας.

Passion Narrative, the Gospels are compelled to press language to the limits to express Jesus' description of his experience as he looked toward Calvary. The soul of the cross-bearing Savior began "to be deeply distressed and troubled . . . overwhelmed with sorrow" (Mk 14:33-34). Mark's verb ἀδημονεῖν ("troubled") "describes the confused, restless, half-distracted state, which is produced by physical derangement, or by mental distress, as grief, shame, disappointment."[15] This vivid, poignant, but profoundly realistic portrayal of Christ's sin-bearing humanity, facing the dissolution of his life on the cross with a holy revulsion is, surely, part of the apostolic preaching that Paul describes as a "placarding" of Christ crucified before the very "eyes" of the Galatians (Gal 3:1).

When Christ's atonement is preached thus, it becomes clear that we do not believe we are saved by a mere mathematical equation (or by a theological "theory"), but by the all-demanding, all-consuming, Son-in-the-flesh forsaking activity of the God of grace. In the very act of proclaiming this, "the love of Christ controls" the preacher (2 Cor 5:14 ESV). For it not to would be tantamount to unbelief in the reality we proclaimed. It is "as though God were making his appeal through us. We implore you . . . be reconciled to God" (2 Cor 5:20). This objective exchange—he takes our sin and gives us his righteousness—is the heart of the atonement.

Polyvalent atonement. But the great exchange is not the only aspect of Christ's work. For the atonement is multidimensional, polyvalent. In the context of 2 Corinthians 2:14—7:4, Paul does not major on the other dimensions. But they are implicit in his teaching. While the aspect of reconciliation is central here, the necessity of forensic justification is also implied ("We must all appear before the judgment seat of Christ," as 2 Cor 5:10 states), as is the principle of redemptive deliverance from bondage. Unbelievers are held in the grip of Satan (2 Cor 4:4). Only once delivered from the cavernous maze in which the Evil One imprisons them can they ever be brought out into the light of Christ. Implied, then, in Paul's teaching is the *Christus Victor* motif that he spells out in Colossians 2:14-15. But here, as there, it is the atoning exchange of our guilt for his righteousness as the basis for reconciliation that simultaneously grounds both forensic justification and spiritual emancipation.

---

[15]J. B. Lightfoot, *Saint Paul's Epistle to the Philippians* (London: Macmillan, 1913), 123.

Person and work. In addition, it needs to be stressed that in our preaching the work of Christ must never be abstracted from the person of Christ. We do not preach "the atonement" as such, or "salvation," "redemption," or "justification" as such, but Jesus Christ and him crucified. These blessings were accomplished *by* Christ and are available only *in* Christ, never abstracted from him. We must learn to avoid the contemporary plague of preaching the benefits of the gospel without proclaiming Christ himself as the Benefactor in the gospel. We do not offer people abstract blessings (peace, forgiveness, new life) as commodities. Rather we preach and offer Christ crucified and risen, in whom these blessings become ours and not otherwise. We preach the person in the work, never the work and its blessings apart from the Savior himself.

Yet, having thus emphasized the objective character of the gospel, we must not lose sight of the fact that the objective exchange that has taken place in the work of Christ produces a radical subjective exchange in the lives of those who receive it.

The Great Exchange, Dimension 2: The Continuing Work of Christ— Reconciliation Applied

Laying down our arms, surrendering in faith to God in Christ, responding to the exhortation to "be reconciled to God" (2 Cor 5:20) means trusting in Christ crucified. But Paul no more divides the message of Christ the Savior from Christ the Lord than he separates the benefits (salvation) from the Benefactor (Christ). For Christ is one Christ, Savior and Lord. He does not save other than in his identity as Lord; he is not trusted as Savior if his lordship is suspended for later response.

Savior and Lord. Jesus himself spells out the implication of this: to belong to him by faith involves taking up the cross. Woven into his dying is our dying. This is the point Simon Peter resisted so stubbornly. He had an instinctive sense that Jesus' death and his dying to himself were two sides of a coin. As he would later see with great clarity, Christ's death, while unique in its atoning character, is also paradigmatic for the shape of the Christian life of every future disciple (1 Pet 2:21).

Preaching the atonement must therefore include expounding its implications in our lives. The objective exchange is radically applied in the ongoing exchange it effects in our lives. For Paul did not preach ef-

438 The Glory of the Atonement

fectual atonement without spelling out its actual effects. He describes this in terms of a series of concentric exchanges.

The epicenter of these lies in the way the old creation order is exchanged for the new: "If anyone in Christ—new creation" (2 Cor 5:17, literally). In view is not so much that "I am a new creature in Christ" but that I have entered into a new order of reality. In the death of Christ as second man and last Adam (1 Cor 15:45-47), my connection with the old order of humanity in Adam has been dissolved; in his resurrection, the new order of humanity has emerged in Christ. To be in Christ means the exchanging of the old for the new.[16] In regeneration/conversion the old person was stripped off, the new person embraced (Col 3:9-10; cf. Eph 4:22-24). Again we should note the spiritual vigor in the strong objectivity of the apostle Paul. He does not think of conversion in terms of adding to what we already are; rather, it involves entering into what we are not, getting "into" (εἰς) Christ. We are no longer "in" Adam, but we are "in" Christ (cf. Rom 5:12-21). This radical exchange of the old for the new then works itself out in a variety of ways.

Exchanging the old view of Christ for a new and true view of him. Like Paul, we knew Christ "from a worldly point of view [κατὰ σάρκα]" (2 Cor 5:16); we judged him from the perspective of the blind men and women of this age (cf. 2 Cor 4:3-4). Now we know him as he really is, the Son of God, the Savior, the Lord of glory (1 Cor 2:8). Paul himself is a vivid illustration of this exchange. Peter also serves us by way of example. He viewed Christ κατὰ σάρκα, resisting with a stubborn passion the notion that Jesus could be Christ only as the Suffering Servant, the Crucified One. But κατὰ πνεῦμα he comes to see that the new order of reality emerges out of a cross-shaped mold (cf. 1 Pet 2:21, 24; 4:1, 12-14).

Exchanging the old attitude toward others for a new attitude toward them. We "regard no one from a worldly point of view [κατὰ σάρκα]" (2 Cor 5:16). Such a new view involves a recognition of their present condition (spiritually blind and perishing, 2 Cor 4:3-4) and their appointed destiny ("we must all appear before the judgment seat of Christ, that each one may receive what is due him for the things done while in the body, whether good or bad," 2 Cor 5:10). This creates a great sense of awe in Paul's heart in the light of that judgment; in turn, this becomes a major motivation in his life as he tries to persuade people of their need

---

[16]A fact emblematized by baptism, Colossians 3:12.

for, and the power of, the gospel of Christ (2 Cor 5:11).

Exchanging the old way of life for a new way of life. Formerly, unbelievers lived "for themselves"; they do so "no longer." Now they live "for him who died for them and was raised again" (2 Cor 5:15). The result of the atonement is that believers' lives become externally focused, not internally devoted; no longer egocentric, but Christocentric.

Two Implications

But this question "How should we preach the atonement?" has further dimensions. For the apostles the nature of the atonement, the substance of their message, carried implications for the way in which its heralds announced it. Two aspects only can be touched on here.

The free offer of the gospel. We have stressed that the atonement is both completed (and therefore perfect) and efficacious (it actually saves). The implication of this is that *all those for whom Christ died will be reconciled.* Unless one is a universalist (holding that Christ died for all and therefore all will be reconciled whether they hear and believe the gospel or not) this implies both a definiteness and a limitation of a certain kind to the atonement. Its corollary is that Christ died efficaciously for the elect alone (whatever impact his atoning work may or may not make on others).

The alternative, of course, is not an unlimited atonement, but an atonement limited in another way, namely in its efficacy. This involves holding that while Christ died for all, that death does not actually accomplish reconciliation for anyone, but only the *potential* of reconciliation for everyone. For all practical purposes, this implies that faith completes the *saving* character of Christ's work.

This latter view inherently carries potentially disastrous consequences. It weakens the atonement's efficacy. (If Christ died for some who are not saved, in what sense can his atonement itself be said to be saving?) In addition, it cuts the nerve of assurance of salvation based on the atonement. For if Christ's atonement was made for someone who is never saved by it, how can I look to it with confidence that I will be "saved by his precious blood"?

Nevertheless, this view of the atonement—the Reformed view—has often been seen to carry with it the insurmountable problem of limiting to the elect alone the offer of the gospel and the command to faith and repentance. This is a serious issue that has long dogged the heels of

churches that are Reformed. It continues to do so to this day and therefore requires at least brief comment.

We have already seen that the preaching of the atonement is the
preaching of Christ crucified—this, better *he,* is the message of the
cross. In Calvin's beautiful expression, we preach "Christ . . . as he is
offered by the Father: namely clothed with his gospel."[17] We do not offer merely the benefits of Christ's work to the elect; we offer Christ
himself to all, the person himself, the Savior, believing that "he is able
to save completely those who come to God through him" (Heb 7:25).
When we understand that to preach the gospel is to preach Christ as
Savior, not to preach his benefits, then, with the high Calvinist Samuel
Rutherford, we are set free in our preaching of the gospel, knowing
that even "reprobates have as fair a warrant to believe in Christ as the
elect have."[18]

In fact, it is this view of the atonement—Pauline, apostolic, reformed, confessional—that creates confidence in the preaching of the
gospel. It is the means by which God brings into his kingdom those
whom he gave to his Son before the foundation of the world and for
whom his Son shed his precious and effectual blood.

The preacher of the gospel. When the gospel is preached in the
power of the Holy Spirit, there is a symbiotic relationship between
proclamation and preacher, which Paul eloquently describes in his *ap-
ologia pro suum ministerium* in 2 Corinthians 2:14—7:4. Especially in
2 Corinthians 5:11-21, the characteristics of the authentic preacher of
the cross can be virtually lifted off the page *seriatim.*

The preacher of the cross is marked by the fear of the Lord. This injects
such urgency into the preacher's life that every effort is made to "persuade men" (2 Cor 5:11). We do not often regard godly fear as a central
motive for evangelistic preaching, but it was clearly one for Paul. His
emotions were akin to those of Robert Murray M'Cheyne who wrote in
his diary toward the end of a life of only twenty-nine years: "As I was
walking in the fields, the thought came over me with almost over-

---

[17]John Calvin, *Institutes of the Christian Religion,* trans. F. L. Battles, ed. J. T. McNeill (Philadelphia: Westminster Press, 1960), 3.2.6.
[18]Samuel Rutherford, *Christ Dying and Drawing Sinners to Himself* (London, 1647), 442. For a
fine popular statement, see J. I. Packer, *Evangelism and the Sovereignty of God* (Downers
Grove, Ill.: InterVarsity Press, 1961) and also his sturdy introductory essay to J. Owen, *The
Death of Death in the Death of Christ* (1647; reprint, Edinburgh: Banner of Truth Trust, 1959),
3-25, esp. 15ff.

whelming power, that every one of my flock must soon be in heaven or hell. Oh, how I wished that I had a tongue like thunder, that I might make all hear; or that I had a frame like iron, that I might visit every one, and say, 'Escape for thy life!'"[19]

Behind and beyond everyone to whom we preach lurks the shadow of a future judgment before Christ's throne. With such a perspective (no longer κατὰ σάρκα, since "from now on we regard no one from a worldly point of view" according to 2 Cor 5:16) the heart is melted with a sense of compassion, and the conscience is gripped by a sense of responsibility.

There is another side to this "knowing the fear of the Lord" (2 Cor 5:11 ESV), however. For Paul recognized that believers will also be assessed by Christ ("*we* must all appear before the judgment seat of Christ," 2 Cor 5:10). The fear here is of a different complexion: filial fear and awe—the fear of disappointing one who has so signally loved us, a fear caused by the knowledge of grace. For the principle on which Christ exercises his judgment on the works, service, witness and ministry of his people is one of grace as well as absolute integrity.

Jesus illustrates this in his parable of the minas (Lk 19:11-27). To those who have—those who have grace—more will be given (Lk 19:26)! In the parable, one servant is faithful in his stewardship of his master's mina by making ten more. In the judgment he experiences, there is an integral connection between what he has done with what he received and the reward he is given. Having made *ten* minas, he is put in charge of *ten* cities. The correlation of service and assessment is expressed numerically.

But what is the relationship between making ten *minas* (the equivalent of two-and-a-half years wages) and being made mayor of ten *cities?* Surely there is disproportion here? What did the servant do to deserve such largesse? But this is the whole point! The reward is a reward of grace, not of inherent merit. This master, whom one servant feared to the point of paralysis, faithlessly describing him as "a hard man" (Lk 19:20), is in fact generous beyond calculation. Having given his Son for his people, he will stop at nothing to lavish his blessings on them (Rom 5:10; 8:32). The preacher who has grasped that Christ is thus immea-

---

[19]*Memoirs and Remains of R. M. M'Cheyne*, ed. Andrew A. Bonar (1844; reprint, London: Banner of Truth Trust, 1960), 148.

surably gracious to his people from first to last will soon be driven by
a passion to persuade others to trust such a gracious Savior.

The preacher of the cross is stripped of a desire for human position or admiration. A further bon mot of James Denney was an adage now inscribed
behind many pulpits in his native country of Scotland: "No man can
show at one and the same time that he himself is wise and that Christ
is mighty to save." The only legitimate ambition that can accompany
preaching the cross is the desire to live with a clear conscience before
God and humanity. Such preachers care little if their commitment is so
radical that those whose perspective is κατὰ σάρκα regard them as
having lost the place (2 Cor 5:12-13).

This is what it means to glory in the cross (cf. Gal 6:14). For Paul it
was a profound reality with implications that ran through the core of
his being and gave shape to his entire life. He describes these implications poignantly (notice the significant chiastic structure of his words,
expressing the chiastic structure of his experience):

(a^1) We always carry around in our body the *dying* of Jesus,
(b^1) so that the *life* of Jesus may also be revealed in our body.
(b^2) For we who are *living*
(a^2) are always being given over to *death* for Jesus' sake,

(b^3) so that his *life* may be revealed
(a^3) in our *mortal* body.
(a^4) So then, *death* is at work in us,
(b^4) but *life* is at work in you. (2 Cor 5:10-12)

As Paul preaches the cross, God providentially creates a cruciform
structure in his life. Of course, he literally bore on his body the marks
of Jesus (Gal 6:17). In that he was distinctive. But the shape of the cross
was true of the underlying rhythms of his life: preaching Christ as a
cross-bearer meant that he too shared in afflictions, trials, opposition,
misunderstandings, privations, loneliness and rejection—as well as in
fruitfulness, joy and the triumphs of grace. The life of the preacher is
death-and-resurrection shaped.

If, as Phillips Brooks's definition claims, preaching is (among other
things) "the bringing of truth through personality,"[20] then the lives of
the preachers of the cross will be marked by the cross: they will be cru-

---

[20]Phillips Brooks, *Lectures on Preaching* (London: Griffith, Farrar, Okedea & Welsh, 1885), 5.

ciform, themselves christophers—Christ-bearers—in life, and Christ crucified placarders as they "try to persuade men" (2 Cor 5:11).

The preacher of the cross is compelled to preach by the love of Christ (2 Corinthians 5:14). Paul's logic here is significant: it is not simply Christ's death, *but his death interpreted as a sacrifice* that grips us ("Christ's love compels us *because* we are convinced that one died for all, and therefore all died"). The love of Christ crucified as atonement is preached with integrity only by those who have been gripped by that love and left with no choice but to say with Paul, "Woe to me if I do not preach the gospel" (1 Cor 9:16). Paul's point is essentially the one famously expressed by Isaac Watts:

> When I survey the wondrous cross
> On which the Prince of Glory died,
> My richest gain I count but loss,
> And pour contempt on all my pride.

> Were the whole realm of nature mine,
> That were a present far too small;
> Love so amazing, so divine,
> Demands my life, my soul, my all.

When the preaching of the cross has become the power of God to us personally, and the cross itself the demonstration of God's love for us (Rom 5:8; Gal 2:20), an obligation arises to go and preach the gospel to every creature. As John Owen once noted: "A man preacheth that sermon only well unto others which preacheth itself in his own soul. . . . If the word do not dwell with power *in* us, it will not pass with power *from* us."[21] When we are thus gripped and compelled by the love of Christ at the heart of the message of the cross, then the aspiration of Charles Wesley will also become our life-long ambition too:

> Happy, if with my latest breath
> I might but gasp his name;
> Preach him to all, and cry in death:
> Behold, behold the Lamb![22]

---

[21]John Owen, *The True Nature of a Gospel Church*, in *The Works of John Owen*, 16:76.
[22]From Charles Wesley's hymn "Jesus! The Name High over All," verse 6.

postscript on
penal substitution

Roger Nicole

It is somewhat unusual for someone who is honored by a volume of essays—and you can be sure that I feel both honored and humbled by the quality of this book—to be included among the contributors. The two editors, my colleagues and friends, had intended to keep this project as a surprise for me until the volume was available in print. InterVarsity Press, however, in their academic catalog for 2002-2003, had a column in which the prospective publication of this book was announced, together with a partial list of the contributors! The topic fit so well with one of the major emphases of my ministry that I boldly approached one editor, asking him whether there was a possibility of including one essay from my pen (I don't yet know how to use a computer!). They then acquainted me with their project. This manifestly explained why they had not approached me previously, but they permitted me to write a brief essay concerning an issue that has been dominant in my study and teaching.

My purpose is to stress the crucial importance of substitution as the major linchpin of the doctrine of the atonement.

That the atonement is at the center of the Judeo-Christian revelation has long been recognized. In the second century A.D., Justin Martyr, by a hermeneutical process that stretches the stringent rules of a proper exegesis, compared the scarlet cord that Rahab tied to her window (Josh 2:18) to the continuity of the scriptural reference from Genesis to

Revelation to sacrificial blood required by God for the atonement. Both
the Jewish and the Christian religions are redemptive religions, and it
is not surprising that redemption should be at the very center of the
faith. Therefore Paul could exclaim, "I resolved to know nothing . . . except Jesus Christ and him crucified" (1 Cor 2:2), and again, "May I
never boast except in the cross of our Lord Jesus Christ" (Gal 6:14); and
the author of Hebrews writes, "Without the shedding of blood there is
no forgiveness" (Heb 9:22).

This central doctrine of the atonement has its own center in the substitutionary interposition of a sin-bearer who absorbs in himself the
fearful burden of the divine wrath against our sin and secures a renewal of access to God and of the reception of his wonderful grace.
This was figuratively foreshadowed in the Old Testament sacrifices,
particularly the sin offering and the guilt offering (Heb 4—7), and was
factually accomplished in one all-sufficient and effective sacrifice of the
God-man, Jesus Christ, on Calvary (Heb 9:12, 14, 24-28). Substitionary
sacrifice is the fundamental basis of the whole process of salvation according to Scripture.

Now this substitution of a sinless person in the place of sinners is a
concept that causes considerable dismay to the mind. Paul anticipated
this when he wrote that Christ crucified is "a stumbling block to Jews
and foolishness to Gentiles" (1 Cor 1:23). Human justice does not allow
substitution, but insists that the guilty party and no one else bear the
sanctions of the law. "Penal substitution," Vincent Taylor observed, "is
a notion which modern Christianity has no option but to discard."[1]

In an effort to bypass this difficulty, many have structured their conception of the atonement by emphasizing the benefit of the sacrifice of
Christ in an area other than penal sanctions, and thus avoiding the
scandal of a just one's suffering in the place of the sinners. In doing this
they hope to stress some real advantages of Christ's work that would
not involve a substitution of persons. However, this effort is futile; a rejection of substitution carries in itself the ruin of other benefits that are
truly flowing from Calvary but that could not be properly sustained if
Christ had not died in the place of the sinner.

A linchpin in a mechanical contrivance makes possible the unified
function of several other parts. If the linchpin is removed, the other

---

[1]Vincent Taylor, *The Atonement in New Testament Teaching* (London: Epworth, 1940), 10.

parts no longer perform their own functions but float away in futility. This, I believe, is precisely what occurs in the doctrine of the atonement. Take the view that envisions Christ's work as being merely an example of a courageous and uncompromising death.[2] The Scripture indeed represents the death of Christ as an example (1 Pet 2:21). Yet for any action to be truly exemplary, it is necessary that it have an appropriate motivation. If I should die in attempting to save a drowning child, my action may be judged heroic and exemplary. But if I thrust myself in the water to give an example to those present, my act will be seen as insane and far from a paragon of virtue. Thus if Christ had as his purpose "to give his life as a ransom for many" (Mk 10:45), what he did would be a challenge to imitation. But if his death was caused by the mere desire to serve as our model, it is not exemplary! The denial of substitution ruins the exemplary nature of the death of Christ.

One significant way to avoid the vicarious nature of the atonement is to focus the attention exclusively on the human predicament as centering in a wrongful understanding of and attitude toward God. It is wrong, some say, to conceive of God as the sovereign judge who will avenge himself by punishing evildoers. This approach, by contrast, centers on God's marvelous benevolence even toward rebellious sinners. The attitude of the father in the parable of the prodigal son (Lk 15:11-32) stands as the supreme expression of divine mercy: he does not require anything from his repentant child but a return to his fatherly home. The obstacle to be surmounted, therefore, is the human attitude of distrust and hatred toward God. The way of doing this is in sending Jesus Christ in order to prove in an unmistakable manner the godly concern for humans by sharing with their plight, their diseases, even their death. This should convince sinners of the superlative love of God for them and thus reorient them to faith and love for him. Abelard's view in the twelfth century may be the first representative of that posture, often called the moral influence theory.[3]

The parable presented by Jesus was certainly not a full expression of

---

[2]Holders of this view include Pelagius, Faustus Socinus, J. A. L. Wegscheider, James Freeman Clarke and many liberal thinkers.

[3]Holders of this view include Abelard, Horace Bushnell (in *Vicarious Sacrifice*), Frederick William Robertson, John Young, Frederick Denison Maurice (in part), Albrecht Ritschl, G. A. F. Ecklin, George Barker Stevens, William Newton Clarke, Hastings Rashdall and Robert S. Franks.

the redeeming process since it has no place for Christ himself. A death that is not specifically required for the relief of the loved ones cannot be interpreted as an expression of love. Mother Teresa showed her love for the outcasts of India by sharing in their plight. It would not have added anything to her expression of it to throw herself in the Ganges shouting, "See how much I love you." To his surprise, Horace Bushnell (1802-1876), the great promoter of the moral influence view in America, found that those who preached of the substitution of Christ in atonement seemed to achieve greater moral improvement among their hearers than he himself succeeded in doing. He, therefore, with great honesty, sought to revamp his treatise *Vicarious Sacrifice* (1866) into a view where the Godward relation of the death of Christ is the basis of its necessity (*Forgiveness and Law,* 1874). Unless the necessity of the atonement be grounded in eternal principles, even the death of Christ cannot be seen as a moving expression of God's love.

What has been known as the mystical view of the atonement does manifest a clearer understanding of the human predicament than the two positions previously mentioned. Here the depth of human corruption reaching out to all the human faculties and activities is seen as an apparently insurmountable obstacle for true fellowship with God whose "eyes are too pure to look on evil" (Hab 1:13). Humanity can be seen as a sullied river whose water cannot be purified. Jesus Christ, the sinless one, in entering humanity has provided for a brand new purifying stream, and human beings in faith union with him can be regenerated, sanctified and ultimately fitted for the beatific vision of our fellowship with God.[4]

This approach rightly perceives that a supernatural transformation is necessary if sin-infected humans are ever to enjoy the beatitude of heaven. What is missing in this presentation is a consideration of our judicial predicament. Granting that a radical change must occur in our sinful nature, we are not receiving here any light concerning God's dealing with our past sins. How could God be called just if he simply disregarded the reality of our transgressions at the judicial level (Rom 3:25-26)? Abraham was right: "Will not the judge of all the earth do

---

[4]Holders of this view include Kaspar Schwenckfeld, Friedrich Schleiermacher, Richard Rothe, Hans Lassen Martensen, Frederick Denison Maurice (in part), Brooke Foss Westcott and Vincent Taylor (in part).

right?" (Gen 18:25). The situation may be compared to that of a prisoner jailed for life who is rehabilitated in their orientation while in prison. This is not a sufficient warrant to cancel their condemnation! If the interests of justice must be safeguarded at a human level, how much more is this true at the divine level! The language of Scripture makes it plain that this is one of the dominant features of the salvation of sinners and that a mere improvement in our nature is not all that is required for a complete salvation: a penal substitution is necessary. This mystical view appears to center in the incarnation but fails to account for the New Testament's great emphasis on Christ's death.

Some authors have recently emphasized victory as the fundamental element to be considered in the atonement. The sinner is pitted against hostile forces that he or she is incapable of overcoming: Satan and sin, disease and death, the law and the wrath of God. Utterly helpless in the presence of any of these enemies, let alone the combination of them, he or she needs a champion to take the cudgels to provide victory over each of them.[5]

Surely the element of victory rightly resounds in the Scripture perhaps nowhere more vibrantly than in 1 Corinthians 15:54-57; 1 John 5:4-5 and Revelation 6:2. A difficulty arises, however, when one notes the difference between the adversaries noted and the victory required. The following classification may clarify this point:

1. Disease and death are physical impairments of our being.

2. Sin and Satan relate to our predicament in the corruption of our soul.

3. Law and God's wrath are enemies because of the judicial impairment of our standing.

The type of victory that we need differs considerably in each case, although all can be subsumed in the victory achieved for us by Christ.

In the third category, law and the wrath of God, it is plain that this is not a struggle against a hostile power. A guilty person does not face a fight against the law properly administered. The only recourse is to

---

[5]Holders of this view—including Irenaeus, Origen, Gregory of Nyssa, Augustine, Bernard of Clairvaux and other thinkers—have emphasized a ransom to Satan in the atonement. More modern advocates include Gustaf Aulén, Jacob Tanner, Ragnor Leivestad, Sydney Cave and J. S. Whale.

cast oneself on the mercy of the court. It is here that a substitute is needed at the spiritual level if the sinner is to escape the sanctions of the divine law and the wrath to come (Mt 3:7; Jn 3:36). Unfortunately, those who advocate this victorious view of the atonement often fail to give sufficient attention to this category. Then even deliverance in the other areas would not really help one who remained exposed to God's judicial wrath. The biblical representation of Christ's death as a sacrifice manifests the incompleteness of this view.

It remains for us to consider two positions in which more attention is given to divine justice and the way in which the solution to the sinner's predicament is presented.

The governmental or rectoral position, anticipated by Duns Scotus in the thirteenth century and vigorously articulated by Hugo Grotius in the seventeenth century, emphasized that as the supreme judge God has a concern to manifest his justice even though he may forgive the repentant and believing sinner. This does not occur as a transfer of the sinner's guilt to the sinless Christ but is achieved by virtue of the fact that in Christ's suffering and death the true divine hatred of sin is made so apparent that one cannot doubt it when God freely forgives the sinner. The death of Christ leaves God free to forgive sin on any term he chooses without creating ambiguity with respect to justice. The conditions that God chooses for forgiveness are repentance and faith. When these are present in the gospel age, God freely forgives.[6]

It must be at once apparent that a fundamental flaw afflicts this view. How can the suffering and death of Christ be an expression of divine justice unless he is seen as burdened with sin, with real, not hypothetical, sin? Under the conditions stated, the death of Christ appears as an act of flagrant injustice. How can justice be manifested where it is not exercised?

If Christ is indeed seen as the substitute of the sinner, he may be charged with the full burden of the sinner's guilt and therefore be struck with God's own wrath as an act of justice. But unless this substitution takes place, there is no way for the Lord's suffering to be an expression of divine justice. The governmental view fails precisely at

[6]Holders of this view include Duns Scotus, Hugo Grotius, Ralph Wardlaw, Frédéric Godet, Joseph Gilbert, R. W. Dale, Marcus Dods, Alfred Cave, Jonathan Edwards Jr., Edward A. Parks, Albert Barnes, William Bart Pope, Marshall Randles, Joseph Agan Beet, John Miley, Horace Bushnell (in *Forgiveness and Law*).

the point it had been thought to validate.

The last view to be considered here is the view of vicarious repentance or penitence. The point of departure here is a profound conviction that the atonement is universal, with an identical reference to all the members of the human race. This is in contrast to definite atonement, in which Christ is portrayed as having borne the guilt of everyone who is saved but only those who are saved. McLeod Campbell started with the premise that the only thing that God requires from a sinner is a sense of repentance that echoes God's own abhorrence of sin. Since we are unable to sense penitence at that depth, Christ has taken our place on the cross to express in an ultimate manner the repentance that God demands. The atonement as a whole has a double reference: to us by God and to God by us. It must also be seen prospectively and retrospectively. The vicarious penitence is the retrospective part of our relation to God.[7]

Here we do indeed see substitution, but in an area in which it cannot be exercised. No one can repent of a sin except the one who committed it. Christ who suffered under the burden of our guilt and thus bore our punishment (Is 53:5) did not and could not repent in our place; even in accepting the baptism of John he did not exercise penitence, but merely expressed his union with his covenant people. Thus the Scripture never tells us that Christ repented. Furthermore, it is clear that God requires us to repent even after the death of Jesus, so it is evident that Christ did not repent in our place. This approach would also fail to manifest the basic unity between the foreshadowing sacrifices of the Old Testament and the final, effectual sacrifice of Jesus on the cross. In failing to include the penal substitution of Christ for the sinner, the vicarious penitence theory shows its own inadequacy to account for the fullness of his work.

Thus penal substitution of Christ is the vital center of the atonement, the linchpin without which everything else loses its foundation and flies off the handle so to speak. When substitution is acknowledged, the courage and obedience of Christ in his suffering and death are exemplary. The spectacle of God's immense love for us melts the fear and hostilities of our hearts to God and exercises a wholesome moral influ-

---

[7]Holders of this view include John McLeod Campbell, R. C. Moberly and Vincent Taylor (in part).

ence on us. The work of Christ induces in us a spiritual renewal by the power of the Holy Spirit, so that in union with him we are increasingly delivered from the attachment to and smudge of sin and renewed into his image (2 Cor 3:17). Victory replaces defeat, and justification, condemnation (Rom 5:18). The interests of God's justice and holiness are safeguarded, and the ineffable greatness of his mercy is evidenced (Rom 5:8).

Moved by his immeasurable love to humankind, the Triune God, Father, Son and Holy Spirit, devised a marvelous plan to bring deliverance for a race of rebellious sinners who are born in iniquity, inclined toward evil and who transgress every day and in several ways his holy commandments. God designed to save from the midst of this sin-cursed race a great multitude of sinners, who were in no way deserving of this grace.

To accomplish this, the Son, who is consubstantial with the Father and the Holy Spirit, did not insist in retaining his eternal glory, but he assumed a complete and sinless human nature, consubstantial with ours except for sin. He thus entered into humanity and united himself in the deepest manner with an innumerable number of sinners, taking on himself the guilt and punishment due for all their sins and providing them with his own immaculate righteousness before the divine tribunal. This effected the propitiation of the triune God's anger against the sinners; the reconciliation of God to us and us to God; the substitutionary sacrifice needed for expiation of sin; the redemption of guilty debtors enslaved to sin; and the ultimate victory over the enemies of our soul and the predicament of our broken relationship with God. This immense blessing of salvation is bestowed on repentant and believing sinners, who are no better than others but who are graciously moved by God to turn to him. This is the gospel, the good news, which must be proclaimed to every man, woman or child whom we can reach by the ministry of the Word, without discrimination against anyone.

To him who loved us and has freed us from our sins by his blood, and has made us to be a kingdom and priests to serve his God and Father—to him be glory and power for ever and ever! Amen (Rev 1:5-6).

seLect BIBLIOgRaphy

Abelard, Peter. "Exposition of the Epistle to the Romans (An Excerpt from the Second Book)." In *A Scholastic Miscellany, Anselm to Ockham,* ed. Eugene Fairweather. The Library of Christian Classics, vol. 10. Philadelphia: Westminster Press, 1956.

———. *A Dialogue of a Philosopher with a Jew, and a Christian.* Translated by Pierre J. Payer. Toronto: Pontifical Institute of Mediaeval Studies, 1979.

Allen, P. S., and H. M. Allen, eds. *Opus Epistolarum Des Erasmi Roterodam.* Vol. 7. Oxford: Oxford University Press, 1928.

Alsup, J. *A Commentary on 1 Peter.* Grand Rapids: Eerdmans, 1993.

Alter, Robert. *The Art of Biblical Narrative.* New York: Basic Books, 1981.

Anderson, A. A. *The Book of Psalms.* New Century Bible. Greenwood, S.C.: Attic Press; London: Oliphants, 1972.

Anderson, Bernhard. *Out of the Depths: The Psalms Speak for Us Today.* Philadelphia: Westminster Press, 1983.

Anselm. *Cur Deus Homo.* In *Anselm of Canterbury,* 4 vols. Translated and edited by Jasper Hopkins and Herbert Richardson. Toronto: Edwin Mellen Press, 1976.

Aquinas, Thomas. *Summa Theologica.* Translated by the Fathers of the English Dominican Province. 5 vols. New York: Thomas More Publishing, 1948.

Aries, Philippe. *The Hour of Our Death.* Oxford: Oxford University Press, 1981.

Attridge, Harold W. *The Epistle to the Hebrews.* Hermeneia. Philadelphia: Fortress, 1989.

Auerbach, Erich. *Literary Language and Its Public in Late Latin Antiquity and in the Middle Ages.* Translated by R. Manheim. Princeton: Princeton University Press, 1965.

Augustine. *Letters.* In *Fathers of the Church,* vols. 12, 18, 20, 30, 32. Translated by W. Parson. Washington, D.C.: Catholic University of America Press, 1951-56.

———. *Enarrationes in Psalmos.* Corpus Christianorum Series Latina, vols. 38-40. Edited by D. Eligius Dekkers, O.S.B., and Johannes Fraipont. Turnholt: Brepols, 1956.

———. *De Civitate Dei.* Translated by Henry Bettenson. New York: Penguin, 1972.

———. *Tractatus In Iohannis euangelium.* Corpus Christianorum Series Latina, vol. 36. Edited by R. Willems. Turnholt: Brepols, 1984.

—————. *Sermones ad Populum.* In *The Works of Augustine for the Twenty-first Century,* Part 3, vols. 1-11. Translated by Edmund Hill. New York: New City Press, 1990-98.

Aulén, Gustaf. *Christus Victor: A Historical Study of the Three Main Types of the Idea of the Atonement.* Translated by A. G. Herbert. London: SPCK, 1931.

Ayo, Nicholas, ed. *The Sermon-Conferences of St. Thomas Aquinas on the Apostles' Creed.* Notre Dame: University of Notre Dame Press, 1988.

Bailey, Daniel P. "Jesus as the Mercy Seat: The Semantics and Theology of Paul's Use of *Hilasterion* in Romans 3:25." Ph.D. diss., Cambridge University, 1999.

—————. *Jesus as the Mercy Seat: Paul's Use of Hilasterion in Romans 3:25.* Wissenschaftliche Untersuchungen zum Neuen Testament, 2nd series. Tübingen: Mohr Siebeck, forthcoming.

Balthasar, Hans Urs von. *Theo-Drama: Theological Dramatic Theory.* Vol. 4, *The Action.* San Francisco: Ignatius, 1994.

Barth, Karl. *Church Dogmatics,* 1/2—3/2. Edinburgh: T & T Clark, 1956-60.

Barnett, Paul. *The Second Epistle to the Corinthians.* Grand Rapids: Eerdmans, 1997.

Barrett, C. K. *The Epistle to the Romans.* Black's NT Commentary. New York: Harper, 1957.

—————. *The Gospel According to St. John: An Introduction with Commentary and Notes on the Greek Text.* 2nd ed. Philadelphia: Westminster Press, 1978.

Bauckham, Richard. *The Climax of Prophecy: Studies on the Book of Revelation.* Edinburgh: T & T Clark, 1993.

Bavinck, Herman. *Gereformeerde Dogmatiek,* 4th ed. Kampen: Kok, 1928-30.

—————. *The Doctrine of God.* Translated by William Hendriksen. Grand Rapids: Eerdmans, 1951; reprint 1977.

—————. *Our Reasonable Faith.* Translated by Henry Zylstra. Grand Rapids: Eerdmans, 1956; reprint 1977.

—————. *The Last Things: Hope for This World and the Next.* Translated by John Vriend. Edited by John Bolt. Grand Rapids: Baker, 1996.

—————. *In the Beginning: Foundations of Creation Theology.* Translated by John Vriend. Edited by John Bolt. Grand Rapids: Baker, 1999.

—————. "The Catholicity of Christianity and the Church." Translated by John Bolt. *Calvin Theological Journal* 27, no. 2 (1992): 220-51.

Becker, Jürgen. *Paul: Apostle to the Gentiles.* Louisville, Ky.: Westminster John Knox, 1993.

Beeke, Joel R. *The Quest for Full Assurance: The Legacy of Calvin and His Successors.* Edinburgh: Banner of Truth Trust, 1999.

Benson, Larry D. "Courtly Love and Chivalry in the Later Middle Ages." In *Fifteenth-Century Studies: Recent Essays,* ed. Robert F. Yeager. Hamden,

Conn: Archon Books, 1984.

Bolt, John. "The Imitation of Christ Theme in the Cultural-Ethical Ideal of Herman Bavinck." Ph.D. diss., St. Michael's College, Toronto School of Theology, 1982.

Bonar, Andrew A., ed. *Memoirs and Remains of R. M. M'Cheyne.* Original 1844; London: Banner of Truth Trust, 1960.

Bonner, Gerald. "Augustine's Doctrine of Man: Image of God and Sinner." *Augustinianum* 24 (1984): 495-514.

———. "Augustine's Conception of Deification." *Journal of Theological Studies* 37 (1986): 369-86.

———. "The Doctrine of Sacrifice: Augustine and the Latin Patristic Tradition." In *Sacrifice and Redemption: Durham Essays in Theology,* ed. S. W. Sykes. Cambridge: Cambridge University Press, 1991.

Brederveld, J. *Hoofdlijnen der Paedagogiek van Dr. Herman Bavinck, met Critische Beschouwing.* Amsterdam: De Standaard, 1927.

Bremmer, R. H. *Herman Bavinck als Dogmaticus.* Kampen: Kok, 1961.

———. *Herman Bavinck en Zijn Tijdgenoten.* Kampen: Kok, 1966.

———. "Bavinck, Herman." In *Biografisch Lexicon voor de Geschiedenis van het Nederlandse Protestantisme,* vol. 1. Edited by D. Nauta. Kampen: Kok, 1978.

Brooks, Phillips. *Lectures on Preaching.* London: Griffith, Farrar, Okedea & Welsh, 1885.

Brown, Peter. *Augustine of Hippo: A Biography,* 2nd ed. Berkeley: University of California Press, 2000.

Brown, Raymond E. *The Community of the Beloved Disciple.* New York: Paulist Press, 1979.

———. *The Epistles of John,* Anchor Bible. Garden City: Doubleday, 1982.

Bruce, F. F. *The Gospel of John.* Grand Rapids: Eerdmans, 1983.

———. *The Epistle to the Hebrews,* rev. ed. Grand Rapids: Eerdmans, 1990.

Burns, J. Patout. "The Economy of Salvation: Two Patristic Traditions." *Theological Studies* 37 (1976): 598-619.

———. "Augustine on the Origin and Progress of Evil." In *The Ethics of St. Augustine,* ed. William S. Babcock. Atlanta, Ga: Scholars Press, 1991.

Byrne, Brendan. *Romans.* Sacra Pagina. Collegeville, Minn.: Liturgical Press, 1996.

Caird, George. *Principalities and Powers.* Oxford: Clarendon, 1956.

Calvin, John. *Commentaires sur le Nouveau Testament.* Paris: Ch. Meyrueis, 1854.

———. *Refutatio errorum Michaelis Serveti.* In *Calvini opera,* ed. G. Baum, E. Cunitz, E. Reuss. Brunswick & Berlin: Schwetschke, 1863-1900.

———. *Institutes of the Christian Religion.* Translated by F. L. Battles. Edited by J. T. McNeill. The Library of Christian Classics, vols. 20 and 21. Philadelphia: Westminster Press, 1960.

Cameron, Averil. *Christianity and the Rhetoric of Empire: The Development of Christian Discourse.* Berkeley: University of California Press, 1991.

Caputo, John D. *Deconstruction in a Nutshell: A Conversation with Jacques Derrida.* New York: Fordham University Press, 1997.

Caputo, John D., and Michael J. Scanlon, eds. *God, the Gift, and Postmodernism.* Bloomington: Indiana University Press, 1999.

Carroll, James. *Constantine's Sword: The Church and the Jews.* New York: Houghton Mifflin, 2001.

Carroll, J. T., and J. B. Green. *The Death of Jesus in Early Christianity.* Peabody, Mass.: Hendrickson, 1995.

Carson, D. A. *The Difficult Doctrine of the Love of God.* Wheaton, Ill.: Crossway, 2000.

Cave, Sidney. *The Doctrine of the Work of Christ.* London: University of London Press, 1937.

Charry, Ellen. *By the Renewing of Your Minds.* Oxford: Oxford University Press, 1997.

Childs, Brevard. *Isaiah.* Old Testament Library. Louisville, Ky.: Westminster John Knox, 2001.

Chilton, Bruce D. *The Temple of Jesus: His Sacrificial Program Within a Cultural History of Sacrifice.* University Park: Pennsylvania State University Press, 1992.

Clines, David J. A. *I, He, We, and They: A Literary Approach to Isaiah 53.* JSOTSup 1. Sheffield: Sheffield Press, 1976.

Cranfield, C. E. B. *The Epistle to the Romans.* International Critical Commentary. Edinburgh: T & T Clark, 1975-79.

Cress, Donald. "Augustine's Privation Account of Evil: A Defense." *Augustinian Studies* 20 (1989): 109-28.

Cullmann, Oscar. *Christology of the New Testament,* rev. ed. Philadelphia: Westminster Press, 1963.

Dalglish, Edward R. *Psalm Fifty-One in the Light of Ancient Eastern Patternism.* Leiden: E. J. Brill, 1962.

Dalton, W. J. *Christ's Proclamation to the Spirits: A Study of 1 Peter 3:18—4:6,* 2nd ed. Rome: Pontifical Biblical Institute, 1989.

Denney, James. *The Death of Christ.* London: Hodder & Stoughton, 1911.

Derrida, Jacques. "The Force of Law: 'The Mystical Foundation of Authority.'" In *Deconstruction and the Possibility of Justice,* ed. Drucilla Cornell et al., 68-91. New York: Routledge, 1992.

———. *The Gift of Death.* Chicago: University of Chicago Press, 1995.

———. *On Cosmopolitanism and Forgiveness.* London: Routledge, 2001.

Deterding, Paul. "Exodus Motifs in First Peter." *Concordia Journal* 7/2 (March 1981): 58-65.

Djaballah, Amar. "Calvin and the Calvinists: An Examination of Some Recent Views." *Reformation Canada* 5/1 (Spring 1982), 7-20.

Dodd, C. H. "Ἱλαστήριον, Its Cognates, Derivatives and Synonyms in the Septuagint." *Journal of Theological Studies* 32 (1931): 352-60.

——. *The Epistle of Paul to the Romans.* New York: Harper & Row, 1932.

——. *The Bible and the Greeks.* London: Hodder & Stoughton, 1935.

——. *The Interpretation of the Fourth Gospel.* Cambridge: Cambridge University Press, 1958.

Dosker, Henry Elias. "Herman Bavinck." *Princeton Theological Review* 20 (1922): 448-64.

Douma, J. *Christian Morals and Ethics.* Winnipeg: Premier, 1983.

Doumergue, Emile. *Jean Calvin: Les hommes et les choses de son temps. T. IV La pensée religieuse de Calvin.* Lausanne: Georges Bridel, 1910.

Duffy, Eamon. *The Stripping of the Altars: Traditional Religion in England 1400-1580.* New Haven, Conn.: Yale University Press, 1992.

Dunn, James D. G. *Romans 1—8.* Word Biblical Commentary. Dallas, Tex.: Word, 1988.

——. *The Theology of Paul the Apostle.* Grand Rapids: Eerdmans, 1998.

Eckardy, Burnell F., Jr. *Anselm and Luther on the Atonement: Was It "Necessary"?* San Francisco: Mellen Research University Press, 1992.

Edwards, David, and John Stott. *Evangelical Essentials: A Liberal-Evangelical Dialogue.* Downers Grove, Ill., InterVarsity, 1988.

Ellingworth, Paul. *The Epistle to the Hebrews: A Commentary on the Greek Text.* New International Greek Testament Commentary. Grand Rapids: Eerdmans; Carlisle: Paternoster, 1993.

Elwell, Walter, ed. *Baker Commentary on the Bible.* Grand Rapids: Baker, 2000.

Fatio, Olivier. "La Conception du salut chez Calvin." In *Le Salut chrétien: Unité et diversité des conceptions à travers l'histoire,* ed. Jean-Louis Leuba. Académie internationale des sciences religieuses; Paris: Desclée, 1995.

Feinberg, John. "1 Peter 3:18-20, Ancient Mythology, and the Intermediate State." *Westminster Theological Journal* 48 (1986): 303-36.

Fiddes, Paul. *Past Event and Present Salvation: The Christian Idea of Atonement.* Lousisville, Ky.: Westminster John Knox, 1989.

Fiorenza, Elisabeth Schüssler. *The Book of Revelation: Justice and Judgment.* 2nd ed. Minneapolis: Fortress Press, 1998.

Fitzmyer, Joseph A. *Romans.* Anchor Bible. New York: Doubleday, 1993.

Fitzpatrick, P. J. "On Eucharistic Sacrifice in the Middle Ages." In *Sacrifice and Redemption: Durham Essays in Theology,* ed. S. W. Sykes. Cambridge: Cambridge University Press, 1991.

Forde, Gerhard O. *On Being a Theologian of the Cross: Reflections on Luther's Heidelberg Disputation, 1518.* Grand Rapids: Eerdmans, 1997.

Frend, W. H. C. "Heresy and Schism as Social and National Movements." *Studies in Church History* 9 (1972): 37-56.

———. *The Donatist Church: A Movement of Protest in Roman North Africa*, 2nd ed. Oxford: Clarendon Press, 1985.

Furnivall, Frederick J., ed. *The Fifty Earliest English Wills*. Edited by Frederick J. Furnivall. Early English Text Society Series. London: Oxford University Press, 1882.

Gaffin, Richard. *Resurrection and Redemption: A Study in Paul's Soteriology*. Phillipsburg, N.J.: Presbyterian & Reformed, 1987.

———. "Paul the Theologian." *Westminster Theological Journal* 62 (2000): 136-37.

Garnet, P. "Atonement Constructions in the Old Testament and the Qumran Scrolls." *Evangelical Quarterly* 46 (1974): 131-63.

Geelhoed, J. *Dr. Herman Bavinck*. Goes: Oosterbaan & Le Cointre, 1958.

George, Timothy. *Theology of the Reformers*. Nashville, Tenn.: Broadman & Holman, 1988.

Gerstenberg, Erhard. *Leviticus*. Old Testament Library. Louisville, Ky.: Westminster John Knox, 1996.

Gilson, Etienne. *L'Esprit de la Philosophie médiévale*. Gifford Lectures Second Series. Paris: J. Vrin, 1932.

———. *The Mystical Theology of Saint Bernard*. London: Sheed & Ward, 1940.

Goldingay, John, ed. *Atonement Today*. London: SPCK, 1995.

Goppelt, L. *Der Erste Petrusbrief*. Göttingen: Vandenhoeck & Ruprecht, 1978.

Green, Joel B., and Max Turner, eds. *Jesus of Nazareth: Lord and Christ, Essays on the Historical Jesus and New Testament Christology*. Grand Rapids: Eerdmans, 1994.

Green, Joel B., and Mark D. Baker. *Recovering the Scandal of the Cross: Atonement in New Testament and Contemporary Contexts*. Downers Grove, Ill.: InterVarsity Press, 2000.

Greer, Rowan. *Broken Lights and Mended Lives: Theology and Common Life in the Early Church*. University Park: Pennsylvania State University Press, 1986.

Grensted, L. W. *A Short History of the Doctrine of the Atonement*. Manchester: University of Manchester, 1920.

Grosheide, F. W. *Het Heilig Evangelie volgens Mattheus*. Commentaar op het Nieuwe Testament. 2nd rev. ed. Kampen: Kok, 1954.

Gruenler, Royce Gordon. *Victory from Defeat: Christology in Biblical, Systematic and Historical Perspective*. Wheaton, Ill.: Crossway Books, forthcoming.

Gunton, Colin. *The Actuality of Atonement: A Study of Metaphor, Rationality and the Christian Tradition*. Grand Rapids: Eerdmans, 1989.

Guthrie, Donald. *The Letter to the Hebrews: An Introduction and Commentary*. Tyndale New Testament Commentary. Leicester, England: Inter-Varsity Press; Grand Rapids: Eerdmans, 1983.

Hall, Charles A. M. *With the Spirit's Sword: The Drama of Spiritual Warfare in the Theology of John Calvin.* Richmond: John Knox, 1970.

Hallam, elizabeth, ed. *Chronicles of the Crusades: Eye-Witness Accounts of the Wars Between Christianity and Islam.* Godalming, Surrey: CLB International, 1989.

Hand, Seán, ed. *Lévinas Reader.* Oxford: Blackwell, 1989.

Harmless, William. *Augustine and the Catechumenate.* Collegeville, Minn.: Liturgical Press, 1995.

Harnack, Adolf von. *History of Dogma,* vol. 7. New York: Dover Publications, 1961.

Harris, William. *Ancient Literacy.* Cambridge, Mass.: Harvard University Press, 1989.

Hartley, John. *Leviticus.* Word Biblical Commentary. Dallas, Tex.: Word Books, 1992.

Hays, Richard B. "PISTIS and Pauline Christology: What Is at Stake." In *Society of Biblical Literature 1991 Seminar Papers,* ed. E. H. Lovering Jr., 714-29. Atlanta: Scholars Press, 1991.

Heideman, Eugene P. *The Relation of Revelation and Reason in E. Brunner and H. Bavinck.* Assen: Van Gorcum, 1959.

Hepp, Valentijn. *Dr. Herman Bavinck.* Amsterdam: W. Ten Have, 1921.

Hill, C. E. *Regnum Caelorum: Patterns of Millennial Thought in Early Christianity,* 2nd ed. Grand Rapids/Cambridge: Eerdmans, 2001.

Hillyer, N. "'The Lamb' in the Apocalypse." *Evangelical Quarterly* 39 (1967): 228-36.

Hodge, Charles. *Systematic Theology.* New York: Scribner, Armstrong, 1877.

Hoekema, Anthony A. "Herman Bavinck's Doctrine of the Covenant." Ph.D. diss., Princeton Theological Seminary, 1953.

Hofius, O. "Sühne und Versöhnung. Zum paulinischen Verständnis des Kreuzestodes Jesu." In *Paulusstudien,* 33-49. Tübingen: Mohr, 1989.

———. "Das vierte Gottesknechtslied in den Briefen des Neuen Testaments." In *Der leidende Gottesknecht. Jesaja 53 und seine Wirkungsgeschichte,* FAT 14, ed. B. Janowski and P. Stuhlmacher, 107-14. Tübingen: J. C. B. Mohr, 2000.

Hughes, Philip Edgcumbe. *A Commentary on the Epistle to the Hebrews.* Grand Rapids: Eerdmans, 1977.

Hultgren, Arland. *Paul's Gospel and Mission.* Philadelphia: Fortress Press, 1985.

Jaarsma, Cornelius. *The Educational Philosophy of Herman Bavinck.* Grand Rapids: Eerdmans, 1936.

Jaeger, C. Stephen. *Ennobling Love: In Search of a Lost Sensibility.* Philadelphia: Pennsylvania University Press, 1999.

James, Frank A., III. *Peter Martyr Vermigli and Predestination: The Augustinian Inheritance of an Italian Reformer.* Oxford Theological Monographs. Oxford: Oxford University Press, 1998.

Janowski, Bernd. *Sühne als Heilsgeschehen: Studien zur Sühnetheologie der Priesterschrift und zur Wurzel KPR im Alten Orient und im Alten Testament*, WMANT no. 55. Neukirchen/Vluyn: Neukirchener Verlag, 1982.

Johnson, Luke Timothy. "Romans 3:21-26 and the Faith of Jesus." *Catholic Biblical Quarterly* 44 (1982): 77-90.

Jones, L. Gregory. *Embodying Forgiveness: A Theological Analysis*. Grand Rapids: Eerdmans, 1995.

Käsemann, Ernst. *Commentary on Romans*. Grand Rapids: Eerdmans, 1980.

Kistemaker, Simon J. *Exposition of the Epistle to the Hebrews*. Grand Rapids: Baker, 1984.

———. *Exposition of the Book of Revelation*. New Testament Commentary. Grand Rapids: Baker, 2001.

Kline, Meredith G. *Kingdom Prologue: Genesis Foundations for a Covenantal Worldview*. Overland Park, Kans.: Two Age Press, 2000.

Kluit, M. Elizabeth. *Het Protestantse Réveil in Nederland en Daarbuiten, 1815-1865*. Amsterdam: Paris, 1970.

Knight, G. W. *The Pastoral Epistles*. New International Greek Testament Commentary. Grand Rapids: Eerdmans, 1992.

Knight, Henry J., III. *A Future for Truth: Evangelical Theology in a Postmodern World*. Nashville, Tenn.: Abingdon, 1997.

Kok, A. B. W. M. *Dr. Herman Bavinck*. Amsterdam: S. J. P. Bakker, 1945.

Kruithof, Bastian. "The Relation of Christianity and Culture in the Teaching of Herman Bavinck." Ph.D. diss., University of Edinburgh, 1955.

Ladner, Gerhart. *The Idea of Reform: Its Impact on Christian Thought and Action in the Age of the Fathers*. New York: Harper Torchbooks, 1967.

Lambrecht, Jan. "Paul's Logic in Romans 3:29-30." *Journal of Biblical Literature* 119 (2000): 526-28.

Landwehr, J. H. *In Memoriam: Prof. Dr. H. Bavinck*. Kampen: Kok, 1921.

Le Goff, Jacques. *The Birth of Purgatory*. Translated by Arthur Goldhammer. Aldershot, England: Scolar Press, 1990.

Léonard, Emile G. *Histoire générale du protestantisme: I/ la Réformation*. Paris: Presses Universitaires de France, 1961.

Levine, Baruch A. *In the Presence of the Lord: A Study of Cult and Some Cultic Terms in Ancient Israel*. Leiden: Brill, 1974.

Leslie, Elmer A. *Psalms: Translated and Interpreted in Light of Hebrew Life and Worship*. New York and Nashville: Abingdon, 1939.

Lewis. C. S. *Allegory of Love*. Oxford: Oxford University Press, 1936.

———. *God in the Dock: Essays of Theology and Ethics*. Grand Rapids: Eerdmans, 1970.

Lightfoot, J. B. *Saint Paul's Epistle to the Philippians*. London: Macmillan, 1913.

Lindbeck, George. *The Nature of Doctrine: Religion and Theology in a Postliberal*

Age. Philadelphia: Westminster Press, 1984.

Lincoln, Andrew T. "From Wrath to Justification: Tradition, Gospel, and Audience in the Theology of Romans 1:18—4:25." In *Pauline Theology*. Vol. 3, *Romans*, ed. David M. Hay and E. Elizabeth Johnson, 130-59. Minneapolis: Fortress, 1995.

Litowitz, Douglas E. *Postmodern Philosophy and Law*. Lawrence: University Press of Kansas, 1997.

Lohse, Bernhard. *Martin Luther's Theology*. Minneapolis: Fortress Press, 1999.

Longenecker, B. W. *Eschatology and Covenant: A Comparison of 4 Ezra and Romans 1-11*. Sheffield: JSOT Press, 1991.

Louw, J. P., and E. A. Nida, eds. *Greek-English Lexicon of the New Testament Based on Semantic Domains*, vol. 1. New York: United Bible Societies, 1988.

Lowe, Walter. "Christ and Salvation." In *The Cambridge Companion to Postmodern Theology*, ed. Kevin J. Vanhoozer. Cambridge: Cambridge University Press, 2003.

Luscombe, D. E. *The School of Peter Abelard*. Cambridge: Cambridge University Press, 1969.

Luther, Martin. *Luther's Works*. Edited by Jaroslav Pelikan and Walter A. Hansen. 55 vols. St. Louis and Philadelphia: Condordia and Fortress, 1958-86.

MacKay, James Hutton, *Religious Thought in Holland During the Nineteenth Century*. London: Hodder & Stoughton, 1981.

MacMullen, Ramsay. "The Preacher's Audience (AD 350-400)." *Journal of Theological Studies* 40 (1989): 503-11.

Manson, T. W. "ιλαστήριον." *Journal of Theological Studies* 46 (1945): 1-10.

Marshall, I. Howard. *The Epistles of John*. New International Commentary on the New Testament. Grand Rapids: Eerdmans, 1978.

———. *A Critical and Exegetical Commentary On the Pastoral Epistles*. Edinburgh: T & T Clark, 1999.

Marion, Jean-Luc. *God Without Being*. Chicago: University of Chicago Press, 1991.

Marx, C. W. *The Devil's Rights and the Redemption in the Literature of Medieval England*. Woodbridge, Suffolk: D. S. Brewer, 1995.

Martin, Ralph P. "Reconciliation: Romans 5:1-11." In *Romans and the People of God*, ed. Sven K. Soderlund and N. T. Wright. Grand Rapids: Eerdmans, 1999.

Mayer, W. "John Chrysostom: Extraordinary Preacher, Ordinary Audience." In *Preacher and Audience: Studies in Early Christian and Byzantine Homiletics*, ed. M. Cunningham and P. Allen. Leiden: Brill, 1998.

———. "Female Participation and the Late-Fourth-Century Preacher's Audience." *Augustinianum* 39 (1999): 139-47.

McCormack, Bruce. "Grace and Being: The Role of God's Gracious Election in Karl Barth's Theological Ontology." In *The Cambridge Companion to Karl Barth*, ed. John Webster, 92-110. Cambridge: Cambridge University Press, 2000.

――――. "For Us and Our Salvation: Incarnation and Atonement in the Reformed Tradition." In *Studies in Reformed Theology and History*, ed. David Willis, 25-34. Princeton, N.J.: Princeton Theological Seminary, 1993.

McDonald, H. D. *The Atonement of the Death of Christ: In Faith, Revelation, and History.* Grand Rapids: Baker, 1985.

McGrath, Alister E. *Luther's Theology of the Cross.* Oxford: Blackwell, 1980.

McGuckin, John Anthony. "Introduction" to St. Cyril of Alexandria, *On the Unity of Christ.* Crestwood, N.Y.: St. Vladmir's Seminary Press, 1995.

McIntyre, John. *The Shape of Soteriology.* Edinburgh: T & T Clark, 1992.

――――. *St. Anselm and His Critics: A Re-Interpretation of the Cur Deus Homo.* Edinburgh: Oliver and Boyd, 1954.

Meeks, Douglas. *God the Economist.* Philadelphia: Fortress, 1989.

Meuleman, G. E. "Bavinck, Herman." In *Christelijke Encyclopaedie,* vol. 1, ed. J. C. Rullmann. Kampen: Kok, 1925.

Michaels, J. Ramsay. "Baptism and Conversion in John: A Particular Baptist Reading." In *Baptism, the New Testament and the Church: Historical and Contemporary Studies in Honor of R. E. O. White. JSNTSup* 171. Sheffield: Sheffield Academic Press, 1999, 136-56.

Milbank, John. *Theology and Social Theory: Beyond Secular Reasons.* Oxford: Blackwell, 1990.

――――. "Stories of Sacrifice." *Modern Theology* 12 (1996): 27-56.

――――. *The Word Made Strange: Theology, Language, Culture.* Oxford: Blackwell, 1997.

Milgrom, Jacob. *Leviticus 1-16: A New Translation with Introduction and Commentary.* Anchor Bible. New York: Doubleday, 1991.

Millauer, H. *Leiden als Gnade: Ein traditionsgeschichtliche Untersuchung zur Leidenstheologie des erste Petrusbriefes.* Bern: Peter Lang, 1976.

Mohrmann, Christine. "Saint Augustin Prédicateur." In *Études sur le Latin des Chretiens* (Rome: Edizioni di Storia e Letteratura, 1958): 391-402.

Montefiore, Hugh. *The Epistle to the Hebrews.* Harper's New Testament Commentaries. New York: Harper & Row, 1964.

Moo, Douglas J. *The Epistle to the Romans,* rev. ed. New International Commentary on the New Testament. Grand Rapids: Eerdmans, 1996.

Morris, Leon. *The Apostolic Preaching of the Cross.* Grand Rapids: Eerdmans, 1965.

――――. *The Cross in the New Testament.* Grand Rapids: Eerdmans, 1965.

Mouw, Richard J. "Violence and the Atonement." *Books and Culture* (Jan./Feb.

2001): 12-17.

Mulder, L. H. *Revolte der Fijnen*. Meppel: Boom, 1973.

Murray, A. Victor. *Abelard and St Bernard: A Study in Twelfth Century "Modern-ism."* Manchester: Manchester University Press, 1967.

Murray, John. *Redemption—Accomplished and Applied*. Grand Rapids: Eerd-mans, 1955.

———. *The Imputation of Adam's Sin*. Grand Rapids: Eerdmans, 1959.

———. *The Epistle to the Romans*. New International Commentary on the New Testament. Grand Rapids: Eerdmans, 1959.

Nicole, Roger R. "C. H. Dodd and the Doctrine of Propitiation." *Westminster Theological Journal* 17 (1954-55): 117-57.

———. "Hilaskesthai Revisited." *Evangelical Quarterly* 49 (1977): 173-77.

———. "John Calvin's View of the Extent of the Atonement." *Westminster Theological Journal* 47 (1985): 197-225.

———. *Standing Forth: Collected Writings of Roger Nicole*. Fearn, Ross-shire, Scotland: Christian Focus Publications, 2002.

Norris, Christopher. *Derrida*. London: Fontana, 1987.

Nygren, Anders. *Commentary on Romans*. Philadelphia: Muhlenberg, 1949.

O'Reilly, Marie Vianne. *Sancti Aurelii Augustini De excidio urbis Romae Sermo. A Critical Text and Translation with Introduction and Commentary*. Patristic Stud-ies 89. Washington, D.C.: Catholic University of America Press, 1955.

Oesterley, W. O. E. *The Psalms: Translated with Text-critical and Exegetical Notes*, vol. 1. London: Society for Promoting Christian Knowledge; New York: Macmillan, 1939.

Old, Hughes Oliphant. *The Reading and Preaching of the Scriptures in the Worship of the Christian Church*. Grand Rapids: Eerdmans, 1999.

Orlinsky, Harry M. "The So-called 'Servant of the Lord' and 'Suffering Ser-vant' in Second Isaiah." In *Studies in the Second Part of the Book of Isaiah*. Sup-plements to Vetus Testamentum 14. Leiden: Brill, 1967.

Oswalt, John N. *The Book of Isaiah: Chapters 40-66*. New International Commen-tary on the Old Testament. Grand Rapids: Eerdmans, 1998.

Owen, John. *The Works of John Owen*. 16 vols. Edited by W. H. Goold. 1850-53. Reprint, Edinburgh: Banner of Truth Trust, 1965-68.

———. *An Exposition of Hebrews*, 7 volumes in 4. Evansville, Ind.: Sovereign Grace, 1960.

Packer, J. I. "Calvin's View of Scripture." In *God's Inerrant Word: An Interna-tional Symposium on the Trustworthiness of Scripture*, ed. John W. Montgom-ery. Minneapolis: Bethany Fellowship, 1974.

———. "What Did the Cross Achieve? The Logic of Penal Substitution." *Tyn-dale Bulletin* 25 (1974): 3-45.

———. "The Love of God: Universal and Particular." In *The Grace of God and the Bondage of the Will*, ed. Thomas R. Schreiner and Bruce A. Ware. Grand Rapids: Baker, 1995.

Pannenberg, Wolfhart. *Jesus—God and Man*. Philadelphia: Westminster Press, 1974.

Paul, Robert S. *The Atonement and the Sacraments. The Relation of the Atonement to the Sacraments of Baptism and the Lord's Supper*. New York: Abindgon, 1960.

Pelikan, Jaroslav. *The Christian Tradition: A History of the Development of Doctrine: The Growth of Medieval Theology (600-1300)*. Chicago: University of Chicago Press, 1978.

Peters, Ted. "The Atonement in Anselm and Luther, Second Thoughts about Gustav Aulén's *Christus Victor*." *Lutheran Quarterly* 24 (1972): 301-14.

Peterson, Robert A. *Calvin and the Atonement*, rev. ed. Fearn, Ross-shire: Mentor, 1999; orig. 1983.

Piper, J. *The Justification of God: An Exegetical and Theological Study of Romans 9:1-23*. Grand Rapids: Baker, 1983.

Prigent, Pierre. *Commentary on the Apocalypse of St. John*. Translated by Wendy Pradels. Tübingen: Mohr Siebeck, 2001.

Rainbow, H. *The Will of God and the Cross: An Historical and Theological Study of John Calvin's Doctrine of Limited Redemption*. Allison Park, Pa.: Pickwick, 1990.

Raitt, Jill. *The Eucharistic Theology of Theodore Beza: Development of the Reformed Doctrine*. Chambersburg, Pa.: American Academy of Religion, 1972.

―――. "St. Thomas Aquinas on Free Will and Predestination." *Duke Divinity School Review* 43 (1978): 188-95.

Ricoeur, Paul. *The Conflict of Interpretations*. Evanston, Ill.: Northwestern University Press, 1974.

Ridderbos, Herman. *Paul: An Outline of His Theology*. Grand Rapids: Eerdmans, 1975.

―――. *Redemptive History and the New Testament Scriptures*. Phillipsburg, N.J.: Presbyterian and Reformed, 1988.

Ritschl, Albrecht. *Die christliche Lehre von der Rechtfertigung und Versöhnung*, 3d ed. Bonn: Adolph Marcus, 1889.

Robinson, D. W. B. "'Faith of Jesus Christ': A New Testament Debate." *Reformed Theological Review* 29 (1970): 71-81.

Rolston, Holmes, III. *John Calvin versus the Westminster Confession*. Richmond: John Knox, 1972.

Rombouts, Fr. S. *Prof. Dr. H. Bavinck, Gids Bij de Studie van Zijn Paedagogische Werken*. 's-Hertogenbosch-Antwerpen: Malmberg, 1922.

Rousseau, Phillip. "'The Preacher's Audience': A More Optimistic View." In *Ancient History in a Modern University*, vol. 2, ed. T. W. Hillard et al., 391-400. Grand Rapids: Eerdmans, 1998.

Rubin, Miri. *Corpus Christi: The Eucharist in Late Medieval Culture.* Cambridge: Cambridge University Press, 1991.

Rutherford, Samuel. *Christ Dying and Drawing Sinners to Himself.* London, 1647.

Sanders, E. P. *Paul and Palestinian Judaism.* London: SCM, 1977.

Schaff, P., ed. *Creeds of Christendom.* 3 vols. Grand Rapids: Baker, 1993.

Schreiner, T. R. "Does Romans 9 Teach Individual Election unto Salvation?" *Journal of the Evangelical Theological Society* 36 (1993): 25-40.

———. *Romans.* Baker Exegetical Commentary on the New Testament. Grand Rapids: Baker, 1998.

Schwager, Raymund. *Must There be Scapegoats? Violence and Redemption in the Bible.* San Francisco: Harper & Row, 1989.

Schwartz, Baruch. "The Prohibitions Concerning the 'Eating' of Blood in Leviticus 17." In *Priesthood and Cult,* ed. Gary A. Anderson and Saul M. Olyan. Sheffield: JSOT Press, 1991.

Seifrid, Mark A. *Christ Our Righteousness: Paul's Theology of Justification.* NSBT. Leicester: Inter-Varsity Press, 2000.

———. "Righteousness Language in the Hebrew Scriptures and Early Judaism." In *Justification and Variegated Nomism.* Vol. 1: *The Complexities of Second Temple Judaism,* ed. D. A. Carson, Peter T. O'Brien and Mark A. Seifrid, 415-42. Tübingen: Mohr-Siebeck, 2001.

Singer, Irving. *The Nature of Love: Courtly and Romantic.* Chicago: University of Chicago Press, 1984.

Smalley, Stephen. *1, 2, 3 John.* Word Biblical Commentary. Waco, Tex.: Word, 1984.

Smeaton, George. *The Apostles' Doctrine of the Atonement.* Reprint, Edinburgh: Banner of Truth, 1991.

Smilde, E. *Een Eeuw van Strijd over Verbond en Doop.* Kampen: Kok, 1946.

Speculum Sacerdotale. Early English Text Society Series. Edward H. Weatherly, ed. London: Oxford University Press, 1936.

Sproul, R. C., ed. *Soli Deo Gloria: Essays in Reformed Theology.* Festschrift for John H. Gerstner. Phillipsburg, N.J.: Presbyterian and Reformed, 1976.

St. Patrick's Purgatory. Early English Text Society Series. Robert Easting, ed. Oxford: Oxford University Press, 1991.

Stauffer, Richard. *Dieu, la création et la providence dans la prédication de Calvin.* Bern, Frankfurt am Main, Las Vegas: Peter Lang, 1978.

———. *Interprètes de la Bible: Etudes sur les Réformateurs du XVIe siècle.* Paris: Beauchesne, 1980.

Sternberg, Meir. *The Poetics of Biblical Narrative: Ideological Literature and the Drama of Reading.* Bloomington: University of Indiana Press, 1987.

Stott, John. *The Cross of Christ.* Downers Grove, Ill.: InterVarsity Press, 1986.

Strehle, Stephen "The Extent of the Atonement and the Synod of Dordt." *Westminster Theological Journal* 59 (1989): 1-23.

Strobel, A. "Macht Leiden von Sunde frei? Zur Problematik von 1 Petr, 4:1f." *Theologische Zeitschrift* 19 (1963): 412-25.

Stuhlmacher, Peter. *Paul's Letter to the Romans: A Commentary*. Trans. Scott J. Hafemann. Louisville, Ky.: Westminster John Knox , 1994.

Sykes, Stephen. *The Story of Atonement*. London: Darton, Longman & Todd, 1997.

Tanner, Norman P., ed. *Decrees of the Ecumenical Councils*, vol. 1. London: Sheed & Ward; and Washington, D.C.: Georgetown University Press, 1990.

Taylor, Vincent. *The Atonement in New Testament Teaching*. London: Epworth, 1940.

Tentler, Thomas N. *Sin and Confession on the Eve of the Reformation*. Princeton, N.J.: Princeton University Press, 1977.

TeSelle, Eugene. "The Cross as Ransom." *Journal of Early Christian Studies* 4 (1996): 147-70.

Thiselton, A. C. *The First Epistle to the Corinthians*. Grand Rapids: Eerdmans, 2000.

Torrance, J. B. "The Incarnation and 'Limited Atonement.'" *Evangelical Quarterly* 55 (1983): 83-94.

Torrance, T. F. *The Trinitarian Faith*. Edinburgh: T & T Clark, 1988.

Travis, Stephen. "Christ as Bearer of Divine Judgement in Paul's Thought About the Atonement." In *Atonement Today*, ed. John Goldingay. London: SPCK, 1995.

Trueman, Carl. *The Claims of Truth: John Owen's Trinitarian Theology*. Carlisle: Paternoster, 1998.

Trueman, Carl, and R. S. Clark. *Protestant Scholasticism: Essays in Reassessment*. Carlisle: Paternoster, 1999.

Turner, H. E. W. *The Patristic Doctrine of Redemption: A Study of the Development of Doctrine During the First Five Centuries*. London: Mowbray, 1952.

Turretin, Francis. *Institutio Theologiae Elencticae*. In *Francisci Turrettini Opera*. 4 vols. Edinburgh: J. D. Lowe, 1847-1848.

Van Asselt, Willem J., and Eef Dekker. *Reformation and Scholasticism: An Ecumenical Enterprise*. Grand Rapids: Baker, 2001.

Van den Berg, J. *De thora in de thora*. Aalten: de Graafschap, n.d.

Van der Zweep, L. *De Paedagogiek van Bavinck*. Kampen: Kok, 1935.

Van der Walt, S. P. *Die Wysbegeerte van Dr. Herman Bavinck*. Potchefstroom: Pro Rege-Pers, 1953.

Van Klinken, L. *Bavincks Paedagogische Beginselen*. Meppel: Boom, 1937.

Van Os, Henk. *The Art of Devotion in the Late Middle Ages in Europe, 1300-1500*. London: Merrell Holberton, 1994.

Van Unnik, W. C. "The Critique of Paganism in I Peter 1:28." In *Neotestamentica et Semitica: Studies in Honor of Matthew Black,* ed. E. E. Ellis and M. Wilcox. Edinburgh: T & T Clark, 1969.

Vanderlaan, Eldred C. *Protestant Modernism in Holland.* New York: Oxford University Press, 1924.

Vanhoozer, Kevin J. *Is There a Meaning in This Text? The Bible, the Reader, and the Morality of Literary Knowledge.* Grand Rapids: Zondervan, 1998.

Veenhof, Jan. *Revelatie en Inspiratie.* Amsterdam: Buijten en Schipperheijn, 1968.

Vermigli, Peter Martyr. *Loci Communes.* London: Thomas Vautrollerius, 1583.

Vos, Arvin. *Aquinas, Calvin and Contemporary Protestant Thought.* Exeter: Paternoster, 1985.

Vos, Geerhardus. *The Pauline Eschatology.* Grand Rapids: Baker, 1979.

———. "The Priesthood of Christ in Hebrews." In *Redemptive History and Biblical Interpretation: The Shorter Writings of Geerhardus Vos,* ed. Richard B. Gaffin Jr. Phillipsburg, N.J.: Presbyterian & Reformed, 1980.

Waltke, Bruce K., and M. P. O'Connor. *Introduction to Biblical Hebrew Syntax.* Winona Lake, Ind.: Eisenbrauns, 1990.

Ward, Graham, ed. *The Postmodern God: A Theological Reader.* Oxford: Blackwell, 1997.

Warfield, B. B. *The Saviour of the World.* 1916; reprint, Edinburgh: Banner of Truth Trust, 1991.

———. "Calvin's Doctrine of God." In *Bibliography of Benjamin Breckinridge Warfield, 1851-1921,* ed. John E. Meeter and Roger Nicole. Phillipsburg, N.J.: Presbyterian & Reformed, 1974.

Watson, Phillip S. *Let God be God.* Philadelphia: Fortress, 1947.

Weber, Otto. "Calvin, II. Theologie." In *Die Religion in Geschichte und Gegenwart,* 3d ed., ed. Hans von Campenhausen et al. Tübingen : J.C.B. Mohr, 1986.

Weber, Otto. *Foundations of Dogmatics.* Translated by Darrell L. Gruder. Grand Rapids: Eerdmans, 1983.

Weingart, Richard E. *The Logic of Divine Love: A Critical Analysis of the Soteriology of Peter Abelard.* Oxford: Clarendon Press, 1970.

Wendel, François. *Calvin: The Origins and Development of his Religious Thought.* Translated by Philip Mairet. London: William Collins, 1963; Fontana Library, 1965.

Wenzel, Siegfried, ed. and trans. *Fasciculus Morum: A Fourteenth-Century Preacher's Handbook.* University Park: Pennsylvania State University Press, 1989.

Westphal, Merold, ed. *Postmodern Philosophy and Christian Thought.* Bloomington: Indiana University Press, 1999.

Wilckens, Ulrich. "Was heisst bei Paulus: 'Aus Werken des Gesetzes wird kein

Mensch gerecht'?" In *Rechtfertigung als Freiheit: Paulusstudien*, 77-109. Neukirchen: Neukirchener Verlag, 1974.

———. *Der Brief an die Römer*. Evangelisch-katholischer Kommentar zum
Neuen Testament, vol. 6. Zürich: Benziger Verlag, 1978.

Wilson, R. McL. *Hebrews*. New Century Bible Commentary. Grand Rapids:
Eerdmans; and Basingstoke: Marshall Morgan & Scott, 1987.

Whale, Peter. "The Lamb of John: Some Myths about the Vocabulary of the Johannine Literature." *Journal of Biblical Literature* 106 (1987): 289-95.

Whybray, R. N. *Thanksgiving for a Liberated Prophet: An Interpretation of Isaiah
Chapter 53*, JSOTSup 4. Sheffield: JSOT, 1978.

Williams, James G., ed. *The Girard Reader*. New York: Crossroad, 1996.

Williams, George Huntston. *Anselm: Communion and Atonement*. Saint Louis,
Mo.: Concordia, 1960.

Williams, Rowan. *Resurrection*. New York: Pilgrim, 1982.

Wright, N. T. *Jesus and the Victory of God*. Minneapolis: Fortress, 1996.

———. *What Saint Paul Really Said: Was Paul of Tarsus the Real Founder of Christianity?* Grand Rapids: Eerdmans, 1997.

Yearly, Lee H. "St. Thomas Aquinas on Providence and Predestination." *Anglican Theological Review* 49 (1967): 409-23.

Young, N. H. "C. H. Dodd, 'Hilaskesthai,' and His Critics." *Evangelical Quarterly* 48 (1976): 67-78.

Zanchi, Jerome. *Commentarius in Epistolam Sancti Pauli ad Ephesios*. A. H. de
Hartog, ed. 2 vols. Amsterdam: J. A. Wormser, 1888.

List of contributors

Joel R. Beeke is president and professor of systematic theology and homiletics at the Puritan Reformed Theological Seminary, as well as pastor of Heritage Netherlands Reformed Church in Grand Rapids, Michigan. He is editor of *Banner of Sovereign Grace Truth* and has authored or edited forty books. He most recently edited *The Path of True Godliness* (Baker Academic, 2003).

Raymond A. Blacketer is senior pastor of the Neerlandia Christian Reformed Church in Alberta, Canada. He studied under Richard A. Muller at Calvin Theological Seminary, where he wrote his doctoral dissertation on the doctrine of the atonement at the Synod of Dort.

Henri Blocher is a longtime friend and colleague of Roger Nicole and currently holds the Knoedler Chair of Systematic Theology at Wheaton College. He is professor of systematic theology at the Faculté Libre de Théologie Evangélique in Vaux-sur-Seine, France. His two most recent publications in English are *Original Sin: Illuminating the Riddle* (InterVarsity Press, 2000) and *In the Beginning: The Opening Chapters of Genesis* (InterVarsity Press, 1984).

D. A. Carson is research professor of Old Testament at Trinity Evangelical Divinity School in Deerfield, Illinois. Author of scores of publications on biblical subjects, he has recently coedited and contributed to the two-volume *Justification and Variegated Nomism* (Baker, 2001).

Sinclair B. Ferguson, a longtime friend of Roger Nicole, is professor of systematic theology at Westminster Theological Seminary in Dallas, Texas. His works include *The Holy Spirit* (InterVarsity Press, 1996), *The Christian Life* (Banner of Truth, 1996) and *Grow in Grace* (Banner of Truth, 1996). Most recently he has published *The Big Book of Questions and Answers: A Family Guide to the Christian Faith* (Christian Focus, 2001).

Richard Gaffin is the Charles Krahe Professor of Biblical and Systematic Theology and chairman of the systematic theology department at Westminster Theological Seminary in Philadelphia, Pennsylvania. He is the author of several books, including *The Centrality of the Resurrection* (Baker, 1978) and *Perspectives on Pentecost* (Presbyterian & Reformed, 1993).

Timothy George, a longtime friend and colleague of Roger Nicole, is the founding dean and professor of divinity at Beeson Divinity School in Birmingham, Alabama. A prolific author, his book *The Theology of the Reformers* (Broadman, 1988) is a standard textbook in many schools and seminaries. More recently he was coeditor with Alister McGrath of *For All the Saints: Evangelical Theology and Christian Spirituality* (Westminster John Knox, 2003).

J. Alan Groves is professor of Old Testament at Westminster Theological Seminary in Philadelphia, Pennsylvania, and executive director of the Westminster Hebrew Institute. He is the author of *The Gospel According to Isaiah: God with Us* (Presbyterian & Reformed, forthcoming) and *Judges,* Two Horizons Commentary (Eerdmans, forthcoming).

Royce Gordon Gruenler, a former colleague of Roger Nicole's at Gordon-Conwell Theological Seminary in South Hamilton, Massachusetts, is Professor Emeritus of New Testament there. He is the author of *New Approaches to Jesus and the Gospels* (Baker, 1982) and "Mark," in *Baker Commentary on the Bible,* ed. W. Elwell (Baker, 2000).

Charles E. Hill, a colleague of Roger Nicole's at Reformed Theological Seminary in Orlando, Florida, serves there as professor of New Testament. He is author of *Regnum Caelorum: Patterns of Millennial Thought in Early Christianity,* 2nd ed. (Eerdmans, 2001) and *The Johannine Corpus in the Early Church* (Oxford University Press, forthcoming).

Frank A. James III, a colleague of Roger Nicole's at Reformed Theological Seminary in Orlando, Florida, serves as vice president for academic affairs and professor of historical theology. He is the author of *Peter Martyr Vermigli and Predestination: The Augustinian Inheritance of an Italian Reformer* (Oxford University Press, 1998) and coeditor with the late Heiko Oberman of *Via Augustini: The Recovery of Augustine in the Later Middle Ages, Renaissance and Reformation* (Brill, 1992). Since 1996 he has been general editor of the Peter Martyr Library and senior editor of *Ad Fontes: Digital Library of Classical Theological Texts.*

Simon J. Kistemaker, a colleague of Roger Nicole's at Reformed Theological Seminary in Orlando, Florida, is Professor Emeritus of New Testament there. He has written several volumes in the New Testament Commentary series, including his *Exposition of the Epistle to the Hebrews* (Baker, 1984) and, most recently, his *Exposition of the Book of Revelation* (Baker, 2001).

Dan G. McCartney, a student of Roger Nicole's in the 1970s, is professor of New Testament at Westminster Theological Seminary in Philadelphia. He is coauthor with Charles Clayton of *Let the Reader Understand: A Guide to Interpreting and Applying the Bible* (Baker, 1994; 2nd ed. Presbyterian & Reformed, 2002) and is writing the volume *James* in the Baker Exegetical Commentary on the New Testament series. He is known to many as the horn player of the Westminster Brass.

Bruce L. McCormack is Frederick and Margaret L. Weyerhaeuser Professor of Systematic Theology at Princeton Seminary. His book, *Karl Barth's Critically Realistic Dialectical Theology: Its Genesis and Development, 1909-1936* (Oxford University Press, 1995), won the Karl Barth Prize in 1998—the first book by an American scholar to receive this award.

J. Ramsey Michaels, a former colleague of Roger Nicole's at Gordon-Conwell Theological Seminary, is Professor Emeritus of Religious Studies at Southwest Missouri State University in Springfield, Missouri, and adjunct professor of New Testament at Bangor Theological Seminary in Portland, Maine. Among his many books are *John*, NIBC (Hendrickson, 1989) and *Revelation*, IVPNTC (InterVarsity Press, 1997).

Emile Nicole, who is a nephew of Roger Nicole, is professor of Old Testament at Faculté Libre de Théologie Evangélique in Vaux-sur-Seine, France. He is author of "Un sacrifice de bonne odeur" in *Esprit et vie*, ed. F. Bassin, Hommage a S. Benetreau (Excelsis, 1997), pp. 55-70.

Roger Nicole, in whose honor this book has been written, is Emeritus Visiting Professor of Theology at Reformed Theological Seminary in Orlando, Florida. He also taught for over forty years at Gordon-Conwell Theological Seminary in Massachusetts. He was a founding member of both the Evangelical Theological Society and Christians for Biblical Equality. His collected works have recently been published as *Standing Forth: Collected Writings of Roger Nicole* (Christian Focus, 2002).

J. I. Packer, a longtime friend of Roger Nicole, is the Board of Governor's Professor of Theology at Regent College in Vancouver, British Columbia, Canada. He serves as senior editor and visiting scholar of *Christianity Today*. Well known for his classic work, *Knowing God* (InterVarsity Press, 1973), he has more recently written *A Quest for Godliness: The Puritan Vision of the Christian Life* (Crossway, 1994) and, with Carolyn Nystrom, *Never Beyond Hope: How God Touches & Uses Imperfect People* (InterVarsity Press, 2000).

Stanley P. Rosenberg is director of the Centre for Scholarship and Christianity in Oxford and dean of the Council for Christian Colleges & University Students at the Centre for Medieval & Renaissance Studies, also in Oxford. A tutor and affiliated member of theology faculty at the University of Oxford, he is also codirector for the John Templeton Oxford Seminars on Science and Christianity held in conjunction with Wycliffe Hall. His principal research interest is the cosmology of Augustine.

Kevin J. Vanhoozer is research professor of systematic theology at Trinity Evangelical Divinity School in Chicago. His most recent books include *First Theology: God, Scripture and Hermeneutics* (InterVarsity Press, 2002) and *The Drama of Doctrine: A Canonical-Linguistic Approach to Theology* (Westminster John Knox, 2003). He also served as the editor of the *Cambridge Companion to Postmodern Theology* (Cambridge University Press, 2001).

Gwenfair M. Walters, a former student of Roger Nicole, is assistant professor of church history at Gordon-Conwell Theological Seminary, teaching primarily in the areas of medieval and Reformation studies. She completed her dissertation, "Dreams, Visions and Visionaries in Late Medieval England," at Cambridge University. She has been an editor and author for numerous historical, theological and homiletical publications.

Bruce K. Waltke, a colleague of Roger Nicole's at Reformed Theological Seminary, serves there as professor of Old Testament, and is Professor Emeritus of Biblical Studies at Regent College in Vancouver, British Columbia, Canada. Most recent in a long list of significant publications is his *Genesis: A Commentary* (Zondervan, 2001), which was awarded the gold medallion by the Evangelical Christian Publishers Association for best commentary and reference work in 2002.

Subject Index

atoning sacrifice, 107
Attridge, Harold W., 165
attrition, 250
Auerbach, Erich, 229
Augustine, 221, 300,
 308-10, 232-33, 399,
 449n.5
  on Donatists, 381-82
  on grace, 223
  sermons, 223-24, 227,
   228-29
Augustinianism, 265,
 313, 322
Aulén, Gustaf, 222, 264,
 267, 272-73, 275, 278,
 289, 449n.5
Aune, David E.,
 196nn.27,32
autobiographical jus-
 tice, 377
Ayer, A. J., 15
Babylon, 30, 192, 193-94
Bailey, Daniel P., 91n.1
Bailey, David W., 10
Baker, Mark, 155n.77,
 370, 376, 377, 383,
 398n.102
Balthasar, Hans Urs
 von, 370, 386n.58
baptism, 105, 185n.24,
 248, 253, 423
Baptist tradition, 13,
 117-18
Barnes, Albert, 450n.6
Barnett, Paul, 428
Barrett, C. K., 165,
 196n.32
Barth, Karl, 12, 14, 305,
 348-49, 356-66
Bathsheba, 54
Bauckham, Richard,

177, 199n.44
Bauerschmidt, Freder-
 ick Christian, 391-92
Bavinck, Herman, 324-
 45
bearing guilt, 62-64, 69-
 89
beast, 206-7
beauty, 238
Beet, Joseph Agan,
 450n.6
being-in-act, 359,
 360n.20
Belgic Confession, 337
Bell, M. Charles, 315n.44
Bellarmine, Cardinal,
 343
benefits, of the atone-
 ment, 416-17
Benson, Larry, 247
Berkhof, Louis, 347
Bernard of Clairvaux,
 241, 251-52, 261, 449n.5
Beza, Theodore, 280,
 306, 307, 317
Bible
  inerrancy, 10
  inspiration and au-
   thority, 12
biblical theology, 97,
 270, 346-47
blessing, 403, 412
blind man, 110, 112
Bliss, Philip, 422
Blocher, Henri, 370n.5,
 389, 395n.90
blood, 35-37, 57-58
  and life, 39-40
  shedding of, 24, 51,
   94, 283
  and substitution, 46

that whitens, 202-4
blood sacrifice, 15, 43,
 416
boasting, 139
  in the atonement,
   142, 414
Bolt, John, 325
bondage, 18, 149, 186-
 87, 192-93, 207, 411,
 436
Bonner, Gerald, 223n.8
book of life, 200, 207
born-again movement,
 432
Boston Theological In-
 stitute, 90
Boston Theological So-
 ciety, 90
Boyd, Greg, 99n.15
Bramley, H. R., 271
Bremmer, R. H., 325
Briggs, Charles, 329
Brooks, Phillips, 442
Brown, Joanne Carlson,
 373
Bruce, F. F., 166
Brunner, Emil, 18
Bucer, Martin, 17, 315
burnt offerings, 42
Bushnell, Horace,
 447n.3, 448, 450n.6
Cain, 336
Caird, George, 376
Calvin, John, 142, 175,
 209-10, 211, 272, 279-
 303, 363, 397, 419, 428,
 440
  on definite atone-
   ment, 305-6, 313
  on descent into hell,
   343

hypostatic union, 349,
351
hypothetical necessity,
299, 300
hypothetical universal-
ism, 280
hyssop, 53, 57-58
idolatry, 132, 147
image of God, 146, 147,
335
imagery, 154-56
immanent Trinity, 359,
363
immorality, 178
imputation, 134n.53, 283
inadvertent sin, 54
incarnation, 270, 296,
341, 357, 358-59
inclusive substitution,
144-45
individualism, 370
individuation, 362
indulgences, 258, 259-60
Innocent II, Pope, 252
intuition, 393, 394n.86
Irenaeus, 222, 235, 389,
449n.5
Irving, Edward, 375n.16
Isaac, sacrifice of,
386n.59, 392
Isidore of Seville, 221
Jerome, 269, 308
Jerusalem, 102-3, 193
Jesus Christ
    as accursed, 269-70,
    273
    as advocate, 114-15,
    206
    alienation, 435
    on the atonement, 91,
    94-98

baptism, 99
blood, 28, 58, 108,
136, 185, 187, 191-
94, 283, 382, 386,
398
body broken, 397-98
crucifixion, 28, 427,
440
death, 94, 108-9, 136,
156-60, 184n.21,
339, 373, 434
death and resurrec-
tion, 96, 142-44, 417
as deconstructor, 373
deformity, 234-35
descent into hell, 171,
188n.33, 253n.46,
287n.27, 343-44
exaltation, 188
as example, 145, 182-
83, 212, 422, 447
faithfulness, 125, 136
flesh, 108
humiliation, 343-44
indwelling, 431-32
as Lamb, 203
and the law, 95-97
life on earth, 168
mediatorial role, 177,
225
as Messiah, 100, 102-
3
nonviolence, 386-87
obedience, 126, 145,
181, 189, 214, 215,
286, 287, 293-94,
341-42
as object of faith, 125,
136
opposes reign of Sa-
tan, 101-2

person and work,
347-48, 418, 432-37
priesthood, 30, 163,
168, 175, 212-15, 292
repentance, 451
righteousness, 211,
214, 433, 436
as Savior and Lord,
437
as Shepherd, 203
spiritual death, 171-
74
submission, 293
as substitute, 211
suffering, 94, 169-71,
175, 176, 181-84,
189, 214, 339, 343-
44, 402n.111, 435-36
testing in wilderness,
100
threefold office, 213,
292
two natures, 175,
270-71, 349-56
as victim, 161n.95
as victor, 275-76, 278,
289-91
*See also Christus Vic-
tor*
Jewett, Paul K., 11, 167
John the Baptist, 190,
196-97
John, on the atonement,
106-18, 190-208
Jones, L. Gregory, 373
Jordan, Clarence, 273
Josephus, 130
Judaizing, 412-13
Jude, 176
judgment, 283
judicial system, 283,

Scripture Index